Black Garden Aflame

Black Garden Aflame

The Nagorno-Karabakh Conflict
in the Soviet and Russian Press

Edited by Artyom Tonoyan

East View Press
Minneapolis, USA

Black Garden Aflame: The Nagorno-Karabakh Conflict in the Soviet and Russian Press

Published by East View Press,
an imprint of East View Information Services, Inc.
10601 Wayzata Blvd
Minneapolis, MN 55305 USA
www.eastviewpress.com

Library of Congress Cataloging-in-Publication Data

Names: Tonoyan, Artyom H., 1975- editor. | East View Information Services.
Title: Black garden aflame : the Nagorno-Karabakh conflict in the Soviet
    and Russian press / edited by Artyom Tonoyan.
Other titles: Nagorno-Karabakh conflict in the Soviet and Russian press
Description: First edition. | Minneapolis, MN : East View Press, an imprint
    of East View Information Services, Inc., 2021. | Includes
    bibliographical references.
Identifiers: LCCN 2021043004 (print) | LCCN 2021043005 (ebook) | ISBN
    9781879944558 (paperback) | ISBN 9781879944541 (ebook)
Subjects: LCSH: Nagorno-Karabakh Conflict, 1988-1994--Press
    coverage--Soviet Union. | Nagorno-Karabakh (Azerbaijan)--Press
    coverage--Russia (Federation) | Nagorno-Karabakh (Azerbaijan)--Foreign
    public opinion, Russian. | Azerbaijan--Politics and government--Sources.
    | Azerbaijan--Foreign relations--Sources. | Armenia (Republic)--Foreign
    relations--Sources. | Russia (Federation)--Foreign relations--Sources.
Classification: LCC DK699.N34 B55 2021 (print) | LCC DK699.N34 (ebook) |
    DDC 947.54--dc23
LC record available at https://lccn.loc.gov/2021043004
LC ebook record available at https://lccn.loc.gov/2021043005

Front cover photo © 2020 Scout Tufankjian
Cover design by Carol Dungan Logie
Map prepared by East View Geospatial (geospatial.com)
Composition by Ana K. Niedermaier

Printed in the United States of America

First Edition, 2021
1 3 5 7 9 10 8 6 4 2

Contents

Part One | Outbreak of Conflict in Late Soviet Period

Part Two | Initial Resolution and Subsequent Mediation

Part Three | Geopolitical Interests in Karabakh – Four Main Vectors

Part Four | Revived Conflict and Ramifications

Nagorno-Karabakh and Surrounding Region

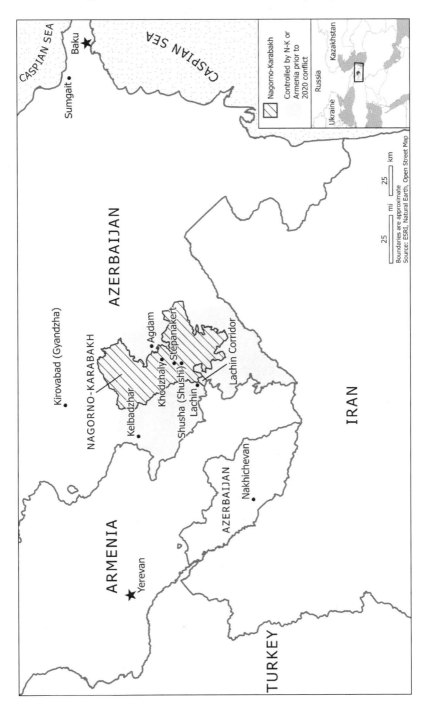

Foreword

When Azerbaijan, abetted by Turkey, attacked areas of Nagorno-Karabakh in September 2020, several obvious questions emerged. Why now? What were Azerbaijan's (or, more precisely, the Aliyev regime's) goals in launching the war? How would Russia (read Putin) respond? Most pressing, of course, were questions as to how the war would proceed. The purely military and immediate territorial questions were answered rather quickly. By November 10, the date of the Russian-brokered ceasefire, Armenia had endured a crushing military defeat. It lost control of long-contested territories in Nagorno-Karabakh. Many thousands of Armenian refugees fled now Azeri-controlled territories. Thousands of Armenian fighters were killed, along with dozens of civilians.

Azerbaijan also suffered a not yet publicly or precisely acknowledged high rate of casualties. Given that the Aliyev regime decisively won the war, these losses will pose no political trials to the Azeri government. Indeed the Azeri war dead will inevitably be commemorated as national heroes lost in a victorious cause against the hated Armenians. Add the economic effects of a lost war on Armenia, coming at a time when the COVID-19 pandemic had already undermined the Armenian economy. Armenia's swift and total military defeat, not surprisingly, ignited political and social turmoil at home. Armenia quickly went from a case study of an apparently successful transition to democratization, under Prime Minister Nikol Pashinyan's populist guidance, to a country facing existential crises challenging its economic, political, and social health. A demoralizing factor for the Armenians is that internally they had developed an overriding arrogance, believing that they could not be defeated militarily by Azerbaijan. This complacency cost them dearly.

Azerbaijan will continue to loom as a threat. Not only to Armenia's control of its remaining territory in Nagorno-Karabakh, but ultimately to Armenia's existence as an independent polity in the South Caucasus. Pashinyan has to rely on agreements with the Azeri government, not an enviable position for any Armenian political leader. Even more so, he must rely on the goodwill of the Russian government, which of course, means Vladimir Putin. Pashinyan's nebulous Russophobia was quickly discarded during the war. Despite some beliefs held in Armenia that Russia would come to its aid in the conflict, no direct aid was proffered. Since the Armenian defeat and the subsequent appearance of Russian peacekeepers in areas of Karabakh, Armenian public opinion would seem to have coalesced around a consensus that Armenian's long-term survival is predicated on Russian support. Russophilia, in all things, is the order of the day. Therefore, an understanding of Azeri-Armenian relations, in the context of the long-simmering conflict in Nagorno-Karabakh, must take into account the overarching presence of Russia/Putin.

Nagorno-Karabakh in the Russian and earlier Soviet gaze, as it were, is the subject of this valuable and timely volume, *Black Garden Aflame*, published by East View Press. This work, divided into four parts containing fourteen chapters, constitutes select Russian-language press coverage of the persistent "Karabakh crisis" from its first Gorbachev-era stirrings in Sumgait to Russian coverage of Nikol Pashinyan's triumphant return to office in June 2021. It is fair to assert that Soviet and Russian press coverage primarily reflects official Moscow-centered views of the conflict. This is not to say that the coverage is monolithic, especially given the chaotic political transformations in the Soviet Union and then Russia from 1988 to 2000.

There has been no easily defined Soviet/Russian position on the South Caucasus. Moscow's interests have evolved, and Nagorno-Karabakh was worthy of attention to Soviet (and later Russian) authorities only as it affected their security position. After Putin's consolidation of power soon after 2000, examining Russian press coverage is the best way to perceive Russia's approach to Armenian-Azeri relations generally. That Russia had no clear public position on the 2020 war in Nagorno-Karabakh is an obvious conclusion from a reading of the Russian press in that period.

The compilation of translated articles in *Black Garden Aflame* offers the reader comprehensive coverage of Soviet and Russian press accounts of Azeri and Armenian political disputes over Nagorno-Karabakh since the late 1980s. Internal Karabakh political questions, and the critical roles of Turkey and Iran vis-a-vis Azeri-Armenian relations, are well covered in the Russian media, and numerous articles on the subject are included herein. Indeed, how Iran and Turkey might respond to further escalating crises in the South Caucasus remains opaque. *Black Garden Aflame* greatly aids in filling this lacuna in expertise in the region. How Soviet and Russian newspapers addressed the (admittedly negligible) US stance on Nagorno-Karabakh is also incorporated into the collection. Given the comparatively little attention given to the issue in the US press, Russian coverage is invaluable for a better understanding of how American policy evolved on the issue over the past three decades.

I well remember a course on late Soviet ethnic conflict, held in Finland in 1989-1990, where the escalating crisis that was Nagorno-Karabakh dominated weekly meetings. Much of our discussion was based on reading the Russian press, including articles of the type and tenor included here. Soviet and Russian press accounts remain an essential source base. In the so-called Western press, the 2020 war and its immediate aftermath were addressed widely, if not as in-depth as in the former Soviet Union. Less filtered coverage appeared in various unmediated online journals and Twitter accounts. Social media speed up access to information; however, it might not be accurate information. The financial inability of traditional media outlets to maintain cohorts of international correspondents with on-the-ground, textured knowledge of a region in conflict leaves the field open for legions of bloggers, amateur foreign policy experts, indeed anyone with access to Twitter, Instagram, and

Facebook – which means everyone – to assume the guise of an expert. This volume offers a persuasive rejoinder to the facile foreign policy reasoning found in social media accounts of the long Karabakh crisis.

The present volume also provides a powerful corrective to the deafening silence on the Karabakh issue outside of the former Soviet Union between the collapse of the USSR and the 2020 Nagorno-Karabakh war. *Black Garden Aflame* powerfully demonstrates that although open disputes between Armenia and Azerbaijan over Karabakh receded into a less violent interlude in recent decades, the intransigence of both sides remained and indeed worsened. In this light, the recent war seems far less surprising. More ominously, reading the articles in this work, it is hard to envision an optimistic solution to the present crisis in the South Caucasus. The translated Russian-language articles found herein provide ready access for scholars, foreign policy experts, and students, as well as those simply interested in a fascinating region of the world, to three decades of often excellent Soviet and Russian reporting on Nagorno-Karabakh and on the fraught state of Azeri-Armenian relations.

Steven A. Usitalo
Professor and Chair, Department of History
Northern State University

Publisher's Preface and Acknowledgments

The volume you are now reading represents the first English-language collection in book form of articles, communiqués, reports, interviews and commentaries on the Nagorno-Karabakh conflict that have appeared in the Soviet and Russian media since the late 1980s.

All of the above materials are translated from Russian and appeared in the weekly periodical *Current Digest of the Russian Press*, previously known as *Current Digest of the Soviet Press* (1949-1991) and *Current Digest of the Post-Soviet Press* (1992-2010). Some of this content was condensed for brevity, either by the original selectors or the present editors. Text omitted by East View Press editorial staff is designated with an ellipsis (...). In other cases, the staff of the Russian publication chose to condense certain text – for example, a quotation from a public speech; such omissions are indicated by asterisks (***).

We wish to acknowledge the following Soviet and Russian publications that provided material used in this collection:

Bakinsky rabochy
Izvestia
Kommersant
Kommunist
Krasnaya zvezda
Meduza
Moskovskiye novosti
Nezavisimaya gazeta
Novaya gazeta
Pravda
RBC Daily
Rossiiskaya gazeta
Republic.ru (formerly Slon.ru)
Segodnya
Sobesednik
Sovetskaya Rossia
Vedomosti

Some additional information that may be helpful to the general English-speaking audience can be found in annotations within the articles. All such additions are indicated in brackets, and some longer annotations are attributed to *Trans*. Supplemental information provided by the editors of the original publication is included in parentheses, with the attribution *Ed.* or the abbreviated title of the publication. More detailed clarifications, as well as other background information, are provided in endnotes following the main text.

All transliterations in this book are based on the Russian spellings of proper nouns using a system that is a compromise between strict orthographic equivalence and phonetic equivalence. The aim is to establish consistency in the presentation of proper nouns throughout the text and on the map, and to enable readers who do not know Russian to approximate the pronunciation of transliterated words, while still allowing readers familiar with Russian to identify the words in question.

For internal proofreading of the above material, we thank Matthew Larson. We also acknowledge our staff in Moscow who downloaded and compiled much of the original material from East View's database; and Matthew Dick of East View Geospatial, who carefully produced the custom-made map of the region that appears here.

We would also like to extend gratitude to Scout Tufankjian for granting permission to use her spare but eloquent photo on the front cover. She explains the image as follows: "A family in Martakert, Nagorno-Karabakh, returned home after the war to find their garden littered with fallen pomegranates and unexploded ordnance. Noting the similarity between the two, they placed them side by side."

This collection has benefited significantly from Carol Dungan's inspired work on the cover design as a whole; Ana K. Niedermaier's adroit composition and layout of the voluminous text; and Mike Bennett's compilation of the extensive index.

In addition, we would like to thank Steven Usitalo for writing the Foreword to this edition; and Laurence Broers, Christopher Marsh, Kevork Oskanian and Ronald Grigor Suny for agreeing to read and comment on the advance copy.

Finally, we express appreciation to Artyom Tonoyan for his enormous efforts in reviewing close to a million words of East View Press material, from which he carefully selected, organized and helped proof the content that ended up in the final edition. This ground-breaking publication could not have existed without the care of such a dedicated and well-informed scholar.

We hope that *Black Garden Aflame* will serve the needs and interests of countless other dedicated scholars, teachers, students and other readers for many years to come.

Laurence Bogoslaw
Chief Editor and Publishing Director, East View Press

Introduction

After Azerbaijan with Turkish support began a military offensive to retake Nagorno-Karabakh in September 2020, Russian president Vladimir Putin was silent for 10 days. Finally, he appeared in an interview with the TV channel Rossia 24 on October 7. Calling the unfolding war "a great tragedy," Putin reminded the viewers that a combined 4 million Armenians and Azerbaijanis live in Russia, adding that "Azerbaijan, Armenia, Nagorno-Karabakh are all territories inhabited by people who are not strangers to us."[1] If this statement was meant to convey that Russia was worried about the conflict, it certainly achieved its goal. But perhaps more than that, Putin's primary message was that Russia, interested as it was in tranquility along its southern borders, was not going to interfere in the conflict militarily on the side of its regional ally Armenia.

He would make this much clearer further in the interview by pointing out that although Russia has treaty obligations with Armenia both within the framework of the Collective Security Treaty Organization (CSTO) as well as a mutual treaty, these obligations have a limited scope and mandate: They can be activated if and only if Armenia itself comes under attack. Since the military operations were happening in Nagorno-Karabakh – a region internationally recognized as part of Azerbaijan – Russia, and by extension the CSTO, could not get directly involved, despite their concerns. In short, Russia was loath to put its finger on the scales, one way or another. For those in Armenia, it was a vexatious development, if not altogether catastrophic. To many observers of the region, Russia's actions (or lack thereof) were difficult to decipher, presenting as it were a giant puzzle. But it need not be so.

The Nagorno-Karabakh conflict is one with which Moscow is intimately familiar. It has loomed large in the Russian-language media and general discourse since it exploded into the public consciousness in 1988. A harbinger of the rising nationalist tide across Soviet space, it accelerated the irreversible political processes that would bring down the Soviet Union. Nevertheless, for Western analysts, the fact that Putin was citing the letter of the law – after Russia's annexation of the Crimea and the chaos wrought by Russian paramilitaries in Ukraine's Donetsk and Lugansk Provinces – was markedly cynical. The leader of the country that was responsible for the "greatest interstate security crisis in the European continent since the collapse of the Berlin Wall,"[2] the argument went, had seemingly just discovered international law. Putting aside Putin's obfuscations, many wondered, what were the real reasons for Russia's reluctance to intervene?

Was this hesitancy Putin's way of punishing Armenia's fiery revolutionary leader Nikol Pashinyan for prosecuting former Armenian president Robert Kocharyan, a close friend of Putin's? Was this retaliation for Armenia's perceived westward geopolitical reorientation, however improbable this was given Armenia's long economic, political, and military dependency on Russia? Alternatively, was this a reprise of the century-old Russo-Turkish (read Bolshevik-Kemalist) political dalliances that effectively carved the South Caucasus into its present form? Others wondered still whether this was a sign of Russia's growing awareness of its own limitations, meaning that its reluctance to help a friend in need was, in reality, a reluctance to spread itself too thin militarily. After all, Russia's Syrian adventure is not exactly a *cause célèbre* in the country. Perhaps Putin was simply caught by surprise? The truth, as it often does, lies quite likely somewhere in the middle and contains elements of all these factors in their varying shades of grey. Yet one thing that can be safely argued is that far from being wholly subject to Putin's whims, Russia's engagements in the South Caucasus are not as *ad hoc* as they seem at first glance.

The Caucasus is hardly new in the Russian imagination. As political scientist Robert Nalbandov notes in his book on Russian foreign policy, "The South Caucasus has traditionally occupied a significant place in Russia's vital national interests and its identity. Caucasus had always some sort of a mysteriously romantic attraction for Russia: its greatest poets (Pushkin, Lermontov, to name a few) wrote their best pieces here."[3] Yet, to anyone unfamiliar with South Caucasus regional conflicts or Russian foreign policy along that vector[4] in the age of Putin, this latest Russian maneuver may indeed seem rather whimsical and desultory. Nevertheless, for those paying close attention to the region, it is anything but. True, Russia appears to lack a neat, standard blueprint for tackling various conflicts on its periphery. The Abkhazian and South Ossetian conflicts were dealt with much differently, as Russia had no qualms about putting one finger on the scales and a few in the cookie jar, as it were. In those instances, Russia did not hesitate to demonstrate support for its clients. However, the fact that Russia addresses different conflicts in different ways does not necessarily mean it lacks either a strategic vision or the ability to execute strategy effectively. Insofar as the Nagorno-Karabakh conflict in concerned, far from being original, or exceptional, or even provocative, Putin's decision-making is rather prosaic in its cold pragmatism. In fact, it can be safely situated within the logic of Soviet (and now post-Soviet Russian) views of how the Armenian-Azerbaijani conflict should be resolved; as Moscow's leaders, have stated frequently since the late 1980s, any solution to the conflict must be "acceptable to both sides."[5]

The question then becomes: What is a solution (or *the* solution) acceptable to both sides? Is this merely diplomatic doublespeak for what is acceptable to Russia and its long-term security interests in the region? To come to a reasonable answer, a brief historical excursus into the origins of the conflict and the peace negotiations is in order.

From the Origins of the Modern Nagorno-Karabakh Crisis to 2020:
A Brief Survey

On March 1, 1988, Soviet readers woke up to yet another set of grandly trivial and inconsequential headlines from *Pravda*'s front page. Soviet leader Mikhail Gorbachev was headed to Yugoslavia, and Soviet farmers were doing their utmost to contribute to the welfare of the fatherland. Yes, the economy was struggling, yet the country's economic foundations were solid, and in case anyone was curious, the Central Committee of the Communist Party was sending its heartfelt congratulations to the newly elected Secretary-General of the Communist Party of Spain, Julio Anguita. Buried in the headlines on page 2, at the very bottom of the page, was a four-sentence news item from the Azerbaijani industrial town of Sumgait. Here, according to the vaguely worded report, certain hooligans had done what many hooligans are wont to do: They disturbed the town's peace. According to the report: "On February 28, in Sumgait (Azerbaijan SSR), a group of hooligan elements provoked riots. There have been cases of outrage and violence. Measures were taken to normalize life in the city, ensure discipline and public order. An investigation by the law-enforcement organs is under way."[6]

If the prominence given to the report was any indication, the situation did not appear to be dire. This effort by *Pravda* to uphold the status quo failed, as the subsequent chain of events would demonstrate.

What the editors of Pravda did not suspect, and what their readers could not imagine, was that one of the most consequential events in the history of the USSR had just taken place. What was initially thought to be a stress test of the system – in the form of a minor set of localized ethnic grievances – evolved into a regional interethnic crisis, and at the most inopportune of times. These grievances, managed or rather repressed for nearly seven decades, were now shaking the very foundations of the empire, exposing its structural weaknesses and a very real "policy void in the center's toolkit for addressing interethnic conflict."[7] No amount of sloganeering would be able to contain the emergence into the open of radicalized national groups. The much-vaunted Soviet concept *druzhba narodov* (friendship among peoples) was on its way to being empirically falsified, in the process mortally wounding a geopolitical superpower.

There was certainly an element of irony in all of this. Events that would destabilize the country happened not in Moscow but in a faraway Transcaucasus town that was barely visible on the Soviet map and entirely absent in the cognitive map of Soviet citizens. Not known for anything spectacular (or, for that matter, anything in particular), Sumgait would become associated with pogroms and wanton violence, where official estimates recorded that 32 Soviet citizens, most of them ethnic Armenians, were murdered.

Although unexpected, the unrest in Sumgait did not happen in a vacuum. If anything, it was the antithesis to the months-long peaceful demonstrations in neighboring Armenia and Stepanakert, the capital of the Nagorno-Karabakh Autonomous Oblast (NKAO). There, taking advantage of Gorbachev's *glasnost* and *perestroika* policies, a group of Armenian intellectuals with roots in Nagorno-Karabakh had begun a coordinated campaign to redress what they considered a historic and historical injustice: the transfer of overwhelmingly Armenian-populated Nagorno-Karabakh under Azerbaijani jurisdiction by Stalin soon after the Sovietization of the region in 1921.[8] The reversal of that fateful decision was the paramount aim of the campaign.

What started as the efforts of a few soon ballooned into a nationwide mobilization with masses of Armenians pouring into the streets, forcing a response from the Kremlin. The Armenian demands were largely motivated by two overarching grievances: economic and cultural. They argued that the Armenian population of Nagorno-Karabakh was subject to myriad discriminatory economic, demographic, and cultural policies that had the ultimate goal of either driving the Armenians out of Nagorno-Karabakh or reducing their numbers enough to preclude any future Armenian claims to Karabakh. The current leader of Azerbaijan, Ilham Aliyev, acknowledges the consequences quite openly.[9]

As reports of rising tensions in Nagorno-Karabakh continued apace, CPSU General Secretary Mikhail Gorbachev addressed "the working people and peoples of Azerbaijan and Armenia." In an impassioned plea that quoted famous Armenian poet and victim of Stalinist purges Yeghishe Charents and Azeri poet Samad Vurgun, Gorbachev implored Armenians and Azeris "to display civic maturity and restraint, to return to normal life and work, and to maintain public order."[10]

But by then it was already too late. The Armenians of Nagorno-Karabakh had already upped the ante on February 20, 1988. Everything indicated that there was no turning back to their demands. On that day, the NKAO Soviet, in an unprecedented move, formalized their demands by passing a resolution calling for unification with Soviet Armenia. Blindsided and enraged by the decision, Moscow displayed a swift but also almost cartoonishly Soviet reaction, where altiloquence and bombast stood in for policy. Perhaps nothing could illustrate this point better than the February 24, 1988 declaration by the CPSU Central Committee regarding the developments in Nagorno-Karabakh that appeared on the pages of *Pravda* and *Izvestia*:

> After reviewing information on the events in Nagorno-Karabakh Autonomous Province, the CPSU Central Committee believes that the actions and demands aimed at a revision of the existing national-territorial structure are at variance with the interests of the working people of the Azerbaijan and Armenian Republics and harm relations between nationalities. Consistently guided by the Leninist principles of nationalities policy, the CPSU Central Committee has appealed to the patriotic and internationalist feelings of the Armenian and Azerbaijani population not to succumb to provocations by nationalistic elements and to strengthen in every way that great asset of socialism: the fraternal friendship of Soviet peoples.[11]

Mere days after Central Committee's declaration, violence broke out in Sumgait. The pogroms against Armenians were shocking in their brutality and led to the exodus of the town's Armenian population. Their muted coverage in the Soviet press and the lack of transparent investigation would in turn raise the stakes, feeding into Armenian fears of a new genocide against their ethnic compatriots in Nagorno-Karabakh and Azerbaijan proper. If there was any hope, however faint, to resolve the conflict by peaceful means, Sumgait shattered them unceremoniously. More than the shock of what transpired, however, Sumgait portended that violence as a method of conflict resolution was a useful tactic. The ghosts of the past, long thought buried, were once again haunting the land in search of new victims. Succeeding events only served to confirm these fears.

A second anti-Armenian pogrom, this time in Azerbaijan's second-largest city Kirovabad (now Gyandzha) in fall 1988, then the massacre of Armenians in January 1990 in the capital city of Baku, followed by the reciprocal violent expulsion of Azeris from Armenia, became the death knell of the peaceful coexistence of the two communities. In retrospect, the events of 1988-1990 led both Armenians and Azeris to believe that armed conflict between them was inevitable. These events also fundamentally redefined the centuries-old interethnic relational dynamics in the region. With the so-called population engineering of 1989-1990, the stage was set for a larger confrontation, which was only a matter of time given the rapid nationalist mobilization in Armenia, Nagorno-Karabakh and Azerbaijan. Moscow, after first losing the thread, was now losing the plot. The Armenian-Azeri confrontation had become a tragedy that was writing its own libretto. What started out as a localized "violence in peace" was fast turning into a "violence in war,"[12] propelling itself with an unmanageable inner logic toward an all-out war and ever greater human misery.

Following the breakup of the Soviet Union in 1991, Moscow's influence over the conflict dynamics diminished as Russia turned more or less inward, seeking to solve its many domestic problems and deal with new foreign policy challenges that would account for its weakened international standing. But not for long. If observers thought Russia was putting its backyard on the back burner, they were soon to be proven wrong. Mistaking regrouping for withdrawal, many thought that Russia would soon abandon the South Caucasus. But Russia was merely performing a foreign policy recalibration, one that would allow Russia to continue to project power in its near abroad despite the creeping overtures of outside actors (or even because of them). Russia was determined not to acquiesce to second-tier status.

Meanwhile, the conflict in Nagorno-Karabakh continued to destabilize the region and distort the internal politics of both Azerbaijan and Armenia. The collapse of the Soviet Union and the emergence of independent Armenia and Azerbaijan transformed what was a badly managed internal Soviet matter into a badly managed international one, broadening the pool of interested parties and opening the doors for the involvement of international organizations in peace negotiations and conflict settlement. Awash with deadlier and more potent weapons abandoned to Armenia and Azerbaijan by the withdrawing Soviet/Russian troops, what was once a Soviet monopoly soon became an international liability. Gone were the days of a conflict waged with angry shouts, stones and hunting rifles, giving way to "the technological and destructive scope of a modern war."[13] Larger weapons brought larger body counts, among them hundreds of civilians in places like Khodzhaly and Maragha, where Azerbaijani and Armenian civilians respectively were killed by advancing troops.

Although Azerbaijan enjoyed both quantitative and qualitative advantages in terms of weaponry and personnel, it would be unable to turn these advantages into battlefield success, plagued as it was by internal political divisions. Poorly planned and executed military operations all but nullified their military gains of 1992, allowing Armenian irregulars and more formal military units to turn the tide of the war by the following year. By the spring of 1994, Armenians had taken nearly full control of the formal territories of Nagorno-Karabakh, except for Shahumyan District, including seven Azerbaijani regions either partly or fully adjacent to the region, and the strategically crucial towns of Kelbadzhar and Lachin.

Exhausted by the cascading defeats on the ground and fearful of continuing political instability and social unrest, Azerbaijan pressed for a Russian-brokered ceasefire in May 1994. Although fragile, the ceasefire would largely hold for the next two decades, with occasional cross-border skirmishes along the line of contact throughout Nagorno-Karabakh and on the Armenian-Azerbaijani border.

International mediation efforts led chiefly by the Organization for Security and Cooperation in Europe (OSCE) Minsk Group cochairs (representing Russia, the US and France) tried unsuccessfully to bring the conflicting parties to the table to negotiate a lasting peace. Though these efforts were successful in managing (or rather freezing) the conflict, a stable peace based on reciprocal concessions would remain a distant dream. In a sense, the closer the parties got to a resolution the further it receded, bringing to mind a passage from Franz Kafka's *The Castle* in which the story's protagonist K. endeavors in vain to reach the eponymous Castle: "So he set off again, but it was a long way. The street he had taken, the main street in the village, did not lead to the Castle hill, it only went close by, then veered off as if on purpose, and though it didn't lead any farther from the Castle, it didn't get any closer either."[14]

The positions of the conflicting sides, diametric opposites since the conflict first began, only became more ossified over time and more entrenched – a Venn diagram with little to no overlap. Armenia, victorious in the war, maintained that any agreement that did not acknowledge the independent status of Nagorno-Karabakh was simply out of the question. Azerbaijan meanwhile insisted that its territorial integrity and sovereignty over Nagorno-Karabakh were nonnegotiable.[15] The emergent status quo dubbed "no war, no peace"[16] can only be described as a slowly intensifying "dynamic tension." It was only a matter of time before the tension gave way to a full-blown armed confrontation.

Unhappy with the status quo and flush with a windfall of oil revenue, Azerbaijan began amassing an impressive array of sophisticated Israeli, Turkish and Russian weapons systems with an eye toward changing the facts on the ground. Increasingly belligerent and dismissive of Western mediators, the government of Ilham Aliyev first tested the waters in 2016 in what came to be known as the Four-Day War. As a result of this rapid conflagration, Azerbaijan managed to claw back a sliver of its former territory: a strategic height overlooking Armenian positions. The fighting, the most violent incident since the cessation of hostilities in 1994, led to the deaths of hundreds of combatants on both sides. In essence, it was a reconnaissance by fire initiated by Azerbaijan to test the battle readiness of its troops and streamline command and operational capabilities of its army. It was also a prelude of what was to follow in the fall of 2020.

If the results of the more recent Karabakh war are anything to go by, Azerbaijan and Armenia drew qualitatively different lessons from the 2016 conflict. The four-day skirmishes were also Azerbaijan's loudest-ever disavowal of the status quo: It was no longer tenable. Accordingly, if there were no meaningful international pressure on Armenia to concede territories, Azerbaijan was willing to take matters into own hands, by fair means or foul.

Despite the violence and Azerbaijan's threats (both vocalized and tacit) to resort to violence-based means of conflict resolution, along with the growing arms race between the two countries, international diplomatic efforts continued in the same vein as before. They consisted largely of sterile declarations and ineffectual finger-wagging, and – in the best traditions of polite diplomatic equivocations – instigators would remain unnamed. Meanwhile, cross-border clashes were becoming increasingly frequent, deadly and ominous, a harbinger of things to come.[17]

In April 2018, exactly thirty years after the launch of the Karabakh Movement, mass protests once again gripped Armenia, recalling the heady days of the late 1980s. This time around, however, what the protesters were demanding redress for was not the legacy of Stalin's pen stroke transferring Karabakh to Azerbaijan, but the legacy of "[a]uthoritarianism, corruption, emigration and injustice" that had plagued Armenia under the leadership of Robert Kocharyan and Serzh Sargsyan.[18] Led by the mercurial opposition MP Nikol Pashinyan, Armenians took to the streets in unprecedented numbers. Within days of the protests, President Serzh Sargsyan would resign, paving the way for snap parliamentary elections and the installation of Pashinyan as Armenia's new prime minister.

The "Velvet Revolution" – as this change of rule in Armenia would subsequently be dubbed – apart from changing the political climate inside Armenia, brought to power a new breed of political actors long outside the country's traditional power structures who were keen on shaking up, albeit cautiously, Armenia's long-term foreign policy objectives. To distinguish themselves from the government of Serzh Sargsyan, whom they toppled, these new more or less Western-oriented elites claimed to derive their legitimacy not from Moscow, but from the Armenian people. A large claim – but one that seemed empirically verified by the mass protests in support of Pashinyan and the subsequent results of the snap elections that cemented their assumption of power.

Although Pashinyan came to power on the promise to reform Armenia's political life and sagging economy, the result left much to be desired. Reform often meant a badly concocted mix of populist sloganeering, some democratic initiatives (and some clearly undemocratic ones), and made-for-TV arrests of long feared politicians and oligarchs, which would prove popular and electrifying. Emboldened by this newfound confidence and a mandate from the people, Pashinyan subsequently set out to tackle Armenia's foreign policy elephant in the room – the conflict over Nagorno-Karabakh with neighboring Azerbaijan.

Having long criticized the negotiating stance of Armenia's earlier governments, Pashinyan set out to rewrite the script of the negotiations – without, however, jettisoning the OSCE Minsk Group framework but lauding its importance.[19] Furthermore he insisted that any negotiated deal must be equally acceptable to both Armenians and Azerbaijanis, something that previous governments were loath to voice publicly, especially in the wake of the 2016 war. Thus, his initial overtures to Azerbaijan were received positively but ever so cautiously, pending further actions on Pashinyan's part and further developments within Armenia (and to a degree within Azerbaijan). These would come soon enough.

Looking to "democratize" the negotiations, Pashinyan first attempted to shake them up by insisting on bringing Nagorno-Karabakh to the negotiating table, citing the fact he himself had not been born nor held an office in the disputed region and therefore he could not speak on behalf of its population.[20] Soon thereafter, Pashinyan would commit perhaps the biggest unforced diplomatic error of his early career as prime minister, providing Azerbaijan and its allies fresh grounds for a renewed diplomatic onslaught. During a speech delivered at the opening of the 2019 Pan-Armenian Games in Stepanakert, he would (with characteristic bombast) declare "Artsakh is Armenia, period!"[21] Although he would later try to play down the remarks, the reaction in Baku and from diplomatic quarters was unforgiving.

Next came the brief but bloody cross-border clashes in July 2020 near the Armenian village of Movses, in Tavush Province, where Azerbaijani troops tried unsuccessfully to take over an important military outpost overlooking essential roadways and a network of Azerbaijani frontline trenches. These clashes killed nearly two dozen Armenian and Azerbaijani soldiers and high-ranking military officers, among them popular Azeri general Polad Hashimov, causing mass demonstrations in Baku with protesters demanding all-out war against Armenia.[22] The intensity of the clashes, coupled with the unprecedented protests in Baku that saw the ransacking of the Milli Mejlis (National Assembly) building, served as an unmistakable indication of the inevitability of the 2020 war, and indeed its prelude.

The diplomatic efforts in the wake of the skirmishes were no different from the routine, sterile and largely featherweight declarations of the previous two decades,[23] a fact readily admitted by Richard Hoagland, the former American diplomat and US Co-Chair of the Minsk Group.[24] The widely shared (though not as widely discussed) belief was that "only a war would finally settle the problem of Nagorno-Karabakh."[25] The war of fall 2020 was the actualization of that belief. It remains to be seen, however, whether the conflict is settled or whether the current iteration of the "peace" also has an expiration date. Given the new realities on the ground and the increasing Russian presence in Armenia and Nagorno-Karabakh, this is the stuff of augury.

Why This Book?

The South Caucasus is not the center of the attention of Western media, to say the least. The occasional coverage of the region falls largely into two categories – tourism (more often than not, commissioned advertorials by local ministries of tourism) or war, as in the case of Georgia/South Ossetia in 2008. When it comes to the South Caucasus, "Journalism largely consists in saying 'Lord Jones is dead' to people who never knew Lord Jones was alive," in the words of the inimitable G.K. Chesterton.[26] People usually do not know (or perhaps do not care) about the region until and unless something of note takes place.

In general, it's something of a blessing to the Western audience when Russia is involved, in which case a ready-made geopolitical framing of the issues of concern can be pulled out of the drawer and given a new shine. Such a verdict may sound overly dolorous or unduly cynical (with apologies to those tireless journalists who risk life and limb to cover the region in times of profound crises for little personal gain), but it may not be *that* far from the truth. This is another way of saying that Western journalistic interests probably match the general or even the precise contours of Western geopolitical interests in the region.

Be that as it may, the Russian media's footprint in the region has been far larger and far deeper, if not more storied. The point made here does not mean that it was better, but that it was more. Infinitely more. As such, the output of Soviet and Russian journalists on the happenings in the region in general, and on the Nagorno-Karabakh conflict in particular, is a veritable mountain next to a veritable molehill. We can only hope that the book the reader is holding will prove to be a worthy sherpa as the reader tries to climb that mountain.

As we wrote above, Russian knowledge of the region is as vast as it is intimate. It is with this "intimate familiarity" in mind that East View Press has made available to specialists and general readers alike this carefully selected, translated, and edited collection of articles that have appeared in the Soviet and the post-Soviet Russian media since the Nagorno-Karabakh conflict first began. The goal of the book is to provide both the broadest and the deepest context of Russian understanding of the conflict as it has been dissected, litigated, and re-litigated on the pages of the Soviet and Russian press. To be sure, there is no such thing as "the" Russian view of the Armenian-Azerbaijani conflict. There are, and always have been, multiple views on how to settle it. Depending on the political (and increasingly geopolitical) winds blowing in the region, Moscow has at times favored Yerevan and at other times Baku, but in all circumstances, it has favored Moscow. To no one's surprise!

Structure of the Book

When presenting such a collection, the immediate question that needs answering is: "What is so special about Soviet and Russian press coverage of the conflict?" The importance of this press material can be summed up in the words of Bernard C. Cohen, when he wrote way back in 1964 that "the press is significantly more than a purveyor of information and opinion. It may not be successful much of the time in telling people what to think *about*." With this in mind, it is our purpose to introduce to readers the most comprehensive press coverage of the conflict apart from the press in the conflicting countries, hoping that readers will learn and study the entire range of issues that Russian commentators, analysts, and politicians considered worth examining and commenting upon – in short, what people should think and think about.

More than anything else, we envision our book *Black Garden Aflame* to be a ready-made tool for historical, political, and social analysis for scholars and historians specializing in the late Soviet period and the South Caucasus, as well as students of nationalism and ethnopolitical conflicts. Divided thematically into four parts and consisting of fourteen chapters (each in turn chronologically structured), the book begins with the first stirrings of what political scientist Mark Beissinger has called "nationalist mobilization" in the NKAO and the Armenian Soviet Social-ist Republic. It moves from the heady days of the Karabakh movement to the counterdemonstrations in Azerbaijan, to the anti-Armenian violence that broke out through Azerbaijani cities, setting the stage for the unraveling of the Soviet Union. Part One also covers early Soviet efforts to manage the conflict (largely un-successful ones), which resulted in the emergence of guerrilla warfare and its rapid transformation into a larger regional war.

Part Two segues into press coverage of the international dimensions of the conflict. If in late 1980s the conflict was mostly an internal Soviet matter, with the collapse of the USSR it was no longer so. What was initially a dispute within a Union republic, then between two Union republics, had become an interstate conflict. The international dimension of the Nagorno-Karabakh conflict also meant a new set of ground rules that involved a new set of international actors with clashing interests and political objectives. Covered in Part Two is also the interwar period, focusing mostly on the decades-long international diplomatic efforts led by the OSCE Minsk Group to resolve the conflict.

Part Three focuses on the involvement of what we may term "external regional actors" in shaping the conflict dynamics. Divided into four chapters devoted to Tur-key, Russia, Iran and the US respectively, the articles cover the evolving regional dynamics in the South Caucasus following the disintegration of the Soviet Union, thus situating the Nagorno-Karabakh conflict in the broader context of regional power play. Especially important for the Russian commentariat were the Turkish and US overtures occasioned by the conflict and the emergence of newly independent countries who sought to chart a foreign policy that reflected their national priorities.

Lastly, Part Four provides extensive coverage of the prelude to the 2020 Karabakh conflict ("Karabakh War 2.0"), concluding with reportage of the war itself and the aftermath. These three chapters take readers from the April 2016 Four-Day War to the military, political and diplomatic developments in Armenia, Nagorno Karabakh and Azerbaijan. If Chapters 12 and 13 focus on the growing military imbalance between the conflicting parties, the last chapter focuses on the actualization of that imbalance through war.

At the time of this writing, the second Armenian-Azerbaijani war over Nagorno-Karabakh has ended, but the conflict is still ongoing. Despite Azerbaijan's and Turkey's insistence that the status of the region is no longer an issue, the truth of the matter is quite different: It was and still is an issue.[27] What remains to be seen is whether it will be resolved any time soon, and whether the envisioned solution will be acceptable to both sides.

NOTES

1. "Ogromnaya tragediya": Putin – o konflikte v Nagornom Karabakhe ("Great Tragedy": Putin on the Conflict in Nagorno-Karabakh." *Novaya gazeta*, October 7, 2020. Accessed on October 7, 2020, https://novayagazeta.ru/news/2020/10/07/164749-ogromnaya-tragediya-putin-o-konflikte-v-nagornom-karabahe.

2. Gerard Toal, *Near Abroad: Putin, the West and the Contest over Ukraine and the Caucasus* (New York: Oxford University Press, 2017), 17.

3. Robert Nalbandov, *Not by Bread Alone: Russian Foreign Policy under Putin* (Lincoln: Potomac Books, 2016), 248.

4. The reader may consult Nikolas K. Gvosdev and Christopher Marsh, *Russian Foreign Policy: Interests, Vectors, and Sectors* (Washington, D.C.: CQ Press, 2013), for a useful discussion on various Russian foreign policy vectors.

5. Igor S. Ivanov, *The New Russian Diplomacy* (Washington, D.C.: Brookings Institution Press and the Nixon Center, 2002), 90.

6. "Soobshchenie," *Pravda*, March 1, 1988, p. 2.

7. Laurence Broers, *Armenia and Azerbaijan: Anatomy of a Rivalry*, (Edinburgh: Edinburgh University Press, 2021), 28.

8. Much ink has been spilled by historians trying to understand the circumstances surrounding the transfer of Karabakh to Azerbaijan, but in the absence of clear documentary evidence Stalin's decision has given rise to a plethora of opinions, some of them informed and some conspiratorial. Stalin's decision-making remains a subject of conjecture. For the best treatment of the topic, the reader may consult: Arsène Saparov, "Why Autonomy? The Making of Nagorno-Karabakh Autonomous Region 1918–1925," *Europe-Asia Studies* 64, No. 2 (March 1, 2012): 281–323.

9. "President Aliyev: Under Great Leader Heydar Aliyev, Percentage of Azerbaijani Population in Nagorno-Karabakh Increased Sharply, Doubled," *Trend.Az*, November 25, 2019, https://en.trend.az/azerbaijan/politics/3153675.html.

10. Address by M. S. Gorbachev, General Secretary of the CPSU Central Committee, to the Working People and Peoples of Azerbaijan and Armenia, *Bakinsky rabochy*, February 27, 1988, p. 1.

11. "On Events in Nagorno-Karabakh," *Pravda*, February 24, 1988, p. 2.

12. On the difference between the two the reader may consult Stathis N. Kalyvas, *The Logic of Violence in Civil War* (New York: Cambridge University Press, 2006), 22–23.

13. Broers, *op. cit.*, 32.

14. Franz Kafka, *The Castle*, trans. Mark Harman (New York: Schocken, 1998), 10.

15. For a more extensive discussion on the early stages of the diplomatic efforts to settle the conflict the reader may consult Vicken Cheterian, *War and Peace in the Caucasus: Russia's Troubled Frontier* (New York: Columbia University Press, 2008), 320–26.

16. See, for instance, Laura Baghdasarian and Arif Yunusov, "War, Social Change and 'No War, No Peace' Syndromes in Azerbaijani and Armenian Societies," *Accord: An International Review of Peace Initiatives* 17 (2005): 52–55.

17. "Nagorno-Karabakh's Gathering War Clouds" (International Crisis Group, June 1, 2017), https://www.crisisgroup.org/europe-central-asia/caucasus/nagorno-karabakh-azerbaijan/244-nagorno-karabakhs-gathering-war-clouds.

18. Gaïdz Minassian, *The Armenian Experience: From Ancient Times to Independence* (New York: I.B. Tauris, 2020), 170.

19. See Al Jazeera English, *Ready to Negotiate with Ilham Aliyev: Armenia PM Pashinyan | Talk to Al Jazeera*, accessed July 20, 2021, https://www.youtube.com/watch?v=3CU9gU_RpLU.

20. See CIVILNET, *Democratizing Karabakh Negotiations: Arsen Kharatyan*, accessed July 20, 2021, https://www.youtube.com/watch?v=dPEvBIrgQIM.

21. Nikol Pashinyan, "Heghapokhutyan arzheknere hamahaykakan arzhekner en … ," August 5, 2020, https://www.primeminister.am/hy/press-release/item/2019/08/05/Rally/. The word "Artsakh" is the Armenian name for Nagorno-Karabakh. Curiously, the English version of the speech omits the emphatic expression "period."

22. "Azerbaijan Protesters Demand War after Armenia Clashes," *BBC News*, July 15, 2020, https://www.bbc.com/news/world-europe-53415693.

23. See, for example, "Press Statement by the Co-Chairs of the OSCE Minsk Group," accessed September 21, 2021, https://www.osce.org/minsk-group/457225.

24. Richard Hoagland, "Does the Minsk Group Still Have a Role?," *International Conflict Resolution Center* (blog), March 26, 2021, https://icrcenter.org/does-the-minsk-group-still-have-a-role/. In this article, penned not long after the 2020 war, Hoagland declared that "to be blunt, very, very little ever got accomplished."

25. *Ibid.*

26. Gilbert K. Chesterton, *The Wisdom of Father Brown* (New York: John Lane Company, 1914), 175.

27. Astghik Bedevian, "U.S. Calls for Negotiated Settlement of Nagorno-Karabakh Conflict, Raises Status Issue," *Radio Free Europe / Radio Liberty*, accessed September 22, 2021, https://www.azatutyun.am/a/31424253.html.

Part One |

Outbreak of Conflict in Late Soviet Period

Chapter 1 | Demonstrations in Armenia and Nagorno-Karabakh

NAGORNO-KARABAKH AUTONOMOUS PROVINCE'S PARTY AKTIV MEETS

Bakinsky rabochy, Feb. 23, 1988, p. 2.

The province's Party aktiv met in Stepanakert on Feb. 22. It discussed urgent measures to overcome the negative phenomena that are taking place in the Nagorno-Karabakh Autonomous Province.

G. P. Razumovsky, candidate member of the Politburo of the CPSU Central Committee and Secretary of the CPSU Central Committee, spoke to the aktiv.

He said that recently the CPSU Central Committee, the Presidium of the USSR Supreme Soviet and other central agencies have been receiving letters and statements from the Armenian population of the Nagorno-Karabakh Autonomous Province asking that the province be joined to the Armenian Republic. Demonstrations are taking place in Nagorno-Karabakh itself, during which the same demands are advanced. I must say that the CPSU Central Committee assesses the actions and demands aimed at revising the existing national-territorial structure as at variance with the interests of the working people of the Azerbaijan Republic and the Armenian Republic. These actions and demands harm the republics' national relations and may, if responsible measures are not taken now, lead to serious consequences.

All this became possible as a result of irresponsible appeals and actions by certain individuals, as well as of the passive, temporizing position of the Party and Soviet agencies of the indicated republics, whose leaderships have taken a superficial approach in assessing the situation.

The CPSU Central Committee has instructed the Bureau of the Azerbaijan Communist Party Central Committee and the Bureau of the Armenian Communist Party Central Committee to take the necessary coordinated measures to normalize the situation and to channel all means of political and ideological influence into explaining the Leninist nationalities policy and its essence at the present stage. In all work, we must proceed from the premise that the national question requires close and constant attention to national features and psychology and consideration for the vital interests of the working people. Full responsibility for the normalization of the situation rests with the Bureaus of these republics' Communist Party Central

Committees and with Comrades K. M. Bagirov and K. S. Demirchyan, the First Secretaries of those Central Committees, personally.

The formation of the Nagorno-Karabakh Autonomous Province was a great achievement of the Leninist nationalities policy. The brotherhood of peoples proclaimed by the October Revolution became a reality, and the best sons of both the Armenian and the Azerbaijani peoples have given their efforts, knowledge, health and even their lives to it....

The Nagorno-Karabakh Autonomous Province is developing dynamically. The railroad, the power-transmission lines, the gas pipelines – all this links the Nagorno-Karabakh Autonomous Province to the Azerbaijan Republic in a very close way.... Of course, not all questions in the republic or in the province have been resolved, and there are still many shortcomings in the economic and cultural spheres, but that's the way life is. Urgent problems should be solved by work and concrete deeds. If necessary, the USSR government is prepared to examine proposals on these questions....

Comrade Razumovsky went on to say that it is to our ideological adversaries' advantage to shake our unity. Their work is directed toward this end. If we now allow ourselves to be drawn into various sorts of debates, this will only slow the accomplishment of urgent social and economic tasks in our society. Consequently, we must display restraint, prudence, true Party spirit and wisdom and think about the future of the homeland. This is our civic and patriotic duty. It is our firm position....

Z. M. Movsesyan, First Secretary of the Stepanakert City Party Committee, ... B. S. Kevorkov, first secretary of the province Party committee, ... [and 14 others] who spoke at the aktiv meeting noted that the province's Communists and working people are deeply concerned about the existing situation, which is the result of the actions of irresponsible individuals, as well as of a loss of political vigilance on the part of a number of Party committees, Communists, officials of Soviet and Young Communist League organizations and economic managers and their passive, temporizing position.

The speakers made a self-critical analysis of the situation in the province and gave a principled assessment of the activity of the Party committees and local bodies of power that have not managed to show maturity and foresight.

Instead of conducting active organizational, political and ideological-upbringing work in this difficult situation, many executives let themselves get carried away by slogans that divert the working people, young people and the whole population from solving urgent problems of social, economic and cultural life.

The province Party committee, its bureau and secretariat and the first secretary of the province Party committee, Comrade B. S. Kevorkov personally, have not taken an aggressive stance on these questions. It was pointedly said that over many years, urgent questions of a social and economic nature and concern for the development of culture and education in the province were lost sight of by the province Party committee and the Azerbaijan Communist Party Central Committee. A number of other problems requiring concrete solutions were also raised.

The Party aktiv assured the CPSU Central Committee and its Politburo that the province's Communists understand the very crucial nature of the situation and emphasized that they have enough experience, strength and Party conviction to normalize the situation and to channel people's efforts into the accomplishment of the first-priority tasks of the province's social and economic development.

P. N. Demichev, candidate member of the Politburo of the CPSU Central Committee and First Vice-Chairman of the Presidium of the USSR Supreme Soviet, and K. M. Bagirov, First Secretary of the Azerbaijan Communist Party Central Committee, spoke at the aktiv meeting.... (Azerbaijan News Agency)

ADDRESS BY K. S. DEMIRCHYAN, FIRST SECRETARY OF THE ARMENIAN COMMUNIST PARTY CENTRAL COMMITTEE, ON ARMENIAN TELEVISION FEB. 22, 1988

Kommunist, Feb. 23, 1988, p. 2.

Dear comrades! Circumstances dictate that I address you.

As you know, rallies have been taking place in the past few days in Yerevan's opera theater square in support of the request by the population of the Nagorno-Karabakh Autonomous Province that it be included in Soviet Armenia. The rallies have adopted appeals on this question to republic and Union leadership bodies.

The situation that currently exists around Nagorno-Karabakh is of a politically serious nature. A superficial approach to it might do great harm to relations between nationalities and to the friendship among our peoples. The situation that has come about is cause for concern, and it demands from all of us a high degree of responsibility and the taking of very vigorous measures to prevent a development of events that might lead to unpredictable or even hard-to-rectify consequences.

The CPSU Central Committee has held a comprehensive discussion of the events in Nagorno-Karabakh. Actions and demands aimed at revising the existing national-territorial structure in that region are at variance with the interests of the working people of the Armenian and Azerbaijan Republics. We have been instructed to take the necessary coordinated measures to improve the situation....

I would like to bring it to your attention that the Azerbaijan and Armenian Communist Party Central Committees and those republics' Councils of Ministers have been instructed to work out the social and economic measures that it is necessary to take in Nagorno-Karabakh.

The Armenian Communist Party Central Committee calls on the republic's labor collectives, their Party organizations and all Communists, working people and our young people to display a high level of political and civic awareness....

We appeal once again to all citizens of Soviet Armenia to display, at this critical moment, courage, vigilance, patience, political maturity and a high degree of organization, and to join more actively in constructive work to restructure all aspects of our public life and to strengthen the internationalist brotherhood of the Soviet peoples.

ON EVENTS IN NAGORNO-KARABAKH

Pravda, Feb. 24, 1988, p. 2.

In Nagorno-Karabakh Autonomous Province, Azerbaijan Republic, there were demonstrations in the past few days by part of the Armenian population demanding that Nagorno-Karabakh be included in the Armenian Republic. As a result of irresponsible appeals by certain extremist-minded individuals, violations of public order were provoked.

After reviewing information on the events in Nagorno-Karabakh Autonomous Province, the CPSU Central Committee believes that the actions and demands aimed at a revision of the existing national-territorial structure are at variance with the interests of the working people of the Azerbaijan and Armenian Republics and harm relations between nationalities.

Consistently guided by the Leninist principles of nationalities policy, the CPSU Central Committee has appealed to the patriotic and internationalist feelings of the Armenian and Azerbaijani population not to succumb to provocations by nationalistic elements and to strengthen in every way that great asset of socialism the fraternal friendship of Soviet peoples.

The CPSU Central Committee has instructed the Azerbaijan and Armenian Communist Party Central Committees to take the necessary measures to remedy the existing situation and to direct all means of political and ideological influence toward the elucidation of the Leninist nationalities policy and its essence at the present stage. All work is to proceed from the premise that the national question requires close and constant attention to national features and psychology and consideration of the vital interests of the working people.

The republics' Party and Soviet agencies have been instructed to normalize the situation concerning Nagorno-Karabakh, ensure public order and the strict observance of socialist legality, and work out and implement measures for the further social, economic and cultural development of the autonomous province. – (TASS)

PLENARY SESSION OF THE NAGORNO-KARABAKH PROVINCE PARTY COMMITTEE

Bakinsky rabochy, Feb. 24, 1988, p. 2.

On Feb. 23, 1988, a plenary session of the Nagorno-Karabakh Province Party Committee was held to consider an organizational question.

The plenary session relieved B. S. Kevorkov of his duties as first secretary and member of the bureau of the province Party committee for shortcomings in his work. G. A. Pogosyan, who had been working as first vice-chairman of the province Soviet executive committee and Chairman of the Nagorno-Karabakh Autonomous Province Agro-Industrial Committee, was elected First Secretary of the Nagorno-Karabakh Province Party Committee.

K. M. Bagirov, First Secretary of the Azerbaijan Communist Party Central Committee, spoke at the plenary session. Taking part in the plenary session's work were V. N. Konovalov, T. Kh. Orudzhev and R. V. Akhundov; V. A. Kondratyev, head of a sector of the CPSU Central Committee; and V. M. Yashin, a high-ranking official of the CPSU Central Committee....

* * *

Genrikh Andreyevich Pogosyan.Genrikh Andreyevich Pogosyan, born in 1931 in the city of Stepanakert, Nagorno-Karabakh Autonomous Province, Azerbaijan Republic, is an Armenian, has been a member of the CPSU since 1961 and has a higher education – in 1955, he graduated from the Moscow Institute of Agricultural Mechanization and Electrification. After graduating from the institute, he worked as senior mechanic at the Gadrut Machine and Tractor Station, as an engineer for and deputy manager of the Nagorno-Karabakh Winemaking Trust, as head of the Stepanakert section of the Azerbaijan Sanitary Engineering Installation Trust, as chief engineer for the Nagorno-Karabakh Province Soviet Executive Committee's department of local industry, and as Director of the Nagorno-Karabakh Province Administration of the Azerbaijan Republic Farm Equipment Association. In 1971, he was elected Chairman of the Stepanakert City Soviet Executive Committee. From 1974 to 1979, he was manager of the Nagorno-Karabakh Autonomous Province State Farm Winemaking Trust, and from 1979 to 1985 he was general director of the Nagorno-Karabakh Agro-Industrial Association.

Since 1985, he has been First Vice-Chairman of the Nagorno-Karabakh Province Soviet Executive Committee and Chairman of the Nagorno-Karabakh Autonomous Province Agro-Industrial Committee.

He is a member of the Bureau of the Nagorno-Karabakh Province Party Committee of the Azerbaijan Communist Party and a Deputy to the Nagorno-Karabakh Province Soviet.

ADDRESS BY V. I. DOLGIKH, CANDIDATE MEMBER OF THE POLITBURO OF THE CPSU CENTRAL COMMITTEE AND SECRETARY OF THE CPSU CENTRAL COMMITTEE, ON ARMENIAN TELEVISION

Kommunist, Feb. 25, 1988, p. 1.

Dear comrades! This is the second day that Comrade A. I. Lukyanov and I have been in your republic on assignment from the Politburo of the CPSU Central Committee.

This is connected with the well-known events in Nagorno-Karabakh and Yerevan, the aim of which is a revision of the national-territorial structure in this region that has existed since the 1920s. Despite the exceptional complexity and delicacy of this question, groups of people are demanding that it be resolved immediately.

We would like to tell you the CPSU Central Committee's position on this problem.

Yesterday and today, we had long conversations with representatives of those who were at the rallies and with working people on the streets and in the squares.... I will say frankly that the Politburo of the CPSU Central Committee is seriously concerned by the current impermissible aggravation of passions and emotions around the Karabakh question.

Holding rallies and disrupting the rhythm of work at enterprises, as well as classes in educational institutions, is completely unacceptable for the study and resolution of these questions.

In Nagorno-Karabakh, things have gone as far as clashes between groups of Armenians and Azerbaijanis, and there have been casualties.

This development of events may lead to unpredictable consequences and, of course, it clouds the fraternal relations between the Armenian and Azerbaijani peoples.

For that reason, on Feb. 21 the Politburo of the CPSU Central Committee adopted a decision on this question that gives a principled assessment of what has happened.

The Politburo of the CPSU Central Committee has demanded that the Azerbaijan and Armenian Communist Party Central Committees take all measures to normalize the situation....

The situation in the Nagorno-Karabakh Autonomous Province is stabilizing, thanks to the restraint and political responsibility shown by Communists and the overwhelming majority of the population....

The situation in Yerevan is not improving; crowded rallies continue to be held in which representatives of various strata of the population are participating, and this is complicating the lives of the city's residents and evoking legitimate protests from them....

Restructuring is under way in the country, and democracy is expanding. But this does not mean encouragement for a wild outburst of passions, violations of public order, or actions not in the interests of socialism.

The meeting of Armenia's Party aktiv that was held on Feb. 23, 1988 ... asked the CPSU Central Committee to give comprehensive consideration to the problem of Nagorno-Karabakh in conjunction with other questions of this sort during preparations for a plenary session of the CPSU Central Committee.

We have been instructed to announce that this problem will be studied and examined most attentively and in the appropriate form. But this will take time.

The situation that has come about in Yerevan may impede, not facilitate, this study and examination. We call on all of you to show maturity and to restore the normal rhythm of life and work in the city of Yerevan and in the republic....

THE NECESSARY STEPS ARE BEING TAKEN

Pravda, Feb. 26, 1988, p. 2.

Stepanakert (Nagorno-Karabakh Autonomous Province, Azerbaijan Republic), Feb. 25 (TASS) – USSR Deputy Prosecutor General A. F. Katusev is in Nagorno-Karabakh, Azerbaijan. In an interview with a TASS correspondent who asked him to describe the current situation in the Nagorno-Karabakh Autonomous Province, he said:

"At present, explanatory work aimed at normalizing the situation and establishing a businesslike atmosphere is under way among the autonomous province's population.

"A study of the state of affairs in the area shows that none of the many conjectures and rumors that are being spread, primarily outside the Nagorno-Karabakh Autonomous Province, rumors to which gullible people frequently succumb, have any basis in fact. For example, a story about an alleged assault by State Motor Vehicle Inspectorate personnel on a car owned by a resident of Stepanakert was widely circulated, but it has proved to be false. Moreover, a rumor was spread that 60 citizens of the Armenian nationality had been murdered, although in fact not one person of the Armenian nationality has been murdered.

"Unfortunately, there are still quite a few gossip-lovers. To hear them tell it, it's impossible to live in the province. I won't deny that there have been instances of lawbreaking that are criminally punishable. Each of them is under investigation.

"At the same time, I can flatly state that the rights and legitimate interests of the working people are being reliably protected."

MAINTAIN CALM AND ORDER

Kommunist, Feb. 26, 1988, p. 1.

Editors' Note. – A correspondent for the Armenian News Agency met with V. P. Trushin, USSR First Deputy Minister of Internal Affairs, and asked him to answer a number of questions.

* * *

Question. – Vasily Petrovich, how do you assess the situation in Yerevan?

Answer. – I must say that in this difficult atmosphere, the city's population is showing restraint and is not committing any violations of public order.

At the same time, the large gatherings of people on the streets and in the squares inevitably impede the city's life. On many streets, the movement of municipal transport is interrupted, traffic jams are created, and the situation is conducive to accidents. This is making it difficult to maintain uninterrupted deliveries of foodstuffs and basic necessities to stores and is hampering the work of medical first-aid squads and other municipal and consumer services. After all, a good many instances of sudden fits and indisposition occur when people have been standing for many hours or walking in processions for a long time.

Something else worries us, too. The participants in the rallies include quite a few teenagers, whose behavior sometimes gets out of the control of adults and parents. Alarmed parents often telephone borough police stations in the evenings. And there is reason for anxiety. Thus, on Feb. 24 about 70 people climbed onto a truck carrying building materials that was parked in the street. It was only by good fortune that the vehicle didn't tip over.

It is not ruled out that in the present situation certain irresponsible people and hooligan elements might at any moment provoke people into actions that could lead to serious consequences. This must not be allowed. Staff members of internal affairs agencies are taking every measure to prevent any incidents.

Q. – Couldn't you tell us about the real state of affairs in Nagorno-Karabakh Province?

A. – There are all kinds of people. Some, out of naivete, others with malicious intent, are spreading various cock-and-bull stories and rumors about the events that have taken place in Nagorno-Karabakh. There are also specific examples of exaggerated rumors. Yesterday I was approached by a man who demanded that I urgently look into and intervene in events that were supposedly taking place in a district of Karabakh. There, my conversational partner asserted, malefactors had overturned buses filled with people. We checked it out and found that nothing of the kind had happened in the province; the situation in the province is returning to normal. All communities and roads are under our control. No crimes against individuals or instances of malicious hooliganism have been registered in the past few days....

ADDRESS BY M. S. GORBACHEV, GENERAL SECRETARY OF THE CPSU CENTRAL COMMITTEE, TO THE WORKING PEOPLE AND PEOPLES OF AZERBAIJAN AND ARMENIA

Bakinsky rabochy, Feb. 27, 1988. p. 1.

Dear comrades! I am addressing you in connection with the events in and around Nagorno-Karabakh.

The question of transferring this autonomous province from the Azerbaijan Republic to the Armenian Republic has been raised. A crucial and dramatic character has been imparted to this matter, which has led to tension and even to actions going beyond the law.

I will say frankly that the CPSU Central Committee is concerned by this development of events, which is fraught with some very serious consequences.

We are not in favor of evading a frank discussion of various ideas and proposals. But this must be done calmly, within the framework of the democratic process and legality, without allowing the slightest damage to the internationalist solidarity of our peoples. Very serious questions of a people's fate must not be made subject to uncontrolled feelings and emotions.

It is very important that people assess their concerns not only in the context of local conditions but also with consideration for the processes of revolutionary renewal that have gotten under way in the country.

Yes, there are unsolved problems in our life. But fanning discord and mistrust among peoples only impedes the solution of those problems. That would run counter to our socialist principles and our morality and to the traditions of friendship and brotherhood among Soviet people.

We live in a multinational country; moreover, all the republics, many provinces, and even cities and settlements in our country are multinational. The point of the Leninist nationalities policy consists in achieving a situation in which every person and every nation can develop freely and every people can satisfy its requirements in all spheres of sociopolitical life, in its native language and culture, and in its customs and religious beliefs.

Socialist internationalism is the source of our enormous strength. The genuine brotherhood and unity of peoples that is our path.

The great Armenian poet Ye. Charents[1] said it well when he addressed Soviet Azerbaijan: "In the name of a past of immeasurable suffering, in the name of the life that appeared before us amid victories, in the name of an amicable union we send a fraternal people greetings, greetings."

And how this is echoed by the words of that great son of the Azerbaijani people, S. Vurgun:[2] "We do not live as neighbors but as the closest of friends. Since olden times, our peoples have taken from each other fire for their hearths and their daily bread."

No mother will consent to a situation in which her children are threatened by national discord where there should be strong bonds of friendship, equality and mutual assistance – truly a great gain of socialism.

A good many shortcomings and difficulties have accumulated in the Nagorno-Karabakh Autonomous Province. The province's new leadership must take urgent measures to correct the situation. The CPSU Central Committee has issued clear-cut recommendations on this score and will directly monitor their fulfillment.

The most important thing now is to concentrate on overcoming the situation that has come about, on solving the concrete economic, social, ecological and other problems that have accumulated in Azerbaijan and Armenia, in the spirit of the policy of restructuring and renewal that is being carried out throughout our country.

The traditions of friendship between the Azerbaijani and Armenian peoples that have evolved during the years of Soviet rule must be cherished and strengthened in every way. Only this approach corresponds to the genuine interests of all the USSR's peoples.

You know that it is intended to devote a plenary session of our Party Central Committee especially to the development of national relations. A broad range of questions in this highly important social sphere will be discussed, and paths toward the concrete solution of social, economic, cultural and other problems will be mapped out on the basis of the fundamental gains of the Leninist nationalities policy.

We are all Soviet citizens. We have a common history and common victories, and we have in our past great labor, sorrows and losses. We are engaged in the great endeavor of restructuring, on the success of which the fate of socialism, our homeland and every one of us depends.

I appeal to you, comrades, to your political awareness and sense of responsibility, to your good sense. In this test, too, we will uphold our Soviet internationalism, our unshakable faith that we can ensure the progress of our society and the prosperity of all its citizens only in a friendly family of all our peoples.

I call on you to display civic maturity and restraint, to return to normal life and work, and to maintain public order.

The time has come for reason and sober decisions. – M. GORBACHEV.

A TIME FOR REASON AND SOBER DECISIONS

Pravda, March 5, 1988, p. 2.

A TASS correspondent met with Genrikh Andreyevich Pogosyan, First Secretary of the Nagorno-Karabakh Province Committee of the Azerbaijan Communist Party, and asked him to answer some questions:

Question. – How have the province's Communists and working people received the address by the General Secretary of the CPSU Central Committee to the working people and peoples of Azerbaijan and Armenia?

Answer. – With understanding and a sense of gratitude. M. S. Gorbachev's address is convincing evidence of very close attention to, deep concern for and sincere interest in solving the basic social and economic problems that have arisen at the new stage of the development of the Nagorno-Karabakh Autonomous Province. We fully share his thought that a carefully considered and democratic approach is necessary in resolving these questions.

The address clearly indicates that new approaches and new guidelines are needed in overcoming the difficulties of growth. To this end, a calm and businesslike atmosphere must be established in the province. The main thing, as M. S. Gorbachev said in his address, is to display civic maturity and restraint and to return to normal life.

The situation in Nagorno-Karabakh is returning to normal. People are going to work in an organized fashion. Industrial enterprises are approaching the planned rates. The Nagorno-Karabakh Autonomous Province's collective farms and state farms are beginning to perform spring field work and are increasing output on livestock sections. Transportation, municipal-service enterprises and all vital services were operating normally to start with.

Nagorno-Karabakh is multinational in its makeup.... Of course, there are also unresolved problems in our life. But it would be a mistake to think that one can gain some sort of capital by exaggerating them. Today, it is important not to allow certain people to play on this. Democracy must not be understood one-sidedly, with rights separated from responsibilities. That would harm the social and economic development of society and the friendship of peoples.

I want to note that, through the fault of the former leadership of the province Party committee, artificial difficulties were created involving cultural exchanges, the provision of belles lettres and school textbooks in the native language, and other aspects of the multifaceted and traditional ties between the working people of Nagorno-Karabakh and fraternal Armenia. These problems can and must be solved promptly and efficiently.

Q. – What measures are being taken for the further normalization of the situation in the Nagorno-Karabakh Autonomous Province?

A. – Extensive ideological, propaganda and explanatory work is now under way in workers' collectives, on state farms and collective farms and in educational institutions. It is aimed at making every resident of the province thoroughly aware of the great clarity and precise position of the CPSU Central Committee, making this a time of reason and sober decisions for every individual, and bringing to the fore a sense of civic duty and responsibility for the common cause.

The Nagorno-Karabakh Autonomous Province's industrial enterprises are linked by close economic bonds with many related enterprises in the nation. In conditions of economic accountability, every lost hour will damage not only the province's enterprises but also our partners in various regions of the country.

Party, Soviet, trade union, economic and Young Communist League agencies are doing everything they can to completely stabilize the province's economic and political life, so that the toilers of Nagorno-Karabakh will make up for the arrears that have been created and will fulfill their contractual commitments....

NOTES FROM A DIARY: THE FRUITS OF COMPLACENCY AND INACTION –
A Few Days in Nagorno-Karabakh

By Karen Khachaturov, Vice-Chairman of the Board of the Novosti Press Agency. *Moskovskiye novosti*, March 20, 1988, p. 10.

Stepanakert and Baku... Back in the 1920s, two national formations with different prerogatives were created in regions of Azerbaijan with a primarily Armenian population: the Nakhichevan Autonomous Soviet Socialist Republic (it has its own Constitution and ensures comprehensive economic and social development on its territory) and the Nagorno-Karabakh Autonomous Province. Unfortunately, neither the Constitution of the USSR nor the Union-republic Constitutions specify the rights of autonomous provinces....

Over a period of several days, I had a great many conversations and discussions with representatives of various strata of the population. They put forth essentially the same kind of arguments. They emphasized that the matter at hand now is the restoration of justice, since in the 1920s Nagorno-Karabakh had been declared an integral part of Soviet Armenia. They also emphasized the uniqueness of the situation in the Nagorno-Karabakh Autonomous Province, the only autonomous formation in the Soviet Union for which there is a Union republic whose national makeup is similar and numerically predominant. But there is also a counterargument: Several generations of inhabitants of Azerbaijan do not agree with this viewpoint. Moreover, the Nagorno-Karabakh Autonomous Province does not share a common boundary with Armenia and has been integrated into the economic complex of Azerbaijan.

At the same time, one cannot brush aside the demographic problems in the Nagorno-Karabakh Autonomous Province (which accounts for 2.6% of the population and 5% of the territory of Azerbaijan), where, according to census data, over two decades (1959-1979) the proportion of Armenians decreased from 84.4% to 75.8%, while that of Azerbaijanis grew from 13.8% to 22.9%. In this context, consider the fate of the Nakhichevan Autonomous Republic, where since the beginning of the century the Armenian population, which once comprised nearly half of the inhabitants of Nakhichevan, has decreased to less than 2%.

I would look for the reason for this situation not so much in higher growth rates for the Azerbaijani population as in the deformation of the social, economic and cultural conditions of life for the autonomous province's population. According to all indices, statistics have prepared a place in the sun for the Nagorno-Karabakh Autonomous Province. But there are serious grounds for doubting these optimistic calculations. The rights of autonomy have been infringed, and sometimes they are a mere fiction. Job assignments, even for physicians or teachers, are sanctioned by an [Azerbaijan] Republic ministry. A thick curtain has been hung between the Nagorno-Karabakh Autonomous Province and Armenia, which could at least provide books in the native [Armenian] language. After all, even the curricula of the humanities division of the Stepanakert Teacher-Training Institute – the only higher educational institution in the Nagorno-Karabakh Autonomous Province – lack a course in the history and geography of Armenia.

The social sphere has been especially neglected....

The events in Nagorno-Karabakh, despite their specific nature, are only one of the sore spots that have been discovered recently in national relations. This is why a plenary session of the CPSU Central Committee will be devoted especially to the development of national relations. In my opinion, one important question is guaranteeing the social, economic and cultural rights of the autonomous province against anticonstitutional, unlawful actions....

EMOTIONS AND REASON – On the Events in and Around Nagorno-Karabakh

By Yu. Arakelyan, Pravda Correspondent for the Armenian Republic; Z. Kadymbekov, Pravda Correspondent for the Azerbaijan Republic; and G. Ovcharenko, Pravda special correspondent. *Pravda*, March 21, 1988, p. 3.

At this point, while the events that riveted the attention of the entire country on Azerbaijan and Armenia are still weighing heavily on our hearts and minds, it is difficult to fully grasp what has happened. Anything said in haste or without forethought can evoke, and indeed has evoked, new outbursts of emotions, passions and even crimes. On the other hand, we mustn't remain silent: The incredible rumors that are making the rounds, largely at the instigation of Western "radio voices" whose information comes from people with a stake in inflaming emotions, can also lead to serious consequences.

So, just what is going on in and around Nagorno-Karabakh?

On Feb. 20 an event occurred that was unprecedented for our country with respect to relations among the nationalities. By a majority of votes the Deputies of the Nagorno-Karabakh Autonomous Province Soviet adopted an appeal to the Azerbaijan and Armenian Republic Supreme Soviets requesting that the province be transferred from Azerbaijan to Armenia, and to the USSR Supreme Soviet requesting that it consider this issue....

The problem of Nagorno-Karabakh is not as simple as it may appear at first glance, and its roots go back many centuries. The territorial affiliation of this region is probably the most complicated in the history of nationality relations among the peoples of the Transcaucasus. In the past it led to many tragic conflicts, aggravated by religious differences. Just between 1918 and 1920, before the establishment of Soviet power in Azerbaijan and Armenia, almost one-fifth of the population of Karabakh was exterminated in a fratricidal war unleashed by the Musavatists and Dashnaks.

There were conflicts over the resolution of the region's territorial affiliation during the first years of Soviet power as well. Suffice it to say that the Nagorno-Karabakh Autonomous Province was not made a part of the Azerbaijan Republic until July 1923. That might have seemed to close the matter.

On the contrary, the problem of Nagorno-Karabakh continued to come up again and again. As a rule, this happened when Armenian leaders stood to benefit by distracting public attention from the numerous unresolved economic and social problems and from the improper operating style and methods employed by the Party organization. At times like these the suggestion would be made that the autonomous province be transferred to the Armenian Republic on the grounds that the majority of the region's population is Armenian and the agricultural conditions there are similar to the conditions in Armenia's mountainous regions. In turn, the leadership of Azerbaijan would put forward counterproposals calling for a change in the administrative boundaries of the Armenian Republic, as well as of Georgia and Dagestan, based on the national composition of a number of districts in these republics.

Scholars from both republics joined the dispute. They "dug" back through the centuries in an effort to determine which people this land had originally belonged to. Unfortunately, the battling scholars did not distinguish themselves with their meticulousness or objectivity, nor did they clarify the issue, but only succeeded in confusing it further....

When the territorial affiliation of Nagorno-Karabakh was being decided, the Communists of the Caucasus Bureau of the Russian Communist Party (Bolsheviks) took into consideration first and foremost which republic would enable the region to develop more rapidly in economic and social respects, so that the lives of the people would be improved. These conditions turned out to be more favorable in Azerbaijan, with its industrial and multinational complex. So this was what determined the choice. It was not a question of which republic to live in, but of how to live. So as not to offend the national feelings of the majority of the population – Armenians – the province was granted autonomy.

Unfortunately, although the style and methods used during the period of the personality cult did get condemned, for some reason the issue of the further development of Leninist traditions of nationality policy was self-consciously skirted. And during the years of the stagnation phenomena, an effort was made to avoid the issue entirely. Thus, many of society's ills were pushed out of sight and laboriously concealed....

And while all efforts to inculcate high standards of national feeling were abandoned, the first signs of national egoism appeared. In the end, it was this that brought thousands and thousands of people to the streets and squares of Armenia. But let's ask ourselves: What were they after? What were they seeking? National separatism, exclusivity.

The past decades have seen Nagorno-Karabakh Autonomous Province form thousands of bonds with the Azerbaijan Republic. Are they to be broken now? Is this smoothly running mechanism to be shut down? But that would have a negative effect on the socioeconomic situation not only in Nagorno-Karabakh and Azerbaijan but throughout the entire country. And what if the rest of the regions started to take similar steps to promote their own interests at the expense of other peoples? What would happen then to the union of fraternal people and to the country's economy? And finally, what about the non-Armenian residents of Nagorno-Karabakh, their concerns and needs? Are they supposed to be ignored?

Were these issues even considered by the people on Yerevan's Theater Square who welcomed every speaker calling for the unification of Nagorno-Karabakh Autonomous Province with Armenia? It's unlikely....

From all appearances, some people aren't interested in taking a sober and businesslike approach to the problem. They are substituting mob and street democracy, in which emotions and passions play the leading role, for genuine, consistent democratization of society. Hence the attempts to exert forceful pressure on the state leadership by means of mass rallies, demonstrations and strikes. There were several days when some 60 enterprises were shut down in Armenia and work in Nagorno-Karabakh was virtually at a standstill.

The people who came out onto the streets and squares of Yerevan, arrivals from all over the republic, were well-organized and disciplined. The organizational procedures for carrying out "popular unrest," which were thought out long ago and carefully planned, played a role here. Leaders "suddenly" turned up at enterprises, institutions and higher schools, and they knew ahead of time where they were to take the people and by what time, and what slogans to shout along the way. What's more, if people refused to go to the rallies, they were humiliated publicly, were practically called traitors of their nation, and were forced to go to the demonstrations.

There was an efficient system set up for providing water, beverages and food to the people who were on their feet for many hours. "Suddenly" it became known that there was a substantial monetary fund. Speakers who had little training in history and science "suddenly" stunned listeners with a cascade of quotations, economic calculations and digressions into centuries long past. It all sounded rather convincing, although the reliability of what they were saying was quite doubtful. In any case, when we talked with some of the speakers, they had trouble telling us in which book or scientific paper they had found the quotations and figures. One was left with the impression that the people were using secondhand information.

By now, though, we know that all the public appearances in Armenia and Nagorno-Karabakh were organized by people who for years have been insisting on the unification of the autonomous province with the Armenian Republic. Recently they organized themselves into the so-called "Karabakh" committee, and they are trying to gain official recognition.

We had an opportunity to attend the meeting of the committee at which its program of action was being readied for approval. We believe that if everything that was discussed that day at the House of Writers, whose hall was obligingly placed at the disposal of the committee members, had been said on Theater Square, the speakers would not have won any applause. For example, the following demand was voiced: The heads of enterprises and Party organizations should be dismissed and new ones elected, the people's Deputies should be recalled, and they should all be expelled from the Party if they interfere with the creation of primary "Karabakh" committees. But what are these committees for?

We did not get a clear answer to this question. The idea that the committees should campaign for the socioeconomic development of Nagorno-Karabakh and a higher standard of living for the population was rejected at the same meeting. For example, when someone started to read off the items in the program for the socioeconomic development of Nagorno-Karabakh, he was cut off abruptly:

"If the leadership of Azerbaijan carries out these demands, Armenia will never see Nagorno-Karabakh."

So there you have it. As it turns out, the committee is not the least bit concerned about the needs of the Armenian population of Nagorno-Karabakh. What it does care about can be seen from these unequivocal lines in its anthem: "Karabakh needs living idols today, too," and "We'll scoff at death and fear of prison to save our Karabakh." In other words, idols are needed whom the people can obey blindly, whom they can follow even into mortal danger, perhaps even committing crimes – what else can "death and fear of prison" mean here? One gets the impression that the members of the newly revealed committee, whether they like it or not, are under the direct influence of those foreign Sovietologists who hold that socialism in the USSR can be defeated only if it is broken up into national factions.

This tactic is not new, by the way. Back in 1905, and again in 1918 and 1920, reactionary forces fanned internecine feuds between the Armenians and Azerbaijanis for the purpose of defusing the revolutionary excitement among the proletariat in both republics. Today the country is engaged in restructuring, a process that is revolutionary in its essence, and in order to weaken it, once again some people are artificially inciting national dissension, this time under the banner of democratization and openness. So, as we can see, the "noble" idea of "reunification" has a clearly antisocialist cast....

In recent years the CPSU Central Committee has repeatedly called the attention of Party and Soviet leaders in Azerbaijan and Armenia to serious shortcomings in the inculcation in the working people of a class-based approach to social phenomena and a spirit of Soviet patriotism and socialist internationalism. But no appreciable changes have taken place so far. Both regions still lack a sufficiently self-critical approach to analysis of the situation in the ideological and moral sphere, there is not enough political acuity in the assessment of negative phenomena, and expectations are too low. An attitude of indifference and appeasement is hindering the restructuring of ideological work. Many shortcomings and omissions in the work of ideological upbringing have not been dealt with for years on end. Party committees and many economic management agencies have failed to recognize the vital necessity of taking a new approach to their work under the conditions of openness and the candid exchange of views, criticism and self-criticism.

This was discussed at a special plenary session of the Armenian Communist Party Central Committee. The Communists criticized actions taken by the republic's Central Committee Bureau, and they spoke about the loss of its link with the masses, its indecisiveness, the unacceptable practice of hushing up negative phenomena in Armenia, and attempts to conceal the problems of nationality relations, which all taken together led to a loss of trust among the masses.

The speakers at the plenary session also discussed why the explanatory work that was done in labor collectives and among students came to naught. The main reason was that the agitators and Party activists were ill-informed about the issue at hand. Therefore, at enterprises one heard general appeals for patience and calm, but no constructive solutions were offered.

The Azerbaijan Party organization, particularly its leadership, also deserves sharp criticism. After all, it was not just a desire for territorial unification with Armenia that brought tens of thousands of Armenians out into the streets of Stepanakert. What brought them there first and foremost was discontent over shortcomings in the socioeconomic development of Nagorno-Karabakh and violations of their national and other rights....

The trouble is that when the April winds of change began to blow, they scarcely touched Nagorno-Karabakh. We were told that even now, just as during the years of stagnation, Azerbaijan's executive agencies still stifle local initiative, that capital investments in Nagorno-Karabakh are lower per capita than in other parts of the republic, that an arbitrary order "from above" in Baku eliminated the study of the history of the Armenian people in Armenian-language schools, and that even the program of cultural ties with Armenia has to be approved by republic departments.

These problems exist. And, we should say, not in Nagorno-Karabakh alone. Unfortunately, the laws on each autonomous province that were adopted 10 years ago are not fully enforced by any means, and sometimes they are ignored outright by republic authorities. And this only reinforces the point that the problem needs to be dealt with in a comprehensive manner, countrywide. Efforts in this direction are already under way in advance of the forthcoming CPSU Central Committee plenary session on nationality problems....

But let's return to the events in and around Nagorno-Karabakh. If at first they didn't go beyond the bounds of the democratic processes taking place in the country, before long they had escalated into open displays of nationalism....

The first outburst occurred in Azerbaijan's Agdam District, adjacent to Nagorno-Karabakh. Nationalistically inclined elements managed to assemble a crowd and lead it to Askeran District in Nagorno-Karabakh "to establish order." As a result of the clash two people were killed and many were hospitalized with injuries. If decisive action had not been taken by the police and conscientious citizens, the number of victims here could have been much higher.

The events in Sumgait were more awful. Taking advantage of the explosive situation, criminal elements intent upon burglary broke into several apartments occupied by Armenians. Lawbreaking, violence and harassment assumed far-reaching proportions in this multinational city....

[At the same time] many of the Azerbaijani residents of Sumgait displayed true internationalism, even putting their own lives at risk. They selflessly saved Armenian families – their fellow workers, neighbors and relatives. They hid them from the rampaging crowd in their homes and factory shops.

"There would have been more casualties," said General V. Krayev, "if the residents hadn't helped us. For example, one Azerbaijani bus driver immediately took 10 Armenians to his hometown of Sheki. Another Azerbaijani family kept some hooligans from entering an apartment building. A worker was riding a bus with an Armenian friend of his. All of a sudden a group of people stopped the bus and demanded that the man be turned over to them. The Azerbaijani himself got injured, but he saved his friend."

Many internationalist-minded Azerbaijanis responded in this manner....

But there were also some people who did not extend a helping hand to their countrymen during their hour of need. They should be ashamed....

We still need to sort out who incited the unstable, irresponsible segment of the population and how they did it, who led this group, and who fomented the nationalistic hysteria. The investigation now being conducted in Sumgait will answer these questions. One thing is clear: The criminals will get what is coming to them, and their every action will receive a proper assessment in accordance with Soviet laws. And Pravda will report on this....

IMPRUDENCE

Izvestia, March 22, 1988, p. 3.

... The so-called "Karabakh Committee" held its latest meeting in Yerevan on March 19, on the premises of the House of Film. The meeting lasted almost eight hours. Seven hundred people listened to speakers in the hall, and another 3,000 listened in the adjacent square, where loudspeakers had been set up.

For the most part, the speakers were representatives of the intelligentsia: scholars, writers, instructors. They spoke not on their own behalf but "in the name of the Armenian people," and they talked exclusively "about the interests of our people." ...

They demanded that rallies and meetings be held at enterprises everywhere, meetings at which new Party committees, trade union committees, etc., could be elected; they called for Yerevan to be declared a "dead city" – i.e., that people not leave their homes, that they go on hunger strikes – and they even called for Armenia to be declared a "non-Party Soviet republic." What's more, it became clear right then and there who might be the leaders of such a republic when two of the speakers present in the hall, I. Muradyan and G. Safaryan, were cited by name and described as "excellent politicians."

S. Kaputikyan, a poetess, tried to make the speakers see reason, called upon them not to stage a rally, and reported that Moscow State University Prof. G. Yepiskoposov and S. Mikoyan, members of the delegation from Nagorno-Karabakh that had been received by Ye. K. Ligachev, were of the same opinion. She read an appeal from V. Ambartsumyan, President of the Armenian Republic Academy of Sciences, for calm in order to give the authorities an opportunity to consider the Karabakh question.

Unfortunately, the voice of prudence was not heeded. The same Candidate of Sciences I. Muradyan, a leader of the "Karabakh Committee," again set forth his demands, which consisted of several points....

We set forth these points exactly as they were presented in the House of Film. According to Muradyan, there is nothing more important now than demanding that the CPSU Central Committee "stop the slander of the Armenian people." This was the first point. In the words of I. Muradyan, "the Armenians in the Nagorno-Karabakh Autonomous Province have no faith in Moscow, in the Central Committee, in higher justice, in the Russian people, or in anything." ...

They demanded that a "state program" be adopted for the resettlement of the Armenian population of the Nagorno-Karabakh Autonomous Province, as well as for "the refugees from Sumgait" (and what fate awaits that part of the population who are not Armenians?). They even demanded that an accusation be lodged against the Azerbaijan Republic with the International Court of Justice in The Hague "with regard to the annexation of Armenian territories." They demanded that appeals be directed to governments, parliaments and public organizations on the question of "the tragedy of Karabakh." Just imagine – these points were adopted virtually unanimously.

The press has already reported about the surprising degree of coordination and organization that was shown at previous rallies, and it has mentioned the fact that it was known ahead of time when and where people were supposed to be brought together and what slogans were to be chanted. At the meeting in question, one could see for oneself how this is done. I. Muradyan issued some straightforward recommendations for organizing the rally: Create protective detachments; cooperate closely with the Ministry of Internal Affairs, to prevent possible provocations; don't bring children to the rally; set up a coordinating council. In conclusion, he talked about money: Accounts have been opened at one of the city's savings banks for collecting money for the "Karabakh Committee."

The following incident is also indicative of the atmosphere that reigned in the hall. When N. Agalovyan, Director of the Armenian Republic Academy of Sciences' Institute of Mechanics, proposed that the instructions of the Politburo of the CPSU Central Committee to the Secretariat to examine the problem of the Nagorno-Karabakh Autonomous Province be approved, he was hissed and driven from the rostrum.

The press was assailed, too. A great deal was said about openness, but a boycott of the Armenian press was agreed upon. Demands for a boycott of the central newspapers had reached us earlier. For the champions of openness, apparently openness is a one-way street on which only their own people are allowed to travel.

All the same, they decided not to declare Yerevan a "dead city" but to hold a rally and to designate March 26 as "a very explosive day." Again, there was glaring irresponsibility in both words and thoughts: "We are facing catastrophic events" and "We will fight to the death."

The journalist Z. Balayan, although expressing doubt about the efficacy of the adopted "program," at the same time reported that "there is no turning back," that "it is unlikely that the promised social and economic transformations in the Nagorno-Karabakh Autonomous Province will produce any effect." So that's how it is! These transformations are still only in outline form, but they're already being rejected, in essence.

It's painful and bitter to read about such things. Against the background of the tragedy that occurred in Sumgait, it's not at all difficult to arouse in oneself and in one's compatriots anger and a thirst for revenge, and to bring oneself and those around one into a state of temporary insanity. But sensible solutions are not arrived

at in fits of anger. However, sensible solutions are precisely what this question requires. The final say here will still belong to the Armenian people, not those who are
trying to speak on their behalf.

IN THE ARMENIAN COMMUNIST PARTY CENTRAL COMMITTEE

Kommunist, March 23, 1988, p. 1.

On March 20, the Bureau of the Armenian Communist Party Central Committee
considered urgent measures to normalize the situation in the republic. It was noted
that...the situation in the republic remains tense and explosive. The "Karabakh
Committee" is resorting to threats and blackmail, directing attacks at Party and
Soviet agencies, and going beyond the bounds of legality. The rally announced
for March 26 in the city of Yerevan may bring an exacerbation of the atmosphere
and unpredictable consequences. The situation is complicated in many respects
in connection with the tragic events that took place in the city of Sumgait. At
present, 595 families2,364 people in all – who have come from Sumgait and other
communities in Azerbaijan have been registered. As a result of various provocative
rumors and fabrications that are being spread, the outflow of persons of the
Azerbaijani nationality across the [Armenian] Republic's borders has not ceased....

The Bureau of the Armenian Communist Party Central Committee has
instructed city and district Party committees and primary Party organizations to
take the necessary measures with a view to preventing rallies on March 26, 1988....

Party committees have been instructed to increase exactingness toward Party
members and their responsibility for the state of the moral and psychological atmosphere in labor collectives and devotion to principle in assessing incorrect actions by
individual Communists who show insincerity or duplicity in their behavior. They are
to channel the efforts of primary Party organizations into neutralizing the activity of
the Nagorno-Karabakh "committees," in view of the fact that at present it is politically
harmful and is at variance with the interests of the people....

ADDRESS BY K. S. DEMIRCHYAN, FIRST SECRETARY OF THE ARMENIAN COMMUNIST PARTY CENTRAL COMMITTEE, ON ARMENIAN TELEVISION MARCH 22, 1988

Kommunist, March 24, 1988, p. 1.

... Very serious questions of a people's fate must not be made subject to uncontrolled
feelings and emotions, whatever they may be.

Unfortunately, not everyone understands this truth. The entire complexity of
the situation and responsibility for a people's fate in an extremely difficult hour of

trial have not been recognized in depth. What's more, as you know, certain elements are even now organizing rallies and giving them a nature that is incompatible with our national interests and is alien to the ideas of socialism. It is also apparent that a considerable number of people cannot display the civic maturity and patience needed to overcome the situation that has been created....

The atmosphere that has come about today requires that each of us display a lofty sense of civic responsibility, political foresight, willpower and restraint, so that new complications will not be created around this question as a result of ill-considered steps and demonstrations....

The rally that certain unwise and unrestrained people propose to hold on March 26 will lead, without a doubt, to a new stirring up of emotions and passions, and it is fraught with unpredictable, and possibly tragic, consequences.

For this reason, each of us and all of us together must once more declare today to be a day of reason and sober decisions....

Do we have the right – political, moral and human – to ignore the danger that exists, the danger that the stainless reputation of a people, built up over many centuries, could be lost in a single hour? No, we do not. Future generations will not forgive us for this. History will not forgive us.

Our civic, patriotic and internationalist duty is to do everything we can to put an end to the tension in the republic, which has lasted for about a month.

The Armenian Communist Party Central Committee, addressing all of you once again today, calls on you in this difficult moment to display prudence, wisdom, restraint and political maturity, to restrain unhealthy emotions and outbursts, to curb ill-considered acts, and to administer a resolute rebuff to all actions that provoke people to engage in disturbances and other unlawful actions....

[*Kommunist* for March 24, p. 5, also published the Armenian Republic's temporary regulations governing the holding of demonstrations. *Bakinsky rabochy* (March 25, p. 3) carried the Azerbaijan Republic's regulations, plus the penalties for violating them.]

MEETINGS AFTER THE RALLIES – Our Correspondents Report From Nagorno-Karabakh

By S. Dardykin and R. Lynev. *Izvestia*, March 24, 1988, p. 6.

We, a group of journalists from central newspapers, went to Nagorno-Karabakh ... having set a single goal for ourselves: to be objective and to rule out any one-sidedness or bias....

In Azerbaijan, the reaction to the very idea of posing the question of transferring the Nagorno-Karabakh Autonomous Province to the neighbor-republic [Armenia] was different from what it was in Armenia: What, aren't we a sovereign republic? And when groups of Azerbaijanis, succumbing to provocative rumors, left Karabakh and a number of districts in Armenia and moved to Azerbaijan "seeking refuge," talk started about some sort of "Armenian threat." In Sumgait, events took such a turn that troops had to be brought in....

For us writers, the difficulty is not in telling the truth but in the fact that it is not to everyone's liking – that the same facts are evaluated differently in Yerevan and in Baku, and that they are viewed differently in Stepanakert and in the neighboring districts of Azerbaijan.

One of our very first meetings in Stepanakert was with a large group of Party and Soviet personnel, journalists and instructors from the teacher-training institute. What they shared with us – expressing themselves heatedly and with conviction – about the problems that have accumulated in Nagorno-Karabakh can be described succinctly: The problems were painful.

On our way here, we asked responsible comrades in Baku, in the Azerbaijan Communist Party Central Committee, where, in their view, the question of changing the status of the autonomous province had come from; the explanation we got consisted of the claim that, in principle, no such question existed. And if it did exist, they said, it had been created by machinations of subversive centers abroad who are trying to play the card of Armenian nationalism.

We won't argue about for whom abroad the events around Karabakh are an outright gift enabling them to reap a propaganda windfall for a certain time. But we will be frank: Is it really as a result of someone's schemes that in the local Nagorno-Karabakh schools there are just two Armenian-language textbooks for an entire class? No, this is the result of the "foresight" of certain republic agencies. The history of the Armenian people has been removed from the curriculum of the local schools, and the question of constructing a television transmitter so that television programs from Yerevan can be viewed in Nagorno-Karabakh, which has been resolved in principle, has been dragged out for an extremely long time. Whose idea was it to draw up documents in such a way that in Deputies' credentials and in local Armenians' internal passports not a single word is in Armenian? Or was this done in the struggle against manifestations of nationalism?

Why, we were asked further, does every arrival of a touring group of performers from Armenia – which, let us note, is only a few kilometers from here – have to be cleared with Baku? Why is it that even a nurse for the polyclinic here, in the autonomous province, cannot be hired without, again, the approval of Baku?

The list of distortions that they cited in the economy and in the social and other spheres seemed endless.

One cannot fail to note that the problems mentioned have much in common with the problems of any out-of-the-way area – not just one where a specific nationality is dominant. On the one hand, here we see the center's chronic habit of exploiting the provinces, taking more from them than it gives for development; on the other hand, we see that the rights of local and province agencies are very limited. In and of themselves, such relations became outmoded long ago – local Soviets must be given more rights, more real power. And when there is a national factor at work too, as there is in our specific case, restrictions on rights are not just a hindrance to development but also grounds for resentment. This seems to us to be the basic real aspect of the problem here....

The processes that were overlooked by the leadership of the republic and the province gradually found their own interpreters, and some directors as well – outside the Party and Soviet agencies, although right next to them, in plain sight of everyone. Guests from Yerevan became constant visitors to Nagorno-Karabakh. Letters were composed, signatures were collected, and delegations were sent to Moscow to gain support there for the idea of uniting the Nagorno-Karabakh Autonomous Province with Armenia. Rumors spread to the effect that Moscow was almost ready to say "yes" – that all that had to be done was to voice the demand more resolutely.

So, starting around Feb. 10, the process that had been gathering force for a long time found an outlet – in the square in front of the province Party committee. The number of people who came there grew. First small groups came, then whole shops, departments and classes. Various people spoke, and various slogans were voiced, but the primary focus was always the same: "Karabakh."

But still, there are questions that were not discussed there, in the square. These were questions that our conversational partners didn't much like, we were given to understand. For example: What would the concrete pluses be if the Nagorno-Karabakh Autonomous Province were to be turned over to Armenia? Who has figured out what they would be, and how? Has any consideration been given to how this would affect the neighbors, their interests and the country as a whole?

In response, we heard: How can you reduce everything to some sort of figures and calculations when we're talking about a sacred cause!...

Slogans about friendship were proclaimed constantly, some of them there, in the square. But here is a question: Was there even one Azerbaijani at those rallies? Did any Azerbaijani speak? After all, Azerbaijanis make up one-fourth of the population of the Nagorno-Karabakh Autonomous Province....

When we questioned our conversational partners about this, we heard something strange:

"What does all that have to do with anything?"...

They tried to show us that supposedly it would be enough just to explain to the Azerbaijanis that the transfer of the Nagorno-Karabakh Autonomous Province to Armenia would not make things worse for them. That's exactly how they put it: not ask, explain. But how will the Azerbaijanis take this explanation? Won't they put forth something of their own in reply, something that will also be convincing? Then what?

One more detail is missing from the stories told by the participants in the February events. It's a rather important detail – how a session of the Nagorno-Karabakh Province Soviet was held, a session that the people in the square had been pressing for. That is to say, people talk about how ridiculous the attempts from above to prevent it were, and about how the chairman of the province Soviet executive committee "lost" the official seal, so that the results of the voting were "uncertified," and therefore some people are now using this point to declare them invalid. All this is true. But here, we repeat, is a detail that is missing from the stories: Indignant at the very fact that the question was posed, the Azerbaijani Deputies did not even vote.

"So what?" our conversational partners said excitedly. "The majority voted 'yes' anyway!"

You can't answer all questions with arithmetic. After all, there is another body in which, in accordance with the USSR Constitution, the question should be examined – the Azerbaijan Supreme Soviet.... It must be respected as the embodiment of the law and democracy. But in response, we heard something quite strange from our Armenian comrades:

"Then we'll turn in our Party membership cards!" said retired Lt. Col. A. Lachichan, a member of Krunk [Stepanakert's "Karabakh Committee" – *krunk* is the Armenian word for the crane, a symbol of yearning for one's native land]....

"A guerrilla war will begin!" predicted another Krunk activist, G. Grigoryan, an assistant professor at the Stepanakert Teacher-Training Institute.

Against whom?

"If there's not going to be a Karabakh, then we don't need any restructuring," said S. Khanzadyan of Yerevan, echoing the others. He is a writer and a Hero of Labor.

And after all this, they are protesting the word "extremism," which the mass news media is applying to them, they are demanding a boycott of the press as a sign of protest, and they are declaring TASS and the State Committee for Television and Radio to be "criminal organizations," just as the "Karabakh" leader I. Muradyan did in calling for new strikes. Excuse me, but just what is extremism, then?...

WHO VIOLATED JOURNALISTIC ETHICS? – Concerning an Office Memorandum From Yu. Arakelyan

Pravda, March 25, 1988, p. 8.

Pravda's editors have received an office memorandum from Yu. Arakelyan, our correspondent for the Armenian Republic, in which he dissociates himself from the article "Emotions and Reason," published on March 21, 1988, accuses the editors of violating journalistic ethics, and claims that he did not see the galley proofs, and hence the content, of the article to which his name was put. We have learned that Yu. Arakelyan's office memorandum, which was transmitted over the telephone, has been photocopied and is now circulating in Yerevan and that it has found its way into the hands of certain Western correspondents accredited in our country.

In this connection, we consider it necessary to state the following. Yu. Arakelyan, together with other comrades, gathered the material for this article from Feb. 23 to March 11, 1988, in the Armenian Republic and turned it in to the editors, and from March 11 to 17 he was in Moscow preparing the article, together with other journalists. He made a number of suggestions that were taken into consideration. The editors have in their possession the original texts of the suggestions and the corrections to the article, made in Yu. Arakelyan's own hand.

On the morning of March 21, the editors had a telephone conversation with Yu. Arakelyan in which he did not dissociate himself from the article but only briefed us on the initial reaction to the article in Yerevan. The text of the aforementioned office memorandum arrived at the editorial offices that evening.

Yu. Arakelyan's act compels the editors to suspend him as Pravda's correspondent for the Armenian Republic until he provides an explanation on the substance of the matter at a meeting of the newspaper's editorial board. – [signed] THE EDITORS OF PRAVDA.

SPONTANEOUS OR ORGANIZED? – On the Events in and Around Nagorno-Karabakh

By special correspondent L. Polonsky. *Bakinsky rabochy*, March 26, 1988, p. 3.

Baku, Stepanakert and Baku – It took the Stepanakert Electrical Equipment Plant 10 days to make up for the time lost during rallies and the strike. It was decided that people would work in three shifts, would make up for the arrears, and would resume the delivery of output that is being awaited in various parts of the country....

But a signal was given from outside, and the workers, as if their promises had been forgotten, left the shops in order once again to hold a rally from morning until midnight in the city's central square. At the deserted plant, only the director and two or three shop superintendents awaited the arrival of a Union Minister.

I saw hundreds of people pour into the square, filling the adjacent streets as well. At first they were silent or talked quietly among themselves. Then they started to yell out their demands, chanting in unison.

The enterprises, and virtually all the institutions, stood idle. Whereas earlier, in late February, people had behaved in a more or less restrained way, now, in the middle of March, the heat of passions had risen sharply.

The new round of demonstrations, like those that preceded it, was far from spontaneous. I became convinced of this while I was in the square and in places where masses of people had gathered. A thorough and precise organizational scheme could be discerned; the scenario for the "expression of the people's will" had been thought out and drawn up ahead of time. With lightning speed, memorandums and declarations appeared, and signatures were collected on petitions and appeals. It was striking how, at regular intervals, a small group of activists would appear in no time at the very same spot near the square; after receiving instructions, the agitators would dive into the crowd, shouting various slogans and adjusting people's behavior. The demonstrators were provided with food, and earlier, on damp, chilly days, chunks of wood that had been prepared ahead of time were brought to the square for bonfires....

An unofficial [*neformalny*] association with the romantic name of Krunk (Crane) was created in Nagorno-Karabakh. This society had its own charter, in which a completely obvious parochial, nationalistic diktat shows through the democratic veil and the innocent intentions. Here, among other things, is what was proclaimed in the charter of Krunk, which was created for the purpose of "stimulating political activity among the intelligentsia and the workers":

"The tasks of the society are: analyzing the ecological, demographic and economic problems of Nagorno-Karabakh; conducting wide-ranging propaganda on these problems, so as to prevent the out-migration of the province's Armenian population; restoring and achieving prosperity for villages that are becoming depopulated and are dying out; preserving the language, traditions and ceremonies; and establishing and consolidating close ties with institutions and public organizations of the Armenian Republic that deal with questions of the language, culture, ecology, economy and historiography of the Armenian people."...

To carry out its program, Krunk intended to collect money and open its own bank account. The charter served only as a screen for the achievement of its main goal – a change in the national-state structure of the province.

Krunk was headed by a "Committee of 55," with a chairman and vice-chairmen. Applying pressure, they tried to shape public opinion in the province. By no means everyone in Stepanakert and in Nagorno-Karabakh's district centers and villages shares Krunk's aims. In conversations with a wide range of people, I heard: "We want tranquility," "We were tired, we hadn't been able to sleep for so many nights," and "I wouldn't go out into the square, I wouldn't give up my job, and I'm afraid." In dealing with some stubborn individuals, Krunk's leaders resorted to unequivocal threats and accusations of betraying the interests of the common cause and of the nation. S. Mamunts, director of the 22nd Party Congress State Farm in Mardakert District, who dared to disagree with Krunk's views and openly condemned them, was shouted down, and he wound up in a hospital bed....

Why, one asks, were children taken out into the square in the rain, so they could hear adults in a frenzy chanting slogans? What will these youngsters carry with them throughout their lives, what sort of scars will be left on their hearts?! ...

In view of the fact that Krunk is taking on inappropriate functions, that its activity is at variance with the goals of communist construction and the principles of socialist internationalism, and that it is inciting the population to mass disturbances, the Presidium of the Azerbaijan Republic Supreme Soviet has resolved to disband the Krunk society and its governing bodies – its committee and council – and to prohibit illegal activity by unauthorized formations of any kind.

Agencies of the prosecutor's office have been instructed to see to it that this decision is carried out without delay. The leaders of Krunk must answer for what they have done. But something else must also be taken into account, without fail.

Many of those who were attracted by such declared goals of Krunk as environmental protection, the identification, preservation and restoration of monuments of olden times, the history of their native area and cultural contacts did not at all link these goals to a change in the status of the province. These people were unable to recognize, behind the publicly declared and seemingly harmless and good aspirations, the skillfully camouflaged parochial tendencies, which led to, among other things, a challenge to socialist internationalism. Among those who joined Krunk, one can also find some who became members only "to be sociable," not wanting to be left out of things, and to avoid the disapproval of zealous activists. It will take time for them to realize their error, their mistake, and to rid themselves of their gullibility and shortsightedness. It is important that these people be treated with understanding....

STEPANAKERT: THE TIME FOR DECISIONS IS HERE

By special correspondent P. Gutiontov. *Izvestia*, March 30, 1988, p. 6.

My report today will be brief: The city's enterprises are at a standstill, the workers are at home....

From their mailboxes, city residents are taking out typewritten leaflets signed by the Krunk Committee (Krunk itself categorically asserts that they're forgeries), which has been dissolved by a decree of the Presidium of the Azerbaijan Supreme Soviet. On the evening of March 28, I was present at the committee's final meeting – its leaders gave a unique accounting of the work they had done. I'll be blunt: It pains me that, in the very difficult situation in which Stepanakert finds itself today, people laying claim to the role of spiritual leaders wasted two hours on questions related basically to the wordings in which the republic Supreme Soviet had evaluated Krunk's activity. Only one person remembered that people aren't going to work....

I suggested that several members of the leadership of the former Krunk, authoritative people in the city, express their attitude toward the situation that had come about. It was agreed that I would pass on their handwritten text to the editors. At the appointed hour, only one person came to my hotel – Gamlet Grigoryan, an assistant professor at the teacher-training institute.

Here's the text he gave me:

"... I appeal to my colleagues, to parents, students and schoolchildren....

"The problem that the Karabakh Committees have raised remains to this day, and the millions of rubles allocated by our government are still, in my view, not completely removing it. Your correct decision – to attend classes – will certainly accelerate the solution of this problem."...

Grigoryan refused to appeal to the workers. Nevertheless, I am passing his text on to the editors, hoping that all residents of Stepanakert will read it and draw positive conclusions for themselves....

JUST WHAT WAS IT? – Reflections on the Events in Yerevan

By special correspondent A. Chernenko. *Pravda*, April 2, 1988, p. 3.

Yerevan – We had a long conversation yesterday with Gevorg Bagratovich Garibdzhanyan, member of the Armenian Republic Academy of Sciences. The conversation was inevitable, since the recent events in Yerevan need serious, sober and honest interpretation.... How do the events that took place in front of the Yerevan Opera House fit into the framework of restructuring processes? And the rallies, attended by thousands of people, and the spirited polemics conducted through microphones The leaflets, the appeals, the open letters to the leaders of the state and the Party Let's be frank: This is the first time that we have come up against this phenomenon on such a large scale, so there is a natural need to understand it....

Answer. – ... The events in Yerevan are a classic example of how people who have completely different motives are brought together, side by side, by one common idea in this instance, by the difficult problem of the Nagorno-Karabakh Autonomous Province. And then personal first causes take a back seat, and people are cemented together in a common impulse. The most valuable thing here is sensible words spoken at the right time. It's no accident that the appeal by M. S. Gorbachev, General Secretary of the CPSU Central Committee, found an immediate response in people's hearts and minds. But a number of one-sided newspaper articles in both the central and the local press have only caused irritation and whipped up emotions....

Question. – The articles were in some way insulting from the standpoint of national relations?

A. – No, I'm talking about something else. Huge numbers of people believed that everything they were doing was in the spirit of restructuring. What is under way is a debate, even if it has taken unusual forms. But in response, we get antiquated labels.

Q. – I have to take issue with you. These "antiquated labels," as you call them, were applied to only a certain number of people. If you will allow me, we will return to them. Now I would like to express my viewpoint on something. I agree: Restructuring and openness are unthinkable without debate. But abandoning your machine, shop and plant – what is that? An element of debate? Of polemics? It's one thing to demonstrate your viewpoint, but measures that involve the undermining of plan and production discipline are something else again....

A. – ... We often say that so far we are only learning democracy. Mistakes are inevitable here.

Q. – But what a price must be paid for these mistakes!

A. – An enormous price. Because the main thing that could happen on the square is the discrediting of the ideas of restructuring and openness. The ideas of the renewal of our society. Yerevan's workers were well aware of this: On the date set in the anonymous leaflets – March 26 – no one supported these "appeals." A healthy class instinct was at work. By that time, it had become clear to the working person and the creative person that people who are immature, as we say, had quietly, imperceptibly but persistently begun to bridle the sincere upsurge of feeling.

Q. – I'll put it in clearer terms: political careerists and adventurers. From among those who have been proposing that Armenia be made a "non-Party republic," etc.

A. – Precisely....

Q. – ... I would like to touch on a question that in the minds of many people seems still to be forbidden. I refer to the units of the Ministry of Internal Affairs that arrived in Yerevan to safeguard order. The police [*militsia*] concentrated forces in the city during those days. Military patrols walked the streets of Yerevan for several nights. What can you say on this score?

A. – ... This crowd of people in a limited space harbors more surprises than an inexperienced person might suppose. I'll call things by their proper names. Were provocations a possibility during those days? Certainly. I don't want to conceal my opinion to the effect that provocateurs are a reality. Frankly, I slept peacefully in the knowledge that our fighting men were in the city. I emphasize the word our....

Were any of those people arrested? Were any submachine guns fired? Were any general searches conducted? No Yerevaner can cite a single abusive instance on this score. Moreover, the boys with shoulder boards were given carnations by our young women and cigarettes by our young men. They brought them lemonade and rolls during the hottest part of the day – you saw that yourself.... I think that the process of democratization should include the element of a guarantee of order....

Q. – Some representatives of the Armenian intelligentsia with whom I happened to talk viewed these measures, in the words of one venerable writer, as "a slap in the face." Incidentally, aren't you afraid that someone will accuse you of making an opportunistic evaluation of the moment?

A. – I am an Armenian, and I won't hide the fact that my heart is still full of pain for the tragedy in Sumgait. My heart also aches for my compatriots from Nagorno-Karabakh.... In my opinion, the Armenian intelligentsia has truly underestimated its colossal spiritual role in restructuring. I won't conceal the fact that I am proud of how sincerely and openly they raised a number of painful problems during those days. But raising a problem is only half the job. Sober assessments, constructive options for solving a problem and the creation of models that must be mulled over more than once, twice or even five times in order to determine the best options – that's the most important thing in restructuring. But this hasn't happened. I can apply this to myself as well....

Q. – Gevorg Bagratovich, in Yerevan today nothing reminds one of the recent events.... This outward calm in your view, to what extent does it correspond to the emotional state of the rank-and-file Yerevaner? Not, of course, for the person for whom the "fermentation process" is an end in itself, and not for the person who has been trying to play a dubious political game. There aren't so many of them, anyway. But primarily for the person who, for just a moment, lost his bearings, while believing that he is participating in measures vitally connected with the spirit of restructuring. Hasn't he lost faith in its genuineness and reality? Doesn't this affect his social activeness?

A. – That's a difficult question. No, I daresay that the Yerevaner has not lost the faith in restructuring that gave you the opportunity – for the first time – to speak out so openly without apprehensions, but rather has gained that faith. But he has been thinking.

Q. – About what?

A. – About many things. For instance, about why it is that someone has been trying to take advantage of his sincerity and openness....

Q. – And are you among those who feel that way?

A. – Absolutely. To be perfectly frank, I am pained very much by the fact that this powerful emotional upsurge, based precisely on the guarantee given to us by restructuring, has not worked in its favor. And all together, in the same breath – how many of the most urgent problems of the city and the republic could have been resolved! Thus, we have no right not to draw lessons from what we have experienced – above all, lessons for the restructuring of Party and ideological work. After all, it's no secret that there were a good many Party members among those gathered in the opera house square. Well, we must learn to live in a new way. Restructuring will not tolerate political dilettantism.

Q. – But there aren't so many dilettantes among the segment of the intelligentsia we have been talking about. They are people who have made a name for themselves, who have produced well-known literary and scientific works....

Rumors are inevitable companions of these unusual events. They are now being stirred up very actively by Western "voices" and in private conversations. The predominant notes are allegations that the true state of affairs in Yerevan is being hushed up, that people are "full of fear because of what happened" and repressions are only a step away. Supposedly, the building of the republic Communist Party Central Committee is crammed full of staff members of the special services.

A. – All this is preposterous and an outright lie.... I am deeply convinced that the republic's Communists will be able to get a Leninist understanding of what happened on the opera house square. I am talking about fundamental social problems – demographic and ecological problems, problems of social justice. What came together on the square was not just people – hundreds of questions came together that at the time could not be answered by, let's say, the secretary of some borough Party committee or a plant director, a shop superintendent or the head of a borough social security service. In short, those who were unable to satisfy human needs or to assuage someone's pain. Those whose job it was to do this.

REPORT: THEATER SQUARE, JUNE 8

By A. Bagdasaryan and S. Nuridzhanyan. *Kommunist*, June 9, 1988, p. 4.

Despite the scorching sun, Yerevan's Theater Square is crowded. People huddled in small groups are heatedly discussing one subject and one only: Nagorno- Karabakh and the events surrounding it....

[Numerous placards] call for inclusion on the agenda of the forthcoming republic Supreme Soviet session the question of a response to the decision taken by the session of the Nagorno-Karabakh Autonomous Province Soviet on Feb. 20 [regarding transfer of the province to Armenian jurisdiction. – *Trans.*] and for proper application of the law to the organizers of and participants in the excesses and pogroms in Sumgait.

Thousands of people from various walks of life are asserting these demands at rallies these days in Theater Square. The rallies take different forms. For example, the students have shown a preference for staging sit-ins. A. Berberyan, a student at the Yerevan conservatory, took it on himself to explain their collective platform to us.

"We resolved to demonstrate until our demands are met....

"No one has given us a guarantee that the Nagorno-Karabakh question will be examined. But guarantees are what we need."...

R. Ovanesyan, a chief economist for the State Agro-Industrial Committee [and part of another group of demonstrators, told us]:

"These rallies wouldn't be so huge if the central and republic mass media had reported the events truthfully from the outset. The lack of objectivity and one-sidedness of the information got people even more worked up. As a result, the course of events is becoming unpredictable."

The people who have been staging a hunger strike on Theater Square since June 4 didn't want to have anything to do with us. But after conferring among themselves, they decided to give the journalists a few minutes after all.

Those we spoke with – Garnik Khachaturovich Manasyan, an outstanding construction worker and Hero of Socialist Labor, and three of his comrades – said only this:

"We don't trust the press. So we'll give an interview only if we are guaranteed that our position will be stated with absolute accuracy."

Here is what was said:

"Our demands are no different from those of the people. But we have chosen this form of protest, and that is our right. We resorted to this extreme measure, and we will abandon it if the session of the Armenian Republic Supreme Soviet adds to its agenda consideration of the decision taken by the Nagorno-Karabakh Province Soviet on June 15 of this year (sic). That is our main objective. In addition to this, we are protesting the way the trial in Sumgait is being conducted and demand that the USSR Supreme Court hear the case. We oppose the distorted, unobjective reporting of events by the mass media, especially the central media, which for some reason have created a zone of silence around what is going on." ...

QUESTION AND ANSWER: TODAY IN NAGORNO-KARABAKH

By special correspondent N. Demidov. *Pravda*, June 10, 1988, p. 3.

Editors' Note. – The torrent of letters to the editors asking what is going on now in Nagorno-Karabakh has recently increased considerably. Our readers ask whether the situation there has returned to normal.

* * *

Stepanakert – It seemed like just yesterday that nearly all the central newspapers were vying with each other to report on February's events in the Nagorno-Karabakh Autonomous Province of the Azerbaijan Republic. The events were also discussed on Central Television. There was a lot of conversation and discussion at that time, but then passions seemed to cool, and since then there have been fewer and fewer references to these areas in the press. But the tension level in the province remains as high as it was.

The majority of industrial enterprises and institutions and public transportation in Stepanakert and the district centers of Martuni, Mardakert and Askeran are not operating at present. Virtually all the restaurants and department stores are closed, and the sale of food is sharply curtailed: Food supplies are not getting in, and economic and other ties with Baku have been severed. The strike – how unusual and unexpected this word sounds to us! – is in its third week. The Armenian population of Nagorno-Karabakh has issued an ultimatum that the possibility of its secession from Azerbaijan and incorporation into Armenia be given immediate consideration.

Every morning in the center of town tens of thousands of people march along the streets in formation, chanting slogans and carrying banners, and they hold rallies. Their sole purpose is "to stand firm until the end." And when night falls, small lights burn uneasily in specially equipped booths on the streets and in alleys. Here is where the so-called "self-defense sentries" have taken up their positions. The small detachments keep their eyes peeled until morning in the belief that they are ensuring their families' peace and security. Who are they protecting themselves against? The answer is simple: "From the Azerbaijanis." And although no attacks are occurring, although there are people whose job, so to speak, is to protect the residents' peace and quiet, the volunteer "watchmen" peer into the darkness, suspiciously eyeing anyone who passes by.

These sentry posts are not only failing to reassure people, they are actually turning into sites of conflict. Several clashes have already occurred there.

The current emotional state of the province's residents and the depressing mood here have developed over a period of months. Practically every day some new event, whether real or imagined, has occurred in the province. These events, enmeshed in rumors and conjectures, have taken possession of people's minds and emotions and have disrupted the normal flow of life. In March and April the psychological climate in Nagorno-Karabakh was heavily influenced by stories told by Armenians who had fled Sumgait. Facts got interspersed with fabrications. The tragedy that did occur was embellished with horrifying details that bore no relation to reality.

The city's May Day demonstration, which turned into a virtual "pro-annexation rally," was followed by a demonstration held by Armenians to protest the appointment of an Azerbaijani to the post of province deputy prosecutor. Then came the first dismissals of Azerbaijanis from jobs in Stepanakert and of Armenians from their jobs in Shusha, as Pravda has already reported. At the same time, some people took illegal actions that were meant to complicate the situation.

On May 14 and 15, A. Mamedov and A. Gasanov, residents of the province capital, fled to Shusha after being severely beaten. A rally ensued in the town square, at which the Azerbaijani residents of Stepanakert condemned the events that had occurred in their town and categorically opposed territorial redistricting. Similar statements were made at rallies in Baku as well.

After the plenary session of the Azerbaijan Communist Party Central Committee, a strike began on May 23 and continues to this day. Farm work is being done, however. And despite the appeals of certain individuals that the dairies and bakeries be shut down, these enterprises are operating.

The province's Party bodies are not in control of the current situation. The Azerbaijan Communist Party province committee's appeals to the populace to normalize the situation and return to work have fallen on deaf ears. A similar appeal made by the famous Armenian writer Silva Kaputikyan in the pages of the province newspaper has also failed.

Nevertheless, the rallies and demonstrations are being carefully organized and very skillfully orchestrated. There are grounds for asserting that the Krunk committee, which was dissolved by a decree of the Presidium of the republic Supreme Soviet, is continuing its activities. By playing on Armenians' nationalist feelings and their desire to live together with their countrymen, the organizers of the mass demonstrations are helping to maintain the tension.

The public is weary from the months of turmoil. The depressing food situation is making their lives more difficult. Despite this, some people are proposing that "the issue that has been raised be pressed with even greater urgency."

According to data from the Azerbaijan Republic State Statistics Committee, in the period from February through June 1 of this year the enterprises in the Nagorno-Karabakh Autonomous Province have had a shortfall of 25.4 million rubles' worth of output. This figure continues to grow.

SESSIONS OF THE UNION-REPUBLIC SUPREME SOVIETS: ARMENIAN REPUBLIC

By special correspondents S. Bablumyan and Ye. Vostrukhov. *Izvestia*, June 17, 1988, p. 2.

Yerevan – The days and even weeks before the regular session of the Armenian Supreme Soviet again proved to be a very difficult time for the republic. In Yerevan and other cities, rallies and demonstrations involving many thousands of people were held. Deputies to the Supreme Soviet held meetings with their constituents everywhere. These meetings took place not just out of duty, to check off on a form, but at the demand of the constituents themselves.

On the eve of the session, there were rallies, demonstrations and even strikes. Yes, that's exactly what happened – although, based on the recent unanimous silence of the central newspapers, one might have supposed that the situation in Azerbaijan and Armenia had finally been normalized, that the events connected with Nagorno-Karabakh are receding into the past, and that, as a result of the steps that have been taken, this question had been resolved once and for all....

But one must not pass off desire for reality.... The question persistently arose: Why has the petition of the extraordinary session of the Nagorno-Karabakh Autonomous Province Soviet to the Azerbaijan and Armenian Republic Supreme Soviets about transferring the autonomous province from the one republic to the other still not been considered? After all, the appeal was adopted in Stepanakert back on Feb. 20.

The voters of the Armenian Republic displayed initiative here, giving the Deputies to the Supreme Soviet instructions to put the question of the decision made by the Deputies to the Nagorno-Karabakh Autonomous Province Soviet on the agenda of the next session of the Armenian Supreme Soviet. And the Presidium of the republic Supreme Soviet did so.

Let us be frank: The growing tension in the past few days was also facilitated by something else – the extraordinarily skimpy reports on what was taking place at the trial in Sumgait. On this point reproaches to the press, especially the central press, are completely justified. The local mass news media finally broke their long silence in covering the problems in Nagorno-Karabakh....

The local press helped to begin advance discussion of the Supreme Soviet's draft resolution concerning the appeal of the Deputies from Nagorno-Karabakh. The day before the session began, all the local newspapers published the draft. It had already been made public on Theater Square in Yerevan. Discussion of the document began right there, on the spot, and it continued the same evening at a televised round-table meeting.

Let us also mention that...there was a live telecast from the hall where the republic Supreme Soviet session was meeting....

A frank discussion of accumulated problems – and by no means all of them were economic problems – was a distinctive feature of this session.... Why was the autonomous province's appeal shelved both in Yerevan and in Baku? was the question heard at the session. And the answer followed: Because, although the plenipotentiary Deputies to the two republics' Supreme Soviets knew about it, they still waited for instructions from above....

The session adopted a resolution saying, in particular, that in view of the tense situation in and around Nagorno-Karabakh, as well as of the expressed will of the Armenian population of the Nagorno-Karabakh Autonomous Province and Armenia, and guided by Art. 70 of the USSR Constitution on the right of the free self-determination of nations, consent is given to the entry of the Nagorno-Karabakh Autonomous Province into the Armenian Republic. A decision was adopted to request that the USSR Supreme Soviet examine and positively resolve this question. An appeal to the Azerbaijan Republic Supreme Soviet expressed the hope that this decision will not disrupt the traditional good-neighbor relations between the two republics and will be received with understanding by the Azerbaijani people. Deputies spoke with great concern about the possible consequences of firing up emotions over the problem of Nagorno-Karabakh....

The Armenian Republic Supreme Soviet condemned the crimes committed against the Armenian population in February 1988 and expressed profound condolences to the families and relatives of those who perished.

A permanent commission on questions of relations between nationalities and internationalist upbringing was formed and confirmed by decrees of the Presidium of the republic Supreme Soviet. S. Arutyunyan, First Secretary of the Armenian Communist Party Central Committee, spoke at the session.

SPEECH BY G. M. VOSKANYAN, CHAIRMAN OF THE PRESIDIUM OF THE ARMENIAN REPUBLIC SUPREME SOVIET, ON ARMENIAN TELEVISION JUNE 19, 1988

Kommunist, June 21, 1988, p. 1.

Dear comrades! The situation in Masis District dictates the need to address you once again.

As reported, on June 17 disturbances and instances of hooliganism took place in the settlement of Masis and the village of Sayat-Nova; windows in a number of houses belonging to Azerbaijanis were broken, and damage was done to household goods in some of these houses. It seemed that, thanks to the measures taken, the situation had normalized; however, yesterday evening the situation in the district was exacerbated once again when a group of irresponsible young people who had gone to Masis District from Yerevan succeeded in provoking several local Armenian residents to commit hooligan actions. As a result of clashes, eight residents of the Armenian nationality and eight of the Azerbaijani nationality received bodily injuries. There were no fatalities. The appropriate organizations are taking effective and resolute measures to restore order so that life in the district can return to normal. An investigation is under way, and the culprits will be severely punished. Party and Soviet agencies in the district are taking every measure to normalize the situation once and for all and to stop provocations and disturbances....

I appeal to the republic's Armenian and Azerbaijani populations to show restraint and common sense, not to succumb to excessive emotions and feelings, and not to listen to those who are sowing distrust and strife between nationalities....

DETAILS: NAGORNO-KARABAKH AGAIN

By special correspondent N. Demidov. *Pravda,* June 23, 1988, p. 6.

Stepanakert, Azerbaijan Republic – In the past few days, the atmosphere in Nagorno-Karabakh has become even more strained. One would have thought that there was no room for further exacerbation, but the Armenian population of Stepanakert, as if under mass hypnosis, keeps holding demonstrations and rallies day after day. From all indications, personnel of enterprises and institutions have no intention of resuming work until the "Karabakh question" is resolved....

Whereas in February 1988 those who attended the rallies in Stepanakert called social and economic questions the impelling motive for Nagorno-Karabakh to leave Azerbaijan, today those questions seem to have been forgotten. Demagogic statements are papered over with slogans about restructuring. But is a situation in which working life in the province is virtually paralyzed conducive to restructuring? Who needs these marches that exhaust people?... Many realize the senselessness and absurdity of the methods of self-exhaustion but can do nothing about it: Things have gone too far.

On June 21, a session of the province Soviet examined the question of the situation in the province and measures to stabilize it. The decision notes disagreement with the response from the session of the Azerbaijan Supreme Soviet concerning the unacceptability of the demand that the Nagorno-Karabakh Autonomous Province be transferred to another republic. In addition, it was decided to make another direct appeal to the USSR Supreme Soviet asking that it consider this question....

People have gathered at the office of the province Soviet executive committee, demanding that a point stating "firm resolve" to transfer the Nagorno-Karabakh Autonomous Province to Armenia – i.e., to continue putting pressure on state agencies – be included in the document adopted by the session of the province Soviet.

In short, the situation is still not returning to normal. The migration of Armenian families to Armenia and of Azerbaijani families from Armenia to Azerbaijan continues. Troops have been sent to a number of cities, including those in Nagorno-Karabakh....

THE SITUATION REMAINS COMPLICATED

By staff correspondents S. Bablumyan in Yerevan, R. Talyshinsky in Baku. *Izvestia*, July 7, p. 6, 1988.

Yerevan – Yerevan can be called a working city this morning only by greatly stretching a point. Even those who tried to get to their machines and take their places at them could not do so: City transport was not operating. I called around to many borough Party committees and got in touch with executives of industrial enterprises. How are things going? Responses varied, but basically most of the assessments boiled down to the conclusion that today the situation is worse than it was yesterday.

And how was it yesterday? According to more precise data, 26 enterprises and organizations did not work on July 5 in the republic as a whole, six of them in Yerevan....

But let us return to an account of today's events. Yerevan's Theater Square is closed off.

The authorities have even had to resort to help from the military. As of 10 a.m. Moscow time, Zvartnots Airport was still not operating. The Armenian News Agency has reported on what happened there yesterday. Let me cite several lines since I myself was unable to get to Zvartnots – the traffic jams were simply impenetrable. The report reads: "On July 4 and 5, 1988, groups of people who had participated in rallies in the city of Yerevan, following the urging of irresponsible persons, blockaded Zvartnots Airport and the roads leading to it. The disrupters of public order demanded that the airport collective stop working. When they got a refusal, they penetrated the work areas of the air terminal, paralyzing its operation and creating a threat to flight safety.*** Numerous attempts to persuade the offenders to stop their unlawful actions were unsuccessful. The situation compelled intervention by the forces for the safeguarding of public order.***"

Unfortunately, several disrupters of order and a few policemen [*militsionery*] were injured in the skirmishes that broke out....

* * *

Baku

On the collective farms and state farms of the Nagorno-Karabakh Autonomous Province, haymaking is under way and the grain harvest is continuing.

However, industrial enterprises, the construction industry, transportation and the consumer-service sphere are still not working in Stepanakert, the center of the Nagorno-Karabakh Autonomous Province. With the exception of groceries, the stores are closed.

According to data provided by the Azerbaijan Republic State Statistics Committee, the total output not produced by the province's enterprises as a consequence of the strikes has already exceeded 41.5 million rubles....

"The situation in the republic as a whole remains complicated," said A. Mamedov, Azerbaijan Republic Minister of Internal Affairs. "A total of more than 18,000 Azerbaijanis who left the Armenian Republic recently have now been housed temporarily in various districts. But there have been no rallies or demonstrations recently."

ON ASSIGNMENT IN STEPANAKERT

By special correspondent A. Kazikhanov. *Izvestia*, July 12, 1988, p. 3.

Stepanakert – I didn't come here of my own volition. But it wasn't against my will, either. I came from another region, on assignment from the editors....

All I knew about the Krunk Committee was that it had disbanded. That's what the newspapers wrote. In my opinion, that information is incorrect. In many places, I saw for myself that a wide variety of aspects of life in the autonomous province are being directed by unofficial leaders....

On the first morning, I had occasion not only to observe but also to talk with participants in a mass rally. Unshaven young fellows pushed their way through the enormous crowd of excited people surrounding this correspondent, literally shouting: "We're condemned men; if they don't detach us [i.e., detach the Nagorno-Karabakh Autonomous Province from Azerbaijan], we won't stop at anything!"

By the way, there are only a few such people, about 100. All are young men. All are unshaven. Almost all of them that I saw were next to the city's Party and Soviet leaders, who were speaking at the rally (my impression was that they were practically the leaders' bodyguards), or at one of the headquarters of the supposedly disbanded Krunk organization. These are the people in the crowd who are filling the role of loudmouths. They make up part of those who are exerting influence on the population, deciding (with threats of "excommunication from the people" or with violence, I was told) whether people should go to work or not. For example, many (not just the old and the sick) residents of Stepanakert admitted to me that they are fed up with (or find intolerable) making the daily 6-kilometer walk – the procession through the city streets before the rally). But they can't refuse....

The most frightening and dangerous thing is that people are working themselves up, as if deliberately bringing themselves to a state of hysteria: It's either-or; either they detach us, or we're ready for anything.

As is known, the city has not been working for several months now. The machines stand idle, and the pay offices at enterprises are closed, too. But people are living, consuming, buying. What are they consuming? And more importantly, what are they buying goods with?

Strong support is coming from Armenia. Hundreds of people leave every day for Yerevan and, similarly, hundreds arrive in Stepanakert (an air bridge has been organized between the two cities for this purpose; there are sometimes as many as four to eight flights per day). And most of them are the same people.

In this complex situation, which is simply unprecedented for us, events and phenomena are taking place that are very difficult to blame on any specific persons. All the same, a considerable part of the blame lies with the mass news media. All the reports, all the analysis is constructed on the principles of proportionality, so to speak. If a critical view of the Armenian claims is cited, then right there, a paragraph down, there has to be a report about the Azerbaijanis. Compliments are also strictly dosed out.

This prescription, which in my view is based on a false understanding of objectivity and impartiality, is interfering greatly with reporting of the truth as it is. This sort of coverage of events has become the only acceptable and tolerable kind for many residents of Stepanakert. They are firmly convinced: They should either write something good about us, or write nothing. And how do you report the bad things? The answer is: Report bad things only about the Azerbaijanis.

Another consequence of this harmful inertia is rumors.

The city is full of rumors about killings and beatings of Armenians and other machinations against them. In the headquarters of the Ministry of Internal Affairs and the Nagorno-Karabakh Autonomous Province Prosecutor's Office, I rechecked all the instances that residents of Stepanakert had told me about: Many of them could not be confirmed, and the rumors about killings were nonsense. But press organs and the province and city Party committees are silent, making no effort to explain to people what is truth and what is fantasy....

In talking with workers (I emphasize, workers), I very often heard: "If it comes to clashes, our 'moneybags' – those who have lived well here and made money – will ditch us, and we simple people will be left to pick up the pieces." I think there's some basis for this thought.

On Saturday, June 25, I heard defiance from Party and Soviet officials: "We'll go all the way with our demands, we'll strike, over what doesn't matter!" On Sunday the 26th, there was a striking change in mood: "We don't know what to do, these blankety-blanks don't want to go to work. Somebody is thwarting us."

On Monday there was real panic in the offices of the province and city Party committees: "What are we going to do? We're helpless."

Meanwhile, on the empty central square, surrounded by troops, members of Krunk gathered and quietly talked among themselves. They talked, although there was a procession of thousands of people not far away. They seemed to be showing everyone: Look, we have nothing to do with this, they're wasting their time trying to blame their "unfinished business" on us."

I could be mistaken, but it seemed to me that fermentation has set in "at the top" of the movement. Isn't someone there getting ready to abandon ship? That would be dangerous. Not only because the mass of people, stirred by rallies and demonstrations, cannot stop just like that, all at once – it would seem to everyone that by stopping they would be betraying "their own people." Something else is more dangerous: Before fleeing, the "leaders" might try to slam the door: to provoke a conflict between Armenians and Azerbaijanis, or, as a last resort, between the military and the Armenians in the Nagorno-Karabakh Autonomous Province....

REPORT FROM YEREVAN: AT THEIR WORKPLACES

By special correspondents G. Ovcharenko and S. Oganyan. *Pravda*, July 21, p. 6, 1988.

Armenian Republic – In Armenia's capital, all enterprises and organizations, public transportation and stores are operating for the third day....

Certainly, the termination of the strike is a major factor making for normalization. But it is just as important to restore good relations between representatives of the Army and the population. They became complicated after the incident at Zvartnots Airport....

Here is what R. Stepanyan, Chairman of the Armenian Republic Council on Tourism and Excursions, told us:

"From February, when the Karabakh events began, through June, 300 tourist groups canceled agreements for trips to Armenia. In July we've received another

150 cancellations, and we're short 35 groups for August.*** We are incurring sizable losses, although none of our staff members participated in the strike. Excursions proceeded even on those days when the streets were clogged with people. When that happened, we simply altered our route. And now we're getting cancellations. Many people think the airport is still occupied, that armed patrols are walking the streets. It's not so."...

However, one must admit that there are forces in Yerevan and the republic that would like to prevent the normalization of the situation and that are continuing to stir up people. Thus, on the eve of the meeting of the Presidium of the USSR Supreme Soviet members of the "Karabakh Committee" called for meetings to be held at enterprises and in institutions and organizations at which new councils of labor collectives and new Party and trade union committees would be elected. Tuesday evening, at a rally at the Matenadaran Library, personnel of internal affairs agencies detained several persons who had "picked up" 32 bottles with incendiary mixtures.

The situation in Stepanakert remains tense, the Nagorno-Karabakh Autonomous Province Party Committee reports. There, strikers have not even let newspapers carrying the resolution of the Presidium of the USSR Supreme Soviet come out on time....

The republic's Party organization, which, to put it bluntly, was only recently out of touch with the masses and was not in control of events, is beginning to administer a resolute rebuff to the antirestructuring forces. The Party apparatus is being strengthened. Persons who followed the lead of the "Karabakh Committee" are being punished strictly, up to and including expulsion from the CPSU. The Armenian Communist Party Central Committee has brought serious complaints against the republic's law-enforcement agencies. For example, it is incomprehensible why they are winking at the activity of the same "Karabakh Committee," which was disbanded by a decree of the Presidium of the Armenian Supreme Soviet....

A rally was held in Yerevan on the evening of July 20; it took place without any serious excesses. The situation in the city is calm.

PREVENT A DANGEROUS DEVELOPMENT OF EVENTS

Kommunist, Sept. 23, 1988, p. 1.

The situation in the [Armenian] Republic, which has become sharply exacerbated in connection with the recent events in Nagorno-Karabakh, remains extremely tense and explosive.

On Sept. 21 the Armenian Communist Party Central Committee, the Presidium of the republic Supreme Soviet and the republic Council of Ministers issued an appeal to the republic's Communists and working people. The people have comprehended the import of this appeal,... which contains a call to exhibit vigilance, self-control, restraint and foresight and to recognize the great danger that could face our brothers and sisters and our children if passions continue to intensify, if the people fall under the power of spontaneous actions.

Party and Soviet agencies and public organizations have used and are using all the political means at their disposal to normalize the present situation as quickly as possible and to return life and work to their usual course. The action headquarters that have been set up in all districts are taking steps to stabilize the situation in the republic.

Despite this, however, people in Yerevan and in several other cities and districts of the republic continue not to show up for work, to boycott classes in [general-education] schools, technicums and higher schools, and to hold unsanctioned rallies at which irresponsible and politically harmful calls for dangerous actions are voiced.

The unsanctioned rally held in Yerevan on Sept. 21 is indicative in this respect. What kind of madness has overtaken the individuals who called for an "armed struggle"? Against whom? In this instance, political flippancy, a passion for cheap effects and recklessness are turning into a new quality – malevolence. Into whose hands does all this play? Those of the Armenian people, who have shed more than enough of their blood? Those of our brothers in Nagorno-Karabakh?

Some of the speakers at the rally tried to sow distrust between children and parents by inciting the latter to strike and take part in ill-considered actions. One gets the impression that the highest concern of these persons is not the problems of Nagorno-Karabakh as such but only the destabilization of the situation....

These calls and ill-considered actions pursue the aim of pitting the people of Soviet Armenia against the country's other peoples, who are watching what is happening with alarm. Politically immature individuals are resorting more and more actively to unlawful actions, creating considerable difficulties in the vital activity of the republic's capital. Thus, on the night of Sept. 22 a group of people blockaded fleets of the capital's urban passenger vehicles and obstructed transport operations, in order to create artificial obstacles to people's going to work and to foment an atmosphere of alarm, fear and animosity....

Careful consideration of the present situation and the possibility of an extremely dangerous development of events have compelled the introduction of forces to safeguard public order, which are called upon to ensure the tranquility and safety of the population and to prevent or cut short all unlawful actions leading to anarchy and an "everything is permitted" situation.

In this difficult and anxious hour, every inhabitant of the republic is required to exhibit the utmost restraint, self-discipline and sense of civic responsibility. No rash steps and no excesses – even fortuitous ones – can be permitted....

A catastrophe must be averted. – (Armenian News Agency.)

ON THE SITUATION AROUND NAGORNO-KARABAKH

Pravda, Sept. 23, 1988, p. 8.

With the introduction, in accordance with powers granted by the Presidium of the USSR Supreme Soviet, of a state of emergency and a curfew in the Nagorno-Karabakh Autonomous Province and Agdam District of Azerbaijan Republic, the situation in the city of Stepanakert and in several nearby communities has begun to improve, to a certain extent. Agencies for safeguarding public order are carrying out measures to ensure the safety and constitutional rights of citizens. Curfew violators have been detained, and firearms and knives have been confiscated.

Stepanakert's industrial enterprises, construction organizations, transportation facilities and educational institutions did not operate on Sept. 22.

In connection with the tension that has arisen in the Armenian Republic, tension caused by actions of the leaders of the so-called "Karabakh Committee," which the Presidium of the republic Supreme Soviet has disbanded, the Armenian Communist Party Central Committee, the Presidium of the Armenian Republic Supreme Soviet and the Armenian Republic Council of Ministers have appealed to the republic's Communists and working people to show a high degree of civic awareness, restraint and responsibility....

In Yerevan and several other Armenian cities, however, the endeavor of bodies of power and Party organizations to defuse the situation by methods of persuasion has not yet met with a proper response. On Sept. 21 and 22, certain irresponsible elements began to make unconstitutional demands on the Armenian Republic Supreme Soviet and government and to call for the organizing of strikes, rallies and hunger strikes. On Sept. 22, work stopped at a number of enterprises in Yerevan, Leninakan, Abovyan and Charentsavan, as well as in Echmiadzin District. Urban transportation schedules were disrupted.

Additional measures are being taken to maintain public order and to curb criminal actions. In the city of Yerevan on Sept. 22, military units participated in these measures, along with police agencies.

The necessary work for the maintenance of order and the observance of socialist legality is being conducted in the Azerbaijan Republic, especially in districts inhabited by citizens of both the Armenian and the Azerbaijani nationalities.... – (TASS)

ON THE SITUATION AROUND NAGORNO-KARABAKH

Pravda, Sept. 24, 1988, p. 6.

The measures that agencies for safeguarding public order are taking in the Nagorno-Karabakh Autonomous Province and in Agdam District of Azerbaijan have made it possible to ease tension and to prevent new nationality-based clashes.

Individuals who set houses afire have been detained, and firearms and knives have been confiscated from certain citizens. An investigation is under way. Representatives of Party and state agencies and public organizations and the mass news media are conducting explanatory work among the population.

A normal work pace is being maintained in the autonomous province's rural districts. At the same time, industrial enterprises, construction organizations and educational institutions in Stepanakert are still not operating....

The appeal of the Armenian Communist Party Central Committee, the Presidium of the Armenian Republic Supreme Soviet and the Armenian Republic Council of Ministers to the republic's Communists and all its working people is having a positive impact on the development of the situation in the Armenian Republic.... Most labor collectives have comprehended the import of the measures that the law-enforcement agencies are carrying out. A large part of the enterprises and organizations in the republic's capital and in its other industrial centers were operating on the morning of Sept. 23. Urban transport operations are returning to normal.

At the same time, the stabilization of the situation is being hindered by rallies organized by irresponsible elements in the center of Yerevan, rallies at which provocative statements are made and rumors aimed at artificially exciting people are floated.

The situation in the city is being monitored. – (TASS)

WHO BENEFITS FROM THIS?

By special correspondents G. Ovcharenko and A. Chernenko. *Pravda*, Sept. 28, 1988, p. 6.

Yerevan and Moscow – Once again there is an explosion of passions and emotions in Armenia. Blood has been shed in the Nagorno-Karabakh Autonomous Province. There are refugees. The last Armenian families are being forced to leave Shusha. Theater Square in Yerevan is filled with people once again. True, there are far fewer people at the rallies now than there were in February, but their mood is much more aggressive....

The present situation in Armenia, like that in Nagorno-Karabakh itself, developed several days before the clash in the Karabakh settlement of Khodzhaly that was its "official" cause. Just what did bring about this situation?

Yes, it must be admitted that the Party and government decisions on providing social and economic assistance to the population of the Nagorno-Karabakh Autonomous Province are being fulfilled slowly. This is drawing justified criticism from people in both Azerbaijan and Armenia. But what can be done, when for all practical purposes people have not been working and emotions and passions have not calmed down in the autonomous province for such a long time? No, I think that the real reasons for the new wave of strikes in the autonomous province lie elsewhere. This has been confirmed, albeit indirectly, by their organizers, members of the so-called "council of directors," which is essentially the "Krunk Committee" that was dissolved by the Presidium of the Azerbaijan Republic Supreme Soviet. While continuing to insist that Nagorno-Karabakh be annexed by Armenia, they have put forth new ultimatums: Stop all checkups and inspections of enterprises, close all criminal cases that have been instituted, including cases against those who made grenades, expel representatives of the Azerbaijan and USSR Prosecutor's Offices from the Nagorno-Karabakh Autonomous Province, appoint a new province prosecutor – who would have to be an Armenian and a native of Nagorno-Karabakh – and withdraw the troop units.

We agree that the demands are unambiguous. They appeared right after the prosecutor's office finally made a serious attempt to get at the sources of corruption, bribery and embezzlement, and, incidentally, quite some time before the Khodzhaly tragedy. We will return to the events in Nagorno-Karabakh and finish talking about why and for whom the attack on the province prosecutor's office, for instance, was necessary.

For now, however, let's talk about the events in Yerevan. There, it turns out, the current situation was preceded by stepped-up activity on the part of law-enforcement agencies. In August and the first 10 days of September alone, when a special operations group of the USSR Ministry of Internal Affairs' Chief Administration for Combating the Embezzlement of Socialist Property and Speculation began to operate, over 200 crimes were brought to light, including 57 instances of the embezzlement of socialist property (on a large scale), 49 instances of speculation (22 of them on a large or an exceptionally large scale), about 10 instances of bribery, and others. The number of crimes is measured in the hundreds, and the losses in millions of rubles!

What is the connection between this and the strikes in support of the annexation of the Nagorno-Karabakh Autonomous Province by Armenia?

"One can't talk about a direct connection as yet," noted the head of the operations group of the USSR Ministry of Internal Affairs' Chief Administration for Combating the Embezzlement of Socialist Property and Speculation (whose name will not be given, for understandable reasons), "but the very disruption of law and order plays into the criminals' hands. It's no accident that in July, when the strikes last reached a peak, only one-fourth (!) as many crimes were brought to light as in August."

Is inaction in the struggle against corruption really in the interests of those tens of thousands of people who even now, as these lines are being written, are holding a rally in Theater Square?

With the advent of the new leadership, a cleansing process began. A number of Party and economic executives were forced to leave their cushy jobs....

It must be said that the authorities do not always behave resolutely and consistently. This is especially true with respect to the leaders of the "Karabakh Committee," who, as time goes on, are more and more apt to resort to confrontations and to hold unauthorized rallies, at which they sometimes proclaim provocative demands, insult Party and government bodies, and even raise the question of seizing power. So as not to be accused of making unfounded statements, let us quote some things we heard in Theater Square in recent days. We will give the speakers' names.

V. Siradegyan. – "The chief mistake made on Feb. 26 was to end the strike from a position of strength.*** We are not a whining nation but a fighting, belligerent one.*** We must stop holding explanatory talks and speak only from the position of strength given us by our unity."

L. Ter-Petrosyan. – ... "***We need Armenian military units."

M. Georgisyan. – "Ladies and gentlemen! We stand on the brink of destiny, and from here on let us not hear the word 'comrade.'*** Moscow's stooges cannot rule Armenia, they are the enemy's local staff.*** It has long been known that Moscow's interests are at variance with our interests. This means that we must openly declare war...."

A. Manucharyan. – "Those who are sending the Army here again should know that the Armenian people regard that Army as a colonial force."

I think that's enough. There you have it, that's how far things have gone! And this activity, which cannot be called anything but subversive, has been going on for nine months now. Frankly, all this has been going on with impunity. That's why one has to talk about the inconsistency and irresolution of the state and law-enforcement agencies. After all, if measures of persuasion don't produce results, measures of co-ercion should be applied, in accordance with Soviet law. But Yerevan's police are doing virtually nothing, and the police chief, K. Kazaryan, was merely given a severe reprimand "not to be entered in his permanent record" at a meeting of the bureau of the city Party committee, on the grounds that the director of the city internal affairs administration has been able to dump his mistakes onto the republic Ministry of Internal Affairs, even though it is he who is responsible for law and order in Yerevan. The republic's law-enforcement agencies deserve special mention. In the past few months, they have shown their inability to cope with the emergency conditions that have arisen. It is logical that a new Minister of Internal Affairs has been appointed in the republic. But this is just the first step, I think. Police agencies must be reinforced with principled, incorruptible people who are experts in their work.

We repeat once again: What is happening today is not the Armenian people's fault, but it is their misfortune. In accepting the idea of Armenia's annexation of the Nagorno-Karabakh Autonomous Province as a national idea, people have not noticed that they are being used as a cover by ambitious, corrupt individuals in order to maintain an unhealthy moral atmosphere in the republic. Isn't it time that we looked around and asked ourselves: Who is benefiting from this? And it's time that we chose our own position in this difficult, complex situation....

LET'S GET A GOOD UNDERSTANDING – Of What We're Striving For, and How

By S. Beglaryan and G. Bozoyan, excavator operators for the Zaktruboprovodstroi [Transcaucasian Pipeline Construction] Trust. *Kommunist*, Oct. 4, 1988, p. 1.

We'll say it right at the start: We, like many of our fellow citizens, are for the reunion of Nagorno-Karabakh with Armenia....

Just what are we against?

Today, life in Yerevan is following a normal course, at long last.

The occasion for the new wave of strikes, rallies and ostentatious hunger strikes in Theater Square was the marauding attack on trucks carrying freight from our republic to Stepanakert that occurred in Askeran District of Azerbaijan. Unfortunately, this was not the first such incident. Vehicles with Armenian license plates had been damaged and windows broken on cars of the Yerevan-Baku and Yerevan-Kafan passenger trains earlier, long before the current events associated with Nagorno-Karabakh. However, whereas earlier we ascribed these hostile escapades to the irresponsibility of some Azerbaijani fans of the Neftchi soccer team and explained the failure to punish them by citing the "everything goes" attitude during the period of stagnation and the protection of Geidar Aliyev [First Secretary of the Azerbaijan Communist Party Central Committee from 1969 to 1982 and a member of the Politburo of the CPSU Central Committee from 1982 to 1987 – *Trans.*], today these misdeeds are taking on a completely different coloration.

We also understand very well those who link the gunshots in Khodzhaly with Sumgait. In reality, if the Sumgait pogrom were to receive a proper evaluation, it would be condemned by the general public of the country and by official authorities, and its participants would be denounced publicly and would receive the full measure of punishment, and, possibly, there would be no new outburst of unlawful actions. This is why we join our voices to those who demand solid guarantees of security for the Armenian population of Nagorno-Karabakh, as well as a public trial of the culprits in the Sumgait tragedy.

At the same time, we are deeply indignant that these just demands of the Armenian people are debased and discredited at our rallies by irresponsible, provocative statements and unlawful actions by certain shortsighted individuals.

Let's start with the strikes. We believe that they were not the best means of attaining the goal. Furthermore, this is a harmful method in all respects....

We find something else extremely alarming....

Today there are provocateurs (it's hard to find another word for them) who are sowing anti-Russian sentiments and calling for secession from the USSR. Do they realize where, into whose embrace, they are pushing the Armenian people? Only a person devoid of reason would chop off the bough he's sitting on! ...

INSTIGATORS

By special correspondent Maj. O. Vladykin. *Krasnaya zvezda*, Dec. 14, 1988, p. 2.

Yerevan – ... On the morning of Dec. 10, a crowd suddenly began to gather... outside the [Armenian] Republic House of the Writers' Union.... Officers entered the building...and in one room found a group of people holding a businesslike discussion. Asked who they were, they replied: "We are members of the Karabakh

Committee." ... [Lt. Col. R.] Karpov suggested that the committee members...advise the citizens to disperse.... Ashot Manucharyan, one of the leaders of the unofficial organization, went into the street and read out the commandant's demand. People actually began to disperse, but half an hour later they returned in even larger numbers.... Yerevan's Military Commandant, Lt. Gen. A. Makashov, demanded that the gathering disperse.... Again they dispersed, but some time later gathered again.

By 7 p.m. the crowd had reached a size of approximately 1,000. People were uttering provocative shouts and insults addressed to the USSR government and Armed Forces. The [Karabakh] Committee's functionaries began collecting signatures on petitions of some sort. Leaflets appeared. Some fell into the hands of officers, who were startled by their contents....

"We call on the agitation and propaganda agencies and the mass news media to act decently; they must stop the cheap and senseless propaganda of internationalism and stop trumpeting the Azerbaijani government's decision to provide assistance to Armenia."...

"We call on the central government not to use the Armenian people's tragedy to declare an all-Union construction project – not to try to change Armenia's ethnic composition."...

Levon Ter-Petrosyan, Samvel Gevorkyan, Karen Vartanyan, Aleksan Akopyan, Bobken Araktsyan, Vozgen Manukyan, Ashot Manucharyan. It was they who, along with their underlings, gathered in the House of Writers on Dec. 10 and prepared the bundles of provocative leaflets. It was they who did not shrink even from taking advantage of sacred maternal feelings for their own unseemly purposes. They concocted the text of a letter to the USSR government on behalf of the republic's women and went into the crowd to collect signatures. What was in the letter? It complained about sluggishness and inadequate technical outfitting of rescue work in the disaster zone, and then came the statement: "We resolutely reject any assistance from the Azerbaijan Republic," talk about an unfavorable ecological situation in Armenia, and another statement: "We demand that the rescued children be placed in accommodations only within our republic."...

Eighteen people apprehended while engaging in provocative actions were detained, in accordance with Art. 1 of the Decree of the Presidium of the USSR Supreme Soviet dated Nov. 23, 1988. It states that in localities and communities in which a curfew has been imposed, persons who incite national strife through their actions***may be detained by administrative procedure for up to 30 days....

Ashot Manucharyan made no secret of his membership in the Armenian Karabakh Movement Committee. He had edited the texts of the aforementioned provocative leaflets. However, he filed a protest with respect to his detention. He explained that he is a Deputy to the Armenian Republic Supreme Soviet and enjoys the right of Deputy's immunity.... The sector commandant...made a phone call and ascertained that he was indeed a Deputy. Then Ashot Garnikovich was informed that the military administration had no authority to hold him any longer....

The next morning, soldiers found on the walls of many houses notices calling on

Yerevaners to take part in unauthorized rallies. Starting at 10 a.m., the commandant's office began to receive alarming reports about attacks on military patrols. Groups of rowdy thugs were throwing stones and sharpened sticks at them. Four soldiers of the Ministry of Internal Affairs' internal troops were taken to the hospital with marks left by severe beatings. Then a report was received that an infuriated crowd of several dozen people had stopped a military gasoline truck in the city. First they had thrown stones at the vehicle and broken the glass, then they had pulled Warrant Officer E. Minosyan and Pvt. A. Biknadze out of the cab and started beating them. As a result, both of them had to be taken to the hospital, too.

By noon, the military commandant's office received a report about a large gathering of people at the railway terminal. Someone had spread the inflammatory rumor that a train bound for Yerevan had been destroyed in Baku. The officer on duty in the commandant's office at once telephoned the neighboring republic's capital, then representatives of the military communications service. The rumor proved to be false. A group of officers and soldiers went to the terminal to restore order and calm people. Suddenly, a new report came in. A column of demonstrators up to 2,000 strong was marching from the House of Writers to V. I. Lenin Square. They were shouting the slogans contained in the leaflets confiscated the day before....

I couldn't help wondering who was leading them. Most of the Karabakh Movement Committee's members had been detained for 30 days, and only one of them had been released.... Then Lt. Col. Yegorov told me...: "I have just been informed by one of the posts that Ashot Manucharyan has been seen among the demonstrators."

A PUBLIC AFFAIRS WRITER'S NOTES: A CHALLENGE TO REASON AND HONOR

By Miroslav Buzhkevich. *Pravda*, Dec. 16, 1988, p. 8.

Yerevan – At a regular morning planning session, one of those conducted daily by N. I. Ryzhkov, chairman of the commission of the Politburo of the CPSU Central Committee, a speaker said:

"Yesterday in Leninakan, people appeared who not only are trying to persuade residents not to allow their children to be taken away from the disaster site to outside Armenia but are also advising adults not to leave the disaster-destroyed city for other republics, where they will be provided with housing at health resorts, hotels and dormitories. They say that no one will be allowed to return to Armenia."

It has been ascertained that once again provocateurs from the disbanded "Karabakh Committee" are speaking out.... Whispering, aggravating fear in the hearts of those who still have not recovered from the shock caused by the tragedy, the death of loved ones and the destruction of their homes, they are dooming those who believe them to new and unwarranted suffering. And all this is being done under the motto of "saving" the Armenian nation....

No one expected the cruel blow from nature – science still cannot see into the future, it cannot predict the actions of the elements. Therefore, with all the will in the world, it was not possible to establish a front of rescue work in an hour, a day or two days. There were disruptions, blunders and lack of coordination. The leaders of the "Karabakh Committee," pointing their fingers at Party and Soviet agencies in the republic, and later at the commission of the Union government, raised a fuss: "You see, either they don't know how to help the Armenian people or they don't want to, so we'll do it." They are demonstrating activeness in every way. The republic newspaper Kommunist reports many such instances.

Their representatives have set up their own headquarters in the Armenian Writers' Union; this headquarters has begun to send commands and instructions to subordinate subcommittees on how to organize rescue work, it has tried to direct freight shipments, and it has reported to the Ministry of Public Health unverified, inaccurate information which for all practical purposes disoriented the organization of assistance for the victims.

But not only have the arms of the "headquarters people" proven to be short, their hands are simply empty. They are not doing anything.... So the "Karabakh Committee" has begun to change its tactics.

Rumors began to spread, each one more scathing than the next. On the first night after the catastrophe, large numbers of Yerevaners were driven out of their homes into the streets: They had been telephoned and warned that a new earthquake was expected. Then the "expose of the century" followed: A nuclear bomb had been exploded under Leninakan! ...

Residents gathered in the center of Yerevan. They were asked to disperse and to observe established procedures. However, the "Karabakh Committee" leader A. Manucharyan shouted, "We'll make them shoot us." As the saying goes, he suffered a memory lapse: He seemed to have forgotten about those who were buried in the ruins of Spitak and Leninakan and thirsted for blood on the streets of the republic's capital. Many of those who heard him realized this. People took exception to Manucharyan from the sidewalks and balconies: Come to your senses, don't disgrace the Armenian people! He was unable to provoke a disturbance....

Oh, how they "look out for" the people, put out news bulletins and appeals and send petitions to the UN.... Their statements about the friendship among peoples are especially hypocritical. The leaders of the disbanded "Karabakh Committee" have worked out the program of an "Armenian National Movement." It contains words to the effect that the movement is "not directed against other peoples. Our principle is to live in peace and harmony with all the neighboring peoples." But at the same time, "Karabakh Committee" activists organized a demonstration in the village of Amasia in which 30 schoolchildren demanded the dismissal of Azerbaijanis.

Let's look behind the scenes of current events. The "Karabakh Committee" leaders are at work, but corrupt wheeler-dealers of various sorts, the godfathers of the local mafia, are skimming the cream. They are very cozy and comfortable hiding behind the backs of political demagogues. The local prosecutor's office and the police have virtually no time to deal with these crooks: The nationality-based clashes must be extinguished, and order must be maintained in the cities and villages. But at the rallies, the statement is made: If you are with the "Karabakh Committee," that means you're a patriot. If you're a bribetaker or a plunderer of public property, that makes no difference....

How long will the activists from the officially disbanded "Karabakh Committee" be allowed to capitalize on restructuring and glasnost? ...

Whoever has challenged the reason and honor of the people is no fellow traveler of the people! It is time to stop them, using both the political and the administrative strength of our people's power.

RALLY AT MATENADARAN

By staff correspondent A. Sarkisyan. *Pravda*, May 13, 1989, p. 6.

Yerevan – A sanctioned rally was held in Yerevan the evening of May 11 at the institute of ancient manuscripts – Matenadaran. The organizers – representatives of an unofficial organization calling itself the Armenian National Movement – announced that they propose the convening of a special session of the Armenian Republic Supreme Soviet, which should discuss the situation that has taken shape in the Nagorno-Karabakh Autonomous Province, develop a guiding policy for the republic in this area, and discuss the progress of efforts to deal with the aftermath of the earthquake, as well as the questions of lifting the curfew and releasing the arrested members of the Karabakh Committee.

Party and Soviet executives, the city's military commandant and a representative of the republic prosecutor's office were invited to the rally. Unfortunately, none of the Party officials spoke at the rally. On the other hand, the military commandant, N. Pishchev, answered all questions calmly and in a businesslike manner. Here is an excerpt from the dialogue.

"By the decision of what agencies was a curfew instituted in the republic?"

"By the decision of the Presidium of the USSR Supreme Soviet with the consent of the Armenian Republic Supreme Soviet." ...

"Can republic agencies lift the curfew?"

"They must go to the Presidium of the USSR Supreme Soviet with a petition, and it will make the decision."

The representative of the republic prosecutor's office was asked on what basis Ministry of Internal Affairs agencies are detaining individual citizens, taking them into administrative custody for up to 30 days, and whether the lawfulness of such actions by the police is being monitored by the prosecutor's office.

"Of the 30 cases presented," A. Arutyunyan, a department head at the republic prosecutor's office, answered, "only three have been found not to have sufficient grounds."

The representative of the prosecutor's office also reported that, according to available information, the investigation of the case involving members of the Karabakh Committee has been completed, and the case will soon be turned over to the court....

RESOLUTION OF THE ARMENIAN REPUBLIC SUPREME SOVIET AND THE NAGORNO-KARABAKH NATIONAL COUNCIL ON THE REUNIFICATION OF THE ARMENIAN REPUBLIC AND NAGORNO-KARABAKH

Kommunist, Dec. 3, 1989, p. 1.

... 1. The Armenian Republic Supreme Soviet recognizes the fact of the self-determination of the Nagorno-Karabakh Autonomous Province, a fact established by the Feb. 20, 1988 and July 12, 1988 decisions of sessions of the Nagorno-Karabakh Province Soviet, as well as by the Aug. 16, 1989 decision of the Congress of Authorized Representatives of the province's population and the Oct. 19, 1989 decision of a meeting of the National Council.

2. The Armenian Republic Supreme Soviet recognizes the Congress of Authorized Representatives of Nagorno-Karabakh and the National Council it elected as the only legitimate authorities currently existing in the province.

3. The Armenian Republic Supreme Soviet and the Nagorno-Karabakh National Council proclaim the reunification of the Armenian Republic and Nagorno-Karabakh. The rights of Armenian Republic citizenship extend to the population of Nagorno-Karabakh....

6. The Presidium of the Armenian Republic Supreme Soviet, the Armenian Republic Council of Ministers and the Presidium of the Nagorno-Karabakh National Council are instructed to take all necessary measures arising out of this resolution to effect a real merging of the political, economic and cultural structures of the Armenian Republic and Nagorno-Karabakh into a unified state-political system.

G. VOSKANYAN,
Chairman of the Presidium of the Armenian Republic Supreme Soviet.
V. GRIGORYAN,
Chairman of the Nagorno-Karabakh National Council.
N. STEPANYAN,
Secretary of the Presidium of the Armenian Republic Supreme Soviet.
Dec. 1, 1989, Yerevan.

TER-PETROSYAN'S FIRST PRESS CONFERENCE

By N. Andreyev. *Izvestia*, Aug. 9, 1990, p. 2.

As already reported in Izvestia, Levon Akopovich Ter-Petrosyan has been elected Chairman of the Armenian Supreme Soviet. He is 45 years old, and is a specialist in oriental studies and a Doctor of Philology by education. He became head of the Karabakh Committee in 1988. On Dec. 10 of that year he was arrested along with other activists of that movement. Thanks to the support of the country's democratic forces (Academician A. Sakharov, among others, came forward in his defense), he was released.

The election of Levon Ter-Petrosyan is yet another indication of a trend in the democratic process: The opposition is coming to power....

Ter-Petrosyan is now in Moscow, where he has met and talked with N. Ryzhkov, V. Bakatin and V. Kryuchkov. At a press conference on Aug. 9, Ter-Petrosyan told Soviet and foreign correspondents about the results of these talks, as well as the problems facing the republic.

Three subjects took precedence: Compliance with USSR President M. Gorbachev's Decree on the disarming of illegal armed groups, the problems of Armenia's state independence and the problems surrounding Nagorno-Karabakh. L. Ter-Petrosyan stated that figures on the size of the Armenian National Army are greatly exaggerated; according to him, it has no more than 5,000 members. He wondered why neither the Ministry of Internal Affairs nor the State Security Committee [KGB] is refuting rumors about an army alleged to be 170,000 strong. On the subject of disarming the ANA, L. Ter-Petrosyan said that he needs time to take control of this process. He affirmed that the USSR President's Decree will be carried out, but stressed that this will be done by the republic on its own....

The Chairman of the Armenian Supreme Soviet favors direct ties with the outside world and with other Union republics. He sees no need for a Union Treaty, but if there is one, he believes it should be some kind of coordinating document, while a Union Constitution and Unionwide laws are not necessary at all.

"We are ready to hold talks with Azerbaijan," said Ter-Petrosyan. "There are grounds for compromise." In his opinion, the first step in this direction should be to restore Soviet power in Nagorno-Karabakh and put Soviet laws back into effect there. He believes that there are favorable prospects for establishing good relations with Armenia's neighbors – Georgia, Turkey, Iran and Azerbaijan. When asked what he thinks of the idea of a common Caucasian home, L. Ter-Petrosyan said that this proposal advanced by Georgia's "greens" is a noble concept, but under current conditions seems romantic....

Ter-Petrosyan said that he has reached an agreement with V. Kryuchkov that the republic KGB will not conceal information from the republic's leaders.

LEVON TER-PETROSYAN: CONFRONTATION HAS EXHAUSTED ITS POTENTIAL

Izvestia, Oct. 9, 1990, p. 3.

Editor's Note. – On Oct. 8, on his way to Yerevan after his trip to the US, Levon Ter-Petrosyan, Chairman of the Armenian Supreme Soviet, made a stop in Moscow. Renat Abdullin and Armen Arushanov, special correspondents from the Interfax agency, talked with him.

* * *

Question. – First of all, we'd like to know about the results of your trip to the US.

Answer. – My visit did not pursue any practical goals. It was of purely political significance, first of all as a display of the republic's sovereignty, an act of breaking its political isolation and starting to conduct an independent foreign policy, and second, it was a coordination of our efforts with the Armenian diaspora in building a new Armenian state.

Q. – What problems did you touch on in your meetings with representatives of Congress and the administration?

A. – ... I tried to show that very significant changes are under way in the Soviet Union, that real power is shifting from the center to the republics, and that American policy should be reoriented in accordance with these changes....

People in the US assess the status of the Baltic republics in an entirely different way, since their occupation in 1940 was not recognized by the world community. When it comes to the other republics, the Americans are showing more restraint and caution, waiting until the status of the center and the republics becomes clearly defined in the USSR....

Q. – In this connection, we'd like to know your opinion of the idea of a new Union Treaty....

A. – ... Ideally, we see the Soviet Union in the same form as the European Community, where every country enjoys complete independence and the central agencies have only consultative functions.

To be specific, we don't rule out the possibility of concluding a new Union Treaty provided that there is no new all-Union Constitution and Union legislation and no Union government. Those are superfluous agencies.

Q. – What is the shape of relations right now between the republic authorities and the military personnel in Armenia?

A. – ... No conflicts are arising between the Army and the people. [The Army leadership] welcomes the fact that we are conducting all operations to stabilize the situation in Armenia using our own forces.

Q. – The most critical question right now is the problem of Nagorno-Karabakh and the relations between Armenia and Azerbaijan. Are there prospects for settling the conflict?

A. – The position of the Armenian leadership is very clear. The strategy of confrontation that was pursued by both sides has exhausted its potential.... At the very beginning of my work as Chairman of the Armenian Supreme Soviet, I stated that we were ready to sit down at the negotiating table with Azerbaijan. I had a telephone conversation with Azerbaijani President Ayaz Mutalibov. Then we had a meeting in Moscow in the presence of Mikhail Gorbachev. So there is a basis for compromise....

Both sides have an interest in a peaceful settlement [of the Karabakh problem]. The point of departure for a compromise could be the restoration of the legitimate authorities in Karabakh and the ensuring of normal life activity for the people of the Nagorno-Karabakh Autonomous Province. To begin with, normal life must be restored in the autonomous province.

NOTES

1. Yegishe Charents (1897-1937), whose original last name was Sogomonyan, was a purge victim.

2. Samed Vurgun (1906-1956), whose original last name was Vekilov, was a prominent Azerbaijani writer.

Chapter 2 | Demonstrations in Azerbaijan

AN ALARMING SPRING

By Famil Mekhti, poet, and Khudu Mamedov, corresponding member of the Azerbaijan Republic Academy of Sciences. *Bakinsky rabochy*, April 2, 1988, p. 3.

... Today it is perfectly clear that these events [in the Nagorno-Karabakh Autonomous Province] were preceded by a great deal of work, and emotions were whipped up. As a result, thousands and thousands of people in Nagorno-Karabakh were torn away from their work and drawn into the events that were taking place. Every day, hundreds of buses (this was an illegal use of state vehicles and fuel) brought people who had left their workplaces to Stepanakert's central square. There, various noisy slogans and appeals could be heard. In an attempt to capitalize on the concepts of "democracy" and "openness," slogans of a provocative nature were used: "Karabakh weeps, but Moscow is silent," "Neither bread nor water – only annexation to Armenia," etc. Was there anything the speakers – representatives of a wide range of occupations, including writers, scholars and journalists – didn't say?! One heard the names of Western countries to which appeals for help in solving the "Karabakh problem" were addressed.

Since when is it possible to live in a single family with fraternal peoples and call on outsiders for help?...

We believe that all peoples have common sense, which dictates the kind of behavior, system of upbringing and standards of communication that should prevent discord between people. Our old men and elders have never conducted discussions inciting hostility toward others, stirred the embers of past times of strife, or cultivated feelings of enmity. For that reason, an opposite position is cause for surprise. We have in mind the article headed "From the Standpoint of Truth" in the newspaper Sovetsky Karabakh [Soviet Karabakh] for March 15, 1988, by the veteran journalist G. Aivazyan. The author calls himself a journalist, but his actions are at variance with the norms of journalistic ethics. He doesn't stop to think that, by calling up the memory of tragic events, he is arousing a feeling of bitterness in people. Passions and emotions prevent him from analyzing what happened soberly and in a well-considered way, finding the sources of the trouble, and helping to create peace and quiet in the present difficult atmosphere. Moreover, he expresses decided dissatisfaction with those who object to the dissemination of Z. Balayan's book "The Hearth" [Ochag], which was written from nonclass positions and is harmful to internationalist upbringing, a book that has been condemned by a resolution of the USSR State Committee for Publishing, Printing and the Book Trade.

Azerbaijanis and Armenians live together on Karabakh soil and have done so from time immemorial.... So why should we divide up our honest meal, our hospitality, the water of our springs, the refrain of the song that we sing together? So why should we divide up the gas burning in our homes, the electricity, the cotton? Let us think about the sacred bonds that unite us, let us try to grasp their essence, let us do everything to strengthen them....

SESSIONS OF THE UNION-REPUBLIC SUPREME SOVIETS: AZERBAIJAN REPUBLIC

By special correspondents A. Sabirov and R. Talyshinsky. *Izvestia*, June 19, 1988, p. 2.

Baku – Last month, before the regular session of the Azerbaijan Republic Supreme Soviet opened, an unusual stirring of passions was noted in Baku.... Alarm began to grow after the central and republic newspapers and other news media, for some reason, fell silent all at once.

However, information leaked out one way or another. It became known that Stepanakert was seething, as before. The stories told by Azerbaijanis who had recently left Armenia were especially disturbing. A rally was held in the city. The next day, there was a second rally. And then V. I. Lenin Square, the largest in Baku, kept filling with thousands and thousands of people.

Overly emotional voices were heard there, too. But city residents asked the basic questions in a completely reasonable way. What, specifically, is being undertaken to normalize the situation in the [Nagorno-Karabakh] Autonomous Province? Is assistance being provided to people who have come to Azerbaijan from the neighboring [Armenian] Republic recently?... And finally, the voters wanted to know why the [Azerbaijan] Republic Supreme Soviet has still not definitely and publicly stated its attitude on the question, posed by the Nagorno-Karabakh Autonomous Province, of transferring the province from one republic to the other.

In short, it was demanded that the mechanism of openness "get working." The republic press and television returned again to this crucial subject. Numerous meetings in labor collectives and meetings between Deputies and their constituents were held.

On June 13, the Presidium of the Azerbaijan Republic Supreme Soviet examined the petition by seputies to the Nagorno-Karabakh Autonomous Province Soviet asking for the transfer of the province from the Azerbaijan Republic to the Armenian Republic. The discussion was wide-ranging. Nearly all the members of the Presidium spoke....

After discussing the petition from the deputies to the province Soviet in conformity with Art. 78 of the USSR Constitution and Art. 70 of the Azerbaijan Republic Constitution, according to which a republic's territory cannot be changed without its consent, the Presidium of the Azerbaijan Supreme Soviet deemed it unacceptable. But it decided to put this question on the session's agenda.

At the suggestion of voters, the session's proceedings were carried live on republic television and radio, for the first time....

Acting on the results of its discussion, the session unanimously approved the resolution of the Presidium of the republic Supreme Soviet. The Deputies noted that the resolution adopted by the CPSU Central Committee and the USSR Council of Ministers, "On Measures to Accelerate the Social and Economic Development of the Nagorno-Karabakh Autonomous Province of the Azerbaijan Republic in 1988-1995," and the measures carried out by the republic Communist Party Central Committee and Council of Ministers are creating favorable conditions for accelerating the development of productive forces and satisfying the economic and spiritual requirements of the Armenian and the Azerbaijani population and of other nationalities in the autonomous province. It is necessary to unite the efforts of representatives of all nationalities to fulfill this resolution, normalize the situation in Nagorno-Karabakh, and ensure the most favorable living and working conditions for people.

In response to an appeal from the Armenian Republic Supreme Soviet, the Azerbaijan Republic Supreme Soviet, proceeding from the interests of maintaining the existing national-territorial structure of the country as fixed by the USSR Constitution and guided by the principles of internationalism and the interests of the Azerbaijani and Armenian peoples and the other nations and nationalities of the [Azerbaijan] Republic, deemed the transfer of the Nagorno-Karabakh Autonomous Province from the Azerbaijan Republic to the Armenian Republic impossible. In doing so, the session emphasized that this would not be in keeping with the goals of strengthening friendship among the peoples of our country or with the tasks of restructuring....

CURRENT TOPIC: RALLY IN THE CITY

By E. Movludzade and A. Kerimov. *Bakinsky rabochy*, Nov. 20, 1988, p. 3.

For three days now, columns of demonstrators have been streaming into V. I. Lenin Square. They are primarily young people and students, but during the rally one can see among the gathering some middle-aged people, and at times even white-haired elders.

This time one could probably have predicted the mass expression of public indignation: It was a really quite unprecedented incident that drew this reaction. The report, published by the Azerbaijan News Agency, that in the area of Topkhana, near Shusha, in an ecologically clean zone known as a site of historical interest, cooperative members from Armenia are felling valuable and rare species of trees – that plots of land are being cleared for construction – and the rumors preceding this activity have disturbed the people in the republic; they are demanding that effective measures be taken to stop the construction and to punish the culprits.

Everyone can understand the feeling of concern expressed by those who spoke in the square: Shusha is one of the most beautiful parts of Azerbaijan, it is an all-Union health resort, and attempts, unsanctioned by the authorities, to build something there are viewed by the rally's participants as a violation of the republic's sovereignty and interference in its internal affairs....

While expressing what is on the whole a natural concern over what has happened in Topkhana, one can hardly consider as reasonable the demand that the problems that have arisen be solved within 24 hours, as was stated here. The same thing can be said of the fact that, along with slogans expressing support for the decision of the Presidium of the USSR Supreme Soviet concerning the Nagorno-Karabakh Autonomous Province, one can see posters the sense of which is very far removed from the questions under discussion.

Besides, one must bear in mind here that the resolution of the conflict that has arisen requires both time and persistent work along these lines. It is hardly reasonable to create a field of public tension and exert forceful pressure over a particular case....

ANXIOUS DAYS AND NIGHTS – Report From the Rally in V. I. Lenin Square
By E. Abaskuliyeva and R. Mustafayev. *Bakinsky rabochy*, Nov. 23, 1988, p. 3.

Nov. 21-22... In the main square of the republic's capital,... many thousands of people are in a state of agitation.

What brought them to the square?

The speeches from the rostrum, conversations with participants in the rally, and the reaction of the gathering to various proposals voiced here indicate one thing unequivocally: The last drop that caused the cup of long-suffering to overflow was talk that began as rumors, later confirmed by reports in the mass news media, about unauthorized attempts by workers from a cooperative formed at the Kanaker Aluminum Plant in the Armenian Republic to carry out a construction project in the small town of Topkhana, near Shusha....

The public of the [Azerbaijan] Republic cannot fail to be worried about the fate of the Azerbaijani population of the Nagorno-Karabakh Autonomous Province (this concern has been manifested with special clarity in the speeches at the rallies here). For many months now, the Azerbaijanis living in Stepanakert and in nearby villages have been deprived of the opportunity to work. They have been reinstated in their jobs by agencies of the prosecutor's office, but nevertheless they have, to all intents and purposes, been deprived of their constitutional right to work. The press has already reported that Azerbaijani villages in the province are not being provided with food, medical supplies and other prime necessities....

There are still quite a few incidents indicating the hostile attitude that the leadership of the Nagorno-Karabakh Autonomous Province takes toward the republic. The position of G. Pogosyan, the Party leader of the Nagorno-Karabakh Autonomous Province, can serve no end except the kindling of national strife.

Those who have gathered in the square continue to be greatly worried over the fate of the Azerbaijanis living in Armenia. It is not by chance that calls are heard, both from the rostrum and in the square, that firm guarantees be demanded from the Armenian Republic's government for these people's safety, that assistance be provided to them, and that the problems they are facing be solved promptly and effectively.

It will soon be a year since we first witnessed, as we now have many times, this bitter picture: Time after time, humiliated, insulted people who have been treated unfairly and driven from their homes in peacetime crowd around the building of the Azerbaijan Communist Party Central Committee.

Refugees

Over the past year, each of us, after hurrying to the refugees with food or with clothing, carried away in our hearts yet another bitter drop of truth....

The speakers at the rally are putting forth more and more new demands. The demand that the safety of the Azerbaijanis living in Armenia be guaranteed, which is essentially fair, ends in a form that is very much an ultimatum, suggesting that if it is not met relations with the Armenian Republic should be broken off....

The feelings that have now seized a large part of society are based on a realization that the July 19 decision of the Presidium of the USSR Supreme Soviet [that the Nagorno-Karabakh Autonomous Province is to remain part of the Azerbaijan Republic – *Trans.*] is being fulfilled only pro forma, and this cannot help but evoke legitimate indignation from people....

The people are listening with interest to a large part of the demands made by the unofficial association Varlyg, demands that have to do with the strained ecological situation in the republic and inattention there to questions of the native language and history....

An extreme situation is, understandably, giving rise to extreme demands. And how can this be avoided, when yesterday alone information circulating in the square about the state of affairs in the Topkhana forests changed three times? The tension is growing, and some speakers are suggesting a shift to more drastic methods of influence, including republic-wide strikes. Since a resolution of the main question has not been forthcoming, these speeches, as a rule, are welcomed by tens of thousands of people....

The unanimity and will of the people in favor of the earliest possible resolution of the "Karabakh problem" are manifested not only in the large scale of the rallies. A truly endless flow of food and clothing is coming into the square....

The name of the national poet of Azerbaijan, Bakhtiyar Vagabzade, enjoys deserved respect. His calls for wisdom and sober assessments always find a response in the hearts of people whose feelings have become especially exacerbated in the current difficult situation. At the rally yesterday, he proposed that an appeal be sent to the Presidium of the Armenian Republic Supreme Soviet suggesting the creation of autonomy for the Azerbaijanis who live in compact groups in Armenia. Otherwise, in his opinion, the autonomy of the Nagorno-Karabakh Autonomous Province in Azerbaijan should be abolished....

Here in the square, there is no room for hypocrisy and lies. Here everyone demands and expects only the truth.

LEARNING DEMOCRACY: WHY THE NEWSPAPER WAS LATE

Izvestia, Nov. 26, 1988, p. 2.

Moscow – On Nov. 25, Izvestia subscribers in the Azerbaijan Republic received that day's issue of the newspaper very late. The reason was that the entire Azerbaijan press run – 134,000 copies – had to be printed in Moscow and delivered to Baku by plane: The Baku printers had refused to print Izvestia. What happened?

The day before, at 3 p.m. on Nov. 24, a representative of our publishing house in Baku reported by telephone that the workers at the local print shop had announced that they were not going to print the central newspapers, since they were not reporting anything about events in Azerbaijan. They issued an ultimatum: If the newspapers get off with silence today, too, we aren't going to print them.

The director of the Azerbaijan Communist Party Central Committee's publishing house and print shop urgently called a meeting of the labor collective, at which key officials of the apparatus of the Azerbaijan Communist Party Central Committee and representatives of the public were present. The debate went on until 7 p.m., but attempts at persuasion got nowhere. By that time, right on schedule, page images of the new issue of Izvestia, which published information on the rallies in Baku and Yerevan, had been transmitted by facsimile machine from Moscow. However, this time the printers were indignant over the fact that mention of the construction of a shop at the aluminum plant in the health resort of Topkhana, which was the reason for the new flare-up of passions around Nagorno-Karabakh, was not detailed enough, while the events taking place in Baku had not been given objective coverage, in their opinion. Moreover, the text called the town Topkhan, not Topkhana, which is the correct spelling. The latter was apparently the "deciding argument" in their refusal to print the newspaper at all.

We apologize to our readers for the inaccuracy. But we cannot fail to note the very unusual understanding of glasnost and democracy under the banners of which complaints are being made against the newspaper. As you see, the essence of the demands is just this: The newspaper should reflect only our viewpoint, and no other. However, this position has been sharply condemned more than once in numerous letters to Izvestia from Azerbaijan.

* * *

Izvestia's staff correspondent in Baku, R. Talyshinsky, reported at 4 p.m. on Nov. 25 that the print shop workers are continuing to insist on their refusal to print the newspaper today, too.

A WOMAN'S WORD, A MOTHER'S WORD

By S. Mirzoyeva. *Bakinsky rabochy*, Nov. 27, 1988, p. 3.

... In these days of extreme situations, many women [in Baku] on their own initiative and at the call of their hearts – have formed the organization Ana (Mother).

With maternal tenderness and special women's words, they come to the square to see those who have been there for 10 days now and who have been most resolutely and categorically putting their demands to the government and to the leaders of the republic Party organization. They are women of deep refinement grown wise with life's experience; among them are actresses, musicians, scientists, educators, physicians, cultural-enlightenment personnel and architects....

These women approach the bonfires late in the evening, when "rally" life is calming down, the fervor of argumentation is slacking off, and there is time to discuss events unhurriedly and to thoughtfully analyze previously unheard-of phenomena....

Doctor of Philology Dilyara Aliyeva says:

"Of course, these young people are right when they demand the formation of an autonomous province in the Armenian Republic for the population of Azerbaijani nationality. How can people be driven away from their homes with no one really standing up for them, no one demanding that their rights be observed? After all, that's essentially what happened to many of the refugees from Armenia. One has to support these young people, who are demanding that human rights – the age-old right to a place to live – be upheld."

"How can we put up with the fact that such an authoritative body as the Presidium of the USSR Supreme Soviet has taken no firm measures to implement its own decisions on Nagorno-Karabakh?" asks republic People's Artist Gyulkhar Gasanova.

"But a great many things in the square's demands are not reasonable or justified," she says. "Can one really demand the immediate implementation of something that takes time and money? Can you really allow yourself to leave your workplace and go on strike? Who is it that suffers from this? It's the people close to you, your own family...."

"Their children's absence from home gives mothers enormous concern and grief. Look at how many women come here every day and stay through the night because they're worried about their sons and daughters who are at the rally."

The singer talked about this, about the need to retain prudence and tranquility in this difficult hour for the republic....

FEWER EMOTIONS, MORE WISDOM!

By special correspondents A. Romanov and A. Teplyuk. *Komsomolskaya pravda*, Dec. 1, 1988, p. 4.

... Baku – Strikes and demonstrations, the impetus for which was the erection of an industrial facility in the Nagorno-Karabakh Autonomous Province without Baku's permission, are continuing in the Azerbaijani capital.

The young Bakuan N. Zeinalov has ended his protest hunger strike. Our Azerbaijani readers have asked us to give the reasons for the hunger strike. They were the demands that the hearing of the Sumgait case be transferred to Sumgait, that the Krunk leadership be prosecuted, and that the work at Topkhana be stopped.... Construction has been halted there, and materials and equipment have been removed.

If you have money, you can get anything in Baku. The exception today is plane tickets. There is a great deal of milling around at Aeroflot ticket counters. To prevent abuses and ensure fairness, the military commandant's office has taken control of ticket distribution. The military is also monitoring railway stations, the airport, and communications, trade and public-catering enterprises.

The number of people wanting to withdraw money from their savings deposits has risen sharply. Most of them are Armenians. Savings-bank employees urge the depositors to use letters of credit, but most clients prefer cash.

In a conversation with us, A. Velibekov, general director of the republic Center of Hygiene and Epidemiology, scotched rumors that Baku's main square has become the site of an extensive dysentery epidemic. But, Abbas Soltanovich said, disaster is only one step away. Food is being trucked to the rally participants from outlying districts, but sanitary physicians are unable to inspect it. Demonstrators bring their own food with them. Elementary conditions for receiving food are lacking. We can confirm that the unsanitary conditions on the square are appalling. Sheep carcasses are cut up in a nearby public garden. In the past few days, the weather has turned sharply colder. The threat of a flu epidemic has grown. T. Kasumov, the republic Minister of Public Health, has talked about this with alarm. There are hundreds of thousands of people on the square every day. Among them are a great many children.

But there is a virus more dangerous than the flu. Thousands of children have happily joined their older brothers and sisters at the rallies. They see the events as an entertaining game and skip their classes. Older people are moved when a little boy yells out slogans.

We were astounded by an article in the newspaper Pioner Azerbaidzhana [Azerbaijan Young Pioneer] bearing the subhead "The Determination of the Sons of the Land of Fires" (Nov. 25, 1988). "Your coevals are among the demonstrators, too," the author, A. Aslanogly, writes with delight. "Classes have been canceled in most Baku schools. Groups of youngsters run to the square, not wanting to fall behind their parents or their older brothers and sisters. These wonderful children-patriots' anger, anxiety and resolve and the innocent and serene looks on their faces – all of which seem not in keeping with their ages – touch the heart, and we say with pride: 'Well done!'" Later on is a passage that is downright inflammatory: "When the homeland is in trouble, when encroachments are made on its land, the descendants of Babek, Kyorogly, Dzhevanshir, Nabi and Khadzhar are prepared for struggle and exploits in the name of the people." Not a word about the fact that schoolchildren are required to attend classes....

The tension in the republic is being exacerbated by the group of refugees from Armenia. To elicit sympathy, some of them tell inaccurate, clearly exaggerated stories of cruelty toward them in Armenia....

More than 600 people have been detained for curfew violations. Instances of wrecking have come to light in the Lenin Borough oil fields. Criminals have cut 300 drive belts on oil-well pumping jacks....

COMMUNIQUÉ FROM THE MILITARY COMMANDANT OF THE BAKU CITY SPECIAL DISTRICT

Bakinsky rabochy, Dec. 3, 1988, p. 4.

The situation in the city of Baku has grown increasingly tense in the past few days as a result of the continuing influx of refugees of the Azerbaijani nationality.

Overnight on Dec. 1-2, disturbances were provoked on the square near the railway station and in Ordzhonikidze, Nasimin, Azizbekov, Nizami, Lenin and other boroughs of the city.

In the vicinity of the railway station, a crowd of as many as 1,500 people tried to beat up a citizen of the Armenian nationality. Attempts at disorderly actions were stopped by troops, using measures that have been adopted. In five instances, warning-type weapons were employed to restore public order.

In all, 417 people and 63 vehicles have been detained and 31 people arrested for violating curfew regulations. Nine firearms and two knives have been confiscated.... – [signed] Col. Gen. M. Tyagunov, Military Commandant of the Baku City Special District.

LESSONS - Our Special Correspondent Reports From Baku

By Lt. Col. O. Falichev. *Krasnaya zvezda*, Dec. 24, 1988, p. 6.

... The Lt. Shmidt Machinery Plant holds a special position among the over 30 different industrial enterprises in Baku's Narimanov Borough.... Recently, when Lenin Square was seething with the crowd that besieged it for many days, this plant was one of the first to pour oil on the fire, as the saying goes, by actively supporting the demonstrators. Moreover, its workers brought forth from their ranks a leader who laid claim to the role of "son of the people" – Neimat Panakhov. To be frank, at first he achieved considerable success. It is said that when the seething square refused to listen to Party or Soviet officials, Neimat Panakhov would come out onto the rostrum, raise his hand over his head – and the crowd of half a million would fall silent.

How was it that he, a worker from Shop No. 12 at the Lt. Shmidt Plant, was able not only to win such popularity but also to manipulate the consciousness of the masses and inflame nationalistic sentiments? ...

During the long years of stagnation, as we call them, people at the plant became alienated, as it were, from the means of production, from participation in the plant's management and, finally, from the distribution of benefits and housing.... Many workers live in dormitories, including some men with families....

"It used to be that men coming from outlying areas to work at the plant would live in dormitories, and their wives and children couldn't even get residence permits to join them," said M. Vaskanov, vice-chairman of the plant's trade union committee....

"Gradually, other problems snowballed as well. There was a demand that those responsible for this situation be found. And found they were – in the person of representatives of the Armenian nationality, who were said to be undeservedly using things that there wasn't enough of for the Azerbaijanis themselves.... In that situation, a spark was enough to set off an explosion. It appeared in the form of nationality problems stirred up by 'well-wishers,' problems that have always been complicated in this region."...

However, Panakhov must be given his due. Thus, ultimately it began to seem to people that he had been able to "wangle," so to speak, what neither the trade union, the Party organization nor the plant's director had managed to get over many years.

When the strikes began, when the plant ran up against the fact of massive discontent among the workers, who lived from hand to mouth and without their families, and when people, through rallies, demonstrations and absences from work, began trying to get their often legitimate rights, the city authorities were forced to give residence permits to family members. That's what they told me at the plant.

Sensing his strength and support, Panakhov managed to get an audience with A. Kh. Vezirov, First Secretary of the republic Communist Party Central Committee. Soon more than 80 apartments were allotted to the workers, although earlier they had been allotted only 23 apartments a year, and those were given out very reluctantly. Certainly this was the result not of Panakhov's visit to the First Secretary but of a serious analysis by the republic's leadership of the situation that had developed. But certain people backing Panakhov presented this as his personal achievement....

Quite a bit is being done at the plant to normalize the situation.... Explanatory work is being conducted with everyone who files an application to leave. Those who took part in the mass disturbances have been recommended for dismissal for leaving work and causing substantial material damage to the plant's collective.... Some of those who left the plant have returned, and others are coming back now....

As for Panakhov, he has been detained by law-enforcement agencies in accordance with Art. 1 of the Nov. 23, 1988, decree of the Presidium of the USSR Supreme Soviet. The investigatory group of the USSR Prosecutor's Office has reported that he is accused of disturbing public order and fomenting national discord. An investigation has begun with respect to a number of other participants in the disturbances who have been detained.

SERVE THE TRUE INTERESTS OF THE PEOPLE – Who Wants to Destabilize the Situation and Stir Up Strife Between Nationalities?

Pravda, Dec. 26, 1988, p. 4.

Trans. Note. – This article is reprinted from the Azerbaijan Republic press – Kommunist (in Azerbaijani), Bakinsky rabochy (in Russian) and Kommunist (in Armenian). Some minor cuts have been made.

* * *

... Today the situation in Baku and the [Azerbaijan] Republic is stabilizing. This is attested to by the full-strength work of industrial enterprises, construction projects and transportation, the resumption of operations as usual as regards the educational process at higher schools, technicums and [general-education] schools, and the return of thousands of Armenians to their homes in Azerbaijan. In order to more quickly overcome the lag caused by rallies and people's failure to show up for work, many labor collectives are working on both Saturdays and Sundays....

It will take us a long time to fully comprehend what happened and to overcome the political and moral setbacks stemming from the events that disrupted the republic's normal work rhythm and our constructive life. But even now, without procrastinating, we should be analyzing what happened and trying to find out where it all began, what led us to the brink of danger, and who aggravated the situation, how and why. Unhealthy speculation around Nagorno-Karabakh, unauthorized rallies and demonstrations, the rampages of hooligan groups, sometimes reaching the point of physical violence and encroachments on the honor and dignity of individuals, blackmail, threats and the use of weapons revealed the presence in Azerbaijan and in Armenia of serious anti-restructuring forces and laid bare the scope and acute nature of their opposition to the Party's course aimed at restructuring.

An odd assortment of social and antisocial elements – exponents of the petit bourgeois ideology and a narrow-minded, philistine, anarchistic morality, who worship the golden calf of gain and enrichment, and the big shots of the "shadow economy" and the corrupt clans – have united in a sturdy alliance on the common antirevolutionary basis of political, economic, social and ideological-moral sabotage of restructuring....

Events on Theater Square in Yerevan and on V. I. Lenin Square in Baku, spreading in ripples and engulfing region after region, sometimes seemed to develop according to a common, jointly conceived and carefully coordinated scenario....

What sort of individuals ruled the roost on the square in Baku, and what ideas did they use to stir up the crowd? Leadership at the rallies was very quickly gained by Neimat Panakhov, a lathe operator at the Lt. Shmidt Machinery Plant. He impressed a large part of the gathering: In his very first speeches, this worker from a respected major enterprise declared himself a fervent supporter of revolutionary transformations and restructuring. He speaks from the rostrum without notes, looking for a kindred spirit in each of his listeners. Few people guessed that this passionate champion of "renewal," the "turbulent" Neimat, was a straw man, a spokesman for the opinions and a vehicle for the aims of the anti-restructuring forces and the corrupt clans, those who yearn to again lord it over the republic and see it as their private domain.

The speeches of N. Panakhov, instigator and dangerous demagogue, contained appeals and slogans that cannot fail to arouse indignation among honest toilers and the Azerbaijani people. They also included a "bouquet" of slanderous passages against the fighting men, sons of the Soviet people, who have risked their lives to defend the honor, dignity and lives of the working people, as well as the base manipulation of fabrications concerning the nationalities policy of the Soviet state and appeals for secession from the USSR. This hysterical character, posing as the "hero" of an ancient epic, reveled in his commands: "We aren't afraid that we'll freeze here on the square. We'll cut down all the trees growing around the square, set the House of Government on fire, and warm ourselves that way!" And this from someone who expressed outrage at the felling of trees in Topkhana.

Panakhov was often replaced on the rostrum by Gatami, an obscurantist and reactionary who urges people to return to the darkness of the Middle Ages. He has always been known for his malice and aggressiveness. Gatami has been warned more than once, he has promised that he will restrain himself, but once again he has spoken out as a fierce instigator of disturbances and a preacher of national discord. These people found not only emotional support from the crowd. A special booth stood on the square where money could be brought, supposedly for those attending the rallies. Typewriter-duplicated receipts were given out. I. Alekperov – head of the Kedabek District Soviet Executive Committee's organizational department – alone brought in large sums of money collected from more than 70 enterprises and organizations in the district, receiving an appropriate receipt....

The instigators of antisocial actions are in effect emissaries of criminal clans that are linked by bonds of mutual support and mutual assistance. In other words, what we have here is a kind of mafia, a form of organized crime.

It is no secret that the homegrown "mafiosi" often use national enmity as a screen to cover up their dirty dealings. A very indicative example is Manucharov, who proved to be a hardened criminal, wallowed in corruption, profited from the misfortune of simple toilers, and is a double-dyed nationalist. Another graphic example: Stirring up nationalistic passions, the mafia in Sheki, threatened with exposure for committing large-scale theft and other very grave offenses, organized armed attacks against the police and the prosecutor's office in order to steal documents incriminating it.

It has yet to be ascertained why firearms and ammunition were stored in the basement of the Children's World department store in Baku and at the homes of personnel of the extradepartmental guard. Day after day, these facts disclose more and more clearly the crafty and insidious designs of criminals who use destabilization and a tense atmosphere to divert the crushing blow of justice from themselves.

Major forces of the Union Prosecutor's Office and over 100 experienced investigators and operations personnel from all over the country were mobilized for the investigation of criminal cases after the February events in Sumgait. A good many specialists were forced to tear themselves away from routine business for work in Stepanakert and Yerevan. A representative of the USSR Prosecutor's Office's Investigations Department noted that the new flare-up of activity by extremists and hooligan elements in Armenia and Azerbaijan occurred during a period of work in both republics by special groups of investigators to discover the threads leading to the mafia's brain center. But instead of untangling this web, the highly skilled legal experts were compelled to spend their time investigating brawls, robberies and pogroms that took place during the days of unauthorized rallies....

The anti-restructuring forces are essentially colluding with the bureaucratized managers who were nurtured during the years of stagnation and are clinging to their privileges and their conservative, accustomed command-administrative methods of leadership.... When the very first symptoms of disturbances emerged, A. Radzhabov, First Secretary of the Sheki City Party Committee, was unable to take control of the situation, and then he fled in disgrace. Leaders of the Party organizations of the Nakhichevan Autonomous Republic and Kirovabad proved unequal to the situation. In Kirovabad, a military patrol detained the first secretary of a district Party committee, forcing him to stop only after shots were fired at his car, which was racing from Kedabek to Baku; a large sum of money, in excess of several years' salary, was found on him....

Quite a few executives [of republic enterprises] displayed unscrupulousness, ideological bankruptcy and shaky moral positions.

For committing unlawful actions, including negative nationality-based manifestations, in Baku alone 213 Communists – including 130 officials – have been brought up on Party charges, and 13 have been expelled from the Party. Some 715 people, including 138 officials, have been punished by disciplinary procedure. A total of 121 people have been dismissed.

A good many employees of law-enforcement agencies also went astray, got confused and found themselves following in the tail of events. Now these agencies, which are called upon to stand guard over legality, order and citizens' safety, are being purged of the moral bankrupts, of staff members who compromised themselves. Various units of the Ministry of Internal Affairs, the State Security Committee, the courts and the prosecutor's offices are being reinforced, and steps are being taken to strengthen and improve the activity of the people's volunteer police aide detachments [*druzhiny*].

Some members of the intelligentsia, who lay claim to a monopoly position in science and culture and are unable to give up the moss-covered dogmas in which their dissertations and pseudoscientific opuses are grounded or the traditionally high pay they receive for works that produce zero return for the national economy or ideology, have also proved to be far removed from the true interests of the people. Their professional and general cultural narrow-mindedness is often accompanied by a staunch elitism, frequently developing into national conceit....

These people, who consider themselves spokesmen for the thoughts and aspirations of the people, who imagine themselves to be "the nation's conscience," have willy-nilly, with their names and prestige, strengthened the position of the instigators of disturbances and the organizers who stand behind them. The speeches and arrogant conclusions of some cultural figures have frequently sounded in unison with the inflammatory appeals of Armenian extremists.

Did any members of the intelligentsia feel responsible, directly or indirectly, for the rampage of emotions and for the acts of hooliganism, even vandalism, that occurred on Dec. 5? Or did they look on with indifference as groups of unrestrained thugs broke the windows of houses and stores, smashed up enterprises, overturned and set fire to vehicles, and beat up bus and taxi drivers and passengers?! Among these hooligans were the so-called "hunger strikers" who had previously occupied special tents on the square.

The position of a certain segment of the intelligentsia (which is supposed to be the people's spiritual mentor), a position embodied in the appeal from the general meeting of the republic Academy of Sciences to the Politburo of the CPSU Central Committee, the Presidium of the USSR Supreme Soviet, the Azerbaijan Communist Party Central Committee and the Azerbaijan Republic Supreme Soviet, is cause for perplexity and resolute condemnation....

While criticizing the extremists operating in Armenia and the Nagorno-Karabakh Autonomous Province, the appeal "tactfully" – or, more accurately, unscrupulously – circumvents the question of the sowers of nationalistic passions in Azerbaijan, whose guilt is just as great....

This discreditable position inevitably snowballed to absurd dimensions in the speeches of some participants in the unauthorized rallies in Baku, those who raised the question – in the form of an ultimatum – of depriving Nagorno-Karabakh of its status as an autonomous province. In essence, this demand is directly allied to the destructive appeals of the illegal "Karabakh" organization.

Perhaps the most destructive consequence of the unauthorized rallies and demonstrations in Azerbaijan and in Armenia and of the noticeable influence of anti-restructuring forces on them was the inclusion in these pernicious "happenings" of pupils of general-education and vocational-technical schools and higher-school students....

It should be said bluntly that television, radio and certain newspapers have not been up to the tasks confronting us, that often they have not provided truthful information about events in the region, adhering to the tactic of keeping silent and lulling people with hackneyed, pompous phrases from the propaganda arsenal of the period of stagnation and with impassive general appeals for strengthening the friendship and solidarity of peoples. Items have appeared in newspapers and on radio and television broadcasts that have disoriented the population and demonstrated the political immaturity both of the individuals who spoke out in the interviews and before the microphones and of the writers of the programs and articles themselves....

A number of broadcasts on republic radio and television were the fruit of political thoughtlessness and careless myopia. Broadcasting a rally at which inflammatory appeals were made without providing any commentary or evaluation was a very flagrant mistake....

The Azerbaijan Communist Party Central Committee has examined the question of serious shortcomings in the work of the republic's mass news media.... The pages of the newspaper Molodyozh Azerbaidzhana [Youth of Azerbaijan] were made available to random authors, who made irresponsible, dangerous statements. The newspaper Azerbaidzhan pioneri [Azerbaijan Young Pioneers] carried an article calling upon schoolchildren to participate in unauthorized rallies.

Television and radio speeches by some cultural figures were ideologically harmful and opportunistic, and certain television and radio broadcasts essentially supported the ultimatum-style demands made at unauthorized rallies.

Flagrant mistakes were made by a number of branch and factory newspapers.

For publishing politically erroneous materials and giving tendentious coverage to events, N. Nadzhafov, editor of the newspaper Molodyozh Azerbaidzhana, was given a strict reprimand, to be noted in his permanent record. He was dismissed from his post. A. Balayev, editor of the newspaper Azerbaijan pioneri; E. Kuliyev, Chairman of the Azerbaijan Republic State Committee for Television and Radio; and F. Tariverdiyev and A. Babayev, vice-chairmen of the committee, were also brought up on strict Party charges....

A decisive turn onto the path of restructuring is now taking place in the activity of the Azerbaijan Party organization and the Azerbaijan Communist Party Central Committee....

THE EPICENTER: ALARMING DAYS IN APSHERON

By special correspondent Konstantin Mikhailov. *Sobesednik*, January 1989, p. 6.

Baku, Agdam and Stepanakert... A rally began on Baku's central Lenin Square, in front of the enormous House of Government, on Nov. 17, 1988. It lasted almost three weeks, until the early morning hours of Dec. 5....

The last morning

"Are you a journalist? Please interview me! I am Rasim Shikhizade, a mathematics instructor at Rural Vocational-Technical School No. 86. Why am I here? Really, it's not just me! We are all indignant: Our republic's sovereignty is being violated. The point is not just Karabakh. We live in Azerbaijan: Leaders at every level should know the Azerbaijani language – if they don't want to learn it, let them leave. And education? I, a teacher, know how to teach Azerbaijanis mathematics better than outsiders; why are the textbooks for our children approved in Moscow?"

An enormous signboard bearing slogans. "Return the Name of Nizami Gyandzhevi[1] to Kirovabad!" and "Restore Soviet Power in the Nagorno-Karabakh Autonomous Province!" Next to them: "Free the Azerbaijani Land From Extremists and Armenians!" On the other side of the square, above the rostrum, is a prominently displayed portrait of Akhmed Akhmedov, who has been sentenced to death for atrocities in Sumgait. If you recall that in the first days of the rally Lenin Square also saw the green flags of Islam and portraits of Ayatollah Khomeini, you can understand how different the people who gathered there were. What united them? It seems to me that it was the square itself – with the rostrum and the microphone. In other words, Hyde Park, but with a triple cordon of internal troops.

A week after Nov. 17, the "Numaishi Komitesi" – the "Rally Committee" – came into being. The most active participants in the events on the square became committee members....

We don't support the anti-Armenian slogans, they [several of the committee members] told me; the Armenian people themselves have been deceived, and we must clearly distinguish them from the Armenian extremists. The Nagorno-Karabakh Autonomous Province must be eliminated, because autonomy isn't justifying itself: Instead of normalizing relations between nationalities, it serves as a constant source of discord. Azerbaijani refugees from Armenia must be settled in the Nagorno-Karabakh Autonomous Province – the climate there corresponds to the conditions of their former homeland; furthermore, the more Azerbaijanis that settle in Nagorno-Karabakh, the more difficult it will be to implement an "autonomy" policy.

All these arguments, which were repeated in the Baku newspapers during those days, were irreproachable in the system of reckoning whose center was Lenin Square in Baku. What the Armenians of Nagorno-Karabakh would think and do when they heard that people in Baku wanted to eliminate their autonomy and artificially populate the province with Azerbaijanis was outside the system; they didn't need to be asked....

Refugees!

That seemingly forgotten concept has become an everyday reality in Azerbaijan and Armenia. As of Dec. 8, there were 119,094 Azerbaijanis who had left their homes in Armenia. The number of Armenians who had left Azerbaijan since the beginning of the events in the Nagorno-Karabakh Autonomous Province was 89,641. Azerbaijanis reached their native republic on trains, airplanes, military helicopters, buses, horseback and simply on foot. It wasn't Topkhana, it wasn't Nagorno-Karabakh, it was the refugees' stories that for so long prevented the anger and indignation of those gathered on the square from dying down....

There were hundreds of stories – about abandoned and ransacked homes, about crossings on foot through snow-covered passes, about threats and arson.

The state of emergency that was instituted in those days in 17 districts of Armenia was a forced, extreme measure – the communiques evoked in one's memory images of a guerrilla war: "On 01.12.88 at about 03:00 hours, a column of military trucks and private automobiles proceeding from Stepanavan District, Armenian Republic***was fired upon with shotguns and pelted with stones.***" And where the border between Azerbaijan and Armenia crosses the Kazakh-Idzhevan Highway, refugees "meeting head-on" were exchanged like prisoners of war, "one for one."...

In late December, at a meeting between residents of the Nagorno-Karabakh Autonomous Province and Andrei Sakharov, the academician uttered these bitter but just words: "In these events, neither the Armenian nor the Azerbaijani people has managed to keep to the moral high ground."...

WHERE ARE WE GOING? – Our Correspondent Interviews Academician Z. M. Buniyatov, Hero of the Soviet Union

Bakinsky rabochy, Dec. 1, 1989, p. 3.

... People should understand that no nation can live in isolation from other nations. The Azerbaijanis were driven out of Armenia, but has life gotten any better there? No. There are the same social and economic problems, the same corruption, bribery and favoritism. And some other problems have been added, too.

We drive out the Armenians, and what happens? Construction projects are left hanging, not one roofer is left ... and enterprise managers cry that there aren't enough specialists. And so forth and so on. On the other hand, crowds of refugees are roaming Baku, lecturing Azerbaijani girls on how long to wear their skirts and how to use cosmetics and starting fights with the "city boys"; and, please note, it's not just "nationality-based," it's also because we are "well off," don't you see, while they are enduring deprivation. Also note that, although we have been going to Altyagach for vacations all our lives, they don't want to live there. It's in Apsheron District, you see. Give us the central city, they say, and good jobs. But after all, in terms of vocational training and in terms of social dynamics they cannot just "fit right into" life in one of the country's biggest cities. The rhythm of life is different here; it has its own specific features and traditions. The result is animosity toward urban Azerbaijanis, who retaliate with disparaging nicknames.... And what about the rise in crime caused by these same refugees?!... The republic is doing everything it can to give them at least some help. The Yardym Society and a committee for providing assistance from the [Azerbaijani] people to Karabakh have been in operation for several months now. Work is under way, but one continues to hear calls to "Beat up the Armenians!" All right, let's assume that we become a mononational republic, a sovereign state, and that we secede. What happens after that? After that, it becomes clear that the structure of our economy is such that we can't live in isolation. Would we sell petroleum, given the current prices for it? Anyone who is the slightest bit knowledgeable, who has any grasp of economic matters, understands that all these demands are absurd. And then, of course, we would have to work, but we don't want to work; professionalism is not respected in our country today. The Arabs have an excellent saying on this score: "I'm an emir and you're an emir. Who's going to look after the donkeys?" Believe me, life isn't any sweeter for the Armenians....

On the evening of Nov. 26, an old friend telephoned to tell me about a rally in Sumgait.... One of the last people to speak at the rally was a certain Vagif Akhmedov, a local "militant" of the People's Front.... He used to work at the Sumgait Museum of History.... First, he enlightened his audience about the situation in the republic's districts bordering Armenia. So you see, he told them, these are the outrages and horrors that are going on there. The situation there is difficult, everyone knows this.... But the speaker relied mainly on rumors and his own conjectures.... He even made an outright call for "Death to the MVD [Ministry of Internal Affairs] and KGB [State Security Committee]!" We know from Moldavia's sad "experience" what such calls bring.

I want to ask him: Toward what kind of abyss are you, Vagif Akhmedov, the son of an Azerbaijani mother, pushing your people?! Wasn't last year's tragedy in Sumgait enough for you? I'm not a young man, and I'm a Hero of the Soviet Union: Answer me!... Whose side are you on? Are you still one of us?...

What the Azerbaijan People's Front was and what it has now become are two fundamentally different things. There has begun to be discord on the board now, a struggle for power.... The unfortunate thing is that the real intelligentsia was squeezed out when the seats were parceled out. There aren't enough intellectuals in the APF. That's why one sees continual shifts in position, absurd demands, extremist slogans and processions around the city featuring shouts and threats....

The fact is, people don't know their history. Therefore, most of them take at face value whatever these uneducated commentators offer them, especially from rally rostrums. That's why there are shouts about "Russian imperialism," "the enemies of the Azerbaijani people," "the empire," etc. At the same time, it is emphasized at these rallies that the APF "takes a Leninist stance." Isn't it absurd? ...

What is needed is a strategy line capable of first halting and then reversing the process of the spiritual and moral impoverishment of people, above all of young people. What is needed is a well-thought-out program of propagandizing the Moslem religion as a culture (after all, the Christian religion and others are propagandized), its history and ideological essence. What is needed is the teaching of the Koran as an elective course and its interpretation as a code of principles of good and rules for people's coexistence in friendship and peace; in the final analysis, this should instill in young people thoughts about the great spirituality of their nation. A spirituality that consists in perceiving Islam not as a religious dogma but as a bearer of moral and ethical values and the culture of a whole group of peoples of the East, united in terms of harmonious ethnic features and a community of languages, that has made its way through the layers of history. But now we have lived to see a time when elders are no longer respected....

It is necessary to do all this now, immediately, before something irreparable occurs....

'THE CAUCASUS IN FLAMES'

Kommunist, Dec. 16, 1989, p. 4.

Editors' Note. – A series of reports from Armenia, Nagorno-Karabakh and Azerbaijan by special correspondents Audrius Azubalis and Audrius Zdanavicius was published under the above headline in the Nov. 30 issue of the Lithuanian newspaper Atgimimas (Accord).

We present for your attention an interview that they recorded with Gamid Kherishchi, an ideologue from the Azerbaijan People's Front and a staff member at the republic Academy of Science's Institute of Literature.

* * *

The Azerbaijan People's Front views the USSR as a dualistic state: Moslem-Christian or, more accurately, Turkic-Slavic. Therefore, we have entirely different tactics than the Baltic peoples. We don't even consider the possibility of seceding from the USSR, since for us that would mean seceding from Turkic unity. But the possible secession of the Baltic republics would benefit us: There would be three fewer European Christian peoples. That would strengthen Moslem influence in the Soviet Union. Proceeding from this standpoint, we should regard your efforts with understanding. The Moslems would not benefit from the breakup of the USSR and, consequently, the disintegration of Turkic unity. Azerbaijan, Kirgizia, Kazakhstan, Bashkiria, the Volga region, Tataria, Yakutia, Turkmenia, the Crimea, the Northern Caucasus – these are all Turkic lands. And we have no intention of giving them up to anyone. But when the existing pseudo-democratic movements were coordinating their tactics for struggling against the totalitarian USSR, they didn't ask for our opinion, so now we aren't cooperating with them....

The Turkic peoples are much worse off than you in the Baltics. You have a paradise compared to us. Just walk a kilometer on Uzbek soil and you'll be able to feel the tragedy and to sense the kind of anger that is building up. A people of 25 million has reached its limit. And the Kazakh people? We keep saying "Karabakh! Karabakh!" But three times as much territory has been taken away from Kazakhstan to use for test sites. Those are autonomous regions, too, in their way, only military ones.... I've been in the Fergana valley, Ashkhabad, Kazan and Tashkent, and I don't have the strength to describe what I saw there. They have made a hell out of our lands. The enterprises are bad, the conditions are hazardous. But look at the [textile] plants in Ivanovo: cleanliness, order, trade union vacation passes, women in smocks. They're living at our expense; they work with Uzbek cotton. But someday we'll take them by the throat: "So, you've arranged a good life for yourselves? Look how our women work in 40-degree [Celsius] heat, when even dogs crawl into the shade, but people are out under the blazing sun!"... Our main tools are strikes and civil disobedience. The economic decline that they try to scare us with doesn't frighten us: 93% of industry in Azerbaijan is subordinate to Moscow and only 7% to the republic. The Russians thought that we would suffer, but they themselves have ended up in a trap. I was a member of the strike committee, and I saw with my own eyes the telegram signed by Ryzhkov and Yazov. Back there in Moscow there was panic. We produce almost all the petroleum, 95% of lubricants and the main component of aircraft fuel, including fuel for military aircraft. On Aug. 16 the intelligentsia appealed to the people to gather all forces – political and religious – into a united, concentrated force. And the People's Front did this. Yes, our struggle contains elements of a jihad (Arabic for a holy war prescribed by the Koran – *Ed.*): gathering as an entire community and swearing that we will stand until the end, and that if we lose, it would be better for us not to live. But it's just the Russians' imagination that the Azerbaijanis are on the point of declaring a jihad at any moment. So far there is no need for such a mighty weapon, in which everyone, great and small, and women too, goes to battle and, according to our faith, ends up in paradise if he dies. More peaceful and democratic methods of influence can be used. For example, a blockade of roads and especially railroads, or an economic embargo. Notice how our struggle resembles the Arab people's struggle against Israel: For instance, both of us have an oil embargo (we have declared one against Georgia, Armenia and Russia). On July 13 the Armenians began a blockade of Nakhichevan and Azerbaijani villages in the Nagorno-Karabakh Autonomous Province. But they lost this war when we started a blockade of our own. They'll globalize the Karabakh problem; they'll say to the Russians and the Baltic peoples: Let's join the province to Armenia, and then there'll be a precedent for doing away with unfairly established borders. But what if we define the problem and globalize it as a conflict between Christianity and Islam, what then? It's the Armenians who are seeking outside assistance: They've sent letters to the UN, the Pope, the American Congress. But we, in accordance with our religion, are relying only on ourselves. Although we know that the entire Moslem world, Iran and Turkey stand behind us. The main thing for the Armenians is not to sit down at the negotiating table, face to face. For them it's absolutely essential that there be an audience: that the Baltic peoples take part, or the Muscovites. But the two peoples alone should handle it. The Armenians have lost their battle, but they will never say so openly to the people. The basis of all their actions is sheer adventurism. Zory Balayan spoke at the recent session of the Armenian Republic Supreme Soviet; he sang the praises of Slavic-Armenian ties and said that Armenia has always been Russia's outpost in the Caucasus. Who are the Armenians to be an outpost?

In general, the West is on the decline. Spengler was essentially right. And revival is coming from the East. Some Arab states have created a paradise on earth. In Iran, for example, the standard of living is considerably higher than in Europe. I've been in that country, and I've seen how high the cultural level is there, what a sense of responsibility the people feel for their homeland, and how sincerely religious they are. If the development of world history continues this way, I think that in about 20 years, the picture will have changed a lot. Right now people have gotten hysterical over Armenia. But notice that Armenia's defeat coincided with the defeat of all Christian forces in general. People who talk about the idea of a common European home simply want to eliminate the East-West confrontation and establish a new one – North-South. And to link the USSR with themselves. Who is proposing this? Francois Mitterrand, who from 1954 through 1958 was the French Minister of Internal Affairs and was directly involved in the mass murders of Algerian Moslem freedom fighters. This man, who is up to his elbows in Moslem blood, is talking about human rights! The idea of a common European home will be a fiasco, since this home will create a rift in the USSR. There'll be no avoiding tragedies. As for the internecine conflicts in the Moslem world, they promote the unification of the Turkic peoples and the consolidation of Islam.

EMERGENCY SITUATION: MALICIOUS VANDALISM ON THE SOVIET-IRANIAN BORDER

By R. Ignatyev. *Izvestia*, Jan. 3, 1990, p. 6.

Editors' Note. – On Dec. 31, 1989, local residents committed outrages on the Nakhichevan section of the Soviet-Iranian border. Here is what I. Petrovas, troops commander of the USSR State Security Committee's Transcaucasus Border District, told an Izvestia correspondent.

* * *

On Dec. 4, 1989, long before this unprecedented and barbarous action, a group of people came to the border and lined up in the form of a chain. People lit bonfires, organized rallies and, with the aid of loudspeakers, talked across the border with residents of Iran. They called upon the Iranians to unite South and North Azerbaijan, to take joint actions. That day everything was relatively peaceful.

The pickets were warned that they were acting illegally.

However, there was a similar incident on Dec. 12, and two weeks later the border guards received an ultimatum from the Nakhichevan Autonomous Republic People's Front. The ultimatum demanded that all barriers be removed from the border by Dec. 31, 1989. Otherwise, everything would be destroyed.

To prevent an undesirable incident, the leadership of the Transcaucasus Border District made some concessions. The local population was given permission to engage in economic activity along certain sections of the border. In places where there are cemeteries, we removed the barriers.

On Dec. 30, leaders of the Nakhichevan border troops detachment spoke on local television and radio. The district command met with representatives of the People's Front. However, the talks led nowhere. Before everyone's eyes, the extremists were preparing for an illegal action: They were stocking up on fuel, vehicles were being driven to designated spots, and a campaign was being conducted among the population.

The action began on the morning of Dec. 31....

To all intents and purposes, border protection along a 164-kilometer section of the Nakhichevan Autonomous Republic's border was paralyzed by these disturbances. In some places, the enraged crowd managed to reach the border itself. Iran's border troops were immediately put on combat alert. Their units took up defensive positions. Iranian border commissars issued a protest pointing out that the Soviet side was violating the May 14, 1957 treaty between the USSR and Iran on Soviet-Iranian border regulations.

"We took every measure we could to relieve the situation on the border," I. Petrovas continued. "Our units acted properly, realizing that it would be extremely undesirable to permit the use of weapons in this situation. The local population continued its illegal actions on Jan. 3. Border protection had to be reinforced, and reserves had to be brought into the area....

"We have received reports that similar disturbances were observed in Zangelan, Pushkino and other districts," I. Petrovas said in conclusion. "There are warning signals from Lenkoran. That is, a difficult situation is taking shape along almost the entire section of border between Azerbaijan and Iran. That's about 790 km. The situation may become worse. The extremists are demanding that a number of border posts be removed altogether, and they are provoking the border guards. We are trying to restore order on the border."

OUTRAGES ON THE BORDER

Pravda, Jan. 3, 1990, p. 8.

Between Dec. 31, 1989 and Jan. 2, 1990, unprecedented barbarous actions to destabilize the situation on the Nakhichevan section of the Soviet-Iranian border were conducted on the territory of the Nakhichevan Autonomous Republic, under the direction of extremist-minded persons....

As a result of the outrages committed by the crowd they organized, part of which was under the influence of alcohol and narcotics, engineering-and-technical structures, signaling and communications lines, towers and border markers were burned and destroyed for over 137 kilometers of the Nakhichevan section of the Soviet-Iranian border. There were threats to set fire to border posts and to do violence to their personnel and to border troops' family members. Defiant actions were undertaken with the aim of provoking the use of violence in response. The material damage done to the state comes to millions of rubles.... – (TASS)

NAKHICHEVAN: WHAT ARE THE CAUSES OF THE CONFLICT?

Izvestia, Jan. 6, 1990, p. 1.

... Everyone with whom we spoke in Baku, Nakhichevan and various districts and villages about the main reason for what happened cited the long, drawn-out process of resolving questions relating to Nagorno-Karabakh and the refugees from Armenia. Among the basic problems that worry people and make them attend rallies again and again, the desire to develop cultural and kinship ties and contacts with Iran and trade with that country was cited, as well as the desire for freer use of the border zone for livestock pasturing and other agricultural needs.

These desires, demands and hopes are justified, in large part. And, as was ascertained during a concrete investigation, their implementation is completely realistic and they can be solved gradually at the republic or departmental level.

The Jan. 5 meeting between A. N. Girenko, Secretary of the CPSU Central Committee; R. N. Nishanov, Chairman of the USSR Supreme Soviet's Council of Nationalities; and A. Kh. Vezirov, First Secretary of the Azerbaijan Communist Party Central Committee, and representatives of Party and Soviet agencies, border troops and labor collectives and leaders of unofficial organizations in various districts of the Nakhichevan Autonomous Republic and spontaneous conversations with people on the streets once again convincingly demonstrated that a constant dialogue, a trusting and concerned dialogue, between representatives of the authorities and the people is necessary.

The causes of what happened are clear, and we hope that the problems they engendered will be solved soon. But can restructuring be conducted in a country and a republic using extreme measures and ignoring the law? – (TASS)

DIALOGUE IS NEEDED, WITHOUT UNNECESSARY EMOTIONS

By special correspondent F. Ivanov. *Izvestia*, Jan. 8, 1990, p. 1.

Editors' Note. – The situation in the Nakhichevan Autonomous Republic remains complex. An Izvestia special correspondent reports from the site of the events.

* * *

Dzhulfa and Nakhichevan... I am in Dzhulfa, on the grounds of a border post. Signs of destruction are visible here, as they are everywhere on this section of the border. Together with the post's chief, Border Guards First Lt. V. Afanasyev, I went to the bank of the Araks River, the natural boundary separating the USSR and Iran....

"Valery Vladimirovich, why did the border guards take no action, and why are they taking no action now? After all, everything that happened here was in direct violation of the Law on the USSR State Border, wasn't it?"

"We were given orders to try to use persuasion. And we did try to stop people and explain to them that their intentions were unlawful. But what effect can you have on an excited, uncontrollable crowd? I was struck by the restraint my soldiers showed," First Lt. Afanasyev said.

I went out into Dzhulfa's streets. The appearance of a stranger in the small town did not go unnoticed, and a crowd promptly gathered around me.

"For decades, barbed wire has cut us off from a part of our homeland – southern Azerbaijan, which is inside Iran," said one of the people with whom I talked, "and for decades we have been unable to see our relatives. But after all, many people have sisters and brothers on the other side of the Araks. We wish no ill to the border guards, but why have they forbidden us to walk on our land and to use it? – after all, there is 17,000 hectares of land on the other side of that barbed wire, land that is in such short supply in our rocky Nakhichevan! It has been extremely difficult for us to visit the graves of our ancestors and to see the ancient monuments, since they, too, are within the border strip."

"But is there really no other way but to take all this by force?"

The crowd exploded: "Do you know how many times we asked the authorities about this?! We sent letters to all levels of power requesting these things, and finally we set a deadline – Dec. 31. But no one listened to us."

V. Zhukov, chief of the Nakhichevan border guards detachment,... said: "A section of the border almost 150 km long has been stripped bare and is being guarded with difficulty. We are sending reinforced border guard details, but they are unable to provide a reliable defense....

"Thousands of parents whose children are serving here are worried about their sons' fate. I can report that as of today no unlawful actions have been committed with respect to the border guards, and that the local population gives us assurances of friendship. But, alas, many servicemen have heard threats against them. We have had to evacuate the border guards' families from the posts in order to guarantee their safety."

On the afternoon of Jan. 7, the situation on the border became aggravated again. A group of residents of Ilyichevsk District attempted to cause more destruction, this time on a section abutting the border with Turkey. Border guards tried to stop the crowd. Using armored personnel carriers, trucks and several dozen soldiers with dogs, they blocked a small bridge leading to the undamaged part of the system.

A spontaneous rally sprang up on the spot, at which V. Allakhverdiyev, the leader of the local people's front, said that the border troops were deliberately provoking a conflict and pushing the people toward a skirmish. After a short conference, an ultimatum was issued: Either the border guards would clear the road, or in 20 minutes the crowd would open the way itself, and maybe cross the Araks too. The situation became explosive, and the border guards decided to let the crowd pass, so as to avoid bloodshed. A minute later, the barrier system along a 250-meter-long section had been torn down.

Unfortunately, virtually all barriers on the border of the Nakhichevan Autonomous Republic have now been destroyed. The border remains a conflict zone.

G. ALIYEV BIDS FAREWELL TO THE CPSU

Komsomolskaya pravda, July 23, 1991, p. 1.

Geidar Aliyev, former member of the Politburo of the CPSU Central Committee, has decided to leave the Party's ranks. In a statement given to the Interfax news agency, he cites three reasons for taking this step: The authorities are doing their utmost to conceal "a monstrous crime – the military aggression against the Azerbaijani people that was committed by the center's political leadership and the Azerbaijan Communist Party Central Committee on Jan. 20, 1990"; the conflict in the Nagorno-Karabakh Autonomous Province, which "arose through the efforts of Armenian nationalists under the patronage of the CPSU Central Committee" (Aliyev asserts that "the political center had a need for this conflict"); and the suppression of democratic freedoms by Azerbaijan's Communists under the direction of Moscow's Central Committee and the falsification of the results of elections to the republic parliament and of the referendum on preserving the Union.

"I sincerely believed in the ideals of the Communist Party and actively participated in the implementation of its plans," writes the man who used to be one of its leaders. "Now all that faith has been destroyed. These endless statements about a renewed Party and a renewed Union of republics are just another means of deceiving the people."

AZERBAIJAN: MUTALIBOV TRIES TO JUSTIFY HIMSELF. – Message to the People Replaced by Congratulations for Yeltsin

By Vladimir Sergeyev. *Nezavisimaya gazeta*, Aug. 24, 1991, p. 3.

Evidently, Azerbaijan President Ayaz Mutalibov now regrets that he didn't manage to restrain his emotions after the *coup d'état* in Moscow. The news of Mikhail Gorbachev's removal from power found Mutalibov in the Islamic Republic of Iran. According to Iran's Islamic Republic News Agency, while standing by the boarding ramp in Tehran before flying to Baku, Mutalibov answered reporters' questions about his attitude toward what had happened by saying: "What transpired was the logical result of Gorbachev's poorly thought-out policy. We welcome the development of events in the Soviet Union."

Tehran radio confirmed the accuracy of this report on the evening of Aug. 19. However, on Aug. 22 the Azerbaijan News Agency stated that Mutalibov had said nothing of the sort in Iran. The republic's communist newspapers reported this.

Perhaps Mutalibov would have gotten away with it if he hadn't made another mistake after returning from Tehran to Baku. At approximately 12 noon on Aug. 21, the text of a message from Ayaz Mutalibov to the Azerbaijani people was read on republic radio. The editors of Azadlyg (Freedom), the newspaper of the Azerbaijan People's Front, provided the editors of NG with a dictaphone recording of this message:

"Dear compatriots! Perestroika, which has lasted six years, has in actual fact proved to be a difficult and unusual experiment during which it has been impossible to avoid serious mistakes and violations.

"I have stressed repeatedly that the anarchy and lawlessness in the country could not go on any longer. This has been confirmed by both our own experience and the experience of history. Our people view the event that has occurred as an effort by the Soviet leadership to restore legality and law and order. The introduction of a state of emergency in certain regions of the country is a temporary measure. We link our hopes for a prompt resolution of the Karabakh problem, an end to the fratricidal war and normalization of the situation in the country with the State Committee for the State of Emergency (SCSE) that has been formed."

After it became clear on the afternoon of Aug. 21 that the junta had been overthrown, personnel from the republic State Security Committee destroyed the tape recordings of the message's text at the Azerbaijan television and radio committee's offices....

APF activists had managed to tape record the message as broadcast on the radio and intended to print it in opposition newspapers on Aug. 23. Imagine their surprise when the newspapers that were to carry the sensational text of the message did not come out at all that day. The director of the printshop attributed this to alleged technical factors....

So as to somehow salvage his reputation, Mutalibov sent a congratulatory telegram to Russian President Boris Yeltsin on Aug. 22.

On the evening of Aug. 22, the republic program "The Day in Review" [Ekran dnya] showed a tape of an interview with Ayaz Mutalibov on the "Time" [Vremya] program, in which the republic president said in a trembling voice that "the reports from Iranian sources regarding my support for the SCSE are an insinuation."

AZERBAIJAN: PRESIDENT MUTALIBOV ELECTED PRESIDENT – Now He Will Reform the Economy and Solve the Karabakh Problem

By Aidyn Mekhtiyev. *Nezavisimaya gazeta*, Sept. 10, 1991, p. 3.

According to data from the Central Electoral Commission, more than 80% of the voters took part in the Sept. 8 general election for president of Azerbaijan, and of these, 83.7% cast their votes for the current president, Ayaz Mutalibov. The elections, as everyone knows, were held against the backdrop of a general strike that had been going on the whole past week, demanding that the elections be postponed. The opposition held numerous rallies one after another under the slogan of boycotting the elections.... Without waiting for the People's Front to succeed in seizing the initiative, Mutalibov went on a counteroffensive. His emotional speech at the extraordinary session of parliament made an impression on voters. In his address to the nation on Friday evening, Mutalibov set forth his plan of action in the event that he was elected: radical reforms in the economy and prompt resolution of the Karabakh problem. He declared that individuals both within and outside the republic who wished the people ill were trying to sow discord and prevent the unification of the nation at this difficult hour.

The previous day, Mutalibov instituted the post of Azerbaijan defense minister and appointed 64-year-old Lt. Gen. Valekh Barshadly to fill it.

On the eve of the election, striving to win over the voters once and for all, Mutalibov signed a decree on Saturday under which all nonworking women with at least three children will receive a monthly subsidy of 50 rubles. A report on the Russian Republic "News" [Vesti] program concerning an alleged attempt on the President's life helped to raise Mutalibov's rating to a certain extent, eliciting compassion for the victim among ordinary voters. Finally, on election day, the still-ruling Communist Party managed to show that it was still in control of the situation.

The voting at the polling places proceeded in accordance with a script written in advance by the Party apparatus. All attempts by observers from the People's Front to monitor the course of the elections were skillfully headed off....

At a rally held on election day, the Azerbaijan People's Front called on the workers to end the general strike. This is understandable: For now, Mutalibov has overcome the opposition and become president. However, it is doubtful that the People's Front will recognize the election as legitimate.

AZERBAIJAN: COMMUNIST PARTY DISSOLVED – Political Crisis Continues

By Aidyn Mekhtiyev. *Nezavisimaya gazeta*, Sept. 17, 1991, p. 3.

Ayaz Mutalibov's victory in the Sept. 8 general presidential election has not ended the political crisis in Azerbaijan....

Before the August revolution, the chief guarantor of stability in Azerbaijan was the Soviet Army troops that were sent into the republic on Jan. 20 of last year to save the communist regime. Reliance on the State Security Committee [KGB] and the Army allowed Mutalibov to achieve at least two goals: to weaken the powerful opposition presented by the People's Front and to strengthen Azerbaijan's positions in the Karabakh conflict.

After the failure of the putsch, however, the situation changed fundamentally: The CPSU virtually ceased to exist, and the reactionary elite at the top of the military-industrial complex collapsed. This forced the Azerbaijani leader to distance himself immediately from the republic Party nomenklatura and to seek an alliance with the democratic opposition. That is why the President has begun to carry out, essentially one after the other, all the main demands of the People's Front, while trying at the same time, however, to "save face." First the state of emergency in Baku, which had been in effect for more than a year and a half, was lifted. Then, at an extraordinary session of parliament, the restoration of Azerbaijan's state independence was announced. This past Saturday, Sept. 14, one of the main conditions for beginning talks with the People's Front was met: The Azerbaijan Communist Party, which had assembled for its last congress, announced its self-dissolution and the transfer of all its monetary resources and property to local Soviets....

Naturally, the change in Ayaz Mutalibov's political orientation evoked dissatisfaction among several figures in his entourage. Vagif Guseinov, chief of the republic KGB, presented the greatest danger among them. Realizing this, Mutalibov instructed the republic prosecutor's office to disclose facts that compromised the KGB and Vagif Guseinov personally, after which a decree was issued removing him from his post....

Finally, there is the problem of the Nagorno-Karabakh Autonomous Province. After the possible withdrawal of Soviet Army troops from Nagorno-Karabakh, the power of the Organizing Committee for the Nagorno-Karabakh Autonomous Province in this autonomous unit will become ephemeral. The People's Front will try to derive dividends from this by attempting to convince the masses that Mutalibov is incapable of solving the Karabakh problem....

NOTES

1. Nizami Gyandzhevi was a 12th-century Azerbaijani poet. His surname is derived from the Azeri toponym for the city of Kirovabad (Gyandzha).

Chapter 3 | Anti-Armenian Pogroms in Azerbaijan

Sumgait

COMMUNIQUÉ
Bakinsky rabochy, March 1, 1988, p. 3.

On Feb. 28 a group of hooligan elements provoked disturbances in Sumgait. There were instances of outrages and violence. Measures have been taken to normalize life in the city and to ensure discipline and public order. Investigative agencies are conducting an inquiry.

The Azerbaijan Communist Party Central Committee has called on the residents of Sumgait and all the republic's population to show a high sense of responsibility, good sense and the utmost restraint and discipline, and to mobilize efforts to ensure discipline and order everywhere and to strengthen the internationalist atmosphere in labor collectives. (Azerbaijan News Agency)

ADDRESS BY K. S. DEMIRCHYAN, FIRST SECRETARY OF THE ARMENIAN COMMUNIST PARTY CENTRAL COMMITTEE, ON ARMENIAN TELEVISION FEB. 29, 1988
Kommunist, March 1, 1988, p. 1.

Dear comrades! First of all, I would like to report to you that the situation in the republic has been normal for three days now and that a normal work rhythm has been restored at all enterprises and in the educational institutions. Unanimously approving the address of Comrade Mikhail Sergeyevich Gorbachev, General Secretary of the CPSU Central Committee, to the working people and peoples of Azerbaijan and Armenia, the republic's toilers expressed their willingness to make up for lost time and worked on Saturday and Sunday.

Now I want to call your attention to one circumstance that alarms us. As you probably already know, the situation that has developed in our republic in connection with the events in Nagorno-Karabakh has caused concern among some of the Azerbaijani population. Some Azerbaijani families have left the republic. This was a consequence of all sorts of rumors that were spread in a number of areas, as well as of inattention to needs and to questions that worry us. Not all that many people have left, of course. Nevertheless, this fact cannot help but pain our hearts, it cannot leave us indifferent. Thanks to the measures that are being taken, some of these families are already returning to their homes.

However, the events around Karabakh, the population moves I have noted and the spread of various rumors, in turn, could not help but affect the situation in Azerbaijan. According to information in my possession, clashes have taken place there. In particular, a group of hooligan elements provoked disturbances in Sumgait on Feb. 28. Instances of outrages and violence took place.

Now the situation there has been brought under control. Measures have been taken to normalize life in the city and to ensure discipline and public order. Investigative agencies are conducting an inquiry.

All this requires that we give more and more attention to the state of relations between Armenians and Azerbaijanis in our republic.

The Bureau of the Armenian Communist Party Central Committee has examined this question and has instructed city and district Party committees, city, district and rural Soviet executive committees and trade union and Young Communist League organizations and their leaders personally to conduct the necessary work in every city and district, in every village, at enterprises, on farms and in families aimed at curbing such instances, and to do everything they can to see to it that the Azerbaijani population has no reason for concern. In the course of explanatory work, they must resolutely curb all rumors and provide broad, truthful and up-to-date information. Those who take an inattentive, irresponsible attitude toward our people's needs must be held accountable in the strictest way.

The most important task is to establish everywhere an atmosphere of friendship, mutual understanding and genuine brotherhood between Armenians and Azerbaijanis....

The brotherhood of the Armenian and Azerbaijani peoples goes back many centuries. It has been tested more than once on the steep roads of history. But nothing has been able to undermine or shake it. And I think that in this hour of new tests for our brotherhood no Armenian and no Azerbaijani will damage it, darken it or cast aspersions on it....

COMMUNIQUÉ

Bakinsky rabochy, March 2, 1988, p. 3.

Sumgait, March 1 (Azerbaijan News Agency) – According to our correspondents, the disturbances that took place in the city have ended. Industrial, transportation, trade, public-catering and consumer-service enterprises are operating normally, and classes are being held in educational institutions. Order and calm are being ensured for the city's residents.

Law-enforcement agencies have detained persons who were caught engaging in outrageous acts.

G. N. Seidov, member of the Bureau of the Azerbaijan Communist Party Central Committee and Chairman of the Azerbaijan Republic Council of Ministers, is in the city.

BRING LIFE INTO A NORMAL CHANNEL

Bakinsky rabochy, March 2, 1988, p. 3.

Unanimously approving the address by M. S. Gorbachev, General Secretary of the CPSU Central Committee, to the working people and peoples of Azerbaijan and Armenia, the working people are taking an understanding and responsible attitude toward the situation that has come about and are exerting the maximum effort to bring life into a normal channel more quickly.

At the same time, the arrival in Azerbaijan of groups of people of the Azerbaijani nationality who live in Kafan, Dilizhan, Idzhevan and certain other districts of Armenia is affecting the situation in the republic. They are concentrated in Baku and Sumgait and in Apsheron, Imishli, Zangelan and a number of other districts of the republic. The newcomers, wittingly or unwittingly, are peddling various rumors and absurd conjectures that do not correspond to reality.

The Azerbaijanis who have come to the republic from Armenia have been received in the Azerbaijan Communist Party Central Committee. Their wishes and critical comments were listened to attentively by high-ranking officials of the CPSU Central Committee and the Azerbaijan Communist Party Central Committee. They were informed that the Azerbaijan and Armenian Communist Party Central Committees are keeping a close eye on the development of the situation and are taking measures to ensure order and the safety of citizens.

An Azerbaijan News Agency correspondent reports that, speaking on local television, K. S. Demirchyan, First Secretary of the Armenian Communist Party Central Committee, said, among other things, that the Bureau of the republic Communist Party Central Committee has instructed city and district Party committees, city, district and rural Soviet executive committees and trade union and Young Communist League organizations and their leaders personally to do everything they can to see to it that the Azerbaijani population has no reason for concern. Party agencies have set up monitoring procedures and are holding to very strict accountability those who take an inattentive, irresponsible attitude toward people's needs.

Measures along these lines are being carried out, explanatory work is being conducted, and those who have arrived in Azerbaijan are being given assistance in returning to their homes. After returning home, some residents of Kafan District, Azerbaijanis by nationality, have seen for themselves that the situation is returning to normal. Now their families are also returning to their places of permanent residence. – (Azerbaijan News Agency)

ON THE SITUATION IN SUMGAIT

Bakinsky rabochy, March 3, 1988, p. 1.

As reported earlier, on Feb. 28 a group of hooligan elements provoked disturbances in Sumgait. Unstable and immature people who fell under the influence of provocative rumors and inflammatory talk about the events in Nagorno-Karabakh and Armenia were drawn into illegal actions. Taking advantage of a situation marked by a wild outburst of uncontrolled feelings and passions, criminal elements committed bandit actions. Tragic events occurred, and there were fatalities. Party, Soviet and law-enforcement agencies have taken resolute measures to normalize the situation. Law-enforcement agencies have detained persons caught in criminal actions.

A government commission has been created, headed by G. N. Seidov, Chairman of the Azerbaijan Republic Council of Ministers. All questions related to ensuring the uninterrupted functioning of municipal services, the repair of residential and public buildings and the maintenance of public order are being resolved. The necessary assistance is being provided to victims. Citizens' requests and appeals are being considered, and measures in response are being adopted promptly.

The city's working people are displaying restraint and are strengthening an internationalist atmosphere in their collectives. Labor rhythm has not been interrupted for a minute. Industrial, transportation, trade, public-catering, consumer-service and other enterprises are operating on their regular schedules, and classes are being held in educational institutions.

P. N. Demichev, candidate member of the Politburo of the CPSU Central Committee and First Vice-Chairman of the Presidium of the USSR Supreme Soviet, and K. M. Bagirov, First Secretary of the Azerbaijan Communist Party Central Committee, have met with the working people of Sumgait and are looking into basic questions of the city's life, the safeguarding of public order and measures to investigate the antisocial manifestations.

An investigative group of the USSR Prosecutor's Office is taking measures to investigate the crimes and to bring charges against the persons involved. – (Azerbaijan News Agency[1])

AN INVESTIGATION IS UNDER WAY

Bakinsky rabochy, March 11, 1988, p. 3.

... Correspondents from the Azerbaijan News Agency and the newspaper Vyshka [Watchtower] met with Senior Counselor-at-Law I. Gaibov, Sumgait City Prosecutor.

During the conversation, he said, among other things, that law-enforcement agencies detained persons caught in the act of violating public order.... During the investigation, it has been ascertained that some of the hooligans are criminal elements, individuals with previous convictions, and parasites. They include persons of various nationalities. The average age of those detained is about 20. Most of them are immature young people who fell under the influence of provocative rumors and inflammatory talk concerning the events in Nagorno-Karabakh and Armenia. Thirty-one people died at the hands of criminal elements. They included people of various nationalities....

The city's public is giving the investigative agencies important help. Among the volunteer helpers, I. Gaibov said, are an especially large number of Azerbaijanis who intervened at difficult moments on behalf of persons of Armenian nationality who were in danger. They not only made their apartments available to neighbors, acquaintances and relatives of the victims but also administered a resolute rebuff to the unbridled gangster elements.

I. Gaibov went on to note that during the search for missing persons of Armenian nationality, it was ascertained that many of them had been given refuge by Azerbaijani families and that some of them had gone to Baku. This led to a great many rumors of all kinds. I can officially state, he said, that these rumors are unfounded, are greatly exaggerated, and are full of cock-and-bull stories.... – (Azerbaijan News Agency)

THE SITUATION HAS RETURNED TO NORMAL

Kommunist, March 8, 1988, p. 2.

V. P. Trushin, USSR First Deputy Minister of Internal Affairs, and A. S. Shaginyan, Armenian Republic Minister of Internal Affairs, spoke on Armenian television on March 5. They talked about the state of law and order in the republic.

V. P. Trushin. – The report that was broadcast on television and published in the press talks about the sources, nature and consequences of the disturbances provoked by a group of hooligan elements in Sumgait.

A few days ago I was in that city and acquainted myself firsthand with the state of affairs and the measures that have been taken and that are being planned to maintain public order.

I would like to say firmly that the personal safety of the city's residents and the security of their property are being reliably safeguarded. All the necessary conditions have been created so that people can work in peace and so that life in the city will quickly return to its usual, normal pattern.

Some very energetic work is under way to investigate the crimes that have been committed. The investigation has been entrusted to a group of investigators for especially important cases from the USSR Prosecutor's Office. They are under the direct supervision of a USSR Deputy Prosecutor General. Working along with the investigators are the most qualified experts, police detectives and operational staff members of the USSR Ministry of Internal Affairs' Chief Administration for Criminal Investigations.

Naturally, time will be needed to disclose the full picture and bring to light all the circumstances involved in the crimes. But even now it is clear that among those detained are individuals with previous convictions, alcoholics, drug addicts, persons who lead a parasitic way of life, and other criminal elements.

Recently, the USSR Ministry of Internal Affairs has received a number of telegrams from residents of Armenia expressing concern in connection with the absence of information about relatives from Sumgait. In order to efficiently ascertain the reasons for each such instance, internal affairs agencies have been instructed to immediately look into the essence of questions and provide information to concerned citizens as soon as possible.

Questions are being asked about the state of affairs in Kirovabad. I can say that the situation in this city is calm, on the whole. Isolated attempts to provoke fights by hooligan groups were immediately stopped. There have been no injuries, let alone deaths, among the population.

The situation in Stepanakert is also returning to normal. All enterprises are operating, and schools are holding classes. No excesses or group violations of public order are being noted.

We are paying very close attention to every warning signal that agencies of the Ministry of Internal Affairs receive about crimes or alleged crimes. Checkups offer convincing proof that many rumors and conjectures that have nothing to do with reality are being spread.

Please do not use rumors and dubious sources of information to answer questions that may arise. At any time, one can turn to state law-enforcement agencies and receive all necessary explanations from them....

A. S. Shaginyan. – I can say with confidence that at present public order is being maintained at the proper level in the city of Yerevan and in other cities and districts in the republic. All enterprises, schools, collective farms, state farms and educational institutions are operating. All municipal services are functioning normally.

At the same time, there are instances in which certain irresponsible persons are spreading various fabrications.

Just how close such rumors correspond to reality can be judged from the following example: A rumor was spread among a certain part of the population to the effect that clashes had occurred in Amasia District and several people had wound up in the hospital....

The crime rate has undergone no substantial changes from Feb. 19 to today.

At the same time, the situation remains difficult. The republic's population should display restraint and calm and not commit violations of public order. – (Armenian News Agency[2])

TIMELY INTERVIEW: DEMOCRACY AND PUBLIC ORDER

By A. Eberlin. *Bakinsky rabochy*, March 12, 1988, p. 2.

Editors' Note. – USSR Deputy Prosecutor General A. F. Katusev answers questions from Bakinsky rabochy.

* * *

Question. – In connection with the events in Nagorno-Karabakh and Sumgait, one can sometimes hear statements asserting that democracy and openness are largely "to blame" for what happened. Tell us, Aleksandr Filippovich, is it right to draw the conclusion that freedom in social relations can give rise to disturbances and violations of socialist legality? Doesn't it seem to you that a certain part of the population is confusing democracy with anarchy?

Answer. – ... True democracy does not exist outside the law or above the law.... Those who connect the disturbances that have been noted in certain places during the past few days with democracy and openness are cruelly mistaken. Expressing one's opinion openly in conditions of democracy is one thing. Organizing disturbances is something quite different....

Q. – Certain citizens and even groups of citizens have now received the opportunity to openly conduct demonstrations. What are the mandatory requirements for organizing them? How is public order to be ensured during the holding of these events?

A. – Yes, our Constitution guarantees USSR citizens the freedom to hold street processions and demonstrations.... Needless to say, these peaceful processions have nothing in common with unorganized and spontaneous demonstrations accompanied by violations of public order, let alone those involving massive disturbances.

Therefore, as democracy, which people sometimes try to use as a cover for such actions, has expanded, it has become necessary to regulate the procedure for conducting processions and demonstrations. This question was resolved first in Moscow, where the Moscow City Soviet Executive Committee adopted a special resolution. Since then, the question has been settled in a number of other cities, including Baku....

Q. – Hasn't the time come to change our attitude to public order, and in the first place the attitude of law-enforcement agencies? What lessons should they draw from what happened in Sumgait?

A. – ... Speaking of the events in Sumgait, it must be said that it is necessary to draw lessons from them, including some very serious lessons. It must be said bluntly that the warning mechanism was spinning its wheels there. What should have been done was to foresee the events and to take all measures and apply the power of the authorities in good time; this could have prevented the well-known consequences....

Q. – What sanctions does the law provide for outrages like those that took place in Sumgait? Can you tell us anything now about the progress of the investigation into the occurrences in Sumgait?

A. – Massive disturbances took place in the city of Sumgait, accompanied by pogroms, arson and other outrages. In view of the great social danger of these acts, lawmakers have placed them in the category of state crimes entailing severe penalties. But during these disturbances, the hooligan elements also committed murders, for which the law provides even harsher measures.

At present, an investigatory group from the USSR Prosecutor's Office is conducting an investigation into the events in Sumgait. A number of active participants in the disturbances have been arrested. Measures are being taken to reveal all aspects of the crimes and to identify the persons involved in them.

What can one say about the motives for these terrible crimes? They were committed by young people, including juveniles, who, on the basis of unfounded rumors, gave in to passions kindled from outside, became ungovernable and, incited by hooligan elements who joined their ranks, committed extremely grave crimes....

COMMUNIQUÉ

Kommunist, March 18, 1988, p. 2.

As already reported, since the well-known events in the city of Sumgait, families and citizens of Armenian nationality have been arriving in the [Armenian] Republic.

At present, 1,761 people (435 families) have arrived in the Armenian Republic. Some of them have moved in with relatives, while others have been temporarily put up in boardinghouses in the republic.

A commission headed by Comrade V. M. Movsisyan, First Vice-Chairman of the Armenian Republic Council of Ministers, is at work with the aim of examining questions pertaining to citizens who have come from the city of Sumgait.

By decision of the republic's government, families and needy persons who have arrived are being given prompt material and other assistance. Citizens' requests and appeals are being examined, and appropriate measures are being taken in response.

A special group from the USSR Prosecutor's Office is conducting an investigation into the Sumgait events. On instructions from the USSR Prosecutor's Office, the Armenian Republic Prosecutor's Office has set up an investigative group to identify victims and eyewitnesses who have left Sumgait and are now in the republic, in order to conduct the necessary investigatory actions, in accordance with criminal-procedural legislation, to establish the circumstances in which crimes were committed. – (Armenian News Agency)

IN THE AZERBAIJAN COMMUNIST PARTY CENTRAL COMMITTEE

Bakinsky rabochy, March 19, 1988, p. 2.

The Azerbaijan Communist Party Central Committee has discussed the question "On Major Shortcomings in Organizational Work Among the Population by the Sumgait City Party Committee and Its Political Shortsightedness and Inaction With Respect to Preventing the Tragic Events in the City."

The resolution that was adopted notes that the Sumgait City Party Committee displayed political shortsightedness and irresponsibility in organizing the fulfillment of the instructions of the CPSU Central Committee and the directives contained in the address by M. S. Gorbachev, General Secretary of the CPSU Central Committee, to the working people and peoples of Azerbaijan and Armenia. The bureau of the city Party committee and its secretaries and the city Soviet executive committee underestimated the complex situation that had taken shape in the republic, took no concrete measures to heighten vigilance and safeguard public order in the city, and adopted a wait-and-see position, which led to tragic consequences....

In this complex situation, a number of the city's Party, Soviet and economic officials, members of the Party aktiv and Communists displayed indecision and confusion and underestimated the full danger of the consequences of the events that had broken out. Labor collectives were not rallied to curb the outrages, and the people's volunteer police detachments [*druzhiny*] did nothing, to all intents and purposes. Emergency, extraordinary measures were required to restore and establish order in the city....

A large share of blame for the tragic events that occurred rests with Comrade D. M. Muslimzade, First Secretary of the Sumgait City Party Committee, personally. Despite repeated warnings, he did not carry out instructions that he return from vacation immediately, and he ignored the republic Party aktiv's decision to immediately organize work to implement the CPSU Central Committee's demands.

In this critical situation, Comrade Muslimzade was unable to mobilize the Party aktiv for a struggle to normalize the situation in the city, displayed inexcusable presumption, and did not measure up to the demands made on a political leader. Comrade Muslimzade's actions in the past as well had displayed elements of a superficial approach to the resolution of urgent questions, a lack of self-control, a predilection for window dressing, and a desire to call increased attention to himself. He reacted incorrectly to critical comments, considering his actions faultless.

The resolution emphasizes that Comrades M. A. Bairamova and A. Kh. Samolazov, Secretaries of the Sumgait City Party Committee; Comrade T. Ya. Mamedov, chairman of the city Soviet executive committee; and other members of the bureau of the city Party committee did not display the qualities proper to Party members and, in the complex situation, acted listlessly and without initiative or the necessary persistence and devotion to principle. Lacking information on the state of affairs at the local level and knowing little about people's state of mind, they did not take timely measures to prevent the events that were about to happen.

Departments of the Azerbaijan Communist Party Central Committee did not exercise proper supervision over the activity of the Sumgait City Party Committee.

The city department of internal affairs (Comrade Kh. Kh. Dzhafarov) also proved professionally unprepared to counteract the elements that were committing outrages. The unconcerned and irresponsible attitude of many personnel of the city's law-enforcement agencies toward the performance of their official duties made it impossible for them to prevent the disturbances in time....

For the political unconcern that he displayed and the major shortcomings that he committed in organizational and political work and his behavior, unbecoming a Party member, which led to the tragic consequences in Sumgait, as well as for his improper behavior before the Bureau of the Central Committee and his un-self-critical assessment of the incident, Comrade D. M. Muslimzade has been relieved of his duties as First Secretary of the Sumgait City Party Committee and expelled from the CPSU.

For the serious shortcomings that he committed in organizing work to ensure proper order and discipline in the city, the political shortsightedness he displayed and his failure to take timely measures to prevent negative phenomena that led to the tragic consequences, it has been decided to consider it inadvisable to allow Comrade T. Ya. Mamedov to remain in his post as Chairman of the Sumgait City Soviet Executive Committee, and he has been given a strict reprimand, to be entered on his permanent record as a CPSU member....

For his irresponsible attitude toward safeguarding public order in Sumgait, which led to disturbances and outrages with tragic consequences, Comrade Kh. Kh. Dzhafarov, the acting head of the city internal affairs department during that period, has been expelled from the CPSU....

To examine and conduct an in-depth study of the causes of and circumstances behind the disturbances in Sumgait, a commission has been set up, headed by Comrade V. N. Konovalov, Second Secretary of the Azerbaijan Communist Party Central Committee. The results of its work will be examined by the Azerbaijan Communist Party Central Committee....

The Azerbaijan Communist Party Central Committee has demanded that the republic Ministry of Internal Affairs (Comrade A. I. Mamedov) take urgent measures to reinforce the personnel of the Sumgait City department of internal affairs and to improve the professional training of police officers. The Sumgait City Party and Young Communist League Committees have been instructed to send the best Communists and Young Communists to replenish the ranks of policemen....

WITH ALARM AND HOPE – We Think Today About the Events in and Around Nagorno-Karabakh

By special correspondents A. Afanasyev, D. Muratov, A. Mursaliyev and A. Sarkisyan. *Komsomolskaya pravda*, March 26, 1988, p. 4, and March 27, 1988, p. 4.

Baku and Yerevan – ... In Stepanakert, we were told that under the former secretary of the province Party committee – let us note that his nationality was Armenian – it was not the custom to mention Armenia in the local newspaper. We were also told that enterprises preferred to hire individuals who had not been educated in Yerevan ("they're not part of our cadres"). If such people were hired, it was only after they had worked for several years in the Nagorno-Karabakh Autonomous Province (a "key element" in a person's biography; then they would be "our" cadres). Is this plausible? It seems that this is how it was: The policy of unwritten taboos is very familiar. It's a policy of roadblocks: Don't mention this, don't step over that line....

Human consciousness is most readily aimed at forbidden fruit....

Although, needless to say, this was not the only factor at work....

For almost two years signatures were collected among the population of the Nagorno-Karabakh Autonomous Province, meetings took place in labor collectives, and some district Soviets held sessions. In Armenia during those same two years, signatures were collected on petitions. Hundreds of letters and telegrams were sent to Moscow asking that the Nagorno-Karabakh problem be considered.

And what did the bodies of power do? Did they react? Did they try to explain and discuss things, to change the course of events, to take the initiative into their own hands? No. They tried to enforce prohibitions – on collecting signatures, for example. In Yerevan, at rallies lasting for many hours, not one official invested with power managed to win over the audience. There was no frank and open discussion. The people in the square were seething because they had received no answers to the questions they had raised.

They were waiting for an answer – a frank, honest, open answer. And the longer the answer was in coming – the last days of February are evidence of this – the more crowded it became in the square. The reasonable people went over to the camp of the moderates, and they in turn joined the extremists. Can we accuse them of political shortsightedness? No, stop and think about it. They tried – even if loudly, in a way unaccustomed to our ears, and some of them were very noisy indeed – to openly discuss some extremely serious problems, perhaps for the first time in their lives. Was it really impossible then – and is it too late today – to devise a sensible, civilized form of debate so that basic solutions, acceptable to the two peoples and to the entire country, can be worked out for the social and economic problems that have accumulated in the Nagorno-Karabakh Autonomous Province?

But let us return to Yerevan....

People's social activeness was awakened by restructuring, something that became particularly noticeable after the June (1987) plenary session of the CPSU Central Committee. On the one hand, there was the just Party criticism, long-awaited and accepted by the people of Armenia. On the other hand, there was the wait-and-see attitude or even resistance of those who "had lived the good life during the stagnant era." Two positions. At the time, they were not reconciled. Here is a characteristic detail that explains a great deal. After the June plenary session of the CPSU Central Committee, sharply critical articles on the social, economic, ideological, moral and ecological problems of Armenia were published in the central press, one after another. Facts were cited, and some extremely serious conclusions were drawn. But at that time, it is hardly likely that anyone could have interpreted this criticism as an attempt to "wound" national dignity and to present the Armenian people in a false light to readers all over the country. Why? Because the social thrust of the criticism was in complete accord with the social expectations of broad strata of the population. Everyone was waiting for renewal.

But, alas, the people's social dissatisfaction remained. The extremely acute problems that were posed remained unsolved. At the same time as all this, the "movement to unite Nagorno-Karabakh with Armenia" developed and gathered speed. Even a few months ago, this was just a tiny stream. At the first demonstration, in October 1987, the movement's leaders were able to gather together only a couple hundred people.

And then the time came when the tiny streams changed course and merged in a different, broader river. It was passivity, the absence of the necessary arguments, an unwillingness to interact with people in a straightforward way and the (in many respects) lost prestige of officials that facilitated rapid growth in the influence of the newly hatched "leaders" on the masses.

We are by no means thinking of accusing the people, who were united by an idea. We especially do not want to pin labels and make premature assessments. At the same time, let us note that an idea may be one thing, but those who interpret it, translate it and carry it out may be something else again. For instance, what were some of the leaders calling for? In essence, their position can be expressed as follows: Whoever is not with us is against us. Why else would they "stifle" everyone who tries to raise objections or to express another point of view? ...

Or this: As a sign of protest, we should declare an hour-long strike. This will not harm the state. We will make up the work we would have done during that time later. The fact of the strike is what's important.

What attitude should be taken toward this?

We have to give them their due: In response to extremist, rather venturesome statements in other instances, here are the sober, sensible voices, let's say, of representatives of a council of elders. But where is the guarantee that the voice of reason will be heard by an often-agitated audience? ...

Are the people whose opinion is being reckoned with here sufficiently aware of their personal responsibility to those who are following them? ...

* * *

Before visiting Sumgait, Agdam and Stepanakert, we spoke in Baku with those on whose actions, in particular, the course of events in the republic largely depended.

We were told that in the emergency situation, habitual methods of work had proved ineffective. During the days following the events in Sumgait, when all sorts of rumors were snowballing in a threatening way, what proved effective was not all kinds of measures but an around-the-clock "confidential telephone hot line," which refuted rumors. Up-to-the-minute information helped to ease the tension.

How did the events develop?

Let's imagine the atmosphere of those first few days. Here is what is important. The nature of the rallies changed as events developed. At the first rallies, the questions raised were addressed to the republic's leadership. The sense of these questions was: We have no information. Tell us: What is your position on Nagorno-Karabakh? Why are you keeping silent? A reasonable explanation was given: The republic's sovereignty is at issue.

A little bit later, the mood changed. There were rumors. And in the wake of the rumors from the Nagorno-Karabakh Autonomous Province and Armenia came refugees. They appeared suddenly, with children and hurriedly packed bundles; it must be said that they heated the atmosphere.

An effort was made to persuade the new arrivals to go back; they were housed in sanatoriums and rehabilitation centers that were empty for the winter, and it was understood that in the existing conditions they might serve as a catalyst for further events....

Whom to follow, whom to believe?

We reached Sumgait by evening. On the sidewalk in front of the city Party committee's building there is a little table with a telephone. If you call inside on it, someone will write out a one-time pass for you, which will be carefully checked by the guard at the entrance. The streets were already empty. Soon the curfew would go into effect. There were sleeping bags in the reception room of the city Young Communist League committee – both administrative-apparatus personnel and members of the operations detachment had spent the night there. There were hand-lettered signs on office doors: "Office for Receiving Citizens With Applications, Complaints and Requests" and "Headquarters of the Azerbaijan Communist Party Central Committee."

At night, we sat and talked with D. Muslimzade, who used to be first secretary of the city Party committee but is now the former first secretary.... Sumgait is only 40 years old, and it exhibits all the contradictions of the difficult growth of socialism. With a population of 250,000, we have 55 dormitories [Muslimzade said]. About 20,000 people live in unauthorized buildings....

The city is literally overflowing with problems: from a housing shortage to gas-polluted air, plus the abundance of chemical enterprises, with the specific social conditions stemming therefrom....

The rallies started on Saturday, Feb. 27. Muslimzade did not return from vacation until the 28th, even though prior to this, at a meeting of the Party and economic aktiv, everyone had been warned about the extraordinary nature of the situation. At 1:30 p.m., he was unable to drive his car to the city Party committee's building – the crowd was too great. He ... said: I realized that this was fate. I mounted the rostrum, went to the microphone, and started to work to restrain the crowd. And then, as he tells it himself, the first secretary, having decided to "give the demonstration a peaceful character," went to the head of the crowd and tried to lead it to the embankment.

This was a mistake. While the first secretary was stepping along at the head of the column, people in the back broke away from the procession. In the very minutes when the secretary was taking part in the rally, an "uncontrollable situation," to use the official language, was being created in the city. Breaking up into several groups, people who had lost their human qualities – among whom, it was ascertained later, were some recidivists – committed crimes. Yes, it was not hooliganism but crimes, and those responsible for them must be punished very severely.

At approximately 8 p.m., a bus carrying Young Communists from the Khimprom [Chemical Industry] Association was returning to the city from an excursion. No one on the bus knew anything about what was going on. Elshad Akhmedov, the secretary of the YCL committee, said: "We were stopped at the edge of the city by a crowd armed with knives.

"They started to beat and threaten us. Vika Akopyan, a computer operator, was with us. They put a knife to my chest. One of the girls fainted. The bandits climbed on top of the bus and yelled that they would set it on fire if we didn't hand someone over to them. We all held firm. Then one of them said: 'There's nothing here, let's go.' Later, we hid Vika in the YCL committee's offices."

In several apartment buildings (in Block 36, for example), Azerbaijanis protected their friends and neighbors and put up defenses around the buildings. Young Azerbaijani men from the YCL operations detachment saw Armenian girls home from enterprises, pretending that they were their wives.

It was important to calm people down, help them and provide them with moral support. Especially since many Armenian families fled the city during those difficult days....

Some Azerbaijani families from the Nagorno-Karabakh Autonomous Province turned up in Agdam. Their appearance there aggravated the situation. Rallies began.

Agdam District, Azerbaijan Republic, Feb. 22.

During a skirmish along the border with Askeran District (which is part of the Nagorno-Karabakh Autonomous Province), two young residents of Agdam died. How? Why? Who was to blame? Why did the group of young people from Agdam go there at all? Was it really just out of curiosity, to see the demonstration in Stepanakert, or did they have other, less innocent intentions? Where did the other group at Askeran come from? An investigation will answer these questions. But at the time, on Feb. 22, thousands of worked-up people left Agdam and headed for Askeran. It's difficult to imagine how this mob law might have ended. The police [*militseiskiye*] guardposts that had been placed along the road and the posts manned by Party, Soviet and YCL personnel were pushed back. The border between the districts was literally a few minutes' march away. An Uazik 91-34, making its way through on the shoulder, drove on ahead and took up a position athwart the highway.

The column had moved right up to the vehicle, when a small woman got up on the hood. People recognized her – she was Hero of Socialist Labor Khuraman Abbasova, chairwoman of the Lenin Collective Farm.

What happened next sounds like a legend. Khuraman-khanum [*khanum* is a Turkish and Persian word indicating a woman of rank or position – *Trans.*] took off a light-colored scarf decorated with golden threads and raised it over her head. According to an ancient custom, a woman's scarf, a symbol of a mother's honor, has prevented bloodshed when thrown down in front of men. Khuraman-khanum does not now remember word for word what she said then. Others do remember. We recorded these words from what many people said: "Kill me!" Khuraman-khanum shouted. "Trample on the scarf! Only then can you go and fight! If you can step over me, go ahead!"

The crowd turned back. It is said that men wept. One fellow tried to slip by her, and she boxed him on the ear. Later, in the meeting hall of the district Party committee, Khuraman-khanum fainted.

Murtuzayev, First Secretary of the Agdam District Party Committee, went out onto another road and stood in front of cars heading for Stepanakert. In Baku, the legend has been making the rounds that he went down on his knees in front of the cars and at the last instant they swerved to the side. Murtuzayev has demolished the legend. He did not go down on his knees. He did not beseech anyone. He went out onto the road. He stood there. They stopped....

Unfortunately, there are only a few such examples. There are more examples of another kind.

Party, Soviet and YCL personnel spoke at a student demonstration in Baku. But their speeches had no effect. Anar, a poet and an authoritative person, rectified the situation. "Let Anar speak, we trust him!"

We are pondering this: When the difficult situation arose, when it was necessary to work every minute with stirred-up people, those who by virtue of their positions were responsible "for working with people" right away turned to informal authorities – poets, writers. Did they sense that their own authority was insufficient? That was apparently the case: After all, before this young people did not know even by sight many YCL personnel in Azerbaijan, including the secretaries of the central committee....

What is the solution?

... It is known that the rights of autonomous provinces are not defined in detail in the USSR Constitution. So perhaps they should be defined, and not simply in detail but in an up-to-date, progressive way.

So that these rights will really guarantee the fulfillment of the tasks that have been formulated today. And perhaps some more extensive tasks, too. So that these rights, not infringing the republic's interests and not erasing the principles of autonomy, can be radically improved, while legally codifying social and economic relations that have been filled with new content – relations both with the republic of which the autonomous province is part and with public organizations and institutions in the other republic....

The ability to seek out and find suitable alternatives, a desire to avoid driving the situation into an impasse, a striving for a solution, for something constructive – these are not signs of weakness, they are signs of sensible strength....

SUMGAIT: RUMORS ARE IMPEDING THE INVESTIGATION

By staff correspondent R. Talyshinsky. *Izvestia*, March 30, 1988, p. 6.

As already reported, an investigation is continuing in Sumgait in connection with the disturbances that took place there on Feb. 28. The investigation is being conducted by a special investigatory group from the USSR Prosecutor's Office. Our correspondent met with the leaders of the group, V. Nenashev, Deputy Director of the Chief Investigations Administration of the USSR State Prosecutor's Office, and V. Galkin, investigator for especially important cases under the USSR Prosecutor General.

Question. – What stage has the investigation reached?

Answer. – The group began its work on March 1....

The volume of work is enormous. At the same time, the duration and thoroughness of the investigation take on special political importance in light of the events that have taken place in the Nagorno-Karabakh Autonomous Province and in Yerevan. Therefore, several dozen of the country's best investigators – from Moscow and various provinces of the Russian Republic, the Ukraine and Belorussia – have been brought in to participate in the work of the investigatory group. In addition to staff members of the prosecutor's office, the group includes – we want to emphasize that its makeup is multinational – investigators from internal affairs agencies, psychiatrists and other specialists.

Q. – Is anything impeding the investigation?

A. – Rumors, above all. They are still being generated, and they are continuing to poison the atmosphere.... The investigation has firmly established that not one child suffered during the disturbances in Sumgait. There were not 400 victims and not 500 but precisely 32 persons, as the published report of the USSR Prosecutor's Office states. Of those 32 persons, 26 were Armenians and 6 were Azerbaijanis....

Q. – When will the first results of the investigation be known?

A. – ... We hope that the first results of the investigation will be known as early as the first half of April.

The city Party committee has informed us that the curfew has been lifted in Sumgait as of March 29.

ALARMING DAYS: A STATE OF EMERGENCY

By special correspondents Vladimir Larin and Yury Makartsev. *Sobesednik*, April 20, 1988, p. 12.

'Internal Refugees'

R. Safaryan, director of the Shushan boardinghouse, where refugees from Sumgait have been put up, told us that, in the opinion of physicians, many of the newcomers are suffering from nervous and psychological disorders and that one of them has died of a heart attack....

"The outrages could have been prevented back on Feb. 27, when stores and workshops were looted and nationalistic slogans were being proclaimed," said Zaven Badasyan, an installation mechanic who was helped by an unknown Azerbaijani. "And as for the city's leaders – why didn't they ask for help immediately? Why did they allow throngs armed with metal bars to loiter about the streets? After all, it wasn't just anywhere but in public places that they yelled about death and violence." ...

When the soldiers arrived in Sumgait, many of the victims emerged from whatever hiding places they had found and tearfully begged to be taken to the airport immediately. They were still wearing the outer clothing they had on when they left their homes just before these events. Of what importance are things, possessions or apartments at such a time! Some of those with whom we talked in the boardinghouse insistently asked that we write the following in the newspaper: They will not return to Sumgait – that is more than any human strength can bear.... For the second time in the history of recent years (the first was Chernobyl), groups of "internal refugees" have formed. Only now they are people shaken by the horror of crimes committed out of national enmity....

SUMGAIT A MONTH LATER

By special correspondent Viktor Loshak. *Moskovskiye novosti*, April 17, 1988, p. 13.

... On walls, you still see this announcement: "The circumstances of the mass disturbances that occurred on Feb. 27-29 are being investigated. We appeal to all citizens who were eyewitnesses to crimes or have knowledge of the circumstances of crimes to notify the prosecutor's office. – [signed] The USSR Prosecutor's Office's Investigatory Group." But the order concerning the regulations in effect in the city and imposing a curfew has been rescinded.

It's a warm April. The sea sits motionless at the end of the street. Grapevines curl around the facade of the city Party committee's building. Next to it is a police patrol: helmets, walkie-talkies, truncheons. How does all this fit together? ...

The USSR Prosecutor's Office has gathered more than 100 investigators and crime specialists in Sumgait. Brigades of medical experts from Moscow are at work. In the largest office, the investigators have drawn a map of the blocks of housing. The map is speckled with spots of various colors. Each color denotes a category of crime: pogroms, murders, rapes. Ismet Gaibov, Sumgait's prosecutor, has already authorized more than 60 arrests....

Those three days came as a shock to everyone here.... Here is what Vagif Kakhramanov, head of the city department of public health, had to say:

"That night I had trouble getting to the hospital. The crowd wouldn't let me through – they were overturning cars or stopping them. All 20 of the emergency squads were operating. How? You can get some idea from the fact that after these events eight vehicles had to be written off – they had been smashed by rocks. In the House of Culture, to which we evacuated Armenians who were apprehensive about their safety, minimal conditions for people had to be created. We brought over everything we had in the hospitals: diapers, blankets and pillows, 500 children's chamber pots.... In those days alone we received 81 injured persons, 16 of whom are still undergoing treatment in Baku." ...

How could such a thing have happened today among us, in our city?

Melek Bairamova, secretary of the city Party committee, sighed: "The proper significance wasn't attached to the Azerbaijani refugees from the Armenian city of Kafan, but they were the match that touched off the whole conflagration." ...

Where did this human gunpowder that burned for several days in Sumgait originate?...

Just how much balm has been poured on this workers' city in the 40 years of its existence?...

While friendship among the delegations [of workers from other republics] flourished, monuments were erected and odes were composed to the working hands of Sumgait's chemical, metallurgical and construction workers, these very people, while producing aluminum, pipe and, it seems, all the products of big chemistry, lived mainly in dormitories, raising their number in this small city to 55. But they seemed fortunate, because others had to move into "shantytown" – in the triangle between plants that spew smoke, blacken the skies and cover everything with dust, a city made of old tinplate, pieces of shell rock and defective concrete blocks arose, unbeknownst to anyone....

How many people live there? You hear figures of 14,000, 16,000, even 18,000.... The smokestacks of the giant factories belch black smoke, and young people from all over the republic are invited to work there, but how they will live once they arrive, and where – that didn't concern the enterprises' bosses, the ministries in far-off Moscow.

It goes without saying that even the most difficult living conditions are no excuse for killing and maiming one's neighbors. But tell me, if officials had seen what really exists in Sumgait, rather than what they wanted to see, wouldn't it have been possible in good time to have eliminated at least some of the underlying factors behind the disturbances, such as disbelief in change, bitterness and discontent? ...

Sumgait officials have now returned from Stavropol, Yerevan and Stepanakert – they have been trying to persuade refugees to return. But so far only a few have agreed to return to the "single family." According to data from the Azerbaijan Communist Party Central Committee, there are now 5,120 Azerbaijani refugees from Armenia in the republic....

SUMGAIT: EPILOGUE TO A TRAGEDY

By special correspondent Viktor Loshak. *Moskovskiye novosti*, May 22, 1988, p. 4.

The first trial of participants in the disturbances in Sumgait has come to an end....

Every day of the trial the small courthouse of Sumgait's Microborough No. 9 was cordoned off by numerous police units. Two machine-gunners in helmets and special vests were stationed not far from the entrance, with bayonets fixed to their barrels. The fears were understandable. But this conspicuous combat readiness and the exemplary cordon, in the absence of a single person wanting to break through it, reminded us of something quite different – the powerlessness of the Sumgait police during the first and most difficult days of the disturbances. Still to come is the trial of the people who, for seven hours and with merciless brutality, besieged an apartment where two people were defending themselves with boiling water, electric current and their fists – the end of this savage siege was horrible. Yet throughout the seven hours the victims kept phoning and calling for the police!

It still remains to be explained why many telephones in the city were disconnected on Feb. 28 and 29, and who was responsible for issuing the soothing advice "Stay at home" when people should have been evacuated immediately. One thing is obvious: The inaction of those from whom people had a right to expect protection encouraged the mob. It encouraged them to commit murders and rapes, to devastate 200 apartments and 50 stores and kiosks, and to set fire to 20 cars and trucks.

More than 10 officers, all Sumgait police supervisors, have now been fired from Internal Affairs Ministry agencies. The USSR Prosecutor's Office is conducting a special investigation....

More than 80 people have already been arrested: The majority are workers; the majority are Young Communist League members. The overwhelming majority are recent migrants from the village who live in factory dormitories and shacks....

Even the church experienced fear and constraint after what happened.

"There are substantially fewer parishioners," David Dilanyan, senior priest of Saint Gregory the Teacher Armenian Church in Baku, told us. "Many were distressed that someone had tried to set fire to our church. Recently, at Easter, we took a count: There were one third as many people as usual." ...

The center of all the Sumgait events was the bus station; the hooligans and pogromists assembled there, and they began their processions there. The chairman of the city Soviet executive committee has come up with the idea of building a new building and removing the old bus station from the center of the city, mainly because it is a reminder of the events.

But forgetting isn't that easy....

Sumgait's bad reputation will not be easy to dispel. But isolating the city would also be a mistake. Twenty-six cities have notified Sumgait's tourist office that they will not work with it. Granted, no one is going to drag visitors here by force. But then, with such a refusal on all sides, Sumgait residents will also be deprived of the opportunity to travel around the country and visit other cities and republics. It's too bad, for isolation is not the best method of internationalist education....

IN THE ARMENIAN REPUBLIC COUNCIL OF MINISTERS

Kommunist, June 1, 1988, p. 1.

The Armenian Republic government has been receiving a great many letters from the republic's working people expressing their concern over the matter of allocating housing in the republic for the Armenian families that have moved here from Sumgait.

From March 2 to today, 802 families, or 3,189 people, have moved to Armenia. Some of them have been given temporary accommodations in the republic's vacation hotels, while others are staying with relatives in various cities. Some 489 people have already returned, mainly to Nagorno-Karabakh.

Recently, on the instructions of the Armenian Communist Party Central Committee, the Armenian Republic Council of Ministers discussed in detail the question of making arrangements for the Sumgait residents who are in Armenia and of creating the necessary social and everyday conditions for them.

Steps are being taken to find accommodations in our republic for the citizens from Sumgait.... The problems of finding jobs for them in their occupations, providing schooling for their children and other vitally important questions will be resolved at the same time.

Executive committees of the appropriate district and city Soviets in the republic have been ordered to assist the arrivals from Sumgait by organizing the exchange of their state-owned apartments for the apartments of citizens who live in the Armenian Republic but have expressed the desire to leave Armenia. In exceptional cases, permission has also been given to exchange state apartments for private houses.

Moreover, plots of land are to be given to those who wish to build their own homes on farms in the Bagramyan, Talin, Ashtarak and Nairysky Districts. They will be granted state credit on preferential terms for this purpose as needed.... – (Armenian News Agency)

SUMGAIT: PROSECUTOR'S OFFICE CONTINUES INVESTIGATION

Exclusive Interview with Aleksandr Filippovich Katusev, USSR Deputy Prosecutor General, by TASS correspondent V. Itkin. *Izvestia*, Aug. 20, 1988, p. 2.

As the press has already reported, the USSR Prosecutor's Office has brought criminal charges in connection with the mass disorders in Sumgait. Trials have already been held to determine the measure and degree of guilt, and fair sentences have been handed down. The investigation is continuing. A group of experienced investigators, forensic experts, doctors and psychologists is now in Sumgait and is making a painstaking analysis of what happened in February....

We met with Aleksandr Filippovich Katusev, USSR Deputy Prosecutor General, and asked him to respond to a number of questions....

Question. – If you could, refresh our readers' memories of the sequence of events on those February days.

Answer. – ... On Feb. 27, a large crowd, mainly young people, gathered on V. I. Lenin Square. There were calls to attack people of Armenian nationality. Of course, there were also those who objected to the violent, physical actions. But the nationalist slogans of the frenzied speakers took effect: Groups of youths in various boroughs of the city began smashing store windows and beating Armenian citizens. On the following day, Feb. 28, these events reached a culmination point. Violations of public order assumed an especially malicious character. Groups of Azerbaijani citizens armed with clubs, stones and other objects began attacking the apartments of Armenians, committing brutal acts of violence and destroying property. As we have been able to ascertain in the course of the investigation, the instigators included people with more than one conviction.

You know the results: Thirty-two people died, 26 of them Armenians. About 200 apartments were devastated, over 50 service establishments were smashed and burned, and several buses and cars were damaged. The out-of-control mob, preventing the performance of services to preserve public order in the city, stoned soldiers and policemen. Over 100 members of internal-affairs agencies and soldiers received bodily injuries of varying degrees of severity.

By March 1, the authorities were able to quell the disorders. As a result of a painstaking investigation of the events, 94 ringleaders and participants were arrested....

Q. – It is cause for concern that the city and republic police personnel were not up to the task during those days. They proved unable, at first, to deal with the instigators and, subsequently, to handle the frenzied mob.

A. – You're right, the police were not up to the task. They were unable to take prompt, decisive steps to restore order and protect the safety of citizens in extreme conditions. One could say frankly that some of them displayed a callous attitude toward the fates of people who were in trouble. Only after decisive intervention by the USSR Ministry of Internal Affairs were additional forces brought into action. To stop the disorders, detachments of the USSR Ministry of Defense and internal troops of the USSR Ministry of Internal Affairs had to be brought into the city. As already reported, the USSR Prosecutor's Office was forced to bring criminal charges against policemen who were negligent in the performance of their official duty. An investigation is under way....

This is a truly unprecedented case. It would not be a misstatement to say that in late February the entire city – its neighborhoods, blocks and many of its apartments – was the scene of the crime....

In view of the nature of the case, its great sociopolitical importance and the volume of work involved, an investigatory working group has been created, consisting of the most qualified investigators of the prosecutor's office, the KGB and the USSR Ministry of Internal Affairs. In the course of our work, we must uncover the organizers and active participants in the mass disorders and determine the circumstances of the criminal violations. There are many difficulties. It's no simple matter to determine the role and actions of those who participated in the excesses, to break down everything that happened into episodes, and to work up the possible versions of what took place....

There is no doubt that some of the people who committed violent acts found themselves in the crowd by dint of circumstance. But there were also savage provocateurs and thugs. And we must now determine who is who....

All manner of trumped-up stories are still impeding the investigation. In particular, rumors are circulating to the effect that on the eve of the mass disorders lists of Armenians slated for physical destruction were compiled in the city. There are rumors to the effect that metal bars and other objects were especially made at a number of enterprises, that workers at communications centers deliberately turned off the telephones in Armenians' apartments, and so forth. To check these and other such reports, investigators have interrogated a large number of Sumgait residents, workers at enterprises, and employees of housing offices, communications centers and other services. And not one of these statements has been confirmed....

Q. – It is a known fact that, in order to accommodate working people's wishes, it has been decided that a number of the criminal cases are to be heard in courts of the Russian Republic.

A. – That decision was made in the interests of ensuring the greatest possible objectivity. In each particular instance, the venue of the case will be determined by the USSR Supreme Court.

Q. – There are rumors to the effect that the investigation has reached a dead end. Is that so?

A. – The USSR Prosecutor's Office is taking steps to ensure that the investigation is conducted as intensively as possible. I have already said that, as of today, criminal charges have been brought against 94 people. Nineteen criminal indictments involving 29 defendants have already been handed down. Since the Ismailov case, which was reported in the press, the court has heard six more cases. These include the case of Aidyn Ibishov, an assistant locomotive engineer who organized hooligans, urged them to commit acts of violence against Armenians, and led his accomplices, armed with metal bars, in attacks on soldiers. Yashar Garibov, a student at Special Vocational-Technical School No. 7, who inflicted bodily injuries on citizen V. Sarkisyan, has been found guilty of hooligan actions and sentenced. Several other cases of murders and other crimes that took place in Sumgait have been turned over to the courts and will soon be heard.

The USSR Prosecutor's Office is continuing the investigation.

Kirovabad

THE SITUATION REMAINS TENSE – Our Correspondent Reports From Transcaucasus

By Col. N. Mulyar. *Krasnaya zvezda*, Nov. 26, 1988, p. 6.

... Extremists have provoked serious incidents in Kirovabad. On Nov. 22, at approximately 5 p.m., hooligan elements surrounded the city Party committee's building and committed an outrage. On behalf of the first secretary, Yu. Pashazade, head of a department of the city Party committee, called for help. When soldiers arrived and cordoned off the building, they were met with insults and threats. Then stones began flying. Someone in the crowd hurled a combat grenade. As a result of the explosion, Lt. Boris Mikhailovich Gusev, Pvt. Anatoly Nikolayevich Kosenko and Pvt. Oleg Anatolyevich Yurchenko were killed. Others were wounded. During the night, small groups of youths tried to set houses and automobiles afire in various parts of the city.

"The situation hasn't eased up in the days since then," says Maj. Gen. V. Omelchenko. "More than 70 attempts to stage pogroms in houses and apartments of the Armenian population have been recorded. Local Party and Soviet agencies are not fully in control of the situation. As has happened before, the local police are doing nothing. The soldiers are shouldering a large and important burden.... With the help of senior officials of the Azerbaijan Communist Party Central Committee, we managed to assemble a conference of executives of the city's enterprises and to set up workers' volunteer police aide detachments [*druzhiny*]. Now they are patrolling the streets along with the servicemen. More than 150 people have been detained for violating law and order, and several firearms have been confiscated."...

The situation in Yerevan and Baku remains very complex. It is uneasy in Stepanakert and in Agdam District of Azerbaijan, where a curfew is in effect and industrial enterprises are not operating.... Weapons have been confiscated there too, from persons of both the Armenian and the Azerbaijani nationality.

BAKU, NOV. 26

By R. Lynev and A. Stepovoi. *Izvestia*, Nov. 27, 1988, p. 2.

Editors' Note. – Izvestia special correspondents arrived in Azerbaijan on Nov. 25. Below is their first report.

* * *

The very first impression is that everything in the city is as it always is: Stores and institutions are open, and many people are on the streets hurrying about their business. But here at the first intersection are armored personnel carriers, and nearby are soldiers with submachine guns. The closer one gets to the center, the more distinctly one feels that the city, alas, is not as it always is. Public ground transport in the center of the city has stopped.

All approaches to Government House and the adjacent Lenin Square are closed, and an unending flow of groups of people carrying flags and banners is moving on foot and by car right up to the square. Many, especially the young people, have red bands with the inscription "Karabakh" around their heads. Immediately in front of the square is another cordon. Actually, there are two: a chain of soldiers, and in front of it one of young people controlling access to the square. Several wear their symbol – labels from Karabakh cigarettes – on their lapels. They check out everyone who, in their view, is suspicious: They inspect bags and ask us to show our [internal] passports....

There are wounded in Kirovabad. Three servicemen have been killed. In this connection, a state of emergency has been established in Baku, Kirovabad and Nakhichevan. An appeal by S. B. Tatliyev, Chairman of the Presidium of the Azerbaijan Republic Supreme Soviet, says that rallies, demonstrations and strikes are forbidden at any time of the day.

But, alas, all these warnings remain only on paper.

During these days, the Azerbaijan News Agency has refuted a rumor to the effect that the disturbances in Kirovabad began with the death of a small girl who fell under an armored personnel carrier. It is not difficult to imagine how such a rumor disturbed the public and aroused indignation....

Gusein Mamedov, the 28-year-old chief of a fire-fighting unit at a plant, [said]: ... "We demand that the law be observed. I don't want a repetition of Sumgait, or of Kirovabad, where blood was shed a few days ago. This time it was Russian soldiers who had come to maintain order." ...

RESPONSIBILITY BEFORE THE LAW

Sovetskaya Rossia, Dec. 3, 1988, p. 3.

Editors' Note. – ... TASS correspondents V. Ternovsky and L. Kanashenko asked A. F. Katusev, USSR Deputy Prosecutor General and State Counselor-at-Law (First Class), to answer some questions relating to the events in and around Nagorno-Karabakh.

* * *

... **Answer.** – To our great regret, hooligan elements have provoked mass disturbances in a number of places – in Nakhichevan, Kirovabad, Sheki and Zakataly, for example. Incited by nationalistic and other inflammatory slogans, uncontrolled groups have committed a number of crimes involving the loss of life. All these incidents are being investigated by an investigative group of the USSR Prosecutor's Office headed by A. I. Kondratyev, an investigator of especially important cases under the USSR Prosecutor General. I should say that prosecutors, investigators and staff members of other law-enforcement agencies have come to the [Azerbaijan] Republic from almost every region of the country. A number of cases are being investigated by Azerbaijan Republic prosecutors and investigators. Several criminals have already been arrested.

I would like to note that mass disturbances entailing the loss of life have also occurred in certain communities of the Armenian Republic. Criminal proceedings are being instituted there as well....

Question. – It was announced from the rostrum at a rally on Baku's central square that agencies of the prosecutor's office have arrested Manucharov, the founder and leader of the Krunk society. Is this report accurate?

A. – Yes, A. M. Manucharov has been arrested. Not for being the leader of Krunk, but for completely different reasons. An investigation established that he headed an organized group of plunderers of public property who managed to pocket especially large amounts of state money. Manucharov's accomplices were also arrested.

I should say that these people transformed the building-materials combine in Stepanakert where Manucharov served as director for 10 years, as well as the bureau of civil services, into sources of unearned income. They stole marble and granite.

In view of the need to preserve the secrecy of the investigation, I will refrain from giving a more detailed survey of this case. But I must emphasize that Manucharov and his accomplices were making money on people's grief by stealing expensive building materials and taking bribes for putting up tombstones.

Baku

AZERBAIJAN REPUBLIC: THE SITUATION HAS BECOME EXACERBATED

By S. Mostovshchikov. *Izvestia*, Jan. 12, 1990, p. 7.

Editors' Note. – The situation in the Azerbaijan Republic has become exacerbated. On Jan. 12, a group of officers of the USSR Ministry of Internal Affairs' internal troops flew to Baku to make an on-the-spot assessment of the situation. An Izvestia correspondent contacted the command of the USSR Ministry of Internal Affairs' internal troops and received the following information:

* * *

On Jan. 11, a rally was held in Baku demanding the resignation of the republic government, which, in the opinion of the gathering, is unable to solve the problem of Nagorno-Karabakh. Speakers also demanded that Armenians be evicted from Baku and called for a mass march to the Nagorno-Karabakh Autonomous Province if the authorities do not take immediate measures.

The situation in the cities of Lenkoran and Dzhalilabad is very complex. In Lenkoran, in particular, power is completely in the hands of representatives of the People's Front, and officials of the district Party committee, the district Soviet executive committee and the military registration and enlistment office, as well as staff members of internal affairs agencies, have been kept from their workplaces. The local radio has been seized. A "provisional defense committee" has been created and has assumed responsibility for maintaining law and order. As of now, no unlawful actions have been observed in Lenkoran. As far as Dzhalilabad is concerned, actions in support of the Baku population's demands are also taking place there, but, according to available information, Party and Soviet agencies are in operation there.

There is now a tense situation in Shaumyanovsk and Khanlar Districts of Azerbaijan as well.

* * *

Our staff correspondent has reported from Baku that the "unofficials" are explaining their actions by citing the protracted resolution of the Karabakh question and the unconstitutional action of the session of the Armenian Republic Supreme Soviet, which adopted a resolution on including in the state plan for the republic's social and economic development a corresponding plan for the Nagorno-Karabakh Autonomous Province.

A communique of the Azerbaijan Republic Council of Ministers on the events that took place in Lenkoran, published in republic newspapers for Jan. 12, says: "The Azerbaijan Republic Council of Ministers resolutely condemns the attempt by the People's Front to forcibly disorganize the work of the local bodies of power and complicate the situation in the region.

"All this is being done in defiance of the efforts by the republic's leadership to strengthen the unity of the people and consolidate actions with the People's Front and other public movements."

THE SITUATION IN TRANSCAUCASUS HAS BECOME EXTREMELY EXACERBATED

By S. Mostovshchikov. *Izvestia*, Jan. 15, 1990, p. 3.

A communiqué received by the editors from the USSR Ministry of Internal Affairs' Press Bureau indicates that the pogroms and attacks on Armenians are continuing in Baku on Jan. 15. According to preliminary information, a total of 33 people have died as a result of clashes in the past three days. However, this figure cannot be considered definitive, since some of the apartments to which the thugs went in Baku have still not been checked.

Using two ferries, 660 Armenian residents of Azerbaijan's capital have been evacuated across the Caspian Sea to Krasnovodsk. The evacuees are mainly women and children.

Reports from Khanlar and Shaumyanovsk Districts of Azerbaijan do not inspire optimism. Real battles are under way there, in which the parties at conflict are using up-to-date equipment – helicopters with no identification marks, as well as seized armored personnel carriers. For example, in a clash between Azerbaijanis and Armenians in Khanlar District, the extremists had two armored personnel carriers at their disposal.

Anti-Armenian rallies are being held in many cities of the republic. They have taken place in Sumgait (20,000 people) and in the cities of Masally (2,500), Akhsu (200), Divichi (600), Agdam (1,000), Belokany (5,000), Zakataly (3,000), Sabirabad (1,000), Pushkino (4,000), Mingechaur (1,000) and Kusary (1,000).

After a rally in the city of Gyandzha [Kirovabad], at which about 7,000 people gathered, the crowd destroyed a monument to S. M. Kirov. A group of unidentified persons went to the local agricultural institute. According to reports, they used force to take training weapons from the insti-tute80 submachine guns, two machine guns, an RTK mortar and 27 bayonets. And then the head of the Gyandzha station of the republic internal security troops, apparently without putting up any resistance, gave representatives of the People's Front who came to him three revolvers with 80 cartridges and two small-bore rifles. Twenty-five subordinates of this commander went to Khanlar District with their standard-issue weapons.

No freight or passenger trains have moved between Azerbaijan and Armenia on the Azerbaijan Railroad recently. According to available information, there are currently 224 trains on the Azerbaijan Railroad. A total of 109 trains are temporarily standing idle without locomotives.

The blockade of motor roads leading to Nagorno-Karabakh continues. According to the communique, no freight trains are coming into the Stepanakert railroad station.

These are the events of the past 24 hours. Assessing them, a spokesman for the USSR Ministry of Internal Affairs said that the situation in Azerbaijan remains extremely complex and in a number of places is not amenable to control.

Baku

In connection with the events that took place on Jan. 13, Ye. M. Primakov, candidate member of the Politburo of the CPSU Central Committee and Chairman of the USSR Supreme Soviet's Council of the Union; A. N. Girenko, Secretary of the CPSU Central Committee; and V. Kh. Doguzhiyev, Vice-Chairman of the USSR Council of Ministers, have arrived in Baku.

Through the efforts of the republic's Party, Soviet and law-enforcement agencies, the situation in Baku is being kept under control.... – (Azerbaijan News Agency and TASS)

Stepanakert

... Reports of deaths are spreading through the country again, this time from Karabakh. In just the past few days, Lt. I. Tsymbalyuk and Pvt. M. Mantayev have died, and five internal-troops servicemen have been wounded. Today an officer and three soldiers who responded to a distress call from a village in the Azerbaijan Republic's Shaumyanovsk District, which borders on the Nagorno-Karabakh Autonomous Province, have been declared missing.

This is the third day that nationality-based clashes involving the use of submachine guns and machine guns have been taking place there, as well as in neighboring Khanlar District of Azerbaijan. Additional internal troops have been assembled there, but the situation remains extremely tense. The gravest possible situation has developed near Armenian villages in these districts. A large concentration of militants – members of armed detachments – has been observed, people coming from other districts. According to some estimates, there are several thousand of them.

The Special District Commandant's Office has announced that on Jan. 14 military helicopters carrying paratroopers flew in to support the group of internal troops that is keeping the warring sides apart. As they approached the Azerbaijan village of Adzhikend, they were subjected to a hail of antiaircraft fire, and small-arms fire opened up as well. One of the choppers was hit, and the navigator, First Lt. N. Pavlov, was wounded.

The fresh units of internal troops that arrived at the airport in the city of Kirovabad to replace and back up the units in and around Nagorno-Karabakh were blocked by the local population. Roadblocks were set up, hundreds of vehicles were concentrated on the roads, and crowds of people blocked the way. Representatives of unofficial organizations in Azerbaijan threatened violence against pilots and their families if helicopters from the local regiment took part in transporting these troops.

There are dozens of dead and injured of both nationalities among the local population of Shaumyanovsk and Khanlar Districts. Nothing is known about the fate of the Armenian hostages, who include the entire leadership of Shaumyanovsk District, nor is there any information about the Azerbaijani hostages that the Armenians took in response.

"The situation today is such that it is extremely necessary to declare a state of emergency. All possible urgent measures must be taken to protect the civilian population, including old people, women and children," believes Maj. Gen. Yu. A. Kosolapov, Commandant of the Special District. – (TASS)

Yerevan

A citywide rally in which over 300,000 people took part was held in Armenia's capital on Jan. 14. The arrival in the republic's capital of N. N. Slyunkov, member of the Politburo of the CPSU Central Committee, and I. S. Silayev, Vice-Chairman of the USSR Council of Ministers, was announced at the rally.

In connection with reports on the pogroms in Baku and the armed attack on Armenian villages in the Getashen subdistrict of Azerbaijan's Khanlar District, the speakers at the rally called on people to maintain self-control, discipline and calm and not give in to panic or provocations. They demanded that emergency measures be taken and that additional troops be sent to Khanlar District to ensure the population's safety. – (Armenian News Agency and TASS)

THE SITUATION IN AZERBAIJAN AND ARMENIA
By special correspondent V. Litovkin. *Izvestia*, Jan. 16, 1990, p. 6.

Baku, Jan. 16 – ... Groups of 10 to 15 people equipped with bags and motor vehicles have appeared in the city. They are robbing Armenians' apartments. In order to haul away their victims' possessions, they stop trucks and make the drivers, under threats, transport the stolen goods. Violence continues to escalate. And here are the terrible figures on these bandits' "work" – the number of plundered apartments in the city is approaching 1,000....

Late yesterday evening an emergency plenary session of the Baku City Party Committee was held here, in which Ye. M. Primakov, candidate member of the Politburo of the CPSU Central Committee and Chairman of the USSR Supreme Soviet's Council of the Union; A. N. Girenko, Secretary of the CPSU Central Committee; and A. R. Kh. Vezirov, First Secretary of the Azerbaijan Communist Party Central Committee, took part. The plenary session discussed urgent measures to normalize the situation in the city....

Safety stations have been organized in the city, places where the necessary conditions have been created for Armenian-nationality victims and medical assistance is being provided. One of these stations is located in the Shafag movie theater. About 100 people are housed in it. The theater building is under police protection....

[Azerbaijan] People's Front leaders are speaking on radio and television, condemning the thugs' actions and calling on people to be calm and vigilant.

But there is other news as well. This morning, part of the headquarters building of the Red Banner Caspian Fleet collapsed as a result of a mudslide. According to preliminary information, 16 people died; rescue operations are under way. During the night, ships from the Caspian Fleet participated in the evacuation of refugees from Baku. The fleet's training ship carried 165 people to Makhachkala.

Many Armenian families are asking the military for protection. They are being housed in the Baku Garrison's military installations and given all kinds of assistance. This is not always easy to do – sometimes extremists blockade the installations. They are threatening the military with reprisals for helping the Armenians.

Baku's major enterprises have conducted rallies and open Party meetings at which the vandalism, looting and violence that have occurred in the city have been condemned. Special working groups have been set up and have gone into the streets to confront the rioting crowd. Nonetheless, the situation remains extremely complicated.

* * *

Staff correspondents A. Pokrovsky and S. Mostovshchikov report from the USSR Ministry of Internal Affairs:

Yerevan

The situation in the republic is extremely tense. In 24 hours, there have been 16 recorded instances of armed attacks on guarded facilities. They have a single purpose – to capture weapons. One such incident was recorded in Artashat District, where at 2 a.m. on the night of Jan. 15-16 about 3,000 people broke into a room in the building of the city police department and seized 106 training submachine guns, 30 carbines, 27 TOZ rifles, 11 revolvers, 3,232 cartridges and a training grenade launcher....

Stepanakert

Since the conflict broke out, 20 people have died here, and more than 260 have sustained bodily injuries. There have been cases of arson and malicious vandalism. Communities are being fired on continually, as are security-force posts and details, and hostages are being taken. Trains and motor vehicles are being fired on or pelted with stones....

The highway blockade continues. No freight trains have arrived at Stepanakert station in the past three days.

Since the conflict began, internal affairs agencies and internal troops have prevented several dozen acts of sabotage and group manifestations of hooliganism and have detained about 26,000 citizens for various violations of the law. Almost 3,000 firearms and knives have been confiscated....

Nakhichevan

... In Ilyichevsk District, Nakhichevan Autonomous Republic, about 3,000 people completely blockaded the village of Kerki at 7:50 a.m. Five houses belonging to Azerbaijanis were burned. The local population has left the village. Fortunately, the situation here is under the control of internal troop units that have arrived on the scene.

Baku

... Here are the latest data. From Jan. 11-16, 1990, a total of 56 people have died, including nine identified as Azerbaijani by nationality, 28 identified as Armenian by nationality, and two representatives of forces for safeguarding public order. The nationality of the other dead persons has not yet been established. A total of 156 people have sustained bodily injuries, and there have been 167 cases of malicious vandalism and arson.

THE USSR MINISTRY OF INTERNAL AFFAIRS' PRESS CENTER REPORTS

Izvestia, Jan. 22, 1990, p. 6.

Azerbaijan Republic – ... Local radio in Baku has broadcast a speech by E. Kafarova, Chairman of the Presidium of the republic Supreme Soviet, expressing disagreement with the introduction of a state of emergency in Azerbaijan's capital. A crowd has gathered at the dock where the tanker Ivan Zemnukhov is moored and is threatening to blow up the ship....

In the city of Barda, the first secretary of the city Party committee has resigned at the demand of leaders of the People's Front. In the city of Mingechaur, a mass rally was held outside the building of the city Party committee. At the crowd's demand, the first secretary of the city Party committee, the chairman of the city Soviet executive committee and the heads of the local internal affairs agency and the local State Security Committee agency burned their Party cards.

The situation in the Nagorno-Karabakh Autonomous Province remains complex.... In Shusha, a rally was held in front of the building of the city Party committee; the rally participants demanded that the Azerbaijani hostages be released, that mixed-marriage families leave the city, and that the supplying of food to servicemen be stopped. Twenty people publicly burned their Party documents. The flag of the People's Front was raised above the building of the city Party committee.

Armenian Republic – Armed attacks for the purpose of seizing weapons are continuing....Work is under way to confiscate weapons that were seized earlier....

BAKU, JAN. 24

By special correspondents Viktor Litovkin and Sergei Mostovshchikov. *Izvestia*, Jan. 24, 1990, p. 1.

It's 11 a.m. on Jan. 24....

The streets have become quieter. However, this does not inspire complete optimism in the authorities. Military specialists assert that events are taking the form of "guerrilla warfare." People who ride around the city on motorcycles have begun to appear at night. They attack the foot patrols and then immediately hide. Sometimes gasoline bombs are thrown from the windows of buildings at armored vehicles transporting military men. Leaflets with photographs of soldiers and officers and the inscription "murderers" have been stuck up on some buildings.

However, the most unpleasant thing today is the panic. The city is literally shaking with a terrible rumor: It is alleged that the Russian population will "be made to answer" for the dead, and that those Bakuans who are not members of the People's Front will not escape retribution either.

Combating the panic is perhaps the military authorities' greatest concern. The head of the commandant's office and Moslem and Orthodox clergymen are making periodic appeals to the population on local radio. They are calling on people to remain calm and not to succumb to provocations....

Special note must be taken of the fact that the military are showing the greatest possible restraint and tact and are trying to avoid any conflicts whatsoever with the population....

A few words about the session of the Azerbaijan Republic Supreme Soviet. It was held on the night of Jan. 21-22.... In brief, the session recognized as legitimate the retention of a state of emergency in Nagorno-Karabakh and on the border with Armenia, but it assessed the introduction of troops into Baku as an illegitimate action. Right then and there, a demand was made that the troops be withdrawn from Baku and the state of emergency there be lifted; otherwise, the question of the Azerbaijan Republic's secession from the Soviet Union might even arise.

Those are the steps that are being taken under the pressure of events. Time will show how carefully considered or hasty these statements were....

If one recalls how the tragic events unfolded before the introduction of troops and the blood that was spilled in Transcaucasia back before the state of emergency was introduced, it becomes clear that the Army and the internal troops are there to stabilize the situation. Their goal is to stop the bloodshed.

EMERGENCY: ON THE SITUATION IN THE AZERBAIJAN AND ARMENIAN REPUBLICS

Pravda, Jan. 28, 1990, p. 6.

... No serious violations of public order were recorded in Baku overnight.... The printing of central newspapers began. At 7 p.m., Moscow time, on Jan. 27, republic television resumed broadcasting. It opened with a speech by A. N. Mutalibov, First Secretary of the Azerbaijan Communist Party Central Committee....

One indicator showing that tension is abating is the sharp reduction in departures of the Russian-speaking population from Baku. It is significant that at rallies posters have begun to appear bearing the inscription "We don't want the Russians to leave!"...

The elimination of the criminal military structure of the Azerbaijan People's Front is continuing. Many Bakuans were relieved to hear that a number of ringleaders of terrorist groupings have been detained. But some of the organizers of terror are still in hiding.

In Lenkoran, the APF division has announced that it is giving up power. The population was asked over the local radio to turn in weapons to bodies of state power. Three hundred firearms and 180,000 cartridges were turned in. However, the so-called "Lenkoran Defense Committee" knocked together a group of militants who refused to turn in their weapons and tried to hide in the mountains. In a Lenkoran suburb, a battle broke out with a detachment of servicemen. A Soviet

Army officer was killed in the exchange of fire. Five terrorists were killed. Fifty-two firearms were confiscated, along with a large quantity of ammunition and three mortars. More than 50 armed terrorists were detained.

Hostages taken earlier by opposing groupings are returning home. In Khanlar District, 17 Armenians and 22 Azerbaijanis have been released....

Tension is lessening in Armenian communities. Enterprises, transportation and the service sphere are operating normally....

At the same time, the knocking together of groups of militants has not stopped in the republic.

At a rally on Theater Square in Yerevan on Jan. 25, leaders of unofficial organizations attempted to distort the meaning of the measures that are being taken to stabilize the situation in the Nagorno-Karabakh Autonomous Province.... – (TASS)

THE DAWN AFTER THE NIGHT – This Is How the Current Situation in Azerbaijan's Capital Can Be Described

By special correspondents A. Gorokhov and V. Okulov. *Pravda*, Feb. 2, 1990, p. 1.

Baku – This city of 2 million has not yet cooled down from the blow, has not yet recovered from the shock of the events on the night of Jan. 19-20....

A commission of the Azerbaijan Republic Supreme Soviet is at work investigating what happened. A commission of the Azerbaijan Communist Party Central Committee has been set up....

Assessing the situation

Ramiz Akhmedov, First Secretary of the Kutkashen District Party Committee, spoke from the rostrum of the republic Party Central Committee's plenary session.

The plenary session met on the night of Jan. 24-25.... Ramiz Akhmedov said from the rostrum:

"I don't know how it is in other districts or in Baku, but in our remote district there are people in the People's Front who have never worked and have never been of any use to Soviet power, to their own family or to society. They don't want political dialogue, they want power. The Communist Party is the greatest obstacle to this, and they are doing everything possible to destroy it. Unless the Azerbaijan Party organization takes some concrete measures, a week from now there won't be a single Party membership card left in a number of districts.

"People with guns came to me at the district Party committee's office and said: 'You ought to burn your Party card.' I replied: 'I'd rather burn myself than my Party card.' The aktiv sat by and watched me. Some respected people said to me: 'Ramiz-muellim, maybe we should get rid of our Party cards. At least they'll leave us alone then.' I said: 'That's desertion, that's treachery.... You have to be a man, you have to be bold.' "

Akhmedov continued: "... You say the troops should leave. But it's an illusion, comrades, that we'll be able to keep power in our hands, because the extremists have created detachments so powerful that tomorrow they would launch a reign of terror in the city....

"We must make some very crucial decisions right now. If we don't resolve the Karabakh question through urgent measures, we won't deprive the extremists of their main trump card, and we'll subject ourselves to new troubles. But if we do resolve that problem, we'll unite people around ourselves and we'll be able to take power into our hands."

It would seem that the Kutkashen secretary assessed the situation accurately....

When power is lost

To call things by their right names, by Jan. 18-19 the state structures of power in Baku had lost any influence on the course of events. The extremist forces in the Azerbaijan People's Front, the APF, having taken the initiative in this unofficial organization, had brought things essentially to the point of a revolt, of a *coup d'état*....

There are quite a few sensible people among the leaders of the APF. A dialogue could have and should have been conducted with them; cooperation should have been established. For a long time, the authorities made no move to do this. The time for building bridges was lost....

The unresolved state of the Nagorno-Karabakh problem enabled the APF to attain organizational unity, to create cells and structures parallel to those of the state, and essentially to become an opposition party struggling for power in the republic....

Karabakh seemed to separate the Communists from the Central Committee and the broad masses of the republic's population from the republic leadership, which distanced itself from the problem of the Nagorno-Karabakh Autonomous Province and dumped its solution on the center. It was as if the leadership of Azerbaijan had created a vacuum between itself and the people. The APF radicals took advantage of this. The vacuum of influence was filled with "Fronters." The growing distrust of the center merged with distrust of the local authorities, and things that had literally an explosive impact on people were removed from the forefront of the republic's problems by unrealistic and sometimes simply ridiculous programs such as "the universal computerization of the republic" and "a bathhouse for every village," which were widely pushed in the local press. To a large extent, this became possible as a consequence of the work style of the Bureau of the Azerbaijan Communist Party Central Committee, and above all of A. R. Kh. Vezirov, First Secretary of the Central Committee, who acted under cover of "restructuring" phraseology but without the proper collective leadership and consideration of public opinion, and who neglected the democratic process of resolving personnel questions....

Thus, by Jan. 20 power in Baku had shifted to the People's Front, for all practical purposes. The Central Committee building was blockaded, insulting graffiti had been written on its base, the approaches were overflowing with rally participants, and a symbolic gallows, intended, one can assume, for the leaders of the republic's Communist Party, had been erected above the crowd....

We were told by military men, whom there is no reason not to trust, that, according to current information, the troops forestalled the extremists by no more than 24 hours. A storming of the Central Committee had been set for Jan. 20. Lists had been prepared of those who were to have been put in isolation after a successful revolt.

Shock

It can be said without exaggeration that the bringing of troops into the city put Bakuans into a state of shock. Not knowing the serious causes of the crisis, they felt insulted, as if a foreign army had entered the city....

Anar, First Secretary of the Board of the Azerbaijan Writers' Union, a People's Deputy and member of the USSR Supreme Soviet, said: "I believe that the tragedy could have been prevented. After all, the authorities have a very powerful apparatus – the pogroms ought to have been prevented. I also blame those who sent unarmed people against tanks. But close contacts should have been established with the Front's healthy forces, thereby isolating the 'hawks.' I said this often to Vezirov, but he just brushed me off: 'They're bandits and CIA agents.'" ...

"Let me put it this way," [the 52-year-old] Anar continued. "My boyhood ended in 1956, when our troops went into Hungary. My youth ended in 1968, when it was Czechoslovakia. Now I feel that my life has ended with the Baku January." ...

'Democracy in danger'

... That was the headline on an editorial in a recent issue of the Azerbaijan People's Front's newspaper, Azadlyg (Freedom), which was banned after the commandant of the city of Baku introduced a state of emergency....

[The editorial says:] "First of all, we need technical means of self-defense. Every collective should think about possibilities of producing them. Think, and then do! We need people who have experience in waging a defensive struggle and who have theoretical knowledge in this field. The defenders of our native land need warm clothing, they need means of transportation, they need many other things, and every collective, every village and every home should provide them. Everyone must come to the defense of the fatherland."

Those are the open appeals. But allow me to ask: ... Since when did the development of events in Baku between Jan. 10 and 20 start being called "defense of the fatherland" instead of an anarchic revolt, with all the attributes characteristic of that sort of "democracy"? ...

TODAY IN AZERBAIJAN

By special correspondent Ruslan Ignatyev. *Izvestia*, Feb. 10, 1990, p. 6.

Baku and Moscow – On Feb. 10, 1990, the situation is still tense in Baku and certain other cities in the republic.

Here is what Lt. Col. A. Drozdov, an operations-group officer, told me:

"The People's Front has sharply stepped up its activity in the capital and a number of districts in Azerbaijan. Using blackmail, threats and bribery, Front representatives are trying to maintain their influence among part of the population. Thus, according to the Ministry of Internal Affairs, in [Baku's] Nizami Borough workers in the Kishlinsky Machinery Plant's dormitory who supported a strike were given sums of money ranging from 20 to 40 rubles. The number of workers at plants and factories has decreased sharply. Only 42% of Baku's enterprises are operating, and another 35% are in partial operation. In the cities of Nakhichevan, Lenkoran, Dzhulfa and Sumgait, 20% to 30% of the enterprises are functioning. No more than 45% of all workers and office employees are on the job. The strike in the Nagorno-Karabakh Autonomous Province is continuing."

Judging from the reports, the most complex situation now is in the sphere of material production. Losses already amount to hundreds of millions of rubles. Ordinary people, workers and office employees, are waiting to hear open, honest talk from the local leadership, but so far only People's Front activists are visibly at work among the population. I spoke about this with R. Zeinalov, Secretary of the Azerbaijan Communist Party Central Committee....

Question. – Don't you think that representatives of the Azerbaijan People's Front are ahead of you in work with the population?

Answer. – I wouldn't call it being ahead of us. Rather, it's a continuation of their inflammatory activity. We're trying to neutralize this activity. I think the people understand that they must work. They have to find the inner strength to go back to work....

Q. – In your view, who is to blame for the fact that a state of emergency had to be introduced? Who should answer for the tragic events that occurred before Jan. 20?

A. – Commissions formed by the Presidium of the Supreme Soviet and the Azerbaijan Communist Party Central Committee, as well as USSR People's Deputies, are now at work. An independent investigation is also under way. I think we'll get the answer when they complete their activity....

Q. – I was in the office of Maj. Gen. A. Kirilyuk, deputy commandant of Baku for political affairs, and there I saw a bag full of discarded Party members' and candidate members' cards. Most of them had been torn up. All of them had been found in a building in the city. Our newspaper published a photograph from Gyandzha, where Party cards had been burned on the square – true, they were burned not by the city's leaders, as Izvestia's caption incorrectly stated, but by rank-and-file Party members. USSR People's Deputy S. Mamedov, First Secretary of the Gyandzha City Party Committee, pointed out this mistake in a letter to the editors. I would like to take this occasion to convey the editors' apologies. Nevertheless, it is an irrefutable fact that people are leaving the Party. How do you assess this?

A. – In the first minutes of general grief, many ill-considered and emotional actions were taken. But later on many thought better of it. There have been quite a few instances in which people have come in and taken back their Party cards. There are many examples of people joining the Party.

Q. – How many people have left the Party's ranks?

A. – About 18,000.

Q. – How do you assess the APF's activity?

A. – I don't think anyone would take a positive view of the actions of the extremist wing of the People's Front. As regards my own attitude toward the People's Front, since this movement operates throughout the country, we need to separate out its healthy elements and work with them, bring APF representatives into our structure and operate in the direction that was stated in the Front's program when it was registered: on behalf of restructuring, not against it.

Q. – Was there a period when neither you nor the Soviet bodies were in control of the situation in the republic?

A. – ... There was only a partial loss (well, maybe more) of real power. This could be sensed particularly during the last day or two before the situation became critical.

Q. – What do you see as the way out of the situation as it now stands?

A. – Above all, it's a matter of consolidating the healthy forces of our society and, of course, finally resolving the question of Nagorno-Karabakh.

———————————

NOTES

1. The TASS version of this report (*Pravda*, March 5, 1988, p. 2; *Izvestia*, March 6) gave a figure of 31 killed, "among them people of various nationalities, old men and women." It did not include the references to "a situation marked by a wild outburst of uncontrolled feelings and passions," "bandit actions" and "the repair of residential and public buildings," and it omitted the final two paragraphs. *Bakinsky rabochy* carried the TASS version two days later (March 5, p. 2).

2. *Bakinsky rabochy* (March 8, 1988, pp. 3-4) carried a 3,700-word article blaming the crisis on foreign subversion.

Chapter 4 | First Clashes and Guerrilla War

ON EVENTS IN NAGORNO-KARABAKH

Pravda, Sept. 20, 1988, p. 6.

After the Presidium of the USSR Supreme Soviet adopted its July 18, 1988 resolution in connection with the events in and around Nagorno-Karabakh, the situation began to change for the better, and life started to become more normal. Work to fulfill the decision of the CPSU Central Committee and the USSR Council of Ministers on accelerating economic and social development in the autonomous province got under way on a broad front. The atmosphere in labor collectives and educational institutions is improving gradually. Party committees and Soviet and public organizations have begun to take more active positions. The strengthening of the leadership of the Azerbaijan and Armenian Communist Parties and the examination at plenary sessions of their Central Committees of resolute measures to eradicate negative phenomena, strengthen legality and develop democracy and openness have been of considerable importance in this respect.

The investigation of criminal cases related to the events in Sumgait has been completed, in the main; all the individuals who were involved in the murders and in organizing the pogroms and violence have been identified and have had charges brought against them. More than 30 cases have been turned over to the courts for consideration.

At the same time, one cannot help but see that the processes of improvement that have gotten under way in Armenia and Azerbaijan clearly are not to the liking of those who are involved in corruption, bribery and embezzlement. Fearing exposure, they are trying to distract the public from the actual problems of restructuring and the real struggle against negative phenomena, to shift attention to questions of national relations, and to use any pretext to inflame nationalistic passions.

This has led to conditions in which the situation in Stepanakert has become heated once again in the past few days. Strikes have been provoked at industrial enterprises, in construction organizations and in public transportation. School classes have been canceled. An attack was staged on the province prosecutor's office, and there have been instances of the infliction of bodily injuries on servicemen of the USSR Ministry of Internal Affairs and police engaged in the safeguarding of public order.

On Sept. 18 a rally was held in the city, one authorized by the city's bodies of power. At the rally, people voiced concern over the situation that has come about in the Nagorno-Karabakh Autonomous Province and their desire to normalize it. After a while, however, the rally was broken off, in connection with inflammatory news about nationality-based clashes between the Armenian and the Azerbaijani population in the village of Khadzhaly, near Stepanakert. When many of the rally's participants moved toward that village, firearms and knives were used by both sides in widespread fighting. As a result, 25 people received injuries of varying severity, and 17 were hospitalized. Appeals for medical assistance have been made by both the Armenian and the Azerbaijani population.

The further development of this clash was prevented by the efforts of the police and the Internal Troops. The necessary steps are being taken to ensure public discipline and the safety of citizens and to stop the disturbances. Officials of the USSR Prosecutor's Office have instituted a criminal case and are conducting an investigation. A headquarters is in operation in the province under the leadership of A. I. Volsky, a representative of the CPSU Central Committee and the Presidium of the USSR Supreme Soviet.

In an appeal broadcast on radio and television, the province Party committee and the Nagorno-Karabakh Autonomous Province Soviet have condemned the antistate and unlawful actions of individuals who are seeking to aggravate tension in relations between nationalities. The holding of rallies, demonstrations and processions has been banned.

The Armenian Republic Communist Party Central Committee and the Azerbaijan Republic Communist Party Central Committee are taking the necessary steps to normalize the situation and establish public order in the republics. Party and workers' meetings are being held.

The situation that has come about cannot help but cause serious anxiety and concern. The situation demands that it be resolutely stated that this situation is sharply at variance with the interests of the working people of both republics, and therefore must no longer be tolerated. The state cannot permit any infringement whatsoever of the rights of citizens of any nationality or the whipping up of animosity among peoples, which is forbidden by the Soviet Constitution and our laws. The further deepening of socialist democracy is unthinkable without the strict observance of legality and of state and public discipline. – (TASS)

ON EVENTS IN NAGORNO-KARABAKH: DISTURBANCES CONTINUE

Pravda, Sept. 21, 1988, p. 6.

As already reported, in the past few days the situation in the Nagorno-Karabakh Autonomous Province has become exacerbated significantly; clashes have taken place between individuals of the Armenian and the Azerbaijani nationalities, clashes that have led to grave consequences. Party and Soviet agencies in Azerbaijan and Armenia, enterprise collectives and the public are striving to prevent further complications in the situation. The working class and rural toilers, exhibiting a high level of responsibility and self-control, are ensuring the normal operation of enterprises, transportation, collective farms and state farms. Nevertheless, irresponsible elements, first of all in the Nagorno-Karabakh Autonomous Province, are continuing to whip up tension, to provoke disturbances, and to resort to arson and other unlawful actions. In Yerevan, a number of rallies have been held at which inflammatory appeals were sounded. Similar appeals have been made in certain communities in the Azerbaijan Republic.

The antisocial manifestations are giving rise to well-founded anxiety and alarm among many citizens of both republics. Party and Soviet agencies are receiving numerous appeals and requests from working people for the taking of resolute measures to ensure the safety of the population, an end to the outrages, and the curbing of actions by irresponsible individuals that threaten the normal life of the population. People are demanding that legality and law and order be ensured everywhere.

The necessary measures are being taken by the agencies of law and order, together with the public. – (TASS)

ON EVENTS IN NAGORNO-KARABAKH: STEPANAKERT

Pravda, Sept. 22, 1988, p. 6.

The situation in the Nagorno-Karabakh Autonomous Province, which has become exacerbated as a result of clashes between persons of the Armenian and the Azerbaijani nationalities, remains tense. Despite measures taken to prevent nationality-based incidents, on the night of Sept. 21 there were new instances of arson to individual homes and automobiles and other unlawful actions.

Gunshots were heard in certain places. There were no casualties. However, all this has created an atmosphere of disquiet; many residents of the city of Stepanakert and rural districts are showing concern for their safety.

In Stepanakert, enterprises, construction organizations, transportation and educational institutions were not in operation.

Party and Soviet agencies, in conjunction with public organizations, are striving to get economic activity going again and to normalize the situation in the Nagorno-Karabakh Autonomous Province and neighboring districts.

In connection with the existing situation, A. I. Volsky, the representative of the CPSU Central Committee and the Presidium of the USSR Supreme Soviet in the Nagorno-Karabakh Autonomous Province, spoke on local television and radio. He said, among other things: "The Party and the government have adopted a number of important decisions regarding the development of the Nagorno-Karabakh Autonomous Province and the earliest possible settlement of the problems of various sorts that have accumulated here. But, obviously, this does not suit a certain group of individuals.

"In the past few days, the situation in the province has become much more complex. Strikes have been started at industrial enterprises, in construction organizations and in public transportation. Schools have canceled classes. There have been unsanctioned rallies and processions. An attack on the province prosecutor's office has been provoked. Verbal insults have been made against bodies of power. There have been instances in which the dignity of servicemen of the USSR Ministry of Internal Affairs' troops and policemen engaged in the safeguarding of public order has been humiliated."

In view of the existing situation, a state of emergency is being instituted and a curfew established in Stepanakert and Agdam District as of Sept. 21. All necessary measures are being taken to ensure the tranquility and safety of the population and to maintain public order and the strict observance of socialist legality. – (TASS)

APPEAL FROM THE BUREAU OF THE NAGORNO-KARABAKH PROVINCE PARTY COMMITTEE AND THE NAGORNO- KARABAKH AUTONOMOUS PROVINCE SOVIET EXECUTIVE COMMITTEE TO THE PROVINCE'S COMMUNISTS AND ALL ITS WORKING PEOPLE

Izvestia, Sept. 23, 1988, p. 2.

On Sept. 18, the situation in our province became sharply exacerbated: As a result of mass disturbances provoked by certain irresponsible individuals, undesirable and deplorable incidents took place, which led to casualties. Material damage was done. Law-enforcement agencies have taken measures to curb the mass disturbances. The USSR Prosecutor's Office is conducting an investigation....

We appeal to your reason. All the questions and problems that have come up must be resolved in an atmosphere of legality. The events of the past few days are developing according to a scenario written by provocateurs who seek to destabilize the situation and to aggravate tension, by those who pursue the goal of discrediting restructuring and democracy and diverting us from the true path....

The notorious formula "an eye for an eye, a tooth for a tooth" is leading us into a blind alley from which there is no exit.

So that our mothers will shed no tears, we call on you to be vigilant and to administer a fitting rebuff to those who are leading us down a discreditable path.

In the present situation, any kind of rallies, demonstrations, processions or meetings could aggravate the situation still more. Consequently, the province Party committee and the province Soviet executive committee deem the holding of such events to be impermissible at this time.... – [signed] Bureau of the Nagorno-Karabakh Province Party Committee and the NKAO Soviet Executive Committee

APPEAL TO THE ARMENIAN COMMUNIST PARTY CENTRAL COMMITTEE

Pravda, Sept. 25, 1988, p. 2.

On Sept. 24, the Nagorno-Karabakh Province Party Committee and the Nagorno-Karabakh Autonomous Province Soviet Executive Committee sent the following appeal to the Armenian Communist Party Central Committee, as well as to newspaper editors:

The Nagorno-Karabakh Province Party Committee, the Nagorno-Karabakh Autonomous Province Soviet Executive Committee and the province's public resolutely condemn the rumors and conjectures that are being spread at rallies in the city of Yerevan in connection with the events of the past few days in Nagorno-Karabakh.

The province's population perceives the introduction of a state of emergency and a curfew as an extreme measure, but a necessary one.

The situation in the Nagorno-Karabakh Autonomous Province, and in Stepanakert in particular, is gradually stabilizing. Relations between the population and the military units are becoming more normal. Necessary measures are being taken to restore the proper work pace in the city's enterprises.

The province Party committee and the province Soviet executive committee regard as impermissible references to dubious sources of information, which radically distort the essence of what is happening in the province. The kind of information that is being given out at rallies in Yerevan misleads people and is conducive to the whipping up of passions.

In order to curb absurd rumors that are far from reality, rumors the spreading of which only plays into the hands of the opponents of restructuring, and to find a just solution to the Karabakh problem, we are prepared to present daily news summaries about events in the province.

We ask that the text of this telegram be read out at a rally in the city of Yerevan. – [signed] G. Pogosyan, Secretary of the Nagorno-Karabakh Province Party Committee, and S. Babayan, Chairman of the Nagorno-Karabakh Autonomous Province Soviet Executive Committee

---

THE SITUATION IS COMPLICATED

By special correspondents N. Demidov and Z. Kadymbekov in Baku, A. Sarkisyan and V. Khatuntsev in Yerevan. *Pravda*, Dec. 1, 1988, p. 8.

Baku – ... What is the current situation in the republic? A. Mamedov, Azerbaijan Republic Minister for Internal Affairs, tells us:

"It's tense; large-scale rallies are under way in a number of cities and districts. At all the rallies, people are demanding the fulfillment of the July 18, 1988 decision of the Presidium of the USSR Supreme Soviet, considering it the only fair solution.

In a number of places, emotions have been heated to a fever pitch. The over 55,000 refugees from Armenia that have gathered in the republic since February 1988 are an additional impetus that is stirring up tension."

* * *

Yerevan

A curfew is in effect in the city from 10 p.m. to 6 a.m. Rallies and demonstrations have been banned, and Yerevaners are observing these conditions....

About 22,000 refugees have left Azerbaijan for Armenia. The counterflow of Azerbaijanis is substantial. The Armenian Council of Ministers has given instructions for the creation of commissions on the refugee question in all cities and districts.

It is clear from a report of the Armenian Republic Ministry of Internal Affairs that, for the first time in the nine months of events, a number of districts in the republic have reported incidents with grave consequences. In the city's enterprises, every morning begins with heated discussions of the current situation....

On the whole, according to data provided by the city Party committee, 125 enterprises in the republic's capital were in full operation on Nov. 29, 58 were operating partially, and 43 were not operating at all....

* * *

Commentary by B. Mikhailov, director of the USSR Ministry of Internal Affairs' Press Bureau

... Underlying the situation is the antirestructuring, antisocialist activity of a number of corrupt individuals. More than that, it is a synthesis of their activity and the activity of ambitious political adventurists. The national aspect of the events is an extremely advantageous camouflage for them....

Question. – How do you assess the situation: Is real control over it possible?

A. – In general, the units that safeguard order are coping with their tasks. The USSR Ministry of Internal Affairs and Army units have permitted no large-scale disturbances in recent days....

Things are more complicated with local, unforeseen conflict situations, such as attacks on individual automobiles, clashes on remote streets, etc. Isolated and unconnected tragic incidents are possible here.

Q. – How many deaths have been confirmed as of today?

A. – Twenty-eight. This figure includes victims of circumstances not directly associated with conflict situations. The number of deaths directly linked to the clashes is considerably lower. Some have been wounded.

Q. – What nationality? In which regions?

A. – Representatives of the Azerbaijani and Armenian nationalities, as well as Russians, Belarussians and Ukrainians, have been killed in both Armenia and Azerbaijan. These deaths were the result of provocative clashes and even exchanges of gunfire.... Although a certain number of weapons have been confiscated, they are not scarce among immature people in Armenia and Azerbaijan. They have homemade pistols, sawed-off rifles and explosive devices....

Unfortunately, we can verify the fact that nationalist movements in Armenia and Azerbaijan quickly found leaders and initiative groups, which, in a number of instances, enjoy firmer prestige than representatives of the local authorities, who sometimes take openly amorphous positions. An example is the Nov. 7 demonstration in Yerevan, when a group of thugs trampled the flags of the Soviet republics, while the authorities had no response whatsoever. This creates the impression of omnipotence for the unofficial "patriot-leaders." The local press is heating up passions; in a number of cases, it has openly propagated nationalistic concepts that distort Party and government documents. The nationalistic virus has led to a situation in which the economic life of Baku and Yerevan has been largely destabilized. Moreover, there has been obvious reciprocal economic sabotage.

Q. – And what is the situation in this respect in the Nagorno-Karabakh Autonomous Province?

A. – Yesterday morning enterprises and institutions were not operating, with the exception of those ensuring the vital activity of the population. Public transport is functioning only in part....

OUR PAIN AND TRAGEDY: AGAINST A BACKGROUND OF MISFORTUNE

Pravda, Dec. 15, 1988, p. 6.

Editors' Note. – A Pravda correspondent interviews Lt. Gen. V. S. Dubinyak, Chief of Staff of the Internal Troops....

* * *

Question. – The first few days after the terrible tragedy showed that the situation in a number of districts of Armenia and Azerbaijan will require the diversion of some of the military units (and, consequently, of both equipment and machinery) that the disaster areas need so badly. What made this necessary?

Answer. – ... Even this terrible tragedy, which has befallen not only Armenia but all of our Soviet people as well, has not, even for a short time, put on the back burner the extremist groups' ambitious calculations and their inflammatory, double-dyed nationalistic goals. Equipment sent by the people of Azerbaijan has "bogged down" at the Armenian border. On the other hand, there has been no lessening of the degree of difficulty in districts with a mixed population from both republics. The fact that in a number of places in Azerbaijan "congratulatory telegrams" to their neighbors – just think of it! – were concocted has also added fuel to the fire. Some people even celebrated this tragedy.

Q. – We have telegrams whose content is just the opposite, too. Ones in which people have refused to "trust the Azerbaijanis to provide assistance."

A. – ... Those renegades were inflaming the situation. They are still inflaming it today. And the Armenian Council of Ministers' poorly organized record-keeping of incoming cargo is an immense help to them.

Q. – … Truck drivers' passes still flaunt the stamp of the long-banned "Karabakh Committee."…

A. – … They affix that stamp to make it seem that it is they who are sending cargo to the stricken areas, that it is not the Soviets and the Party committees but "Karabakh" that is actually heading up the rescue work. It's a dirty farce against a background of tragedy. And again there is slander, rumors, conjectures….

People involved in the "Karabakh Committee" are putting out rumors to the effect that the Army and the Ministry of Internal Affairs' troops are using the situation to completely enslave Armenia. They say that the soldiers are working not with shovels but with rifle butts.

Q. – But in these days, are significant forces really having to be diverted to perform law-enforcement functions?

A. – Exactly. Here are a few facts and figures. In the vicinity of Spitak and Kirovakan, criminals from whom valuables worth 130,511 rubles were taken were detained in a fairly short period of time – and they certainly weren't detained by members of the "Karabakh Committee." Pvt. V. Bushlakov alone took 30,000 rubles from one detainee….

The number of looters has been established at slightly more than 150. All told, we have returned valuables worth more than 250,000 rubles….

It's no secret that all kinds of scum in search of easy gain have started to gather in places hit by the tragedy.

Q. – Yes, it can't be easy for fellows who are so young. And there are still these provocative slogans like the ones heard on the square in Yerevan on Nov. 7, when soldiers, as they were risking their lives, were compared to the fascists, and when some artist depicted a Soviet soldier holding an Armenian while others killed him. The inscription above all this was "Friendship of the Peoples of the USSR."

A. – And during this time we have to safeguard order in a very wide range of areas in both republics. I'd be going against my conscience if I failed to mention the fact that we have confiscated thousands of firearms. Many rifles, sawed-off shotguns and other deadly "items" have been surrendered voluntarily, but thoroughgoing law-enforcement work was a contributing factor.

Q. – How do you assess the situation in the Nagorno-Karabakh Autonomous Province?

A. – It's critical and tense. Many people's attitudes remain basically unchanged. Several citizens have been beaten up in Martuni, there have been threats to use weapons, and livestock have been stolen.

Q. – But enterprises are operating, aren't they?

A. – Yes, for several days now. However, the situation is such that Azerbaijanis are not going to work – they're afraid to. But our units do have the situation under control and are maintaining order in the communities and on the roads….

In one area ravaged by the earthquake, we discovered a tunnel while clearing away debris. There were 27 weapons in it! Including a machine gun, 16 submachine guns, seven TT pistols and some other items….

WHOSE HANDS DOES THIS PLAY INTO?

By staff correspondent D. Melikov. *Sotsialisticheskaya industria*, Dec. 16, 1988, p. 4.

Baku – ... Our correspondents' office got a telephone call from the Azneft [Azerbaijan Petroleum] Association: Some truck drivers and gas welders who had been sent to the disaster zone to provide assistance to victims had come back.

"What do you mean, they've come back?" I asked in bewilderment....

The situation was one of those that you had to see and hear for yourself. We went to the small office of the Azneft Association's Bibi-Eibat Technological Transportation Administration....

"Maybe we should begin at the beginning," said [the driver] Mikhail Areshev. "A column of cranes and heavy-duty trucks from Azerbaijan formed up at the border between the two republics. We were the last ones in the column. We had an escort: Up front was an armored personnel carrier, there were police on each side of us, and State Motor Vehicle Inspectorate personnel brought up the rear. Why such a convoy was needed became clear soon after we entered Armenian territory. We got curses and open threats from passenger cars that passed us, people shook their fists at us, etc. It took us all night to get to Leninakan. The road between Spitak and Leninakan had caved in, and our column stopped to let vehicles coming from the other direction get by. Our vehicles were immediately attacked by thugs with shovel handles shouting: 'Get out of here! Go back to Azerbaijan! We don't need your help!' It was a good thing that the column soon got moving again, and we could get away from the hooligans for a while."

"The column approached Leninakan in the morning," said [gas welder] Vladimir Lozovan, continuing the story. "They took the cranes right away. We were told: 'Wait.' But the military escort had to leave, and thugs surrounded our trucks immediately. They had figured out from the trucks' license numbers that we were from Azerbaijan.

"'If you try to work, we'll kill you!' One of them turned to me and said: 'You're lucky you're a Russian. If you don't try to work, we won't touch you.'

"Then they went after [another gas welder] Rafik Kuzakhmedov. 'You have a dark complexion,' they said. He answered that he's a Tatar, but they took their sticks to him anyway. 'You're still a Muslim,' they said. 'We're going to kill you.'...

"Some soldiers came up from their post: 'Fellows, you're creating tension here. You'd better leave.'

"We turned to a policeman and asked him to show us the way to the commandant's office. He got in the cab with us, and we drove off. But when he found out we were from Baku, he stopped the truck: 'I have to get out here.'

"We stopped, and right away the truck was surrounded by thugs. We decided to have a heart-to-heart talk with them.... They didn't want to hear anything.... They grabbed sticks and stones. So we turned around and came back."

"... What surprises me,..." says Rafik Kuzakhmedov, "is that this isn't being rebuffed...."

ON EVENTS IN NAGORNO-KARABAKH: ETHNIC DISCORD CONTINUES

Pravda and *Izvestia*, May 10, 1989, p. 2.

Stepanakert, May 9 (TASS) – The atmosphere of relative calm that had set in from January to April in the territory of Nagorno-Karabakh has again been replaced by tension. Nationality-based conflicts, instances of reciprocal insults and threats on the part of the Armenian and Azerbaijani populations and cases in which cars and buses with passengers from Azerbaijan or Armenia have been pelted with stones on the roads have become more frequent of late.

For example, on May 5, in the settlement of Kirkidzhan on the outskirts of Stepanakert, three Armenians got into a fight with some Azerbaijanis, a fight that ultimately involved about 200 people. To break it up, warning shots were fired into the air. Police and internal troop details restored order, but in the process three civilians and four servicemen were injured. Four cars and a motorcycle were damaged. Criminal proceedings have been instituted with regard to this incident.

On May 6, ... unknown persons damaged a multichannel communications cable in Shusha District.

These and other manifestations of interethnic discord that have taken place in several communities in the Nagorno-Karabakh Autonomous Province are happening against the background of a strike in Stepanakert and a partial strike in district centers. Workers and office employees of Azerbaijani nationality are not being allowed into enterprises and institutions in Stepanakert to perform their jobs, while those of Armenian nationality are afraid to work in Shusha. The strike involves industrial enterprises, construction sites, some automotive transportation and some institutions.... On the whole, work is still proceeding at its normal pace in Shusha District and at the province's collective and state farms....

According to a statement by strike participants, the main cause of the strike was the accelerated construction of industrial, social and consumer-service facilities in Azerbaijani villages at a time when this is not being done in the province's Armenian communities. In actuality, according to the plan for 1989, the volume of construction in the Nagorno-Karabakh Autonomous Province amounts to 96 million rubles, including 4 million rubles' worth in Azerbaijani communities. The Committee for Special Administration, in conjunction with the leaders of Party and Soviet bodies, has reviewed the list of construction projects not included in the plan.

Passions were also aggravated by a number of statements in the local and republic media, particularly with regard to the "Azerbaijanification" of the autonomous province that is allegedly under way. The Armenian side fears that as a result of this process, the demographic situation will change in favor of the Azerbaijanis.

The problem of refugees remains the most acute source of the population's unrest. In Stepanakert the number of refugees has reached 20% of the native population, and in the province as a whole, 10%.

A significant portion of the Armenian population of Nagorno-Karabakh is expressing distrust of the Committee for Special Administration and demanding the restoration of the province bodies of power, as well as the virtual removal of the Nagorno-Karabakh Autonomous Province from the jurisdiction of the Azerbaijan Republic. This is also stated in an open letter to M. S. Gorbachev published in the newspaper Sovetsky Karabakh and signed by the first secretaries of the city and district Party committees, the chairmen of city and district Soviet executive committees (except Shusha) and some of the USSR People's Deputies from the Nagorno-Karabakh Autonomous Province. After the situation began to become heated, the same officials signed an appeal to the working people of Nagorno-Karabakh, in which they call on the population to show restraint and calm.... But voices calling for the strike to be extended indefinitely and to be turned into a "campaign of civil disobedience" are ringing out ever louder.

Taking into consideration the fact that there is still tension among most of the Armenian population and that the Azerbaijani population is also stirred up, the Committee for Special Administration of the Nagorno-Karabakh Autonomous Province and the military command of the special district have taken vigorous measures to strengthen the safeguarding of public order, avert and stop clashes based on interethnic discord, and ensure citizens' safety. These measures include an extension of the curfew in the city of Stepanakert and the district centers of the special district, intensified monitoring of the roads, and military patrols of the boundaries where Armenian and Azerbaijani communities meet. Law-enforcement agencies and internal troop personnel in the special district are doing everything possible to ensure people's safety....

On the whole, the situation is under control, although it remains tense and complex.

ON EVENTS IN NAGORNO-KARABAKH: OUTBREAKS OF SHOOTING

Pravda, July 14, 1989, p. 3.

Stepanakert, July 13 (TASS) – The situation in Nagorno-Karabakh remains complex. The past 24 hours were marked by provocative firing of hunting weapons in a number of communities by irresponsible people trying to stir up tension and create an atmosphere of increasing fear of an attack by the other side....

Yesterday, a citizen of Armenian nationality was found shot to death in Mardakert District. In Askeran Borough, a rampaging crowd demolished a household goods store and the air traffic control station at the Stepanakert airport. In the town of Shusha, a group of Azerbaijanis tore up an Armenian family's apartment and beat up the head of the household, who was hospitalized. These and other incidents are being investigated....

Despite the fact that [the roads] are being patrolled continuously by details of internal troops, groups of hooligans tried repeatedly over the course of the day to set up roadblocks on various sections of road and stop the flow of traffic. Bus service between Stepanakert and other communities has been interrupted. To all intents and purposes, motor vehicle access to the autonomous province has been cut off, as has telephone service between Stepanakert and Mardakert District. There has been an alarming increase in the number of acts of provocation directed against internal troop and police personnel who have the job of preventing clashes between nationalities in the special district. Last night a checkpoint in Askeran District was fired upon. Yesterday, during an attempt to check the documents of a driver whose truck had no license plates, unidentified individuals fired on the police squad from inside the vehicle.

S. G. Lisauskas, USSR Deputy Minister of Internal Affairs; Col. Gen. Yu. V. Shatalin, Commander of the USSR Ministry of Internal Affairs' Internal Troops; and B. A. Koryakovtsev, director of the USSR Ministry of Internal Affairs' Chief State Motor Vehicle Inspectorate Administration, have come to Stepanakert to clarify the situation in the province and coordinate the activities of the forces maintaining law and order.

In the heat of emotion, attempts are being made to interfere with the work of surveyors and prospectors who have come to Nagorno-Karabakh, and this could significantly postpone implementation of the autonomous province's construction program....

The Committee for Special Administration and the special district's military command are taking the necessary steps to stabilize the situation. At a staff meeting chaired by A. I. Volsky, additional measures were outlined for putting a decisive halt to the hooligan activities and displays of hostility between nationalities and for ensuring the safety of the general public.

EXACERBATING THE SITUATION

Pravda, Jan. 13, 1990, p. 3.

Stepanakert, Jan. 12 (TASS) – Gunfire continues to be heard in and around Nagorno-Karabakh. During the suppression of unlawful actions in the Azerbaijani village of Akhullu, Gadrut District, Nagorno-Karabakh Autonomous Province, on the night of Jan. 11, Lt. I. Tsymbalyuk was seriously wounded and Master Sgt. E. Sapilov sustained bodily injuries. According to preliminary information, an Azerbaijani policeman who was in the village shot the internal troops lieutenant.

Lt. I. Tsymbalyuk died today in a military hospital in Tbilisi. Criminal proceedings have been instituted with respect to the incident.

In the afternoon, an armed attack was made on the village of Manashid in the Azerbaijan Republic's Shaumyanovsk District, which is contiguous to the Nagorno-Karabakh Autonomous Province. Eight internal troops repelled the attack by militants of the Azerbaijani nationality, who were equipped with bulletproof vests and armed with submachine guns. There were casualties on both sides.

The situation in Shaumyanovsk District of the Azerbaijan Republic is extremely tense. Additional forces of internal troops have been assembled there.

SITUATION WORSENS

Pravda, March 26, 1990, p. 3.

The reports coming in from the Armenian and Azerbaijan Republics continue to cause concern and inspire a certain degree of alarm.

On the morning of March 22, as a group of Armenian militants were trying to adapt a hail-suppression artillery piece to fire at communities in the Azerbaijan Republic, a shell exploded. Two of the militants died, and others were wounded.

On that same day 15 people, members of a district organization of the so-called "association for national self-determination" in Armenia's Artashat District, broke into district Party and Soviet offices. They were armed with assault rifles and pistols, and they threatened officials with physical violence.

The situation on the border between Armenia's Noyemberyan District and Azerbaijan's Kazakh District has deteriorated sharply. On March 23-24, firearms were used by both sides in a number of villages in these districts; vehicles and dwellings came under fire. Armenian militants attacked the communities of Aksipira and Baganis Airum. According to preliminary reports, seven Azerbaijanis died, including two children and a policeman. An Armenian woman and a child were injured in the clashes. There were some hostage-taking incidents.

On March 24 a homemade explosive device with a timing mechanism blew up at a gas station on the road between Yevlakh and Lachin in the Nagorno-Karabakh Autonomous Province's Shusha District, putting the station out of service. That evening in Armenia's Megri District there was an explosion beneath one car of a passenger train on the Norashen-Baku route. The explosion derailed the engine and two cars. No lives were lost. A reserve engine that was sent to the Megri station to clear the way so that a repair train could reach the site of the accident was fired upon by militants. Train traffic was halted.

These are bitter, tragic reports, made doubly bitter by the fact that recently, thanks to prodigious efforts by the authorities and the public, the situation in the region had improved somewhat; transport service had resumed, as had deliveries of freight to the Armenian Republic. It seems, however, that these developments are not to the liking of certain extremist forces. They want to disrupt the first results of stabilization and spark more conflict, without regard for casualties and destruction. The actions of Armenian militants in particular serve only to undermine the interests of the Armenian people. In order to avert a new outbreak of violence in the region, law-enforcement agencies have been ordered to carefully investigate all the incidents cited above, find the guilty parties and bring them to strict account. – (TASS)

SITUATION IN THE NAGORNO-KARABAKH AUTONOMOUS PROVINCE: ROAD TO NOWHERE?

Kommunist, June 3, 1990, p. 4.

The shots that rang out in Stepanakert the night of May 24-25 were echoed in Yerevan two days later.

The relevant agencies still have quite a bit of work to do in seeking the specific reasons for what happened both in Yerevan and in Stepanakert, but the true reasons, i.e., the political ones, are well known to everyone today: the delay on the part of the country's top echelons of state power in solving the problem of Nagorno-Karabakh....

The adamant position taken by Armenian public forces on the question of Nagorno-Karabakh has come into profound conflict with the position of the center, which in no way wants to go any farther than numerous resolutions, decrees and appeals for "common sense." Today the Karabakh movement aims primarily at separation from Azerbaijan, whose public forces, using the interethnic conflict as a cover while actually inflaming it further, simply want to secede from the USSR when a convenient political moment arrives. Well, that's their business, but what does Nagorno-Karabakh, an age-old Armenian province that was forcibly included in Azerbaijan, have to do with it? ...

The economic blockade, which has long kept Nagorno-Karabakh under tension and made the province's overwhelming Armenian majority tighten its belt, has today been transferred to a different plane – one of political pressure on the people of Karabakh, pressure that is supported, unfortunately, by the internal troops that have been stationed in the province since the very beginning of the Karabakh events.

In and of itself, the presence of troops in a territory threatened by its own explosiveness due to conflicts between nationalities is a noble thing, needless to say. This is the position that people in Nagorno-Karabakh – the Armenian part of the population, at any rate – had taken toward the presence in their home of gallant lads in gray-green uniforms. But lately, since the adoption of the well-known Nov. 28, 1989 resolution of the USSR Supreme Soviet ["On Measures to Normalize the Situation in the Nagorno-Karabakh Autonomous Province."], this noble mission has begun to take on a clearly one-sided nature, and the Armenians of Karabakh have felt themselves under double pressure.

Even for the most extreme liberals, the last doubts on this score evaporated after March 27 of this year, when at the order of Maj. Gen. V. Safonov, the new commandant of the emergency district, an attempt was organized to prevent the holding of a planned session of the province Soviet – a session that, incidentally, stemmed from the aforementioned Nov. 28 resolution. It was to have considered the question of restoring the functions of the province Soviet and its executive committee in connection with the stepping down of the Committee for the Special Administration of the Nagorno-Karabakh Autonomous Province.

The attempt to keep the session from being held was not successful, but to this day Maj. Gen. Safonov does not want to acknowledge the restored body's Soviet authority and is essentially imposing military authority in the province, authority that goes beyond the bounds of the decree on the state of emergency. This is the source of all the problems having to do with the building of social and economic facilities in the cities and villages of Nagorno-Karabakh. That is, in the Armenian part of the province, of course; there are no problems at all in building planned and, to a large extent, unplanned facilities in the Azerbaijani communities....

The humiliation and slow deportation of Nagorno-Karabakh's Armenians continue, now in undisguised form, shamelessly and with militant cynicism.

All the roads leading to Nagorno-Karabakh and connecting it with the civilized world are closed today. Only one road is open – the one to Baku....

All the rest are closed. Closed, unfortunately, by the soldiers of Maj. Gen. Safonov....

BOOMERANG

By T. Akopyan. *Kommunist,* June 5, 1990, p. 4.

On May 29, a day of national mourning, the teletype machine in the newspaper office tapped out an appeal to the country's president.[1]...

The first shot fired at a soldier in Armenia rang out this year. But the bolt of an assault rifle clicked back much earlier. Was it perhaps on March 25, 1988, when military hardware filled the peaceful squares and streets of Yerevan? But at that time girls gave the soldiers flowers, grandmothers treated them to baked goods, and young men generously shared cigarettes with them.... No, it wasn't then.... The people considered it a moral victory that they didn't respond to Sumgait [anti-Armenian pogroms in February 1988] with violence, and the first refugees from Azerbaijan were grateful to the soldiers for rescuing them.

But some time later, a gallant officer – a participant in the "March action" in Yerevan – claimed in a newspaper that Armenian men had offered the soldiers "money, drugs and their women" to divert their attention from their weapons for at least a little while. Attacking the moral principles of any people leads to alienation. Surely the numerous special correspondents and other "experts" should have thought about that when they were sowing lies and disinformation on the pages of newspapers, shouldn't they?

Then in July. we lived through the events at Zvartnots Airport.[2] Without assessing them emotionally, let's admit nonetheless that this was a political act whose participants were trying, after the 19th Party Conference's silence on the "Karabakh problem," to draw the attention of the country's public to the events in the region, which were starting to move in a threatening direction. It was a naive and unnecessary step, but it was also nonviolent. Yet it was answered with violence. Boys in uniform (colleagues of the very servicemen who have now held a meeting and appealed to the president of the USSR for truth and objectivity) fell upon the demonstrators with truncheons and with malice in their eyes. They beat and kicked the unarmed, defenseless picketers, as well as passengers and women who happened to be there. Photographer Kh. Zakaryan, who dared to record the atrocities on film, was killed. This single death shocked Armenia, because the man was not killed by a criminal or a crowd of riffraff – he was shot by the Army, that very same "heroic," "liberating" Army that "guards the interests of the people." Yet Central Television showed a soldier whimpering over a scratch on his ear that he had received from an Armenian "extremist." How do you like that! ...After Zvartnots, a policy of "parity," of dividing the blame for the blood and violence between the two peoples, came into use. That was how the September events in Khodzhaly (Nagorno-Karabakh Autonomous Province) were interpreted, while the beatings of Armenians in Kirovabad and other Azerbaijani cities simply went unmentioned.

But again, in Armenia no one crossed the line of bloodshed....

Starting last November, attacks on Armenian villages bordering on Azerbaijan became more frequent, and the first casualties among Armenians on their own land were recorded. Armed Azerbaijani militants blockaded Armenian villages in Shaumyanovsk District and Getashen, and began to gather on the border with Nagorno-Karabakh. Our valiant border troops were not able to prevent the 600-kilometer border from being torn down in the Nakhichevan Autonomous Republic, and combat weapons...were brought across into Azerbaijan from Iran. The troops, as always, arrived too late or showed up in the wrong place.

There were pogroms in Baku for seven days, and riffraff in Kirovabad brutally killed Armenians – elderly residents of a home for the aged. No matter what anyone says, it looks as if the state totally "forgot" about its duties to protect the safety and the very lives of its citizens.

It was then that people in Armenia began spontaneously seizing weapons. Because violence begets violence. Because every people should know how to defend itself. That's the truth, although for a long time we haven't wanted to talk about it....

I am not trying in any way to justify the senseless shots fired at soldiers, nor am I trying to deny the right of the latter to repulse an attempt on their lives. I simply want to explain why this tragedy happened....

For a long time, a very long time, our historical memory kept our entire people from engaging in violent acts. We knew the price of violence and terror, and we did not and do not want to build a temple on blood.

Today the link between times has been broken, for the "psychological rehabilitation" of a spiritually and physically desperate people who endured a terrible earthquake with hundreds of thousands of refugees has been carried out with the assistance of blockades, sieges, truncheons, a curfew, political arrests and a cynical newspaper and magazine campaign. The boomerang effect has started to operate.

I am not going to talk about the hypocrisy of the appeal by servicemen calling for "truth and objectivity" from the territory of Azerbaijan itself, where dozens of soldiers and officers were killed and where a genuine terror was unleashed against women and children solely because they were members of servicemen's families. No such appeals came through TASS channels then....

We've been under provocation for two years now. We'll survive. We'll survive the hypocritical appeal to the president, too....

SITUATION IN NAGORNO-KARABAKH

By Azerbaijan Information Agency Correspondent V. Shulman. *Izvestia*, June 28, 1990, p. 3.

Stepanakert, June 27 (TASS) – ... The [Azerbaijan] Republic Committee for the Nagorno-Karabakh Autonomous Province has been operating for five months now.

"Our committee's basic task," said V. Polyanichko, Second Secretary of the Azerbaijan Communist Party Central Committee, "is to normalize the situation in Nagorno-Karabakh and to restore people's hope in the reestablishment of peace and calm."

By no means everyone wants to see peace in Nagorno-Karabakh. And that is why it's so hard for the USSR Ministry of Internal Affairs' internal troops. The office of the military commandant for the area under a state of emergency reported that 67 special operations have been carried out in 43 communities this year, and that 350 kilograms of explosives, more than 1,200 rifles and shotguns, tens of thousands of rounds of ammunition, 180 cloud-seeding cannons and almost 4,000 shells for them have been confiscated.

But a considerable quantity of weapons remain in the terrorists' hands, and they are using them. And not just in the Nagorno-Karabakh Autonomous Province, but also in the adjacent areas of Azerbaijan, which armed groups from Armenia are infiltrating with increasing frequency.

"A few days ago, in Kelbadzhar District, an attempt was made to attack a military outpost high in the mountains," said Maj. Gen. G. Malyushkin, deputy commander of the internal troops administration for the Northern Caucasus and Transcaucasus. "Our troops returned fire, and one of the attackers, a resident of Yerevan, was killed. But hopes that common sense will prevail have not been lost. Many people in the Nagorno-Karabakh Autonomous Province understand that efforts to solve the problem with arms in hand will not succeed for either side, but will bring only grief, bloodshed and more senseless victims."

Representatives of the province's Armenian population are more and more often entering into dialogue with the organizing committee. The first contacts have shown just how much can be achieved through joint efforts. In the past few days, people have been compensated for lost housing and property, benefits and pension matters have been transferred, and Armenian refugees have been given jobs....

"There are a good many problems in the province," V. Polyanichko said. "We must make up for the losses caused by numerous strikes, totally revise the infrastructure, sharply increase the pace of construction of housing, schools, hospitals and polyclinics, and create thousands of new jobs. Resolving these questions requires peace and calm. But it's unlikely that peace and calm will come to the long-suffering land of Nagorno-Karabakh until the unconstitutional decisions that the Armenian Supreme Soviet has taken on the Nagorno-Karabakh Autonomous Province are rescinded."

TRANSCAUCASUS: CHRONICLE OF THE PAST FEW DAYS

Reports received by I. Andreyev. *Izvestia*, Aug. 22, 1990, p. 1.

The protracted Transcaucasus drama, which has been keeping the whole region and the whole country tense, has opened a new page, one that, alas, is just as bloody as before. Weapons that Armenian militants have obtained by criminal means are being fired again, both in the [Armenian] Republic itself and in Azerbaijan....

The situation is causing concern among the authorities in Armenia and Azerbaijan. Speaking to a meeting of the Armenian parliament on the new escalation of the Armenian-Azerbaijani conflict, L. Ter-Petrosyan, Chairman of the republic Supreme Soviet, said, in particular, that this is a very real provocation by armed groups, some of which, one has to say bluntly, are backed by mafia elements for whom the stabilization of the situation in Armenia by no means serves their purposes. It is no accident that every night gunshots are fired in Yerevan itself, cars are stolen and police stations are attacked, Ter-Petrosyan continued. The only gratifying thing is that in the past few days the police have finally begun to administer a fitting rebuff to the bandits.

Addressing the Union-republic Supreme Soviets on republic television and radio, A. Mutalibov, President of the Azerbaijan SSR, said, among other things:

"The failure to put real levers of disarmament into operation is the political reason for the instability in the region and essentially means that the Union is, to all intents and purposes, refusing to fulfill its constitutional commitments with respect to a member of the federation – namely, Azerbaijan."

Now for a brief summary of the events of the past few days....

Several hundred Armenian militants blockaded four Azerbaijani villages.

Internal troops took part in an operation to lift the blockade of the communities, with the support of two helicopters. One of them was shot down....

A real battle was joined during the seizure of the Azerbaijani community of Baganis-Airum.... The terrorists, who had four artillery pieces, mortars, grenade launchers and automatic sniper rifles, launched an attack on the village. Servicemen... successfully repelled the attack. But, after receiving reinforcement from three unidentified helicopters that arrived on the scene, the militants were able to take the village.

Additional manpower, tanks and armored personnel carriers were sent to border villages....

The body of Police Maj. G. Abasyan, a staff member of the Soviet Borough department of internal affairs in the city of Yerevan, who had been taken hostage a few days before, was discovered near the village of Garni, Abovyan District.

Attacks on local internal affairs departments in Armenia for the purpose of seizing weapons are continuing....

According to the USSR Ministry of Internal Affairs' summary reports for Aug. 21, on that day guns were seized in the Georgian SSR [as well]....

The situation in the Nagorno-Karabakh Autonomous Province and adjacent districts remains complicated....

SHAUMYANOVSK DISTRICT – A War at the Working People's Request?

By special correspondent Mikhail Shevelyov. *Moskovskiye novosti*, Feb. 3, 1991, p. 5.

On Jan. 14, 1991, the Presidium of the Azerbaijan SSR Supreme Soviet adopted a decision to unite two neighboring districts of the republic – Shaumyanovsk and Kasum-Ismailov. Both districts are located next to the Nagorno-Karabakh Autonomous Province. About 20,000 people live in Shaumyanovsk District, of whom 82% are Armenians; Kasum-Ismailov District's population of 50,000 consists mainly of Azerbaijanis.

* * *

Prehistory

On July 25, 1989, a session of the Shaumyanovsk District Soviet appealed to the Azerbaijan Supreme Soviet, asking that the district be made part of the Nagorno-Karabakh Autonomous Province.

On Aug. 1, Baku replied with a refusal.

On Jan. 15, 1990, a state of emergency was declared in Shaumyanovsk District and was simultaneously instituted in the Nagorno-Karabakh Autonomous Province and adjacent districts.

On Aug. 29, 1990, the Bureau of the Azerbaijan Communist Party Central Committee suspended the activity of the Shaumyanovsk District Party Committee and expelled its First Secretary, Vladimir Agadzhanyan, from the CPSU for nationalism and separatism.

On Sept. 2, the Azerbaijan News Agency disseminated a story that questioned the need for Shaumyanovsk District to exist as an administrative unit.

On Sept. 28, the Presidium of the Azerbaijan Supreme Soviet canceled elections to the republic and local Soviets in the district, suspended the activity of the existing Soviets, and transferred their powers to a temporary organizational bureau directly subordinate to the republic authorities.

* * *

The district is divided by an unofficial but strictly observed border. The four Azerbaijani villages located on the outlying edges of the district receive supplies from Azerbaijan. Shaumyanovsk and the Armenian villages have severed relations with the republic. There are no telephone, postal or telegraph services, and no newspapers are received. Few people dare to travel to Stepanakert through the Azerbaijani villages. Round-the-clock patrolling of villages and farms by volunteers has become a way of life. You can travel through one of "the other side's" villages only if accompanied by soldiers; otherwise, you could wind up as a hostage, at best. According to the military's information, there are a great many weapons in the district – from hunting guns to cloud-seeding cannon – and there are people who know how to use them.

Once a day, weather permitting, a helicopter flies in from Yerevan (the pilots who fly to Shaumyanovsk refuse to part with the weapons they were issued at one time). Gasoline, lubricating oil and diesel fuel are the chief form of currency. The meager amounts that can be obtained with incredible difficulty are distributed drop by drop. When the helicopter lands people dash toward it, jerricans in hand, to get kerosene for lamps, since electricity is regularly shut off. Homes are heated by small wood-burning stoves and homemade electric heaters: There is no fuel oil at all. The medicine situation is very bad. Only six physicians are working (there are supposed to be 68). People in Shaumyanovsk start lining up for bread at 7 a.m., and it is all sold out by 8:30 a.m. But there is plenty of wine, because there is nowhere for the local winery to ship it. The gypsum mine, the district's largest enterprise, has been shut down: Its output used to be sent through the Geran railroad station in Kasum-Ismailov District. People who used to receive their salaries from republic organizations have been left without pay. But money is the last thing in people's minds here; all conversations are about an imminent war.

I think a war will begin as soon as the republic authorities decide to implement the decision on merging the two districts. What will life be like if the police, the prosecutor's office and the court are located in Kasum-Ismailov? Who will govern the district? Who will distribute money, building materials and apartments? But these arguments are used only in conversations with Moscow journalists. The Armenians in Shaumyanovsk District have no doubts that submitting to the decree would mean abandoning their land. "This land is worth fighting for and dying for," said Shagen Megryan, a man who now enjoys unquestioned authority in Shaumyanovsk District, expressing the general mood.

Armenians will be in the minority in the new district, which is to be named Geranboi. They are convinced that they will not be forgiven for the present confrontation, and that sooner or later they will be forced to sell their homes to Azerbaijanis or Meskhetian Turks, who have been permitted to settle in these parts. But even this takes second place in the thoughts of people in Shaumyanovsk. The immediate future is more frightening: If the troops leave for the new district center, the police detachments based in the Azerbaijani villages, detachments that call themselves special police units, will begin to operate more boldly. On Jan. 22 one such unit, which controls the airport in Stepanakert, detained some Russian SFSR

People's Deputies who had come to study the situation in the Nagorno-Karabakh Autonomous Province and sent them to Baku.

An appeal from the Azerbaijan SSR Supreme Soviet to the population of Shaumyanovsk District says: "The tense situation that has developed in the district and the critical state of the economy, as well as numerous requests and petitions from district residents, have forced the leadership of the Azerbaijan SSR, taking into account the measures that are being implemented to restructure the economy and improve the financial situation and the actual economic and geographic ties linking the two districts, to unite Shaumyanovsk and Kasum-Ismailov Districts." The republic has the right to change the borders of districts on its own territory. But should this right be exercised when such a step will lead to bloodshed?

The inevitable armed clashes in Shaumyanovsk District will certainly have repercussions in the Nagorno-Karabakh Autonomous Province and in other places in Azerbaijan and Armenia. The Armenian Supreme Soviet has already stated that it "will take all necessary steps to safeguard the lives and property of the district's Armenian population."

"I fear Feb. 5," said Col. Nikolai Chernovol, the commandant of Shaumyanovsk District during the state of emergency. That is the opening day of the session of the Azerbaijan Supreme Soviet, to which the decision on the merger of Shaumyanovsk District [with Kasum-Ismailov District] will be submitted for confirmation.

NAGORNO-KARABAKH: WILL THE LIVING WALL STAND FOR LONG?

By special correspondent V. Reshetnikov. *Izvestia*, Feb. 5, 1991, p. 2.

Stepanakert – For several years now, soldiers and officers of the internal troops have been standing between Armenians and Azerbaijanis in Nagorno-Karabakh, standing as a third force in the protracted conflict between the two neighboring peoples, as a living wall that prevents large-scale carnage from breaking out – carnage that would be merciless and senseless....

In Agdam, several officers said they would give me a lift to Stepanakert. They were clearly in no hurry to leave a town outside the "zone," a place where they could "get hold of" evaporated milk, butter, fruit and everything else that brightens the service routine, if just a little. In Stepanakert, they told me, such things are nowhere to be found. And military grub is not known for its variety....

Along the way, our vehicle sped by an Armenian settlement, then an Azerbaijani community. In both, people along the roadside looked longingly at the speeding armored personnel carrier. The lieutenant colonel explained that it is common for people to beg soldiers to give them rides to places they need to go, under armored protection. Money is offered in return, often sizable sums.

Stepanakert's appearance is depressing. Terribly neglected, it looks less like a city than a fortified area – in a combat zone. The entrances have checkpoints with trenches, sandbags, antitank obstacles and other "engineering structures."...

The city has no water, most of its enterprises are not operating, and lines for bread form at 6 a.m. In front of the province Party committee building is a standard-design, several-ton monument to Lenin, just like the one in Gyandzha. In a period of accentuated hostility between the two peoples, this monument seems to be practically the only unifying symbol. The province Party committee building is closed, as is that of the Soviet executive committee. The officials have all gone. And they seem to be in no hurry to come back. On paper, the representative of legitimate authority is the Committee for Special Administration, but the Armenian population doesn't feel even a shade of confidence in it. Its decisions are not recognized and are not carried out.

The upshot is that the only real authority in Nagorno-Karabakh is the military. Today the military is the province Party and Soviet executive committees combined. It now shoulders all concerns for vital services in the city. Military personnel repair and guard the water line that militants periodically blow up, and they unload freight coming in from Baku, since the local population refuses to do it. Military personnel fight fires, deliver the mail, supply fuel to municipal transport, obtain firewood and nails, haul refugees' belongings, issue them labor booklets, and even try to take on a peacemaking mission. In other words, the military is doing everything it shouldn't be doing.

When darkness falls, off-duty officers move through the streets only in groups. If an officer does go alone, he takes along a loaded pistol, with the safety on, in the pocket of his pea jacket.

And that's how it is day after day, with no days off.... Servicemen are convinced that those "on top" either can't change the situation or don't want to. The over-whelming majority are sure that the troops who were sent here to maintain order while the conflict is being settled will be bogged down here for many years. They are convinced that a better solution to the problem than keeping thousands of soldiers in Nagorno-Karabakh has not been found and is not being sought.

The passivity of the supreme authorities in solving the Karabakh problem and their clear disregard for those who are made to do their service here – this is what makes the officers indignant. Coming to a meeting with representatives of the USSR Supreme Soviet's monitoring commission, they wanted to hear the Deputies say whether Moscow sees a way out of the Karabakh impasse. Their opinion is that the Committee for Special Administration has not justified the hopes that were pinned on it. The republics are not seeking paths to a compromise. The internal troops are now viewed with hostility by both parties in the conflict. The Armenians believe that the troops, invited here at the request of the Azerbaijan government, are preventing them from setting up their own bodies of power. The Azerbaijanis, meanwhile, are convinced that the military is protecting the Armenians. More and more often the soldiers, instead of hearing words of gratitude for saving lives, are being met with bullets. Troop details are being fired on; armored personnel carriers and checkpoints are being fired on....

Outposts in the mountains on the Armenian-Azerbaijani border are being subjected to outright assaults. Now, during the snowy season, conditions are especially hard for our boys there. A duty shift sometimes stays on post two weeks instead of one, living on no more than dried crusts by the end. The militants make special targets of military commanders and special forces officers. They set cash rewards on the heads of some. They promise 70,000 rubles for the commanding officer of an internal troops regiment, 50,000 for a district commandant.... On a Stepanakert street on Jan. 19, someone in a passing car fired point-blank on the Niva [automobile] of V. Kovalyov, director of the Nagorno-Karabakh Autonomous Province internal affairs administration. The general was miraculously saved, thanks only to his instantaneous reaction.

Twelve military personnel were killed last year, and five have lost their lives this year....

Nevertheless, they [military personnel] understand that Karabakh is a knot that cannot be untied overnight. But they are simply terribly, inhumanly tired. They are tired of living in wretched conditions, in tents, dugouts and gymnasiums converted into barracks....

But they do not feel that they are getting either moral or material support from those who sent them to Nagorno-Karabakh. Spending a year there, instead of a year and a half – this is their nominal "material incentive" for service in a high-risk zone, for the constant threat of being killed.

It is by no means an accident that there are virtually no young officers in Karabakh. The overwhelming majority are colonels and lieutenant colonels. Many have just a few years left before they can retire on pension "after long service." But those for whom a pension is not in the foreseeable future are kept in the Army, in their own words, only by existing legislation, which does not allow them to resign their commissions. Because of their nomadic Army life, they have not acquired many belongings. On being transferred to their new "place of permanent deployment," many lost their apartments....

I dare say the reader has noticed that not one last name has been given. Anonymity was an invariable condition stated by the officers who agreed to talk to this journalist. This is very indicative. Punishment for candor can be harsh.

Their missions, I repeat, are to prevent bloodshed between the two neighboring peoples, to block the movement of armed groups, to escort convoys, to control the roads, to confiscate weapons, and to maintain public order in the cities. But, in the general opinion of military personnel, unless full-fledged bodies of power are set up in the near future, of all the missions that have been set for the internal troops only one may remain – self-protection.

In January, there were 14 killed and 19 wounded in the Nagorno-Karabakh Autonomous Province.

SOVIET-FRENCH DIALOGUE

Pravda, May 8, 1991, p. 1.

Moscow, May 6 (TASS) – **Editors' Note.** – The following is an excerpt from a press conference with M. S. Gorbachev and [French President François] Mitterrand.

* * *

Correspondent from Agence France-Presse, France. – We know that domestic problems in the Soviet Union were also touched on during the meeting. Did you talk about Armenia? In particular, about the actions of Soviet Army units and their operation against Armenian volunteers, which resulted in civilian casualties, including people from an Armenian village on the territory of Armenia itself?

M. S. Gorbachev. – ... We did touch on the critical situation that has arisen, only I would say it is not in Armenia but in Azerbaijan, on whose territory Nagorno-Karabakh, an area where a large part of the indigenous residents are Armenians, is located....

The presence in both republics of armed groups of bandits that are terrorizing the people – both Armenians and Azerbaijanis – is hindering the political process, including the restoration of full autonomy and all its attributes in Nagorno-Karabakh. The way things stand, unless all these detachments are gotten rid of, the political process won't get off the ground.

On my way to the meeting with the French President, I asked for information on just what has happened from March to May. There have been 235 shooting attacks in Nagorno-Karabakh and in border districts, and that's just for March, April and May. Of this number, 153 came from the Armenian side and 82 from the Azerbaijani side. Twenty Azerbaijanis and 10 Armenians were killed or died. The USSR internal troops that are there were fired upon 115 times. If they hadn't been there, a real war, a slaughter, would have broken out. Nine soldiers of the internal troops died, and 15 were wounded. Since we were faced with such a situation, it was deemed necessary to fully implement the President's decree, disarm the illegal formations and confiscate their weapons. There are weapons there from literally all over the world, from homemade weapons to modern flame-throwers, to say nothing of assault rifles, machine guns, armored vehicles, etc. It's a complex situation. It has to be defused; otherwise it could lead to events that will result in great bloodshed.

A disarmament operation is currently under way, within the limits of constitutional provisions, laws and the President's decree. It is being carried out community by community. Some people don't like this; some have used this distressing nationality-based drama to earn political capital for themselves and want to exploit it further. We cannot allow this. Constitutional order must be restored. The Nagorno-Karabakh autonomous unit and all the attributes that belong to it must be completely restored. Moreover – and it seems to me that such intentions do exist on the Azerbaijani side – we must make the autonomous unit's status such that people feel themselves to be the object of concern and attention.

The country's leadership cannot be accused of failing to make efforts along political lines. This was done from the very first days of the conflict. We intend to continue adhering strictly to the law and acting within legal bounds....

TOPICAL INTERVIEW: BACK TO THE STARTING POINT

Interview conducted by G. Ovcharenko. *Pravda*, June 26, 1991, p. 3.

Editors' Note. – For several years now, the attention of the country, and even the world, has been riveted on the Azerbaijani-Armenian conflict that has arisen over Nagorno-Karabakh. These events reached a tragic culmination in May, when blood was spilled again on the border between the two republics. And, as always in such instances, rumors began spreading that defame both peoples and make insulting, wrongful accusations against the Soviet Army and the internal troops.

But what really happened on the Azerbaijani-Armenian border? It was this question, which many readers are asking, that began a Pravda correspondent's interview with the following officials: I. Shilov, USSR First Deputy Minister of Internal Affairs; A. Vasilyev, USSR First Deputy Prosecutor General; and V. Vorotnikov, Director of the USSR State Security Committee's Administration for the Protection of the Soviet Constitutional System, who have recently returned from the scene of the events.

* * *

I. Shilov. – I will begin with some terrible figures: Since February 1988, when the well-known events began in and around Nagorno-Karabakh, 816 people have been killed in strife between nationalities and more than 5,000 have been wounded. In effect, a war between nationalities has been going on for the past few months in that region, a war in the flames of which, let me note, 123 employees of internal affairs agencies and servicemen have been killed and 675 wounded while attempting to stop unlawful actions....

It was in this critical situation that the Azerbaijan leadership asked the USSR Ministry of Internal Affairs for assistance in conducting an operation on the republic's territory to carry out the USSR President's well-known decree on the disarming of illegal armed formations and the confiscation of illegally held weapons.

Question. – Can one already talk about the results of the operation and draw some conclusions?

I. Sh. – In general terms, yes. During the operation, which was conducted in an especially vigorous way from April 30 to May 17, 240 firearms were confiscated, including 115 assault rifles and pistols, explosives, mines and antiaircraft guns. A total of 413 people were detained on administrative charges, and criminal proceedings were instituted against 64 people. As a result, the situation on the border between the two republics and in Nagorno-Karabakh is calmer today.

Q. – It has been reported in a number of media outlets that the operations aimed at disarming the militants turned into punitive actions against Armenian civilians and that legality was violated. Can you confirm or deny these reports? ...

I. Sh. – There has been a great deal of talk about outrages and looting committed by members of Azerbaijani special police units. I can testify that yes, special policemen were involved in the disarmament operation, but most of them were held in reserve or stayed on the border. Those who were put into operation in the communities themselves were internal troops, reinforced by staff members of agencies of the Azerbaijan Ministry of Internal Affairs. Nevertheless, an official investigation is being conducted into every complaint, and there have been somein one place, the public was treated roughly, in another, furniture was broken.

A. Vasilyev. – The newspapers wrote that people are being detained indiscriminately and without legal grounds. Perhaps there were isolated cases of this during such a large-scale operation. But careful checks were made on all those who were detained, and the innocent were released once their identity had been established. At the same time, I can say that more than 100 of the 413 people who were detained are individuals who were wanted for committing various types of crimes.

Q. – Staff members of the Azerbaijan Prosecutor's Office are conducting an on-the-spot investigation, in accordance with the law. But many readers have their doubts: Can the republic Prosecutor's Office be objective?

A. V. – We are monitoring the course of the investigation, and so far there is no reason to distrust our Azerbaijani colleagues.

But since there is this talk, I think it would be useful to have the criminal cases that were instituted after the tragic events on the Armenian-Azerbaijani border investigated jointly by the two republic Prosecutor's Offices with the participation of the Union Prosecutor's Office. The Azerbaijani side has no objection to this, but the Armenian Prosecutor's Office has made no move in response.

Q. – Now let's return to the events in the village of Voskepar, which is on Armenian territory. There, Soviet Army units detained a group of Armenian policemen but for some reason turned them over to the Azerbaijan Prosecutor's Office.

A. V. – Criminal proceedings have been instituted in connection with these events, and the matter is not as simple as it might seem at first glance. After all, before the group of policemen was detained in the village of Voskepar, there had been a bloody incident involving another group of Armenian policemen who had gone to that village. Preliminary information indicates that it was they, not the military men, who began the exchange of fire. Moreover, the men detained in this case had not only standard-issue weapons but also homemade ones – grenades, mines, etc. And besides, the law establishes no territorial borders that have to be observed during the pursuit of criminals....

Q. – One cannot pass over in silence the question of the forcible eviction by internal troops and Azerbaijani police of the population of Armenian villages in the Azerbaijan Republic. There are numerous statements from eyewitnesses, including their comments on Armenian television, indicating that this is not a fabrication.

I. Sh. – Here are two thick bundles of handwritten requests from Armenian residents to our staff members asking that they be resettled in other republics. People are tired of the war, they are caught between the devil and the deep blue sea. I categorically affirm that we moved no one by force. As far as the eyewitnesses who appear on Armenian television are concerned, I think that they are simply being made to do this, that they are being intimidated. Just as militants intimidated the Armenian population that wanted to leave Azerbaijan voluntarily, by the way....

Q. – Now a question for you, Valery Pavlovich: Which aspects of the conflict between nationalities in the Transcaucasus attract the attention of the State Security Committee, and particularly of the Administration for the Protection of the Soviet Constitutional System, which you head?

V. **Vorotnikov.** – There are several things.... The repercussions of the tragic events are rather widespread and affect interests going beyond those of the two republics' populations. A wide variety of political forces, both inside the country and abroad, are seeking to use the conflict in their own interests, which includes attempts to discredit our constitutional system, undermine confidence in legitimate authority and smear the measures that are being taken by the state and society to stabilize the situation in the Transcaucasus....

And finally, something else that cannot be ignored: In point of fact, terrorist groups are operating in the region.

Q. – As I understand it, what we're talking about is terrorist groups on both sides, right?

V. V. – Violent encroachments have occurred on both sides. The proof of this is that both Armenians and Azerbaijanis are dying. At the same time, one cannot ignore the fact that the Azerbaijani side does not have support bases and groups of militants permanently stationed in the neighboring republic. Moreover, it is obvious that such groups are sent from Armenian territory to Azerbaijani territory, supposedly to protect the Armenian population. Here is the testimony of one of the detained militants: In his words, every Armenian village in Azerbaijan is supposed to be defended by a group from a certain area of Armenia, and the militants take an oath that they will fight to the bitter end....

Q. – ... And now this question: A number of media outlets are spreading the story that the center, along with law-enforcement agencies, has taken the side of Azerbaijan completely, supposedly because Communists are in power there, while democrats are in power in Armenia.

A. V. – I heard a similar question in the Nagorno-Karabakh Autonomous Province: Why don't the Communists want to give up Nagorno-Karabakh? – they asked. This is the answer they received: If capitalists were in power in Azerbaijan, would they give up the territory? It seems to me that in this conflict, talking about the type of regime distracts people from the heart of the problem. And that is: Who wants to extinguish the flames of the war between nationalities, and who doesn't?

Our task as representatives of law-enforcement agencies is to see to it that legality is observed. That's why the central law-enforcement agencies responded to the Azerbaijani leadership's request for assistance in implementing the decree of the country's President.

Q. – And the Armenian leadership has not made a similar request?

I. Sh. – No, as far as I know, we have received no such requests from Armenia.

Q. – Give me your personal opinion: Which side is trying harder to settle the conflict, which has already brought so much grief to these two peoples and to the whole country?

I. Sh. – What is needed here are not inferences but facts. Here is one. The year before last, the center proposed that so-called five-kilometer security zones be created on the border between the two republics. Such a zone has been created in Azerbaijan, but not in Armenia.

V. V. – Here's a second fact: the Armenian Supreme Soviet's unconstitutional decision on the annexation of Nagorno-Karabakh. It has done nothing but aggravate the situation.

Q. – But there is yet another fact: Constitutional bodies of power have still not been restored in Nagorno-Karabakh.

V. V. – True. And this, unfortunately, indicates that neither republic is trying very hard to show goodwill toward the other....

Q. – My final question: What's the way out of this deadlock? We can't seriously expect it to be resolved by the internal troops, can we?

I. Sh. – Of course not. It's not up to the soldiers, but to the political leaders of the republics and the center. They must finally sit down at the negotiating table and put aside their pride.

A. V. – More than that, it seems to me that everyone should return to the starting point of February 1988, and then gradually and unemotionally resolve all the problems that have led to the current confrontation.

ARMENIA PREPARED FOR GUERRILLA WARFARE AND IS NOW PREPARED TO SAY GOODBYE TO THE USSR

By Gagik Karapetyan. *Nezavisimaya gazeta*, Aug. 24, 1991, p. 3.

At a press conference on Aug. 22, Levon Ter-Petrosyan, the head of the Armenian parliament, noted that the blame for what happened in the country rests with President Gorbachev: His personnel blunders, indecisiveness and concessions to rightist forces made it possible for the coup to occur. Sumgait in 1988, Tbilisi in 1989, Baku in 1990 and Vilnius in 1991 – there you have a list of crimes to which Mikhail Gorbachev was a party. The coup was organized by the very people upon whom the President had relied for six years, whom he trusted and who had served him faithfully. For this reason, Gorbachev was not the victim of a plot; the coup's organizers were his diligent pupils. He should be held just as responsible for what happened as the plotters, not share the laurels that were earned by Boris Yeltsin alone – although Yeltsin and the country's democratic forces do need Gorbachev today.

Levon Ter-Petrosyan noted that while Gorbachev was occupied with the preparation of the Union Treaty, in a matter of only 17 days in late April and mid-May, with the complicity of the same plotters – Kryuchkov, Yazov and Pugo75 Armenians died in Nagorno-Karabakh and Armenia's border districts, and [residents of] 23 Armenian villages in the Nagorno-Karabakh Autonomous Province were deported. And only a few democrats shared this tragedy with us: the People's Deputies to the Russian Republic parliament, the Moscow City Soviet and the Leningrad City Soviet. Levon Ter-Petrosyan recalled that during that same period, Armenia appealed to the country's Supreme Soviet and asked that an extraordinary Congress of People's Deputies be convened. However, the session voted almost unanimously against this legitimate demand. At the same time, Armenian law-enforcement agencies filed suit against Pugo, demanding that criminal charges be brought against him. The democrats got a laugh out of this unlikely undertaking.

Levon Ter-Petrosyan reported that, according to more accurate information he had obtained, Armenia was in fact among the localities where a state-of-emergency regime was to have been introduced. On Aug. 19 Armenia's leaders learned that fully authorized representatives of the junta were flying there. Ten generals did in fact arrive in Yerevan and attempt during a meeting with Ter-Petrosyan to persuade him to introduce a state of emergency in Armenia.... Levon Ter-Petrosyan admitted that during the days of the conspiracy, the republic Defense Committee had adopted a secret resolution: All the republic's lawful armed formations were to have gone underground and prepared to wage guerrilla warfare....

PILOT ERROR OR SABOTAGE?

By V. Belykh. *Izvestia*, Nov. 21, 1991, p. 7.

On Nov. 20, a helicopter of the internal troops of the USSR Ministry of Internal Affairs crashed in Azerbaijan. The tragedy occurred at 4:30 p.m., three kilometers from the village of Karakend in Martuni District. Twenty-one people were killed.

According to eyewitness reports, the MI-8 was flying at a low altitude when it entered an area of thick fog and slammed into a 700-meter-high mountain. The crash scattered wreckage and passengers' remains over a huge area. There were no survivors. Among the victims were Gen. N. Zhinkin, commandant of the Nagorno-Karabakh Autonomous Province special district; Gen. V. Kovalyov, director of the Nagorno-Karabakh Internal Affairs Administration; T. Ismailov, Azerbaijan's State Secretary; I. Gaibov, Azerbaijan's Prosecutor; Z. Gadzhiyev, Vice-Chairman of the Azerbaijan Council of Ministers; M. Asadov, state counselor; S. Ivanov, chief of the KGB's Nagorno-Karabakh division; I. Plavsky, the Nagorno-Karabakh Prosecutor; USSR People's Deputies V. Dzhafarov and V. Mamedov; O. Milzoyev, the Azerbaijan President's chief of staff; S. Serikov, Deputy Minister of the Kazakhstan Ministry of

Internal Affairs; M. Lukashov, representative of the Russian Ministry of Internal Affairs; O. Kocherov, representative of the Union Ministry of Defense; Azerbaijani television correspondents, officials and crew members.

As our correspondent V. Samedov reports from Azerbaijan, virtually everyone there regarded these tragic events as sabotage. Crowds of agitated people are gathering in various parts of Baku. Tension is growing.

Representatives of the internal troops, however, are more inclined right now to consider an error by the helicopter's pilot to be the cause of the crash. But they are also not ruling out the possibility of a terrorist act.

A special commission that has flown to the site of the tragedy is supposed to ascertain what really happened.

AFTER THE HELICOPTER CRASH IN NAGORNO-KARABAKH, RELATIONS BETWEEN ARMENIA AND AZERBAIJAN HAVE WORSENED DRASTICALLY

By staff correspondent S. Bablumyan. *Izvestia*, Nov. 23, 1991, p. 1.

The Armenian government has issued a statement in connection with the Nov. 20 helicopter crash in Nagorno-Karabakh.

Among other things, the statement condemns the position of certain representatives of the mass media and political circles who, even prior to the investigation into the causes of the tragedy and the final conclusions of the commission of experts, hastened to express their theories in this regard. The Armenian government views such reckless and biased commentaries as an attempt to organize a new round of escalation of tension between Armenia and Azerbaijan....

The Armenian government is proposing and insisting upon the creation of an authoritative, independent international commission to conduct an objective investigation into the crash. It proposed that while the investigation is being conducted, public reports on its progress should be issued by a joint news team that would be set up in accordance with the Zheleznovodsk communiqué.

The Armenian government has called on the government of the Azerbaijan Republic, in order to avoid an escalation of the confrontation, to refrain from any actions that could carry the threat of further destabilization of the situation, including blockades of railroads and other communications lines.

Nevertheless, on Nov. 21, the crew and passengers from a Yerevan-Kafan train, including women and children, were taken hostage on Azerbaijani territory, and rail traffic from Azerbaijan was been cut off.

On the evening of Nov. 22, in his brief statement to reporters, Armenian President Levon Ter-Petrosyan described the situation that has developed as an emergency. He noted that judging by everything that is known about the agenda of the Azerbaijan Supreme Soviet session that is expected next week, the issue of declaring war against Armenia will be discussed.

A decree by the Armenian president was announced at the press conference: The duties of republic prime minister have been assigned to Armenian Vice-President Gagik Arutyunyan.

NOTES

1. *Kommunist* for June 6 (p. 1) carried a lengthy open letter to President Gorbachev from seven USSR People's Deputies from Armenia, calling the military and political pressure on the Armenian populace of Nagorno-Karabakh in recent months "monstrous," and charging that the servicemen's appeal to Gorbachev published in Pravda was part of a "well-planned campaign" to keep Azerbaijan's "apartheid regime" in place in Karabakh.

2. Demonstrations at Yerevan's Zvartnots Airport disrupted its operations from July 4-6, 1988.

Chapter 5 | Soviet Efforts to Calm the Crisis

CONFERENCE IN THE CPSU CENTRAL COMMITTEE

Pravda, March 10, 1988, p. 2.

On March 9, a conference in the CPSU Central Committee heard reports from Comrade K. M. Bagirov, First Secretary of the Azerbaijan Communist Party Central Committee, and Comrade K. S. Demirchyan, First Secretary of the Armenian Communist Party Central Committee, on the situation that has come about in those republics in connection with the events in Nagorno-Karabakh.

It was noted at the conference that the situation in the indicated republics is returning to normal, although there continue to be some difficulties. Enterprises and educational institutions are operating. The industrial output that was lost in production facilities is being made up. Public order is being maintained. The investigation is continuing in cases involving the crimes that took place in the city of Sumgait on Feb. 28, 1988.

The address to the working people and peoples of Azerbaijan and Armenia by M. S. Gorbachev, General Secretary of the CPSU Central Committee, has received warm support from the republics' population....

Speaking at the conference, M. S. Gorbachev emphasized that the main thing now is to consistently implement the Leninist principles of nationalities policy and to strengthen the friendship of the Azerbaijani and Armenian peoples, of the peoples of Soviet Transcaucasia and the whole country. Any exacerbation of the situation may throw us back from the great gains of friendship among peoples that our country has achieved in the seven decades of its existence.

By decision of the Politburo, the Secretariat of the Central Committee has been instructed to organize a thoroughgoing and comprehensive study of the problems that have accumulated in the Nagorno-Karabakh Autonomous Province and of the causes of the exacerbation of relations between nationalities over that area and the study of relevant proposals, and, as they become ready, to submit them for consideration by the CPSU Central Committee and the USSR government.

At the same time, it has been recommended that the Azerbaijan and Armenian Communist Party Central Committees work out a set of long-term measures to improve the internationalist upbringing of the working people and that they resolve in a coordinated way immediate questions having to do with the social, economic, everyday-life, scientific, cultural, linguistic and other aspects of relations between these republics, on the basis of the Leninist principles of internationalism.

In concluding the conference, M. S. Gorbachev once again emphasized that no question of restructuring can be resolved today without taking into account its impact on national relations and that the progress of restructuring requires harmonious, persistent and united work by all the working people and by representatives of all nationalities of the Soviet Union.

Taking part in the discussion of questions at the conference were Comrades A. A. Gromyko, Ye. K. Ligachev, N. I. Ryzhkov, A. N. Yakovlev, P. N. Demichev, V. I. Dolgikh, G. P. Razumovsky and A. I. Lukyanov, as well as G. N. Seidov, Chairman of the Azerbaijan Republic Council of Ministers; G. M. Voskanyan, Chairman of the Presidium of the Armenian Republic Supreme Soviet; and F. T. Sarkisyan, Chairman of the Armenian Republic Council of Ministers.

THE ECONOMY OF THE NAGORNO-KARABAKH AUTONOMOUS PROVINCE OF THE AZERBAIJAN REPUBLIC: PROBLEMS AND PROSPECTS – Meeting With Academician T.S. Khachaturov on the Azerbaijan Republic Council of Ministers' Institute of the Management of the Economy

Bakinsky rabochy, March 11, 1988, p. 2.

Editors' Note. – ... An exchange of opinions among officials of planning agencies and scholars on the problems of accelerating the development of the productive forces of Azerbaijan's [Nagorno-Karabakh] Autonomous Province was held in the republic Council of Ministers' Institute of Economic Management. Materials from this meeting are published below.

* * *

... **T. Khachaturov, member of the USSR Academy of Sciences and Chairman of the Scientific Council on the Problem of the Economic Efficiency of Fixed Assets, Capital Investments and New Equipment.** – The question has been posed correctly here – the branches of the economy that require highly skilled employees are the ones that should be developed. The very structure of the province's development should be such that it stimulates scientific and technical progress.

Candidate of Economics S. Guseinov, senior research associate at the republic Academy of Sciences' Institute of Economics. It must be said that, in terms of industrial output per capita over 1,400 rubles the Nagorno-Karabakh Autonomous Province holds the leading place among the Azerbaijan Republic's economic regions (with the exception of Baku's industry).

Moderator. – Why do you set apart industry in the city of Baku?

S. Guseinov. – An apt question. The point is that, under the influence of a number of objective factors, Baku historically took shape predominantly as an industrial center. It contains more than half of the republic's production apparatus, which is connected to a large extent with what has traditionally been the leading branch of the republic's industry fuel. The overwhelming majority of capital investments has been channeled into this capital-intensive branch. In these conditions, there is no justification for comparing Baku with other regions in whose structure branches of the agro-industrial complex make up a large percentage in particular, with the Nagorno-Karabakh Autonomous Province....

Moderator. – We haven't heard anything about the province's interregional economic ties. But, as is known, they are a kind of indicator of economically warranted areas of economic cooperation that have formed over a long time.

V. Akhundov, prorector of the Azerbaijan Institute of Economic Management. – Nagorno-Karabakh has a rather high index of intensiveness when it comes to economic ties.... The other regions of the Azerbaijan Republic play a key role in the formation of the Nagorno-Karabakh Autonomous Province's economic ties and are vitally important to the functioning of the province's economy (fuel and power resources, cooperative deliveries of light-industry products, etc.)....

B. Budagov, acting director of the Azerbaijan Republic Institute of Geography and corresponding member of the republic Academy of Sciences. – Nagorno [i.e., upland] Karabakh, together with lowland Karabakh (Agdam, Mir-Bashir, Agdzhabedi, Fizuli and Dzhebrail Districts) and the republic's western regions (Kelbadzhar, Lachin and Kubatly Districts), forms an integral natural-geographic region, a complete ecological system, a single river network, and an interconnected economy and system of communications.

Karabakh's geographic and economic unity and the inevitability of its interconnections with other regions are underscored by the location of vitally important communications arteries – the Agdam-Stepanakert rail line, the highways, the gas pipeline and the power-supply lines, which are very necessary to the effective functioning of the autonomous province's economy.

In other words, the economy of the autonomous province and the economy of the other regions of the republic are mutually complementary, and the intensification of economic ties between them is objective in nature and involves a whole series of fundamental prerequisites for the systemic planning and management of this single natural-economic complex.

V. Akhundov. – All this indicates once again that the stable functioning of the province's economy and the efficiency of its economic life depend to a decisive extent on ties with the republic's other economic regions and its economic complex as a whole....

T. Khachaturov. – ... It is necessary to intensify the restructuring of industry in the area of the priority development of progressive branches, above all machine building. In doing so, special attention must be given to those branches that require the application of skilled labor. More vigorous work must be done to raise the technical level of production and to accelerate the pace of the updating of the equipment inventory....

Capital construction is the weak link here, as it is throughout the country. I have in mind, first of all, its inadequate material and technical base and the presence of "overdue" construction projects. The development of a highway network and the construction of paved roads is also an important task. In view of the province's difficult terrain, it would be a good idea to find opportunities for developing irrigated farming.

There are problems in the social sphere, too. In my view, thought should be given to expanding the scope of the training of personnel. I am not asserting this categorically, but perhaps there is some point in thinking about organizing a number of educational institutions with an eye to future changes in the province's economy. And, of course, in keeping with the spirit of restructuring and democratization, the rights of local agencies should be expanded.

It seems to me that it would be a good idea to reflect all these points in the measures that the republic is now preparing for the further social and economic development of the Nagorno-Karabakh Autonomous Province.

Z. Samedzade, head of the Azerbaijan Communist Party Central Committee's Economic Department and corresponding member of the republic Academy of Sciences. – ... It must be recognized that some republic ministries and departments and local Soviets do not always resolve questions raised by the republic's autonomous province in a thoroughgoing and comprehensive way. Sluggishness, inertia and old approaches are still making themselves felt. The questions that have been raised and the current difficulties and problems should be resolved in the spirit of the policy of restructuring and renewal that is being implemented in our country.... – (Azerbaijan News Agency)

NAGORNO-KARABAKH: A DEVELOPMENT PROGRAM

Izvestia, March 25, 1988, p. 3.

Editors' Note. – ... Recently a group of key officials from the USSR Council of Ministers and the USSR State Planning Committee and executives from a number of ministries and departments went to the Nagorno-Karabakh Autonomous Province. V. P. Lakhtin, First Vice-Chairman of the USSR Council of Ministers' Bureau for Social Development, was among them. Today he answers questions from an Izvestia correspondent.

* * *

Question. – ... The newspaper Bakinsky rabochy recently published an extensive roundtable article, in which many scholars participated. The point of the article was to show that the Nagorno-Karabakh Autonomous Province is one of the most prosperous areas in the [Azerbaijan] Republic. In your opinion, don't such conclusions suffer from one-sidedness?

Answer. – These conclusions are based on precise data....

Q. – Then why was it necessary to set up an additional program of social and economic development, which is why you went there? To create even more advantages?

A. – Two circumstances must be taken into account here. The first is this: Along with the achievements in the social sphere noted above, there are also a number of deficiencies in the province. There are considerable difficulties with water supply. The network of hard-surface roads has been developed to a lesser extent than the average for the republic. The cultural sphere is lagging. For example, the Palace of Sports in Stepanakert has been under construction for more than nine years. That city is the province center, but it still does not have a Young Pioneers' Palace. Or take the largest enterprise in the province – the silk combine in Stepanakert, which I had an opportunity to visit. It creates the impression that no one is in charge.... Food service for the combine's workers is really bad. This is just one example of inattention to human needs.

The second circumstance is that, if the deficiencies are to be corrected, the existing advantages must be developed, not left at the achieved level....

Q. – Have there been difficulties in work on the program?

A. – ... I think that something ought to be said about one – perhaps the only one – difficulty in this respect. Surprisingly, it has to do with the position taken by the province leadership. First of all, that of the Party leadership, headed by G. Pogosyan, the new first secretary of the province Party committee, which does not consider these to be major questions....

Q. – We have been talking about the material sphere. But after all, in their demands many residents of the Nagorno-Karabakh Autonomous Republic are putting just as much emphasis, and perhaps even more, on the spiritual factor, on the establishment of broader, closer and freer ties with Armenia.

A. – ... A special point in the program has to do with work in schools in which instruction is in the Armenian language. It has been proposed that, beginning this year, places be set aside in the Armenian Republic's higher schools specifically for the admission and instruction of young people from the Nagorno-Karabakh Autonomous Province....

Correspondent. – ... When this interview was being prepared, the writer Z. Balayan came to the editorial offices. He didn't just happen to drop by – he came in connection with a recent article in Izvestia stating that he had doubts about the efficacy of the program that has been worked out for the social and economic development of the Nagorno-Karabakh Autonomous Province.

On this score, Z. Balayan asked that his explanation be published as follows:

"When I said that there is no turning back, I meant that it is impossible to continue to operate using the old methods. It is necessary, as was stated correctly at the conference in the CPSU Central Committee, to resolve in a coordinated way immediate questions having to do with the social, economic, everyday-life, scientific, cultural, linguistic and other aspects of relations between the Azerbaijan and Armenian Republics on the basis of the Leninist principles of internationalism.

"I think that the program described above can be a fundamental step in this direction."

Editors' Note. – On March 24, the Party leadership examined and approved this program.

FOR CALM AND WISDOM

By Academician Andrei Sakharov. *Moskovskiye novosti*, April 3, 1988, p. 4.

On March 21, 1988, I sent a letter to M. S. Gorbachev, General Secretary of the CPSU Central Committee, in which I set forth my viewpoint on two critical national problems: the return of the Crimean Tatars to the Crimea, and the reunification of Nagorno-Karabakh with Armenia. I have called and am calling for decisions based on a calm consideration, in as impartial a way as possible, of the interests of each of the peoples of our country.

A resolution of the Presidium of the USSR Supreme Soviet concerning the situation in Nagorno-Karabakh was published on March 24. However, this resolution did not express a stand on the decision of the Nagorno-Karabakh Province Soviet. I hope that this is not the last word from the Supreme Soviet and its Presidium.

It seems to me that it is necessary, in accordance with the USSR Constitution, for the Azerbaijan Supreme Soviet and the Armenian Supreme Soviet to consider the petition from the Nagorno-Karabakh Province Soviet. In case there is disagreement, the USSR Supreme Soviet should hand down a decision by way of arbitration....

ADDRESS BY THE REPRESENTATIVE OF THE CPSU CENTRAL COMMITTEE AND THE PRESIDIUM OF THE USSR SUPREME SOVIET IN THE NAGORNO-KARABAKH AUTONOMOUS PROVINCE

Kommunist, Sept. 25, 1988, p. 2.

... The situation in the province has become much more complicated in the past few days.

Strikes have begun at industrial enterprises, in construction organizations and on public transportation. School classes have been canceled, unsanctioned rallies and processions have been held, an attack on the province prosecutor's office has been provoked, and verbal insults have been made against bodies of power. There have been instances in which the dignity of servicemen of the USSR Ministry of Internal Affairs' troops and policemen working to safeguard public order has been humiliated.

On Sept. 18 some residents of Stepanakert, provoked by irresponsible people, headed for the village of Khodzhaly with the aim of "punishing" the residents of that village for having damaged some automobiles. Firearms and knives were used in the melee that took place.

Then disturbances were provoked in Stepanakert, Shusha and other places, accompanied by arson to homes, pogroms and beatings of citizens. Things went as far as looting. A total of 49 citizens have received bodily injuries in the past few days, including 33 Armenians and 16 Azerbaijanis, 17 people have been hospitalized, and the citizen Shakhramanyan has died from the injuries he received. Over 30 houses and other buildings have been burned down....

The events that are taking place have created serious tensions and instability and have engendered in people a sense of fear, uncertainty and the feeling that they lack protection against arbitrary action and the flagrant violation of their rights and legitimate interests. A real threat has emerged in Nagorno-Karabakh to people's safety, health and dignity and to the personal property of citizens....

Despite the actions that Party, Soviet and law-enforcement agencies are taking and their appeals for restraint and prudence, the situation not only is not improving but has become extremely menacing, with unpredictable consequences....

The drawing of young children into unlawful actions and various kinds of processions and rallies is cause for special indignation. Instructors and teachers are involving schoolchildren in their strikes. As a result, children are being deprived of the opportunity to study, something that is doing enormous harm to their education and moral upbringing....

In essence, the unlawful actions have taken on the nature of a confrontation with the law and with bodies of power....

In these conditions, only one path is left – the path of taking resolute action to counter the provocateurs who are drawing the population into violations of law and order.... When blood is being shed, the state cannot remain on the sidelines.

As a measure to protect the interests of the state and society and to ensure public order and safety, a state of emergency has been introduced and a curfew established in Nagorno-Karabakh Province and Agdam District of the Azerbaijan Republic.... – [signed] A. Volsky, Representative of the CPSU Central Committee and the Presidium of the USSR Supreme Soviet in the Nagorno-Karabakh Autonomous Province.

SEEK PATHS TO MUTUAL UNDERSTANDING – Meeting of the CPSU Central Committee

Pravda and *Izvestia*, Dec. 4, 1988, p. 1.

... On Dec. 1, M. S. Gorbachev, General Secretary of the CPSU Central Committee and Chairman of the Presidium of the USSR Supreme Soviet, met in the CPSU Central Committee with Deputies to the USSR Supreme Soviet who are representatives of the Azerbaijan Republic and the Armenian Republic and with the leadership of both republics and of the Nagorno-Karabakh Autonomous Province of the Azerbaijan Republic. Comrades N. I. Ryzhkov, N. N. Slyunkov, V. M. Chebrikov, A. N. Yakovlev, A. I. Lukyanov and G. P. Razumovsky took part in the meeting.

After a brief introductory speech by M. S. Gorbachev, there was an exchange of opinions concerning the reasons for the acute conflict between nationalities in the region and ways of settling it....

M. S. Gorbachev spoke at the conclusion of the meeting....

[He said:] In discussing the question, those who spoke said with alarm that the crisis that has been going on for months around Nagorno-Karabakh has recently become sharply exacerbated and that both republics have reached an extremely dangerous point. In a number of instances, events have gotten out of control and have resulted in deaths and suffering for women, old people and children. If those who are responsible don't stop now, if they don't think better of what they are doing and renounce the psychology of confrontation, tomorrow may prove to be immeasurably more tragic, and it may threaten the loss of much of what has been achieved during the years of Soviet power....

It was noted that in this extreme situation the leadership of Azerbaijan and that of Armenia have failed to implement legal guarantees and to ensure the safety of the Armenian population in Azerbaijan and of the Azerbaijani population in Armenia. Businesslike steps toward improving relations between nationalities are frequently supplanted by perfunctory calls for brotherhood and good-neighborliness. Instead of an uncompromising struggle against those who incite the people to engage in disturbances, who sow all kinds of rumors and who stir up strife between nationalities, what is basically taking place – even at the level of the leadership of the two republics – is an effort to ascertain the reasons why one side or the other is more to blame for what is happening. In essence, the republics have been completely unable to agree on coordinated actions with respect to any of the questions related to the normalization of the situation....

On the whole, there is no clear political line in the work of the republics' political organizations and aktivs that is based on reality and the genuine interests of the working people rather than on the ambitious aspirations of a small group of people.

In discussing ways of solving the problem of Nagorno-Karabakh, which continues to be a hotbed of tension, the participants in the meeting have emphasized that redrawing the borders is impermissible in current conditions, that one can't just plow under people's fates. At the same time, one cannot justify the position of Azerbaijan's former leadership, which committed numerous deviations from the Leninist principles of nationalities policy with respect to the Nagorno-Karabakh Autonomous Province. The situation that has been created must be resolutely corrected, and everything must be done to see to it that people's lives return to normal.

A detailed analysis of the situation that has taken shape has been given at the meeting. It has been noted that the Party and Soviet agencies of the Nagorno-Karabakh Autonomous Province, Armenia and Azerbaijan have, to one extent or another, lost control of events. This is a result not merely of confusion but of a lack of principle. Fear of "losing the people's confidence," as well as assenting to nationalistic sentiments, has led to a situation in which part of the Party aktiv has departed from internationalist positions.

But the essence of what is taking place does not hinge solely on the problem of Nagorno-Karabakh. It has more clearly elucidated serious shortcomings in political, social and economic life, violations of socialist legality and distortions in personnel policy in general in both Armenia and Azerbaijan, and major miscalculations by the former leadership of both republics.

The CPSU Central Committee, the Presidium of the USSR Supreme Soviet and the USSR Council of Ministers are doing everything they can to correct the situation. The leadership of both republics has been strengthened. Certain decisions have been adopted on the Nagorno-Karabakh Autonomous Province and on the region as a whole. To implement those decisions, patience and tranquility, complete mutual understanding and mutual assistance, and persistent work by all Party organizations and labor collectives are required.

But this approach is not acceptable to everyone. It is becoming increasingly obvious that for some people the Nagorno-Karabakh problem is a convenient screen for criminal, antistate activity.... Under cover of demands for a just resolution of the Karabakh question, an open struggle for power is going on. Elements of this sort, taking advantage of the mechanism of democracy, are trying to gain the upper hand. There are antirestructuring forces and corrupt elements in both republics.... It is their efforts that have drawn thousands of people into strikes, rallies and demonstrations. They have on their conscience the tragedy of many families who are leaving their homes today, and they have people's deaths on their conscience. The working people insistently demand that these madmen be stopped and held to account.

One of the most serious deficiencies in the activity of the Party organizations has been a slighting attitude toward work with the intelligentsia, especially with writers, scientists and workers in the mass news media, something that has had an effect on their political and civic positions. The influence of the intelligentsia in shaping public opinion is great, but it frequently turns out to be disastrous, when it is exercised by politically immature people....

The principle of a solution is: There should be neither "victors" nor "vanquished," and neither side should bear a grudge....

What is needed is a firm position by all of our cadres on the key questions – what should be done now, and on what basis? The atmosphere will not change without a change in the cadres' position, since in the final analysis the cadres have an impact on the situation in labor collectives and on people's mind-set. It is especially important that the republics' Central Committees, the Presidiums of their Supreme Soviets and their governments, all executives and eminent figures in science and culture take a responsible civic position dictated by the interests of the peoples....

A steady work pace must be restored everywhere....

It is necessary to use all measures to ensure people's safety. Here the labor collectives and the administrative agencies should have an important say. The problem of the people that have been forced to leave their places of permanent residence must be dealt with immediately. All local agencies must provide assistance to these people – feed them, house them, show attention to their children. Everything possible must be done so that they can return to their own homes. Attempts to use people's suffering as a pretext for whipping up passions and manipulating public opinion must be resolutely curbed. Both republics must have a keen sense of their guilt before these people....

Waging an uncompromising struggle against those who incite the people to engage in disturbances, sow rumors and stir up enmity between nationalities is an important task. The scandalous instances of nationality-related dismissals of people should be combated in a very resolute way, up to and including expelling the culprits from the Party and bringing criminal charges against them. In eradicating these phenomena, it is necessary to make full use of the power of the law and the authority of public opinion. Restructuring, the life and dignity of Soviet people, and public order must be defended. Lofty demands have been made upon the press. It cannot now take a position that would further destabilize the situation....

It has been deemed advisable to create a commission made up of representatives of the Azerbaijan Republic and the Armenian Republic and members of the Politburo of the CPSU Central Committee. The commission's task, as emphasized by the July 18, 1988, decision of the Presidium of the USSR Supreme Soviet, is to find, in the shortest possible time, an optimal, genuinely internationalist solution to the problems without changing the Nagorno-Karabakh Autonomous Province's territorial affiliation with the Azerbaijan Republic. The proposals that are worked out will be submitted for consideration by the CPSU Central Committee, the Presidium of the USSR Supreme Soviet and the USSR Council of Ministers.... – (TASS)

M. S. GORBACHEV'S INTERVIEW WITH CENTRAL TELEVISION AND ARMENIAN TELEVISION CORRESPONDENTS

Pravda, Dec. 12, 1988, p. 1.

Before flying out of Yerevan, M. S. Gorbachev, General Secretary of the CPSU Central Committee and Chairman of the Presidium of the USSR Supreme Soviet, gave an interview to Central Television and Armenian Television correspondents.

Question. – Mikhail Sergeyevich, what have you come away with from your tour of the disaster areas?

M. S. Gorbachev. – It's a terrible disaster. An utter tragedy. I've seen so many people stricken by misfortune, people who have lost loved ones and entire families. All the things I've seen in these past two days have simply astounded me.

In human terms, it's hard to bear this – it's simply unbearable. I want to express once more, on behalf of the leadership, myself and our entire people, words of the deepest and most heartfelt sympathy to the families stricken by this disaster and to the entire Armenian people....

I learned here how on that first, most difficult night, in the first hours, when the city of Leninakan was cut off, the airport destroyed, the railroad out of commission and the highway destroyed, too, how in that situation Yerevan – its physicians, workers, construction workers, young people and students, especially medical-school students – how everyone immediately left Yerevan to come to people's assistance. Pilots made landings in absolute darkness, picked up the gravely injured and brought them out, and physicians here performed operations and saved lives. Now I see how the entire country has responded to this common misfortune of ours with such deep warmth, with such sincerity, and I feel proud of all our people....

Organizing the effort will now be of decisive importance. Above all, we must help sort through this rubble more quickly, since many people are still alive under it. After all, people are being freed every day. I met with some of them. Therefore, the first task that must be undertaken, the first thing to be done, is to rescue the people who are still alive. We must also bring out, in a humane way, the bodies of those who were killed and bid farewell to them. This is only natural.

By 8 a.m. there will be 700 cranes here, and the next day there will be 900, to sort through all this.

Now everything has entered a businesslike phase. Work goes on day and night. Power is being restored, and hot water is being supplied to the homes that remain. Enough heated tents to accommodate 300,000 people, to house them temporarily, have now been brought in. Of course, special concern must be shown for women and children. Therefore, here in Armenia, in Georgia, in Stavropol Territory and in the Kuban, accommodations for tens of thousands of people have been opened in boardinghouses and sanatoriums, which are awaiting these people. They have already started to leave Leninakan and Spitak. They are moving as classes, with their teachers and their mothers....

I should say that perhaps those who are acting most skillfully are the doctors, headed by Minister Chazov. Things are being organized better and better. These areas have been closed off, because there are too many people there, for understandable reasons. Relatives and loved ones have gone there, and this has impeded the organization of work. Now everything has been taken in hand. I think that greater order and results will come more quickly now. Of course, people are interested in what will become of the cities. This question has been discussed and considered. We must rebuild these cities, of course. On behalf of the country's leadership, I have said this to people in all the cities, so they know. This is their ancient land, their roots are here, all generations of them have lived here. It is clear to us that people should receive an answer to this question....

I have found the Armenian people to be courageous in their hour of trial. The weeping, the tears, the demands – none of this has taken away from what we have seen: how people – selflessly, in spite of everything, and without waiting for everything to be organized – have acted and used everything at their disposal to come to the assistance of others....

Q. – But here in Yerevan yesterday, the Nagorno-Karabakh slogans were heard again. What kind of blindness is this? ... These slogans will bring nothing good, only new mishaps.

M. S. Gorbachev. – I'll tell you honestly, I was struck by one incident yesterday. We were returning from Leninakan to the Armenian Communist Party Central Committee last night to start reviewing practical questions – how to increase the scope of rescue work and of the effort to find accommodations for people, how to resolve practical questions and alleviate this disaster. Residents of Armenia were standing on the street. I stopped, and we had a good conversation. The people were all worried, very worried. They were taking it hard. I shared with them the fact that I had been simply astounded by what I had seen, by the magnitude of the disaster that had befallen people. And suddenly, right here in Yerevan, I was asked: What kind of relations are we going to have, what kind of dialogue are we going to establish with the unofficial organizations? Again, the subject was Karabakh. You know, I told them just what I thought, in rather sharp language, perhaps. First of all, I said to them: Stop. Look at the calamity that has befallen both the Azerbaijanis and the Armenians, look where they are being pushed and at the point they've already reached – blood is being spilled. Now so great a disaster has struck that the whole country, the whole world, is stunned by what has happened in Armenia, by what has befallen the Armenian people. And here's a person in the capital of Armenia asking me what kind of dialogue we're going to set up with unofficial organizations. Only a person devoid of all morality could do such a thing.

Today I talked about this frankly with working people in Kirovakan, and they agreed with this and asked: Mikhail Sergeyevich, all this has to be stopped.

I think that there is such a thing as a Karabakh problem. The problem has roots, and it has become exacerbated because at a certain stage the former Azerbaijani leadership took an incorrect attitude toward the Karabakh population, an attitude that was not in the spirit of Leninist traditions and sometimes was simply inhuman. This offended people. We condemn this. That is why we came to their assistance, why we adopted a resolution to help their social and economic development – we allocated 500 million rubles for this tiny province in order to build it up, to remove all of the people's problems, to create better living conditions, to resolve questions of culture and the development of their native language and teaching in it, and to establish normal ties with Armenia.... Recently, after the session of the USSR Supreme Soviet, I and other comrades in the leadership called in members of the Central Committee and Deputies from both sides.

We sat down and talked. There were about 100 of us. I said bluntly: You know, we're at the brink of a precipice. Any further, one more step, and we plunge into the abyss.... We agreed to let both sides think about how to calm Nagorno-Karabakh for a while. But now this situation has put us off the track somewhat.

So, this is a problem. But, you know, the subject of Karabakh is now being taken advantage of by unscrupulous people, political demagogues, adventurists and, more than that, by a corrupt clique. They see that restructuring is under way, it is coming to Armenia and Azerbaijan, the leadership is changing and is taking up restructuring positions. This means that a blow against this whole clique is in the offing, against this whole parasitical clique that is keeping the people under its thumb and intimidating them. Black shirts, white shirts, bearded ones[1] have been set up here – both in Azerbaijan and in Armenia. They are putting pressure on Deputies and on the government.

They profess Karabakh slogans. On the Azerbaijani side, the slogan is "We'll die before we give up Karabakh," while on this side the slogan is "We'll die to take Karabakh." They haven't needed Karabakh for a long time, and it has never worried them. They're waging a struggle for power, they need to retain power....

I talked about this to everybody in Leninakan and Kirovakan. People supported me: They said I was right....

We have already set about this task, we will see it through to conclusion and, together with the working people of both republics, we will institute order. The Karabakh problem will take its proper place. People should live on this land, where they have lived for centuries. One scholar tries to prove that the Armenian nation has roots in Karabakh, while another scholar, no less successfully, tries to prove that the Azerbaijani nation has roots there. Bear in mind that both of them base their arguments on facts and historical documents. What does this tell us? I say to these scholars: This tells us that these two peoples have always lived there, that they are intertwined, that they have common teachers and pupils. They have many common songs, and there are mixed, internationalist families. How can these people be treated like this?

They are political adventurists, and they must be branded as such, people must know this. Look what they're doing now. The people have been stricken by a great calamity, but these adventurists are trying to intimidate them by saying that the earthquake is going to continue, that it may lead to who knows what, that we are acting irresponsibly. We brought in five scientists from the USSR Academy of Sciences. We asked them: Do you have any such information? There is no scientific information. But workers everywhere are asking me this. I tell them: You know, there is no center – not to my knowledge, at least – that can predict today whether or not an earthquake is going to occur. That's the opinion the scientists expressed. Or take another major topic, women and children. They are now spreading rumors that someone wants to take the children off to Russia and never return them to Armenia, to tear them away from their people, and that the Armenians will now be resettled in Siberia. Can you believe it, to say such a thing at a time like this! What kind of morals do these people have, I ask? People should know what sort of clique it is that uses concern for the people and for the nation to conceal what it is doing. This clique is grabbing for power. It must be stopped using all our strength, both political and administrative.

But forget about them – it will not be they that will determine the fate of this land, but the people, and I want to assure the Armenian people, on behalf of the Central Committee and the government, on behalf of the entire Soviet people, that they can and must count on our help and support in this difficult period, in this hour of trial. We will do everything we can to emerge from this disaster even stronger and more united. I am leaving, but the commission headed by N. I. Ryzhkov will remain, Comrade Slyunkov and Comrade Yazov will remain, the three Vice-Chairmen of the USSR Council of Ministers will remain, and they will continue to conduct this work in the way that we have now begun it. – (TASS)

CONVERSATION WITH VAZGEN I

Pravda, Dec. 15, 1988, p. 2; Izvestia, Dec. 16, 1988.

On Dec. 14, N. I. Ryzhkov, Chairman of the USSR Council of Ministers, met with Vazgen I, Supreme Patriarch and Catholicos of All the Armenians, at the latter's residence in Echmiadzin.

During a warm conversation that took place in a spirit of goodwill and mutual understanding, Vazgen I expressed heartfelt gratitude to the Soviet leadership for its magnanimous and truly fraternal attitude toward the Armenian people, who have been the victims of an earthquake of unprecedented scope. He said: "... Everywhere in Armenia people are expressing feelings of great respect for M. S. Gorbachev, who, putting off all other matters, came to Armenia, visited the disaster areas and gave moral support to all the people. It is impossible to forget this."

The head of the Soviet government spoke with respect of the efforts of the Armenian church and of Catholicos Vazgen I aimed at strengthening the steadfastness of believing citizens in this difficult hour of trials....

Sharing reminiscences about the past and about his contacts with representatives of various nationalities of our country, Vazgen I said that he highly appreciates good relations among peoples and hopes that it will be possible to overcome the strife that has come about between nationalities.

N. I. Ryzhkov supported these statements by the Catholicos, emphasizing that the primary aim of the nationalities policy of the CPSU and the Soviet state is strengthening our country's family of fraternal peoples.... – (TASS)

PEACE TO THE LAND OF KARABAKH – From Confrontation to a Struggle for Restructuring

Pravda, Jan. 15, 1989, p. 6.

Editors' Note. – The decree of the Presidium of the USSR Supreme Soviet instituting a special form of administration in the Nagorno-Karabakh Autonomous Province of the Azerbaijan Republic was published today....

At Pravda's request, Arkady Ivanovich Volsky, Chairman of the Committee for the Special Administration of the Nagorno-Karabakh Autonomous Province and head of a department of the CPSU Central Committee, tells what brought about this decision and what tasks confront the Committee for Special Administration.

* * *

The decision that has been adopted is unusual. There is nothing like it in the history of our state. I won't hide the fact that until very recently there was still hope that good sense would gain the upper hand in Azerbaijan, Armenia and Nagorno-Karabakh and that healthy forces would be able to achieve a reconciliation. This did not happen, unfortunately.... Harsh measures were needed to stop the rampage of violence, and a state of emergency was instituted in a number of districts. And now, on the basis of a mutually acceptable and reasonable compromise, a Committee for the Special Administration of the Nagorno-Karabakh Autonomous Province has been created as a forced measure....

With its creation, the province essentially acquires self-government with respect to planning, material and technical supply, and the resolution of personnel and special questions. At the same time, the creation of the committee does not infringe on the province's autonomy and does not signify a change in its territorial affiliation with the Azerbaijan Republic.

In adopting this decision, the Presidium of the USSR Supreme Soviet considered the fact that the urgent questions here had taken on such scope and become so critical that they could not be resolved by the forces of Azerbaijan or Armenia alone. As you know, Armenia's overall possibilities will be severely limited for the next few years following the terrible earthquake of Dec. 7.

Before describing the committee's tasks, I would like to talk about why the Party once again resolutely and unequivocally opposed any redrawing of territorial borders.

Any historical references to age-old possession of the land by one people or the other are absolutely groundless. For many centuries these peoples roamed from place to place, exchanged territories and lived together. One layer of culture was deposited on top of another. Today reality is such that the territorial claims of some peoples cannot be resolved without encroaching on the vital interests of others and trampling on their rights. Taking this path would cause a new outburst of strife and bloodshed....

We do not have any border posts and closed roads within our country, and we are not going to have any. When people start moaning about "sacred integrity" and the "need to preserve every bush, stone, tree and mountain," we must ask in conclusion: Preserve against whom? ...

There is no question that the existing territorial community of a nation or nationality, its Constitution, its cultural traditions and customs, even the dominant religion, are all realities of national life on which no one should infringe. But it is just as indisputable that nowadays all our republics and regions are, without exception, multinational....

There will be no national reservations in our country. On the soil of Nagorno-Karabakh Armenians and Azerbaijanis, Kurds and Russians will live together, work together, raise their children together and care about their happiness. There is no other way! Peace will not come to the land of Karabakh until there is an end to the settling of scores....

V. I. Lenin had some excellent advice on this subject. He emphasized that in disputes between nationalities it is impermissible to strive for formal equality – an eye for an eye, a tooth for a tooth. On the contrary, inequality is even justified here, so that confidence will be restored to the aggrieved: "It is better to overdo pliancy and mildness toward national minorities than to underdo such a policy."

I think that this behest should be addressed above all to teachers, the intelligentsia and the mass news media. Stop fanning the flames of hatred and distrust for another people! Stop lavishing unthinking praise on your own people, because this, too, is the path to chauvinism, to discord between nationalities....

It goes without saying that love for one's people and one's homeland is a sacred and beautiful feeling. But love, not unthinking idolization. Love, not unthinking fanaticism, when one nation begins to describe itself as the most intelligent, the most talented, and the one chosen by God....

There have been quite a few instances recently in which it has been demanded that a thief, a rapist or a robber be excused only because he is "one of us," that his crimes be covered by a "patriotic" screen. When it comes to justice, there can be no nationalities....

Let us cleanse the people's movement for restructuring of all scum, of everything that interferes with the main objective – the renewal of all aspects of our life. It is impermissible to stage a political boycott of restructuring even in a tiny region of the country. What has happened here is precisely that – a boycott! ...

Now for a few words about the committee's basic tasks.

In the economic sphere, they are enlisting the assistance of Union ministries and departments for the accelerated development of the province's productive forces and for the fundamental reconstruction of enterprises, state farms and collective farms. Measures have been mapped out for the transfer of enterprises to the conditions of self-financing and economic accountability and for the large-scale introduction of leasing and of family and collective contracts. The province will have to be helped with centralized capital investments and credits, of course, but in the long run it will live on its own profits.

In the social sphere, the scale of housing construction and that of public health, educational and cultural facilities will have to be sharply increased. We plan, among other things, to sharply increase the capacities of the local construction trust and create a local base for the construction industry. In a short time, a number of roads will have to be repaired, new ones built, and electricity and gas supply organized properly.

In resolving economic and social questions, we will gear ourselves primarily to centralized assistance. In fact, the USSR State Planning Committee is adding a special line – on the Nagorno-Karabakh Autonomous Province – to the national-economic plan for this purpose. But, naturally, traditional economic ties with Azerbaijan will be maintained as well. Disrupting them today would be suicidal for the province. A boycott of this kind would strike a blow not at Azerbaijan but at the population of Nagorno-Karabakh. Only irresponsible windbags who have no understanding of economics could call for such steps.

Another point. All of Karabakh's ties with the outside world – not just with Azerbaijan but also with Armenia, the Russian Federation, the Ukraine, etc. – must be shifted to a solid basis of equal economic cooperation. Not administrative pressure but cooperative interest – that is the solid basis of such relations.

In the implementation of the extensive program for the development of the Nagorno-Karabakh Autonomous Province, a significant place has been assigned to the cultural sphere. Here it will be necessary to carry out a thorough reorganization of the activity of many organizations and institutions – both in the area of culture itself and in education, upbringing and the provision of public services and amenities. Ties with Armenia will be expanded in every way – especially in culture, education, the arts and the training of personnel.

This approach should be applied in equal measure to the Azerbaijani segment of the population. It is unjust, unreasonable and simply stupid to think that the residents of Shusha should not have wide-ranging and diversified national ties with Azerbaijan as well. To deny such ties would mean simply turning the hourglass the other end up – whereas before the Armenian community felt offended and aggrieved, in this case the Azerbaijani community would feel the same.

So, we will encourage and develop the population's contacts with both republics. But the fundamental questions of Karabakh's life can be resolved only through the efforts of the province's population itself.... The province will autonomously resolve everything that it alone can resolve – from personnel questions to self-financing....

IN TRANSCAUCASUS AFTER THE DECREE – Moskovskiye Novosti Correspondents Report on the Attitude in the Armenian and Azerbaijani Capitals Toward the Institution of a Special Form of Administration in Nagorno-Karabakh

By staff correspondents Valery Grigoryev and Asim Dzhalilov in Baku, Levon Dayan in Yerevan. *Moskovskiye novosti*, Jan. 22, 1989, p. 2.

Baku

... "In my view, the decree is good because it suspends the operation of the province's bodies of administration, which have been unable to gain control of the situation," says Zia Buniyatov, a member of the Azerbaijan Academy of Sciences. "New people should come to positions of leadership in the Nagorno-Karabakh Autonomous Province. It is important that the process of searching for and nominating them not go on behind closed doors. Each of the candidates for one post or another should publicly set forth his program of work and provide a guarantee that there will be no return to the old ways.

"One more important factor. The decree says nothing about the problem of refugees. However, this is one of the sorest points of the conflict. People need more than just appeals to return to their homes; they need a guarantee of safety, which would be implemented not by the Army but by acts of law."

"The decree makes it possible to finally begin tackling the economic and social problems of the Nagorno-Karabakh Autonomous Province," noted Doctor of Economics Korkhmaz Imanov, Director of the Azerbaijan Republic State Planning Committee's Institute of Economics. "It will help to implement the July 18, 1988, decision of the Presidium of the USSR Supreme Soviet" [that Nagorno-Karabakh is to remain part of the Azerbaijan Republic].

* * *

Yerevan

... "I wholeheartedly welcome this decision, and I realize that it would have been impossible even five years ago," I was told by Boris Karapetyan, deputy director of a branch of the Optical-Physical Measurements Research Institute. "Of course, it must be considered a palliative measure, since such a form of government cannot continue indefinitely....

"The Committee for Special Administration will have almost unlimited power, and we hope that it will use it with sufficient responsibility."...

Mkrtych Minasyan, First Secretary of the Ordzhonikidze Borough Party Committee in Yerevan, told me: "... I believe that this is one of the first practical results that restructuring has given us in relations between nationalities.

"It's a temporary measure. Life itself and the principles of restructuring will be the prerequisites for solving the problems of the Nagorno-Karabakh Autonomous Province, in its political and economic aspects and in its social and spiritual aspects. But at the same time, some questions are arising. Our borough's Communists and Party aktiv, while welcoming the decision of the Presidium of the USSR Supreme Soviet in general, nonetheless ask: To whom will the province's Party organization ultimately be subordinate?

"I would like to add that the special form of administration will create all the preconditions for the complete and comprehensive fulfillment of the resolution of the CPSU Central Committee and the government on the social and economic development of the province. I think that the Armenian Party organization should actively participate in accomplishing these tasks."...

Sarkis Arakelyan, a heat treater at the Yerevan Electrical Equipment Plant, noted: "... I support this decision, although I don't consider it final but an alternative to the future creation of a new status for the Nagorno-Karabakh Autonomous Province."

NAGORNO-KARABAKH, DECEMBER 1989

Interview by N. Lapayeva. *Izvestia*, Dec. 7, 1989, p. 3.

Editors' Note. – On Nov. 28, 1989, the USSR Supreme Soviet adopted a resolution "On Measures to Normalize the Situation in the Nagorno-Karabakh Autonomous Province." In this connection, a correspondent for the Novosti Press Agency asked Arkady Ivanovich Volsky [Chairman of the Committee for the Special Administration of the Nagorno-Karabakh Autonomous Province for the past year and a half] to comment on the situation in the Nagorno-Karabakh Autonomous Province.

* * *

... **Question.** – There is now a lot of talk to the effect that the central authorities wrongfully dragged their feet on solving the Karabakh problem. What do you think about this?

Answer. – It has practically become fashionable to reproach the country's leadership for slowness and indecisiveness in Nagorno-Karabakh. We have often heard assertions that the region's problems are the result of the Center's position.... Having been in the thick of the events for a year and a half and having been in constant communication with the country's leaders, I can authoritatively declare that such charges are completely groundless....

Q. – ... The question of relations between the nationalities...did not arise just today.

A. – Or even yesterday. The contradictory and ambiguous decisions of the early 1920s on the national-territorial structure of Transcaucasia led, among other things, to Nagorno-Karabakh, with its predominantly Armenian population, being included in Azerbaijan. I think the initiators of this decision were proceeding not from any sort of evil motives but from the ideas prevailing at that time, which held that in a socialist state, the nationalities question as such would quickly fall away due to the complete merging of nations on the basis of class. We also cannot forget the romantic ideas of our state's founding fathers to the effect that a world revolution would occur in a very short time, the proletariat would emerge victorious everywhere, and borders would disappear of their own accord.

Proceeding from this theory, the main factor determining the country's national-state structure was economic. If you analyze the location of the autonomous republics and regions on the map, you will notice that all of them are included in republics or territories that could become economic sponsors of sorts for these small peoples and could provide them with support in their socioeconomic development. Obviously, at that moment this was not the worst decision....

The repeated attempts by representatives of small nations in the 1930s, 1940s and 1960s to raise the question of self-determination were cast aside and ignored, and the bearers of these ideas were severely punished as extremists and nationalists. It has been hard to overcome these errors even under the conditions of restructuring....

I think that among the measures the country's leadership has taken to solve the

Karabakh problem, the most important are the introduction of the special rules and the creation of the Committee for Special Administration....

All local bodies elected by the people are functioning in the province, as everywhere else.... We resolutely embarked on a course of replacing only those people who were mired in corruption and who had lived for years as parasites on the people's misfortunes. Many honest and qualified cadres were brought forward, and there were plans to transfer all powers of authority to them in the coming elections. But it was this process that drew a stormy reaction from the forces of the "shadow authorities" that had been set in place by the "shadow economy." This happened in the Nagorno-Karabakh Autonomous Province, Armenia and Azerbaijan, all three. The shady operators, faced with the looming prospect of being unmasked, launched an attack on the committee under the banner of national unity, and it must be confessed that this card was skillfully played. A hysterical wave of accusations began, to the effect that the committee was pursuing the Azerbaijanization of the province, while the Azerbaijani population accused it of a pro-Armenian policy. It was on the wave of this hysteria that the strikes and blockades began, in many respects canceling out everything positive. Unfortunately, many leaders of unofficial organizations are doing their bit to escalate the conflict. First in one place and then in another, calls are ringing out to join the ranks of "self-defense" detachments, to arm, to rebuff, to punish, etc.

The Azerbaijan People's Front has declared and is "successfully" carrying out a blockade of Nagorno-Karabakh and Armenia. The front's members are not allowing trainloads of food, fuel and other freight into these regions. Unofficial and even official leaders of both communities in Karabakh are organizing sabotage and stone-throwing warfare on the roads, and terrorist acts against completely innocent people.

In such an atmosphere, the outlined plans could not be implemented in full. Distrust of the committee began to increase, first on the part of the Armenian and then the Azerbaijani population. There were demands that the committee take harsher measures against the "coparticipant" in the conflict. The public in Azerbaijan also took a destructive position, declaring that the Karabakh question didn't exist at all, that it was all the intrigues of Dashnak-type forces[2] and that establishing order in the province should be entrusted to the republic itself. The official propaganda is silent about the methods whereby this was to be achieved. But the leaders of the People's Front are openly calling for harsh solutions.

Under these conditions, the question of the very idea of the existence of the Committee for Special Administration has arisen. I continue to hold to the viewpoint that such a form may be used in crisis situations, but a number of conclusions must be drawn, including ones that relate to the sphere of public awareness....

Not only in the Nagorno-Karabakh Autonomous Province, but in Armenia and Azerbaijan as well, we are dealing with a special kind of mass psychological stress, not yet fully understood, in which a persistent image of an "external enemy" has taken shape, in which compromise is perceived solely as capitulation by the enemy, and in which all points of view are divided into two categories: One is ours and all the rest are wrong....

The main difficulty now lies in the fact that we have to seek a compromise between the moral and the political demands of restructuring. The moral imperative as applied to the nationalities sphere means recognizing every people's right to free will and self-determination, and humanizing nationalities policy, which is inconceivable without giving preeminence to human needs. The political approach is conditioned by awareness of the fact that restructuring cannot now run the risk of new state shakeups, which a redrawing of national-territorial borders would inevitably cause. Destabilization in this sphere could strike an irreparable blow to the economic and political reforms in the country as a whole.... It is wrong to reduce the idea of self-determination solely to the possibility of a different kind of state (or republic) subordination. This approach shows a good deal of archaism, stemming from historical experience in which the possession of territory and the existence of one's own state were in fact the sole guarantee of a people's survival....

[A final point:] Territorial, political and cultural isolation lead to a closed-in civilization. Armenia is now turning into essentially a monoethnic republic, which could be fraught with consequences that are clear to see. On the other hand, Azerbaijan's tendencies to affirm its principles through force are no less dangerous. The fundamental principle of the CPSU's nationalities policy is the humanization of relations between nationalities. Following this path means recognizing the values of both one's own people and another people, with the goal of joint self-improvement....

Speaking at the session [of the USSR Supreme Soviet on Nov. 28] and addressing the People's Deputies from Azerbaijan, the Nagorno-Karabakh Autonomous Province and Armenia, I said:

"... Very little is required of each of you: just to try to understand the pain and concern of the other people.... Try to answer the following question yourself: Why are our brothers in our fatherland dissatisfied with my people? Is there something wrong in our behavior?...

"Believe me, everyone sitting in this room is motivated by the same feelings: pain and concern over the fate of your peoples. People who try to find pro-Armenian or pro-Azerbaijani motives in our words, which come from the heart, are fools. There aren't any! ... There is a desire to help both peoples return to peace. Let us follow this path together!"

I am ready to repeat those words now....

A DECISION WAS MADE, BUT QUESTIONS REMAINED

By Prof. Khikar Barsegyan, Doctor of History. *Kommunist*, Dec. 21, 1989, p. 4.

... We were very surprised by A. Volsky's thought [in his Dec. 7 *Izvestia* interview] that "Armenia is now turning into essentially a monoethnic republic, which could be fraught with consequences that are clear to see." Why doesn't the former committee chairman like the idea of monoethnicity for a national republic? And then, is Armenia really monoethnic? After all, Russians, Ukrainians, Kurds, Greeks, Assyrians and others live a full life here....

What does he see as the danger of monoethnicity for the republic? Or perhaps he doesn't know about the historical circumstances that predetermined this monoethnicity of a people who at the beginning of the century were scattered virtually all over the world and finally received an opportunity to gather in their own age-old lands, to return to the home of their fathers. And A. Volsky certainly should not forget that while he was in Nagorno-Karabakh about 300,000 Armenians were deported from the Azerbaijan Republic and many of them fled to Armenia, which raised the percentage of the republic's indigenous population even higher.

Judging from the interview, A. Volsky hasn't noticed the blockade, the sabotage, the banditry or the political erosion that are damaging our common home – a federation of peoples. He hasn't noticed the ideological provocations against the Armenian people, the defilement of monuments to revolutionaries, or the inflammatory articles in the Baku press....

The problem of the reunification of the Armenian Republic and Nagorno-Karabakh has entered a new stage. One can already talk about their cultural and economic fusion into a single organism. Creative unions have united – the Writers' Union, the Journalists' Union – as have societies of labor and war veterans, industrial enterprises, trade unions and the Young Communist League. This process is continuing, but, unfortunately, in conditions of an onerous blockade of the Nagorno-Karabakh Autonomous Province and the Armenian Republic.

Thus, A. I. Volsky and his apparatus set foot on the land of Nagorno-Karabakh 500 days ago. But instead of the well-known "I came, I saw, I conquered," he can only say: "I came, I saw, I left it in an even more difficult situation." ...

I think that the Volsky interview had a definite purpose – to condition public opinion, first of all that of the USSR People's Deputies, one more time before the Congress began.

A PUBLIC AFFAIRS WRITER SPEAKS OUT: ONCE MORE ABOUT POLITICS AND MORALITY – Notes on Comrade A. I. Volsky's Interview

By Azat Yegiazaryan. *Kommunist*, Dec. 26, 1989, p. 4.

... For me, the following words were really the most important point made in the interview: "The moral imperative as applied to the nationalities sphere means recognizing every people's right to free will and self-determination, and humanizing nationalities policy, which is inconceivable without giving preeminence to human needs." At this point, I cannot help exclaiming silently: Thank God! At last we've found a person who, when he considers the Karabakh problem, recognizes a people's right to self-determination and the free expression of its will. But, while recognizing this as a moral imperative, in the interview he immediately dilutes it with a political approach. This is noteworthy in the highest degree and makes you think again and again: "But the political approach is conditioned by awareness of the fact that restructuring cannot now run the risk of new state shakeups, which a redrawing of national-territorial borders would inevitably cause." So, from the standpoint of morality, Artsakh [a historical name for the Karabakh region] and the entire Armenian people have a right to demand reunification. But the political approach rejects that possibility....

First, I want to draw a parallel between what Comrade Volsky says about the current situation and what happened in 1921. After all, people then were reasoning along roughly the same lines that he is now. At that time...it was understood that, out of fairness, Karabakh should be part of Armenia, something that was recognized by Russia's representatives (Chicherin, Legran, Kirov, Ordzhonikidze and others) and even by Azerbaijan's representatives, and at first they even included Karabakh in Armenia. But as soon as the Azerbaijanis began threatening very serious upheavals, Karabakh was transferred to Azerbaijan, at the time in the name of the Revolution's interests (as it stays there now in the name of restructuring). ...

Let's look at the Supreme Soviet's [Nov. 28] decision on Nagorno-Karabakh, which, as I understand it, Comrade Volsky supports. After all, it is Azerbaijan that the decision instructs "to restore order in the province." What is this if not an undisguised concession to Azerbaijan? That is the form that the "political approach," which is opposed to the moral imperative, takes. The decision of the USSR Supreme Soviet is not a compromise between morality and politics but a jettisoning of the former in favor of the latter....

In the context of the arguments made during the interview, it turns out that Moscow had no choice: The existing borders must be preserved at any price. An amazingly inflexible policy! It is especially striking against the backdrop of our flexibility in the international arena.... For decades we have regarded the existence of two German states as an indispensable condition for peace and stability in Europe. But now our leader is no longer giving unequivocally negative answers to questions about the reunification of Germany. The possibility is no longer being rejected, although it lies in the future.... The FRG and the GDR are two different states belonging to opposing military blocs. But for Armenians, the right of reunification seems not to be recognized even as something for the distant future.

If you want to know, the weakest spot in all the decisions that have been adopted on Nagorno-Karabakh to date is that they forget (intentionally or not) the elementary truth that the two parts of a people should live together under the roof of a single state and that this is a people's natural desire, one that needs no justification. Even if Azerbaijan were a paragon of legality, law and order and a normal attitude toward other peoples, the Karabakhers would still seek to be in the bosom of their own Armenian state, because it is unnatural to be subordinated to a different republic when your own republic is right next door! I am convinced that if the agencies that have been deciding the fate of Karabakh had understood this simple truth in time, there would not be the tension that exists today....

For me, the value of A. I. Volsky's interview in Izvestia, despite the inconsistent and equivocating nature of many of his positions, consists in the fact that it demonstrates the contradiction between "the moral imperative as applied to the nationalities sphere" and the political approaches that have been used up to now. This contradiction must be eliminated – there can be no other way out.

BAKINSKY RABOCHY REJOINDER: WAS IT A MISTAKE, ARKADY IVANOVICH?

By E. Namazov, senior research associate at the Azerbaijan Republic Academy of Sciences' Institute of History. *Bakinsky rabochy*, Dec. 10, 1989, p. 3.

On Dec. 8, Izvestia published an extensive interview with A. I. Volsky, who worked for nearly a year as head of the Committee for the Special Administration of the Nagorno-Karabakh Autonomous Province. ...

In this lengthy interview, many very important and correct thoughts were expressed....

But there are also assessments in the interview that evoke objections, and sometimes bewilderment as well.

A. I. Volsky says: "The contradictory and ambiguous decisions of the early 1920s on the national-territorial structure of Transcaucasia led, among other things, to Nagorno-Karabakh, with its predominantly Armenian population, being included in Azerbaijan."...

One need only open the relevant minutes of the July 4-5, 1921, meeting of the Caucasus Bureau of the Russian Communist Party (Bolsheviks) Central Committee to see for oneself: Nagorno-Karabakh was not "included" but "left" in Azerbaijan....

The numerous proclamations and publications by Armenian public-affairs writers nowhere cite the text of these highly important documents but make the unsubstantiated assertion that in 1921 Nagorno-Karabakh was "included" in Azerbaijan. This is not just playing with words, since from the context readers reach the false opinion that Nagorno-Karabakh belonged to Armenia before the Caucasus Bureau adopted its decision and was then "detached."

Of course, this allegation has also exerted a strong influence on the sentiments of the all-Union public. So why does A. I. Volsky, by repeating these "innocent" verbal flip-flops, play up to such sentiments? Does he really not know the true state of affairs?...

Or how about the assertions that the Azerbaijani side is trying to "establish its principles by force"? After all, the Azerbaijani side's principles on the "Karabakh question" are the same as those of A. I. Volsky, as he set them forth in Izvestia.... Can it be that no one besides the Azerbaijanis in interested in defending these principles against the unparalleled pressure that has been exerted for nearly two years now by nationalistic forces, forces that are now in conflict not so much with the Azerbaijanis as with our common principles and the interests of the Soviet federation?

There have been quite a few such "trifles" recently in the practical activity of the Committee for Special Administration and in interviews given by its leaders to the country's mass news media.... It is impossible to achieve stabilization of the situation in one region or another of interethnic conflicts if one doesn't know the historical roots and real causes of a conflict – or, worse yet, if one stands them on their head. One cannot hope to conquer the disease when the proper diagnosis has not been made. The experience of the activity of the Committee for the Special Administration of the Nagorno-Karabakh Autonomous Province is a living example of these simple truths.

KARABAKH DIARY

By Andrei Nuikin. *Izvestia*, Oct. 18, 1990, p. 6.

... The hopes for a peaceful settlement of the Karabakh conflict that had been stirred by Yeltsin's arrival were quickly replaced by disappointment. The very text of the Zheleznovodsk communique, alas, provided a good many reasons for caution. The powers of Karabakh's legitimate authorities remained unrecognized, and hence one of the warring parties (after all, it's Karabakh, not Armenia, that is at war – at least for now) appeared at the talks not as a party but on the sidelines; it did not sign the communique, and it is not obligated to answer for compliance with its provisions. Many things in that communique are unacceptable to the Karabakhers. Even such indisputable, at first glance, formulas as "a cease-fire" and "the withdrawal of all armed formations from the conflict zone." Especially when it comes to "illegal armed formations." Which formations are "legal" is decided in Baku, after all. Hence, for the Armenians all armed formations will be illegal, while for the Azerbaijanis all of them will be "legal." But even if one doesn't resort to this classification, Azerbaijan has someplace to which it can "withdraw" its militants from the conflict zone and keep them in complete combat readiness, but all the Karabakhers live in this zone and, consequently, they would simply have to eliminate their self-defense detachments, relying entirely on the enemy's nobility (which would be folly) or on protection by Union troops.

Alas, it is under cover of these troops that the Azerbaijani special police have been killing, raping, plundering and torturing. How can any trust be put in these troops? – one wonders. But without such trust, the point about a "cease-fire" becomes dubious. The Azerbaijani special police, who recently have been partially deprived of support from the Soviet Army, have exhibited very bad military training and insufficient readiness to sacrifice themselves. But even so, the formation of a regular Azerbaijani Army has begun, a force that is laying claim to all the combat equipment deployed on the republic's territory! Wasn't it as a delaying tactic that the Baku politicians agreed to talks, which are clearly not making quick progress toward completing a peace agreement? Otherwise, why would President Mutalibov have flown with Yeltsin to Karabakh, where the hatred for him might have provoked some very rash actions? Why did he have to bring some odious unaccredited journalists with him and seat an uninvited Azerbaijani representative at the negotiating table alongside Yeltsin and Nazarbayev (against their will)? All this can be explained only by a deliberate desire to thwart an agreement and discredit the mission of the Presidents of Russia and Kazakhstan.

The Karabakhers did me a great honor by including me in their delegation for the talks in Stepanakert, and I can testify as an eyewitness that it was only Boris Nikolayevich's personal charm that saved the mission from a disastrous conclusion. He was able to find some out-of-the-ordinary, humane words to make the Karabakh representatives, who were ready to get up and leave, reconcile themselves to the presence of Tamerlan Garayev. But the attempts to thwart a peaceful resolution of the conflict did not end there.

"I am in complete control of the armed formations in Azerbaijan," Mutalibov said on Sept. 23, when he signed the Zheleznovodsk communique. On that day the Azerbaijan special police killed six residents of the village of Chapar.... The days that followed were not much different: Stepanakert was hit by rocket and machine-gun fire, vehicles were attacked, hostages were taken and killed, etc., etc.

It is very regrettable that some units of the Don Division of the Ministry of Internal Affairs' internal troops and the 23rd Division of the Fourth Army, which is famous for the venality of its officers, are continuing to unabashedly use their combat might to shield the actions of the special police, are transferring to them (not as a gift, needless to say) armored personnel carriers, howitzers, mortars, grenade throwers, ammunition and rifles, are taking hostages (for resale), etc....

True, instances have been recorded of efforts by Union internal troops to stop being the Azerbaijanis' hirelings and to curb attempts at armed attacks by both sides, but on the whole, alas, blood is being shed more thickly than before Yeltsin's arrival. But most importantly, the people's last hope for protection on the part of Russia is in jeopardy.... More than just once or twice, I have heard the bitter comment: "It would have been better if he hadn't come at all!"

This, of course, is both untrue and unfair. As we have said, the position and tactics of the Union internal troops are changing (except for the corrupt and venal troops, but the leadership of the Ministry of Internal Affairs can deal with that problem, if it wants to). The criminal blockade of the railroad has been partially broken (emergency supplies of gasoline and foodstuffs have been brought in). And after all, these are only the first steps. One would like to hope that at least some of the seeds scattered by a kind hand on the war-scorched earth will produce healthy shoots....

From the very outset, it would have been naive, after all, to count on an easy and swift untangling of the Karabakh knot, so a certain amount of disappointment was, as it were, built into the program of the Presidents' peacemaking mission, but nevertheless one has to admit that the disappointment could have been less and the results could have been more substantial, even at the first stage, if "We are only mediators.*** In no way are we encroaching on the sovereignty of independent Azerbaijan," Yeltsin and (especially) Nazarbayev never tired of repeating throughout their tour of the Caucasus.

In view of the active efforts to play on the people's "insulted self-esteem" that have been made by Azerbaijani politicians, it was probably necessary to say this, but this postulate should not have been the internal position of the truce envoys. There was really no point in coming to a region engaged in a life-and-death struggle carrying "only a selection of general phrases about the need for mutual understanding and a peaceful resolution of the question" (as Nezavisimaya gazeta put it).

The Azerbaijani leadership has repeatedly sworn to its people that it will definitely solve the Karabakh problem once and for all this year. How? The formation of a punitive army of special police, plus the 200,000-man regular armed forces whose formation is now beginning, forces in which Mutalibov is demanding, in the form of an ultimatum, that the Fourth Army, which is two-thirds Azerbaijani, and all its weaponry be included – this reveals rather unambiguously how. In fact, in this respect the talks begun by Azerbaijan can be assessed only as an attempt to gain time to accomplish this strategic task. The question arises: Does sovereignty give someone the right to exterminate and deport hundreds of thousands of people of another nation and another religion? ...

Inge Genefke, a Danish physician and specialist in post-torture rehabilitation, believes that, from a formal standpoint, torture is not employed in our country.... But when Genefke began to list just what forms of torture are in fashion in the world, I felt that I was once more in the sovereign state of Azerbaijan....

How many times we have been told about all this...in Karabakh! I don't want to give all the details on paper, but I really have to describe one of them.

In ancient Rome, during the time of Caligula, torturing prisoners to death was an integral part of festivals. Victims of excesses testify that a nice folk custom is evolving now in some districts of Azerbaijan – an Armenian "militant" (a peaceful peasant or schoolteacher) is rented cheap from a prison and taken to – guess what – a wedding! Collective beating of the Armenian – that is now the highlight of the entertainment program given on the threshold of wedded bliss....

Violations of human rights cannot be considered the "internal affair" of any state, and genocide is one of the most repugnant and dangerous crimes against humanity and humaneness. It is with this postulate (an internal one, at least) that all politicians should go to every "hot spot" in our former country. Are there effective mechanisms capable of compelling even the most ardent admirer of the State Committee for the State of Emergency to behave in a civilized manner in an area that, by the will of fate, has ended up in his possession? If not, they must be created as a top priority and rounded into form through use....

Russia's Army and its military equipment have been used above all for the ruthless deportation of Armenian villages and for terror against peaceful inhabitants of Karabakh. The Russian people, misled by false propaganda, have remained outside observers, alas. This guilt must be expiated. The protection of the rights and liberties of residents of this long-suffering region must be ensured through all the diplomatic, economic, intellectual and, in the case of the new large-scale attempts at genocide, military might of Russia, multiplied by its international influence and the moral purity of the set goals.

I am convinced that Russia's democratic leadership craves neither a revision of borders nor the appropriation of new territories. The question of Nagorno-Karabakh's administrative status should be decided primarily by the leadership that was legally elected by its people, a leadership to which all the rights and powers pertaining to the autonomous formation must be immediately restored. Needless to say, it must not decide this question separately but in conjunction with Russia, based on talks with all the parties concerned....

However, the parties must be aware of reality: Both warring camps have gone to such extremes of intransigence and hatred (which at any moment run the risk of causing the conflict between nationalities to develop into a war between religions) that any new attempts to persuade them to walk "hand in hand" into a bright future are now nothing more than pompous nonsense and a dangerous delay in solving the problem.... Everyone will have to live side by side for centuries to come, and at some time the pain of the injuries will probably lose its edge, and trade and cultural exchanges will be put to rights. But this will take a long time! Right now, the task of those who have decided to return peace and legality to Karabakh soil should consist in the firm separation of the warring sides and the strict suppression of all armed and all criminal actions....

The question arises: Are our Armed Forces, 3 million men armed to the teeth, really unable to cope with such a trivial task, and, at the same time, unable to explain where the Azerbaijani militants are getting combat equipment, as well as machine gunners and snipers whose skills indicate clearly that they were not trained in Azerbaijan? ...

Today we must stop engaging in empty peacemaking chatter and finally get down to tough, authoritative actions to bring about democratic order in the country and establish legality and humaneness. While it is still possible for us to do so.

TALKING ABOUT KARABAKH IN ZHELEZNOVODSK – Leaders of Azerbaijan, Armenia and Nagorno-Karabakh Autonomous Province Meet With Yeltsin, Nazarbayev at Negotiating Table

By TASS special correspondent Anatoly Aladinsky in Zheleznovodsk; Izvestia special correspondents N. Andreyev, S. Bablumyan, V. Samedov and V. Oliyanchuk in Baku and Yerevan. *Izvestia*, Sept. 23, 1991, p. 1.

Zheleznovodsk, Sept. 23 – Talks on settling the Karabakh conflict began here today.

As Boris Yeltsin emphasized, the Russian Republic "address" was not chosen by chance. Because of the special delicacy of the question under discussion, it was decided to conduct the talks on neutral territory.

Taking part in the working meeting are: Ayaz Mutalibov, President of Azerbaijan; Levon Ter-Petrosyan, Chairman of the Armenian Supreme Soviet; the leaders of the Nagorno-Karabakh Autonomous Province; and representatives of the Azerbaijani and Armenian communities of that autonomous province. The Presidents of Russia and Kazakhstan – Boris Yeltsin and Nursultan Nazarbayevhave taken the role of mediators in the talks.

* * *

Baku and Yerevan

"We are mediators. We are nothing but mediators" – B. Yeltsin and N. Nazarbayev repeated this statement to journalists like an incantation. The presidents were extremely cautious in their utterances, assessments and proposals. They emphasized that their visit is a goodwill mission, nothing more.

The talks began in Baku on Sept. 21. Three delegations – from Azerbaijan, Kazakhstan and Russia – met in the House of Receptions, which was built by G. Aliyev in his time. Ayaz Mutalibov set forth his program for solving the problem of Nagorno-Karabakh, which provides for restoring the status quo in the autonomous province, recognizing the territorial integrity of Azerbaijan and the inviolability of its borders, and restoring local self-government agencies. Yeltsin and Nazarbayev refrained from any commentary on this program....

The route of Yeltsin and Nazarbayev's trip was worked out with some difficulty. There were apprehensions about the safety of a trip to Stepanakert. Russia's State Secretary G. Burbulis flew there. There was no news from him for some time, and it was rumored that he had been taken hostage. On the evening of Sept. 21, when we met with him, alive and unhurt, in Gyandzha, he said: "They can go, and they must go. The Presidents are awaited in Stepanakert and Shusha."

And so, this was the route: From Baku to Gyandzha, where the presidents spent the night. In Stepanakert and Shusha, they met with representatives of the Armenian and Azerbaijani sides. In Yerevan, they got a clarification of the Armenian leadership's position. Finally, they went to Mineralniye Vody. In this resort city, A. Mutalibov, L. Ter-Petrosyan, Nagorno-Karabakh representatives, B. Yeltsin and N. Nazarbayev will sit down at the negotiating table.

It must be noted that people in Baku are pinning very great hopes on the arrival of Yeltsin and Nazarbayev, although the opinion is also being voiced that this mission is nothing other than interference in the internal affairs of sovereign and independent Azerbaijan....

The question of the presence of Soviet troops in Azerbaijan arises constantly. On this score, Yeltsin said: "Everything depends on the will of the two republics' peoples. We are prepared to withdraw troops in as short as a week's time. Today there are 2,500 soldiers on the border between Azerbaijan and Armenia. They are not conducting combat operations, they are only separating the hostile sides...." In Baku, however, another statistic is cited: 60,000 Azerbaijanis are serving in the Army outside the republic, and it is still unknown which is cheaper for Azerbaijan –

to allocate large sums of money for the Soviet Army or to maintain its own army. In view of the fact that Armenia also intends to create its own armed forces, one can predict how this may turn out.

The participants in the talks are united in the view that M. Gorbachev should not interfere in the situation. As is known, the USSR President is drafting a decree that will attempt once more to resolve the problem of Nagorno-Karabakh. According to Nazarbayev, "there is no need for this decree; the two independent republics should come to an agreement themselves."...

When they arrived in Nagorno-Karabakh, Yeltsin and Nazarbayev understood how difficult it would be to reach agreement. The building of the (now dissolved) province Soviet was surrounded by internal troops, special police units and paratroopers. Thousands of Stepanakerters were chanting "Freedom," "Russia," "Yeltsin," and the flags of Russia, Kazakhstan and Armenia were flying. An incident arose because the Armenian flag had been raised over the province Soviet building: A. Mutalibov refused to enter the building. B. Yeltsin became noticeably agitated. In the end, the Presidents of Russia and Kazakhstan entered the province Soviet building, while A. Mutalibov went to the building of the Committee for Special Administration, over which the Union and Azerbaijani flags were flying....

A. Manucharov, a representative of Nagorno-Karabakh, suggested these possible solutions: enter the Union with the rights of a free republic, or join Russia.

Yeltsin spoke in Stepanakert.... He said that the news media were using the improper tactic of setting peoples at loggerheads. Judging from his words, special censorship of reports and materials on the problem of Nagorno-Karabakh will be set up in Moscow.

Nazarbayev spoke after Yeltsin....

Yeltsin and Nazarbayev arrived in Yerevan on Sept. 22. Work continued at the same fast pace....

So, what did the Yerevan meeting add to the already achieved gains from the talks? The President of Russia noted that on a number of questions the various sides' positions are beginning to coincide. This gives us hope that it will be possible to sign a communique and begin a process of talks among Armenia, Azerbaijan and Nagorno-Karabakh, with Russia and Kazakhstan as mediators....

Confirming the fact that viewpoints coincide on several questions, Levon Ter-Petrosyan, Chairman of the Armenian Supreme Soviet, put special emphasis on the point that perhaps the most important achievement to date is the Nagorno-Karabakh representatives' participation on an equal footing as one of the sides at the talks. In predicting their outcome, the head of the Armenian parliament expressed cautious optimism. "This is only the beginning," he said, "the first step. One should not expect very much, but it is important to take the first step. And it must be to restore constitutional order in Karabakh."

Journalists' attempts to obtain more information were unsuccessful. In Yerevan, as in Baku and Stepanakert, Yeltsin and Nazarbayev were inflexible in their unforthcoming attitude....

So, we will wait for the promised press conference in Zheleznovodsk, which, one has to assume, will enable us to get answers to many questions.

Ye. Shaposhnikov, the country's Minister of Defense, and V. Barannikov, USSR Minister of Internal Affairs, left Yerevan for Mineralniye Vody with the presidents of Russia and Kazakhstan. V. Manukyan, Chairman of the Armenian Council of Ministers, and A. Manucharyan, the republic's minister of internal affairs, will take part in the concluding round of talks.

* * *

Our correspondent reports from Zheleznovodsk that the delegation arrived at the Mineralniye Vody airport on the morning of Sept. 23 and headed for the Oak Grove Sanatorium in Zheleznovodsk. The talks resumed at once....

ARMENIA, AZERBAIJAN BEGIN DIALOGUE WITHOUT WEAPONS

By special correspondent N. Andreyev. *Izvestia*, Sept. 25, 1991, p. 1.

Zheleznovodsk and Moscow – As a result of the talks between Azerbaijan and Armenia in which Yeltsin and Nazarbayev took part, a communiqué has been signed.... The situation in Nagorno-Karabakh had seemed hopeless.... Any contacts between the hostile parties employed Kalashnikov assault rifles, mines, cloud-seeding guns and other lethal weapons.

The presidents of Russia and Kazakhstan proposed that an end be put to this sort of "dialogue." They took on the thankless role of mediators. Thankless because an attempt to be peacemakers between parties that have not listened to each other for a long time could set both sides against Yeltsin and Nazarbayev. The leaders of Russia and Kazakhstan tirelessly repeated that they were nothing more than mediators, that they were in no way seeking to interfere in the internal affairs of sovereign Azerbaijan and Armenia. Nevertheless, the two presidents did have a personal interest in resolving this protracted conflict. Soldiers of the Union Army are dying in Karabakh, among them citizens of the Russian and Kazakhstan Republics. In the second place, Azerbaijan and Armenia are part of the economic space of the former Union. And peace and tranquility are among the necessary conditions for economic activity.

The parties worked out questions relating to a step-by-step settlement of the conflict. They consider the following to be mandatory conditions: a cease-fire, the repeal by Jan. 1, 1992, of all unconstitutional acts adopted by Azerbaijan and Armenia regarding the Nagorno-Karabakh Autonomous Province, recognition of the authority of the lawful bodies of power, and the withdrawal of all armed formations from the conflict zone, with the exception of units of internal troops of the USSR Ministry of Internal Affairs and the USSR Ministry of Defense. After this time period expires, the presence of all armed formations and their operations will be considered unlawful by the parties and will be curbed by internal troops of the USSR Ministry of Internal Affairs, while members of armed formations may be called to account under the law.

A working group of observers has been instructed to work out measures for a cease-fire, the neutralization of all armed formations, and the creation of safety guarantees for all citizens living in the conflict zone.

In order to carry out agreed-upon actions to normalize the situation in the conflict zone, a temporary working group of observers will be formed, a group that will include authorized representatives of the Russian Federation and Kazakhstan.

The Azerbaijan Republic and the Republic of Armenia will ensure the step-by-step return of the deported population, beginning with the villages that have been abandoned. The two sides will guarantee the population's safety in their places of permanent residence.

The parties involved in the conflict will immediately begin the release of hostages. This process is to be completed within a two-week period, at the expiration of which time persons involved in the holding of hostages will be called to account in accordance with the law.

In conjunction with Union agencies, the parties will ensure, within a two-week period, the normal functioning of rail and air transport, communications systems and utility lines.

It has been deemed necessary to ensure the objectivity of information coming from the conflict zone. It has been decided to form an information group, made up of representatives of the Russian Federation and Kazakhstan, that will be authorized to prepare official information about events.

The parties believe that the negotiating process that has begun will be promoted by the preparation and signing in the near future of bilateral treaties between the Russian Federation and the Azerbaijan Republic; the Russian Federation and the Republic of Armenia; the Kazakh SSR and the Azerbaijan Republic; and the Kazakh SSR and the Republic of Armenia.

The working group of observers has been instructed to prepare, within one month, proposals for subsequent stages in the settlement of the conflict...

USSR STATE COUNCIL PROPOSES RESTORING CONSTITUTIONAL ORDER IN NAGORNO-KARABAKH – Now It's Up to the Parliaments of Azerbaijan and Armenia

By G. Alimov. *Izvestia*, Nov. 28, 1991, p. 1.

The acute conflict between Azerbaijan and Armenia, having reached the "boiling point," has demonstrated once again what its consequences could be. The two states were on the verge of war. But the political dialogue that is still possible within the framework of the Union (even if, as they say, it is the former Union), the fact that Presidents Ayaz Mutalibov and Levon Ter-Petrosyan went to a State Council meeting in Moscow, and the interested participation in this dialogue by the USSR President and representatives of other republics made it possible to avert a calamity....

Contrary to pessimistic assumptions, the extraordinary session of the USSR State Council held on Nov. 28 in the Kremlin for the express purpose of discussing the conflict between Azerbaijan and Armenia played an important role in the dialogue between the two republics.

Whatever anyone may say, this new body, created at the last Congress of USSR People's Deputies to govern the country, has once again demonstrated its viability and necessity. How the resolution it adopted will be implemented in practice is another matter. Time will tell....

Mikhail Gorbachev assessed the meeting in Moscow as a "critical moment in the resolution of the conflict over the Nagorno-Karabakh Autonomous Province." "Both parties," the USSR President stated, "demonstrated exceptional responsibility. Both Ayaz Mutalibov and Levon Ter-Petrosyan, I think, needed precisely this kind of dialogue, which convinced them of the complete hopelessness of resolving the conflict through force. Both sides turned completely naturally to the protection of the USSR Constitution, as it were."

The USSR State Council's resolution consists of just four points. The main one involves putting everything back into a constitutional framework – specifically, repealing "all acts changing the legal status of the Nagorno-Karabakh Autonomous Province as set down in the USSR Constitution."

In concrete terms, this means returning the Nagorno-Karabakh Autonomous Province to the status it had before the conflict. This will have to be done by both Azerbaijan and Armenia. The resolution also proposes continuing without delay, in accordance with the Zheleznovodsk communique, the negotiations between duly empowered delegations from both republics with the participation of representatives from Russia and Kazakhstan. It can also be seen as a significant step that the State Council considers it extremely necessary to have direct talks between the Presidents of Azerbaijan and Armenia for the purpose of working out terms for the complete normalization of relations between the two sovereign states.

The leaders of both republics are advised to take measures for a cease-fire and the withdrawal of all illegal armed formations from the conflict zone. They are obligated first of all to do everything possible to ensure the safety of the population. Among specific steps it is also suggested that air traffic between the two republics be regulated and unauthorized flights be barred.

The State Council also discussed the idea of creating a "buffer zone." Unfortunately, this sound idea has gone unimplemented for the past three years. Now the State Council urgently recommends that a security zone be formed along the border between the republics in the areas of greatest tension. The zone's depth and the rules under which it will operate should be determined through negotiations between Baku and Yerevan.

NOTES

1. In an article published in *Izvestia*, Dec. 18, 1988, an official of the Armenian Republic Ministry of Internal Affairs identifies the black shirts as Armenian extremists who are "in mourning" for Nagorno-Karabakh; they are wearing beards until there is a "just solution" of the Karabakh problem. The white shirts are Azerbaijani extremists on the Karabakh question.

2. The Dashnaks were members of an Armenian nationalist party that resisted Soviet rule in the Caucasus.

Part Two |

Initial Resolution and Subsequent Mediation

Chapter 6 | Internationalization of the Conflict

AZERBAIJAN'S PARLIAMENT ELIMINATES NAGORNO-KARABAKH AS AUTONOMOUS UNIT

By staff correspondent V. Samedov. *Izvestia*, Nov. 27, 1991, p. 1.

Baku – As previously reported, an extraordinary session of the Azerbaijan Republic Supreme Soviet opened on Nov. 26....

After a recess, the deputies began discussing one of the most important items on the agenda – the status of the Nagorno-Karabakh Autonomous Province of the Azerbaijan Republic. All the people of Azerbaijan have long awaited a decision on this question, the Deputies noted. A decision is also necessitated by the sharp deterioration in the social, political and economic situation in the republic, the continuing actions of separatist forces in the Nagorno-Karabakh Autonomous Province, which is still the object of territorial claims by Armenia, and the nonobservance on the province's territory of the Constitution and laws of the Azerbaijan Republic.

The Deputies unanimously decided to eliminate Nagorno-Karabakh as an autonomous province. They passed a law making the appropriate changes in and additions to the Azerbaijan Republic Constitution. Stepanakert, the former capital of the province, was given back its ancient name – Khankendi.

With that, the session of the Azerbaijan Supreme Soviet concluded its business....

TROOP WITHDRAWAL BEGINS

Pravda, Dec. 25, 1991, p. 2.

Units and elements of the internal troops have begun withdrawing from the territory of Nagorno-Karabakh.

Gen. Savin, commander of internal troops in the Nagorno-Karabakh Republic [NKR], attributed the hasty withdrawal of the troops to the absence of any legal basis for their continued presence in Nagorno-Karabakh. However, the general said, the command staff of the internal troops realizes that this could lead to an escalation of the conflict in the region and to another deportation of the Armenian population.

According to information now coming in, since the start of the pullout there have been more frequent shellings and attacks on both villages and the NKR's capital, Stepanakert, which is now in its third day of continuous bombardment by Alazan rockets and mortar shells.

* * *

In connection with the withdrawal of the USSR Ministry of Internal Affairs' internal troops from the territory of Karabakh, the NKR Soviet of People's Deputies has issued a statement to the parliaments and presidents of the member republics of the Commonwealth of Independent States, saying, in part: "On behalf of the Armenian population, the NKR leadership declares its readiness to counter any aggression on the part of Azerbaijan and to defend, despite clearly uneven forces, its people's right to live on the territory of their historical homeland."

The NKR leadership called on the peoples and presidents of the CIS member republics not to remain "indifferent to the numerous appeals of the people of Nagorno-Karabakh, who have been suffering for more than three years," and to take prompt and effective measures to prevent possible aggression. – (SNARK)[1]

THE FIGHTING MAN SHOULD SWEAR AN OATH TO THE PEOPLE, AND THE POLITICIANS ONE TO COMMON SENSE

By Vladimir Urban. *Krasnaya zvezda*, Jan. 9, 1992, p. 1.

... There is no doubt that every state has the right to create its own army. This is a legal right. But there is a special situation now in the CIS, one that can be gotten out of in a sensible way only if this is done without haste, on the basis of the transitional period. The new states have inherited from the USSR a vast and unified Army that in the past few years, due to the inconsistent policy of the leaders of the now defunct Union, has acquired an unbalanced, if not explosive, nature. It's no secret to anyone that the Army was used to plug all the holes in the crumbling state, and then it was given peripheral priority. Will the men endure the new adversities? And what flags will they be under?

The problem is not confined to Ukraine alone. Azerbaijan's President A. Mutalibov signed the Agreement on the Armed Forces and the Border Troops with the proviso" – with the mandatory completion within two months of the transfer of general-purpose armed forces to the Azerbaijan Republic."

One doesn't have to be a prophet to answer the question: Why is the republic taking this particular position? The hastily formed national army is battling the Karabakh "self-defense forces" and is taking casualties. In short, the new army needs military specialists. Azerbaijan has promised substantial legal and social guarantees to Soviet Army officers who enter its service. There are already some who want to do so – one mustn't hide that fact. Apparently, it is expected that a new oath will be sworn there, too. It's no accident that Azerbaijan, like Ukraine and Moldova, insisted in Minsk that its personnel be released from the oaths they had taken earlier....

ANOTHER HELICOPTER SHOT DOWN: SOME 40 PEOPLE KILLED

By staff correspondent Sergei Taranov. *Izvestia*, Jan. 29, 1992, p. 1.

On Jan. 28 at 4:20 p.m., a helicopter belonging to Azerbaijan's Azal Airline was shot down by a missile on the territory of Nagorno-Karabakh during its approach to the town of Shusha. According to preliminary information, all the passengers and crew members about 40 people were killed.

The details of this tragedy have not yet been investigated. But unlike the previous such incident, to which there were no witnesses (26 people died in that instance), this time dozens of Shusha residents saw the helicopter burn and explode. Initially, said Rafael Guseinov, first deputy representative of the Azerbaijan Republic in Moscow, a heat-sensitive Stinger missile was launched. The helicopter, already heading for a landing, burst into flames. But there was still a little time before the explosion and complete destruction of the aircraft.... [The captain and his crew] were able to turn the aircraft away from Shusha. The explosion happened in a location that was safe for the town's residents. The pilots' actions can be viewed as a heroic deed....

The town of Shusha is under a blockade of many days' duration. Its only communication with the world is by air, and, of course, without any writing up of tickets, presentation of passports, etc. That is why nobody knows exactly how many passengers were aboard the MI-8. It is known that the regular load was about 40 people, of whom, as a rule, at least half were women and children. This time they had been joined by six members of the OMON special police. So it is not appropriate to say that the helicopter was shot down in the course of military actions.

"We view this as one in a series of terrorist acts," Rafael Guseinov stressed, adding that in two years Armenian militants have attacked the Moscow-Baku train three times with bombs and gunfire (12 people died) and have blown up two passenger buses (50 victims), a ferry (21 deaths) and, finally, two civilian helicopters....

NAGORNO-KARABAKH: THE ARMY IS UNDER AIMED FIRE

By staff correspondent Viktor Litovkin. *Izvestia*, Feb. 24, 1992, p. 1.

More tragic news has been received from Nagorno-Karabakh: All day on Feb. 23, the Azerbaijani army directed aimed fire on Stepanakert (Khankendy) from Grad or BM-21 artillery rocket launchers. More than 110 shells that an international convention bans for use against the population were launched against the city.

Several volleys were fired into the area of the 366th Motorized Infantry Regiment, which is quartered in the city. Eighty high-explosive fragmentation shells of great destructive force landed on the soldiers. We were told at the press center of the CIS Joint Armed Forces' Commander in Chief that 10 servicemen had been wounded, three of them seriously. Pvt. Kovalyov died from his wounds.

Maj. Gen. Nikolai Popov, Commander of the Fourth Baku Army, elaborated in a telephone conversation: The 366th Regiment was shelled for two days, the 22nd and the 23rd. It was fired on by one BM-21 and two BM-13 artillery [rocket] launchers, as well as by large-caliber artillery guns.... The regiment's commander, Lt. Col. Yury Zarvigorov, said that the regiment's personnel are exhibiting self-restraint and patience and are not being drawn into the fighting, although this is very, very difficult for them.

In view of the unsuitable flying weather – there are clouds and rain over Stepanakert – there has been no opportunity to deliver food for three days – no helicopters are flying.

The commander also said that in Azerbaijan the situation involving CIS military units has become sharply exacerbated. There are constant attacks on military camps, and a general "inventorying" of combat equipment and property by local authorities. On the night of Feb. 23-24, there was an attack on a major ammunition dump near the city of Agdam. Thousands of tons of shells of various calibers were seized. The servicemen who were guarding the dump and their families were taken away to an unknown destination.

Attempts to seize automotive equipment have not stopped. In the past three days, more than 20 army motor vehicles have been stolen in Baku. On the morning of Feb. 23, the car of the Fourth Army's Commander was attacked en route to the airport. The attack was made from ambush by 10 militants who opened fire on the car with automatic weapons. The driver managed to get away from the attackers. He and the general were not hurt, but the car was severely damaged.

Marshal of Aviation Yevgeny Shaposhnikov, Commander in Chief of the CIS Joint Armed Forces, has said:

"If we do not achieve peace in the Transcaucasus and in Nagorno-Karabakh through political means, my position is unequivocal – we must withdraw all CIS military formations from there, since, like it or not, the prospect remains that they may be drawn into this conflict. I have already said that if just one shell lands on the area where the 366th Regiment is stationed, return fire will be opened in the direction from which the shell came."

Why has the motorized infantry regiment still not been withdrawn from Stepanakert? According to news agency reports, the city's residents have said that they will lie under the wheels of tanks and combat vehicles in order to prevent the withdrawal from the city of the CIS troops – the residents' only hope for protection against complete destruction.

The aimed fire against the capital of the Nagorno-Karabakh Republic is continuing....

OPINION: PROSPECTS FOR A WAR OF ATTRITION – The Military-Strategic Equilibrium in the Region Will Inevitably Lead to a Protracted War

By Pavel Felgengauer. *Nezavisimaya gazeta*, Feb. 21, 1992, p. 1.

... According to estimates by informed observers, the Azerbaijani Army and special police detachments now have about 20,000 personnel and several hundred armored vehicles, including tanks. Nagorno-Karabakh's self-defense forces consist of poorly trained detachments (*dzhokat*) that come from Armenia to the area of combat operations for two or three months (then they are rotated to give them a chance to rest) and the more numerous but even more poorly trained and more poorly armed local residents. Officially, Armenia has no army, but, judging from certain indirect indications, if there was a general mobilization the Armenian side could put in place forces comparable in numbers to the Azerbaijani forces.

Incidentally, the greatest number of identifiable military clashes are taking place at the battalion level (on both sides), and those units are not at full strength.

Azerbaijan was late in beginning to create its own national army, and its military development is proceeding in an extremely inefficient manner. Incidentally, the sizable special police force, which was created earlier, operates much better than the army, which was formed from volunteers. Military experts give an extremely low rating to the combat capabilities of Azerbaijani units: A combat-ready army cannot be improvised in a few months. Volunteers inspired with the national idea and a certain advantage in arms are not sufficient for real success, either.

Armenia's territory is separated from Karabakh by a cordon of Soviet [sic; Russian] troops: a motorized infantry division, deployed in outposts along the border, that serves as a major obstacle to any large-scale penetration by Armenian detachments into the territory of Nagorno-Karabakh. However, recently attempts to disarm individual small outposts – the Azerbaijanis need weapons – have become more frequent. If the armed buffer between the republics eventually disappears (if the troops are pulled out to avoid unpleasantness), a clash between the Armenian Armed Forces and the Azerbaijani Army will be inevitable. And if Nagorno-Karabakh's self-defense forces get into a truly desperate situation and there is a direct threat to Stepanakert, then a full-scale interrepublic war will be inevitable....

Azerbaijan is potentially the stronger, both in number of inhabitants and economically....

According to estimates by army intelligence, the Armenian armed forces are now much stronger than the Azerbaijani army. The Armenian formations are superior to the Azerbaijanis on an organizational level and in terms of fighting efficiency. Armenia began its military development earlier and, one has to think, did a more successful job. Meanwhile, the Azerbaijani leadership hoped that the Soviet Armed Forces and internal troops would do all the "dirty work" and "solve" the problem of Nagorno-Karabakh. In July and August 1991 matters did come to that point, and under a state of emergency in the USSR the Karabakh problem would have been "solved." But the August putsch was unsuccessful, the internal troops were withdrawn from Karabakh, the troops of the Transcaucasus Military District are now truly neutral, and the two sides have been left to their own devices.

The Armenian Army is the best prepared to fight "guerrilla" style: to infiltrate the enemy's combat formations, set up ambushes, etc. When (and if) things reach the point of a full-scale war between Armenia and Azerbaijan, the Armenian army will undoubtedly be attended by success, at least during the first months of fighting. A land corridor will be created between Karabakh and Armenia proper. Shusha and possibly Agdam will most likely be taken, but further offensive action is improbable. The next completely obvious strategic objective is Gyandzha, but it is the headquarters of two Soviet divisions (a motorized infantry division and an airborne division), which might intervene in the fighting if they were provoked. Moreover, in offensive operations considerable losses are inevitable, and Armenian society would react extremely badly to such losses.

Thus, in the next few years flare-ups of fighting will continue to alternate with long and fruitless talks under general mediation (by the UN, NATO, the CIS, Russia, Turkey, etc.). Azerbaijan's potential is superior, as I have already said, so the correlation of forces will gradually shift in its favor, but a decisive victory will not come soon – it will take many years of efforts, thousands of casualties and billions of rubles.

However, "peace" in the Transcaucasus could be established earlier if some sort of outside force were to undertake this task. The Soviet troops stationed in the region are keeping careful track of the two sides' actions and movements, and they know the disposition of their forces, their routes of travel and their supply bases at any given moment in time (for the past six months, the airborne division stationed in Gyandzha has had the exclusive task of conducting intelligence operations, without interfering in events). According to experts, if these troops received the appropriate order, they could completely rout both of the "armies" opposing each other in Karabakh in a few days. But there will be no such order. At any rate, not until Russia sorts out problems that are closer and more important to it – problems in the Northern Caucasus, in the Crimea, in Ukraine, etc. As a result, the Transcaucasus is open for political and, perhaps, not just political interference by two old rivals: Turkey and Iran.

Turkey is stronger both militarily and economically, but, as a member of NATO and a candidate for entry into the European Community, it is acting (and will continue to act) extremely cautiously, using diplomatic and economic channels for influencing the Transcaucasian republics. Iran is prepared for more rash actions, especially if fighting starts in Nakhichevan Province, but the southern front with Iraq is still the most important sector for Tehran. One can expect deliveries of firearms and ammunition, but it is hardly likely that there will be anything more serious than that, since Iran itself is a major importer of weapons and depends on Russia: It needs regular deliveries of spare parts for its Soviet planes. Moreover, the new Iranian leadership (Khomeini's heirs) is less inclined toward foreign-policy adventures than the previous leadership was.

There is every reason to think that the outside forces (Turkey, Iran and Russia) will continue to counterbalance one another in the next few years, so the war of "attrition" in the Transcaucasus will most likely continue for an indefinitely long time – until the two sides are indeed completely exhausted.

THE 366TH REGIMENT IS LEAVING NAGORNO-KARABAKH – Outposts Between Armenia, Azerbaijan Being Removed

By staff correspondent Viktor Litovkin. *Izvestia*, Feb. 29, 1992, p. 1.

... On Feb. 28, Marshal of Aviation Yevgeny Shaposhnikov, Commander in Chief of the Joint Armed Forces, sent telegrams to Azerbaijani President Ayaz Mutalibov, Armenian President Levon Ter-Petrosyan, and Col. Gen. Valery Patrikeyev, Troops Commander of the Transcaucasus Military District, as well as to the commanders of the Fourth Baku Army and the Seventh Yerevan Army. The telegrams say, among other things, that, despite the measures that have been taken, the situation regarding Nagorno-Karabakh is not improving, unfortunately, and that combat operations are continuing to escalate.

Criminal actions involving the seizure of equipment, arms and ammunition from CIS military facilities are being accompanied by the deaths of and severe injuries to completely innocent people. This year alone eight servicemen have died, 22 have been wounded and 28 have been taken hostage in Azerbaijan. Moreover, those responsible for these crimes remain unpunished, and the republic's law-enforcement agencies are taking a position of noninterference.

Marshal Shaposhnikov has asked that the residents of the two independent states take all possible measures to return the seized combat equipment, weapons and ammunition to the Commonwealth's Joint Armed Forces, to prevent unlawful actions against servicemen and members of their families, and to call to account the initiators and perpetrators of criminal actions.

Shaposhnikov has instructed the troops commanders of the Transcaucasus Military District and the Baku and Yerevan Armies to put military camps, ammunition dumps and other military facilities under increased guard, to prevent outsiders from getting into them, and, if fighting men and Army facilities are attacked, to give the attackers a decisive rebuff. If the seized equipment and arms are not returned, measures are to be taken to destroy them, while trying not to harm civilians.

Marshal Shaposhnikov has ordered that the 366th Motorized Infantry Regiment be withdrawn from Nagorno-Karabakh and that all military outposts be removed from the administrative border between Armenia and Azerbaijan....

There has been no official confirmation of the televised report that an evacuation of servicemen's families from Azerbaijan has begun. The Joint Armed Forces' press center has reported that neither the Commander in Chief nor the army commanders gave such an order. But, according to information available to the editors, this evacuation was organized by the officers themselves, who are concerned about the fate of those who are near and dear to them....

BAKU REPORTS ON TRAGEDY IN KHODZHALY – Yerevan Considers the Storming of the City a Military Success

By staff correspondents Vasif Samedov and Sergei Taranov. *Izvestia*, March 3, 1992, p. 1.

...It is impossible these days to find impartial, accurate and totally reliable information about events in Karabakh. Each of the opposing sides presents its own version, and each has its own "indisputable" arguments that are born of long suffering. And there is no longer a Union center, which would have had its own representatives on the battlefield. One can hardly have complete faith in assessments by the command of the CIS Armed Forces, since it is accused of making use of the 366th Regiment, which is still stationed in Stepanakert (Khankendi). Nevertheless –

Zaur Rustamzade, the Azerbaijan Republic's authorized representative in Moscow, gave the following account:

"According to preliminary reports,... about 1,000 people died and nearly 1,500 disappeared – most of them civilians – [during the storming and capture of the town of Khodzhaly in Nagorno-Karabakh on Feb. 26]. Our greatest woe is that now no one can count the people who were killed on their own land, or even give them a decent burial. Khodzhaly has been occupied and burned down by Armenian militants. Perhaps the film that was shot from a helicopter by foreign and Azerbaijani journalists will make the situation clearer. That film will be taken to Moscow on March 4, and we'll show it to the press and the public there.

"The destruction of the town came as no surprise to us, unfortunately.... As of today, Armenian militants have captured 53 of the former autonomous province's 54 towns and villages. Only the town of Shusha is holding out. In all the other villages that have fallen into enemy hands, there is utter devastation, with houses burned down and their inhabitants murdered." ...

Robert Arakilov, an adviser to the Armenian Republic's permanent representative in Moscow, said this:

"The talk about the 'destruction' of Khodzhaly is no more than an attempt by Azerbaijan to spread propaganda. As a matter of fact, it is not a town of 10,000 people but a small village a few kilometers away from Stepanakert on the road to another Armenian (by population) town, Askeran....

"If you have Khodzhaly, you can totally control the Stepanakert airport and, at the same time, rake all of Stepanakert with fire. Which did in fact happen every day over the past few months. Azerbaijan's special police and other armed units used artillery. From Khodzhaly they adjusted the fire of the Grad rocket launchers firing from Shusha. The enemy also succeeded in blocking the airport, after which we couldn't obtain even medicine or food. That is why the leaders of the Nagorno-Karabakh Republic decided to wipe out that focus of bandit activities...."

"How many civilians were in Khodzhaly when the town was stormed?"

"There were hardly any, because most of them had left the town earlier due to the intense fighting. Khodzhaly, I repeat, had become one of the bases of support for the war. And its capture was dictated by the very logic of war. When the Armenian troops entered the town, the remaining civilians were allowed to leave through a 'corridor' between the opposing sides....By the way, now the bombardment of Stepanakert has quieted down a bit. And that is a direct result of the fact that the bandits were driven out of Khodzhaly."

"Did any soldiers or officers of the 366th Regiment participate in the battle for Khodzhaly?"

"No. The town was taken only by the Armenian self-defense forces."...

NAGORNO-KARABAKH: CIS ARMY SOLDIERS AND OFFICERS ARE FIGHTING ON BOTH SIDES OF THE CONFLICT

By staff correspondents Viktor Litovkin and Sergei Taranov. *Izvestia*, March 4, 1992, p. 1.

(By staff correspondent Sergei Taranov) – What was hidden is coming out into the open. The facts that officials have been carefully concealing but that the whole world is talking about have been confirmed. Individual officers, warrant officers and soldiers of the 366th Motorized Infantry Regiment, quartered in Stepanakert (Khankendi), have participated in military actions on both sides.

Furthermore, according to our information, after the regiment was prepared for withdrawal from the zone of armed conflict, Maj. S. Oganyan, commander of the Second Motorized Infantry Battalion, along with several Armenian officers under his command and soldiers of various nationalities, many of whom are running away from the unit, seized a tank, three infantry fighting vehicles (according to other reports, 20 infantry fighting vehicles) and two artillery pieces and occupied commanding positions four kilometers south of the village of Balydzha, and are not letting two other battalions from Stepanakert pass.

There was also some confusion in the ranks of the paratroopers who were supposed to cover the regiment's withdrawal to a new place of deployment – no one expected that they would have to fight against their own....

The 366th Regiment, which according to plan was to be withdrawn to Gyandzha, will now be transferred to Georgian territory. Azerbaijan has declared that those who shot at its citizens will not be allowed across its borders. The regiment's banner has already been moved to its new place. Time will very quickly reveal what will happen to the soldiers of the troubled unit. Two battalions of the motorized infantry regiment are ready to withdraw but are being hampered by the betrayal, military personnel told us.

* * *

(By staff correspondent Sergei Taranov) – ... Izvestia special correspondent Vadim Belykh transmitted the following report by fax from Baku on [March] 4:

"The 366th Regiment has not been able to move out of Nagorno-Karabakh. It has been blocked by a crowd of women and children who are convinced that with the withdrawal of the last CIS troops, Stepanakert will be completely destroyed and its residents annihilated. The regimental commanders are negotiating with the Armenian residents, so far without results. There are many wounded servicemen. According to unverified information, two paratroopers from the group that was sent to cover the withdrawal have been killed in the last 24 hours. Deserters from the 366th Regiment say that after massive desertions there are no more than 300-350 people left in the unit (the full complement is 1,800), and almost half the tanks, infantry fighting vehicles and trucks are out of order. The operation to withdraw the regiment from Nagorno-Karabakh is being directed by Col. Gen. Gromov, former commander of the 40th Army (in Afghanistan), who has set up his headquarters in Gyandzha.".....

AZERBAIJANI UNITS GO ON THE OFFENSIVE – Ayaz Mutalibov's Resignation Intensifies War

By staff correspondent Sergei Taranov. *Izvestia*, March 7, 1992, p. 1.

The most important event of the extraordinary session [of Azerbaijan's Supreme Soviet], working for the second day in a row without a break, was the resignation of republic President Ayaz Mutalibov. The first popularly elected head of the independent state, elected in September 1991, announced his resignation in an address to parliament on the evening of March 6.

Yesterday's issue of Izvestia quoted a statement by Mutalibov in which the President urged that the Karabakh problem be solved by political means. And he was not planning to resign. But at that very time, a rally that had started on Thursday was raging under the windows of the parliament building where the extraordinary session is being held. According to various figures, there were between 80,000 and 200,000 people demonstrating outside the Supreme Soviet building, demanding the resignation of the President and a military attack on Karabakh to avenge the numerous victims of Khodzhaly.

The opposition is not hiding the fact that if it comes to power, or if A. Mutalibov is at least replaced by a firmer and more uncompromising leader, new impetus will be given to the war in Nagorno-Karabakh....

It is no accident that the current extraordinary session of the Azerbaijani parliament began with a conflict between Deputies from the democratic bloc and the leaders of the Supreme Soviet. The ANI news agency reports that the democratic bloc proposed starting the parliament's discussion of the question of the Nagorno-

Karabakh Autonomous Province by showing a film on the seizure of the city of Khodzhaly by Armenians....

After [the film was shown], the ANI correspondent continues, the president of the republic addressed the meeting. A. Mutalibov acknowledged that he had made a number of mistakes. Specifically, he had not created a national army and had not signed an agreement on economic ties with Russia, and this had heightened tension in the region. The republic's failure to join the Commonwealth of Independent States was also a mistake, in his view. Although the [CIS] agreement was signed at the highest level, the President did not present it to parliament for ratification....

Nevertheless, until the very last minute, A. Mutalibov was not planning to resign. On the contrary, in his speech he accused the opposition of attempting to slander him personally. After that statement the crowd, which was still outside the building, blocked the entrances and exits and announced that no one would leave until Mutalibov resigned.

The Deputies and the President were in the Supreme Soviet building all night. Nevertheless, not until the President officially abdicated his post did it become definitively clear that he had been broken....

After accepting Ayaz Mutalibov's resignation, the republic parliament passed a law on the personal immunity of Azerbaijan's first president. He was given a 10,000-ruble pension, a personal automobile, a dacha and 10 guards.

The President's powers were transferred temporarily pending elections to Yagub Mamedov, Chairman of the republic Supreme Soviet.

Meanwhile, military actions are being stepped up, and thus the number of victims in Nagorno-Karabakh is growing....

TEN OFFICERS TAKEN HOSTAGE IN ARMENIA – Armed Forces Leadership Considers This a Dangerous Provocation

By staff correspondent Viktor Litovkin. *Izvestia*, March 11, 1992, p. 1.

The tragic events of the bloody war in the Caucasus have taken a new dramatic turn, involving a threat to the lives of innocent people: 10 officers of the CIS Army, who are citizens of four of its states – Russia, Ukraine, Kazakhstan and Kyrgyzstan.

On March 8 in the Armenian town of Artik (25 kilometers south of Kumairi, formerly Leninakan), extremists attacked an antiaircraft missile brigade and an antiaircraft technical support base. Armed with assault rifles, they blockaded the military installation and opened fire from inside of vehicles and from the roofs of buildings surrounding the military unit, presenting the antiaircraft gunners with an ultimatum: Lay down your weapons and open the stores of missiles and ammunition.

During the attack on the military unit, which lasted almost 10 hours [two servicemen were killed and two were wounded]....

Before this, the commanding officers of the antiaircraft missile brigade and technical support base were asked to come to the Artik City Soviet on the pretext of a meeting and were then taken hostage....

In exchange for the officers' lives, the militants demanded to be given 5,000 rockets for Grad (BM-21) rocket launchers, the same number of mortar shells for 120-millimeter mortars [and large quantities of other ammunition] within 24 hours, with the countdown to begin at noon on March 9....

Talks on March 10 between Maj. Gen. Fyodor Reut, commander of the 7th Yerevan Army, and Levon Ter-Petrosyan, President of the Republic of Armenia, did not, unfortunately, yield results. The President gave assurances that all measures would be taken to free the hostages, but on the morning of March 11 they were still in the hands of the terrorists....

Our correspondent in Yerevan, Sergei Bablumyan, reports that according to Ashot Manucharyan, the Armenian President's chief national security adviser, the unit was supposed to hand over its weapons to one of Karabakh's military formations – specifically, the "Getashen avengers."[2] The purpose was to rectify the imbalance in weapons. But the unit command violated the agreement. The Getashen avengers were fired upon.

The commanders of the Joint Armed Forces and the Transcaucasus Military District categorically deny the existence of any agreements with the militants. On the evening of March 10, Maj. Gen. of Aviation Nikolai Stolyarov, deputy commander in chief of the CIS Joint Armed Forces for work with personnel, held a press conference for Russian and foreign journalists at which he made a statement on behalf of the command of the Armed Forces.

"The military conflict in Nagorno-Karabakh," he said, "is developing into a dangerous international war. The warring parties should understand that this brings into effect all the protective norms of international law. In this case, the Armenian side has flagrantly violated [the Geneva Convention]...."

Gen. Stolyarov also declared that the Army is prepared, if necessary, to take any actions to protect its honor and dignity. Granted, he did not specify what actions. But depending on how one understands his words, such actions could range from meeting the terrorists' demands ("the lives of officers are dearer than any ammunition") to using weapons against the bandits ("we know the area in which they are hiding, and it will be blocked off").

The deputy commander in chief said that Russian Vice-President Aleksandr Rutskoi had telephoned the President of Armenia in his presence. They had a very strained conversation, in the course of which Levon Ter-Petrosyan once again gave assurances that he would do everything possible to free the officers, and the vice-President stated that our troops had to be withdrawn from the Transcaucasus without delay.

So, upon analyzing the situation briefly, one can draw an unequivocal conclusion. The war in the Transcaucasus has entered a new round of escalation. Militarized formations that do not intend to submit to the official authorities are, with particular insidiousness and refinement, doing everything in their power to exacerbate the situation to the utmost and draw the regular CIS Army into military actions. In the opinion of experts, they are doing this not to achieve military goals and gain victory in the fighting for Nagorno-Karabakh this is impossible by military means but in order to achieve, through these military actions, various objectives in the battle for political and state power.

On the night of March 10-11, the president of Armenia telephoned the command of the Transcaucasus Military District and reported that the hostages would be freed by the evening of March 11. There is no information on the terms of their release.

MOSCOW BETWEEN BAKU AND YEREVAN

By Valery Shuikov, Secretary of the Russian Supreme Soviet's Joint Committee on Defense and Security Questions. *Moskovskiye novosti*, April 12, 1992, p. 10.

... While until August 1991 the Union center unequivocally supported Azerbaijan, which made it possible to deport the residents of 24 Armenian villages in the Nagorno-Karabakh Autonomous Province and wipe the Armenian villages of Getashen and Martunashen from the face of the earth, today it is obvious that part of the Russian leadership has pro-Armenian sentiments. What else could explain the conclusion of a treaty of friendship and cooperation between Armenia and Russia at a time when there have not even been talks along those lines with Azerbaijan? Art. 3 of this treaty, which provoked the most controversy in the Russian parliament, essentially concerns military aid, a fact that prompted the parliament to set aside the treaty without approving it.

This thrashing about demonstrates the ill-considered and inconsistent nature of Russian doctrine in the Transcaucasus. First, the mere fact of concluding a unilateral treaty weakened Russia's already weak positions in Azerbaijan. Second, time has been irretrievably lost for negotiations with Azerbaijan on the fate of weapons and armed forces. Now they are being either uncontrollably misappropriated or "privatized" without Russia's agreement, at the same time as Russia itself is financing these forces, since formally they are part of the CIS Army. And, third and finally, one must not forget the fate of Russians in Azerbaijan, where the increase in anti-Russian sentiments after Khodzhaly and other losses in Nagorno-Karabakh is a fact that threatens to produce a stream of refugees and make the situation explode in Russia itself, since there is nowhere for its indigenous Moslem population to flee.

Not taking these circumstances into account means allowing the Karabakh tragedy to spread. At the time when Secretary of State Baker of the distant United States made the rounds of all the CIS states, the Russian Minister of Foreign Affairs had not been in a single one. And the point, I think, is not that prosperous Finland or exotic Africa is preferable. It is simply that an old Union syndrome – the imperial syndrome – is at work in the new Russian leadership. "These are our people; we'll get it all straightened out."

But the situation has changed fundamentally. The former Union republics have become the "near foreign countries." Meanwhile, the process of developing Russian foreign policy in this area is being delayed. And, it seems, is taking on the features of a crisis.

RUSSIAN DIPLOMACY'S DEBUT IN KARABAKH – The Foreign Minister Failed to Achieve Significant Results, but There Were 'Some Rays of Hope'

By staff correspondent Maksim Yusin. *Izvestia*, April 13, 1992, p. 7.

Shusha, Stepanakert, Baku, Yerevan and Moscow – Russian Foreign Affairs Minister Andrei Kozyrev reached Nagorno-Karabakh only on his second try. He was unable to visit Shusha and Stepanakert on April 5, because the helicopters waiting for him in Gyandzha couldn't take off due to bad weather. There is no other way to get to the zone of combat operations – the roads are mined.

But without a visit to Karabakh, the entire plan for the Russian minister's mediatory mission would have fallen through. So four days later, Kozyrev returned to Gyandzha.... The skies were clear. Kozyrev's eight-day tour through six CIS republics ended on a Karabakh note: Gyandzha, Shusha, Stepanakert, Gyandzha, Baku and Yerevan.

In talking with journalists on the plane on the way back to Moscow, contrary to his custom, the minister did not dwell in detail on either the course of the talks or the possible ways to reach a settlement: "This is a very complex and delicate process. A search for a peaceful solution is under way, and there were some rays of hope. But it is still too soon to make public the alternatives we discussed."

During his trip, Kozyrev met twice each with the leaders of Armenia and Azerbaijan, and in Shusha and Stepanakert he spoke with representatives of both ethnic communities in Karabakh. "The situation is very difficult. But I got the impression that confrontational logic has not taken over the minds of the two republics' leaders, and they are prepared to seek a sensible way out of the situation. And this inspires definite hopes," Kozyrev said, summing up the results of the trip.

But by no means everyone in the Russian delegation is so optimistic. In unofficial conversations, the diplomats admit that a peaceful solution of the Karabakh problem is still a very, very long way off. Kozyrev's talks in both Yerevan and Baku proceeded with difficulty. Armenia's leaders deny that their republic is participating in the conflict. The war, they maintain, is being waged between Azerbaijan and Karabakh's Armenians, so those are the two sides that should participate in peace talks.

Baku categorically rejects this alternative, preferring to do business with Yerevan rather than Stepanakert. Sitting down at the negotiating table with the Armenian leaders of Karabakh is unacceptable to the Azerbaijani leadership – it would mean recognizing their legitimacy. The Russian diplomats tried to find a way out of this impasse, but without success. The compromises that Kozyrev proposed (for example, to have representatives of the Armenian and Azerbaijani communities of Karabakh participate in the talks) were not rejected outright, but they weren't developed any further, either.

No specific agreements, even symbolic ones, were reached during the Russian minister's trip. And they couldn't have been. Kozyrev's visit came at a most unfavorable time – neither side is ready for talks. The military "arguments" have by no means been exhausted, and despite the peace-loving statements by the leaders of the two republics, intensive combat operations will, in all likelihood, continue for at least several more months.

The proposals for a ceasefire are evoking no particular enthusiasm among Karabakh's Armenians. In saying this, I do not in any way mean to depict them as the guilty party. War has its own laws and its own logic. And one can have no doubt that if the Azerbaijanis had the superiority that their opponent now has, they would not agree to a truce either. But at present the Armenians have the undisputed advantage. They are better armed, better equipped and more disciplined. This is not denied in Baku. "I'm surprised that the Armenians haven't yet seized all of Karabakh and our nearby towns," said a staff member of the Azerbaijani Ministry of Foreign Affairs.

The Azerbaijanis' explanation for their military failures is that the 366th regiment of the former Soviet Army, which was stationed in Karabakh, gave the Armenians combat equipment and participated on their side in decisive operations. There is no doubt in Baku that units of the 366th regiment under the command of Armenian officers played the main role in the Armenians' taking of Khodzhaly (the Azerbaijanis' most painful defeat since the beginning of the war). Civilians who fled Khodzhaly assured Kozyrev that they had seen Russian soldiers burst into the village. Army spokesmen categorically deny that the regiment participated in that operation. They say that all the military units had already been withdrawn from Karabakh.

But these arguments are not accepted in Azerbaijan. Anti-Army sentiments (though not anti-Russian ones as yet, fortunately) have gripped the republic....

Only Shusha and a few adjacent villages remain under the Azerbaijanis' control in Karabakh. The Armenians are firmly holding onto the initiative....

What are the Armenians counting on? In all likelihood, in the next few months they will strive to extend their military successes. "We have no other way out," says a detachment commander who met Kozyrev in Stepanakert. "The city doesn't have electricity, water or heat, and food is delivered only by air. We survived the winter with tremendous difficulty. We don't want another winter like that. If the Azerbaijanis don't lift the blockade (which is virtually impossible in the present situation – M. Yu.), we will break open a corridor to Armenia. Even if we lose 10,000 people in the process, the other 190,000 will be saved." The Karabakh deputies spoke in the same spirit during their meeting with Kozyrev.

People in Stepanakert reject even the mere thought of remaining a part of Azerbaijan: "That would be tantamount to a death sentence for our people. In a few months there wouldn't be a single Armenian left in Karabakh, just as there aren't any now in Nakhichevan."

Between Stepanakert and Armenia lies impregnable Shusha. It is located high atop a hill, from which Stepanakert can be seen very clearly (and very easily shot at). All the roads leading to the Armenian part of Karabakh have been mined. It would be extremely difficult to take Shusha by storm. Nevertheless, if hostilities continue, the Armenians will have no other way out.

Their strategic plan is obvious – to seize Shusha and then Lachin (an Azerbaijani district center lying between Shusha and the Armenian border), get across the narrow strip of Azerbaijani territory separating Karabakh from Armenia, and only after that, having broken through the blockade, either sit down at the negotiating table, demanding recognition of their independence, or continue the war but under more favorable conditions.

The Russian diplomats who participated in the talks did not deny that the Armenians are entertaining such a scenario and that they spoke to our minister about it. Speaking with journalists, Kozyrev called this alternative "a mistake and nearsighted": "It's naive to suppose that the other side will sit around doing nothing and watch Shusha be seized. Azerbaijan will create its own army. A new spiral of confrontation will begin, and there will be a war of annihilation. It can't be ruled out that an international coalition will be created to oppose Armenia. I think that realistic politicians in Baku and Yerevan realize the danger of such a development of events."...

The only thing that is within our power is to prevent the formation of the coalition whose possible creation the minister spoke of.

At present its emergence seems unlikely. Both Turkey and Iran, which could potentially be allies of Azerbaijan, are behaving with great restraint. Ankara doesn't want to complicate its already difficult relations with the European Community, and therefore is confining itself to symbolic gestures of solidarity with Baku. Tehran fears an outburst of Azerbaijani separatism in the northern regions of the country.

Azerbaijan bitterly realizes that the republic has no reliable allies at this critical moment. That is why it is reacting so sensitively to pro-Armenian sympathies in Russia.

The most important things that Russian diplomacy can do today to reduce the tension are, first of all, to prevent weapons from the CIS republics from getting into the conflict zone, and second, to prevent our two armies – the Fourth and the Seventh, based in Azerbaijan and Armenia, respectively – from being drawn into the hostilities. Both Mamedov and Ter-Petrosyan asked Kozyrev to do this.

Despite the lack of concrete results from Kozyrev's trip, Moscow does not intend to abandon its mediatory efforts. The emergence of a permanent hotbed of tension on our southern borders is not in Russia's geopolitical interests. Unfortunately, things are heading in precisely that direction. The Armenian-Azerbaijani conflict threatens to become a protracted one.

The Azerbaijanis hope that, over time, their human and economic resources will nullify the Armenians' military superiority, and the tight blockade will stifle the neighboring republic's economy. But for now the warring sides' main argument is still force....

THE RETURN OF AYAZ MUTALIBOV

By staff correspondent Georgy Ivanov-Smolensky. *Izvestia*, May 15, 1992, p. 1.

A sensational report came in from Baku on May 14: At an emergency session, the Azerbaijani parliament rescinded its previous decision regarding the resignation of President Ayaz Mutalibov. The parliament also decided to cancel the presidential elections scheduled for June 7.

As will be recalled, Mutalibov resigned under pressure from radically minded supporters of the Azerbaijan People's Front after they blockaded the parliament building. However, it became clear very soon that forced retirement did not suit Mutalibov. The closer it came to the time of the presidential elections, the more often he was heard to make statements about the forcible and unjust nature of his resignation.

Immediately after he was reinstated in his post, Mutalibov's actions proved to be just as decisive as the statements that preceded them. As the first order of business, Internal Affairs Minister Takhir Aliyev, a supporter of the People's Front, was removed from his post. President Mutalibov issued a decree imposing a state of emergency in Baku for two months. It places restrictions on the movement of transportation, bans rallies and strikes, introduces prior censorship and suspends the activity of public organizations that are preventing stabilization of the situation. By an overwhelming majority vote, the parliament also decided to disband the present National Council – the standing legislative body – in which 25 of the 50 members represented the opposition. (Representatives of the People's Front did not take part in the session.)

According to news agency reports, the situation in Baku is calm, on the whole. However, the leaders of the People's Front have unambiguously assessed what has happened as a "coup," have urged their supporters to engage in acts of civil disobedience, and have declared that "they will wage a struggle until a victorious end." They also claim that they control the airport and a number of other important points in the capital. In light of the statements about "the possibility of civil war in Azerbaijan" that were made by People's Front leaders right on the eve of the emergency session, the situation in the republic does not seem stable.

Unquestionably, the factors that set off the parliament's decision were the approaching presidential elections and the not unwarranted predictions that People's Front leader Elchin [elsewhere referred to as Elchibei – *Trans.*] was likely to win them, which would have legitimized the shift of power in the republic to the opposition. However, in addition to the logic of political struggle, Mutalibov's return also involves the elementary logic of life. The main problem destabilizing Azerbaijani society-the Karabakh problem-not only has not moved any closer to resolution (and this is what was held against Mutalibov), it has grown significantly worse. Defeats on the Armenian-Azerbaijani fronts have become increasingly palpable. But no matter how radical Azerbaijani politicians interpret the combat failures and no matter how they urge their fellow citizens to give "everything for the front, everything for victory," the ravaged post-Communist republic cannot help but gravitate toward stability. It seems that Ayaz Mutalibov is perceived as a figure capable of at least not aggravating the instability and of pursuing a well-considered policy.

KURDISTAN: THE MYSTERY OF LACHIN

By Suleiman Ali, Syrian journalist. *Moskovskiye novosti*, June 7, 1992, p. 9.

After the Armenians' taking of Lachin [in a May offensive] and the opening of a seven-kilometer corridor between Karabakh and Armenia, another event remained in the background: More than 7,500 Kurds disappeared from Lachin and the surrounding area without a trace....

The town has been empty for two weeks now. On its streets there are traces of fires, roofs pierced by shells, and the stench of decomposing animal carcasses, but not a living soul....

"Don't think that we chased the Kurds out of here," Paruir Airikyan, a human rights advocate who is well known in Armenia and with whom I went to Lachin, said to me. "They left on their own. If they want to, they can return."...

The tragedy of the Kurds is that they are caught between a rock and a hard place – between the Armenians and the Azerbaijanis. Each side is trying to use the Kurds in its own interests. The Armenians support aspirations to restore the "red Kurdistan" that existed from 1923 to 1930, since that would be advantageous to them: It would mean continued surveillance over the "corridor" to Karabakh, which will inevitably close if the Azerbaijanis come back.

"We must prepare for victory," believes Uakil Mustafayev, vice-chairman of a Kurdish organization called Yakbun. "We are now gathering volunteers from nine CIS republics to win back the rest of our land – Kelbadzhar, Zangelan, Kobetlya – from the Azerbaijanis and to restore a Kurdish state."

However, Yakbun leader Mukhammed Babayev has flatly refused to lead this movement. He told me that the Azerbaijanis and Kurds are brothers. And he will do everything to avoid bloodshed.

These two mutually exclusive views are evidence of a split within the Kurdish movement. And therefore the "mystery" of Lachin is advantageous to everyone. Both to the Azerbaijanis, who hope to use the Kurds in their fight against the Armenians, and to the Armenians, who are willing to settle absolutely anyone except "Turks" in the empty town....

Although the Azerbaijanis are considered brothers, the Kurds are hiding from them in villages and in the mountains so as not to fight against the Armenians....

The Armenians have suggested to the Yezidi Kurds[3] that they resettle Kurds from Kazakhstan and Central Asia in Lachin....

After the Stalinist destruction of "red Kurdistan," a people numbering almost a million was scattered throughout many republics of the Soviet Union. Now Armenia is proposing a compromise – autonomy in exchange for loyalty with respect to the "Karabakh corridor." The style of any victor is "divide and conquer." This is precisely how Azerbaijan acted in 1990 in expelling the Armenians from Karabakh. The long-suffering settlement of Khodzhaly, in which Azerbaijani refugees from Armenia and Meskhetian Turks from Uzbekistan were settled, was founded at that time. Finding themselves in the role of victor, the Armenians are offering the same fate to the Kurds.

"We have no other way out," Uakil Mustafayev believes. "I've been to Karabakh; they don't mind if the first volunteers from Kazakhstan and Uzbekistan move to Lachin. For us this is a chance not to be lost as a people."...

AZERBAIJAN: PEACE, BUT STILL WAR

By staff correspondents Georgy Ivanov-Smolensky and Vasif Samedov. *Izvestia*, June 10, 1992, p. 3.

Baku and Moscow – ... In Baku, one can frequently hear it said that the new authorities won't last for more than a few months, since reports about their stable and firm "nationwide support" have been greatly exaggerated. It is also being said that the Communists, who had quieted down for a while, have not yet said their last word. Finally, since the People's Front came to power a new opposition has appeared – the influential Party of National Independence. Its radically minded leader, Ekhtibar Mamedov, one of the founders of the Azerbaijan People's Front, enjoys appreciable support in Turkey and, even more important, is coordinating his political efforts more and more closely with Nakhichevan.

The leaders of the APF themselves are optimistic, however. From all outward indications, the position of the People's Front today is indeed more than stable. Whereas previously its social base was active and energetic but not broad enough – refugees and other unfortunate people, some students and an even smaller part of the scholarly intelligentsia – since May 15 this base has grown stronger and broader. Some people have joined it after once again seeing for themselves the APF's determination to achieve its aims in any situation, and others (for example, some of the nomenklatura) have joined out of a sense of self-preservation.

"Our goal," Abulfaz Elchibei told us the day after the election, "is to build an independent, unified and democratic state in which the rights of all citizens, regardless of their religion and nationality, would be observed. In order to achieve this, we will seek to quickly reform our legislation, above all to adopt a new Constitution for sovereign Azerbaijan. It will codify the separation of powers and a mechanism for society to exercise real control over the authorities. A paralysis of power is obvious in the republic today. Therefore, we will have to urgently erect a new edifice of state organization and administration. Finally, we will seek as quickly as possible to create a mixed economy, to begin small-scale privatization, and to bring in foreign investments. However, the most important condition for all this is an acceptable solution of the Karabakh problem."

Well, this program is in fact what has attracted numerous supporters and sympathizers to the People's Front. The whole question is: Are these problems solvable in the foreseeable future? And what are the limits of the time and trust that citizens have given to the APF? ...

The loss of control over Karabakh and the surrender of Shusha and Lachin are painful to people and are having a depressing effect on the mood of society. Every day, hundreds of refugees from border districts reinforce the army of the unemployed and the homeless, of people driven to extremes. You won't meet a person here who doesn't assess what is happening as "aggression by Armenia." Nor is there a person in the republic who doubts that "sooner or later, Karabakh will be returned at any cost." People are waiting for this impatiently, almost fanatically. Karabakh has strained everyone's nerves.

A total of 56 Azerbaijani villages in Karabakh have been destroyed. (For the sake of fairness, let us note that just as many Armenian villages have suffered the same fate; in May 1991 alone, Armenians were evicted from 26 villages at once.) In the past few months, the 200,000 refugees from Armenia have been augmented by another 100,000 from Karabakh, Lachin, Shusha and border districts. (It's true that before the conflict began 500,000 Armenians lived in Azerbaijan, but now there are only 20,000 to 30,000 left, mainly partners in mixed marriages.) Ragim Guseinov, Azerbaijan Minister of Public Health, showed us a report: There are almost 800 wounded people in the republic's hospitals today, of whom only 160 are military personnel; the rest are civilians. All told, more than 3,000 people have died. (About 1,500 Armenians have died during the "conflict.")...

Normal people on both sides agree that things cannot go on like this. The trouble is that everyone has his own view of the conditions for normalization.

"The condition for beginning talks," parliament Chairman Isa Gambarov told us, setting forth Azerbaijan's position, "should be the withdrawal of all troops from our territory and the disarming of all illegal military formations on that territory. Otherwise, the Armenian side will conduct the talks from a position of strength. We will seek to achieve this with the help of the world community's condemnation of Armenia as the aggressor and the application of whatever sanctions are stipulated against it. If this doesn't work, we will be forced to make every effort to reestablish the borders militarily. The return of Azerbaijanis to areas of Armenia where they have lived in concentrated groups and the granting to them of the same status held by the Armenians in Karabakh would be a guarantee of the observance of the

Armenians' rights in Karabakh and their safety on Azerbaijani territory. That is, the achievement of a mirror-image situation. However, I don't think we will be able to achieve this any time soon."

The last proviso set by the leader of the Azerbaijani parliament is symptomatic. Because there is also the position of the second belligerent. It was explained to us in Moscow by Armenia's permanent representative, Feliks Mamikonyan:

"We are in favor of putting down the assault rifles right now and sitting down at the negotiating table. But to achieve a mirror-image situation would mean a start on returning 200,000 Armenians to Baku, where, after all, their apartments have been occupied by others for some time. Beginning talks not simply with a cease-fire but with a return to the starting line is unacceptable to the Armenians. They accounted for 75% of the population of Karabakh. For the past four years they lived under a blockade, which became increasingly harsher day by day. But now, when the blockade has been broken at the cost of hundreds of casualties and endless suffering, the Azerbaijanis want to propose to these people that they voluntarily return to it. On Azerbaijan's word of honor, without 100% guarantees and without a real mechanism for securing their safety and rights. The Armenians don't need Lachin; they will leave tomorrow, but let some international third force guarantee the unhindered delivery of civilian cargo to Nagorno-Karabakh."

Those are the positions, the points of departure. They are incompatible and irreconcilable. We don't want to assess them. We will only note that it will be extremely difficult for the new President and the People's Front to find a way out of the Karabakh impasse, especially given the current economic situation.

Either war or the economy

Here are some figures provided to us by Doctor of Economics Gorkhmaz Imanov, Director of the Azerbaijan State Planning Committee's Institute of Economics. One-third of the republic's territory today (one-fourth, according to another source) has now been affected by military operations, with varying degrees of intensity. Because of this, Azerbaijan has lost 34% of the land sown to wheat, 32% of the land sown to cotton, 72% of its vineyards and 39% of its mulberry trees; the Azerbaijanis used to receive 34% of their meat and 39% of their dairy products from the land that has been lost. Imanov's conclusion is that "it is impossible for Azerbaijan to change over to a market under wartime conditions."

On what can we place our hopes?

On the fact that in the Soviet Union Azerbaijan was one of three republics, along with Russia and Belarus, in which intra-Union exports exceeded imports. Annual amounts of 600,000 tons of raw cotton, 25,000 tons of aluminum and 12 million tons of petroleum – today these are the new politicians' trump cards in the struggle for a truly independent Azerbaijan. But serious economists believe that if they are trump cards, they are sixes and sevens up the politicians' sleeves rather than aces in the hands of the economic managers.

For instance, no more than 50% of Azerbaijan's petroleum undergoes refining there, whereas the figure reaches 80% to 85% elsewhere in the world. The average age of fixed production assets is 25 years, and they cannot reach world standards in cotton processing, in aluminum smelting or even in large-scale winemaking....

So, there is a vicious circle: The state of the economy is making it difficult to stabilize the political situation, but unless the war is ended the economy cannot be put on its feet. This is aggravated by the fact that the People's Front, which in its struggle has spoken out against "the diktat of Moscow" and for liberation from dependence on the "empire," must stick to logic – it must distance itself from the CIS countries, to a certain extent. However, Russia alone accounts for almost 55% of Azerbaijan's imports. According to economists' estimates, Azerbaijan's economy can achieve an adequate degree of autonomy in five to 10 years, at a minimum. That is, if two basic conditions are met: The war ends, and the greatest possible economic pragmatism is employed.

But what kind of State Planning Committee will give the new authorities even one calm five-year period?

On the whole, today everything is still shaping up in favor of the People's Front and its leader, as it is for the other democrats. There is one factor that may force adjustments: the war. For this reason, time periods have been compressed. Everything is happening more quickly and will continue to do so.

NAGORNO-KARABAKH

Nezavisimaya gazeta, June 11, 1992, p. 3.

As expected, the coming to power of the Azerbaijan People's Front in Baku has exacerbated the Azerbaijani-Armenian discord even more.

On its "Morning" [Utro] radio program a few days ago, Radio Baku urged that a holy war (jihad) be declared at the state level against the "Armenian infidels."

In the past few days, there has been an increase in the activity of the Azerbaijani Army along the entire perimeter of the Nagorno-Karabakh Republic. Azerbaijani troops have actively shelled the district center of Martuni, as well as border villages in Mardakert and Shaumyanovsk Districts. Despite this, peaceful life is being restored in Stepanakert and Shusha.

Meanwhile, on the evening and night of June 9 and the morning of June 10, the situation on the northern section of the Armenian-Azerbaijani border worsened drastically; the Azerbaijani side subjected Armenian border villages in Armenia's Idzhevan, Noyemberyan and Taush Districts to intensive shelling. – (NEGA)

GEIDAR ALIYEV: 'NO ONE WILL SUCCEED IN PUTTING PRESSURE ON ME'

By staff correspondent Aleksandra Lugovskaya. *Izvestia*, June 27, 1992, p. 3.

Nakhichevan and Moscow – On his return from a trip to Turkey, Geidar Aliyev repeated in a telephone conversation what he had told me earlier in Nakhichevan on the eve of the presidential election: "These matters have nothing to do with us. I do not want to interfere in them, since I am occupied with the problems of Nakhichevan. I am not personally acquainted with [Azerbaijan's new President] Elchibei, there has been no contact between us, but naturally, I recognize him as the president elected by the people."

Meanwhile, the problems of Nakhichevan itself are becoming more and more acute.

"The shelling continues," Aliyev told me two days ago, "and there are dead and wounded every day.... The railroad that runs from Azerbaijan through Armenia has not been operating for two months, and it is expensive and dangerous to bring food here from Baku by airplane. Nakhichevan is essentially under a blockade, food and fuel reserves are at zero."

However, the future course of events in this region depends to a great extent on Geidar Aliyev himself. Returning after 50 years to his native Nakhichevan and becoming head of the autonomous republic's parliament, the Ali Majlis, he has been able in less than a year to show that it is too soon to write him off as a figure in big-time politics. But now, standing on the verge of war, the autonomous republic and its leader will need to do some high-class political aerobatics to keep the constant border clashes from attaining the critical mass of a military avalanche.

This will depend on several factors. First of all, on successful control over unlawful armed groups within the republic, which are potentially capable of provoking conflict and reducing the efforts of the upper political echelons to naught. The second condition is the immutability of a course aimed at a process of negotiation with the leadership of Armenia and a joint search for a way to end the hostilities.

The third factor is the normalization of relations between Nakhichevan itself and Baku. Let me remind you that the autonomous republic simply boycotted Mutalibov's election, for reasons that included his personal confrontation with Aliyev, and that during his tenure as president the republic behaved very coldly and independently toward greater Azerbaijan, letting it be known that it itself had all the attributes of statehood – its own Constitution, parliament and government. But even the recent changes on the presidential Olympus drew a more than restrained comment from Aliyev: "We'll wait and see." ...

Diplomatic missions, including ones from neighboring Iran, have been appearing in Aliyev's office with increasing frequency, and ties with Turkey are referred to here as fraternal. Prime Minister S. Demirel [of Turkey], who paid a short visit in May, said unequivocally in an Izvestia interview that "without the permission of Turkey, which considers itself a guarantor of Nakhichevan's integrity, no one will be able to change Nakhichevan's status." ...

I asked Aliyev the following question after he spoke with Yerevan:

Question. – What forces in Nakhichevan don't want the conflict [with Armenia] to end?

Answer. – There is one circumstance that worries me: the fact that our People's Front, a political organization, possesses armed formations. They are participating in the conflict between Armenia and Nakhichevan, and participating ineptly.... As for ending the conflict, I have been holding constant negotiations with the leadership of Armenia, which every time reaffirms its desire to stop all this, but Armenia too has people who do not carry out orders. All the same, I think that through joint action we will stop them.

Q. – As far as I know, you have normal relations with President Ter-Petrosyan.

A. – We have never met personally, but we immediately established businesslike telephone contacts.... I would like our contacts to continue, in the name of ensuring peace and tranquility on the border between Armenia and the Nakhichevan Republic.

Q. – Your attitude toward the Karabakh conflict?

A. – ... Nagorno-Karabakh is Azerbaijani territory, and no one will succeed in changing its borders by force. And the sooner the leadership of Armenia understands this and the leadership of Azerbaijan finds a realistic solution, the easier it will be for both our peoples....

Q. – Are you blocked from participation in the political life of all of Azerbaijan?

A. – In many respects, yes. According to my information, the Azerbaijan Supreme Soviet received hundreds of thousands of letters demanding that Aliyev become head of the republic. But there is a tightly interlinked ruling stratum that was unwilling to put power into someone else's hands.

Q. – How do you regard the new president, Elchibei, and the People's Front leaders who have come to power?

A. – I am not going to answer that question. The election results will not change my position here, or Nakhichevan's position, either. No one can put pressure on me.

Q. – Won't it end up that owing to the difficult situation, Nakhichevan will join neighboring Turkey?

A. – No, we are Azerbaijani land and will not break away from Azerbaijan.

Q. – What has dictated the noticeable stepping up of Nakhichevan's relations with Iran?

A. – We have a long common border and long-standing historical ties. Tehran, incidentally, is South Azerbaijan. The very requirement of being civilized dictates equal treatment of all states, particularly neighbors. I think that a time will come when everything will be set right between Azerbaijan and Armenia, too.

Q. – All the same, how do you see your own political future in Azerbaijan?

A. – I have never thought about my own political future: What happens, happens. The most important thing right now is to stop the shooting on the border with Armenia and to establish normal relations. But at the same time, I am also busy with economic problems we have declared the autonomous republic to be a free economic zone and now want to introduce market principles into its life and its economy....

* * *

The large-scale combat operations in Nagorno-Karabakh leave almost no chance for a political and diplomatic settlement of the military conflict. It is obvious that both for Armenia and, particularly, for Azerbaijan, this is fraught with the possibility of internal destabilization. In the event of military failures and large numbers of casualties, the new Azerbaijani President's stock will begin to fall quickly, unlike that of his political opponents, including such strong opponents as Geidar Aliyev.

ARMENIA: CONFLICT OVER KARABAKH BETWEEN PRESIDENT AND OPPOSITION REACHES CULMINATION

By Armen Khanbabyan. *Nezavisimaya gazeta*, July 1, 1992, p. 1.

Armenian President Levon Ter-Petrosyan spoke on the republic's national television on June 29. We believe, he said, that our only significant achievement on the path to independence has been the establishment of stable governmental authority. All our successes in Nagorno-Karabakh have stemmed primarily from this. But today, as a result of the activities of the opposition, which seeks to draw Armenia into war, that stability is in jeopardy. The authorities, by contrast, want a peaceful settlement of the crisis, on the condition that Nagorno-Karabakh's defense is ensured....

On June 28 the president spoke with Georgy Petrosyan, acting chairman of the Nagorno-Karabakh Republic Supreme Soviet, and told him that because of that republic's refusal to participate in talks, not just Nagorno-Karabakh but all of Armenia is in jeopardy. However, Ter-Petrosyan stressed [in his televised speech], the basic problem is that the decision on whether or not the Nagorno-Karabakh authorities should go to the Rome meeting[4] is being made not by those authorities themselves but by the Dashnaktsutyun Party (of which Georgy Petrosyan is a representative), headed by a bureau in Athens that is directed by Grair Marukhyan. The party has large financial resources, the president said. It has collected $5 million for weapons for Nagorno-Karabakh. However, only $40,000 has been spent on 230 Kalashnikov assault rifles. The rest of the money has been used to create party structures inside Armenia, to set up a party press and to hire activists. Ter-Petrosyan reported that Deputies to the Armenian Supreme Soviet from the Dashnaktsutyun Party receive $300 a month, and people are paid between $20 and $30 to join the party.

The Armenian president made a sensational statement, accusing the Dashnak-tsutyun leadership of resorting to the help of foreign intelligence services in its struggle for power. In February 1988, when the Communist leadership decided to create a counterweight to the Karabakh movement, Grair Marukhyan, the head of Dashnaktsutyun's Athens bureau, came to Armenia illegally with the knowledge and approval of Vladimir Kryuchkov, then chairman of the USSR State Security Committee [KGB]. The Dashnaktsutyun bureau and the USSR KGB concluded an agreement on combating the Karabakh movement.

Dashnaktsutyun is directed and financed from abroad, and it has its own armed detachments and primary organizations at enterprises, which is against the law. Grair Marukhyan is already distributing ministerial portfolios to members of his team, saying that the Armenian government has been virtually toppled. I have signed a decree ordering this citizen of Greece to leave the country within 48 hours, Levon Ter-Petrosyan declared. If the things I have said about him are untrue, the President stressed, let him take me to court, and then I'll produce the necessary evidence.

The president officially proposed that a referendum be held on the question of confidence in the parliament. He has decided to resign if the referendum fails....

* * *

(By Liana Minasyan) – ... Up until now, the battle between the authorities and their opponents has been waged in the parliament and on the adjacent squares, where the republic's ruling party and other parties have taken turns gathering their supporters for public debates. This was quite sufficient to allow the expression of political passions, but since the destruction of Karabakh's Shaumyanovsk District, the opposition has gained the opportunity not only to "trample on" the President and his team but to seize the political initiative from them, and with it, power....

Dashnaktsutyun has always considered itself and has always been not so much a party of Armenia as a party of the Armenian nation. This may stem from the fact that the party has spent most of its 102-year history outside its home country and has created its most influential structures in the diaspora, and that in Armenia, in the opinion of politicians who do not sympathize with it, "it hasn't felt at home." It has always been a state within a state, or rather, a state without a state – with its own military detachments and subsidiary youth and cultural organizations. It officially returned to Armenia only after the change in power, after it was "all right" to do so. But by that time, virtually all positions at the helm were already occupied, and the party with such all-embracing pretensions found itself one of many.

But in Karabakh, war was raging, and this party that espouses the ideology of an armed national-liberation struggle found quite a few supporters. It is officially in power there right now, considering that Georgy Petrosyan, the acting head of the Nagorno-Karabakh parliament, serves simultaneously as Dashnaktsutyun's official representative in Karabakh....

With the intensification of the conflict in Artsakh [i.e., Karabakh – *Trans.*], the difference between Stepanakert's and Yerevan's approaches to the problem and the fact that different political forces are in power in the two capitals – a circumstance that, in the opinion of many Yerevan politicians, has made it impossible for the two leaders to subordinate themselves to any common goal – is no longer just one of the conditions governing the political game. The stakes in Yerevan have proved too great, and Dashnaktsutyun has decided to play for keeps....

NAGORNO-KARABAKH: ARMENIAN TROOPS OCCUPY KELBADZHAR –
UN Security Council Will Discuss the Situation
By Aidyn Mekhtiyev. *Nezavisimaya gazeta*, April 6, 1993, p. 4.

As the result of a broad-scale offensive, Armenian armed formations have taken complete control of a large part of Kelbadzhar District, which is in western Azerbaijan, adjacent to Nagorno-Karabakh. On April 2, Armenian troops occupied the district center, Kelbadzhar, and opened a second corridor from Armenia to Nagorno-Karabakh. As we know, the first corridor was opened back in May 1992, through Lachin District. In comparison with the Lachin corridor, the new one shortens the route from Yerevan to the northern districts of Karabakh by almost 200 km, and this will make it possible to increase deliveries of weapons and heavy equipment from Armenia to Karabakh. Armenian forces launched the present offensive from two directions – from Vardenis District of Armenia and from Agdara District of Karabakh. They were able to block the Kelbadzhar-Lachin road and surround the Lachin grouping of the Azerbaijani Army. It was possible to evacuate only about 40,000 of Kelbadzhar District's population of 60,000. The threat of physical annihilation hangs over the remaining residents. Azerbaijan's President Abulfaz Elchibei asked the government of Turkey to send several helicopters to the disaster area for the immediate evacuation of residents. In response, Erdal Inonu, Deputy Prime Minister of the Turkish government, said that it would be very difficult to fulfill this request in view of the absence of a common border between Azerbaijan and Turkey. Meanwhile, according to Azerbaijani sources, more than 100 Azerbaijani residents have been killed in Kelbadzhar District in the past few days, including women and children. After taking Kelbadzhar, the Armenian troops launched an offensive in the northern part of the Karabakh zone in the direction of the district center of Fizuli. Encountering no special resistance, they came close to the district center on April 4....

By decree of President Elchibei, a two-month state of emergency throughout Azerbaijan was declared on April 3. This document, which was confirmed by the National Assembly, gives broad powers to the State Defense Committee. Maj. Gen. Abdulla Allakhverdiyev, Chief of the Baku City Police Administration, has been appointed military commandant of the city. The Presidium of the Supreme Majlis of the ruling [Azerbaijan] People's Front (APF) has issued an order that suspends the political activity of the APF's regional divisions and points out the need for declaring general mobilization in the country....

THE KARABAKH PROBLEM HAS FINALLY BEEN INTERNATIONALIZED – At the
Diplomatic Level, for the Time Being
By Aidyn Mekhtiyev. *Nezavisimaya gazeta*, April 8, 1993, p. 1.

Azerbaijan – According to the Azerbaijan Ministry of Defense, fierce fighting has continued in Kelbadzhar and Fizuli Districts of the republic in the past 24 hours (April 6-7). Since taking Kelbadzhar, Armenian troops have been continuing their offensive deep into communities in western Azerbaijan....

Heavy shelling of Kubatly District, in the southwestern part of the republic, has begun from Goris District of Armenia. Events in the southeast are developing dramatically: Armenian troops are attacking the district center of Fizuli and have managed to seize four of the six hills overlooking the district center, from which rocket shelling of Fizuli has begun. The city has sustained significant destruction and casualties. Fortunately, it was possible to evacuate a large part of the city's population (about 10,000 people).

The Armenian forces' offensive against Fizuli has created a threat to the security of Iran's borders: Fighting is going on only 200 km from the Azerbaijani-Iranian border. An NG correspondent has learned from reliable sources that, by order of the Iranian military command, two Iranian regiments have been put into a state of heightened combat readiness and redeployed to the border with Azerbaijan. Tehran has made it unambiguously clear to the Azerbaijani leadership that if Iran is called upon for help the Iranian government is prepared to take very resolute actions to protect the territorial integrity of Azerbaijan. An April 6 commentary on Radio Tehran, which reflects the viewpoint of the Iranian government, sharply condemned Armenia's actions. "The Armenian troops' actions, for which there can be no justification, create a threat not only to the territorial integrity of Azerbaijan but also to the entire Caucasus and neighboring states," the commentary notes.

However, President Elchibei's administration has not yet attached any significance to Tehran's transparent hints about possible intervention in the conflict. Moreover, it has been learned that during all the preceding days of the Armenian offensive Abulfaz Elchibei did not try even once to get in touch with Iran's President Rafsanjani by telephone, and all contacts between Baku and Tehran took place through Iran's Ambassador to Baku, Nakhvendiani. At the same time, a sharply negative reaction was produced in Tehran by the fact that on April 6 Elchibei asked for help from Israel, toward which Iran has a very hostile attitude. The Azerbaijani President's press service announced that Elchibei, in a telephone conversation with Israel's Prime Minister Yitzhak Rabin, asked Tel Aviv to provide Azerbaijan with diplomatic support. However, the Israeli government has so far refrained from openly condemning Armenia's actions.

Meanwhile, Turkey has toughened its position toward Armenia. Back on April 4, Turkish officials rejected the possibility of open military intervention by Turkey in the Armenia-Azerbaijan conflict. However, the statements made on April 6 by Prime Minister Demirel and Turkey's UN representative Aksin leave no doubt that this time Ankara will hardly be able to confine itself to diplomatic steps alone. Speaking on April 6 at a meeting of the True Path Party's parliamentary group, Demirel said that ... "Turkey is prepared to make any sacrifice" to help Azerbaijan. Mustafa Aksin, Turkey's permanent representative to the UN, made a statement in New York that was even harsher in tone. He recalled that, according to Art. 51 of the

UN Charter, Azerbaijan has the right to collective defense to rebuff the Armenian aggression. Most likely, what he meant by collective defense is the participation of Turkish troops on the side of Azerbaijan. "The Turkish government will take every measure, up to and including military measures, to repulse the Armenian aggression," Aksin said. However, this statement did not affect the UN Security Council's subsequent decision. The UN Security Council rejected a draft resolution, proposed by Turkey, that condemned Armenia's aggression against Azerbaijan. Without naming either side as the aggressor, the Security Council called upon them to stop military operations immediately. UN Secretary-General Boutros-Ghali was instructed to present a report on the situation in the region.

The likelihood that Iran and Turkey will be drawn into the Armenia-Azerbaijan conflict has caused serious concern in the command of the CIS Joint Armed Forces. Marshal Yevgeny Shaposhnikov, Commander in Chief of the CIS Joint Armed Forces, without condemning Armenia's occupation of Kelbadzhar, has proposed that a meeting of representatives of Azerbaijan's and Armenia's defense agencies be held in southern Russia under the good offices of the CIS Joint Armed Forces.

TESTIMONY: KARABAKH CALL-UP

By Vladimir Yemelyanenko. *Moskovskiye novosti*, April 18, 1993, p. A3.

Baku and Khanlar – ... [In Baku] roundups at railway terminals, marketplaces and right on the street have begun – it's called mobilization. I myself got involved in a roundup. My 23-year-old escort, the airport employee Nakhim K. (he asked me not to give his last name), was threatened with being forcibly sent to the front. They wanted to push him into a bus, where five frightened youths were already sitting. His argument about the strategic importance of the airport worked, and they let Nakhim go, after writing out call-up papers for the military registration and enlistment office. He assured me: "I'm not taking one more step into the city."

Even though after the furor at the Technical University, where students were taken for the front right from the lecture halls, President Elchibei banned this kind of "call-up," the police are continuing to act on their own. The additional powers that the Ministry of Internal Affairs has received have turned into another source of income. The going rate for exemption from call-up is well known – from 150,000 to 400,000 rubles, depending on how well off the parents are.

The main source of "cannon fodder" is Azerbaijanis who fled Armenia some time earlier. The fact that they have no connections and, as a rule, no jobs makes it impossible for them to avoid the "mobilization."

The downfall of many Azerbaijani politicians is linked with defeats in Karabakh: the Communist Vezirov; Mutalibov, Azerbaijan's first president; Yagub Mamedov, chairman of parliament; and Mutalibov again.

Finally, the People's Front, which took the republic out of the CIS, became firmly established in power. But the defeat outside Kelbadzhar could have put an end to Elchibei's career. Especially since dissatisfaction with the National Democrats, who had promised to end the war with Armenia, begin privatization and introduce private ownership, has reached a peak. Instead of what was promised, there have only been price increases and reprisals against political adversaries.

But the unexpected happened. After the latest news from the Karabakh front, the opposition canceled its planned rallies, and its real leader, Geidar Aliyev, called on people to "rally around the President." Even the radical Etibar Mamedov, the leader of the Party of National Independence, who had accused the Azerbaijan People's Front and Abulfaz Elchibei of betraying national interests, agreed that differences must be temporarily put aside. This is the reason for the calm in the streets and the wrought-up patriotic sentiments in Baku.

They have proved to be so strong that the formation of women's battalions to be sent to the front has begun, as has the creation of brigades of journalists" – for boosting morale."...

Day and night, Baku TV is showing military-patriotic films – "No Way Back" [Obratnoi dorogi net], "The Old Gun" [Staroye ruzhyo], "Chapayev" and "Rambo." "Rambo" gets especially frequent showings....

GEIDAR ALIYEV URGES THAT THE THREAT OF CIVIL WAR BE ELIMINATED

By Sokhbet Mamedov. *Izvestia*, June 15, 1993, p. 1.

Baku and Gyandzha – The talks between Surat Guseinov – the "rebel colonel," as the authorities call him – and Geidar Aliyev, head of the Nakhichevan parliament, went on, behind closed doors, for virtually all of Sunday night. Aliyev had arrived in Gyandzha Sunday evening on a peacemaking mission. The day before, a rally was held there at which demands were voiced once again that the Azerbaijani leadership, including the President, resign and an emergency session of the republic Supreme Soviet be convened....

The 34-year-old Surat Guseinov is not a military man. Before the Karabakh events began, he was the director of the Yevlakh Woolen Mill. During the period that the Armenian-Azerbaijani conflict was getting under way, he took an active part in providing supplies to the newly created national army. Surat Guseinov's services did not go unnoticed, and last year, by a decree of President Elchibei, he was assigned several duties simultaneously. He became the President's authorized representative in Nagorno-Karabakh, Deputy Prime Minister of Azerbaijan and commander of the corps that last summer liberated Geranboi and Agdera Districts of Upper Karabakh. The republic's highest award National Hero of Azerbaijan was conferred on Surat Guseinov for this operation. He was also given the military title of colonel. According to some military experts, Col. Guseinov showed outstanding abilities in military affairs. The corps commander's prestige increased day by day.

From all indications, this was the reason for the emergence of certain frictions in his relations with the leadership of the republic Ministry of Defense.

The final brick in the wall of this confrontation was set in place by the Azerbaijani Army's failures on the Agdera front early this year a defeat that the Azerbaijan People's Front tried to link to S. Guseinov's name. This was followed by a presidential decree relieving him of all his posts and appointing him general director of the newly created state wool concern. But it turned out that Surat Guseinov was not destined to take over his new post; according to the official authorities, the 709th unit, which remained loyal to him, in effect refused to obey the Ministry of Defense, which is what led to the events in Gyandzha....

One can say in advance that Geidar Aliyev's trip to Gyandzha will disarm Guseinov, who, observers believe, is not so strong in politics and, in addition, sympathizes with Geidar Aliyev....

SURAT GUSEINOV: 'I AM A SLAVE OF MY PEOPLE'

Telephone interview conducted by staff correspondents Georgy Ivanov-Smolensky and Sokhbet Mamedov. *Izvestia*, June 26, 1993, p. 4.

Baku, June 25 – ... The director of a combine for the primary processing of wool, Surat Guseinov became the most well-known figure among those who fought on the Azerbaijani side in Karabakh. By decree of President Abulfaz Elchibei, he was awarded the title of National Hero of Azerbaijan, which corresponds to the title of Hero of the Soviet Union. The president appointed him his authorized representative in Nagorno-Karabakh, Deputy Prime Minister and commander of the Agdera military corps. In the opinion of most observers, it was the rapid growth of S. Guseinov's prestige that was the reason for the discord in his relations with the People's Front and the republic's leadership. Our conversation began with the dramatic storming of the barracks of the 709th Brigade, which was loyal to Surat Guseinov....

Question. – What do think caused this attack? After all, just six months ago the President was bestowing the highest positions and titles on you.

Answer. – ... Politicians are the kind of people who can't stand someone else's popularity. That's why Gyandzha was besieged three times this past spring.

Q. – Do you believe that the President knew about the actions that were being prepared against you?

A. – There are documents that confirm this. There are also witnesses, live ones, whom we took hostage and who confirmed that they had acted on orders "from above." ...

Q. – Are you willing to engage in a political dialogue with Geidar Aliyev and other political leaders of the republic?

A. – This can happen only after they determine their attitude toward the events that occurred in Gyandzha. Today the actions and deeds of every political figure are being weighed in the balance. On this basis, the people will decide who is who....

Q. – What is your attitude toward a possible meeting with Abulfaz Elchibei?

A. – I can't meet with a criminal; he shed the blood of his own people, and that is the main obstacle....

Q. – If new structures of power are formed in Azerbaijan in the next few days, what place do you see for yourself in these structures, and on what political forces will you rely?

A. – I am not thinking about a leadership position. But if the people demand that I participate, I am willing. I will rely on the people, who support me. I think that I am capable of pulling my people out of the situation they are in today.

Q. – In your view, what is the explanation for the fact that essentially no resistance was offered to your troops on their way to Baku?

A. – It's because in the past year the people have lost faith in the leadership, which has impoverished them. The leaders called themselves democrats, but they established a dictatorship in the republic....

Q. – The replacement of the heads of executive authority in the districts is associated with your name, and this is perceived as a coup d'état.

A. – There are no grounds for these assertions. The population of most of the districts, dissatisfied with the local leadership, demanded that these officials resign. When these legitimate demands encountered resistance, these people called on my people for help. So, in no place and at no time were the heads of executive authority replaced on my orders.

Q. – How do you envision a solution to the Karabakh problem?

A. – ... It is not Armenians and Azerbaijanis who must solve this problem, but Armenia and Nagorno-Karabakh. We must all come to our senses! We must not forget that the process of the Union's destruction began with Karabakh. Forces overseas wanted to destroy the Union. It began with Karabakh. The two republics that were one family should be aware of this and not blame everything on "objective processes." We were driven into a swamp; we must get out of it together, and then choose who will take what road....

APPOINTMENTS: NEW DEFENSE MINISTER IN ARMENIA – He Is the Defense Minister of Nagorno-Karabakh

By Gamlet Matevosyan. *Segodnya*, Aug. 27, 1993, p. 4.

Yerevan – Rumors about the impending dismissal of Armenia's acting Defense Minister, Vazgen Manukyan, had been circulating in the press for a long time....

Today we can recall that when the ruling Armenian National Movement (ANM) gradually began "melting away," a large group headed by its former ideologue, ex-prime minister Vazgen Manukyan, split off from it. He created a new party the

National Democratic Union (NDU) around which the opposition forces rallied with a demand to immediately recognize the Nagorno-Karabakh Republic and speed up the formation of a regular army. It was only the appointment of Manukyan to the post of minister of defense that somewhat cooled the opposition's aggressive ardor. But, as can be seen, the differences between the President and the new minister remained.

Thus, there was nothing surprising about the President's decree removing Vazgen Manukyan from his post "in connection with his transfer to other work." But the second part of the decree, whereby Serzh Sargsyan, defense minister of the Nagorno-Karabakh Republic, was appointed minister of defense of the Republic of Armenia, could be called surprising and even sensational.

Sargsyan is a native of Stepanakert and a former Komsomol worker, and was once an assistant to Boris Kevorkov, First Secretary of the Nagorno-Karabakh Province Committee of the Communist Party. From the beginning of the hostilities in Karabakh, he has held leadership posts in the self-defense forces and then in the NKR Army.

In the opinion of observers, the appointment of Sargsyan as Armenia's military minister can be assessed as a manifestation of inconsistency in the policy being pursued by the Republic of Armenia. Throughout the past few years, this policy has been aimed at demonstrating to the whole world Armenia's noninterference in Karabakh's internal affairs and the NKR's independence from Armenia.

Observers believe that the new appointment is associated first and foremost with the fact that the Republic of Armenia's president, Levon Ter-Petrosyan, has decided to put at the head of the state's main power-wielding structure a man under whom there will be no chance of any differences and conflicts between the army, which today represents a real force, and the president's own authority.

MOSCOW READIES COUNTERMEASURES AGAINST ARMENIA AFTER RUSSIAN MISSION IS FIRED UPON

By Boris Vinogradov. *Izvestia*, Nov. 23, 1993, p. 2.

Russian Foreign Minister Andrei Kozyrev held a press conference on Zubovskaya Square in Moscow in connection with the incident involving Vladimir Kazimirov, the personal representative of the Russian president who had been on a peacemaking mission in Nagorno-Karabakh. As reported earlier, the mission was shelled by the Armenian side.

After returning to Moscow, Kazimirov said that the time and place of the mission's crossing of the border had been cleared in advance with Baku and Yerevan. The site chosen for it was the town of Kazakh, far away from the Nagorno-Karabakh Autonomous Province's borders. On the morning of Nov. 20, the lead escort vehicle went on ahead in order to make direct contact with Armenian forces. Some time later, Armenian positions began firing. Two Azerbaijani servicemen were wounded. It became impossible for the mission to proceed any further.

This is not merely an extraordinary incident, Andrei Kozyrev said. One gets the impression that there is politics behind it. I would be happy if this impression were mistaken, [he said,] but everything will depend on swift and unambiguous actions by, first and foremost, the Armenian leadership.

The minister read out a statement issued by the Russian Federation government. It says that Russia decisively condemns this unprecedented action, which flagrantly flouted the norms of international law, and demands that the Armenian government apologize and provide security guarantees for the Russian mission's activities. The Russian government expects the guilty parties to stand trial and reserves the right to take the most resolute measures to prevent such incidents from recurring.

The Russian Federation Foreign Ministry has been waiting for two days now for the Armenian side to provide official explanations. As of today, Moscow has received only one note from Yerevan; it puts all the responsibility on the Azerbaijani side. Last year, Kozyrev pointed out, his helicopter was fired upon in the area of Nagorno-Karabakh between Shusha and Stepanakert. It is still not known which side did the firing. But in the present instance Moscow has no doubt that the firing was initiated by the Armenian side. "I regard the attempt to send me a note in which Yerevan seeks to deflect the accusation from itself as an attack on me personally," Kozyrev declared.

The note hints that if Kazimirov fails to interpret the incident the right way, it will be difficult for him to work in Armenia. "If I were the Armenian Foreign Ministry, I would not engage in personnel selection for the Russian mission but would instead try to defuse the incident in an appropriate fashion," Kozyrev emphasized.

NAGORNO-KARABAKH: ON THE EVE OF TOUGH MEASURES

By Vladimir Yemelyanenko. *Moskovskiye novosti*, Nov. 28, 1993, p. A11.

The firing on the car of Russian Federation special envoy Vladimir Kazimirov on the Armenian-Azerbaijani border provided a reminder of the most chronic conflict in the ex-USSR the Karabakh conflict. Russia has never denied its involvement in the dispute over Karabakh. Azerbaijan's entry into the CIS constituted a firm bid by Moscow for recognition of its interests in the Transcaucasus. After having spurned the Commonwealth for more than a year, Azerbaijan has not merely joined it but has granted Russia the right to have naval bases in the republic and to defend its borders. At the Kremlin's insistence, Baku has dissolved its contracts with British-American and German oil companies and changed the direction of an oil and gas pipeline that was to link it with the West via Turkey; plans now call for the pipeline to run through Russia. Baku has met all of Moscow's conditions in hopes of a settlement of the Karabakh problem. But what is happening is quite the opposite. On Geidar Aliyev's "service record" are the surrender to Armenian forces of Agdam, Agdam District, and Fizuli, Lachin and Agderinsky Districts plus 1.4 million refugees, the largest number in the former Soviet Union. But Aliyev is holding on, propped up by the former mother country....

The leading powers are casting their lot with Azerbaijan, which is rich in oil and other natural resources, rather than with Armenia. Moreover, the annexation of Azerbaijani land confronts Armenia and Karabakh with the threat that the economic blockade (more than four years old) could develop into a geopolitical one: Yerevan and Stepanakert have been on the verge of international isolation since their troops moved up to the Iranian border. And although Armenia separates itself from the Nagorno-Karabakh Republic, seeking to portray the latter as an independent force, the differences between them are minimal.... The continuing war is reaching the stage of professionalization both sides are hiring mercenaries. The Armenians did so first, when the first mercenaries from the foreign diaspora appeared. Then Afghan mujahedeen made their way to Azerbaijan. This sharply increased the chances of religious confrontation, which in turn led to talks between Vazgen I, Catholicos of All Armenians, and Sheikh-ul-Islam Allakh-Shukyura Pashazade, through the offices of Metropolitan Aleksy II of All Rus.

However, religious peace and a ceasefire are attainable if the main issue can be resolved the federalization of Azerbaijan. Karabakh, Lezgistan and the flash-in-the-pan Talysh Republic have already proclaimed their rights. But as the experience of the new states' first years of independence shows, most of them see federalism as the embodiment of Russian imperial ambitions. Russia, for its part, has traversed a path from recognizing these territories as sovereign to acknowledging Russian spheres of influence there. Nagorno-Karabakh, which came first at the beginning of this path, is now the last at its other end. There is one reason for this: If Russia takes one side Armenia's or Azerbaijan's it will lose one of its spheres of influence.

Nevertheless, Russian Foreign Minister Andrei Kozyrev's statement that the "most resolute measures will not be long in coming" signals a Russian offensive against Armenia and Karabakh....

CIS LEADERS MEET IN ASHGABAT, TOGETHER AND SEPARATELY

By Aidyn Mekhtiyev. *Nezavisimaya gazeta*, Dec. 25, 1993, p. 1.

At a closed session of the Council of CIS Heads of State in Ashgabat yesterday, Azerbaijan's leader, Geidar Aliyev, delivered a sharply worded statement in which he demanded that Armenia immediately and unconditionally withdraw all armed formations from occupied Azerbaijani territory. Aliyev called on the CIS heads of state to set up a special commission to determine material damages and give an assessment of the Armenian formations' actions in the seized areas. He warned that if the council fails to adopt a decision on this question the conflict on the

CIS's southern borders may lead to the involvement of neighboring countries, Iran in particular, inasmuch as Armenian troops have moved up to Azerbaijan's state border with Iran. From all indications, the Azerbaijani leader's emotional speech produced an effect: The summit meeting adopted a decision to instruct experts to work out a mechanism for implementing the Collective Security Treaty. The whole problem is that this document provides for measures of collective defense by CIS members against external aggression. Azerbaijan, however, maintains that it does not need protection against neighboring Iran and Turkey, but that the real threat to its interests comes from Armenia, which has now occupied more than one-fourth of Azerbaijan. Before, when Azerbaijan was not a CIS member, the Commonwealth countries were unwilling to take on the role of an arbitration tribunal in this conflict. But now that Azerbaijan has become a full-fledged member of this organization and has signed the Collective Security Treaty, the CIS countries cannot ignore the question of relations between Azerbaijan and Armenia. In the current situation, Armenia will hardly risk political isolation among the CIS countries, and its actions will not be sharply condemned. The reason is Moscow's position. Russia recognizes the conflict as being between Azerbaijan and Nagorno-Karabakh, not between Azerbaijan and Armenia. Consequently, Moscow believes that Azerbaijani territory is occupied not by Armenia but by Karabakh formations. Every time the question of adopting a resolution on the Karabakh conflict has come up in the UN Security Council, Russia, as a permanent member, has categorically opposed attempts to declare Armenia the aggressor. In view of this circumstance, Baku is not inclined to overestimate the possibility that the CIS will resolve the Armenia-Azerbaijan conflict. Despite the fact that Muslim countries make up a majority in the Commonwealth, no attempts on their part to show so-called "Muslim solidarity" with respect to Azerbaijan have been observed. Moreover, the CIS Muslim countries that are simultaneously members of the Economic Cooperation Organization (ECO) are ignoring a resolution that calls for the imposition of an embargo on economic assistance to Armenia. This document was adopted on July 6, 1993, at a meeting of the ECO member-countries' heads of state in Istanbul. Shortly after the Istanbul summit, Turkmenistan, for example, began supplying kerosene to Armenia, which is experiencing an extremely grave energy crisis. All the above allows one to assume that Azerbaijan's success or failure on the diplomatic front will depend on whether Aliyev succeeds in persuading Moscow of the need to put pressure on Armenia. Russia would agree to this, perhaps, only if Baku gave its support to the idea of stationing Russian troops in the conflict zone to perform a so-called "peacekeeping mission."

Observers are calling attention to the fact that the Ashgabat summit revealed a sharp deterioration in the personal relationship between Geidar Aliyev and Levon Ter-Petrosyan. It is noteworthy that on the eve of the Azerbaijan President's aforementioned speech Aliyev and Ter-Petrosyan held a one-on-one conversation during which the two leaders spoke excitedly and agreed on nothing. On the morning of Dec. 24, after Aliyev's speech at the meeting of CIS heads of state, Ter-

Petrosyan took the floor to accuse Aliyev of not wanting to resolve the Karabakh conflict by peaceful means.

CONFLICT: RUSSIA CONCERNED ABOUT BAKU'S MILITARY SUCCESSES – Moscow Feels It's Time for Azerbaijan to Stop

By Aidyn Mekhtiyev. *Nezavisimaya gazeta*, Jan. 29, 1994, p. 1.

... For the first time in many months, the Azerbaijani Army has seized the initiative.... In January, Azerbaijan gained control of towns in Agdary and Kelbadzhar Districts that had previously been occupied by Armenian units, as well as of the highway from Agdary to Ter-Ter and Kelbadzhar. Moreover, according to preliminary reports from the area where the fighting has occurred, Azerbaijani troops have advanced right up to the Kelbadzhar-Lachin road in recent days. On the southern front, the offensive aimed at the district center of Fizuli continues. To all appearances, Yerevan and Khankendi [also known as Stepanakert] clearly didn't expect a large-scale offensive from the Azerbaijani side. According to the Azerbaijani Ministry of Defense, troop units were urgently dispatched to the combat zone from Armenia, but the units were made up mainly of poorly trained Armenian Army recruits. Despite the reinforcements, the Armenian side continues to retreat.

Azerbaijan's military successes have led to a sharp rise in President Geidar Aliyev's approval rating, and it is now clear that the promise Aliyev made in his New Year's message to the nation, in which he pledged to liberate all the occupied areas within a few months, was based on the chief of state's firm conviction that the national army was capable of mounting offensive operations. While Moscow and Yerevan continue to conjecture about how Aliyev managed to strengthen his army in such a short time, official Baku remains silent and is in no hurry to deny reports in a whole series of Russian publications asserting that the backbone of the newly invigorated army consists of Afghan mujahedeen. Moscow's insistent call for an end to hostilities has confronted the Azerbaijani leader with a difficult dilemma: either make concessions and agree to talks with Armenia, or ignore Russia's diplomatic pressure. If he chooses the first option, Aliyev risks losing the support of the republic's population; if he chooses the second, he could force Moscow to seek other ways of bringing influence to bear on Azerbaijan's present leadership.

EPICENTER: THE LAST WAR?

By special correspondent Vladimir Yemelyanenko. *Moskovskiye novosti*, Feb. 20-27, 1994, p. A4.

Stepanakert – Against the backdrop of the semi-peace in the Dnestr region and South Ossetia, and the end of the wars in Abkhazia and Tajikistan, the only place in the former USSR where warfare is still going on is Nagorno-Karabakh.

The latest flare-up occurred on Dec. 16, 1993, when the Azerbaijani Army began an offensive along the entire front. However, the "entry into Stepanakert" that Baku had slated for Jan. 8 ended with the taking of the town of Goradiz to the south of Karabakh, part of Kelbadzhar District to the north, and part of Agdam District to the east. The Azerbaijani troops never actually reached the territory of the Nagorno-Karabakh Republic per se.

Frontline. The "gates" to Stepanakert Agdam and its environs remain impregnable. The long-deserted city has turned into a sort of "guardian of the hearth." Plundered by the victors, who even took latches from gates and birch-twig brooms, it has an unsettled air that scares people away. Even the military prefer to live in dugouts, far from the roofless ruins.

"So what are they saying there? Will the war end soon?" officers from the Karabakh Army ask in greeting me. Artur Grigoryan, commander of an artillery battery, lists where "there" is, counting the places off on his fingers: "In the capital of our former homeland, in Yerevan, in Baku and in the UN." "Actually," Grigoryan explains, "we realized a long time ago that relying on 'there' would mean being driven from our land, down to the last Armenian. I personally try to get it into everyone's head that we must rely on ourselves alone."

This kind of frontline mentality is characteristic of the fighting Karabakhers. So when I asked, "But how is it that you're not shooting in Karabakh but have seized other people's lands: Agdam, Fizuli, Kelbadzhar almost a third of Azerbaijan?," everyone from fighting man to government minister answered, "If we hadn't taken the border districts, we would be shooting on our own land."

I saw a group of captured soldiers, about nine of them, bound with ropes. "So they won't run away," the fighter guarding the captives explained. The young fellows were sitting right in the snow and refused to talk. Only one of them admitted that none of them wants to fight either. "Geidar Aliyev himself said that this would be the last offensive," the captive told me. "The President promised that all the refugees would return to their homes soon. He even named a date no later than January."

But now it's February, and an end to the war is nowhere in sight. At the talks, Baku is asking for another delay. "We are willing to return the seized territories," says NKR Minister of Foreign Affairs Arkady Gukasyan, "but only through negotiations and in exchange for guarantees of peace. If we leave Fizuli or Agdam as the result of a defeat or 'just because,' that will be the beginning of the Armenians' departure from Karabakh. They'll simply drive us out with artillery bombardments."

Human joys

No one from Karabakh intends to live on the land that has been taken: It's been completely plundered, stripped as clean as an operating room. In Lachin, in Agdam, everywhere. "Well, what were we supposed to do, when before that they took everything away from us?" recalls 72-year-old Maksim Ovanisyan. "We didn't invent the laws of war: No victor has ever yet been able deny himself the small joys of victory." One joy came to Ovanisyan's large family ... while I was there. "My nephew's leg was blown off at the front," he shared the news. "He's still alive. His wife and aunts aren't even crying. They're saving their strength for the dead."

From Moskovskiye novosti files

According to unofficial data, from Dec. 16, 1993, through Feb. 16, 1994 (the dates of the Azerbaijani Army's winter offensive in Karabakh), the following numbers were killed: between 3,000 and 6,000 Azerbaijani soldiers, about 500 fighters from the NKR defense army, and 500 to 1,000 soldiers from the Armenian expeditionary corps....

Resource race

The Karabakh conflict has changed qualitatively over the years. Whereas fighters used to go into battle with assault rifles or even hunting guns, nowadays people in the NKR recall this with nostalgia. The war became professionalized long ago. Now a great deal is decided by who is better at handling a tank, an infantry fighting vehicle, heavy artillery and Grad rocket launchers. Who has aircraft and NATO communications equipment. Whose assault rifles are more sophisticated: the Kalashnikovs, the Czech weapons, the Turkish ones, the Chinese, the American or the British.

The war is turning into a war of resources. "We know we are losing this race," says NKR Deputy Prime Minister Zhirair Pogosyan. "Baku has oil, the status of a recognized state, and no blockade. We once had a situation in which we were out of cartridges and were buying gasoline through illegal channels in Azerbaijan."...

He is sure that the resource race can be won by turning it into an intellectual race. "Were we, 150,000 Karabakhers, able to defend our land against Azerbaijan with its population of several million?" he asks me, and answers: "We were. Because we got away from a standard confrontation based on numbers. We have to look for the right moves now, too."

"We are willing to talk with Baku," Robert Kocharyan, Chairman of the NKR State Committee on Defense, told an MN correspondent. "Russia's idea of creating a demarcation line is worth discussing."

Moscow's proposal to deploy peacekeeping troops subordinate to Russia on this line was greeted with hope in Karabakh and with silence in Azerbaijan. But against the backdrop of its failures at the front, Baku was confronted with the need to respond.

Sub-rosa tactics were chosen: NKR Minister of Foreign Affairs Arkady Gukasyan and Azerbaijan Supreme Soviet Vice-Chairman Ismail Dzhalilov met unofficially. That fact itself was unprecedented: For the first time Baku deigned to talk directly, albeit secretly, with the former autonomous entity. The sides admitted the impossibility of the coexistence of a joint Armenian-Azerbaijani peacekeeping battalion on the demarcation line. But the most important thing happened nonetheless talks were held without intermediaries. How the signing of contracts for the development of Baku oil will end and what share of the oil pie will fall to Turkey, Russia and Britain, respectively, depends on those talks.

"I wish they'd hurry up and reach agreement," Zhirair Pogosyan told me in parting. "We and the Azerbaijanis are still going to be neighbors in any case...."

AZERBAIJAN OPPOSES ESTABLISHMENT OF RUSSIAN MILITARY BASES ON ITS TERRITORY

By Sokhbet Mamedov. *Izvestia*, April 7, 1994, p. 3.

Baku – Statements by certain Russian generals that they are "planning to put a military base in Azerbaijan" and Moscow's obvious desire to send Russian peacekeeping forces into the Karabakh conflict zone have prompted an extremely negative response in the republic.

Many Azerbaijanis are saying that the "republic's authorities were unable to withstand the heavy pressure being exerted by the Russian generals and have been forced to agree in principle to their demands."

Azerbaijan is currently the only CIS republic with no Russian troops on its territory, with the exception of a small number of specialists operating the Gabalin radar station.

The last Russian Army units left Azerbaijan peacefully and without hindrance in early 1993. That event, which occurred during Abulfaz Elchibei's presidency, is regarded by his comrades in the People's Front as one of their greatest achievements.... Most observers note a certain inconsistency on the part of the Russian leadership. After completing the hasty redeployment of its troops from Azerbaijan to the Northern Caucasus a year ago, now Moscow is looking for ways to send them back.

"Russia has not officially presented such a proposal to us," Azerbaijani Foreign Minister Gasan Gasanov told Izvestia. President Geidar Aliyev has also spoken categorically on this score: "As long as I am leader of Azerbaijan, there will be no foreign bases on the republic's territory."

The situation involving peacekeeping forces is somewhat different. A well-informed source in the republic's Foreign Ministry told Izvestia that Russia is insisting that only Russian units, under the aegis of international organizations, participate in the process of settling the conflict in Nagorno-Karabakh. Azerbaijan, on the other hand, is naturally taking a cautious approach and suggesting that a mixed contingent of peacekeeping forces from the Conference on Security and Cooperation in Europe or the UN be stationed along the entire Armenian-Azerbaijani border. As the politicians search for mutually acceptable solutions, the republic's opposition forces have made it known that they will not allow Russian soldiers to return to Azerbaijan in any way, shape or form....

KARABAKH SETTLEMENT IS A HEADACHE FOR MOSCOW – Russian Peacekeeping Plan Still Far From Implementation[5]

By Aidyn Mekhtiyev. *Nezavisimaya gazeta*, April 19, 1994, p. 1.

Foreign Minister Gasan Gasanov of the Republic of Azerbaijan assessed the signing of the declaration "On Respecting the Sovereignty, Territorial Integrity and Inviolability of CIS Borders" at the April 15 summit meeting in Moscow as a success for Azerbaijani diplomacy. In an exclusive interview with NG, Mr. Gasanov emphasized that the document, which was submitted by the Azerbaijani side, had been sealed with the signatures of 11 CIS heads of state, and that only Armenian President Levon Ter-Petrosyan had pointedly refused to sign the declaration. Before that, at a meeting of the Council of Foreign Ministers, Armenian Minister Vagan Papazyan did likewise as the 11 other ministers signed the document. "Consequently," said Gasan Gasanov, "the Armenian side is now isolated, having issued a challenge to the entire CIS." In Gasanov's view, Armenia's refusal to recognize the declaration shows once more that Yerevan continues to advance territorial claims against Azerbaijan. In this connection, the Azerbaijani Foreign Minister recalled that not only has Armenia not annulled its parliament's 1988 decision to annex Nagorno-Karabakh, but it also included the territory of Nagorno-Karabakh as a part of Armenia in its 1991 declaration of independence. In Gasanov's opinion, the Armenian side was especially unhappy with two points in the declaration signed at the April 15 summit, the gist of which is as follows: The CIS countries declare that the seizure of territory by force cannot be recognized and the occupation of territory cannot be used as grounds for international recognition, and they pledge to refrain from supporting or using separatism against the territorial integrity of any CIS member country.

The Azerbaijani foreign minister said that the Armenian delegation's attempt at the Moscow meeting to force a discussion of the so-called "Convention on National Minorities" on the talks' participants had failed. The overwhelming majority of CIS member countries rejected the document in the proposed form, and it was decided to postpone discussion of it until the next meeting....

One can agree with Foreign Minister Gasan Gasanov's statement that the summit strengthened Azerbaijan's position within the CIS. At the same time, commentators who followed the Moscow summit meeting are pointing out that the Commonwealth was once again unmoved by Azerbaijani leader Geidar Aliyev's demand to "condemn Armenia's aggression against Azerbaijan and impose sanctions on the aggressor." The CIS heads of state preferred to take the position of outside observers in the conflict and to refrain from passing judgment. Incidentally, the reluctance of the Turkic-speaking CIS leaders (those of Kazakhstan, Turkmenistan, Uzbekistan and Kirgizia) to back Geidar Aliyev's demands for a condemnation of Armenian aggression can easily be explained: Those countries are still taking their cue from their "older brother." And Moscow is not inclined to view Armenia's actions as aggressive. In the end, the CIS leaders limited themselves to supporting the Russian plan for a resolution of the Karabakh problem and urging the world community to back the Kremlin's efforts....

To all appearances, Azerbaijani leader Aliyev's behind-the-scenes talks with Russian officials brought no progress in a discussion of a possible Russian military presence in Azerbaijan. Moscow has yet to persuade Aliyev to allow even one Russian military base in Azerbaijan. Addressing a plenary session of the Council of CIS Heads of State and the Council of CIS Heads of Government, Boris Yeltsin indirectly admitted the lack of an agreement with Azerbaijan on this issue. Following the emergence of a serious threat to the Commonwealth's security in the Caucasus, agreements were reached with the Republic of Georgia and the Republic of Armenia on Russian participation in protecting their external borders, Boris Yeltsin said.

NOTES

1. The next day, *Pravda* (Dec. 26, 1991, p. 1) reported that some 500 armed Armenians had recently raided a military post in Stepanakert and seized a large number of guns and armored vehicles to help them continue their fight against the Azerbaijanis after the internal troops leave Nagorno-Karabakh.

2. Getashen, a village in Azerbaijan that was at one time inhabited by Armenians, was the scene of heavy fighting between the two sides in spring 1991.

3. The Yezidis are a religious division of the Kurds. Many of them migrated from Turkey to Russian-controlled parts of the Transcaucasus in the 19th century to escape persecution by Sunni Muslims, who considered their religion a heretical sect.

4. This meeting among representatives of 11 member countries of the Conference on Security and Cooperation in Europe was convened to discuss the Nagorno-Karabakh conflict in preparation for an international peace conference in Minsk.

5. Twenty days later, Azerbaijan signed the Bishkek Protocol, marking a breakthrough in ending the years-long Nagorno-Karabakh conflict. An article by Pyotr Karapetyan titled "Karabakh Has Never Been as Close to Peace as Today" (*Krasnaya Zvezda*, May 11, 1994) reads as follows:

   Hopes for a turning point in the Karabakh conflict grew after the Azerbaijani side ended up signing the Bishkek Protocol on May 9. [This document had been drafted] at a meeting of parliamentary deputies from Azerbaijan and Armenia and representatives of Nagorno-Karabakh, held with the mediation of the CIS Interparliamentary Assembly in early May. Thus, for the first time in six years of the Karabakh conflict, the groundwork has been laid for settling the problem.

   By stubbornly refusing to recognize NKR as a party to the conflict until May 9, 1994, Azerbaijan automatically relieved its opponents of responsibility for breaking the agreements, since Armenia (as recorded by a number of international organizations) is not in a state of war with Azerbaijan. From the moment that the speaker of the Azerbaijani parliament, Rasul Guliyev signed the Bishkek Protocol (albeit with two provisos), the situation has changed dramatically. The task now is to engage in the gradual settlement of the conflict according to the plan proposed by Russia. It consists of three stages. The first is a ceasefire, an end to hostilities and a separation of the forces (for which six days are allotted). The second is the liberation of the occupied territories, except for Shusha and Lachin, the immediate exchange of prisoners and hostages, the restoration of communications and the return of refugees (34 days). The liberation of Shusha and Lachin is scheduled for special consideration two weeks after the ceasefire. The third stage is negotiations on the status of the NKR.

Chapter 7 | Interwar Period: Regional Leadership Changes, OSCE Mediation

---

ROBERT KOCHARYAN REELECTED PRESIDENT OF NAGORNO-KARABAKH REPUBLIC – Voting in Nagorno-Karabakh Draws Protests From Baku

By Gamlet Matevosyan. *Segodnya*, Nov. 26, 1994, p. 4.

Yerevan – A presidential election was held in the self-proclaimed Nagorno-Karabakh Republic on Sunday [Nov. 24]. The institution of the presidency was established two years ago, when the parliament elected Robert Kocharyan, who was then head of the republic's SDC, to that post. The timetable and procedures for holding elections were also determined at that time.

Three candidates ran for the post of head of Nagorno-Karabakh: Robert Kocharyan, the incumbent president; Boris Arushanyan, former vice-chairman of the Karabakh parliament and an independent candidate; and Grant Melkumyan, leader of the local Communist Party.

Voter turnout was 77.6%. According to preliminary figures released by the NKR's central electoral commission, 42-year-old Robert Kocharyan won a convincing victory in the election; 86.1% of the voters cast their ballots for him. Boris Arushanyan received 6.9%, and Grant Melkumyan 2.6%....

* * *

(By Arif Useinov) Baku – The election in the Nagorno-Karabakh Republic caused a storm of protest in Azerbaijan. About half a million people attended rallies. The Azerbaijani public views the holding of the presidential election as illegal and contrary to international norms, and sees the position taken by the Karabakh Armenians' leaders as a challenge to the world community that is meant to sabotage peacemaking efforts to resolve the Karabakh conflict.

Gasan Gasanov, the head of Azerbaijan's Foreign Ministry, said that the 15 member countries of the European Union and nine member countries of the Organization for Security and Cooperation in Europe's Minsk group have declared the presidential election in the NKR to be illegitimate and its results legally invalid.

ELECTION: PRESIDENT ELECTED IN NAGORNO-KARABAKH – He Is State Defense Committee Chairman Robert Kocharyan

By Dmitry Zhdannikov. *Segodnya*, Dec. 24, 1994, p. 4.

On Thursday [Dec. 22], the parliament of Nagorno-Karabakh elected the first president in the republic's history. He is Robert Kocharyan, chairman of the State Defense Committee (SDC) the republic's emergency executive body during the war with Azerbaijan. He took the presidential oath yesterday.

Over the past two years Mr. Kocharyan has been the de facto leader of the republic, but his move from the rank of chairman of the Karabakh Council of Ministers to the rank of president occurred rather unexpectedly. The decision to institute a presidency was made Dec. 20 at a regular session of the Nagorno-Karabakh Republic Supreme Soviet, during a discussion concerning reorganization of the system of government. Within the framework of the same discussion, several more laws of considerable importance were adopted in the days that followed: The Supreme Soviet will henceforth be called the parliament, and it has been decided to make it a professional, standing body. The SDC, which performed the functions of a government over the past two years, has also been abolished. It has been replaced with a Council of Ministers.

The president, who is to be elected in direct, general elections by secret ballot for a term of five years, has the right to appoint and remove the prime minister and all other members of the government, is the commander in chief of the republic's armed forces, and heads the Security Council. The current president, who was elected not in a general election but by a parliamentary vote, will hold office until the end of 1996, when an election for a new president is to be held.

Robert Kocharyan ... was one of the most active participants in the movement, which began in 1988, to annex the Nagorno-Karabakh Republic to Armenia. In 1988-1990 he was a deputy to the Armenian SSR Supreme Soviet; in 1990 he became a deputy to the Armenian Supreme Soviet, and in 1992, a deputy to the Karabakh parliament.

ARMENIA'S NEW PRIME MINISTER IS NOT TO BAKU'S LIKING – Azerbaijani Politicians Think the Appointment Will Negatively Affect Situation in the Region

By Mekhman Gafarly. *Nezavisimaya gazeta*, March 25, 1997, p. 3.

The appointment of Robert Kocharyan, President of the self-proclaimed Nagorno-Karabakh Republic, to the post of prime minister of Armenia has provoked the wrath of Azerbaijani diplomats. Azerbaijani Deputy Foreign Minister Araz Azimov said that it could have a negative impact on the process of a peaceful settlement of the Armenian-Azerbaijani conflict. He believes that the appointment shows a desire on the part of Yerevan to "consolidate the annexation of part of Azerbaijani territory." The Azerbaijani side is unhappy that no one consulted official Baku about the appointment of Robert Kocharyan, who is officially a citizen of Azerbaijan.... Mr. Azimov thinks that in becoming prime minister of Armenia, Robert Kocharyan should give up his Azerbaijani citizenship and resign as leader of Nagorno-Karabakh's Armenian community. "If that doesn't happen, Robert Kocharyan's appointment as head of the Armenian government will have to be seen as a challenge to Azerbaijan and the world community," the deputy foreign minister said.

Baku is particularly concerned that, as head of the Armenian government, Mr. Kocharyan will do his utmost to help strengthen the NKR's defensive capability and help it secede from Azerbaijan.

To all appearances, the Azerbaijani leaders' concern is rather well founded. While speaking at a press conference immediately after his appointment, Robert Kocharyan said that an improvement in the economic situation in Armenia would have a positive effect on Nagorno-Karabakh as well: "Without economic development in Armenia, Karabakh has no future."

Meanwhile, Azerbaijani President Geidar Aliyev declared that his country will do "whatever it takes" to liberate the territory occupied by Armenian units and that it "will never agree to the occupation of its territory." At the same time, he said that Azerbaijan's strategic policy is still to seek a peaceful settlement of the Armenian-Azerbaijani conflict through negotiations. He said that Azerbaijan will continue to adhere to the terms of the ceasefire.

TRANSCAUCASUS: THEY TALKED ABOUT KARABAKH IN DENVER – Presidents of Russia, US and France Adopt a Joint Statement on Reaching a Settlement in the Region

By Mekhman Gafarly. *Nezavisimaya gazeta*, June 24, 1997, p. 3.

The joint statement on Nagorno-Karabakh that was issued in Denver on Friday [June 20] by Presidents Boris Yeltsin of Russia, Bill Clinton of the US and Jacques Chirac of France has drawn a positive reaction in Baku. The three presidents, whose countries cochair the OSCE Minsk conference on Nagorno-Karabakh, called on all parties to the Karabakh conflict to reach a negotiated settlement as soon as possible. Although the statement by the presidents contains no explicit support of Azerbaijan, Baku regards the very appearance of such a document as a victory for Azerbaijani diplomacy. The increasing initiative of Washington, Moscow and Paris in working toward an Armenia-Azerbaijan settlement can be called a success for Azerbaijan's diplomats, since close attention to the Karabakh problem from the heads of leading world powers precludes any resumption of combat operations on the Armenia-Azerbaijan front, which would dash all of Baku's hopes for implementing the oil projects it has worked out with foreign companies. Moreover, war could harm Azerbaijan's economy, which is only now beginning to get out of crisis. Against this backdrop, the desire of Azerbaijan's leaders to obtain international guarantees of a peaceful resolution to the conflict seems quite logical. To date, President Geidar Aliyev is coping successfully with the republic's problems in the international arena. An additional success for Azerbaijani diplomats was the fact that in Denver the only separate discussion that any of the heads of leading countries had was on the Karabakh question.

The joint statement by the presidents of Russia, the US and France shows that disagreements among Moscow, Washington and Paris on the Karabakh question are diminishing all the time.

After expressing satisfaction with the observance of the cease-fire accords in the conflict zone, the Presidents noted at the same time that "without progress toward a lasting settlement, the cease-fire could be broken." The document goes on to say that the cochairmen of the OSCE's Minsk conference from Russia, the US and France have worked out a whole series of proposals for a peaceful settlement that take into account the legitimate interests of all parties to the conflict.

KARABAKH GETS A LEADER – And Russia, US and France Get a Negotiating Partner

By Leonid Gankin and Gennady Sysoyev. *Kommersant-Daily*, Sept. 3, 1997, p. 4.

The winner of the presidential election held in Nagorno-Karabakh on Sept. 1 is Arkady Gukasyan, the self-proclaimed republic's minister of foreign affairs. Despite their negative attitude toward the election, the mediators in the effort to settle the Karabakh conflict expect to achieve a breakthrough in the negotiating process sometime soon.

The victory of the 40-year-old Gukasyan (he got almost 90% of the vote) was basically a foregone conclusion. As Karabakh's foreign policy chief, he had participated in all the talks on a settlement and convinced the voters of his commitment to the idea of independence. His rivals Artur Tovmasyan, speaker of the Karabakh parliament, and Deputy Boris Arushanyan were not as much in the public eye and could claim little in the way of practical accomplishments.

The cochairs of the Minsk group (Russia, the US and France), which represent the OSCE in the efforts to resolve the conflict, were unanimous in refusing to acknowledge the legitimacy of an election in a republic that no one has recognized. But it appears that they are all disinclined to overdramatize the situation, in the belief that every cloud has a silver lining. Now Karabakh has an acknowledged leader who can be negotiated with. And all the parties involved in the settlement process are in a hurry to resolve the explosive conflict as soon as possible.

Azerbaijan, having concluded contracts worth $30 billion with foreign investors, realizes that it won't get any real money until the Karabakh problem is solved. Its Western partners, who are itching to get the Caspian oil pipeline going, are wary of investing their capital until the situation in the region has been stabilized.

Armenia is choking in the stranglehold of an economic embargo: The main transportation arteries connecting it with the outside world run through Azerbaijan, and Yerevan is also unable to make full use of alternative routes through Turkey, which is sympathetic to Baku.

Russia is caught between a rock and a hard place. Moscow can't afford to fall out with either Baku or Yerevan if only because, in the first instance, it's counting on being involved in the Caspian oil projects very soon. And, in the second instance, because of the commitments that Yeltsin and [Armenian President] Ter-Petrosyan have recently assumed as allies, commitments that have breathed new life into the plan for integration within the CIS that Moscow is carefully nurturing.

People in the Russian Ministry of Foreign Affairs realize that in view of the differences in the Armenians' and Azerbaijanis' positions on Karabakh, the process of solving the problem will be painful for both sides. Moscow likes the current format of mediation in the context of the OSCE's Minsk group, in which collective pressure is being brought to bear on Armenia, Azerbaijan and Karabakh.

In late August, Foreign Minister Yevgeny Primakov said that he thought there should be direct contacts between the leaders in Baku and Stepanakert. Moscow, along with its partners in the Minsk group, is prepared to do its utmost to facilitate this. According to Kommersant's information, soon Yury Yukalov, the chief Russian negotiator on Karabakh, together with his counterparts, American Lynn Pascoe and Frenchman Georges Vaugier, will go to Stepanakert to meet with the new Karabakh leadership.

They face some difficult negotiations. On the eve of the election, Arkady Gukasyan said that he disagreed with the Minsk group's proposals and that the republic would never go back under Azerbaijan's jurisdiction. But the mediators are hoping that those words were addressed to the voters, and that pragmatic politics will take over after the election.

ROBERT KOCHARYAN BECOMES PRESIDENT OF ARMENIA – But This Doesn't Trouble Russia

By Gennady Sysoyev. *Kommersant-Daily*, April 1, 1998, p. 5.

Armenian Prime Minister Robert Kocharyan won a convincing victory in the presidential election held in the republic on Monday [March 30]. If he actually starts implementing his Nagorno-Karabakh program, there will be no avoiding another conflict. But Moscow is hoping that President Kocharyan will be wiser than presidential candidate Kocharyan.

Kocharyan's success was predictable: He was the favorite in the presidential race from the very beginning. His second-round rival, Karen Demirchyan, who held the post of First Secretary of the Armenian Communist Party Central Committee from 1974 to 1988, got only half as many votes. Demirchyan's main trump card –

Soviet-type stability – was not strong enough even to provide real competition for the 43-year-old prime minister.

Kocharyan's victory was also clean in the eyes of international observers. After the first round, they had voiced serious complaints about the organization of the voting, but this time the head of the Council of Europe mission, Lord Russell Johnson, said that "everything went fine." Telman Gdlyan, who acted as an observer from the Russian State Duma, agreed with him.

The world community's interest in the Armenian election is understandable. The fate of efforts to settle the Karabakh conflict hinges on its outcome, and so, accordingly, does the safety of the oil pipeline from Baku to the Georgian port of Poti, which runs in direct proximity to Karabakh. Kocharyan, who was president of Karabakh for several years, vigorously advocates its independence. It should be recalled that the former head of Armenia, Levon Ter-Petrosyan, lost his post in large part precisely because he dared to agree to a solution of the Karabakh problem that preserved the territorial integrity of Azerbaijan.

Therefore, the world fears that Kocharyan's victory could lead to a new conflict in the region. A Kommersant correspondent was told at the Azerbaijani Embassy in Moscow that "Kocharyan's views do not please Baku. He won popularity by making radical statements that smell of gunpowder. If he acts in the same spirit as president, everything that has been achieved toward a Karabakh settlement over the past four years will be in jeopardy."

Baku believes that any Armenian politician today is subject to the "Ter-Petrosyan syndrome": A moderate approach to the Karabakh problem inevitably leads to political death. Nevertheless, Azerbaijan hopes that Kocharyan's position as president will differ from the statements made by Kocharyan the office-seeking politician.

Moscow is counting on the same, to all appearances. In a conversation with a Kommersant correspondent, a high-ranking official in the Russian Ministry of Foreign Affairs expressed the opinion that "in his new post, Kocharyan will have to be guided not by his personal likes and dislikes but by the interests of all Armenia." Therefore, according to this source, "the new president's tough position could very well be combined with a responsible approach toward a Karabakh settlement."

Moscow is also confident that under its new president, Armenia's relations with Russia will not worsen. "Not one serious Armenian politician, including Kocharyan, would jeopardize friendship with Moscow," Kommersant was told at the Russian Foreign Ministry. "Armenia, which is not spoiled by an abundance of allies, has an objective stake in an alliance with Russia."

AZERBAIJAN ELECTS LEADER FOR THE 21ST CENTURY – He Is 75-Year-Old Geidar Aliyev

By Yury Chubchenko [in Moscow] and Irada Agayeva in Baku. *Kommersant-Daily*, Oct. 13, 1998, p. 4.

The presidential election in Azerbaijan on Sunday [Oct. 11] produced no surprises, and Geidar Aliyev will celebrate his 80th birthday as president. In 1993, the end of the war in Karabakh assured him the presidency. Aliyev won this latest election by casting his lot with large-scale Caspian oil production. All that remains is to choose the route by which the oil is to be transported.

The official election results haven't been announced yet, but Azerbaijan's Central Electoral Commission has already said that there won't be a second round. The election had been declared valid by noon, after about 32% of the voters had been to the polls. A total of approximately 4.2 million people (77.9%) participated in the election. According to the president's campaign staff, almost 79% of all the people who voted cast their ballots for him.

This is Geidar Aliyev's second victory in a presidential election. In 1993, the end of the war in Karabakh won him nearly 99% of the vote.

This time, he based his campaign on "national prosperity through oil." Few people doubted that Aliyev would win, and he himself did his utmost to deny his rivals the slightest chance of victory. When he arrived at a polling place to cast his own ballot, he said he was absolutely confident that the man he was voting for would win. Attempts by the opposition to postpone the election ultimately prompted all five opposition candidates, led by former Azerbaijani president Abulfaz Elchibei, to boycott the election because it was "undemocratic." The remaining five candidates from progovernment parties and organizations were no match for Aliyev. His main rival, Etibar Mamedov, who leads Azerbaijan's National Independence Party, got just 13% of the vote.

The losers' charges that the "election results were completely falsified" are unlikely to draw much attention. International observers have already said that they found no flagrant violations that could have "seriously affected" the outcome of the election. Europe and the US see the Caspian region as a long-term source of energy resources for the West. And having assured himself of five more years in power, Geidar Aliyev will continue to implement plans to deliver "Caspian main oil" to the West.

A decision on the route for the main export pipeline will be made on Oct. 29. The most likely choice is the route from Baku to Supsa (a Georgian port on the Black Sea). So it's not surprising that the first person to congratulate Aliyev on his "historic victory," without waiting for the official election results, was Georgian President Eduard Shevardnadze.

BAKU AND YEREVAN ENTER EUROPEAN ORBIT – But They Are Still Speaking Different Languages

By Vladimir Katin and Armen Khanbabyan. *Nezavisimaya gazeta*, Jan. 27, 2001, p. 5.

After their visits to Strasbourg, where, as reported earlier, an official ceremony admitting Armenia and Azerbaijan to the Council of Europe was held, President Geidar Aliyev and President Robert Kocharyan immediately headed for Paris. There they met with President Jacques Chirac, with whose assistance another round of talks on Nagorno-Karabakh was held....

Robert Kocharyan said that he considers the OSCE Minsk Group on Karabakh (one of whose cochairs is France) to be the "optimal format for continued dialogue on a settlement." At the same time, the Armenian leader believes that the peacemaking process has acquired new elements lately; in particular, direct contacts between the leaders of the opposing sides have picked up. Kocharyan is convinced that the "peace process has the potential to succeed, but time and patience are required." "We must take into account the realities of Nagorno-Karabakh, whose authorities are demanding a broader interpretation of the concept of 'sovereignty,' " the Armenian leader said. He reiterated that a settlement must be based on the principles of equal status for the Nagorno-Karabakh Republic and Azerbaijan as subjects of international law, and the impermissibility of Karabakh's existing as an enclave. When asked whether Armenia was willing to affirm Azerbaijan's territorial integrity, the Armenian leader replied, "The question has to be framed differently: Is Azerbaijan willing to recognize the established statehood of the Nagorno-Karabakh Republic?" He added, "For countries making the transition to democracy, territorial integrity often becomes an excuse for genocide."

Geidar Aliyev also set forth his view of the problem. In his opinion, the efforts of the Minsk Group, which was set up in 1992, have been unsuccessful. Aliyev accused Armenia of "aggression against Azerbaijan and the occupation of 20%" of his country. "For more than eight years, a million Azerbaijanis have been banished from their native land and are living in suffering and poverty, while the world community silently observes this tragedy," he said. In the Azerbaijani president's opinion, a just settlement could be based on granting the Nagorno-Karabakh region the "highest status of self-government within the framework of Azerbaijan's territorial integrity."...

The two presidents took equally different views of the French parliament's recent recognition that the Ottoman Empire committed genocide against the Armenians in 1915. Geidar Aliyev reacted negatively to this, saying that such questions cannot be decided by a vote in parliament. "Neither the Council of Europe nor the concept of human rights existed in 1915, so the current situation cannot be equated with what happened at the beginning of the century," he stressed. Robert Kocharyan, for his part, was certain that the French legislators "did a noble thing." He also said that Armenia "has no right to make territorial claims against Turkey based on the fact that***genocide was committed against Armenians there," but added that "the victims of the genocide and their descendants have the right to demand compensation from Turkey."

It's no secret that the French lawmakers' resolution caused noticeable friction in relations between Paris and Ankara. Jacques Chirac noted diplomatically in this regard that he was in no hurry to ratify the parliament's decision with his signature. However, French observers are certain that he will do so immediately after Geidar Aliyev leaves Paris....

KARABAKH HAS NEW PRESIDENT WITH OLD POLICY

Moskovskiye novosti, Aug. 13-19, 2002, p. 9.

Our Yerevan correspondent, Ara Tatevosyan, reports that the recent presidential election in the Nagorno-Karabakh Republic brought no surprises. Arkady Gukasyan, the incumbent president of the unrecognized republic, won handily, garnering more than 88% of the vote. His three rivals split just over 10% of the vote, but none is going to challenge the election results. Gukasyan's opponents admitted that they had lost a fair fight. That opinion is shared by foreign observers who monitored the voting over the protests of Azerbaijan, which doesn't recognize the legitimacy of elections in Nagorno-Karabakh. An independent delegation of American observers, among them former officials of the US State Department and two congressmen, called the Karabakh election "free and transparent." However, the UN and the OSCE did not recognize the election. In the wake of his reelection, Arkady Gukasyan's chief task, as before, will be to try to reach a settlement of the Karabakh problem. To all appearances, Azerbaijan needn't expect any softening of the Nagorno-Karabakh Republic's position. Gukasyan has already said that the only possible alternative to independence for Nagorno-Karabakh would be for the region to become part of Armenia. Meanwhile, in the Nakhichevan village of Sadarak, preparations are under way for a meeting between Armenian President Robert Kocharyan and Azerbaijani President Geidar Aliyev, who last met in Moscow in November 2001. But Arkady Gukasyan said that he wasn't particularly hopeful about the meeting's outcome. He said that hopes of Geidar Aliyev proving to be a more constructive Azerbaijani leader had not panned out. "Aliyev's time is past, and now he's the main obstacle to the negotiating process," the Nagorno-Karabakh president declared.

FAILURE IN RAMBOUILLET

By Arkady Dubnov. *Vremya novostei*, Feb. 13, 2006, p. 2.

Hopes that a two-day meeting late last week between the presidents of Azerbaijan and Armenia at the medieval Rambouillet Castle outside Paris would produce a breakthrough in efforts to resolve the Karabakh conflict have been dashed. Ilkham Aliyev and Robert Kocharyan failed to reach agreement on a plan for a future settlement. A communiqué issued Saturday evening [Feb. 11] by the OSCE Minsk Group on Nagorno-Karabakh states that "despite intensive discussions, the sides' positions on certain aspects of the Karabakh problem remained the same as they had been in recent months." One of the [three] cochairmen of the Minsk Group, American diplomat Steven Mann,... was laconic: "No agreement was reached. We will assess the outcome of the Rambouillet talks and see what steps might be taken next."

What those next steps will be has now been determined: The Minsk Group cochairs will meet, this time in Washington in early March, and will invite the foreign ministers of Armenia and Azerbaijan to join them in an attempt to reestablish a direct dialogue between the heads of the two states involved in the dispute....

Little is known about how the Aliyev-Kocharyan talks went, only that the leaders' first meeting on Feb. 10 lasted for a total of about four hours. For the first 40 minutes, they were accompanied by the three Minsk Group cochairs, who presented the presidents with their proposals for a settlement of the conflict. Then Aliyev and Kocharyan conferred one-on-one for two and a half hours, after which they summoned their foreign ministers, [Elmar] Mamedyarov and [Vardan] Oskanyan, to join them. Before the talks got under way, the Azerbaijani and Armenian presidents were received by French President Jacques Chirac, who remarked afterward that "there is a real opportunity to lay the foundation for a resolution of the Karabakh problem."

What actually kept that from happening can be judged only from certain statements by the international mediators and from the commentary now coming out of Baku and Yerevan. Azerbaijan's ANS Television reported that the presidents had been unable to reach agreement on two of the nine points discussed at the meeting – the return of refugees and displaced persons, and Azerbaijan's territorial integrity. Information that Vremya novostei obtained in Paris yesterday from informed sources close to the Armenian-Azerbaijani talks suggests that this interpretation is close to the truth, although it is presented from the perspective of official Baku.

According to one source, the presidents' dialogue stalled when they began discussing a phased withdrawal by Armenia from several districts it occupies around Nagorno-Karabakh, primarily Kelbadzhar District, and preparations for a referendum in Karabakh on the enclave's future status. This is the so-called "package approach" to a settlement favored by Yerevan. But the referendum idea failed to win the support of Azerbaijani President Ilkham Aliyev. Baku is insisting on a phased resolution of the problem: First Armenia must return the occupied Azerbaijani territories without any conditions, and only then can the subject of Nagorno-Karabakh's status be discussed.

That position stems from domestic political factors. Under the present circumstances, a referendum on Karabakh's status that could result in its proclaiming independence would be opposed by the overwhelming majority of Azerbaijan's population. But that position on Baku's part hardly came as a surprise to those who initiated the Rambouillet meeting....

Informed diplomatic sources told Vremya novostei that the failure of the Rambouillet meeting means only one thing: Another round of talks between the Armenian and Azerbaijani leaders (in hopes that they might be more willing to compromise than they were in February) is unlikely to be arranged in 2006.... And the "golden pause" for a Karabakh settlement created by the absence of domestic political tensions in Armenia and Azerbaijan in 2006, which international mediators spoke of with such hope, will be lost.

IN BUCHAREST AS IN PARIS – Aliyev-Kocharyan Meeting Proves Fruitless
By Arkady Dubnov. *Vremya novostei*, June 6, 2006, p. 5.

The presidents of Armenia and Azerbaijan held another round of talks on a settlement of the Nagorno-Karabakh conflict on June 4-5 in Bucharest, with the mediation of the OSCE Minsk Group. The nominal occasion for the meeting was the presidents' participation in the Black Sea Forum for Dialogue and Partnership. The presidents met on Sunday evening [June 4] at the Polish Embassy, where they conferred for more than three hours. One of those hours was spent with the cochairmen of the OSCE Minsk Group – Yury Merzlyakov (Russia), Steven Mann (US) and Bernard Fassier (France), as well as with [Polish] Ambassador Andrzej Kasprzyk, the personal representative of the OSCE's chairman-in-office. Yesterday's meeting lasted about 40 minutes and was attended by those same OSCE mediators. According to Vremya novostei's sources, the meeting was a pro forma event intended to pin down the results of the previous day's discussions. Or lack of results, to be more precise.

According to VN's sources, Aliyev and Kocharyan were unable to overcome the differences that had led to the failure of the previous round of Armenian-Azerbaijani talks, held on Feb. 10-11 at Rambouillet Castle near Paris. The presidents were unable to come to terms on two issues: an Armenian withdrawal from occupied territories (primarily Kelbadzhar District) and the return of Azerbaijani refugees and displaced persons to die area, and preparations for a referendum in Nagorno-Karabakh to determine the status of the enclave.

The failure to achieve a breakthrough came as no surprise. When he left for Bucharest, Robert Kocharyan made no attempt to conceal his pessimism: "I have very modest expectations for my meeting with Ilkham Aliyev. One gets the impression that the Azerbaijani side isn't exactly inclined toward a peaceful settlement of the conflict, as the bellicose statements coming out of Baku attest." Azerbaijan responded in kind, accusing Armenia of systematically violating the cease-fire in the conflict zone. Two Azerbaijani soldiers were killed in May alone. Nine soldiers have been killed and another nine wounded since me beginning of me year.

The inability to reach a Karabakh settlement confirms predictions made by analysts, who maintain that the situation will not change until parliamentary and presidential elections are held in Armenia in 2007 and 2008, respectively. In the meantime, the dialogue between Baku and Yerevan will remain focused on the terms of a compromise proposed to the two sides by the mediators of the OSCE Minsk Group. The Minsk Group's three cochairmen are to prepare a report for a meeting of the OSCE Permanent Council on June 22, at which the outlook for continuing the talks will be discussed. The presidents of Armenia and Azerbaijan probably won't meet again until September, when a summit of the CIS is to be held in Moscow.

AZERBAIJAN ISN'T QUITTING THE NEGOTIATING PROCESS – OSCE Mediators Persuade Baku to Continue Contacts With Yerevan

By Sokhbet Mamedov. *Nezavisimaya gazeta*, Oct. 4, 2006, p. 5.

The main result of the latest round of talks in Baku between the cochairmen of the OSCE Minsk Group and the Azerbaijani leadership is that President Ilkham Aliyev agreed to continue contacts with the Armenian side.

Specifically, the international mediators from Russia, the US and France were able to reach agreement with the republic's leadership on arranging a meeting between the Azerbaijani and Armenian foreign ministers. At a concluding press conference, Yury Merzlyakov, the OSCE Minsk Group cochair from Russia, said that "the talks in Baku focused on renewing direct contacts on a Karabakh settlement, and we consider this task to have been accomplished with regard to Azerbaijan." After analogous talks with the Armenian leadership, the Russian diplomat said, it will be possible to talk about the time and place of talks between the two countries' foreign ministers, and after that it will be possible to begin arranging a meeting at the highest level, between the presidents. A source at the Azerbaijani Foreign Ministry told NG that such a meeting could take place in late October.

Bernard Fassier, the OSCE Minsk Group cochairman from France, said that the mediators will be working "under difficult circumstances" to set up the new meetings, because Paris, Moscow and Washington "rule out any military option for settling the conflict." Matthew Bryza, the American cochair of the OSCE Minsk Group, said that a recent initiative by the GUAM group [consisting of Georgia, Ukraine, Azerbaijan and Moldova] to discuss at the UN the problem of "frozen" conflicts "could have a positive effect on the Karabakh settlement process."[1]

Meanwhile, President Aliyev, who has come under heavy pressure lately from those who oppose continued peace talks with Armenia, reassured his opponents in an address to the first meeting of the fall session of the Milli Majlis (parliament). He said that not everything in the international mediators' proposals is acceptable to Azerbaijan, which lost approximately 20% of its territory in the war with Armenia. "We have been criticized for not settling the Karabakh problem. But the reason we have not done so is that the settlement options proposed to us are not consistent with Azerbaijan's national interests. Despite the pressure being exerted on us, I will never sign such a document," Ilkham Aliyev declared.

KARABAKH BREAKTHROUGH

By Andrei Odinets in Moscow and Rafael Mustafayev in Baku. *Kommersant*, Dec. 1, 2007, p. 4.

One of the few positive outcomes of the Madrid meeting of OSCE foreign ministers was the presentation of a plan for settling the Nagorno-Karabakh conflict. The plan was conveyed Thursday [Nov. 29] to the foreign ministers of Azerbaijan and Armenia, Elmar Mamedyarov and Vardan Oskanyan, by the countries of the OSCE Minsk Group (Russia, the US and France). "These proposals incorporate all of the positive understandings reached by Baku and Yerevan over the past few years," Russian Foreign Minister Sergei Lavrov said. "The Minsk Group's proposals are fair and objective," agreed US Under Secretary of State Nicholas Burns.

Kommersant learned some of the plan's details from diplomatic sources close to the talks. Under the plan, Yerevan would relinquish the territories surrounding Nagorno-Karabakh, which are currently under Armenian control, in phases. Armenian troops would withdraw from Kelbadzhar District (where only a limited contingent would remain), and the highway from Azerbaijan to Nakhichevan would be opened. Kelbadzhar District would be placed under international administration under OSCE auspices, but the area would eventually be transferred to the full control of Azerbaijan. At the same time, the plan calls for the establishment of a corridor in Lachin District to link Armenia with Nagorno-Karabakh. The territories vacated by the Armenian side would be demilitarized, and international peacekeepers would be stationed in them. Finally, the international community would encourage resettled Armenians to leave these territories and go back to Armenia's internal regions, and Azerbaijani refugees would be able to return to Kelbadzhar District a few years later. The UN Security Council would serve as guarantor of the peace agreement.

Matthew Bryza, the Minsk Group's American cochairman, yesterday urged Baku and Yerevan to "quickly approve the plan before the start of election campaigns in the two countries." Meanwhile, Azerbaijani and Armenian officials declined to comment yesterday on the document they had received. The head of the Azerbaijani Defense Ministry's press service, Eldar Sabiroglu, even said that "there are no guarantees against another war."

BAKU DISRUPTS AGREEMENTS – UN Resolution on Karabakh Provokes Controversy

By Grigory Plakhotnikov and Rafael Mustafayev. *Kommersant*, March 17, 2008, p. 9.

Baku – This past Friday [March 14], the UN General Assembly adopted a resolution on "the situation in the occupied territories of Azerbaijan."...

The Baku-initiated draft resolution on "the situation in the occupied territories of Azerbaijan" was submitted to the UN General Assembly for consideration back in late February, and at first it did not draw much attention from the world media. According to the UN Department of Public Information, the document urged UN member states to express support for the sovereignty and territorial integrity of Azerbaijan within its internationally recognized borders. "The General Assembly reaffirms that no State should recognize as lawful the situation resulting from the occupation of territories of the Republic of Azerbaijan, or render assistance in maintaining that situation," the draft resolution said. It also demanded "the immediate, complete and unconditional withdrawal of all Armenian forces from all the occupied territories."

The document was put to a vote in the General Assembly on Friday, and that's when the scandal erupted. The resolution was opposed by Russia, the US and France, which are the cochairs of the OSCE Minsk Group on Nagorno-Karabakh, which has been trying to negotiate a peaceful settlement of the conflict since 1992. Moscow, Washington and Paris issued a joint statement indicating that the resolution proposed by Baku "does not reflect all approaches to a settlement of the Karabakh conflict." Speaking on behalf of the Minsk Group, US Deputy Permanent Representative to the UN Alejandro Wolff pointed out that the resolution selectively reflects only some of the principles that the group has established as guidelines. "Because of this selective approach, the three OSCE Minsk Group cochair countries must oppose this unilateral draft resolution," Mr. Wolff said.

The rare consensus among the Minsk Group cochairs can be attributed primarily to the fact that the resolution submitted by Azerbaijan does not take into account the agreements that have already been reached within the group – in particular, the agreement on holding a referendum to determine the status of Nagorno-Karabakh. Additional confirmation of this was provided in a statement the Russian Foreign Ministry released after the vote. "The draft resolution included only some of the basic principles for a settlement – those that meet the interests of Azerbaijan alone – without mentioning, for example, the determination of a final legal status for Nagorno-Karabakh by holding a plebiscite among its population for a free and true expression of their will," the statement says.

Meanwhile, within the framework of the Minsk Group, Baku has repeatedly stated that it is amenable to holding a plebiscite, though it links this to the return of Azerbaijani refugees to Karabakh. But in Azerbaijan itself, many members of the establishment regarded that position as an impermissible concession: If a referendum were to be held, residents of Karabakh would certainly vote for independence, not for joining Azerbaijan. Therefore, official Baku assessed the adoption of the resolution as a great achievement, emphatically declaring that the document has full legal and political force. According to Azerbaijani Deputy Foreign Minister Araz Azimov, as a resolution of the UN General Assembly, the document should be viewed as a cornerstone for reaching a settlement of the conflict.

Of the UN's 192 member states, 146 participated in the vote. Thirty-nine of them (including 33 Muslim countries) were in favor of the resolution, and seven were opposed (Armenia, India, Angola and Vanuatu joined Russia, the US and France in saying "no"). But the majority (100 countries) chose to abstain.

Meanwhile, immediately after the vote, Baku threatened Moscow, Washington and Paris, saying that Azerbaijan might "review its relations" with them because of their refusal to support the resolution. "If the cochairs are going to take a selective approach to the resolution, acting solely out of concern for the role of the Minsk Group, their work will only become harder," Araz Azimov said. He added that he does not rule out the possibility of revising the Minsk Group's current operating mechanism, which has been in place since 1997.

LOST IN TRANSLATION FROM ARMENIAN

By Arkady Dubnov. *Vremya novostei*, Sept. 25, 2008, p. 5.

The political elites of Azerbaijan and Armenia have been engaged in heated debates for several days now as they try to discern the hidden meaning in remarks that Armenian President Serzh Sargsyan made in an interview with the BBC. If one believes the version of the interview that was released by the British radio station's Azerbaijani service on Sept. 22, the Armenian president's words appear sensational. Mr. Sargsyan allegedly said: "I proposed to Azerbaijani President Ilkham Aliyev that, as a demonstration of the Azerbaijanis' interest in the welfare and security of the people of Nagorno-Karabakh, he make investments there. Perhaps after that, Armenians in Karabakh would express a desire to live within Azerbaijan."

The Armenian leader's voicing aloud of even the hypothetical suggestion that Karabakh's Armenians might consider it possible to live within Azerbaijan caused a commotion. And even more so in Azerbaijan than in Armenia. Members of Azerbaijan's expert community are split. Some openly hail Sargsyan's statement. "If he keeps his word, he will go down in the history of not just the region, but the entire world," the Day.az news agency quotes Mubariz Akhmedoglu, director of the Center for Political Innovations and Technologies, as saying. "Sargsyan would be creating conditions for the existence of an Armenian community within Azerbaijan and for the existence of Armenian statehood as a whole."...

Vafa Guluzade, a former adviser to the Azerbaijani president who is known for his fierce rejection of Russian policy, holds a diametrically opposed point of view: "It would be far more honest to simply offer the Azerbaijani leadership the opportunity to buy back the parts of our country that are occupied by Armenia. Let

Serzh Sargsyan share the money with his partners in crime and the head honchos from Moscow who installed him as president of Armenia."

A statement released the next day by the Armenian president's press service was intended to stem the tide of emotions. It claims that the Azerbaijani media distorted the interview and that "the president didn't say that Karabakh's Armenians would agree to become part of Azerbaijan." But employees of the BBC's Moscow bureau said that they "take full responsibility" for the translation from Armenian, the language Sargsyan was speaking, to English – "none of the statements he made were distorted." Aleksandr Iskandaryan, a well-known Armenian political analyst and director of the Caucasus Media Institute, commented to Vremya novostei that "you can gauge whether or not a reader has a sense of humor from his reaction to what the Armenian president said," and that basically "there is no reason to stir up a tempest in a teacup over these words." Essentially, Yerevan released a trial balloon to test the reaction to its proposal in both Armenia and Azerbaijan, and then it fell back on standard diplomatic practice, dissociating itself from the remarks and blaming the ensuing uproar on an inaccurate translation.

Negotiations on a Karabakh settlement received a second wind as a result of Turkish President Abdullah Gul's visit to Yerevan on Sept. 6 to attend a soccer match, followed by his visit to Baku on Sept. 10. Ankara actively offered to serve as mediator in the dialogue between Baku and Yerevan. Considering that Turkey is one of the nine countries [sic; there are actually 13 – *Trans.*] that make up the OSCE Minsk Group [on settling the Karabakh conflict], the Turkish initiative seems to have a decent chance of succeeding. A few days ago, Turkish Foreign Minister Ali Babacan expressed hope that the negotiating process would speed up after Azerbaijan's presidential election on Oct. 15: "The Armenians have expressed readiness to resolve their problems not only with Turkey, but also with Azerbaijan." However, according to VN's information, Yerevan has already confined the possible parameters of Ankara's participation in the negotiating process to "assistance," not "mediation," which will continue to be the job of the Minsk Group....

––––––––––––––

KARABAKH POSTPONED

By Yury Simonyan. *Nezavisimaya gazeta*, Dec. 2, 2009, p. 7.

In Athens, where the 17th session of the Ministerial Council of the OSCE is under way, a meeting has taken place between Armenian Foreign Minister Eduard Nalbandyan and Azerbaijani Foreign Minister Elmar Mamedyarov. The ministers discussed the issue of the self-declared Nagorno-Karabakh Republic (NKR), continuing a dialogue that had been resumed by the countries' presidents on Nov. 22 in Munich....

Before the ministers met in Athens, it was announced pointedly that Nalbandyan and Mamedyarov would touch on important questions such as the status of the NKR.

Judging by half-hints from official spokesmen in Baku and Yerevan, one might have speculated that the ministers were even capable of reaching a compromise. That was difficult to believe, though. As of today, it is hard to imagine that the Azerbaijani side would in any way agree to the NKR having the status of an independent state – or, on the other hand, that Armenia would stop supporting Karabakh's sovereignty. After the Athens talks, the skeptics were gloating.

After Nalbandyan and Mamedyarov's meeting, which "took place in a luncheon format" on Monday [Nov. 30], the Armenian Foreign Ministry's press service released a report saying that "the two sides discussed the possibility of approving a statement about Nagorno-Karabakh to be issued by the OSCE Ministerial Council for its 17th session," and also that Nalbandyan had met with the cochairmen of the OSCE Minsk Group – Yury Merzlyakov (Russia), Bernard Fassier (France) and Robert Bradtke (US) – and with Andrzej Kasprzyk, personal representative of the OSCE chairman-in-office, and Goran Lennmarker, the OSCE Parliamentary Assembly's special representative for Nagorno-Karabakh.

In a brief comment for journalists, Elmar Mamedyarov, for his part, expressed optimism. "There is potential for intensifying the negotiation process on the Nagorno-Karabakh conflict next year. The countries cochairing the OSCE's Minsk Group recognize that this is necessary. I believe that the potential is there." Lennmarker went a bit further, specifying that "we can expect positive results in the very near future."

But the "very near future" of those positive results is already seriously irritating the Azerbaijani side. A few days after [Azerbaijani and Armenian Presidents] Aliyev and Sargsyan met in Munich, Azerbaijan's Defense Minister Safar Abiyev made a statement that clashed with Aliyev's positive tone regarding the negotiations. At a meeting in Baku with his Polish counterpart Bogdan Klich, Abiyev said that "the cochairmen of the OSCE's Minsk Group have been unable to solve this problem for 15 years now, and no solution remains other than taking back Karabakh by military means."

Yerevan responded no less pointedly to the Azerbaijani defense chief's statement. At a congress of the Republican Party, at which he was elected its chairman, Armenian President Serzh Sargsyan, touching on Armenian-Azerbaijani problems, demanded categorically that Baku "change its rhetoric and once and for all forget about a possible war in Karabakh," or else "Yerevan is prepared to assist the NKR and give the harshest kind of response."

Nagorno-Karabakh itself also responded to Baku's bellicose warnings. In late November, the National Assembly (parliament) issued a special statement defining for itself the right to "respond appropriately to statements made about Artsakh (the NKR's name for itself – NG)." The statement emphasizes that these periodic threats make Karabakh think of the Azerbaijani side as "an extremely unreliable participant in the peace talks to resolve the conflict." The NKR's Foreign Ministry, at the behest of parliament, sent a copy of that statement to the OSCE secretariat to be disseminated to the participants in the OSCE foreign ministers' meeting in Athens, and sent another copy personally to OSCE Chairman-in-Office George

Papandreou. Observers believe that these actions by the NKR signal not just a desire to attract the attention of the international community to the military threats from Azerbaijan, but also, possibly, the beginning of attempts to return to the negotiating process, which since the mid-1990s has been proceeding without Stepanakert, with only Baku, Yerevan and mediators participating....

BAKU IS TALKING ABOUT WAR AGAIN

By Sokhbet Mamedov and Svetlana Gamova. *Nezavisimaya gazeta*, June 24, 2010, p. 6.

Baku – Nagorno-Karabakh has once again popped up on the international community's radar screen: The presidents of Azerbaijan and Armenia exchanged remarks on the conflict, demonstrating their differing views of the problem. Ilkham Aliyev expressed his opinions at home – at a meeting of the Islamic Development Bank. Serzh Sargsyan spoke out in Germany. The Azerbaijani president reproached Armenia for ignoring resolutions made by international organizations, while the Armenian leader expressed disappointment with "the ambiguous position of European institutions" on incidents in the conflict zone. The exchange of words was caused by an exchange of fire between the two countries' troops on the border.

Addressing the 35th annual meeting of the Islamic Development Bank Group in Baku, Azerbaijani President Ilkham Aliyev said: "Karabakh is indigenous Azerbaijani territory and I have no doubt whatsoever that it will be liberated." He described the occupation of Nagorno-Karabakh and the seven districts around it as "the most painful and serious problem that Azerbaijan has faced during its entire period of independence."

"The conflict can only be resolved under the principle of Azerbaijan's territorial integrity," Aliyev stressed. In his words, a foundation for that is provided by the decisions adopted by international organizations – the UN, the OSCE and the Council of Europe – but Armenia is ignoring these organizations and continues to occupy Azerbaijani territories."

Every day, the Azerbaijani Defense Ministry press service comes out with reports on Armenia's attempts to mount offensive operations; it has also reported the shelling of Azerbaijani army positions, which the defending side has successfully repelled. However, one of the bloodiest clashes took place on the night of June 18-19, as a result of which four Armenians were killed and as many injured. One Azerbaijani army serviceman was also killed in the gunfight.

Commenting on the incident, Azerbaijani Defense Ministry press secretary Eldar Sabiroglu told NG that the incident was a provocation by Armenian armed forces on the front line. "By once again creating tension on the front line, the Armenian side is trying to find a way out of the impasse in the negotiating process. Evidently, President Sargsyan was not satisfied with some aspects of the recent negotiations in St. Petersburg if he decided to resort to such actions," Sabiroglu observed.

In his opinion, the latest events confirm that Armenia is not interested in a peaceful settlement of the Karabakh conflict. Furthermore, the press secretary believes that clashes along the front line could lead to the outbreak of war in the region, given that over the past month, Armenian army subunits violated a cease-fire agreement 101 times.

"I would like to take this opportunity to point out the following: According to our data, 70% of conscripts in the Armenian Armed Forces serve on Azerbaijani territories occupied by Armenia. The majority of those killed and wounded during the gunfight on the night of June 18-19 are Armenian nationals. These facts confirm that Armenia is waging an invasive war against Azerbaijan."

The latest events on the line of separation between the two countries' troops have caused serious worries among international organizations involved in negotiating a resolution to the conflict.

The cochairs of the OSCE Minsk Group expressed serious concern about the use of force and the senseless loss of life in the conflict zone. They noted that "the incident took place immediately after the meeting between the Presidents of Armenia and Azerbaijan, held in St. Petersburg on June 17 at the invitation of the President of the Russian Federation to pursue the negotiation of peaceful settlement of the Nagorno-Karabakh conflict." "The use of military force, particularly at this moment, can only be seen as an attempt to damage the peace process," the statement said....

According to the overwhelming majority of Azerbaijani analysts, the latest incidents should be a warning to Armenia and the mediating countries: The Armenian-Azerbaijani conflict is by no means a frozen one, and war could resume at any moment.

In the opinion of political commentator Rasim Musabekov, Baku has not yet withdrawn from the negotiating process. At the same time, a number of steps it has taken show that it was not just spouting propaganda when it issued previous warnings that the course of events might compel it to use force to restore the country's territorial integrity.

"Contrary to persistent recommendations from Western countries, the Milli Majlis directly indicated [the possibility of using force] in its recently adopted military doctrine, while the day before the St. Petersburg meeting, the parliament allocated additional budget expenditures and increased military spending by one-third. So, our military spending this year will reach $2 billion, which actually exceeds Armenia's entire state budget," the expert says, adding that as the peace process drags on, the risks of recurring clashes run high.

Meanwhile, Armenian President Serzh Sargsyan believes that conflict resolution is impeded by the ambiguous reaction of the international community to various incidents. "Progress is often hampered by the uncertain position of numerous structures, including European structures, their concern being that if they point the finger at anyone, it could affect the negotiating process," Sargsyan said on Tuesday [June 22] in Germany.

According to Armenia's version of events, late in the evening of June 18, an Azerbaijani army scout team infiltrated the territory of unrecognized Nagorno-Karabakh near the village of Chailu, where it ran into Karabakh border guards....

'ARMENIA IS YIELDING TO INTERNATIONAL PRESSURE'

By Ivan Sukhov. *Vremya novostei*, Dec. 2, 2010, p. 3.

Editors' Note. – An OSCE summit is under way in Astana, where – as Dmitry Medvedev suggested at an Oct. 27 Russian-Armenian-Azerbaijani meeting in Astrakhan – the sides involved in the Nagorno-Karabakh conflict "might come to an agreed-upon set of common principles for settling the situation." But such a breakthrough in the settlement process could turn out to be so unacceptable for Armenia that it could threaten the downfall of Serzh Sargsyan, who was elected in 2008, or even a revival of the Karabakh war. Levon Zurabyan, an opposition leader from the Armenian National Congress, talked with Vremya novostei commentator Ivan Sukhov about possible paths toward settlement.

* * *

Question. – Where did the idea come from that a breakthrough in the Karabakh conflict might be possible?

Answer. – Pressure is mounting around Nagorno-Karabakh. The basic reason for it is a growing military-strategic imbalance between Armenia and Azerbaijan in favor of the latter. As long as talks are under way and there are promises from the international community that the conflict will be resolved, Baku won't go to war. But it will get a casus belli if it proves that talks are stalling. Without strong pressure from the international community, it will be hard to avoid war. On the other hand, Russia is inclined to believe that maintaining the status quo any longer is impossible. In the two years since the war in Georgia, interest has grown among all players for a rapid settlement of the Nagorno-Karabakh problem. There is competition between the US and Russia over how to settle the Karabakh problem. Sargsyan hopes that controversy between the US and Russia will impede a breakthrough. But that would be a temporary postponement. It will be very hard for Sargsyan to find a way out: His regime isn't providing an answer to the question of how to maintain a military-strategic balance with Azerbaijan.

Q. – Was extending the agreement on the Russian military base in Gyumri a sufficient response?

A. – As it is, the agreement on the base in Gyumri is effective for another 15 years. But if it comes to war, Azerbaijan will portray everything as an operation against "separatists" on "its" territory. Everyone will be interested in localizing the fighting, and Baku can play off that. Currently, an international security system is in place. The main factor keeping war in check in the region is Russia, which is being supported by the Europeans and the Americans. But the growing imbalance between Armenia and

Azerbaijan is gradually making that system inadequate. The only possible answer for Armenia is modernization. We are in a state of partial blockade. The economy needs to have illegal monopolies broken up, illegal customs and tax benefits must be taken away from the oligarchs close to the president, and we need to return to competition and focus on exports. Currently, Armenia is yielding to international pressure. But it needs to be able to speak from a more secure position. Right now, they are trying to dictate a certain solution for Armenia, and the current regime can do nothing to oppose it. The main diplomatic achievement for Armenia was the acknowledgment at the 1994 OSCE summit that Nagorno-Karabakh was a party to the conflict. That made it possible to lay a foundation for recognizing Nagorno-Karabakh's independence and it protected Armenia from international pressure. All of that was completely lost by [the succeeding] Armenian presidents of Karabakh descent – Robert Kocharyan and Serzh Sargsyan. They made a deal with the international community that facilitated the latest negotiations on Nagorno-Karabakh. In exchange, the world closed its eyes to human rights violations and ballot-rigging in Armenia. By agreeing to represent Nagorno-Karabakh in negotiations, they [Kocharyan and Sargsyan] changed the concept of the conflict: What had been considered a war of the people of Nagorno-Karabakh for self-determination became a territorial conflict between Armenia and Azerbaijan. That was a strategic mistake based on selfish reasons.

Q. – What sort of breakthrough might be achieved in Astana?

A. – Sargsyan could be pressured. Then the possibility would arise of a framework agreement that disregards the interests of Nagorno-Karabakh. A serious battle is being waged between Armenia and Azerbaijan, between mediators, between the real geopolitical interests of many countries.

Q. – But if the Armenian president comes to a compromise that hurts the interests of Nagorno-Karabakh, he'll become a political corpse.

A. – He's been driven into a corner; he needs to choose the lesser of two evils. From his standpoint, that would be the choice that allows him to remain in power. His legitimacy rests on the support of the international community; he doesn't have any domestic legitimacy. Therefore, he is susceptible to international pressure, and losing international support would be fatal for him....

Q. – Is war a possibility?

A. – The only thing preventing it is that not one of the great or regional powers has an interest in it. If war breaks out, Russia, Turkey, Iran and the US will get involved. That's a global escalation of instability that nobody wants. But Azerbaijan is becoming more demanding, and the international community could start showing a trend toward "appeasing the aggressor."

Q. – Many people think Armenia is the aggressor.

A. – No. Everyone understands that Azerbaijan was trying to deal with the Karabakh problem by force and even trying to get rid of the republic's Armenian population. The result was military action, which led to the creation of a security belt. Because of its aggressiveness, Azerbaijan has missed several opportunities to resolve the conflict.

Q. – What became of the Armenian-Turkish initiatives of 2008?

A. – That initiative was basically sponsored by the Americans. At its core was the removal of problems in American-Turkish relations. The Armenian diaspora in America got promises from the Republicans and the Democrats that the US would formally acknowledge the genocide of Armenians [by Turkish authorities of the Ottoman Empire] in 1915. But such a resolution would spoil US-Turkish relations. America, which is involved in two tough wars in the Middle East, doesn't need that. And so they contrived an Armenian-Turkish settlement process: Armenia agrees to Turkey's proposal for a joint review of the genocide, and the US gets an opportunity to allude to a reconciliation process – which would be jeopardized if the US acknowledged the Armenian genocide. That was a crude miscalculation by Armenia's leadership. The essence of the deal is that Armenia "sells" the genocide issue, and in return, Turkey opens its borders....

The genocide issue has been raised in vain in talks – it has turned from an issue of moral responsibility into a political bargaining chip: Turkey got a question mark put on the genocide issue, Armenia didn't get anything, and the border remains closed. Turkey has tied ratification to a breakthrough in resolving the Nagorno-Karabakh problem. That has led to an increased role for Turkey in the settlement process. Until now, Turkey had only formally been a member of the Minsk Group of the OSCE. Today, it is one of the group's key players. That is one of the most grievous consequences of Sargsyan's miscalculation.

Q. – Did Russia want to stop the Armenia-Turkey [Protocols] process?

A. – How could it have stopped the process? The Turks stopped it when they didn't ratify the Protocols, by linking them with Karabakh. I think that Russia, like the US and Europe, wanted the Protocols ratified. But that issue is being addressed by Turkey, which nobody can pressure. It is more interested in entering the Nagorno-Karabakh settlement process than in opening its border.

Q. – If the border is opened, will Russia lose influence over Armenia?

A. – Armenia would get more freedom to maneuver. But the question is a different one: Does Russia need influence over an Armenia that is perishing or an Armenia that is a strong ally? Russia understands that the US is stuck in Iraq and Afghanistan for the time being. But after some time, it will manage to free its hands and become more active in the Caucasus. Now, Russia has a double incentive to settle the Karabakh issue on its own terms. It is interested in becoming the primary guarantor of an agreement between the Armenians and the Azerbaijanis. Russia is inclined to believe that maintaining the status quo is not in its interests and could harm it in the future. Therefore, Russia is playing an even greater role than that of a Minsk Group cochair.

Q. – What is the ideal solution to the Nagorno-Karabakh problem, and how can it be achieved?

A. – First of all, by modernizing Armenia and destroying the stagnant regime that is based on a clan-oligarchy system. That would allow Armenia to negotiate without being on its knees. That could quickly improve the situation. In the 1990's, the gross domestic products of Armenia and Azerbaijan, as well as their military budgets, were comparable. Armenia was the leader, surpassing Georgia and Azerbaijan according to many indicators. That's not true today. Armenia is experiencing an economic decline. Armenia's government machine has been "hijacked" by a few oligarch families; they are using the levers of power for personal enrichment. The country's exports are only a fraction of its imports, and it has been artificially inflating the national currency over the past 10 years. That allows importers to have super-high profits. Incidentally, a change in power would automatically mean that the international community would give Armenia a time-out to seek new proposals for solving foreign policy problems. As for Karabakh, it needs to be stated clearly that this is a conflict between Nagorno-Karabakh and Azerbaijan. Any other position would mean that Armenia is an occupier or an aggressor....

GRAVE RESULT OF THE OSCE SUMMIT

By Yury Simonyan, deputy head of NG's desk for politics in the near abroad. *Nezavisimaya gazeta*, Dec. 6, 2010, p. 11.

Analysts have been quick to call the OSCE summit in Astana that took place on Dec. 1-2 unproductive. At first glance, it was. The declared tasks and objectives – which, you may recall, were predominately centered on the conflicts in the post-Soviet space – turned out to be unattainable. For everyone. Georgia did not succeed in getting the term "occupied territories" used in the OSCE format with regard to Abkhazia and South Ossetia – which it had managed to do earlier at the NATO Parliamentary Assembly. Moldova did not succeed in getting the other member countries to reach an understanding for withdrawing Russian troops from Transnistria. Azerbaijan did not succeed in persuading the community to adopt its interpretation of the Karabakh conflict. And Armenia did not sway them its way, either.

But, although the Georgian and Moldovan conflicts could currently be called "chronic" in nature, with no potential for escalation for the time being, the Armenian-Azerbaijani conflict may have entered the acute phase in Astana. An alarming symptom was that presidents Ilkham Aliyev and Serzh Sargsyan did not meet with one another. And the reason they didn't, frankly, was because it would have been senseless.

The only thing Baku wants to talk and hear about is Azerbaijan's territorial integrity. Yerevan has, perhaps in tougher terms than ever before, made it understood that its patience isn't endless, and that Armenia – which is now officially the guarantor of Nagorno-Karabakh's security – would simply acknowledge the sovereignty of that Armenian republic if faced with foreign political pressure or force from Azerbaijan. Indeed, in that case, war would likely break out. It would hardly last long. Then, more than likely, peace would need to be enforced – maybe with peacekeepers brought in. And, logically, the final demarcation of the geographic layout would stay whatever it is at that moment. That's the worst-case scenario. But one gets the impression that those involved in the conflict – the mediators, who have adopted yet another amorphous document with words of peace – are already prepared for just that. And no longer at the declarative level, of course. Informed sources are certain that Baku is delaying striking the first blow only because it can't be certain of a quick victory. And it couldn't be quick, considering reality. A relatively drawn-out military campaign, if the world community allows it, will inevitably turn into a domestic crisis with unpredictable consequences for the current authorities. And Yerevan, as noted above, has put forth its position: Let there be war, if there is no other way.

The situation surrounding Karabakh has, in the blink of an eye, become reminiscent of that which preceded the Russian-Georgian war of August 2008: frequent provocations between frontline forces, tougher rhetoric, statements about not wanting war but being ready for it, many comments from the expert community about the inevitability of confrontation, etc. We can only hope that the Karabakh situation will be an exception to the "unwritten rule." But the Armenian-Azerbaijani settlement process has shown complete stagnation in Astana, instead of leaving even the slightest glimmer of hope for a peaceful outcome of the confrontation between all sides involved in the conflict.

BAKU EQUATES KARABAKHS WITH TERRORISTS

By Yury Roks. *Nezavisimaya gazeta*, Dec. 8, 2010, p. 1.

On Monday [Dec. 6] and Tuesday, Azerbaijani and Armenian media outlets made public a number of sharp statements by members of the political establishment that bear witness to the two sides' readiness to launch a large-scale war. Baku is talking about the need to conduct a "counterterrorist operation" in Nagorno-Karabakh. Yerevan and Stepanakert are talking about their willingness to respond in kind. The publications claim that the diasporas outside Azerbaijan and Armenia have begun mobilizing and that they are ready, if necessary, to arm 150,000 to 200,000 people from each side.

The escalation, which is so far limited to the information arena, began almost immediately after an OSCE summit in Astana on Dec. 1-2, which was called unproductive by political analysts.

Renewed hostilities from the sides in the Nagorno-Karabakh conflict might seem inevitable. And talk of the impending arrival of tens of thousands of foreign mercenaries is not an exaggeration: "Soldiers of fortune" have fought in Karabakh before. The flames of an already tense situation were fanned by comments (widely publicized in media outlets in both countries) from the chairman of Russia's Islamic Committee, Geidar Dzhemal, to the effect that the Karabakh problem should have been resolved by force long ago instead of holding countless unproductive negotiations. The situation indeed seems at a stalemate. Azerbaijan cannot in any way achieve a breakthrough in the negotiation process and bring to the fore the principle of territorial integrity – which, according to Baku's interpretation, could also accommodate Nagorno-Karabakh's self-determination. Armenia is complaining that its staunchly held arguments – that Karabakh has already gone through a self-determination process, having carried out two referendums, and that the issue is now the republic's international recognition – are not finding the desired support.

"Despite the prevailing opinion, I would not claim that the OSCE summit was a failure. In any case, I feel a step forward has been made toward settling the Karabakh conflict: The presidents of Azerbaijan and Armenia have signed on to the Muskoka Declaration, which proposes a six-step outline of the well-known Madrid settlement principles," Stepan Grigoryan, head of the Yerevan-based Analytical Center for Globalization and Regional Cooperation, told NG.

Readers are reminded that the joint Muskoka Declaration – adopted during a Group of Eight summit in Huntsville, Canada in June by the presidents of the countries that cochair the OSCE Minsk Group (Russia, the US and France) – is devoted to the settlement of the Nagorno-Karabakh conflict. It includes the return of the territories surrounding Nagorno-Karabakh; interim status for Nagorno-Karabakh, guaranteeing security and self-governance; a corridor linking Armenia to Nagorno-Karabakh, final status of Nagorno-Karabakh to be determined in the future by a legally binding expression of will; the right of all internally displaced persons and refugees to return to their former homes; and international security guarantees, including a peacekeeping operation. Plus, it contains recommendations such as refraining from statements and actions capable of adversely affecting the situation.

"Therefore, Ilkham Aliyev and Serzh Sargsyan – and this is the most important thing – have reaffirmed their desire to resolve the problem without resorting to weapons. Another thing is that the populations of Azerbaijan and Armenia are heterogeneous; they include so-called "irreconcilables" who feel that even the slightest concession is inadmissible. Appeals for militarism will peal forth, and we need to be ready for that," Grigoryan told NG. "According to the political analyst – who just recently attended a major conference in Baku -the populations of both Armenia and Azerbaijan are radicalized to the same degree in this regard. Meanwhile, expert circles in both countries feel to about the same extent that negotiations are necessary and so are actions to increase mutual trust. "The meeting of the presidents of Russia, Azerbaijan and Armenia in Astrakhan can be considered a positive example. That meeting was also hastily called inconclusive, but agreements were made there on specific issues whose implementation had a positive impact on the overall atmosphere. Take, for example, the restoration of an Armenian church in Baku. That, of course, is just one trust-building step, and there will have to be many more before anything budges," thinks Stepan Grigoryan.

Rasim Musabekov, a political science professor and an Azerbaijani parliamentary deputy, also thinks that the situation between Baku and Yerevan is not as acute now as it has been in the past. "If you follow the statements and attacks published in the media, you can see an obvious attempt to heat up the situation. Not one official in the days following the summit in Astana has tried to escalate matters or resorted to provocative statements. It seems to me that this is an absolutely unproductive policy by media outlets who are trying to stir things up for their own purposes," Musabekov told NG....

BAKU DISSATISFIED WITH OSCE MINSK GROUP

By Sokhbet Mamedov. *Nezavisimaya gazeta*, March 18, 2011, p. 6.

Baku – In recent years, the lack of results from the OSCE Minsk Group's 15-year mission to mediate a resolution to the Armenia-Azerbaijan conflict has become the subject of sharp criticism in Azerbaijan. Recently, dissatisfaction with the mediators' actions was expressed by Azerbaijan's defense minister, Lt. Gen. Safar Abiyev. Receiving Ukrainian Defense Minister Mikhail Yezhel in Baku, Abiyev lamented that the Minsk Group's actions were not yielding concrete results.

Baku maintains that it is unacceptable when almost 20% of Azerbaijan's territory is occupied by neighboring Armenia and roughly 1 million people have been expelled from their homeland for mediators to do nothing but shuffle back and forth to the region and shrug their shoulders, saying there is nothing more they can do. Resolutions by authoritative international organizations calling for an end of Armenia's occupation policy remain unimplemented.

As Safar Abiyev noted, in a situation like this, Azerbaijan has no choice but to take serious and necessary steps to liberate the occupied territories. "We are stepping up activity in that area," said Abiyev.

"Every time, the mediators come up with some new format for negotiations in order to drag out the process of resolving the conflict. That helps the mediating countries keep the situation in the region under control and exert influence on the states in the region," political analyst Rasim Agayev said on Wednesday [March 16] at the 17th session of the South Caucasus discussion club for political analysts, devoted to the topic of "March activities of the negotiation process for Nagorno-Karabakh settlement."

"As a result, the negotiating process is being unjustifiably delayed, and the situation is returning to that of the late 1980s. In this situation, Azerbaijan may use the option of force to resolve the conflict. This may significantly alter the existing status quo and create a new one," Agayev commented.

Against this background, analysts see the initiatives of regional players Russia and Turkey as more promising. Thanks to the efforts of Russian President Dmitry Medvedev, eight meetings were held between the leaders of Azerbaijan and Armenia, Ilkham Aliyev and Serzh Sargsyan, which led to a resolution of the issue of prisoner-of-war exchanges. On Thursday, according to agreements reached in Sochi, an operation was conducted to exchange Artur Badalyan, an Armenian citizen who had been detained in Azerbaijan, for Azerbaijani Army Sgt. Anar Gadzhiyev, a prisoner of the Armenian side. A similar exchange took place earlier, following a meeting between the leaders of the three countries in Astrakhan. These concrete steps, although humanitarian in nature, demonstrate Russia's special role in the process of resolving the conflict. That, incidentally, was noted by Turkish Prime Minister Recep Tayyip Erdogan after negotiations with President Dmitry Medvedev in Moscow. He said that Moscow's initiatives in resolving the Nagorno-Karabakh problem are capable of exerting a positive influence on the normalization of Armenian-Turkish relations and make it possible to establish peace in the region.

Many analysts believe that the Turkish prime minister was in fact indicating that Moscow has a greater capacity than other mediators to influence the process of resolving the Nagorno-Karabakh conflict – a conflict that, unless resolved, will leave no hope for the normalization of Armenian-Turkish relations.

EUROPEAN 'REALPOLITIK' AND EASTERN BARBARISM

By staff correspondent Aleksandr Mineyev. *Novaya gazeta*, Sept. 7, 2012, p. 9.

Brussels – EU diplomacy is in a stupor from some unexpected craziness to which it must somehow respond. For it, this foreign policy scandal is exceedingly ill timed. So far, we're hearing only barely coherent statements of condemnation. But the EU foreign ministers will find it difficult to act as if nothing has happened during a meeting in Cyprus this Friday [Sept. 7].

The players in this event are EU member Hungary and one of the six member countries in the Eastern Partnership project – Azerbaijan.

In 2004, when Hungary was considered a completely democratic new member of the Western community, a seminar for soldiers took place in Budapest as part of NATO's Partnership for Peace program. Participants were representatives of Azerbaijan and Armenia, among others. The night after yet another discussion, Ramil Safarov, a lieutenant in the Azerbaijani Army, entered the room where his 25-year-old Armenian counterpart, Gurgen Margaryan, was sleeping, and delivered him 16 blows with an axe, practically chopping off [Margaryan's] head.

The stunned Hungarians collared the barbarian, and a court sentenced him to that country's highest form of punishment: life imprisonment.

In July 2012, Hungarian Prime Minister Viktor Orban, during a visit to Baku, reached an agreement with [Azerbaijani] President Ilkham Aliyev whereby the convicted Safarov would be handed over to continue serving his sentence in an Azerbaijani prison. Rumor in Brussels has it that the criminal was exchanged for a promise from Aliyev to buy Hungarian government bonds.

On Aug. 31, Lt. Safarov was put on a plane and flown from Budapest to Baku, where he got a hero's welcome. The president praised him, promoted him directly from lieutenant to major, paid him eight years' worth of wages and gave him an apartment. At a briefing, a highly placed Azerbaijani representative assured the press that in chopping up his sleeping victim with an axe, Safarov "was defending the honor and dignity of his country."

No government of a country that considers itself civilized could fail to condemn such actions. The same day, the White House expressed its bewilderment to Aliyev, and on Monday, the Russian Foreign Ministry announced its "deep concern." In Brussels, Maja Kocijancic, the press secretary of the EU foreign policy body, speaking before journalists, admitted that her leadership was disturbed by the possible negative consequences of this event for the situation in the region, where shooting has started up again in the area of the Nagorno-Karabakh conflict.

European leaders, intoxicated by the aroma of oil and gas, have been turning a blind eye to Azerbaijan's domestic policy, which is far from European standards of democracy and human rights.

Moscow is even farther removed from human rights sentiments. The EU and Russia are both vying for attention from the Azerbaijani leader, and competing over how to transport Caspian gas to Europe – whether through Russian territory or bypassing it. Washington, meanwhile, is counting on Baku's assistance in moving American military forces out of Afghanistan in 2014. And now this! Even Azerbaijan's close ally Turkey could not avoid expressing its concern.

Yerevan has frozen diplomatic relations with Budapest. But Budapest is more indignant than anyone. Hungary was already having difficulty cleaning up its image as the "sick man of Europe," which it has been stuck with since last year, after the adoption of populist laws limiting the autonomy of the Central Bank and freedom of the press. The Azerbaijani ambassador has been called on the carpet at the Hungarian Foreign Ministry, and [Hungary] has even released a letter in which Baku promised the Hungarians that Safarov would spend the rest of his life in prison.

Few believe Budapest. Armenia has logically pointed out that the Hungarians are not so naïve as to be unaware of what Aliyev is like and what would actually happen to Safarov in his homeland.

So far, European Council President Herman Van Rompuy, who shook Aliyev's hand in July in Baku, is keeping quiet. European energy commissioner Günther Oettinger was in Baku last weekend, and also did not make a peep.

Ironically, Aliyev signed the order to pardon and reward Safarov eight days after the EU allotted Azerbaijan 19.5 million euros to conduct democratic reforms of the court system and the immigration service. He completely forgot his manners!

PRICE OF OFFICER SAFAROV'S FREEDOM

By Yury Roks. *Nezavisimaya gazeta*, Sept. 3, 2012, p. 1.

The controversy involving Hungary, Azerbaijan and Armenia is gaining momentum....

Yerevan announced it was halting diplomatic relations with Budapest and recalled its ambassador. There have been emotional protests in the Armenian capital involving the burning of the Hungarian flag. Several publications have reported the price of freedom for Safarov – 3 billion euros, which Azerbaijan will use to buy Hungarian government bonds. And social networks have exploded with curses against Hungary and Azerbaijan.

Budapest may have any number of reasons for extraditing the convict to his homeland, ranging from the theory voiced by Armenian newspapers to [Hungary's] interest in Azerbaijani energy resources. But it had better be an extremely weighty reason – in taking this step, the Hungarian authorities had to have expected a serious negative reaction from internal opponents and from the West, and, most likely, joint backlash in the international arena, which is being successfully lobbied by the global Armenian diaspora.

Azerbaijan, of course, has its own interest in what has transpired. In giving Safarov his freedom – whether he is a national hero or the murderer of a sleeping man is, in the end, a matter for the Azerbaijani people to decide – President Ilkham Aliyev, of course, also would have foreseen the West's reaction. With his act, he seems to have declared his self-sufficiency and demonstrated his willingness to act on certain issues without regard for the international community. In this light, it is curious that Safarov's amnesty took place on the eve of the latest anniversary of the unrecognized independence of Nagorno-Karabakh. In freeing the convicted officer, the Azerbaijani leader was also able to pursue another goal – raising the fighting spirit of both the national army and the people as a whole, giving them clear evidence that the government does not abandon its heroes in distress. And finally, the Azerbaijani authorities themselves, who are growing increasingly uncomfortable with a more proactive opposition, have acquired in the run-up to the [presidential] election next year a decent trump card in their game with the nationalistically inclined segment of society.

Armenia is, of course, incensed. But if we leave emotions aside once again, then it turns out that Yerevan didn't lose much in this escapade. Undoubtedly, state and national pride have been wounded. But by whom? Hungary – a country that does not even have an embassy in Armenia. Yerevan's response, at the government level, has been completely appropriate: Its ambassador has been recalled from Budapest for consultations, and there is a discussion under way to break off diplomatic relations. Armenia's disappointment in NATO and the EU ... evidently will allow Yerevan to expect certain preferences from those institutions. But the main thing is that in negotiations on the Nagorno-Karabakh issue, the Armenian side will now be able to point to the unreliability of Azerbaijan's statements and promises about the shining future of Nagorno-Karabakh and its population as part of a unified state. For the West, where the Azerbaijani government is seen as having pardoned and coddled a common murderer, this is a serious argument. And Baku will not have an easy time putting its spin on the situation, no matter how often it appeals to the fact that its legislation allows for amnesty of the convicted officer.

ARMENIAN PARLIAMENT DOES NOT RECOGNIZE NAGORNO-KARABAKH'S INDEPENDENCE

By Yury Roks. *Nezavisimaya gazeta*, Nov. 14, 2013, p. 6.

The majority of deputies of the Armenian National Assembly (parliament) did not support a bill to formally recognize the independence of the Nagorno-Karabakh Republic (NKR). Only 10 deputies out of 131 voted in favor of the bill, introduced by the opposition party Heritage, which has been calling for years to recognize the NKR's independence. Without waiting for the parliament's decision, Armenian President Serzh Sargsyan traveled to Nagorno-Karabakh and, together with his counterpart, [NKR President] Bako Saakyan, familiarized himself with the conditions of military service in several parts of the breakaway republic.

The fact that Armenian deputies would abstain from recognizing the independence of the NKR was clear even before the bill was yet again submitted. Declaring the NKR an independent state would mean the start of a new war with Azerbaijan. Meanwhile, Armenia's official position is that it does not believe negotiations have run their course. The fact that the issue of recognizing the NKR's independence was broached now should perhaps be viewed as a maneuver in the run-up to a meeting between Ilkham Aliyev and Serzh Sargsyan, which could take place before the end of November. The parliament's decision is intended to show that Armenia wants to resolve the issue by peaceful means.

Speaking in parliament, Deputy Foreign Minister Shavarsh Kocharyan stressed that de jure recognition of the NKR's independence at this point is not a good idea. "But Armenia has long ago de facto recognized the NKR. We have signed roughly 100 bilateral agreements, and these agreements are parity-based," he said. He stressed that the Minsk [Group] conflict resolution process first requires Armenia and Azerbaijan to work out a unified approach to solving it. The NKR will then join in on working out a peace treaty. "Armenia must not stand alone in recognizing the NKR, as Turkey is doing on the issue of Northern Cyprus," said Kocharyan.

The Azerbaijani side did some maneuvering of its own. President Ilkham Aliyev paid a two-day visit to Turkey in order to get on the same page with his strategic ally. The meeting of the leaders of Azerbaijan and Turkey is nothing extraordinary. But this time, the meeting generated buzz because certain forces in Turkey are now demanding that Ankara no longer ensure that all of Baku's interests are met when dealing with the Armenia question. For example, [they are demanding] ending the blockade of Armenia; restoring diplomatic relations; opening borders and resuming rail transit, etc. In an unexpected twist, the sentiments of these experts and members of the public were echoed by [Turkish] Foreign Minister Ahmet Davutoglu, who stated his desire to resume dialogue with Armenia. However, during Aliyev's visit, official Ankara's rhetoric returned to its usual form: There will be no softening on Armenia until Nagorno-Karabakh is again under Azerbaijan's jurisdiction.

At the same time, the influential Turkish newspaper Zaman proposed a series of steps to lead relations between Baku, Yerevan and Ankara out of an impasse.

According to the publication, the Turkish authorities have appealed to Switzerland, the next OSCE chair and a participant in the Turkish-Armenian negotiations, asking it to convince Armenia to return to Azerbaijan at least five of the seven districts that make up the so-called security zone around the NKR.

If Yerevan agrees – and the newspaper is hinting that Armenia is ready to do so – Azerbaijan will not object to Turkey reopening its border with Armenia....

Artak Zakaryan, chair of the Armenian parliament's standing committee on foreign relations, called Ahmet Davutoglu's statement and the propaganda campaign in Zaman part of an attempt to save face before the international community. "Turkey is trying to come up with an excuse as to why it halted the process of normalizing relations with Armenia.*** We never gave Azerbaijan and Turkey cause to tie the settlement of the Nagorno-Karabakh issue to normalizing Armenian-Turkish relations. Turkey cannot be considered a neutral party to the Nagorno-Karabakh problem, especially in light of its pro-Azerbaijan statements and strategic partnership with Baku," Zakaryan stressed....

TRANSCAUCASUS CONFUSION

By Yury Simonyan. *Nezavisimaya gazeta*, Dec. 7, 2015, p. 3.

The situation in the unrecognized Nagorno-Karabakh Republic (NKR) flared up again this past weekend. Clashes between the opposing sides at the line of contact resulted in casualties. The latest violation of the ceasefire was preceded by a visit to Baku by Turkish Prime Minister Ahmet Davutoglu. In a sign of special friendship, he prayed the Friday *namaz* at one of the main mosques in Baku and said that Turkey will always be at Azerbaijan's side until the very last centimeter of land occupied by the Armenians is liberated. Yerevan and Stepanakert viewed the aforementioned subversive attack by Azerbaijani forces as a consequence of such strong support for Baku by Ankara.

Actually, Davutoglu said nothing new. Turkey has always unfailingly supported Azerbaijan in the Nagorno-Karabakh conflict. In a sign of solidarity with Azerbaijan, Turkey broke off diplomatic relations with Armenia, closed the state border [with Armenia] and heeded Baku's call to organize an economic blockade of Armenia. Russia's position on the Nagorno-Karabakh conflict and the presence of the [Russian] 102nd military base in Gyumri, Armenia have barred Turkey from playing a more active role in resolving the conflict on Azerbaijan's side.

The Russian-Turkish conflict has undoubtedly aggravated the situation in the Transcaucasus, [but] not in terms of resuming the war in Nagorno-Karabakh. Lately, the contact line in the NKR has seen stable tension, which the Azerbaijani side will clearly maintain. It is openly advocating for the disruption of the status quo, backing its demands in the diplomatic standoff with military incursions at the line of contact – but without crossing the threshold of war. Baku certainly understands (as do Yerevan and Stepanakert, incidentally) that the initiator of a new war in the NKR between what are universally regarded as equally matched forces (preventing either side from expecting any quick success in a military campaign) would be the loser in the eyes of the international community.

The deterioration of the situation will further limit the parties' room for geopolitical maneuvering in the region. This goes primarily for Azerbaijan. For Armenia and the NKR, the Turkey-Russia conflict has not changed much. It has perhaps only dispelled fears associated with the assumption that for the sake of implementing major joint projects with Ankara, Moscow may require its partner Yerevan to make some concessions on the Nagorno-Karabakh issue in favor of Turkey's ally Azerbaijan.

For Baku, the situation is more delicate. It is important to understand that without Russia, [Baku] can forget about resolving the Nagorno-Karabakh issue in its favor. If the Russian-Turkish conflict escalates any further, Azerbaijan may be faced with a choice. It is not about to turn its back on Ankara, because that would eviscerate the perennial "two states, one nation" philosophy of Azerbaijani-Turkish relations, as well as the entire Cooperation Council of Turkic-Speaking States, in which Azerbaijan has played a prominent role. But the consequences of turning away from Moscow are no less painful, the crucial Nagorno-Karabakh issue aside. They could impact trade, the interests of thousands of Azerbaijani migrant workers, energy projects in the Caspian Sea that are faltering as it is, as well as the difficult situation along the Azerbaijan-Dagestan border. It is no coincidence that Baku was one of the first to express willingness to mediate a dialogue between Moscow and Ankara. But the parties are clearly far from recognizing the need for mediation, and Baku essentially has to balance between the conflicting regional leaders without irritating either of them.

Two other South Caucasus players, Abkhazia and Georgia, are also in an unenviable position. The former because it is entirely beholden to Russia and had (not without reason) certain views toward developing links (albeit not quite legitimate ones) with Turkey, where there is a sizable and relatively influential Abkhaz community. Today, besides Russian companies, only some Turkish firms have flouted international sanctions to have dealings with this partially recognized Black Sea republic. Now, the already minute presence of Turkish capital in Russia's protectorate Abkhazia will vanish. Georgia is very much between a rock and a hard place. If the Turkish-Russian conflict escalates, Ankara may demand that its strategic partner Tbilisi fulfill its obligations as an ally – requiring that it at least close its airspace to Russia in order to cut off Russia's link with its military base in Gyumri. Moscow, conversely, would ask Tbilisi for additional (ground) links to it.

The Turkish-Russian conflict has brought the South Caucasus region into a state of clear confusion. The local capitals realize that events will unfold without their participation, even though they may impact their vital interests.

ALIYEV SENDS MESSAGE TO WORLD'S POLITICIANS

By Sokhbet Mamedov. *Nezavisimaya gazeta*, Feb. 1, 2016, p. 6.

Azerbaijani President Ilkham Aliyev has accused the OSCE Minsk Group of not wanting to settle the Armenian-Azerbaijani Nagorno-Karabakh conflict. Never before has the head of Azerbaijan leveled such severe public criticism against this group.

The charges were made yesterday during a meeting between President Aliyev and a group of young people on the occasion of the 20th anniversary of their first forum.

According to analysts, the president essentially gave what amounted to a policy speech at the meeting and defined the main challenges facing Azerbaijan's young people. After reviewing the post-Soviet period of Azerbaijan's development, Ilkham Aliyev commented that a new post-oil period is beginning for the country. He expressed confidence that it would be just as successful as past years, and commented: "According to our calculations, it was supposed to begin after 2040. But as a result of the sharp drop in oil prices, we have already entered the post-oil period." It became clear from the president's speech that the country's future is oriented toward innovation and the intellectual development of the young generation.

Meanwhile, the only problem the authorities can't solve today is the Nagorno-Karabakh conflict. In this regard, Ilkham Aliyev expressed regret that the cochairs of the OSCE Minsk Group, who are supposed to be directly involved in the issue, are seeking to freeze the conflict, not settle it.

"What they are currently doing is absolutely meaningless. Not only are they putting no pressure on Armenia, but they are also protecting it from potential problems. Look at what their provocative activities at recent Council of Europe hearings have led to," Aliyev said, commenting on the results of a vote in the Parliamentary Assembly of the Council of Europe on a report by Robert Walter titled "Escalation of Violence in Nagorno-Karabakh and the other occupied territories of Azerbaijan."

"Just who do they think they are? In other words, are they going to be pressuring all international organizations? The Council of Europe is putting this issue on the agenda. A rapporteur has been appointed. The Council of Europe is an international organization. Of course, there are all manner of people there. There are people who hold an anti-Azerbaijan position; there are quite a few Islamophobes. There are those who are generally in solidarity with Armenia, who are associated with the Armenian lobby. I have been a member of this organization – I know this. But this organization has now put this issue on the agenda. The Minsk Group cochairs are pressuring them.*** It is because of this provocative activity that the resolution didn't pass by four votes." Therefore, the president commented that the work of the cochairs merits only a negative evaluation.

"I am saying this openly today, so that the public knows this, too. They are the main reason why this issue is not being addressed. Why? Because there are double standards. Why is that? Who knows. But we know the answer is double standards.

The religious factor plays a role here. We are Muslims, so we are treated with double standards. Especially now, when Islamophobia is at a peak in Europe."

At the same time, the president sent a message to key global political leaders. "If double standards are currently a yardstick on a global scale and in world politics, then let them say that. There shouldn't be any more hypocrisy. They shouldn't be saying, 'We support democracy and equality, we believe all people are equal, we advocate human rights.' Do they think about the violated rights of 1 million Azerbaijani citizens? No, they don't care!" Ilkham Aliyev said.

To exit the current situation, Azerbaijan must rely primarily on its own strength and resources. The country must become stronger, so that people live even better and security is safeguarded. People in Azerbaijan are living in security and peace, the president believes.

It should be noted that Aliyev's speech during his meeting with representatives of the country's youth resonated deeply with society. That is because the head of state not only outlined the country's main development paths, but also for the first time revealed certain details of the negotiation process for developing relations with the West.

NOTES

1. In the transcript of the press conference posted on the US State Department's Web site, Bryza denies having made any such statement about the GUAM initiative, attributing it to his predecessor, Ambassador Steven Mann.

Part Three |

Geopolitical Interests in Karabakh – Four Main Vectors

Chapter 8 | Turkey

TURKEY RECOGNIZES AZERBAIJAN'S INDEPENDENCE – What Prompted the Decision

By V. Khovratovich. *Izvestia*, Nov. 12, 1991, p. 5.

Editors' Note. – For an explanation, our correspondent turned to Mr. Volkan Vural, the Ambassador of the Republic of Turkey to the USSR.

* * *

Vural. – In making this decision, the government of my country proceeded first of all from the document adopted at the last Congress of USSR People's Deputies. As you know, it says that all the republics that have declared their independence are henceforth subject to international law and that their sovereignty can be recognized by any foreign state. So Turkey has done nothing unlawful.

The recognition of Azerbaijan's independence took place in the following manner. On Oct. 29, that republic's government declared its decision to join the world community and appealed to the states of the entire world to recognize its independence. On Nov. 3, a note from the Azerbaijan Ministry of Foreign Affairs arrived at our consulate in Baku. It contained a request that we recognize the republic's independence. And finally, Prime Minister [Gasan] Gasanov repeated this request during his recent visit to Ankara.

On the basis of our long-standing cultural and linguistic ties with that republic, which Turkey regards as a fraternal one, and with due regard for the decision of the last Congress of USSR People's Deputies, our government announced its recognition of Azerbaijan's independence.

Question. – But doesn't that announcement add fuel to the fire of the continuing war in Nagorno-Karabakh?

Answer. – No, not at all. In recognizing the sovereignty of the neighboring republic, we simultaneously affirm our noninterference in the internal and foreign affairs of any independent state. Furthermore, we intend to continue to cooperate with Ukraine, Armenia, Moldova and Georgia as well.

Q. – And so if, for example, Armenia were to make a similar request of Turkey tomorrow, would your government grant that request?

A. – That is correct. That no other republic besides Azerbaijan has made such a request of us is another matter. Since we have mentioned Armenia, Izvestia's readers will find it not uninteresting to learn that Turkey plans to open a consulate in Yerevan. This confirms once more our sincerity and impartiality in relations with any republic.

Q. – Are you saying, then, that Turkey is prepared to acknowledge the independence of other republics besides Muslim ones?

A. – My country does not differentiate among Muslim, Christian or, for instance, Jewish countries. And not only because the Republic of Turkey is a secular state. We proceed first of all from civilized, universal human positions.

Q. – All right, then, so Turkey regards Azerbaijan as an independent state. What if, after a certain period of time, Baku suddenly asks you to sell weapons to it?

A. – Naturally, we will not be able to grant such a request. For the simple reason that Ankara knows full well just where such weapons would be sent. And in general, my country strives to promote the resolution of any conflicts solely by peaceful means. This is our firm position. Furthermore, a decision was recently adopted to reduce the strength of the Turkish Armed Forces by 50%.

Q. – One last question, Mr. Ambassador. What about the several thousand deserters from the Nakhichevan Republic?

A. – They have been returned to their homeland.

AZERBAIJAN: RUSSIA'S POSITION ON TRANSCAUCASUS ISSUE STIRS CONCERN – Ayaz Mutalibov on His Visit to the Republic of Turkey

By Aidyn Mekhtiyev. *Nezavisimaya gazeta*, Jan. 29, 1992, p. 3.

On the last day of Ayaz Mutalibov's official visit to the Republic of Turkey, the influential Turkish newspaper Milliyet carried an interview with the president of Azerbaijan. It is clear from the interview that in the course of negotiations with the Turkish side, an agreement was reached under which Azerbaijani officers will receive advanced training at Turkish military academies. It was also reported in the interview that Azerbaijan hopes to obtain assistance from Turkey in establishing a national army. On the same day, however, at Istanbul Airport prior to his departure for Baku, Mutalibov expressed regret and bewilderment to an official representative of the Turkish president's press service. Mutalibov was dissatisfied that the newspaper, in his opinion, had distorted his phrases and misinformed its readers. This resulted in a situation in which, on that same day, television newscasts in the CIS and other countries of the world reported that Turkey and Azerbaijan had agreed on military cooperation. At a press conference in Baku, Mutalibov added that the Armenian side and forces conniving with it had been looking for just this sort of hidden meaning in the Azerbaijani delegation's visit, which, according to Mutalibov, was of an exclusively economic nature.

Mutalibov said he does not seek close cooperation with Turkey in the military sphere. He told journalists that he intends only to borrow the methods of the

Turkish police in establishing a national police force in the republic. The question of Nagorno-Karabakh was raised at the press conference. Mutalibov said this question was also at the center of attention in the talks in Turkey, and it was said that Azerbaijan does not want the conflict to become internationalized and that Turkish mediation could play a positive role. Mutalibov said that he was given to understand during the visit that the development of relations between Turkey and Azerbaijan should not affect relations between Turkey and Russia. Mutalibov explained that the Azerbaijani side has been concerned of late by Russia's position on the Transcaucasus issue. Although Russia concluded a treaty with Armenia, it has avoided a similar step with respect to Azerbaijan. The president of Azerbaijan reported that "in February, perhaps, we will conclude a friendship treaty with Russia. After we presented our complaints to the Russian side, Yeltsin issued a directive." Mutalibov also declared that "we do not intend to pit relations between Azerbaijan and Turkey, on one hand, against Russia and Armenia, on the other. All these countries should work together within the framework of the plan proposed by Turkey for cooperation among the countries of the Black Sea region." The president said that Azerbaijan's foreign minister will discuss a specific program of cooperation in Istanbul on Feb. 3, perhaps with the participation of Armenia's foreign minister.

In response to a question about Turkish investments, Mutalibov answered that "we would like Turkish business circles to become active in rebuilding Azerbaijan's economy. We need Turkish technologies." A discussion on this topic was held with business representatives, and an agreement was reached to open a Turkish trade center in Baku. Mutalibov believes that Azerbaijan should become a kind of bridge linking Turkey and Central Asia on economic issues....

TURKEY DEMANDS PROTECTION FOR MUSLIMS IN KARABAKH – Ankara and Baku Propose a Multilateral Conference

By staff correspondent Konstantin Eggert. *Izvestia*, March 2, 1992, p. 4.

The trip to Azerbaijan and Armenia by Iran's Minister of Foreign Affairs Ali Akbar Velayati caused visible nervousness in Turkey, which regarded the Iranian minister's mediation mission as an attempt to expand Tehran's influence in the Transcaucasus. Late last week, official Ankara took a number of diplomatic actions intended to demonstrate that Turkey is not going to remain on the sidelines of the processes occurring in the region.

On Friday [Feb. 28], Turkey's Minister of Foreign Affairs Hikmet Cetin held talks in Baku with Azerbaijan's Prime Minister Gasan Gasanov, resulting in the announcement that Azerbaijan is ready to enter into a quadripartite conference with Armenia, Turkey and Iran to resolve the Karabakh crisis. Furthermore, Cetin noted, Georgia, Russia and Ukraine may be included as participants if Armenia so desires.

The Associated Press reports that on Sunday Suleyman Demirel, the head of the Turkish government, called for an end to "attacks by Armenia on Muslims in Nagorno-Karabakh." "Turkey cannot remain indifferent to the development of events and the whipping up of tension in the region. The country will undertake all necessary diplomatic efforts to help in the settlement of the conflict," he said. Reuters reports that earlier Ankara asked the US, Russia, Great Britain, France and Germany to use their influence on Yerevan to get talks started on the Karabakh question.

The problem of Turkey's participation in the process of a regional settlement has a complicated historical background. Armenia continues to insist on an admission of responsibility by Turkey for the genocide of Armenians in 1915. In addition, much vagueness remains with respect to the part of Turkish territory that Armenians consider to be their own. Although the Armenian government has repeatedly let it be known that it does not consider the return of this land to be a realistic prospect, official Yerevan has not yet made any statements unequivocally confirming such a position. This is explained in large part by pressure from the parliamentary opposition, in the form of the Association for National Self-Determination and the Republican Party, which refuses to rule out once and for all the possibility of the territories' return.

It is these two questions that prevent Turkey and Armenia from establishing diplomatic relations. It should be noted that until recently Ankara sought to take a neutral position with respect to the conflict in Karabakh. However, the seizure of the city of Khodzhaly by Armenian formations and the simultaneous increase in activeness by Iranian diplomats made Prime Minister Demirel hastily remind all interested parties that Turkish neutrality does not mean indifference. However, ethnic, cultural and historical closeness to Azerbaijan and a desire by Ankara to strengthen its influence on Baku are colliding with its European aspirations: with its membership in NATO and the hope of joining the European Community in the not too distant future. This makes it take into account Europe's sympathies with Christian Armenia. Incidentally, one of the conditions for entry into the EC is Turkey's acknowledgment of the fact of genocide against Armenians in the early part of the century, something that the Turkish authorities are not yet prepared to do, especially since if they did, it would then be logical to expect a demand for financial compensation from Armenia, where thousands of families that suffered in 1915 live.

This is why what Turkey desires is not French, much less Iranian, mediation between Armenia and Azerbaijan, but an active peacemaking role for Russia. Foreign Minister Cetin, who has a high regard for the efforts of his Russian colleague A. Kozyrev in this area, frankly told this to a correspondent. If Ankara, due to objective reasons, is not able to play the role of an "honest broker" in the Transcaucasus crisis, it can always be certain that Moscow, relying on Turkey's active participation in the development of Russia's economy, will not forget its interests....

NAKHICHEVAN IS BEING DRAWN INTO THE CONFLICT – Turkey Intends to Demand That Armenia Set Free the Occupied Areas of Karabakh

Nezavisimaya gazeta, May 14, 1992, pp. 1, 3.

Azerbaijan (By Aidyn Mekhtiyev) – Against the backdrop of the stepped-up combat operations between Armenian and Azerbaijani armed formations in the Shusha-Lachin area and along the border between the two republics, the drastic complication in relations between the leadership of the Nakhichevan Autonomous Republic and that of Armenia has escaped the attention of the Russian news media. However, according to a report by Azerbaijan's Turan News Agency, on May 7 there was a clash between detachments of the Nakhichevan Autonomous Republic's Defense Committee and Armenian troops.... Combat operations continued on May 8 and, Turan reports, spread to the 11-kilometer Nakhichevan-Turkish border. Elman Mamedov, Chairman of the Nakhichevan Defense Committee, reported that a state of emergency was declared in Sadarak on May 10. During a telephone conversation with Turkey's Prime Minister Suleyman Demirel, Geidar Aliyev, Chairman of the Nakhichevan Autonomous Republic Supreme Majlis, expressed concern in connection with the situation that has developed. In addition, the Nakhichevan leader telephoned Armenian President Levon Ter-Petrosyan and demanded an explanation of the Armenian troops' actions. The leader of the neighboring republic replied that the clash had been provoked by fighting men from the Nakhichevan division of the Azerbaijan People's Front (APF). However, at an emergency meeting of the Nakhichevan parliament, deputies from the APF rejected this version of what happened. In the opinion of observers in Baku, the fact that the conflict on the Sadarak border occurred on the eve of the Armenian troops' offensive against Shusha in Karabakh is a weighty argument in favor of a different version: Before beginning a large-scale operation to "open a corridor" between Armenia and Karabakh, the Armenian forces decided to use this means to warn the Nakhichevan self-defense detachments against a possible attempt to open a second front against Armenia in the event that the Armenian troops were successful in the Shusha-Lachin area.

It is important to note that the community of Sadarak occupies a strategically important position: It is there that the Nakhichevan enclave's borders with Armenia, on the one hand, and with Turkey, on the other, come together. According to the treaty that Turkey and Soviet Russia signed in Kars on March 16, 1921, Turkey is the guarantor of the security and unchangeable status of the Nakhichevan autonomous entity. That is why the now obvious fact of expanded fighting in direct proximity to the 11-kilometer Turkish-Nakhichevan border has caused great concern in Turkey's political circles. Moreover, the Armenians' taking of Shusha, which almost coincided in time with the events in Sadarak, has become a no less alarming warning signal for Ankara. Opposition political parties have subjected Suleyman Demirel's government to harsh criticism. In particular, Bulent Ecevit, former Prime Minister and leader of the Democratic Left Party, has de-manded that "before it's too late,

Turkish troops be sent to Nakhichevan" in order to prevent a situation similar to the one that has developed in Nagorno-Karabakh....

Mesut Yilmaz, leader of the most influential opposition party, the Motherland Party (ANAP), has said that "if Demirel's government waits any longer, the Armenians will come right up to the Turkish border." Speaking at a meeting of the parliamentary group of the True Path Party (DYP), Prime Minister Demirel, who is the chairman of that party, replied to the opposition's criticism. "The path of Turkish military intervention in the conflict is futile," he stated. At the same time, he noted that "the Turkish government is using every opportunity to resolve the Karabakh and Nakhichevan questions."... According to Demirel, in the near future a meeting of the UN Security Council will be convened in New York to consider Turkey's demand-that Armenia set free the occupied Azerbaijani areas of Karabakh.

In connection with the stepped-up activity of Armenian militants near the Nakhichevan-Turkish border, Turkish newspapers have recalled that in a statement before the US Senate this March, Manfred Wörner – then NATO's secretary-general – warned that "NATO will be forced to intervene if the Armenian-Azerbaijani conflict spreads to Turkish territory."

* * *

Armenia (NEGA news service) – The military situation on the Armenia-Azerbaijan border has become extremely exacerbated. Fierce exchanges of gunfire are now taking place along virtually its entire length. The Goris District Internal Affairs Department, Armenia, reports that columns of tanks are moving from Kubatly into the Azerbaijani border-district center of Lachin, while a stream of trucks carrying residents is moving in the opposite direction. On May 12-13, the district centers of Goris, Kapan and Berd, as well as dozens of other villages, were struck by Grad [Hail] missiles launched from Lachin, which has been turned into a heavily fortified area. There are dead and wounded.

It has been learned that significant numbers of troops and considerable amounts of equipment are being moved from Baku and Gyandzha to the Nakhichevan Republic. A large concentration of Azerbaijani infantry and armored vehicles has been noted on the Ararat section of the Armenian-Nakhichevan border. Experts believe that Azerbaijan may launch a major offensive from that area against the Ararat Valley of Armenia before long. There are reports that after the taking of Shusha Turkish-made food products, cigarettes and ammunition were found in Azerbaijani Army depots.

In connection with the growing complication of the situation, the authorities in Armenia's border districts are now evacuating women and children from the sites of combat operations.

FOREIGN INVOLVEMENT IN ATTEMPTS TO RESOLVE CONFLICTS ON CIS TERRITORY GROWS

Nezavisimaya gazeta, May 13, 1992, pp. 1, 3.

Armenia (By Armen Khanbabyan) – On the morning of May 9, Armenian self-defense detachments in Nagorno-Karabakh captured the district center of Shusha. During the Soviet years, it was the only city in Karabakh where the Azerbaijani population predominated. After the Karabakh epic began, this fact enabled the Baku authorities, with the help of Union troops, to control the Yerevan-Stepanakert highway, on which Shusha is located, and to begin a blockade of Karabakh. The civilian population was gradually evacuated from the city, and it was turned into a strong point for the Azerbaijani Army.

Over a six-month period, 5,000 rockets and shells were fired from Shusha against Stepanakert, the capital of the Nagorno-Karabakh Republic; 111 people were killed, and 332 civilians were wounded.

On the morning of May 7, after heavy preparatory artillery fire, Azerbaijani infantry began an assault on Stepanakert. At the same time, the city was subjected to a bombing strike from an SU-25 supersonic ground-attack plane that the Azerbaijanis had leased from the CIS strategic forces. The Azerbaijani detachments got as far as the suburbs of Stepanakert. The number of casualties in two days was 30 dead and about 80 wounded. The Nagorno-Karabakh Republic Defense Council was instructed to take measures to avoid the complete destruction of Stepanakert and the killing of the population. Fulfilling this decision, on the night of May 7-8 Armenian self-defense detachments launched a counterattack. At midday, they took the tactically important Dzhangasan hill and burst into Shusha. The Azerbaijani Army tried to save the situation by using its complete superiority in the air.... Nevertheless, by the morning of May 9 the resistance had been crushed. Shusha passed completely into the hands of the Armenians, but the Armenian offensive detachments left corridors through which Azerbaijani soldiers, most of whom fully realized the pointlessness of further bloodshed, were able to withdraw unhindered in the direction of Lachin. The taking of Shusha cost the Armenians more than 20 dead and several dozen wounded. The Azerbaijanis' precise losses have not yet been ascertained. However, it is known that more than 150 people were taken prisoner, among them some mercenary servicemen in the CIS forces. The pay of a rank-and-file mercenary serving in the Shusha garrison was 10,000 rubles.

The fall of Shusha fundamentally changes the entire military-strategic situation in the region and undoubtedly will have far-reaching political consequences.

It is obvious that the military defeat makes Yagub Mamedov's chances of being elected President of Azerbaijan ephemeral. It is also clear that the as yet latent processes of disintegration in Azerbaijan, processes connected with the growth of the national-liberation movement of the Lezgins, the Kurds and the Talysh, may now come into the open. At the same time, according to Vagan Shirkhanyan, adviser to the Armenian President, the Azerbaijani side didn't even make any attempts to reestablish the positions it had lost.... The Azerbaijani Army ... is now clearly avoiding any direct exchanges of fire with the Karabakh defense forces.

During the first hours after the fall of Shusha, Armenia began to be accused of aggression. Meanwhile, the reaction of official Yerevan was far from euphoric. The Shusha events coincided with a visit to Tehran by President Ter-Petrosyan, who, while there, signed a memorandum on a cease-fire [together with the leaders of Azerbaijan and Iran]. Incidentally, the president did this on behalf of his own state, and it should be borne in mind that for a long time now he has avoided making any statements "on behalf of or on the instructions of" the Karabakh authorities, for whom tactical military problems are still more pressing than strategic political accords. This could serve as one more reason for the further exacerbation of Armenian-Turkish relations. It was not by chance that on the evening of May 9, the president of Armenia and Foreign Minister Raffi Ovannisyan spoke by telephone with their colleagues in Washington, London, Paris, Bonn and Tehran, trying to explain to them that since the Nagorno-Karabakh Republic's proclamation of independence, Armenia's opportunities to influence the state of affairs in Karabakh have been greatly reduced. The leaders of the NKR should take a place at the negotiating table at the forthcoming Minsk conference on a peaceful settlement of the Karabakh crisis. Otherwise, it will be pointless even to hold a conference.

* * *

Azerbaijan (By Aidyn Mekhtiyev) – ... The fall of Azerbaijan's last stronghold in Upper Karabakh – Shusha – has caused an outburst of patriotic sentiments in the republic. On May 9, the organizing committee of the Party of National Independence (PNI) urged the people to "rise in a struggle to liberate the occupied Azerbaijani lands." "We approve of any actions aimed at realizing this sacred goal," the statement's authors noted. It is also reported that Etibar Mamedov, the 37-year-old leader of the PNI, who, as is generally known, is a candidate for the post of president, has set off for the area of combat operations at the head of a detachment of volunteers he has created, in order to participate in the fighting. On May 9, Abulfaz Elchibei, chairman of the People's Front, issued an order to all sections and support groups of the Azerbaijan People's Front not to take any actions without the knowledge of the Front's leadership and to carry out all orders of local military authorities. Elchibei issued a call: "Everyone to the defense of the homeland!"...

The Azerbaijan Ministry of Foreign Affairs warned that "Azerbaijan is using all available means to curb the aggression."[1]

The news of the taking of Shusha by Armenian forces has been at the center of attention of the Turkish government. According to Turkish sources, Prime Minister Suleyman Demirel, speaking May 9 at an emergency meeting of the Cabinet of Ministers devoted to the situation in Karabakh, made the following observation: "The events in Shusha are nothing other than one more act of terror by the Armenians against the Azerbaijanis." ... Demirel emphasized that Turkey will not play the role of a detached observer while an attempt is made to resolve the Karabakh conflict by force.... On May 9, Mustafa Aksin, Turkey's permanent representative to the UN, said in an interview with Voice of America that he had talked with the members of the UN Security Council. Aksin expressed the hope that the members of the Security Council would support the initiative by Turkey, which is acting in accordance with the UN Charter and international law. "Any attempts to occupy the territory of another state and to try to change existing borders by force should be condemned by the UN Security Council," Turkey's permanent representative to the UN said in conclusion.

EDITORS' VIEWPOINT: INTERVENTION BY TURKEY COULD LEAD TO CATASTROPHE

Izvestia, May 22, 1992, p. 4.

"We will send troops to Nakhichevan. We must send them there without hesitation-otherwise, the events occurring in Nagorno-Karabakh could be repeated there." This publicly proclaimed intention of Turkish President Turgut Ozal could become the trigger for an explosion in the already unstable Caucasus region. The effect of the threatened intervention would be like pouring oil onto the flames of the undeclared war between Armenia and Azerbaijan.

References to the 1920 Soviet-Turkish treaty under which Ankara is the formal guarantor of Nakhichevan's territorial integrity are no more valid than the Brezhnev Politburo's attempts to justify the invasion of Afghanistan by citing the treaty between Kabul and Moscow.

Today is not 1920. From a legal standpoint, an invasion by NATO member Turkey could be regarded as an invasion of the CIS by the North Atlantic bloc, something that would pose the risk of a clash with one of the parties to the collective security treaty that was just signed in Tashkent. Moreover, before "crossing the Rubicon," the Turkish Army would first have to deal with CIS armed forces guarding the border-with all the ensuing consequences, which would most likely affect more than just the Caucasus.

Turkey is a member of NATO. It is hard to imagine that the Western alliance would be eager to be drawn into a military adventure – even if only technically – whose outcome few would dare predict. Let's hope that Brussels will have something to say about this. There are UN troops for peacekeeping actions. The world community entrusts these troops with an extremely delicate mediatory mission, confident of their impartiality and neutrality.

Turkey is a parliamentary republic, so the real levers of power in the country are in the hands of the Prime Minister, not the President. Many people there believe that the opposition party led by Ozal is trying to use the conflict in the Transcaucasus to further its own narrow and self-serving aims: to undermine the Demirel government, which is pursuing a far more realistic policy. It is not a rarity in politics for party leaders to jeopardize security and peace only to further short-term interests.

NATO AND NAKHICHEVAN

By staff correspondent Vladimir Peresada. *Pravda*, May 26, 1992, p. 3.

Brussels – For the first time in its history, NATO has undertaken a démarche concerning a specific political-military situation within the borders of the former USSR, namely in the Nagorno-Karabakh area.

Only recently, during the era of the Soviet Union's existence, such a thing would have been inconceivable. Not only because situations capable of prompting such a démarche never arose, but mostly because even if, hypothetically, they had, people here would have never doubted for a second, I'm told, that the Soviet Union itself would have found a solution.

But now NATO headquarters has issued a rather tough statement stressing that the dangerous turn of events represented by the spread of violence beyond Karabakh's borders – specifically, to Nakhichevan – "affects all of us." Any attempts to infringe on the territorial integrity of Azerbaijan or any other country, the statement goes on to say, would be a flagrant violation of international legal norms and the principles of the Conference on Security and Cooperation in Europe. Any change in the existing status of Nagorno-Karabakh or Nakhichevan either unilaterally or by force is termed "unacceptable to NATO."

There is no question that in terms of the "big picture," the document is aimed at ending the conflict. However, there is something alarming about the very fact of NATO's démarche, and especially about the circumstances surrounding it.

First of all, this signals considerably greater internationalization of the Karabakh crisis than before. The failure of a number of mediatory efforts, in particular by Russia, Kazakhstan and Iran, is forcing – or perhaps allowing – the West's major political-military organization to move into the "settlement arena." For the time being this movement is occurring on the basis of "appeals for peace"; but as we know, NATO has other capabilities, too.

Second, the "NATO factor" is emerging at a time when the Karabakh conflict has begun to assume the character of a war between Armenia and Azerbaijan. Judging from the wording of its statement, the alliance unambiguously condemns Armenia's military actions in Nakhichevan and supports Azerbaijan. This is unquestionably an objective position, but it comes at a time when a third country in the region – Turkey – is speaking ever more loudly about possible armed intervention in the conflict on Azerbaijan's side.

Finally, the following circumstance merits attention. A general agreement was reached recently among the NATO member countries to the effect that the alliance will promote peacekeeping operations in Europe, participating in them at the request and mandate of the Conference on Security and Cooperation in Europe. Needless to say, we are talking about the participation of armed forces. Could this question be raised at the CSCE conference on Karabakh if the situation has not improved by that time, or if the conference itself fails to devise effective political measures? Why not?

About a year ago, NATO Secretary-General Wörner told me: "The most unpleasant thing that could happen would be a disorderly breakup of the USSR and the formation in its place of a group of states that have little trust in one other and that are even hostile to each other in some respects. The future development of the situation could be so unpredictable as to require unusual and nonstandard decisions by the West."

It's as if he had peered into the future.

TURKEY DOES NOT INTEND TO USE MILITARY MEANS TO SOLVE NAGORNO-KARABAKH PROBLEM

By Gennady Charodeyev. *Izvestia*, May 27, 1992, p. 5.

On Tuesday [May 26], Prime Minister Suleyman Demirel of Turkey concluded a visit to Moscow.

It will be recalled that aside from the signing of a Treaty on Principles of Relations Between the Russian Federation and the Turkish Republic and a large number of protocols of intention in various areas, an important place in Demirel's talks with Russian officials was devoted to examining ways for the two countries to cooperate in settling the situation in the Caucasus. In a special statement on Nagorno-Karabakh, the parties expressed deep regret in connection with the situation in that region. The spread of the conflict beyond the region's borders, in particular the seizure of Lachin and the recent clashes on the border of Armenia and Nakhichevan, are of special concern, Demirel said.

In response to a question from Izvestia, the head of the Turkish government said that no attendant circumstances can justify the armed clashes in Nagorno-Karabakh. At the talks in Moscow, the sides confirmed that in accordance with the principles of the UN and the Conference on Security and Cooperation in Europe, territory may not be acquired through force. Russia and Turkey condemn the escalation of violence and in the most resolute manner call on all the parties involved in the conflict to secure an effective ceasefire and to take the necessary steps to reduce the intensity of confrontation. Demirel reported that Moscow and Ankara are prepared to extend all possible assistance, including joint mediation efforts, with the aim of ending the bloodshed and finding a political solution to the conflict.

The Turkish prime minister emphasized once again that his country does not intend to use military means to solve the problem of Nagorno-Karabakh. He denied rumors of a concentration of Turkish troops on the border with Armenia.

Speaking at a press conference for Russian and foreign journalists, Demirel reported that in his talks in the Kremlin with Russian Deputy Prime Minister Yegor Gaidar, an agreement was reached to increase trade turnover between Turkey and Russia from $2 billion to $10 billion a year.

DIPLOMACY: RUSSIAN-TURKISH FRIENDSHIP – Better a Bad Peace Than a Good Quarrel

By Pavel Felgengauer. *Segodnya*, May 14, 1993, p. 3.

... Well-informed sources in the Russian Federation Ministry of Defense report that in early April 1993, after Armenian forces took Kelbadzhar, the Turks trained the sights of 15 tanks directly on Russia's Leninakan division, which is stationed on Armenian territory. This was followed by several bellicose statements by Prime Minister Demirel and the late Turkish president Ozal. The two countries unexpectedly found themselves on the brink of an armed conflict. But when Moscow, Ankara and Washington became sufficiently aware of the danger of the situation, they quickly began searching for a compromise.

The Turkish tanks maintained their combat posture for several days, then retreated to their bases. A Turkish, Russian and American plan to settle the conflict in the Transcaucasus was quickly drafted, and diplomatic activity was stepped up in the region.

On May 10, Russian Defense Minister Grachev arrived in Turkey to discuss the situation in Nagorno-Karabakh, the possibility of concluding an agreement on preventing military incidents in the Black Sea, the war in Bosnia, possible deliveries of Russian arms to Turkey, etc. But it must be assumed that the visit's most important aim was to try to reach an agreement with the Turkish military directly on a certain amount of mutual restraint during the "transition" period, until the current geostrategic chaos in the Middle East resulting from the USSR's collapse returns to some sort of equilibrium.

So the success or failure of Grachev's diplomatic efforts will have to be assessed on the basis of future communiqués on combat operations in the Caucasus.

TURKEY BUYS WEAPONS FROM RUSSIA – But Doesn't Share Russian Views on Situation in 'Trouble Spots'

By Aleksandr Sychov. *Izvestia*, May 14, 1993, p. 1.

Defense Minister Pavel Grachev's visit to Turkey marks the first time a Russian military chief has visited that country in 200 years.

In Ankara, Grachev and Turkish Defense Minister Nevzat Ayaz signed a memorandum of mutual understanding that, among other things, set in motion a previously concluded contract for supplying Russian weapons. Turkey is buying 25 armored personnel carriers and 20 helicopters from Russia for $75 million, thus becoming the first NATO member country to buy military hardware from us. Ankara will pay $15 million for the deliveries and deduct the rest from Russia's accumulated debt. In addition, Turkey, which is a major arms producer, is showing more and more interest in obtaining licenses to manufacture certain types of Russian weapons domestically.

While Russia and Turkey expressed complete mutual understanding on this aspect of the visit, a discussion of political problems revealed considerable differences in their views on the situation in Bosnia and Herzegovina, as well as on the Armenian-Azerbaijani conflict.

It will be recalled that Ankara strongly supports the idea of using military force to settle the Yugoslav conflict and lifting the embargo on arms supplies to the Bosnian Muslims.

Grachev expressed the view of the Russian Ministry of Defense, which feels that using force would result in enormous loss of life among the civilian population. Lifting the embargo would fan the conflict and give new impetus to the arms race in the region. In Grachev's opinion, the conflict can be settled only by political means. He called for a tighter economic blockade and stepped-up aerial surveillance of areas inhabited by Bosnian Serbs.

As for the Armenian-Azerbaijani conflict, Grachev thinks that Armenia and Azerbaijan are equally to blame for its continuation. However, his remark that the Armenians of Nagorno-Karabakh need corridors to link them with the outside world via Armenia was seen as an attempt to vindicate Yerevan. A statement by the Azerbaijani Ministry of Defense says that Grachev's pronouncements jeopardize the efforts of the US, Turkey and Russia to settle the conflict (Ankara shares this view, incidentally).

Grachev confirmed that there are no Russian troops in the combat zone and that the only airborne division on Azerbaijani territory will be withdrawn over the course of this year. At the same time, he expressed regret that some countries are supplying arms and ammunition to Azerbaijan.

It is not known just what information he possesses. But there have been several reports in the world press to the effect that Turkey is buying weapons from the former Warsaw Pact countries, especially the former German Democratic Republic, and sending them to Azerbaijan. It has been learned that at Grachev's request, some changes were made in his itinerary and he was allowed to visit Turkey's Third Army, based in Eastern Anatolia along the former Soviet border. Western news agencies interpreted this as a demonstration of the seriousness of Moscow's fears that Turkey is involved in supplying arms to Azerbaijan. However, Grachev's entourage characterized the trip as a "friendly get-acquainted visit."

ISTANBUL HAS SPECIAL RELATIONS WITH BAKU – Turkish President's Visit Ends

By Elmira Akhmedly. *Nezavisimaya gazeta*, Dec. 15, 1995, p. 3.

Turkish President Suleyman Demirel paid a three-day official visit to the republic [of Azerbaijan].... He was given a very warm and cordial reception.... Many people in the republic believe that Suleyman Demirel's visit to Azerbaijan marks a new stage in the two states' relations. Politicians are speculating that the visit will provide impetus for a shift from emotions and expressions of brotherhood and friendship to the development of commercial relations. It is noteworthy that Demirel arrived in Baku immediately after Azerbaijan had formed a new parliament and adopted a new Constitution. Demirel addressed the second meeting of the Milli Majlis....

In his speeches, President Demirel emphasized above all how important the fact of Azerbaijan's independence is to Turkey. He said: Turkey has always stood and will continue to stand side-by-side with Azerbaijan in its just struggle for independence and territorial integrity. Demirel was accompanied on the trip by more than 100 ministers, businesspeople and others. The two presidents held a closed-door meeting. The presidents later continued their dialogue in the presence of representatives of the Turkish and Azerbaijani sides. During the visit, discussions centered on political and economic issues on close cooperation and the development of bilateral relations, a settlement of the conflict between Armenia and Azerbaijan, and oil transport via the Western route. A serious discussion of matters pertaining to economic cooperation was held.

It's an interesting fact that Turkey has invested only about $120 million in Azerbaijan, while Russia has invested more than $2 billion in Azerbaijan and $1.5 billion in Turkmenistan. Turkey's Export-Import Bank has stopped extending credits to Azerbaijan because of its debt, which stands at $20 million. Azerbaijan, which is currently experiencing a serious social and economic crisis, is not only interested in Turkish investments and credits, it needs them. And so the Azerbaijani government, at President Geidar Aliyev's direction, put together a package of economic issues and submitted them for discussion. This package, in the opinion of First Deputy Prime Minister Abbas Abbasov, reflects the timeliness of strategic partnership between Azerbaijan and Turkey.

One of the main issues that the document deals with is Turkish help in supplying the Nakhichevan Autonomous Republic with energy....

The presidents of Azerbaijan and Turkey signed a joint communiqué setting forth principles governing the subsequent development and strengthening of cooperation in all sectors. It expresses the sides' commitment to resolving the Armenian-Azerbaijani conflict peacefully within the framework of the OSCE. The communiqué also calls for the return of the Azerbaijani lands seized by the Armenian Armed Forces and for the repatriation of refugees.

The document goes on to note that Turkey is stepping up its role within the OSCE Minsk group. The sides believe that the signed contract of the century creates a favorable basis for political and economic cooperation in the region. The sides also signed an agreement on extending Turkish television and radio broadcasts to Azerbaijani territory, including the Nakhichevan Autonomous Republic. Under this agreement, Turkey will pay Azerbaijan $1 million annually and connect Azerbaijan to its satellite link....

According to [President Demirel], the conflicts in the Caucasus are cause for great concern in Turkey. But Turkey will never tolerate a situation in which someone hurts

Azerbaijan. Turkey will never abandon Azerbaijan in midstream. One guarantee of these words is the 60 million 'brethren of Azerbaijan' living in Turkey. Turkey does not intend to compete with other states for influence in the region. Turkey welcomes joint and mutual regional cooperation, Demirel stressed.... During his visit, Demirel also held meetings with members of the National Independence Party of Azerbaijan, the Azerbaijan People's Front and the Musavat Party and representatives of the Meskhetian Turks and Azerbaijani business circles.... He visited refugees and orphans whose parents were killed in the Karabakh war....

MOSCOW IS COMPELLING YEREVAN TO COMPROMISE WITH BAKU, EXPERTS BELIEVE

By Yury Simonyan. *Nezavisimaya gazeta*, Nov. 26, 2008, p. 5.

The foreign ministers of Turkey and Armenia, Ali Babacan and Eduard Nalbandyan, wrapped up a meeting yesterday in Istanbul....

The Turkish newspaper Cumhuriyet, which is close to government circles, reported that five issues had been submitted for discussion at the foreign ministers' meeting: the formation of a joint commission to study the events of 1915; a time frame for the withdrawal of Armenian troops from the Nagorno-Karabakh Republic (NKR); the opening of the border between Armenia and Turkey; a visit to Turkey by Armenian President Serzh Sargsyan; and the Black Sea [sic; Caucasus] Security and Cooperation Platform. "During a private dinner in honor of Eduard Nalbandyan, Babacan proposed the idea of Turkey's sending an ambassador to Yerevan without the establishment of diplomatic relations," the newspaper writes, speculating that as a reciprocal gesture of goodwill, Armenia might agree to the formation of a joint commission to study the events of 1915, which Yerevan regards as genocide of the Armenian people.

Further developing this topic, another influential newspaper, the Hurriyet Daily News, reported that the reopening of the Turkish-Armenian border, which Ankara closed during the war between Armenia and Azerbaijan, would be preceded by the establishment of regular flights between Istanbul and Yerevan by Turkish Airlines.

The director of the Armenian Academy of Sciences' Institute of Oriental Studies, Ruben Safrastyan, while acknowledging the high level at which the Armenian-Turkish talks were held, says that things only appear to be positive. "In presenting its proposals, Ankara today is taking the same ultimatum-like tone it has used for the past 15 or 16 years – a tone that assumes unilateral concessions by Yerevan. The Turkish side operates on the basis of the following principles: Armenia is not an important country for Turkey, and Armenia has a greater interest in normalizing relations, since it is under a blockade. On the basis of those two principles, concessions can be obtained from Armenia on a number of issues – specifically, it can be persuaded to drop its demands to recognize the genocide or to make compromises regarding Nagorno-Karabakh," Safrastyan told NG. According to him, official Yerevan has clearly defined its position: There will be no concessions on fundamental issues....

"If anything, it is Ankara that should be more interested in normalizing relations with Yerevan and opening the borders, since those things have been demanded by the European Union, which Turkey wants to join," Ashot Manucharyan, a Berlin-based expert on international relations, told NG.

In his opinion, Turkey should look at the example of Germany, which apologized to Israel and regards the establishment of diplomatic relations with that country in 1965 as a colossal success of German diplomacy. "But with Armenia and Turkey, besides Ankara's ultimatums, we are also seeing pressure on Yerevan by third countries. Especially Russia, where high-ranking officials make statements in which they call primarily on Armenia to normalize relations. What they mean by this is that Yerevan should fulfill Ankara's conditions – withdraw its demands that Turkey recognize the genocide, restore Azerbaijan's territorial integrity, etc. The proposals that Turkey has made in response – for example, appointing an ambassador to Yerevan without establishing diplomatic relations or opening an air route – are humiliating to Armenia," Manucharyan said.

In his opinion, the fact that Russia is playing on the side of Turkey – Azerbaijan's official protector – will lead to a change in Armenia's foreign policy orientation. For the past 15 years, Russia has been criticized for its inability to resolve conflicts, and now Moscow is trying to become a peacemaker in the Karabakh conflict. "But the attempts it is making, namely its attempts to convince Yerevan to make concessions, could result in a new war between Armenia and Azerbaijan and the subsequent deployment of foreign military assets in the region, which in turn would be a slap in the face to Russian policy in the South Caucasus," Manucharyan told NG. According to the expert, Moscow needs to realize that Turkey will not give up its role as the champion of the US's and NATO's ideas in the region, and flirting with it will push Armenia straight into the arms of the US as it seeks a new protector. Yerevan will need to find a counterbalance so it won't end up fighting a war on two fronts (Azerbaijan and Turkey), a war it would be unable to win.

Stepan Grigoryan, the director of Yerevan's Analytical Center for Globalization and Regional Cooperation, directly links Yerevan's increased activity on the Turkish front to statements by members of Russia's political beau monde on a settlement of the Karabakh conflict and the need for Armenia to normalize its relations with Turkey.

"All of this means one thing – Russia is trying to persuade Armenia to make concessions. Moscow needs a friendly Azerbaijan: It is interested in the transportation of Caspian hydrocarbons across Russian territory, and that is why it wants to expedite a resolution of the Karabakh conflict. It also needs Turkey as a partner on Black Sea issues. Yerevan is extremely afraid of a repetition of the events of 1921-1923. Back then Russia, albeit Bolshevik Russia, built relations with Azerbaijan and Turkey by giving them Armenian land," Grigoryan told NG.

According to the political analyst, Yerevan might propose a counterplan for settling the Karabakh conflict: Why not let Russia acquire a dominant position in the South Caucasus by ceding to Azerbaijan a portion of its own territory equivalent in area to the NKR, on the condition that Karabakh is at least allowed to maintain its status quo? "Under this scenario, Moscow would acquire two loyal strategic partners at once – Azerbaijan and Armenia – which would do their utmost to uphold Russian interests in the region," Grigoryan told NG.

ARMENIA, TURKEY PUSHING THE BOUNDS OF THE POSSIBLE – Yerevan, Ankara Making Peace at Russia's Expense

By Mikhail Zygar and Vladimir Solovyov. *Kommersant*, April 24, 2009, p. 8.

... Late Wednesday night [April 22-23], the foreign ministries of Armenia and Turkey released a joint statement announcing that they had worked out and agreed on "a road map" for normalizing relations between the two countries, including opening the border. No specific details about what stages the two sides still must go through before the border is opened were given. Turkish sources only conjecture that this could happen before October – that is when the Turkish and Armenian national [soccer] teams are scheduled to play a rematch in a World Cup qualifier. Turkish President Abdullah Gul's visit to Yerevan last year for the first match between the Turkish and Armenian national teams symbolized the beginning of rapprochement between the two countries. Serzh Sargsyan has already said that he would like to travel across an open border for the rematch.

Both sides have stressed that all subsequent negotiations between them will be conducted without any mediators or preconditions. Yesterday, the Armenian Foreign Ministry even issued a protest against the Euronews television channel, which, citing Turkish Prime Minister Recep Erdogan, had reported that a final settlement would be possible only after the problem of Nagorno-Karabakh was resolved. The Armenian Foreign Ministry stated that that was not true.

The date that the two sides chose for announcing that they had drawn up a "road map" clearly was not chosen at random. The fact is that today, April 24, marks the anniversary of the Armenian genocide during the Ottoman Empire....

Back in early April, during the Alliance of Civilizations forum in Istanbul, which was attended by Barack Obama, among others, Armenia and Turkey officially acknowledged that they had been conducting talks on the normalization of relations since 2007. At the forum, Swiss Foreign Minister Micheline Calmy-Rey said that she had been acting as mediator in the talks throughout the entire two years. However, Washington was most likely much more active in prodding Armenia and Turkey toward concluding the just-announced agreement. The US State Department issued a special statement welcoming the "road map" at almost the same time that Turkey and Armenia released their statements. "We look forward to working with both governments in support of normalization, and thus promote peace, security and stability in the whole region," said State Department [acting] spokesman Robert Wood.

On the other hand, the Armenian-Turkish agreement drew a markedly negative reaction from Azerbaijan. Elkhan Polukhov, an official spokesman for the country's Foreign Ministry, said that the opening of the border between Turkey and Armenia would be in conflict with Azerbaijan's interests. Baku remembers very well that Turkey's official position used to be that a normalization of relations with Armenia would be possible only after the Karabakh conflict was resolved. Now Azerbaijan regards the mere mention of a separate peace as betrayal. Mr. Polukhov said yesterday that it was too soon to talk about what kind of sanctions Baku might take against Turkey. But Azerbaijani media outlets are discussing, among other things, the possibility of cutting off energy supplies.

If a decision to open the Armenian-Turkish border is made in the foreseeable future, it will essentially signify Armenia's escape from the isolation it has been in since 1993. During all that time, Yerevan's main economic partners have been Russia and Iran, trade turnover with which has been somewhere on the order of $700 million and $200 million a year, respectively. The opening of the border with Turkey will drastically change this situation. Despite the closed border, trade with Turkey was still conducted during all that time, but in the shadows, and according to unofficial estimates it even reached 25% of Armenia's total trade turnover. Therefore, Armenia will no longer have compelling reasons to orient itself exclusively toward Russia in its foreign policy.

While the Armenian Foreign Ministry was disseminating the statement about the breakthrough in relations with Turkey, Armenian President Serzh Sargsyan was in Moscow. Dmitry Medvedev received him yesterday at his Zavidovo country residence. At the very beginning of the talks, the Russian leader said that the site of the meeting indicated the special nature of relations between Moscow and Yerevan. "We have a tradition – our closest partners are invited here (to Zavidovo – *Ed.*)," Dmitry Medvedev said. Mr. Sargsyan must have been flattered to hear those words. Especially considering that only a week ago, when Azerbaijani President Ilkham Aliyev visited Russia, Dmitry Medvedev received him not at Zavidovo but at Barvikha, just outside Moscow.

Behind closed doors, Mr. Medvedev and Mr. Sargsyan discussed primarily economic issues. One of them, a source at the Russian Foreign Ministry told Kommersant, was Russia's granting Armenia a $500 million loan. According to Kommersant's source, Moscow is ready to sign a loan agreement with Yerevan. Russian financial assistance to Armenia is obviously supposed to encourage Yerevan to be open to Moscow's peacemaking initiatives regarding a resolution of the Nagorno-Karabakh conflict. As Kommersant has already reported, the Kremlin and the Russian Foreign Ministry are currently actively involved in making preparations for talks between the presidents of Armenia and Azerbaijan, Serzh Sargsyan and Ilkham Aliyev, which are to take place in June on the sidelines of an economic forum in St. Petersburg.

If everything proceeds according to Moscow's plan and the meeting in St. Petersburg not only takes place but also produces some agreements, Russia will be able to confirm its leading role in the Karabakh peace process, a role it has been diligently playing since last fall. At that time, Dmitry Medvedev managed to persuade the Armenian and Azerbaijani leaders to sign their countries' first joint document since 1994 – a declaration on a peaceful resolution of the Karabakh conflict. Yesterday Mr. Medvedev made no secret of his hopes to build on last year's peacemaking success. "We're on the right track in our discussion. My contacts, including contacts with the president of Azerbaijan, have confirmed that the sides are ready to move in a constructive direction to resolve this complex problem, so I think that any movement, in this sense, is encouraging," the Russian president said after the talks at Zavidovo.

It is noteworthy that Presidents Medvedev and Sargsyan did not say a single word about the Armenian-Turkish "road map." Kommersant's source at the Russian Foreign Ministry said that Moscow was not inclined to attach particular importance to that event, which, in his opinion, "is nothing more than an empty PR stunt." The Russian leadership will soon be able to determine how far Turkey is prepared to go in its friendship with Armenia: Turkish Prime Minister Recep Erdogan will visit Moscow in May.

DASHNAKS GOING INTO OPPOSITION

By Yury Simonyan. *Nezavisimaya gazeta*, April 27, 2009, p. 6.

The Armenian Revolutionary Federation Dashnaktsutyun (ARFD) refused to participate in a meeting of the National Security Council on Saturday [April 25]. The démarche was prompted by Wednesday's joint statement by the Armenian and Turkish foreign ministries announcing that they had signed a "road map." ...

Armen Rustamyan, one of the ARFD's leaders and chairman of the parliament's standing committee on foreign relations, told reporters that the party is considering withdrawing from the ruling coalition, so "it would be inappropriate to participate in the work of the Security Council." The Dashnaks feel betrayed – even though they are members of the ruling coalition, they learned about the drafting of a road map for reconciliation between Armenia and Turkey only after the Foreign Ministry statement was made public.

Besides the ARFD, the ruling coalition includes the actual party of power – the Republican Party – as well as Country of Law and Prosperous Armenia. The loss of an influential ally ahead of the [May 31] Yerevan mayoral election, which will be a significant event in the country's political life, could result in unpleasant consequences for the Republicans. Especially considering the tough competition from the opposition Armenian National Congress (ANC), which has named the country's first president, Levon Ter-Petrosyan, as its candidate.

The ANC, like the ARFD, is demanding that the authorities make the "road map" transparent. The classified nature of the document is causing concern both among Armenia's political forces and among the public. "We demand that the document be published, since it affects the interests not only of Armenia but of all Armenians," reads a statement by the ANC. But the authorities are in no hurry to meet that demand.

At the aforementioned meeting of the Security Council, President Serzh Sargsyan merely assured the participants that the interests of Armenians would not be betrayed in any way and that the document merely spells out the actions that Yerevan and Ankara will take to improve relations.

The Turkish authorities are not offering any comments on the "road map" either. However, it is known that in Ankara, too, there are forces that suspect the authorities of making "unwarranted concessions to Armenia" and are demanding that the document be declassified....

To date, only the US has officially supported the document signed by the Turkish and Armenian foreign ministries. On April 25, in a traditional message to Armenians in remembrance of the genocide during the Ottoman Empire, President Barack Obama commended the steps that Ankara and Yerevan have taken toward reconciliation. Although he promised during his election campaign to recognize the Armenian genocide, Obama, like all of his predecessors, did not use the word "genocide," replacing it with the Armenian term Meds Yeghern ("Great Calamity" – that is what the Armenians themselves call the 1915 tragedy, since the word "genocide" did not come into international usage until more than 30 years later). But Obama's ploy to keep everyone happy failed.

The Turkish Foreign Ministry described a number of Obama's words as unacceptable and expressed regret that he did not mention the Turks who were killed in clashes with Armenians. Official Yerevan did not respond to Obama's speech, but Armenian diasporas abroad expressed their dissatisfaction with it.

ERDOGAN REASSURES ALIYEV

By Sokhbet Mamedov. *Nezavisimaya gazeta*, May 14, 2009, p. 6.

Baku – Yesterday marked the end of Turkish Prime Minister Recep Tayyip Erdogan's brief official visit to Azerbaijan, an event that was closely watched not only by the public in those two countries, but also by the political establishment in the region as a whole. The fact is that Erdogan's visit to Azerbaijan was intended primarily to relieve some of the tension in relations between Ankara and Baku over Turkey's plans to open its borders with Armenia.

This issue is of fundamental importance to Baku, which is not opposed to a normalization of relations between Turkey and Armenia, provided that this process proceeds in tandem with a settlement of the Armenian-Azerbaijani conflict....

The border between Turkey and Armenia was closed in 1993 because of Armenia's occupation of Azerbaijani territories. Nothing has changed since that time, and official Baku thinks Ankara should keep that in mind. "Our position is neither to promote nor to impede the development of relations between those two countries. These days we've been hearing a lot of conflicting comments on this from various sources. Some say that the 'road map' was drawn up with preliminary conditions. Other sources say that the 'road map' doesn't say anything about preliminary conditions. This is a kind of equivocation. I think the world, the region and the people of Azerbaijan should know what's going on. Has the settlement of the Nagorno-Karabakh conflict been removed from the context of rapprochement between Turkey and Armenia or not? This is a simple question that requires a very simple answer" – that is the message that Ilkham Aliyev conveyed to Ankara when he was in Brussels in late April.

Erdogan arrived in Baku on the evening of May 12. On Wednesday morning [May 13], Erdogan and Aliyev held talks, which were later continued in an expanded format....

According to the APA news agency, the Turkish prime minister declared that the meeting was "the best answer to those who would like to cast a shadow on our historical unity. Azerbaijan's sensitivity on the issue of Nagorno-Karabakh is our sensitivity as well. Trying to profit from this matter is unacceptable to us. There is a relationship of cause and effect here. The cause was the occupation of Nagorno-Karabakh, and the effect was our closing of the borders with Armenia. We closed the doors because parts of Azerbaijan were occupied." Erdogan also reassured Baku that "until the occupation ends, the doors will not be opened."

ARMENIA, TURKEY INCH CLOSER TO OPENING BORDER

By Nikolai Filchenko. *Kommersant*, Sept. 2, 2009, p. 5.

Armenia and Turkey have reached a preliminary agreement on resuming diplomatic relations and opening the border, which has been closed since 1993....

News of the sensational agreements between Armenia and Turkey broke on Monday evening [Aug. 31]. The Armenian Ministry of Foreign Affairs reported that during negotiations between Yerevan and Ankara, with Switzerland acting as mediator, the sides agreed to begin consultations on signing two documents on the normalization of relations. They are a Protocol on the Establishment of Diplomatic Relations and a Protocol on the Development of Bilateral Relations.

The Protocol on the Establishment of Diplomatic Relations includes several points, the main one being to open the border no later than two months after the Protocol on the Development of Bilateral Relations enters into force. The document also calls for the creation of a bilateral working group to draft a program of measures for an intergovernmental commission, which will work on resolving disagreements, including historical disputes.

Negotiations on the two protocols are to be concluded within the next six weeks, i.e., just in time for Armenian President Serzh Sargsyan's visit to Turkey. He is scheduled to visit Ankara on Oct. 14 to attend, together with Turkish President Abdullah Gul, a soccer game between the Turkish and Armenian national teams, which are squaring off in another leg of the World Cup 2010 qualifying round....

Addressing the Armenian diplomatic corps yesterday, Sargsyan said that Armenia is closer than ever before to mending Armenian-Turkish relations. "We have tried to mend relations with our neighbor in a manner befitting the civilized world of the 21st century. I think that these protocols provide such an opportunity," Mr. Sargsyan said. He made particular note of the fact that the agreements do not include any preliminary conditions involving a settlement of the Karabakh conflict or other related issues.

The West is also hoping that Ankara and Yerevan make peace with each other soon. Washington said yesterday that the US supports the normalization of relations between the two countries. A statement released by official State Department spokesman Ian Kelly says that "the United States warmly welcomes the joint statement made by Turkey and Armenia, with Swiss participation, outlining further steps in the normalization of their bilateral relations. We urge Armenia and Turkey to proceed expeditiously, according to the agreed framework."

Meanwhile, Baku takes a different view. Commenting on reports of an imminent breakthrough in Armenian-Turkish relations, official Azerbaijani Foreign Ministry spokesman Elkhan Polukhov said bluntly that opening the border between the two countries without settling the Karabakh conflict would go against Azerbaijan's national interests....

Baku had previously expressed displeasure over the rapprochement between Yerevan and Ankara. In the spring, when it was first reported that Armenia and Turkey were holding negotiations, the Azerbaijani authorities were extremely upset with Turkey. It reached the point that Azerbaijani President Ilkham Aliyev pointedly ignored an invitation to come to Istanbul on April 7 to meet US President Barack Obama. Instead, on April 16 Mr. Aliyev went to Moscow for a meeting with Russian President Dmitry Medvedev.

In that light, yesterday's statement by the Azerbaijani Foreign Ministry should be viewed as a warning to Turkey not to be too hasty in establishing friendly relations with Armenia. And to all appearances, Ankara heeded that warning. In any case, Turkish Foreign Minister Ahmet Davutoglu stated yesterday that, for now, his country has no plans to open its border with Armenia.

ARMENIA, TURKEY AGREE SILENTLY

By Vladimir Solovyov and Igor Sedykh. *Kommersant*, Oct. 12, 2009, p. 7.

Zurich – The foreign ministers of Armenia and Turkey, Eduard Nalbandyan and Ahmet Davutoglu, signed protocols in Zurich on Saturday [Oct. 10] on normalizing relations between their two countries....

The two Armenian-Turkish protocols – "On the Establishment of Diplomatic Relations" and "On the Development of Bilateral Relations" – which envision, among other things, opening the border (closed since 1993), were initialed by the countries back in the spring. And on Aug. 31, Yerevan and Ankara officially announced that preparations were under way to sign the documents, which were promptly pronounced "historic."... The site chosen for the grand public display of reconciliation was Switzerland, which had served as mediator between the countries in talks that lasted more than a year. The protocols were signed by the Armenian and Turkish foreign ministers, Eduard Nalbandyan and Ahmet Davutoglu, on Saturday in Zurich. Officials who had come to town for the occasion included the foreign policy chiefs of Russia, the US, France and Slovenia, as well as European Union High Representative for Common Foreign and Security Policy Javier Solana, who were to give their blessings to the start of friendship between Armenia and Turkey.

The signing ceremony had been scheduled down to the minute. The delegations were to gather at Zurich University at exactly 5 p.m. to listen to a welcoming address by the head of the Swiss Federal Department of Foreign Affairs, Micheline Calmy-Rey. Then Mr. Nalbandyan and Mr. Davutoglu were to sign the protocols, make statements, hear parting words from their counterparts and go their separate ways. But at the last minute, the "historic event" was threatened with derailment.

Mr. Nalbandyan and Mr. Davutoglu had a disagreement, which was described to Kommersant by one of the participants in the Zurich meeting. The two ministers had an unexpected squabble over the content of their final statements, which they had decided to share with each other before making them public. Media reports said that Armenia was upset by Turkey's linking the signing of the protocols to a settlement of the Nagorno-Karabakh conflict. According to Kommersant's source, Armenia did not like the Turkish foreign minister's statement about the need to set up a commission to establish whether the Turks had committed genocide against the Armenians in 1915. In any event, Nalbandyan and Davutoglu did not show up at Zurich University either at the appointed time for the signing or two hours later.

While US Secretary of State Hillary Clinton tried to persuade the sides not to cause a scandal, Sergei Lavrov, Javier Solana and the French and Slovenian foreign ministers, Bernard Kouchner and Samuel Zbogar, passed the time watching a soccer match between Russia and Germany. When the game was over and the wait had exceeded the bounds of diplomatic decorum, Nalbandyan and Davutoglu were given an ultimatum: Either solve the problem by 8 p.m. (Swiss time) and sign the protocols, or the ceremony would be canceled.

A source in one of the delegations told Kommersant: "At that point, Lavrov wrote a brief note to Nalbandyan. It was six words long [in Russian – *Trans.*]: 'Eduard! Agree to a ceremony without statements.' " The note, which was signed not only by the Russian minister but also by Kouchner, Solana and Zbogar, was passed along to the Armenian foreign minister (Kommersant obtained a copy of it). An hour later, Eduard Nalbandyan and Ahmet Davutoglu silently signed the protocols and silently departed.

The signed documents provide for the establishment of diplomatic missions in the capitals of the two countries and the opening of the border "within two months after the entry into force of this protocol." However, the protocols still must be ratified by the Armenian and Turkish parliaments. And problems could arise there....

FRATERNITY OVERSHADOWED BY PROTOCOLS

By Irada Alekperova. *Vremya novostei*, Oct. 14, 2009, p. 5.

Baku – ... Azerbaijan's political elite has reacted strongly to the thaw in relations between Armenia and Turkey. President Ilkham Aliyev remarked: "Some people are of the opinion that normalizing Turkish-Armenian relations and opening the border can help achieve a settlement of the Nagorno-Karabakh conflict. I do not share those views, since I believe that if Turkish-Armenian relations are normalized before there is a resolution of the Karabakh problem, Armenia may take a harder line in the negotiating process." The president feels "absolutely certain" that the settlement of the Karabakh conflict and the opening of the Turkish-Armenian border must occur "concurrently and simultaneously," or else "the status quo in the region may change for the worse."

Azerbaijan's Foreign Ministry also issued a stern statement: "The normalization of relations between Turkey and Armenia before Armenian troops are withdrawn from the occupied Azerbaijani territories is directly contrary to Azerbaijan's interests and casts a shadow on the spirit of its fraternal relations with Turkey, which have deep historical roots. While taking into account the importance of opening all borders and lines of communication in the region, Azerbaijan believes that the unilateral opening of the Turkish-Armenian border will call into question the architecture of peace and stability in the region." Baku refers to previous statements made by Ankara about the impossibility of opening the border with Armenia until the "occupation" of Azerbaijani lands comes to an end....

Turkish Deputy Prime Minister Cemil Cicek stressed yesterday that the establishment of lasting peace in the region depends "on a settlement of the disagreements between Armenia and Azerbaijan with regard to Nagorno-Karabakh." He called the Turkish-Armenian protocols a "serious and sincere manifestation of (Ankara's) desire for peace," adding that only parliament "can decide whether they should be ratified or rejected." According to Mr. Cicek, Turkey's "fraternal" relations with Azerbaijan "are not aimed at deriving benefits for itself." His view was echoed by Turkish Foreign Minister Ahmet Davutoglu, who said that "we are not talking about automatically opening the border." The minister emphasized the importance of creating "the appropriate psychological, political and international atmosphere," which can only come about from "progress toward settling the Karabakh issue." "Turkey will not abandon Azerbaijan. The two countries' fortunes are inextricably linked," the Turkish diplomatic chief stated.

But Azerbaijani politicians were not placated by those words. Mubariz Ahmedoglu, director of the Baku-based Center for Political Innovations and Technologies, thinks that if Turkey "does not offer some kind of reasonable proposal soon, relations between the two fraternal countries could be seriously damaged." Vremya novostei's source does not think that there will be any problem with ratification of the protocols: "Turkey has taken on a commitment, and if its parliament does not ratify these agreements, Turkey itself will suffer for it. After all, this whole thing is an American scenario, and what's important is the end result. Otherwise the US and Armenia will punish Turkey."

In the opinion of Elkhan Kuliyev, an analyst with the Baku-based Atlas Research Center, Turkey is motivated "by more than the desire to strengthen its influence in the South Caucasus." He commented in a conversation with Vremya novostei that, with the signing of the protocols, Turkey "has succeeded in forcing Armenia to abandon its territorial claims, since the agreements confirm the mutual recognition of the two countries' territorial integrity." And the "question of recognizing the 'Armenian genocide' in the Ottoman Empire during World War I is now moving from the international arena to the sphere of bilateral relations between Armenia and Turkey."... "Moreover, thanks to its efforts to normalize relations with its neighbor, Ankara has strengthened its position in negotiations with Brussels on membership in the European Union," the expert observed.

Mr. Kuliyev also pointed out the benefits that could accrue to Armenia: "It will be able to expand its foreign economic and communications ties, which have been in serious jeopardy since the 2008 war between Georgia and Russia. And as a result, it will be able to conduct a more balanced foreign policy, which will facilitate the process of Armenia's integration into the Euro-Atlantic space." If there is a resolution of the conflict over Nagorno-Karabakh, Yerevan "will gain a real opportunity to participate in regional integration processes, including international energy projects like the Nabucco gas pipeline."

The expert added that establishing diplomatic relations and opening the border between Turkey and Armenia will not have any "serious economic consequences" for Azerbaijan, "since its abundant oil and gas resources are already contributing to the country's dynamic development." But in foreign policy "you can expect to see some adjustments – it's possible that Baku might pin its hopes on Moscow on the Karabakh issue."...

MEDVEDEV'S KARABAKH DILEMMA

By Aleksandr Karavayev, deputy general director of Moscow State University's Information Analysis Center. *Nezavisimaya gazeta*, Dec. 1, 2009, p. 3.

The subject of Karabakh has been constantly on the agendas of both regional and international events over the past few days. For example, it might come up for discussion during the meeting of OSCE foreign ministers that is being held in Athens today and tomorrow. It had been anticipated that the day before, or perhaps even during the Ministerial Council session, the foreign ministers of Armenia and Azerbaijan, Eduard Nalbandyan and Elmar Mamedyarov, would meet and discuss the situation surrounding Karabakh. Russian politicians haven't been skirting the subject either.

One of the expectations placed upon the Medvedev-Putin tandem at the very beginning of their administration was the expectation that Russia would develop more sophisticated foreign policy mechanisms....

Perhaps a true indicator of the effectiveness and maturity of that policy will be how active a role Russia takes in settling the Karabakh conflict, which was the first ethnic-territorial conflict to surface after the USSR collapsed. This conflict has always had many dimensions that go beyond the borders of the Caucasus. It is now closer than ever before to moving from discussion to real action. Turkey has begun gradually lifting the blockade in its political relations with Armenia, which were frozen 16 years ago. But the twist here is the difference in the positioning strategies of the US and Russia.

The Americans are actively putting pressure on Turkey for rapprochement with Armenia. Clearly, they have serious geopolitical motives with regard to Turkey and the Caucasus. But then, Russia has at least as much interest in the region from a substantive and historical perspective. Washington, however, unconcerned about accusations of pressure, is clearly stating its position, and by taking part in the outcome of this historical conflict it is also showing the depth of its interest in Turkey and Armenia. We, meanwhile, on our side of this complex problem in the post-Soviet Caucasus, aren't making any direct statements linking the Armenian-Turkish and Karabakh processes. We hesitate to assert our influence on Armenia, as though the process of rapprochement between Armenia and Azerbaijan were not to our advantage.

The logic behind this inhibition is understandable – why should Russia be in a hurry, the Caucasus is complicated, and any openly expressed position could complicate the situation. But this self-removal is fraught with serious limitations on Russia's future presence in the region. Turkey was not afraid to shift its position toward compromise, being aware of Baku's grievances, but also understanding that, as a long-term strategy, Armenian-Turkish rapprochement is advantageous to Azerbaijan and that the geostrategic link between Turkey and Azerbaijan will remain a constant, regardless of circumstances.

Moscow, however, has stopped cold in the face of the dilemma. On the one hand, blocking Armenian-Turkish reconciliation would look doubly strange, considering Russia's economic interests in Armenia, its major investments in transportation and the necessity of extensive trade traffic for developing joint business projects, including projects with companies of the Armenian diaspora. On the other hand, a stereotype prevails: If you support Azerbaijan, you will lose your influence over Armenia. But let's ask this question: Who else would Armenia turn to? Turkish-

Azerbaijani ties, despite all the friction over Karabakh and gas trade, are not being annihilated. The same is true for Armenian-Russian relations. Russia's presence in Armenia cannot be reduced by its taking a clearer position on the Karabakh issue. The conflict will gradually begin to work itself out in the foreseeable future. One can see general agreement among the US, Russia and the EU on a road map for resolution. But the mediator who is the first to establish the need to take practical steps in the occupied areas around Karabakh will play the leading role, for example, in the formation of peacekeeping and police units....

Moscow continues to try to distance itself from a clear-cut public position, indicating that the parties to the conflict must find the solution themselves. The most likely result of this self-withdrawal is that bold Atlantic outsiders will take the lead and compel the sides to take the first step.

TURKEY REFUSES TO MAKE PEACE WITH ARMENIA

By Yekaterina Zabrodina. *Izvestia*, Dec. 3, 2009, p. 5.

The tentative warming that has emerged in relations between Ankara and Yerevan faces the threat of a new diplomatic impasse. Turkish Foreign Minister Ahmet Davutoglu has linked the ratification of Armenian-Turkish protocols with the Nagorno-Karabakh issue.

The minister announced this condition in Athens at a meeting with his Azerbaijani counterpart Elmar Mamedyarov during the 17th session of the OSCE Ministerial Council. "The ratification of the protocols [signed] with Armenia is possible only after it withdraws from the occupied Azerbaijani territories," Mr. Davutoglu stated categorically. This démarche by Ankara essentially negates all attempts to put an end to the age-old enmity between the two peoples.

Readers are reminded that in Zurich on Oct. 10, in the presence of Russian Foreign Minister Sergei Lavrov and US Secretary of State Hillary Clinton, the parties signed documents that the international community was quick to hail as "historic" – namely, Armenian-Turkish protocols on establishing diplomatic relations and normalizing bilateral contacts. Armenian Foreign Minister Eduard Nalbandyan and his Turkish counterpart agreed that their states would exchange diplomatic missions in the foreseeable future. In addition, Turkey promised to open its border with Armenia.

Those arrangements immediately set off a storm of indignation in Baku. The Azerbaijani authorities stated that the opening of the Turkish-Armenian border should be preceded by "the settlement of the Nagorno-Karabakh issue." Otherwise, Turkey "might lose the friendship of Azerbaijan."

TURKISH TREPIDATION – Yerevan Awaits Arrival of Sergei Lavrov

By Gayane Movsesyan. *Vremya novostei*, Jan. 13, 2010, p. 5.

Yerevan – Russian Foreign Minister Sergei Lavrov arrives today in Yerevan, where he was invited by Armenian Foreign Minister Eduard Nalbandyan for a two-day visit. The itinerary includes a meeting between the guest and Armenian President Serzh Sargsyan. Sources at the Armenian Foreign Ministry told Vremya novostei that the talks will address the situation in the South Caucasus region and the process for resolving the problem of Nagorno-Karabakh, as well as cooperation in the political, military, trade-and-economic and humanitarian spheres. Also on the agenda is a discussion of partnership between provinces of Armenia and members of the Russian Federation....

Mr. Lavrov's trip to Yerevan coincides with a visit to Moscow by Turkish Prime Minister Recep Tayyip Erdogan, which began yesterday. This has caused uneasiness in Armenian public and political circles. Against the backdrop of Ankara's unceasing attempts to make normalization of Armenian-Turkish relations contingent on a settlement of the Nagorno-Karabakh conflict on Azerbaijan's terms, and also in light of the rapprochement between Russia and Turkey and Russia and Azerbaijan, people in Yerevan have begun talking about the possibility that Russia, as cochair of the OSCE Minsk Group, might put pressure on Armenia over the Karabakh issue.

Sergei Minasyan, deputy director of the Yerevan-based Caucasus Institute, noted in an interview with Vremya novostei that "Sergei Lavrov's visit is a routine one. Under an agreement between the two countries' foreign ministries, the ministers meet twice a year to exchange opinions. The positive dynamics in bilateral relations will be maintained in the future as well. Lavrov's trip to Yerevan coincides with Erdogan's visit to Moscow, where officials will touch on, among other things, both the Karabakh problem and Armenian-Turkish relations. But I don't think that the apprehensions about this that have arisen in Armenian society can be considered warranted." In the expert's opinion, "when it comes to a Karabakh settlement, nothing major can happen in the foreseeable future."

However, there is another reason why political passions in Yerevan are seething. The Armenian Constitutional Court ruled yesterday that the Armenian-Turkish protocols "On the Establishment of Diplomatic Relations" and "On the Development of Bilateral Relations," which were signed by the two countries' foreign ministers on Oct. 10, 2009 in Zurich, are in conformity with the country's basic law. After Court Chairman Gagik Arutyunyan stated that the ruling was final and not subject to appeal, cries of condemnation rang out in the courtroom. The Armenian Revolutionary Federation Dashnaktsutyun and 10 other parties that see the Armenian-Turkish protocols as a threat to the security of Armenia and Nagorno-Karabakh and oppose their ratification in their current form had tried to get the documents found at least partly unconstitutional. Now, to all appearances, opponents of the protocols will direct their efforts at thwarting their ratification. Meanwhile, Armenian parliamentary speaker Ovik Abramyan recently stated that the deputies would approve the protocols only after they are ratified by the Turkish parliament.

"Russia openly supports the process of normalization of Armenian-Turkish relations, and it itself has a vested interest in this when it comes to transportation. Russian-Turkish relations have a very important economic component, especially in the energy sector. Mr. Lavrov's visit will give Armenian officials yet another chance to impress upon the Russian leadership the need to put indirect pressure on Turkey to open the border with Armenia," Sergei Minasyan told VN....

ANKARA BEGINS SPEAKING TO YEREVAN IN LANGUAGE OF ULTIMATUMS

By Yury Simonyan. *Nezavisimaya gazeta*, Jan. 22, 2010, p. 6.

On Wednesday evening [Jan. 20], Murat Mercan, chairman of the Turkish parliament's committee on foreign affairs, told foreign journalists that the parliament would not even discuss the so-called "Swiss protocols" – the agreements on normalizing relations between Armenia and Turkey that were signed in Zurich on Oct. 10-11 by the two countries' foreign ministers. "That will not be possible until the deoccupation of Azerbaijani territories," Mercan stated. Ankara places the blame for the breakdown in the process on the Armenian Constitutional Court, which allegedly made changes in the protocols before forwarding them to the parliament for confirmation....

Some of the more radical Turkish parliamentary deputies have even demanded apologies from their government, "which, in offending the fraternal Azerbaijani people, have insulted the entire Turkish people as well."

Another of the Turkish side's complaints directly involves the "Swiss protocols." Under Armenian law, prior to the documents' consideration by parliament, the Armenian Constitutional Court had to render a ruling on their acceptability or unacceptability. Ankara claims that the Constitutional Court forwarded amended protocols to the parliament, which is impermissible. The influential newspaper Hurriyet writes that Yerevan was admonished by Prime Minister Recep Tayyip Erdogan, who announced a suspension of the rapprochement process, and by Foreign Minister Ahmet Davutoglu, who spoke by telephone with his counterpart Eduard Nalbandyan on Wednesday evening.

A high-ranking source in Yerevan outlined for NG what actually happened in the past few days. The Armenian Constitutional Court, in studying the "Swiss protocols" on the normalization of relations, did not find anything in them that contradicted the republic's Basic Law and forwarded them to the parliament. At the same time, the court ruling mentions that the protocols may not be interpreted or applied in any way that violates the provisions of the Armenian Constitution or Point 11 of Armenia's Declaration of Independence, which reads: "The Republic of Armenia supports the process of achieving international recognition of the 1915 genocide of

Armenians in Ottoman Turkey and Western Armenia." "It is that statement in the Constitutional Court's ruling that upset the Turkish side. Essentially, Ankara's protest involves the Constitutional Court's commentary, which does not per se propose any changes in the protocols that were forwarded for ratification. The Constitutional Court's ruling was definitely designed for domestic political consumption," NG's source said. He also stressed that in the past few days, on the basis of a number of statements made by official Ankara and prominent Turkish politicians, Yerevan has gotten the impression that Turkey itself is deliberately dragging out the process of ratifying the "Swiss protocols" and is even looking for an excuse to torpedo the process. "In their telephone conversation, the Armenian foreign minister brought this to the attention of his Turkish counterpart," the source said.

Of course, this turn of events should never have been ruled out – if only because, well, let's put it this way: The level of trust between the societies of Armenia and Turkey is not exactly high. But even leaving that aside, literally the day after the signing of the "Swiss protocols," when the two sides had apparently agreed to differentiate Armenian-Turkish problems from Armenian-Azerbaijani problems, Prime Minister Recep Tayyip Erdogan stated that unless Baku's jurisdiction over Nagorno-Karabakh was restored, there could be no reconciliation between Armenia and Turkey. He subsequently repeated that statement many times. However, Erdogan's words could also have been a response to the extremely distressed reaction on the part of Azerbaijan, which officially declared the Armenian-Turkish contacts a betrayal by Ankara and even issued a threat to Turkey, saying that Baku would reconsider the level of strategic relations and create certain energy inconveniences....

MOSCOW, ANKARA VIEW KARABAKH CONFLICT DIFFERENTLY

By Sokhbet Mamedov. *Nezavisimaya gazeta*, Aug. 17, 2010, p. 5.

Turkish President Abdullah Gul arrived in Azerbaijan on an official visit yesterday....

Prior to his visit, Abdullah Gul gave an interview to the Azerbaijani news agency APA, in which he touched upon the influence Russia has on the peace process in the region.

"I know that Mr. Medvedev, Mr. Putin, Mr. Aliyev and Mr. Sargsyan believe that this status quo (the conflict between Azerbaijan and Armenia – NG) will not last long. They, too, want the issue resolved. During the cold war era, great powers used conflicts to their advantage. Today, the situation is different. Everybody is working hard to resolve the problem. In today's world, you can't occupy another country's lands for such an extended period of time. Unless the issue is resolved, uncontrollable problems may emerge," Gul said. He added that it is necessary to work intensely on this problem. This issue requires quiet politics. Last year, when "the mountain started to move," there was too much noise. [Back then], an erroneous assessment of the issue created problems for everybody – Azerbaijan, Armenia and Turkey.

"Now, we have entered a period of quiet yet determined diplomacy. I hope we have a smoother process ahead of us," the Turkish leader said.

Abdullah Gul's visit and the upcoming visit by Russian President Dmitry Medvedev to Azerbaijan are being viewed in the republic today from a standpoint of settling the Armenian-Azerbaijani conflict. According to political analyst Vafa Guluzade, these two visits pursue different goals.

"Russia's strategic goal is to prevent the Karabakh conflict from being resolved. Moscow is unhappy over NATO expansion. It thinks that as soon as the Karabakh conflict is settled, Azerbaijan and Armenia will immediately join NATO. The Turkish president, on the other hand, wants the conflict resolved as soon as possible in a way that would uphold Azerbaijan's territorial integrity and help Turkey retain its influence in our country. Thus, these two visits are polar opposites," the political analyst thinks.

It must be noted that many Azerbaijanis share Guluzade's opinion....

AZERBAIJAN MAY HOST TURKISH MILITARY BASE

By Yury Roks. *Nezavisimaya gazeta*, Aug. 20, 2010, p. 1.

Azerbaijan may host a Turkish military base. It may be deployed in the Nakhichevan Autonomous Republic, an exclave sandwiched between Armenia and Turkey. This was reported on Wednesday [Aug. 18] and Thursday by a number of Azerbaijani media outlets. Supposedly, the subject was discussed during President Abdullah Gul's recent visit to Baku. If the plan goes through, it may be regarded as Baku and Ankara's response to the new treaty Moscow and Yerevan signed recently that extends the lease of the Russian military base in Armenia to 49 years and expanding its functions to include ensuring Armenia's security.

The relationship between Baku and Ankara, described by the late Azerbaijani leader Geidar Aliyev as "two states, one nation," is so close that one can only wonder why Azerbaijan, being officially in a state of ceasefire with Armenia, did not deploy a Turkish military base earlier, and why the issue is getting attention only now. The answer to those questions lies in Baku's expectation that Moscow would render effective assistance in resolving the Nagorno-Karabakh conflict. In other words, Baku was hoping that Moscow would influence its strategic ally, Yerevan, and help restore Azerbaijan's territorial integrity, and because of this, Azerbaijan was hesitant to openly intensify a pro-Turkish bias or any other tendency in its foreign policy.

However, now Baku thinks those expectations were too high. Despite all the summits, Russia's active role in conflict resolution and its avowed readiness to resolve the problem "justly" and quickly, no real progress has been made.

That's why Baku has decided to set a limit to its expectations, and once that limit is reached, it will probably attempt to go for a breakthrough through different means.

That limit is Russian President Dmitry Medvedev's upcoming visit to Baku, which is scheduled for September. Azerbaijan is waiting to see what new proposals the Russian president will bring.... Azerbaijani analysts believe that Moscow used the new treaty to solidify its geopolitical presence in the South Caucasus and simultaneously warn Baku that it shouldn't even think about using force to resolve the Karabakh conflict. At the same time, [analysts] emphasize that the new military treaty between Armenia and Russia cannot be interpreted as a "step that Moscow and Yerevan were forced to take in response to an agreement on strategic partnership and mutual support that Turkey and Azerbaijan signed in Baku recently during the aforementioned visit by Abdullah Gul. This is because the Armenian-Russian treaty was in the works for a long time, whereas Azerbaijan and Turkey simply renewed their old treaty."

Essentially, these comments repeat what the Turkish president himself said. Upon his return to Ankara, he told the press that the treaty signed in Baku was not directed against a third party and that Turkey and Azerbaijan "have been strategic partners for a long time and decided to renew the document signed in 1994." The treaty doesn't contain any fundamentally new provisions....

Nevertheless, most of the experts on the region believe that the unpublished treaty between Turkey and Azerbaijan devotes much attention to military issues and possibly even to concrete plans to set up a Turkish military base in the Nakhichevan exclave as a "symmetrical response to Yerevan." After all, it is no accident that this issue was raised right now. On the other hand, by leaking the story about possibly hosting a Turkish base, Azerbaijan is sending a clear message to Russia – Baku will inevitably and perhaps irrevocably adjust its geopolitical orientation unless there's progress in the near future on resolving the Karabakh issue in terms favorable to Azerbaijan.

Commenting on the situation, Rasim Musabekov, a well-known Azerbaijani political analyst, said that even if the military component does play a dominant role in the renewed agreement between Azerbaijan and Turkey, it shouldn't come as a surprise, since Armenia and Russia are also updating their military agreements. "Why can't Azerbaijan and Turkey do the same? The two countries have an agreement on pipeline security, and this cooperation may be expanded, especially since Armenia and Iran have threatened to blow up the pipelines and Russia's war against Georgia in August 2008 could have easily disrupted supply. Turkey might provide air defense for the pipelines.... It may deploy a mobile force in the Gyandzha area," Prof. Musabekov thinks. In his opinion, a Turkish military base in Nakhichevan is quite possible. Under current circumstances, such a scenario is in Azerbaijan's interests. Having a base practically within Armenia's territory that's capable of receiving uninterrupted supplies from Turkey (unlike, by the way, the Russian base in Gyumri, the logistics of which look very questionable) can at the very least create a serious diversion for the Armenian army in case hostilities break out in Nagorno-Karabakh. Yet, according to Musabekov, "Russia has interests in Azerbaijan as well; that's why Russian President Dmitry Medvedev shouldn't come to Baku in September empty-handed in regard to settling the Karabakh conflict."...

Yerevan reacted fairly calmly to the prospect of a Turkish military base in Na-khichevan. A high-ranking military official who occupied an important position in the Armenian Defense Ministry during the Nagorno-Karabakh war told NG the following: "Do you think that just because there was no Turkish base in Nakhichevan either during the liberation of Karabakh or at present, we felt secure? Today, our positions regularly come under fire from Nakhichevan. If Turkish troops are officially deployed there, that won't really change anything because their presence will be neutralized by the Russian military base, as stipulated in the treaty Dmitry Medvedev and Serzh Sargsyan signed. In the same way, any possible attack on Armenia from that direction was neutralized by our Russian brothers during the war. From a geopolitical point of view, Yerevan will even benefit if Turkey sets up a base there, because this will polarize the situation for Moscow and clearly demonstrate who's on whose side. But I don't think it will get to that point. I think Ankara is smart enough not to look at Russia through the sights of Nakhichevan rifles. Ankara is interested in cooperating with Moscow, not in escalating tensions."

NOTES

1. The newspaper *Nezavisimaya gazeta* reported on May 14, 1992 (p. 3) that a session of the Azerbaijan Supreme Soviet had been convened to discuss the new developments and to consider postponing the presidential election, scheduled for June 7, until autumn. Yagub Mamedov, Azerbaijan's current leader, called for a postponement because of the need to institute a state of emergency in the republic and declare a general mobilization.

Chapter 9 | Russia

NEIGHBORS: RUSSIA STRENGTHENS ITS INFLUENCE IN THE TRANSCAUCASUS –
Military Diplomacy in Tbilisi, Yerevan, Baku and Gudauta
By Pavel Felgengauer. *Segodnya*, June 15, 1994, p. 2.

Last week Defense Minister Pavel Grachev was met in three Transcaucasus capitals more than just cordially, as if he were a head of government: He was greeted by a band and an honor guard, escorted along a cordoned-off route, etc. Only the meeting in Baku was impeccably polite, but cool.

The Russian minister was received by the heads of all the Transcaucasus states, and one member of the delegation reports that Eduard Shevardnadze, in addition to the official meeting, came to see Gen. Grachev twice more (in less than 24 hours) to find out about the results of talks with Mr. Ardzinba and about the timetable for sending in Russian peacekeepers.

The total number of Russian troops in the Transcaucasus is insignificant: approximately 20,000 in the Group of Forces, and 5,500 border guards. But Russia is still the dominant force in the Transcaucasus, and only because of its Army.

Economic ties with the Transcaucasus have weakened considerably, and at this point there is no serious hope of radical changes for the better. Trade has been made more difficult even in a purely physical sense: The railroad along the coast is completely blocked south of Sukhumi, and the line to Baku is partially blocked by Chechen bandits and can't be used to transport freight of any value. Air transportation is expensive and motor transport is unreliable, especially in Georgia. In economic terms, the region is coming to be tied more and more closely to Turkey and Iran, just as it was two centuries ago.

But in time, the Russian military's cooperation with the Transcaucasus republics will evidently be able to help restore trade and other ties, and in any event guarantee that the Transcaucasus will not become a potential military threat to Russia. For instance, Moscow and Yerevan have developed relations that can quite accurately be described as a close military alliance: The 127th Motorized Infantry Division stationed in Gyumri (with one regiment in Yerevan) evidently will eventually be transformed into a brigade, and the amount of heavy weapons and armored vehicles will be reduced somewhat. At the same time, Army aircraft will be sent to Armenia, a move that will sharply increase the real combat potential of Russian troops on the Turkish border. A joint Russian-Armenian antiaircraft defense system will also be deployed. Fighter-interceptors, antiaircraft missile complexes, radar devices, etc. will be sent to Armenia.

In the past two years, Russia's Defense Ministry has been trying to bring home from the Transcaucasus all equipment of any value, and the 19th Air Defense Army has been withdrawn to the Northern Caucasus. Everything that remained has been seized, plundered or destroyed. Only Armenia has managed to develop some semblance of an air defense system, but even it is useful only for the fight against Azerbaijan.

Now, convinced that the situation in Armenia is stable, Russian generals have allowed themselves to be persuaded by official Yerevan that they should beef up their forces with modern equipment. But the Russian side is insisting that an agreement on a base in Armenia be concluded for a lengthy term of 25 years, or for 15 years with an option to extend it for 10 more. Meanwhile, Armenian Defense Minister Serzh Sargsyan told a Segodnya correspondent that "Armenia wants this to be a permanent agreement we are prepared to conclude a treaty granting a lease, free of charge, in exchange for the training of specialists in Russia's higher military schools and certain other kinds of technical assistance. The agreement will be signed and ratified this summer."

The situation in the other Transcaucasus republics is less predictable. Eduard Shevardnadze agrees in principle to both the presence of Russian military bases and Georgia's participation in a single Transcaucasus air defense system. But at this point the government in Tbilisi has little control over the situation in the country, and many Russian garrisons are located in outlying regions that are inclined to act on their own. In particular, Vladislav Ardzinba would like to offer Russia a military base in Abkhazia (in the town of Bombora) on his own, without the involvement of the government in Tbilisi. It's clear that a serious agreement on bases in Georgia can be signed only after the situation stabilizes in Abkhazia and in the country as a whole.

The military alliance with Armenia has somewhat cooled relations between Moscow and Baku, which in principle supports the decision to join a single Transcaucasus air defense system. Geidar Aliyev is also agreeable to letting the Russian military continue to use the rocket-attack early-warning radar station in Gabal, but, emphasizing that "the radar station is Azerbaijan's property," he demands that Russia in return pay rent and provide military and technical assistance.

For that matter, the Russian side made the proposal on participation in a single air defense system mainly out of diplomatic courtesy. The Army hasn't forgotten the seizing of Russian military facilities in Azerbaijan in 1992. Gen. Grachev declared: "We are going to create a single Armenian-Georgian-Russian air defense system in any case, even if they (the Azerbaijanis) refuse."

On the negotiating table in Baku lay the original protocol on the separation of troops in Karabakh and the introduction of Russian peacekeeping forces there, which was signed on May 17 in Moscow by the defense ministers of Russia and Armenia, as well as the head of the Nagorno-Karabakh Republic's Defense Committee. But Gen. Mamedov, Azerbaijan's Minister of Defense, did not sign it this time, either the protocol wasn't even discussed. When he was unofficially shown, prior to the talks, the protocol's last page with its missing signature, Mr. Mamedov told the Russian generals: "What for? There's no need. I'm going to Moscow in a few days, and we'll sort things out then."

The ceasefire in Karabakh is currently being strictly observed. But according to information obtained by Russian intelligence, both sides are amassing equipment and concentrating troops for a resumption of the fighting. Evidently, only new defeats on the front will be able to persuade Baku to seriously accept Russia's help in resolving the conflict.

CONFRONTATION: STAGES OF A MAJOR RETREAT – After Being Forced From Caspian Shelf, Russia Is Being Excluded From Karabakh Settlement

By Leonid Velekhov. *Segodnya*, Nov. 18, 1994, p. 3.

Judging from several indications, the two-day meeting of representatives of the nine member-countries of the so-called Minsk Group of the Conference on Security and Cooperation in Europe that ended the day before yesterday in Moscow failed to accomplish the task that Russia, which aspires to the role of chief participant-intermediary in a Karabakh settlement, hoped it would....

According to [Vladimir] Kazimirov, [who heads the group of Russian diplomats at the talks on Karabakh settlement,] Russian diplomacy expected the recent meeting in Moscow to resolve the question of putting the group's activities in order, and in particular to define its mandate. These matters were not resolved; on the other hand, it is quite clear that the conflicts between the European and American intermediaries, on the one hand, and the Russians, on the other, were sharply aggravated. Although this isn't being said outright, the appearance on Nov. 15, after the first day of the Minsk Group's Moscow meeting, of a joint statement by the Russian Federation Ministry of Defense and Ministry of Foreign Affairs is more eloquent than any commentary.

The joint statement says that any attempts to limit Russia and the CIS in their efforts to settle the Karabakh conflict "in fact undermine the very core of the peace process, no matter what statements about the importance of other international efforts are used to conceal this." The document declares quite sternly that only Russia has managed to participate effectively in efforts to settle the conflict, that full credit for the ceasefire that has lasted six months belongs to Russia, and that this cannot be ignored. "Russia's mediation is not based on expediency," the statement concludes, clearly hinting that those who oppose a dominant Russian role in a Karabakh settlement do take such an approach.

To all appearances, this statement stops just short of a break with the intermediaries from the Minsk group. Just what is fueling this new and perhaps climactic crisis in Russia's relations with its fellow intermediaries from the CSCE? First and foremost, it seems, the situation at the trilateral (Armenia, Azerbaijan and Karabakh) talks on a settlement that are being held with Russia's mediation, a situation that has taken a turn for the worse. The latest, third round of the talks concluded in Moscow on the eve of the Minsk Group's meeting here. And in the opinion of a number of participants, it accomplished absolutely nothing. They "didn't even get around to" working on the text of a political agreement that, strictly speaking, was the reason the delegations had come to Moscow in the first place. It can be concluded from this that the talks have become bogged down in the stubborn particulars of a settlement, on which the sides are still unable to find a common language. According to some reports, the deadlock resulted from the tough and uncompromising position taken by Azerbaijan, which is insisting on the unconditional return of Shusha and Lachin and is not offering any security guarantees for Nagorno-Karabakh in return. Azerbaijan also made some completely new demands for the participation of representatives of Karabakh's Azerbaijani community in the talks and the inclusion of a provision specifying the term of the agreement. Members of the Armenian and Karabakh delegations believe that meeting this last condition, in particular, would lead to a situation in which Azerbaijan, after regaining the territories occupied by the Armenians, would again look for a military solution to the conflict.

Commenting on the toughening of Azerbaijan's position at the talks, Baku's opponents say that it stems from a fundamental reorientation of Azerbaijan's foreign policy. "Baku is now putting greater emphasis on the CSCE," they say.

There is some basis for this conclusion, without a doubt. The Russian-Azerbaijani conflict over Caspian oil, which remains unresolved, could not help but have an impact on the effort to reach a Karabakh settlement. Or rather, a resolution has been found, but in a completely unilateral fashion, something that is by no means to Russia's liking. The agreement whereby an international consortium is to develop the Apsheron fields, which drew a sharp response from the Russian Ministry of Foreign Affairs, was ratified by Azerbaijan's Milli Majlis [parliament] the day before yesterday. At the same time, an Azerbaijani-Iranian agreement on Caspian shelf oil was reached in Baku, meaning that Russia lost the only influential ally it hoped to find in opposing the "contract of the century" namely, Iran.

The "oil conflict" has undoubtedly affected Russian-Azerbaijani relations as a whole. The defeat that Russia has suffered in the conflict has struck a painful blow to its prestige, including its prestige as a mediator. The problem is not only that Baku got the message that it doesn't have to reckon with Russia. What country, in Azerbaijan's place, would trust an intermediary that has a score to settle with it? The instinct for self-preservation is forcing Aliyev to change his points of reference in a Karabakh settlement. Without a doubt, the Minsk Group is prepared to help him do so and to offer an alternative to Russia as the key mediator of a settlement. In turn, it seems that the Minsk Group's aspirations are being regarded with more and more understanding by Boutros-Ghali, who has objected more than once to Russia's claims to the role of chief peacemaker in the CIS. The UN Secretary-General's recent visit to Baku confirms these fears.

Could Russia's being forced from the Caspian shelf have the consequence of its being excluded from a Karabakh settlement?

KARABAKH SETTLEMENT: MOSCOW STILL WANTS TO BE CHIEF PLAYER – Growing CSCE Role Irritates Kremlin

By Aidyn Mekhtiyev and Georgy Plekhanov. *Nezavisimaya gazeta*, Nov. 10, 1994, p. 1.

The Minsk Group of the Conference on Security and Cooperation in Europe is currently making a thorough study of the possibility of creating an international peacekeeping contingent to serve in the region of the Armenian-Azerbaijani conflict. At its next meeting, which will take place Nov. 18 in Budapest, the CSCE Committee of Senior Officials (CSO) will examine all issues having to do with the formation of peacekeeping forces. Swedish diplomat Anders Bjorner, who was recently appointed to serve as the acting chairman of sessions of the CSCE Minsk Group, discussed this with an NG correspondent in an exclusive interview....

During a two-day stay in the Russian capital, Bjorner held consultations with a number of Russian officials. He exchanged views on the Karabakh problem with Russian First Deputy Foreign Minister Igor Ivanov, among others, but the most important part of the program for his visit, needless to say, was the many hours of talks with the Russian Federation President's special envoy for Nagorno-Karabakh, Vladimir Kazimirov.

"I am encouraged by the results of the talks," Mr. Bjorner said in the interview with NG....

Question. – Mr. Bjorner, one can hardly say that there is complete mutual under-standing between Moscow and the Minsk Group on the Karabakh issue at the present time. The Russian mediator, Mr. Kazimirov, recently published an article in a Russian newspaper in which he openly accused certain members of the Minsk Group of attempting to place artificial obstacles in the way of Russia's peacemaking efforts.

Answer. – In my view, Russian participation in the Minsk Group is not only desirable but essential. And ... my conversations with Mr. Kazimirov convinced me that it is entirely feasible.... I think the Russian side shares the view that international involvement, and specifically CSCE involvement, in this peacemaking process is essential. I want to stress that just as Russian involvement in the peace process is desirable and essential, CSCE involvement is also desirable and essential. This is the firm conviction of the majority of the Minsk Group's members....

* * *

... From the comments that Mr. Bjorner, the acting chairman of sessions of the Minsk Group, made in the interview with NG, one can conclude that the question of sending peacekeeping forces to Karabakh is going to be a topic of vigorous discussion between Moscow and Western countries. Observers believe that Stockholm, as the current coordinator of the Minsk Group's activities, is carrying on intensive consultations with the West and the US with the aim of forming a peacekeeping contingent under the CSCE aegis.... The International Operations Group (IOPG) is currently studying the military aspects of a future operation, plans for which have been drawn up by the CSCE Minsk Group under the direction of the Swedish Gen. Bergman. In the opinion of observers, the Minsk Group's sharply stepped-up efforts in this area are a source of concern to the Kremlin. Moscow continues to insist that it be recognized as having a primary role in the process of settling the Karabakh conflict.

* * *

As Moscow sees it, the sharp disagreements between the Russian mediators and the CSCE mission that are engaged in joint and parallel efforts to resolve the conflict in Nagorno-Karabakh stem from yet another attempt to push Russia out of the Transcaucasus.

The Russian Ministry of Foreign Affairs is now criticizing the CSCE publicly and harshly: Moscow thinks that its dissatisfaction with the Minsk Group's activity is warranted in that the group includes countries that have their own political ambitions and geopolitical interests. They are trying to deprive Russia of the right to participate in the peace process on its own. As a result, Russia is in effect questioning the possibility of cooperating with the CSCE on the Karabakh issue.

The disagreements became noticeable last fall, when Moscow succeeded in arranging a fairly long ceasefire and the first meeting of representatives of Azerbaijan and Nagorno-Karabakh. At the time, the CSCE Committee of Senior Officials issued a statement about the "central role of the Minsk process," a statement that did not, strictly speaking, mention Russian mediation. The standoff reached its peak this fall, when a new program for a peaceful settlement of the Karabakh conflict was worked out at an assembly of CSCE member countries in Vienna. One of its main provisions calls for deploying an international disengagement force of 1,600 to 2,000 men between the military combatants.

Since the main issue now is who will play the primary role in this process, and not the settlement plans per se (which basically differ little from each another), the countries involved in the conflict have taken a wait-and-see attitude, while maintaining a truce at the front, by the way. Meanwhile, Azerbaijan, through Foreign Minister Gasan Gasanov, has said ... that the republic insists that the Karabakh problem be solved within the framework of the CSCE and the UN. Armenian Foreign Minister Vagan Papazyan, for his part, has said that the "West is willing to take the risk of a stronger Russian military presence in the Transcaucasus if the proper controls are established." He "can understand Russia's desire to obtain a CSCE or UN mandate to send troop units into the conflict zone, but [he has] no objections to representatives of other countries being involved in that operation, either."

In the opinion of Russian diplomats, the crux of the matter is that primary influence in the region will be determined by whose troops ultimately make up the backbone of future peacekeeping forces. They say that Russia was the first, a year ago, to raise the question of the need for a disengagement force. The CSCE "matured" to this realization only after Moscow achieved some success, and it is through Moscow's efforts that a truce has held for six months now. Perhaps the reason for the stepped-up Western mediation effort was the Baku oil deal and certain commitments on the part of Western partners to provide assistance to Azerbaijan (which insists on CSCE priority in efforts to settle the conflict). This also accounted for the attention that the Washington administration paid to the Karabakh problem during President Yeltsin's visit to the US, as well as for President Clinton's promise of financial support for a peacekeeping operation. It will be recalled that Georgian leader Shevardnadze's attempt to win US support and his speech to the UN General Assembly drew a very harsh reaction from corridors of power in Moscow, despite the fact that Western involvement was limited to a UN observer mission.

With regard to Nagorno-Karabakh, although it was decided, after the September session of the CSCE's Minsk Nine in Vienna and the Prague meeting of the Committee of Senior Officials, to study the question of conducting a peacekeeping operation in the Nagorno-Karabakh region under the CSCE aegis and with CSCE funding and of creating a multinational force, Russia is unlikely to consent to this, so that other countries won't be tempted to do the same thing. Moreover, Moscow considers the CSCE plan a "hoax," since the CSCE has never conducted a peacekeeping operation and has neither the proper mandate nor the money. Conducting such operations in a hasty manner is impermissible, Moscow believes, and it is making clear through its behavior that it does not consider collective efforts to be a guarantee of success and that it sees the CSCE Minsk Group's actions as a jealous reaction to its own mediation efforts....

The primary objective of the Russian plan was a ceasefire, while the aim of the CSCE plan is to keep the negotiation process going and to send CSCE observers to the region at a slack pace and in homeopathically minute doses.

Incidentally, Moscow also refused to agree to a compromise the coexistence of European observers and Russian troops. And so in the absence of the security guarantees that Nagorno-Karabakh links with the presence of peacekeeping forces, Azerbaijan is unlikely to recover the Azerbaijani territory currently occupied by the enemy. Baku rejected an agreement proposed by the Minsk Group's chairman, Jan Eliasson. That agreement was an accord on sending observers. Moscow didn't like the agreement, and neither did Azerbaijan, since it would have frozen the status quo. Baku could have been forced to accept the presence of Russian troops under international control. But Russia had more than that in mind and wanted the peacekeeping forces to consist solely of its own military units under its own command. It also wanted to obtain an international mandate and funding, but without a Western presence in the region. At the time Moscow was actively working on its own draft of a major political agreement that assigned only a nominal role to the CSCE. For its part, the CSCE is now trying to speed the process in hopes that the question of setting up an international force can be resolved by the time the organization holds its next assembly in Budapest in December.

3,000 PEACEKEEPERS ARE SUPPOSED TO CREATE CONDITIONS FOR A SETTLEMENT IN KARABAKH

By staff correspondent Boris Vinogradov. *Izvestia*, Dec. 9, 1994, p. 3.

The operation in Nagorno-Karabakh that was approved in principle at the Budapest meeting of the Conference on Security and Cooperation in Europe should go down in history as the birth of a new peacekeeping institution, second in importance only to the UN.

The tasks of separating the parties, monitoring the ceasefire and preparing conditions for a political settlement will be borne by the 3,000 soldiers who are to be sent to Karabakh. If the operation succeeds, one will be able to say that the CSCE has taken a major step toward increasing its authority in international affairs, thereby putting an end to the accusations, which everyone is sick and tired of, that the organization is "amorphous and overindulgent."

Talk about the need for peacekeeping using armed force in Karabakh has been going on for a long time....

Back at the beginning of this year, Pavel Grachev agreed to send troops into the conflict zone, on condition that the parties not shoot at one another and recognize Russia's status as peacekeeper. As far as the shooting part goes, things seem to be fine: There is no shooting in Karabakh. Recognition has proved to be a more difficult matter. Unlike Yerevan and Stepanakert, Baku is overcautious, fearing reproaches for a "betrayal of national interests" and a "loss of sovereignty." Geidar Aliyev, who has little doubt of Moscow's disinterested stance, nevertheless paid greater heed to the West and said that he preferred multilateral forces.

Boutros-Ghali and US representative to the UN Madeleine Albright, who visited Baku and Yerevan, also said that they had nothing against Russia's participation, but its forces should not exceed 30% of the total. Moreover, they emphasized that the operation would have to be conducted exclusively under the aegis of the CSCE or the UN, which means that generals from other countries would be commanding the Russian units.

This way of putting the question did not suit Moscow, which until very recently was still hoping for a more prominent role in the settlement process, a role corresponding to its authority and influence in the Caucasus. However, as the Budapest meeting has shown, Russia's great-power ambitions have not found proper understanding in the West, where they have not drawn sympathy but caused irritation. The proposal to use CIS countries in the peacekeeping forces changed nothing. The "Russian plan" for a Karabakh settlement is not being discussed in Budapest.

Sam Brown, the American representative to the CSCE, advised that the operation not be delayed but be started quickly, before the cannon open up in Karabakh again.... However, the opposing sides must sign a so-called "agreement on terminating the armed conflict." Only after that will the "blue berets" take up places between them.

One has to have a rich imagination to picture this document in agreed-upon form, considering the current differences among the parties....

DIPLOMACY: MOSCOW, BAKU DISPLEASED WITH EACH OTHER

By Aidyn Mekhtiyev. *Nezavisimaya gazeta*, March 14, 1995, p. 2.

Against the backdrop of the fighting that flared up last week on the Armenian-Azerbaijani border, signs of increased tension have appeared in relations between Baku and Moscow. The Russian Ministry of Foreign Affairs has issued a harsh statement in which it condemns comments by Azerbaijani officials expressing a negative assessment of Moscow's role in the Karabakh settlement: "The assertions that Russia is not interested in a settlement of the conflict and is trying to remove the peacemaking process from under the aegis of the Organization for Security and Cooperation in Europe [formerly CSCE] are absolutely out of line. Aren't they trying by this means to cover up for unrealistic aims that are hindering movement forward?" The document reflecting the viewpoint of Smolensk Square also says that it was with Moscow's assistance that a ceasefire that has now lasted about 10 months was achieved.

Although the statement by the Russian Foreign Ministry does not specifically name the Azerbaijani officials who wounded Moscow's pride, many observers believe that the appearance of this document is linked with an unusually harsh statement by Azerbaijan's State Adviser on Foreign Policy Issues, Vafa Guluzade, who accused Russia of supporting Yerevan's expansionist policy. In late February, during a visit to Turkey, Guluzade said, "Armenia is a Russian military base in the Transcaucasus and is doing Moscow's will."

It is noteworthy that this document's emergence from inside the Russian Foreign Ministry coincided closely with another event the unexpected cancellation of a visit to Baku by Dmitry Ryurikov, the Russian president's adviser on international affairs. Sources in the Kremlin informed an NG correspondent that the visit had not been canceled but postponed indefinitely. But observers are inclined to link this incident with the recent statement by the Russian Foreign Ministry. Official Baku had previously criticized the Russian government's decision to suspend rail traffic between Moscow and Azerbaijan, which caused a sharp deterioration of the economic situation in Azerbaijan. Some Russian generals, for their part, accused the Azerbaijani side of indirectly supporting Dzhokhar Dudayev. It is significant that after the text of an alleged telephone conversation between Dudayev and Iskander

Gamidov, leader of Azerbaijan's "Gray Wolves," appeared in Komsomolskaya pravda, telephone communications between Baku and Moscow mysteriously stopped almost completely.

RUSSIA IS STILL MAIN FORCE IN TRANSCAUCASUS

By Maksim Yusin, Izvestia staff. *Izvestia*, May 13, 1995, p. 1.

Yevgeny Primakov's visit to Armenia, Azerbaijan and Georgia at the direction of Boris Yeltsin appears to have lived up to the president's expectations. After a series of not particularly convincing actions in the international arena (mainly in the Middle East), this time Russian diplomacy presented itself in a better light.

The most visible achievement was the release of Armenian and Azerbaijani prisoners of war. Thanks to Moscow's efforts, all 39 Armenians and 71 Azerbaijanis who had been on a list compiled by the International Committee of the Red Cross gained their freedom. Pushing aside the OSCE Minsk Group and other international intermediaries, Russia demonstrated once again just what country is still the main force in the region and holds the keys to a Karabakh settlement.

Russian diplomacy is having equal success on the Georgian front. A memorandum on confidence- and security-building measures between Georgia and South Ossetia, the former autonomous province that became the scene of bloody fighting five years ago, will be signed in Moscow on the morning of May 16.

Russian First Deputy Foreign Minister Boris Pastukhov told Izvestia that, in addition to its military section, the document also includes an economic section: The sides pledge to help rebuild South Ossetia's economy and to assist in the resettlement of returning Georgian refugees. The most difficult problem is that of defining the province's political status.

The ceremony in the Kremlin will be attended by Boris Yeltsin, Eduard Shevardnadze, North Ossetian President Akhsarbek Galazov and South Ossetian Supreme Soviet Chairman Lyudvig Chebirov. Yeltsin will have a splendid opportunity, a month before the election, to appear before his compatriots as a peacemaker and to take credit for an important diplomatic success, and at the same time to issue a reminder that Russia plays the leading role in the post-Soviet space.

Progress in resolving another conflict the Georgian-Abkhaz one is not quite so evident as yet. The conflict was the central topic during a meeting between Primakov and Shevardnadze. Russian diplomats declined to elaborate on the results of the talks. Eduard Amvrosiyevich [Shevardnadze] was more loquacious, telling journalists that the guest from Moscow had taken an "understanding" view of Georgia's proposal to revise the mandate of the Russian peacekeeping forces in Abkhazia by having them monitor the return of refugees. It may be recalled that the Abkhaz leadership is emphatically opposed to that idea.

RUSSIAN WEAPONS STRIKE AT MOSCOW'S INTERESTS – Azerbaijani Authorities Accuse Russia of Abetting Armenia's Aggressive Intentions

By Arif Guseinov in Baku, Gamlet Matevosyan in Yerevan, and Stanislav Tarasov. *Segodnya*, March 7, 1997, p. 3.

The uproar over what Azerbaijani authorities believe to be illegal deliveries of Russian weapons to Armenia is getting louder and louder in Baku. At issue are 85 T-72 tanks, 40 BMP-2 infantry fighting vehicles, antiaircraft systems and spare parts worth a total of 7 billion rubles.

Azerbaijan's parliament has adopted an appeal to the Russian State Duma asking it to conduct an investigation. On Wednesday, Gasan Gasanov, head of the Azerbaijani Ministry of Foreign Affairs, told the Milli Majlis (parliament) that Mirgamza Efendiyev, Azerbaijan's representative to NATO, had informed the alliance's member countries that weapons were being amassed on a large scale in the region and that Armenia was essentially preparing for war with Azerbaijan. A report on Russian deliveries of weapons to Armenia will also be heard at a meeting of the political council of the OSCE (that organization is acting as the main mediator in efforts to settle the conflict over Nagorno-Karabakh). According to Gasanov, consultations are being held between Azerbaijan and the NATO member countries on preparations to be made in the next few days for a meeting to discuss the actions of Moscow and Yerevan.

Deputy Minister for National Security Galib Khalygov caused a sensation at a meeting of the Milli Majlis when he reported that weapons are being transported from Russia to Armenia by Russian ships crossing the Caspian to the Iranian port of Enzeli, from which they are then taken by truck through Iranian territory. According to Azerbaijani sources, the second way in which arms are transported is by Russian planes based at airfields in the North Caucasus. Baku also maintains that most of the weapons delivered from Russia to Armenia have gone to Karabakh a rather transparent hint that the arms deliveries are a component part of preparations for a new Armenian offensive on the Karabakh front....

One can say with utter certainty that Baku will bring up before the OSCE the question of whether it is right for Russia to continue participating in the process of resolving the Karabakh situation as a cochairman of the Minsk group.

For its part, official Yerevan categorically denies all claims concerning unmonitored deliveries of Russian weapons to Armenia.... Moreover, the Armenian Ministry of Foreign Affairs is awaiting official explanations from Moscow as to how Russian ministers could make such statements.[1]

Both Baku and the Azerbaijani Embassy in Moscow are awaiting a response from Russian authorities. Azerbaijan's Foreign Ministry lodged its first protest against arms deliveries to Armenia on Feb. 21. The Russian Ambassador in Baku was handed a protest note on March 4. There has not yet been any official reaction from Moscow. A Segodnya correspondent was told by the Russian Foreign Ministry's press and information department that at present the department has no information that would enable it to confirm or deny reports of Russian arms deliveries to Armenia.

According to a Foreign Ministry spokesman, the matter is being discussed in the Ministry of Defense. An official response will be given to Baku through diplomatic channels after Russian military officials ascertain just what kind of weapons have been sent to Armenia.

The furor will undoubtedly continue. It could substantially undermine Russia's position in the Transcaucasus, and just when a serious geopolitical struggle to shift control over the routes by which the main flow of Caspian oil will be transported is developing in the region.

BAKU WANTS TO STRIKE AT MOSCOW WITH MOSCOW'S OWN WEAPONS – 'News Leaks' About Arms Deliveries Were Planned

By Stanislav Tarasov. *Segodnya*, March 19, 1997, p. 3.

Segodnya conjectured earlier that the furor over certain allegedly secret deliveries of Russian arms to Armenia (the accusations against Moscow are coming from Baku) would continue. Our predictions are coming true. Vladimir Andreyev, head of the Foreign Ministry's current information department, said in a telephone conversation with a *Segodnya* correspondent yesterday that the matter had been forwarded to the Chief Military Prosecutor's Office and that the Duma had set up a special commission to investigate all the circumstances of the secret deal. At the same time, the Foreign Ministry spokesman stressed that Russia has not yet responded officially to the protest that Azerbaijan lodged in connection with the public allegations of illegal arms shipments, because it needs to make a more careful study of all the circumstances of the incident, which involves dozens of tanks, infantry fighting vehicles and rocket launchers.

Meanwhile, Azerbaijani President Geidar Aliyev, in letters to Boris Yeltsin, is insisting that Moscow proffer an immediate political and legal assessment of the "facts that have come to light," and also take steps to return the illegally delivered arms to Russia and punish those involved in the deal. In addition, Baku has raised the question of conducting an international inspection in Armenia to see if it is complying with the flank limits set by the Paris Treaty on Conventional Armed Forces in Europe (the CFE Treaty). A scandal that could have been defused within the CIS is being elevated to an international level. Why?

If we arrange the events associated with this complex intrigue in chronological order, we can conclude that what is going on is a political maneuver involving several moves.

The first breezes began blowing from the offices of the Duma's defense committee. It was there, a *Segodnya* correspondent has learned, that a draft parliamentary decision on the need to close the Russian Federation's military bases in Georgia and Armenia was drawn up early this year. The gist of the draft was this: The Russian military bases in the Transcaucasus have no strategic importance and would not play an important role in the event of armed aggression by a third country. Meanwhile, however, the bases remain one of the main irritants in relations between Moscow and Baku, which sees their existence as evidence of Russian bias in the Karabakh conflict. Ultimately, the defense committee's chairman, Gen. Lev Rokhlin, urged that Moscow completely change the emphasis of its Transcaucasus policy and pay more attention to Baku, because it is Baku that has recently begun playing an active geopolitical game involving the transit of Caspian oil.

We know that the draft decision on Russian bases was hotly debated at a committee meeting but failed to win majority support. However, it did find its way into the Armenian press, drawing a vehement reaction from Yerevan, which had recently signed a long-term agreement on the Russian bases with Moscow. But be that as it may, many analysts welcomed the initiative by Gen. Rokhlin, who served in the Transcaucasus Military District from April 1987 to mid-1990 and has first-hand knowledge of the situation in the region. Some even speculated that the general would at last reveal certain secrets of that military district, which in the Soviet era was brimming with the most advanced weapons – weapons that later mysteriously disappeared almost without a trace. However, events took a different course.

First, Russian Minister for CIS Affairs Aman Tuleyev spoke publicly of illegal shipments of Russian arms to Armenia. Rokhlin made reference to Tuleyev's comments in a speech in the Duma. Both politicians ignored the sensitivity of the matter, despite the fact that it involves Moscow's attitude toward CIS member countries that are essentially in a state of armed conflict. An uproar ensued. Citing Rokhlin and Tuleyev, Baku lodged its protest with Moscow, and the republic's news media launched yet another anti-Russian campaign. Yerevan did not remain silent either. On the one hand, Yerevan denied Rokhlin's statement, while on the other, it made allegations of illegal arms shipments to Azerbaijan from Ukraine.

In an attempt to somehow untangle the mess, Russian Defense Minister Igor Rodionov spoke out. He essentially confirmed the Tuleyev-Rokhlin report, saying that the Defense Ministry itself had provided Tuleyev with the information about arms shipments.

Next it turned out that the original source was materials prepared by Aleksei Kudrin, head of the Russian President's Chief Oversight Administration, concerning the situation in the Russian military.

Familiar with the Caucasus, Rodionov had to have known what a nasty reaction such a "leak" could cause. And after all, he could have ordered an unpublicized judicial investigation and remedied the situation quietly. That didn't happen. Attempts to explain the motives for the minister's actions that he didn't want to keep silent for fear that suspicions concerning some sort of arms deals would fall on him do not seem very convincing. How could anyone suspect Rodionov, who spent the years 1994-1996 as head of the General Staff Academy? It's obvious that the main suspicions would have fallen on the man who was minister at the time, Pavel Grachev, and, as Baku later added, on the former chief of the General Staff, Gen. Mikhail Kolesnikov.

Another interesting aspect of the matter is also coming to light. If one is to believe recent statements made by the Azerbaijani Ambassador to Russia, Ramiz Rizayev, as well as officials of Azerbaijan's Ministry of National Security, Baku had possessed the information made public by Tuleyev and Rokhlin for a long time. But if that is the case, why did Baku, which never passes up a chance to slam what it calls "certain Russian forces" that seek to destabilize the republic, keep silent until now, waiting until Russian politicians spoke up? There is some kind of intrigue going on; one can see the moves. But the author of the script clearly isn't Baku.

In general, one gets the impression that at this point no one really cares much about the results of the official probe into illegal shipments of Russian arms to Armenia. However, it seems more than coincidental that reports have cropped up in the news media in the past few days to the effect that former Defense Minister Grachev might be appointed chief military inspector in the Defense Ministry. Now, after all the uproar, this is highly unlikely, since the Chief Military Prosecutor's Office has already begun investigating all the nuances of the aforementioned deal. As for Azerbaijan, with another round of talks on a Karabakh settlement coming up, it now stands a good chance of successfully challenging Russia's representative as a "biased party" and pushing Moscow farther away from the settlement process, while more actively drawing in its Western partners and Turkey.

ALIYEV ASKS YELTSIN TO TAKE WEAPONS BACK FROM ARMENIA

By Sergei Gavrilov and Asya Gadzhizade. *Kommersant*, April 5, 1997, p. 2.

Yesterday Azerbaijan's President Geidar Aliyev sent Boris Yeltsin a special message in which he asked the Russian president to take "the most effective measures" to return to Russia weapons that were illegally sent to Armenia.

It had seemed that the uproar over illegal deliveries of Russian weapons to Armenia had ceased to be the dominant theme in Russian-Azerbaijani relations. At the CIS summit it was decided to postpone discussion of the matter until the next summit Moscow was given time to conduct an internal investigation.

But after Deputy Lev Rokhlin's speech at a closed meeting of the State Duma on Wednesday [April 2], the furor flared up anew. Rokhlin reported that the affair was not limited to the tanks and armored vehicles mentioned earlier Armenia had also received missile and antiaircraft systems, multiple rocket launchers and ammunition worth a total of about $1 billion.

On Wednesday Aliyev called a special meeting of the republic's leadership to discuss the situation. The meeting's participants came to the conclusion that the weapons deliveries to Armenia could lead to a destabilization of the situation in the region, and that they pose a threat "not just to Azerbaijan but to all neighboring states as well."

"When we heard the new facts that were discussed in the State Duma, we were astonished," the Azerbaijani president declared. "If we are holding peace talks to resolve the Armenian-Azerbaijani conflict, why are those weapons necessary?" Geidar Aliyev decided to send a letter to the Russian president. Azerbaijani Minister of Foreign Affairs Gasan Gasanov handed Russian Ambassador Aleksandr Blokhin a note from the Foreign Ministry asking the Russian side to clear things up....

Some independent Azerbaijani experts are certain that the weapons could not have been sent to Armenia without the Russian political leadership's knowledge. Russia is accused of pursuing "a deliberate policy of double standards," of not wanting a Karabakh settlement or a stabilization of the situation in the region as a whole and, generally, of preferring a state of "neither peace nor war."

Baku believes that the deliveries violated the Treaty on Conventional Armed Forces in Europe, since the number of weapons on Armenia's territory now exceeds the permissible quota. It's entirely possible that Azerbaijan will insist on an international inspection in Armenia and Nagorno-Karabakh....

At the official level, so far there has been no talk of a break with Moscow. Yesterday [Ramiz Rizayev, Azerbaijan's Ambassador to Russia,] pointed out that based on the results of the first three months of 1997, Russia occupies second place in Azerbaijan's balance of trade, and he expressed confidence that Russia will become Azerbaijan's main economic partner. Nevertheless, it's already clear that Azerbaijan is trying and not without success to derive the maximum benefit from the furor over the arms deliveries.

THE PRESIDENT OF AZERBAIJAN DECIDES NOT TO CONGRATULATE MOSCOW

By Ivan Andreyev. *Kommersant*, Sept. 6, 1997, p. 3.

Following in the footsteps of Georgian President Eduard Shevardnadze, ... Azerbaijan's leader Geidar Aliyev has announced his decision to ignore the celebration of Moscow's 850th birthday. The reason is that he is displeased by the Russian-Armenian treaty of friendship, cooperation and mutual assistance that was concluded on Aug. 29.

In the treaty articles having to do with military cooperation, Russia pledged to protect the sovereignty and territorial integrity of Armenia. Baku did not understand what geographic area this integrity applied to – whether it included Nagorno-Karabakh, which Azerbaijan considers its own, or not – and decided to take offense.

It should be noted that Russia does not have a similar treaty with Azerbaijan, and it is unlikely that Aliyev intends to conclude one. At the same time, the Azerbaijani president fears that now, if the situation in Nagorno-Karabakh becomes exacerbated, Russia will provide support to Armenia especially since the treaty talks about military-technical cooperation between Moscow and Yerevan. Azerbaijan took this to mean an agreement to supply weapons to one of the parties to the conflict.

Therefore, Aliyev's refusal to go to Moscow looks like a vote of no confidence in Russia, a cochair of the OSCE Minsk group on Nagorno-Karabakh, on the eve of an important round of talks on a Karabakh settlement. He hopes to derive an advantage from this, because now Moscow will have to prove that it is unbiased.

Eduard Shevardnadze was evidently guided by similar logic. It turns out that the harsh statement by Russian Federal Border Service Director Andrei Nikolayev regarding the "alcohol crisis" (Nikolayev warned that the border troops are prepared to use weapons if vehicles carrying unlicensed alcohol try to make their way across the border) is only one reason for the Georgian leader's failure to put in an appearance at the Moscow festivities. According to Sergei Yastrzhembsky, the Russian President's press secretary, "there are also other reasons," which the Georgian side has conveyed to Boris Yeltsin.

According to Kommersant's information, one reason is that Shevardnadze had intended to sign a Georgian-Abkhaz protocol during his trip to Moscow. But that protocol is not yet ready. Yastrzhembsky happened to mention that Shevardnadze may pay a visit to Moscow when the process of settling the Georgian-Abkhaz conflict, a process in which Russia is playing "a very appreciable role," reaches the point of signing "specific documents." Thus, in refusing to come to Moscow, Shevardnadze has made it clear that Russia should put pressure on Abkhazia and force it to make concessions.

PRESIDENT OF KARABAKH SEEKS SYMPATHY IN DUMA

By Leonid Gankin. *Kommersant-Daily*, Oct. 14, 1997, p. 5.

Having rejected the proposals of the OSCE Minsk group on settling the Karabakh conflict, Arkady Gukasyan, president of the self-proclaimed Nagorno-Karabakh Republic, came to Moscow yesterday to seek support from the Russian public.

In the wake of the joint statement on a Karabakh settlement that was made by the presidents of Azerbaijan and Armenia at the Council of Europe summit in Strasbourg, Nagorno-Karabakh is now completely alone at the negotiating table. Geidar Aliyev and Levon Ter-Petrosyan agreed to the OSCE Minsk group's new plan as proposed by its three cochairs Russia, the US and France.

This means that a balance of interests has finally been reached between two of the three parties to the conflict, as well as with the representatives of the Minsk group. Azerbaijan is counting on getting back the occupied territories, while Armenia wants to escape from the economic blockade in which it found itself after Baku cut off most of its links with the outside world. The Western countries are ready to immediately start implementing the planned multibillion-dollar projects to develop Azerbaijani oil deposits, but this requires stability in the region. Russia also intends to participate in extracting and transporting Azerbaijani energy resources. This will be its reward for solidarity with the other participants in the Minsk process.

The gist of the OSCE Minsk group's proposals boils down to a two-stage settlement of the conflict. During the first stage, Armenian armed units will vacate the six districts of Azerbaijan adjacent to Nagorno-Karabakh; in the second stage, they will leave the areas of Shusha and the Lachin Corridor, which links Karabakh with Armenia. During the second stage, the sides will also have to resolve the most difficult issue in the settlement process defining the status of Nagorno-Karabakh.

Stepanakert is not in agreement with this plan. Karabakh's leaders fear that if they withdraw their armed units from the captured areas, they will lose their trump card in bargaining with Baku for the status of a self-proclaimed republic.

But it looks as if they have no other choice. Karabakh faces a dilemma: Either accept the proposed terms or be subjected to combined pressure from the great powers and all the states in the region. It knows that the second option is a losing proposition. So all that the Karabakh leadership can do is think about how to save face and Arkady Gukasyan's visit to Moscow is evidently supposed to help accomplish this.

The Karabakh leader does not intend to meet with top officials of the Russian Ministry of Foreign Affairs: He wouldn't be able to influence Russia's official position anyway. Besides, under the Minsk group's terms, its participants may not make separate agreements with any of the parties to the conflict.

But in meeting with faction leaders and committee representatives from the State Duma, the Karabakh leader could very well play on themes that strike a "geopolitical chord" with the opposition the idea of alliance with "brothers and sisters in faith" and the anti-Turkish sentiments of the Duma majority and thereby "raise a wave" in the Russian parliament. And, at the same time, show his compatriots that he does not intend to give up without a fight.

THERE'S NO FRIEND LIKE AN OLD FRIEND – Geidar Aliyev Has Made Several Gestures Toward Russia, Actively Backing the Fight Against Terrorism in the North Caucasus

By Mekhman Gafarly. *Nezavisimaya gazeta*, Oct. 16, 1999, p. 1.

There has been a perceptible warming lately between Baku and Moscow. Right after hostilities began in Dagestan's Botlikh and Tsumada Districts, Azerbaijani President Geidar Aliyev endorsed the Russian leadership's actions and stated that "the military operation by Russian forces against religious extremists in the North Caucasus is Russia's internal affair, and Russia has a right to restore order on its territory." Unlike his Georgian counterpart, the Azerbaijani President also endorsed the Russian forces' combat operations against rebellious Chechnya, calling them, too, a Russian internal affair.

The heads of Azerbaijan's security and intelligence services and border troops, for their part, said they were ready to help their Russian counterparts and would do their utmost to ensure that Chechen guerrillas did not use the republic's territory as a transportation corridor through which to bring mercenaries and weapons into the North Caucasus. Moreover, the Azerbaijani leadership stated that it was willing to allow Russian inspectors into the republic to inspect any and all sites where fighters were allegedly being trained for the Chechen army. The inspections, which were conducted jointly by Azerbaijani and Russian military experts at locations in Azerbaijan that had been identified in some Moscow newspapers as training sites for Chechen fighters, found nothing to indicate that Baku was helping the Chechen guerrillas. This added to the atmosphere of trust between Baku and Moscow.

In addition, the president of Azerbaijan fired several high-ranking republic officials with anti-Russian leanings. In particular, Geidar Aliyev issued a decree dismissing Azerbaijan's state counselor for foreign policy, Vafa Guluzade, who had been the first to speak publicly in favor of siting NATO military bases, and US air bases in particular, on the Apsheron peninsula. The reason for Vafa Guluzade's dismissal was that he called the Wahhabis' guerrilla forays in western Dagestan a "national liberation movement" of the peoples of Dagestan.

On Wednesday [Oct. 13], Konstantin Totsky, the director of Russia's Federal Border Service, announced after two days of talks with top officials of Azerbaijan's border protection agency that in order to cover the Dagestani sector of its border with Russia, Azerbaijan had moved an additional 2,000 motorized infantry troops to the region. The Federal Border Service director said that during the talks with the commanders of Azerbaijan's border troops, the Russian side had received guarantees that not a single convoy carrying weapons or ammunition for Chechnya would get across the Azerbaijani-Russian border....

Meanwhile, the Georgian leadership still refuses to allow Russian border troops to help guard the Georgian-Russian border. Georgian President [Eduard Shevardnadze] is urging Moscow to halt combat operations against Chechnya and immediately begin negotiations with Chechen President Aslan Maskhadov. Shevardnadze feels that the only way to solve the Chechen problem is by political means, at the negotiating table....

[Baku's support for Moscow] is linked to several factors. First, Azerbaijan, like Russia, is fighting for its territorial integrity. Moscow is trying to reestablish its sovereignty over Chechnya, and Baku, over Nagorno-Karabakh. By supporting Moscow's actions with respect to rebellious Chechnya, Baku hopes to enlist Russia's support in resolving the Armenian-Azerbaijani conflict. Baku believes that Moscow has a great deal of influence in Armenia and can put pressure on Yerevan to make it more willing to compromise on the Karabakh issue. It was thanks to Russia's efforts in May 1994 that Armenia and Azerbaijan signed a ceasefire agreement halting hostilities on the Karabakh front. Second, the large Azerbaijani diaspora in Russia is also putting a lot of pressure on the Azerbaijani leadership to take Moscow's interests in the region into account, and sometimes even to defend them. Third,

Baku has become disillusioned with its pro-Western foreign policy, which was conceived and promoted by the aforementioned Vafa Guluzade. Fourth, the threat of Islamic fundamentalism is forcing Azerbaijan to join forces with Russia in order to effectively combat that evil. The main threat to Baku in this respect comes from Iran....

Incidentally, this a matter that Moscow ought to think about seriously. Iran, which on some issues is a Russian ally in the region, has harshly condemned the actions taken by the Russian forces in Chechnya and urged Moscow to end its war against Chechnya and immediately begin negotiations with Maskhadov. Recent events in the North Caucasus show that Tehran ranks the interests of Islamic extremists higher than its relations of alliance with Russia.

Azerbaijan's recent friendly moves toward Russia show that Moscow and Baku now have new chances to establish relations of strategic partnership.

MOSCOW, YEREVAN FULLY SUPPORT EACH OTHER – In Armenia, Vladimir Putin Fleshes Out Russia's Position on Nagorno-Karabakh

By Arman Dzhilavyan. *Nezavisimaya gazeta*, Sept. 18, 2001, p. 5.

Yerevan – The first official visit to Armenia by a Russian president was marked for success from the very beginning, something that neither Yerevan nor Moscow would dispute.... It was not surprising that, on the first day of the visit, Vladimir Putin and [Armenian President] Robert Kocharyan decided to discuss the international situation and the problem of international terrorism in general. According to Russian Defense Minister Sergei Ivanov, the Armenian and Russian presidents agreed on the need to move from condemning terrorism to taking specific measures against it, by which both Putin and Kocharyan meant the use of force in addition to other methods. The Armenian head of state thus became the first president with whom Putin spoke face-to-face about the threat confronting the world community. Naturally, this could only be regarded as a sign of special relations between Moscow and Yerevan, so it couldn't help but have broad resonance throughout the Transcaucasus.

The first real fruits of the Russian president's visit to Armenia will become apparent in the near future. But it can already be said without hesitation that Putin's trip to Yerevan fundamentally strengthened Russia's position throughout the Transcaucasus and clearly demonstrated that Moscow is calling the shots in the region at this particular juncture. And to all appearances, this was the main effect that Vladimir Putin was striving for. On the one hand, he said that Moscow does indeed regard Yerevan as its chief strategic partner in the region, and that Russia recognizes its responsibility to safeguard the security of its Transcaucasus ally. "All our policy in the region will be aimed at ensuring the reliable defense of Armenia," Vladimir Putin said. At the same time, he made it very clear that Russia intends first and foremost to uphold its own interests in the region, interests that extend to the entire Transcaucasus. And this is why the Russian president was extremely restrained in his assessments of the problem of settling the Nagorno-Karabakh conflict. While successfully shifting the immense burden of determining Nagorno-Karabakh's status onto Yerevan's and Baku's shoulders, Putin nevertheless made the key statement that Moscow was willing – and, moreover, intended – to serve as guarantor of a Karabakh settlement, which the Russian president said should be based on a compromise between Armenia and Azerbaijan. "We will aid and facilitate a resolution of this problem. The only thing we don't want is for someone to castigate Russia after the two countries have reached a compromise." Vladimir Putin was alluding to the possibility that one of the parties to the conflict might say after the fact that its decision had been made under pressure from Moscow.

Russia seems to have finally worked out its position on the issue of a Karabakh settlement. While emphasizing that it does indeed have an interest in a resolution of this years-long problem, Moscow nonetheless indicated that it has no intention of putting pressure on either Armenia or Azerbaijan over the issue....

Moscow's decision to reinforce its military presence in Armenia is further evidence of Russia's intention to fundamentally strengthen its position in the Transcaucasus. Russian Defense Minister Sergei Ivanov, who accompanied Vladimir Putin to Yerevan, confirmed the establishment of Armenian-Russian armed units. "We see this approach as one of the main components of our national security," said his Armenian counterpart, Serzh Sargsyan, in this regard. Sargsyan's positive comments were backed up by an Armenian decision to transfer the land occupied by Russia's Military Base No. 102, which is located in the republic, to the base free of charge.

The overall program of economic discussions held during Putin's visit to Yerevan proved to be a breakthrough as well. Based on the outcome of those discussions, Russia and Armenia signed five key agreements on economic cooperation: a Treaty of Long-Term Economic Cooperation Between the Russian Federation and the Republic of Armenia to 2010, and intergovernmental agreements on principles of cooperation between Russian Federation members and Armenian province administrations, cooperation in the tourism sector, mutual recognition of academic titles and degrees, and mutual protection and incentives for investments. Putin said that the documents signed would serve as a "stable foundation for expanding joint business activity." In this context, the Russian president emphasized that the preconditions would soon be in place for establishing Russian-Armenian joint ventures in key sectors of the Armenian economy. Putin said that this would benefit both Armenia, for which it would create new jobs, and Russia, which is "interested in investing in the Armenian economy." Naturally, this prospect is certain to be appreciated by Armenia, which has become alarmingly dependent on loan "infusions" from Western financial institutions in recent years.

It goes without saying that both Russia and Armenia were pleased with the visit's outcome.... The Armenian head of state said exactly what Vladimir Putin had most wanted to hear from him: "Armenia welcomes Russia's economic achievements and its growing role in the international arena and believes that Russia plays an extremely important role in stability and security in the South Caucasus." Obviously, Putin was indeed correct not to postpone his visit to Armenia.

KOCHARYAN UNDERSTANDS PUTIN – Armenia Displeased With Russia's Neutrality in the Nagorno-Karabakh Conflict

By Vladislav Vorobyov. *Rossiiskaya gazeta*, Jan. 18, 2003, p. 1.

... President Robert Kocharyan of Armenia simply could not find a more important and reliable ally than Vladimir Putin. So it is not surprising that, with just a month remaining until [the presidential election in Armenia], he came to Russia for a three-day official visit. "I don't recall our ever having argued about anything. Each of us understands the other before he has even finished speaking," Kocharyan said of his relationship with the Russian president.

The head of the Transcaucasus state did not confine himself to talks at the Kremlin alone. He was also received by Prime Minister Mikhail Kasyanov and by the heads of both houses of the Russian parliament. "You held good talks with the government on economic issues," Putin said. He mentioned that trade between the two countries had risen by 10% in 2002, but he characterized that rate of growth as inadequate.

Kocharyan, for his part, said that more than 500 enterprises with Russian capital are now operating successfully in Armenia. "Within a couple of years, the figure will be even higher," he added....

Robert Kocharyan said that Russia's presence in Armenia and the Caucasus is a stabilizing factor for the region and a major element of its security.

A joint declaration signed yesterday states that the two countries' leaders advocate an early settlement of the [Nagorno-Karabakh] conflict solely by peaceful means and on a basis acceptable to all parties. "We're going to do everything we can to bring about a fair resolution," Putin said.

"We're grateful to Russia for the constructive role it is playing in efforts to resolve this conflict," Kocharyan responded. Still, he did not pass up the chance to criticize Moscow's decidedly neutral stance.

But no one paid much attention to that political nuance. The first part of the meeting was held in a so-called narrow format – i.e., virtually tête-à-tête. After the meeting, the occupant of the Great Kremlin Palace expressed satisfaction with the talks and said there had been a productive exchange of views "on all key issues," including political and international cooperation between the two countries and cultural exchanges between them....

The Russian president also said that Russia welcomes Armenia's decision to participate in the Eurasian Economic Community as an observer. Moscow hopes that official Yerevan will eventually be prepared to join the organization as a full member; this would allow Armenia to establish a qualitatively new level of economic relations not only with our country, but also with the community's other members. "We should take a look at the processes under way there and find a way to link membership in the World Trade Organization with membership in EurAsEC [Eurasian Economic Community]," Kocharyan said.

A total of six documents were signed at the Kremlin yesterday, including an arms sales agreement between the Russian and Armenian governments and an accord between the two countries' central banks on cooperation in monitoring lending institutions....

Today is the final day of Robert Kocharyan's official visit to Russia. The esteemed guest is being received in Krasnodar.

BAKU ALARMED – Azerbaijan Doesn't Like Russian-Armenian Military Alliance

By Mekhman Gafarly. *Noviye Izvestia*, Nov. 20, 2003, p. 5.

Azerbaijan's Ministry of Foreign Affairs lodged a protest Wednesday [Nov. 19] in connection with Moscow's intention to create a Russian-Armenian joint group of forces....

The Azerbaijani Foreign Ministry's protest was prompted by a statement by Russian Defense Minister Sergei Ivanov, who during a visit to Armenia on Nov. 11 announced Russia's plans to create the Russian-Armenian joint military group. The minister said that the strength of the Russian military contingent currently stationed in Armenia (5,000 servicemen, not counting border troops) would be sufficient. In Moscow's view, however, the contingent is underequipped. So plans call for upgrading the Armenian base of Russia's 102nd Army, and eventually for establishing the joint military group.

Officials in Baku say this will lead to a "change in the balance of forces in the South Caucasus and further aggravate the situation in the region." Especially considering that Azerbaijan and Armenia are essentially in a state of war in connection with their dispute over ownership of Nagorno-Karabakh. In a conversation with a Noviye Izvestia reporter, Farkhad Agamaliyev, first secretary of the Azerbaijani Embassy in Moscow, offered the following explanation for his Foreign Ministry's reaction: "The fragile peace that has been maintained in the Armenian-Azerbaijani conflict zone for more than 10 years will be disturbed, making it more difficult to resolve the Karabakh problem. Armenia, after strengthening its military potential with Russia's help, will start making tougher, unreasonable demands at the talks on Karabakh, thereby deadlocking the negotiating process. Before deciding to create a joint military group with Armenia, Moscow should consider the fact that the republic has occupied more than 20% of Azerbaijan's territory, expelling over a million people from that area."

In Yerevan, by contrast, Armenian-Russian military cooperation is seen as a guarantee of peace in the region.

Russian Defense Ministry officials say that the group will be a "purely defensive structure that is not directed against anyone else." They maintain that it will not upset any balance because it will not require an increase in the Russian military contingent in Armenia. The group will not be the first joint group of forces with Russian participation: A Russian-Belarussian group has already been created. Moreover, Russian military officials say that their actions are within the bounds of the Collective Security Treaty Organization....

Baku, which objects to the Russian-Armenian group, is not a member of the CSTO. But if it joins, Russia will eventually be able to form a military group with Azerbaijan as well, Russian Defense Ministry officials said.

FROM ONE BASE TO ANOTHER – Transfer of Russian Weapons to Armenia Piques Azerbaijan

By Gayane Movsesyan. *Vremya novostei*, June 3, 2005, p. 5.

Yerevan – "There's no need to sign any new document or agreement" in order to move Russian military equipment from Georgia to Armenia, the Armenian defense minister's press secretary, Col. Seiran Shakhsuvaryan, said yesterday. The first trainload of military equipment and ammunition left the Russian military base in Batumi for the Armenian city of Gyumri on Tuesday [May 31]. At this point there is no question of transferring Russian servicemen from Georgia to Armenia, the colonel said.

The plans for moving military property to Armenia were known even before Moscow and Tbilisi reached an agreement early this week to end Russia's military presence in Georgia in 2008. It may be recalled that Russia's military base No. 102 been located in Armenia since 1995. Baku is not happy about these plans. Novruz Mamedov, who heads the foreign relations department of the Azerbaijani president's staff, said that "Russia's transfer of weapons to Armenia, which continues to occupy part of Azerbaijan's territory, not only does nothing to strengthen Azerbaijani-Russian relations but, on the contrary, is detrimental to them."

A statement that Pyotr Burdykin, Russia's temporary chargé d'affaires in Baku, handed to officials at the Azerbaijani Ministry of Foreign Affairs yesterday stresses that Russia is transferring Russian military equipment from one Russian base to another. "This doesn't mean that we can give weapons to Armenia," Mr. Burdykin explained. According to the diplomat, speculation along those lines is "a complete fabrication; that's impossible." and in general, the transfer of some weapons to Armenia "will have no influence whatsoever on efforts to settle the Nagorno-Karabakh problem."

Armenian Defense Minister Serzh Sargsyan said that Yerevan is interested in "increasing stockpiles of weapons" at the Russian military base. Nevertheless, the subject is controversial within Armenia as well. David Shakhnazaryan. who was the Armenian president's special envoy for Karabakh during the presidency of Levon Ter-Petrosyan, said flatly in an interview with Vremya novostei that the transfer of additional Russian weapons to the country "will polarize the region even more."

He reminded us that Georgia and Azerbaijan are being actively integrated into NATO structures, while Armenia is a member of the CSTO, which Azerbaijan and Georgia left in 1999. The presence of Russian troops in the region could lead to the emergence of "new dividing lines" there. Shakhnazaryan said. Especially since just recently, the Armenian defense minister affirmed that the country's foreign policy agenda "does not include the question of membership in NATO."...

KARABAKH SETTLEMENT GETS REINFORCEMENTS

By Vladimir Solovyov. *Kommersant*, April 17, 2009, p. 8.

... Meetings of the Council of Foreign Ministers of the CSTO are routine events at which the ministers normally confine themselves to discussing technical issues. In this sense, yesterday's gathering of foreign policy chiefs in Yerevan was no exception. The participants talked about how to jointly counter "present-day challenges and threats" and also discussed the creation of a collective rapid reaction force [CRRF]. The presidents of the countries that make up the "group of seven" (the CSTO consists of Armenia, Belarus, Kazakhstan, Kyrgyzstan, Russia, Tajikistan and Uzbekistan) decided back in February to create a rapid reaction force. But so far the CRRF exists only on paper.

The event in Yerevan didn't get by without a minor controversy. The meeting was ignored by Uzbekistan, which did not send its foreign minister to Armenia. Tashkent declared that it "does not see the expediency of our participating in the work of the meeting," which was taken as yet another sign that Uzbekistan is poised to leave the CSTO. Especially since the Uzbek authorities earlier suspended their membership in another organization led by Russia – the EurAsEC. Nevertheless, officials at the Russian Foreign Ministry assured Kommersant yesterday that Uzbekistan definitely has no plans to leave the alliance.

Unlike Uzbek Foreign Minister Vladimir Norov, Russian Foreign Minister Sergei Lavrov not only went to Yerevan, but he tried to make the most of the trip. He met with Armenian President Serzh Sargsyan and, according to Kommersant's information, secured the Armenian leader's agreement to attend a three-way summit that Russia is planning on a settlement of the Nagorno-Karabakh conflict. The summit is expected to be held in June as part of the economic forum in St. Petersburg and will be attended by Azerbaijani President Ilkham Aliyev, with Russian leader Dmitry Medvedev acting as mediator.

The Armenian president's press service explained to Kommersant that a final decision on Armenia's participation will be made during Serzh Sargsyan's upcoming visit to Russia on April 23. But Moscow, which aspires to play the role of chief reconciler of the Armenians and the Azerbaijanis, already has no doubts that its peacemaking initiative will be successful. Especially in view of the fact that Russia is preparing to give Armenia some financial assistance. The Russian leadership has agreed to grant Yerevan's request for a loan in dollars. Granted, instead of the requested $2 billion, Moscow intends to provide only $500 million. However, a high-ranking Kommersant source at the Russian Foreign Ministry explained that if that isn't enough, Russia is prepared to help Armenia obtain access to money from the "anticrisis fund" that was created by EurAsEC at the beginning of the year (the fund contains $10 billion). Although it cannot be ruled out that in return for this aid, Yerevan, which currently has observer status in EurAsEC, might be asked to more closely integrate itself into the organization.

While Sergei Lavrov was trying to get Yerevan to agree to support Moscow's peacemaking efforts in the Karabakh conflict, Dmitry Medvedev was making a similar effort with his Azerbaijani counterpart Ilkham Aliyev. Mr. Aliyev arrived in the Russian capital yesterday and spent the evening in the company of the Russian president. The presidents will continue their talks today at [Medvedev's] Barvikha residence outside Moscow, and Kommersant has learned that their discussion will not be limited to the subject of oil and gas.

In addition to confirming agreements on Gazprom's purchases of gas from the second phase of the Shakh-Deniz field, the sides will discuss preparations for the aforementioned St. Petersburg summit on Nagorno-Karabakh. To all appearances, the Russian president, who last fall got the Armenian and Azerbaijani leaders to sign a declaration on a political settlement of the Armenian-Azerbaijani conflict (it was the first document to be signed by the leaders of the opposing sides since 1994), plans to build on that success. This is particularly important in view of the fact that Messrs. Aliyev and Sargsyan plan to meet on May 7 in Prague "on the sidelines" of a summit devoted to the EU's Eastern Partnership initiative. Moscow claims to welcome the upcoming meeting in Prague, but it doesn't believe it will be successful, so it is preparing to give the West a peacemaking lesson in St. Petersburg.

Whereas Russia is promising Armenia financial benefits to guarantee its cooperation, the Kremlin has found a different way of approaching hydrocarbon-rich Azerbaijan. According to Kommersant's information, Baku has long been asking Russia to supply it with arms, specifically antitank weapons, surface-to-air missile systems, tanks and artillery. But because of the "Armenian factor," those requests went unanswered in the past. However, Azerbaijan's interest in acquiring Russian weapons might well be satisfied at today's talks between Medvedev and Aliyev.

In any case, officials at [state-controlled arms exporter] Rosoboronexport informed Kommersant that Azerbaijan is on a list of priority partners in military-technical cooperation....

MOSCOW GETS CAUGHT IN KARABAKH IMPASSE

By Svetlana Gamova and Sokhbet Mamedov. *Nezavisimaya gazeta*, July 22, 2009, p. 1.

Baku – ... In the hype that preceded the Moscow meeting between the presidents of Armenia and Azerbaijan, the sides were promised a quick way out of the Karabakh impasse with Russia's assistance.

However, the very first reaction to the meeting from the parties concerned has shown that compromise in solving the Karabakh problem is still a long way off. Whereas Baku welcomes the Madrid principles that have been proposed as a basis for the negotiating process, Yerevan and Stepanakert completely reject them. At a press conference on Monday [July 20] in Baku, Azerbaijani Foreign Minister Elmar Mamedyarov reported that the participants in the well-publicized meeting in Moscow had discussed the possibility that, as a first step in settling the conflict, five of the Azerbaijani districts occupied by Armenian forces be returned, after which the status of Nagorno-Karabakh will be determined. In the opinion of the Azerbaijani minister, this is a positive and promising path. However, on the same day, this path was described in Karabakh as unpromising and even harmful. And yesterday, a number of nongovernmental organizations in the unrecognized republic issued a statement in which they described the mediation talks as explosive for the region.

Many experts say the reason for this vociferous reaction was that, as has become traditional, the direct participants in the talks made mutually exclusive comments about them afterward, once again confusing the two countries' citizens, who are trying to figure out what the leaders of Azerbaijan and Armenia said to each other for roughly three hours and what kind of proposals were actually made by President Dmitry Medvedev.

"Perhaps the results of the meeting between the presidents of Azerbaijan and Armenia did not lead to any breakthroughs, but we are happy about the intensification of the negotiating process, especially the active efforts by the Russian side. During talks with Russian President Dmitry Medvedev, you become confident that the negotiating process will end in success," Azerbaijani Foreign Minister Elmar Mamedyarov said at a press conference in Baku devoted to a visit to Azerbaijan by the European Union troika. He also said that "an unequivocal decision has been made to withdraw Armenian troops from the territory of Nagorno-Karabakh." "Other issues that are currently being discussed are a timetable for withdrawing Armenian armed forces from the occupied territories, the return of forced migrants to their historical places of residence, the provision of proper living conditions for them and reconstruction of the territories," the Azerbaijani minister said. Taking advantage of the fact that Swedish Foreign Minister Carl Bildt, the leader of the EU delegation that had visited Azerbaijan, was present at the press conference, Mamedyarov observed that Baku is counting on financial assistance from the EU in dealing with those problems.

Some of the details that Mamedyarov reported about the Moscow meeting between the two heads of state were denied that same day by his Armenian counterpart, Eduard Nalbandyan.

"The Armenian side has never said at an official level that it approves of the Madrid proposals. We have only said that they are a basis for negotiations," Nalbandyan said. As for the withdrawal of troops and the return of forced migrants to their historical places of residence, according to the Armenian foreign minister, "those issues were not discussed at all during the Moscow meeting." Which of the two ministers is telling the truth and which is not is hard to tell. But it is clear that the negotiations are being held on the basis of the Madrid proposals, which, as was recently learned, include points on the withdrawal of Armenian troops from the occupied territories surrounding Nagorno-Karabakh and the transfer of those territories to the control of Azerbaijan, as well as the return of forced migrants to their historical places of residence.

In the opinion of well-known Azerbaijani political analyst Rasim Musabekov, the participants in the talks "discussed the most important things during the Moscow meeting, but the most problematic issues, those that will determine the fate of a future agreement, remained unresolved. Clearly, making these decisions, decisions that entail risk, is rather difficult." "The heads of state talked for three and a half hours, and I don't think they were getting any enjoyment out of the discussion. There was hard bargaining. Even if, as the cochairmen of the OSCE Minsk Group say, the parties managed to bring their positions closer together without setting down on paper at least some sort of agreements, I still think that each president needs to take a time-out to think things over," Rasim Musabekov told reporters. This is necessary to give them an additional opportunity to weigh and determine how able their countries are to accept the latest mutual decision and what the repercussions might be in terms of image, as well as what kind of political and military consequences could occur. There are many nuances that need to be weighed in a calm, cool and collected manner. The presidents have most likely taken that time-out, the expert believes.

Meanwhile, Armenian President Serzh Sargsyan also commented on this issue, but in Yerevan, during a meeting with Swedish Foreign Minister Carl Bildt. Mr. Sargsyan observed that "in the wake of the Moscow meeting, neighboring Azerbaijan is once again attempting to distort the essence of the negotiations." At the same time, the Armenian president said that progress had been made, "although not without difficulties." He said that at present the sides are discussing the most basic of the so-called Madrid principles, and after that they will discuss the remaining principles. Then, based on the results of those discussions, they will begin drafting the main agreement. "By now everyone should realize that the most important issue is the status of Nagorno-Karabakh, which must be determined through a free expression of the people's will and be legally binding. Once we have managed to properly define this issue, I think the talks will begin moving more smoothly," Sargsyan concluded. Meanwhile, after his remarks in Baku about the possible withdrawal of Armenian forces from the occupied territories, the Armenian opposition demanded his resignation.

BASE VISIT

By Gayane Movsesyan. *Vremya novostei*, Aug. 16, 2010, page number unavailable.

Yerevan – Russian President Dmitry Medvedev is to arrive in Yerevan on an official visit on Thursday, Aug. 19....

The parties are expected to sign an agreement extending the lease of Russia's military base No. 102, which has been operating in Gyumri under a treaty signed in 1995. It has been revealed that the new agreement will change the wording of the treaty to say that the purpose of the base is not only to protect Russia's interests but also to ensure Armenia's security in cooperation with the Armenian armed forces.

The news attracted much attention in Armenia, especially after a Moscow publication reported in late July that Russia had supposedly agreed to sell Azerbaijan two battalion systems of Russian S-300 Favorit surface-to-air missiles. The article quoted an anonymous "CEO at a Russian defense facility."

The news drew mixed reactions from Armenian politicians and experts. Some say that the amendments to the base treaty will only strengthen Russia's influence on the region but won't serve Armenia's interests in any way, and that they actually pose a threat to Armenia's sovereignty. They say that by making the arms deal with Azerbaijan, Russia "betrayed Armenia as a strategic ally." Others, after stating that selling such a powerful weapon to Azerbaijan may upset the balance of power in the region, believe that the new base agreement will serve as a containment factor for Baku, which often threatens to resolve the Nagorno-Karabakh conflict by military means.

Sergei Minasyan, deputy director of the Yerevan-based Caucasus Institute, told Vremya novostei that "in case Azerbaijan launches another attack, hostilities will affect not only Karabakh's territory but the Armenian-Azerbaijani border as well". "Then the Russian base's new legal status will significantly limit Azerbaijan's ambitions," [he said]. As for the possibility of Russia selling S-300 systems to Azerbaijan, Minasyan said that "those reports have not been confirmed, and most likely, such an agreement has not been reached." But even if the deal goes through, Yerevan "will receive from Moscow specific political and military guarantees and compensation in the form of weapons," [he said]. "The Russian leadership obviously believes that this will help redress the military and political balance in the region and prevent war," the expert thinks.

Arman Melikyan, former foreign minister of Nagorno-Karabakh, expressed a different view. He told Vremya novostei that, in his opinion, "the Russian base in Gyumri is a purely symbolic presence of the Russian forces in Armenia and a nominal warning to Turkey lest it suddenly take some irresponsible steps against Armenia." "After all, the combined forces of Armenia and Karabakh would be sufficient to defeat Azerbaijan," he says.

The presence of a military base in Armenia does not help Moscow advance its interests in the region, [Melikyan] thinks. Georgia is now outside Russia's sphere of influence and will be for a long time, so Russia now needs Azerbaijan. Currently,

Russia uses "the lands that are the constitutional territory of the Nagorno-Karabakh Republic" as a bargaining chip in dealing with Azerbaijan. At the same time, Russia realizes that "if it cedes Karabakh with all the territories that were included in it after the 1991-1994 war, Russian will lose Armenia along with Karabakh." That's why Moscow "wants to limit its haggling with Baku to five or six districts that used to be part of Azerbaijan proper and strong-arm Yerevan and Stepanakert into returning those territories to Azerbaijan." As regards Karabakh, "its status will remain in limbo, but it won't be part of Azerbaijan." And as for the reports about S-300 supplies to Baku, regardless of whether the deal goes through or not, they are merely an instrument for putting pressure on the conflicting parties."...

"Moscow is currently playing both sides, putting pressure alternately on Azerbaijan and Armenia to force them to make concessions on the Karabakh issue. But that policy won't get them anywhere," the expert thinks.

GYUMRI, A PLACE TO FIGHT AND DIE FOR

By Vladimir Solovyov. *Kommersant*, Aug. 21, 2010, p. 1.

Editors' Note. – Russian troops will stay at the Gyumri base until 2044. They will equip the Armenian army and fight on Armenia's side in case it has a conflict with any other nation. This agreement was officially concluded in Yerevan yesterday after talks between the Russian and Armenian presidents.... Kommersant correspondent Vladimir Solovyov has been following Russia's attempt to build up its military expansion in former Soviet republics.

* * *

The state visit to Armenia by Russian President Dmitry Medvedev, which started on Thursday [Aug. 19] night, resulted in a packet of five documents. Moscow and Yerevan agreed to cooperate on building new reactors for nuclear power plants in Armenia and to exchange trade missions. They also signed an agreement on readmission and a memorandum saying that the Federal Service for Military-Technical Cooperation would open service centers and set up joint ventures for repairing and servicing Russian weapons and military hardware in Armenia.

But the biggest news was an unprecedented bilateral agreement, according to which Russian troops, together with the Armenian army, will from now on ensure the security of Armenia, which is wedged between two hostile countries – Turkey and Azerbaijan. A provision to this effect is included in Protocol No. 5 of the treaty between the Russian Federation and the Republic of Armenia on the deployment of a Russian military base in the Republic of Armenia (the treaty was originally signed in March 1995 for a period of 25 years).

The protocol, which was signed yesterday by Russian Defense Minister Anatoly Serdyukov and his Armenian counterpart, Seiran Oganyan, significantly alters the earlier agreements concerning the deployment of a Russian base in Gyumri. First, the term of the treaty was extended to 49 years; in other words, Russian troops won't leave Gyumri before 2044. Second – and this is particularly important to Yerevan – Art. 3 of the treaty will no longer contain the clause saying that, in addition to protecting Russia's interests, the base ensures Armenia's security "along the external border of the former USSR."

Also, according to Protocol No. 5, the troops deployed in Gyumri will no longer limit the scope of their potential combat activities to territories strictly outside the former Soviet Union. They will now be ready to operate within the territory of the former USSR, Armenian leader Serzh Sargsyan proudly emphasized.

"This protocol not only extends the period for the base's deployment in Gyumri. It also expands the scope of its geographic and strategic responsibility. Formerly, that scope was limited to the external border of the former USSR, but now that limitation has been eliminated. Russia will now be responsible for protecting Armenia and supplying it with modern weapons," he exclaimed.

The reason why Mr. Sargsyan was so happy is because in the event of an armed conflict with an unfriendly neighbor – like Turkey or Azerbaijan (which is still officially at war with Yerevan), or even Georgia – Russia will be required to protect Armenia. That's the price for keeping Russian troops in Gyumri. Moscow will not pay a single penny for the base directly, Anatoly Serdyukov told Kommersant.

After listening to their president's statement, Armenian journalists probably could not believe their ears, so they asked somebody else – namely, Dmitry Medvedev – to confirm that their country really managed to land such a deal. Both questions addressed to him at the press conference had to do with Moscow's actions in case the simmering conflict between Yerevan and Baku over Nagorno-Karabakh escalates.

"It is crucial to Russia that there be peace in the region," Mr. Medvedev replied with a sigh. "We have assumed certain obligations as allies in the CSTO. Armenia is a CSTO member. The treaty lists everything CSTO countries are allowed to do (in case one of them comes under attack – K). Russia takes its obligations seriously."

Moscow's commitment to fight for its allies if necessary is recorded not only in CSTO agreements. Russia's new military doctrine, which was adopted earlier this year, reads: "The Russian Federation considers an armed attack on a CSTO member-state an act of aggression against all CSTO member states and will respond by taking measures stipulated in the Collective Security Treaty." Incidentally, the doctrine also speaks of the need to enhance "the system of deploying the Russian Armed Forces and other troops, including deployment outside the Russian Federation." Mr. Medvedev achieved impressive results in this area this year. Yesterday's agreement on the Russian base in Gyumri was Moscow's second military-political victory in the post-Soviet space. Earlier, in April, during his visit to Kharkov, Dmitry Medvedev signed an agreement with Ukrainian President Viktor Yanukovich to extend the lease of the Russian Black Sea Fleet base in the Crimea until 2042....

Russia has been actively expanding and strengthening its military presence in former Soviet republics of late. At any rate, this has been Dmitry Medvedev's priority throughout the two years of his presidency. For example, after the war against Georgia in August 2008, Russia set up bases in Abkhazia and South Ossetia. This was Moscow's way of compensating for withdrawing its troops from Georgia after Tbilisi demanded that the bases in Batumi and Akhalkalaki be evacuated.

The next country that the Kremlin may turn to in order to satisfy its militaristic ambitions could be Moldova, which, like Armenia, has its own frozen conflict – in Transnistria....

BAKU'S REGIONAL PHOBIAS

By Yury Roks. *Nezavisimaya gazeta*, Aug. 25, 2011, p. 1.

At present, the primary threats to Azerbaijan's statehood come from Iran and Russia. Security could be guaranteed by a military alliance with Turkey, later followed by the creation of a confederate Azerbaijani-Turkish state. Prominent Azerbaijani political analysts Khikmet Khadzhizade and Vafa Guluzade recently offered up that analysis of the situation on the pages of the Baku newspaper Azadlyg [Freedom].

Khikmet Khadzhizade, analyzing the as yet unsettled situation of Nagorno-Karabakh in an Azadlyg interview, said that the "key to resolving the conflict lies with Russia." As a whole, Azerbaijanis were disappointed with the early August meeting in Sochi between the presidents of Russia and Azerbaijan, Dmitry Medvedev and Ilkham Aliyev, that was devoted to the Karabakh conflict. Expectations were high. Although official sources have called the meeting useful and capable of jumpstarting the negotiation process, a number of indications tell a different story. The most important one is that Azerbaijan will be represented at the upcoming CIS summit on Sept. 3 in Dushanbe by Prime Minister Artur Rasizade. And although this did not create any particular waves among Commonwealth members, who call Baku's decision "common practice," it is obvious that if the Sochi meeting had been productive, the Azerbaijani leader would be the one going to the Tajik capital.

According to Khikmet Khadzhizade, the Azerbaijani government is afraid of Russia, and for good reason. The political analyst highlighted a phrase used by Dmitry Medvedev during the aforementioned Sochi talks: "Aliyev and I spoke frankly." Khadzhizade believes that this expression should be seen as a reminder that attempts to use force to solve the Karabakh problem are unacceptable.

In his opinion, "Such a statement seems to be a warning: If Azerbaijan starts military action," Russia could remind them of what happened in Georgia. "This is a clear anti-Azerbaijani message," believes Khikmet Khadzhizade, remarking in passing that "Russia has hundreds of ways to destroy Azerbaijan***and about 2 million Azerbaijanis live in [Russia]."

Azerbaijani concerns about Iran were laid out in the same issue of the newspaper by former presidential adviser Vafa Guluzade. In his opinion, the latest actions of Iran, which never does anything for no reason, are aimed at creating an Islamic state in Azerbaijan. This is the main factor behind the growth of "religious consciousness" in Azerbaijani society, the intensification of radical Islamic groups (whose activities local security and law-enforcement officials have so far managed to squelch with preemptive strikes), and finally the famous open threat by Iran's chief of staff of the Armed Forces to the Azerbaijani president. "Iran, by using religion in politics, is seeking to expand its influence. Azerbaijan is Iran's primary target because of our country's geographic importance. And since it is hostile toward Azerbaijan, Tehran is not involved in major regional projects such as the Baku-Tbilisi-Ceyhan oil pipeline project," said Guluzade. On the other hand, Iran's anti-Azerbaijan position is in some ways beneficial to official Baku, which is fending off criticism from the West for neglecting democratic values: How can civil liberties be increased when the country is facing the threat of an Islamic revolution?! Guluzade feels that the way out is the creation of a confederation with Turkey. "A military alliance should be forged with Turkey; and then both nations should declare a confederation. Nothing else is needed. This would be a strong signal to Iran that it shouldn't touch Azerbaijan at all, since it would be facing an Azerbaijani-Turkish alliance," the former presidential adviser said.

Aleksei Malashenko, a member of the Carnegie Moscow Center's research council, believes that the confederation scenario is unrealistic both "in the near and distant foreseeable future." "Statements like that are a display of resentment toward Russia over the Karabakh issue. The same goes for Aliyev's opting out of the Dushanbe summit. The Azerbaijani leadership has declared a multivector policy – that's what it is trying to show Moscow. Let's just say that these statements are a way of pursuing a multivector policy," Malashenko told NG. As for Baku's concerns about Tehran, the professor considers them unfounded. "Relations between Baku and Tehran will not be smooth or normal as long as Iran's current regime is in power, since Iran will remain a standard-bearer of revolutionary Shiite Islam, which cannot please Baku," Malashenko told NG. To counter threats from Iran and others, it can be assumed that there will be a further rapprochement between Baku and Ankara, but it won't get to the point of forming a confederation....

SUPERVISED PEACE IN THE TRANSCAUCASUS

By Yury Roks. *Nezavisimaya gazeta*, Sept. 29, 2011, p. 6.

... "Russia is determined to do everything necessary to prevent a use-of-force scenario and an escalation of violence in the Caucasus," Sergei Lavrov said at a session of the UN General Assembly in New York. According to him, if any party unlawfully uses force, "Russia is ready to take all necessary measures to enforce peace in the region."

Can this statement be seen as a warning about a possible repeat of August 2008 if shooting breaks out somewhere in the Transcaucasus? That seems to be the case.

Russia has once again expressed readiness to become a guarantor of agreements on the nonuse of force between Georgia, Abkhazia and South Ossetia. "We would welcome it if the US and the EU assumed similar obligations," Lavrov said. "As guarantors, we will be ready to take measures to prevent the resumption of violence in the region. If any side resorts to force, we're prepared to ensure an early settlement of the situation based on the existing norms of international law."

According to Aleksei Malashenko, a member of the Carnegie Moscow Center's research council, Lavrov's remarks were prompted by an acceptance of the current realities, as well as the desire to avoid casting Russia as an empire, considering Vladimir Putin's likely return as president. "If, for example, the West fails to achieve anything within the Georgia-Abkhazia-South Ossetia triangle, criticism of Russia on these issues will die down," Prof. Malashenko told NG.

Tbilisi responded to Lavrov's remarks about Russia's desire to be a guarantor of peace in the region with a reminder about the losses that Georgia had sustained by trusting its northern neighbor. Tbilisi also indicated in no uncertain terms that it has no intention of signing treaties with "its autonomies," but is ready to consider the possibility of signing an agreement on the nonuse of force with Russia (with the participation of the international community, meaning the West).

Unlike Georgia, the EU showed greater interest in Lavrov's proposal. Maja Kocijancic, press secretary of the high representative for foreign affairs, told reporters that it "concerns some aspects of the complex situation around the conflict in Georgia that we need to study in more detail."

"We will continue to pursue additional opportunities for a peaceful resolution of the Nagorno-Karabakh conflict that have emerged due to Russia's efforts and its mediating role. We will continue to work toward a peaceful resolution of the conflict under the auspices of the OSCE Minsk Group together with our partners – France and the US," Lavrov said on the issue of the Armenian-Azerbaijani conflict. "Together with the other cochairs of the OSCE Minsk Group 'troika' – France and the US – we will be putting forth an array of confidence-building measures, as well as measures to consolidate the ceasefire regime."

Putting it bluntly, the Russian foreign minister basically said that maintaining the status quo was the optimal direction on the Karabakh issue: This boils down to continued negotiations under the aegis of the OSCE Minsk Group with pressure applied alternatingly on each party to the conflict, coupled with a refusal to sign documents proposed by each of the parties. This approach may somewhat suit Yerevan. But not Baku.

Speaking from the same rostrum, Azerbaijani Foreign Minister Elmar Mamedyarov outlined conditions that could facilitate progress. He did not say anything new in listing the demands that the Armenian side would never accept without the recognition of Nagorno-Karabakh's independence: the withdrawal of Armenian troops, the return of refugees, and "the creation of conditions for the peaceful coexistence of Azerbaijanis and Armenians in the Nagorno-Karabakh conflict area within the bounds of territorial integrity." "Azerbaijan still has not lost interest, motivation or patience in this very difficult and sensitive negotiating process.*** We believe that the international community will be able to convince the Armenian side.*** For our part, we are ready to guarantee a high level of autonomy for this region as part of the Republic of Azerbaijan," Mamedyarov said. The foreign minister sounded clearly disappointed in the long but fruitless years of negotiations. His deputy, Khalaf Khalafov, commented more bluntly on the issue at a meeting with an Argentine parliamentary delegation in Baku: "Peace negotiations are producing no results because the Armenian leadership is not ready to free the occupied territories." There is probably no need to explain what the connotations of such an "honest" statement are, considering that Azerbaijan will never agree to cede the territory of Nagorno-Karabakh. From this perspective, the statement about Russia's readiness to be a guarantor of peace could have puzzled Baku and at the same time had a tranquilizing effect on Armenia.

Yerevan has once again emphasized: Compromise implies give-and-take, but Azerbaijan only makes demands and fleeting promises to "hold a referendum on the status of Nagorno-Karabakh at some point," "ensure democratic norms and civil freedoms for the people of Karabakh," and so on. "It is strange to hear this coming from leaders of a country that has repeatedly come under criticism from PACE for regressions in democratic processes," said Naira Zorgabyan, head of the Armenian parliament's standing committee on European integration. "Azerbaijan has approved amendments to the Constitution abolishing the two-term limit for the presidency. In a country***where lifelong rule has been sanctioned, there can be no talk of democracy," she said.

"Of course, it's impossible to interpret Mr. Lavrov's remarks with 100% certainty. A joint approach to the Karabakh problem is possible if Russia, the US and the EU, with the acquiescence of Turkey, formulate realistic conditions and propose a package agreement to Yerevan and Baku as the only possible solution. My position on the issue is well known: Recognize the sovereignty of the Nagorno-Karabakh Republic, give Azerbaijan the land around Karabakh with the exception of the Lachin District, and repatriate refugees," Konstantin Zatulin, director of the Institute of CIS Countries and a [Russian] State Duma deputy, told NG. According to him, the Russian and Western positions on the Karabakh conflict are quite close. "However, if what Lavrov meant to say was that Russia could find a compromise with the West on all South Caucasus issues, I don't believe that. We have a totally different vision of the situation in Georgia, Abkhazia and South Ossetia," Zatulin told NG.

NOT BY KARABAKH ALONE

By Yelena Chernenko. *Kommersant*, April 4, 2012, p. 8.

Yerevan and Baku – ... Sergei Lavrov's visit to Yerevan and Baku was timed to coincide with a holiday – the 20th anniversary of their establishment of diplomatic relations with Moscow. But in both capitals, the guest and hosts had more to say about touchy subjects – most of all Nagorno-Karabakh. The OSCE Minsk group (of which Russia is a co-chair) has been trying for these same 20 years to solve that problem. In recent years, on the initiative of Russian President Dmitry Medvedev, a dozen meetings have taken place with the participation of the presidents of Armenia and Azerbaijan, but no real success has come of them.

In Yerevan, Sergei Lavrov confirmed that Russia is still "prepared to facilitate the achievement of accords." "Taking the wishes of the two sides into account, of course," the minister stipulated. However, it became clear from the statements of Armenian and Azerbaijani officials that their wishes differ strongly.

Armenian Foreign Minister Eduard Nalbandyan complained that Azerbaijan has rejected all of the Minsk group's new proposals, and suggested that Baku does not want to come to an agreement at all. "We are not asking for much from Armenia. We are asking that it remove its occupying troops from seized Azerbaijani territory and create the conditions necessary to restore civil, national and ethnic rights to the Azerbaijanis and Armenians of Nagorno-Karabakh," parried presidential administration spokesman Ali Gasanov from Baku. And one week earlier, that country's defense minister, Safar Abiyev, stated outright that Baku was prepared for a military solution. "We are ready to liberate our lands by military means, and nobody should doubt that Azerbaijan will liberate our territory from occupation," he stated.

In Baku, Sergei Lavrov tried to call on the partners to have patience, stating that "there are problems that have been waiting much longer to be resolved," and reminding listeners about Palestine, Cyprus, and Western Sahara. But the situation in the region is heating up even without Nagorno-Karabakh. The threat of war in Iran is the reason. If Iran closes its borders due to bombing, Armenia would be effectively cut off from the outside world. As that country's prime minister, Tigran Sarkisyan, confirmed to Kommersant, Armenia is preparing for such a scenario. Yerevan also fears an influx of refugees. What's more, the Armenian media are seriously discussing the possibility that Baku will use the situation as a pretext for incursions onto the territory of Nagorno-Karabakh.

Reports that Azerbaijan has purchased $1.6 billion worth of weapons and ammunition from Israel have added fuel to the fire. What's more, the authoritative American publication Foreign Policy, quoting White House and intelligence sources, reported last week that Baku has allowed Israel to deploy several military bases on its territory for the purpose of attacking Iran. Azerbaijani authorities immediately rushed to deny that information. On Monday [April 2], the US State Department denied it as well.

In Yerevan, Sergei Lavrov stated that in the case of war in Iran, Azerbaijan would also have a difficult time. "If the worst happens, Azerbaijan's security will also be affected, not just Armenia's," said the minister, explaining that the beginning of a war in Iran may cause an enormous influx of refugees into Azerbaijan (around 30 million ethnic Azeris live in Iran). "The consequences are hard to predict," he admitted, adding that they would be "very, very serious and negative."

BLACK HOLE OF THE SOUTH CAUCASUS

By Yury Roks. *Nezavisimaya gazeta*, June 15, 2012, p. 1.

A visit by OSCE Chairman-in-Office Eamon Gilmore to Armenia and Azerbaijan, which ended on Thursday [June 13], has not reduced tension between the conflicting countries. Skirmishes continued both along the line of contact in the unrecognized territory of Nagorno-Karabakh and in several border areas. In Yerevan and Baku, Gilmore spoke about the unacceptability of violence. However, judging from reports coming from the aforementioned places, his appeals proved ineffective. Now the hopes for a calmer scenario are being pinned on a meeting between the Armenian and Azerbaijani foreign ministers on June 18 in Paris.

Eamon Gilmore told the conflicting sides all the right things about peace. But they have heard all of that many times over the years. Having found themselves at an impasse, the opponents are ready to blame even the mediators in the negotiating process....

Even if Yerevan is not completely satisfied with the mediators' work, it is more content with it than Baku is. Nevertheless, Gilmore's remarks made during the latest visit have also raised questions from the Armenian side. It is openly disappointed that after the OSCE chairman dodged the question of visiting Nagorno-Karabakh in every possible way in Yerevan, he announced in Baku as soon as he descended the airplane ramp that he had no intention of visiting the unrecognized republic. Another question is not so much about the OSCE but about the way that global players interpret the ongoing events in the North Caucasus.

In particular, the Armenian side cannot help wondering why the West persistently describes the visibly growing Azerbaijani-Israeli military cooperation, including the purchase of some $2 billion worth of arms by Azerbaijan, as a necessary step in the face of the Iranian threat. At the same time, Baku methodically denies that assertion, assuring Tehran that despite the existing contradictions between the two states, Azerbaijan will under no circumstances act as part of an anti-Iranian coalition if one is formed. While accepting these assurances, Iran hardly trusts them, bearing in mind the fact that Azerbaijan has sold Israel several abandoned Soviet-era military airfields.

"Israel, which has embarked on military cooperation with Azerbaijan to its own specific ends unrelated to the Nagorno-Karabakh problem, has begun to be perceived as its ally. Understandably, provided that funds available, weapons can be bought anywhere, and in response, Baku may point out the fact that Moscow provides Armenia with arms supplies at preferential rates, for example. Nevertheless, a shadow has been cast on Armenian-Israeli relations," a Yerevan-based commentator told NG. Evidently, in a bid to rectify relations somehow, Tel Aviv – whose official representatives, particularly Foreign Minister Avigdor Lieberman, had stated that there was no chance of Israel recognizing the of the Armenian genocide in Turkey – suddenly reversed its position.

A few days ago, the Knesset discussed that tragedy. Zahava Gal-On, a deputy of the Meretz party that initiated it, said: "We're close to redressing a historical injustice." The Knesset debate, during which members of seven parliamentary factions spoke for the recognition of the genocide, proceeded at such a level that Archbishop Aris Shirvanian, a representative of Jerusalem's Armenian Patriarchate who attended the discussion, said in a telephone conversation that an affirmative resolution on the issue was very likely. "The very course of the discussion showed that the Israeli government is giving the green light and is not opposed to recognizing the genocide," the archbishop observed.

However, such optimism may be excessive; the reversal of Tel Aviv's position may be linked not only to the wish to fix its relations with Yerevan, but it may also be used to exert pressure on Ankara. This interpretation was offered to NG by a source close to the Turkish Foreign Ministry. "However, the government's position on the Armenian issue will not change, no matter what happens in Tel Aviv. Ankara still believes that the circumstances of those events should be studied by scholars, not politicians," NG's interlocutor said. He also stated that Turkey wants a normalization of relations with Armenia and "work in that direction continues, even though no one is saying anything about it." He says that even though it is not abandoning the principle of Azerbaijan's territorial integrity, Ankara is categorically against a use-of-force scenario in tackling the issue – so much so that according to unconfirmed but very persistent rumors, after the 2008 Russian-Georgian war, Turkish Prime Minister Recep Tayyip Erdogan advised Azerbaijani President Ilkham Aliyev in a friendly way "to forget about recovering Nagorno-Karabakh through war." The interlocutor also said that in light of this, Turkey is concerned by the fact that Azerbaijan is purchasing large amounts of arms from Israel, as well as by its excessive activity on the Iranian front. "Overall, a somewhat distorted impression persists that Turkish-Azerbaijani relations are spotless. We are indeed partners, but there are plenty of rough spots. To give a more accurate impression, relations between Ankara and Baku could be compared to those between Moscow and Minsk, or even between Moscow and Kiev," NG's interlocutor said, hinting that if Baku was at one time unhappy when ties started improving between its ally Ankara and hostile Yerevan, then Ankara, too, has a right to be unhappy with Baku's partnership with Tel Aviv, which is antagonistic toward Turkey.

The tension in the Transcaucasus cannot go unnoticed by Moscow. Readers are reminded that the announcement of a big military deal between Baku and Tel Aviv occurred almost at the same time that Rosselkhoznadzor [Russia's Federal Veterinary and Plant Disease Oversight Service] issued a warning about a possible ban on the import of Azerbaijani fruit and vegetables that this past spring suddenly turned out to be harmful to humans. In the same vein, Georgian and Moldovan wines and agricultural products, as well as Tajik dried fruit, have been banned previously. That may have been simply coincidence, and the warning was never carried out, but in any case, Russia is worried by Azerbaijan's colossal military spending, whomever it might be directed against: Armenia is [Russia's] well-known strategic ally, whereas Iran, in its confrontation with the West, is one by default. And it is no coincidence that according to a number of news agencies, military personnel at the Russian base in Gyumri have intensified firing practice, while pilots have had their flight time increased significantly against the backdrop of mounting tension in the region.

(Editorial) – RUSSIA FINDS GOLDEN MEAN IN NAGORNO-KARABAKH

Nezavisimaya gazeta, Aug. 12, 2014, p. 2.

Nagorno-Karabakh is experiencing a second day of calm. The negotiations over the weekend in Sochi between the presidents of Russia, Azerbaijan and Armenia have stabilized the situation in the volatile region. Of course, this won't last forever. After a time, provocations will resume, as experience has taught us. There are no easy solutions to the Nagorno-Karabakh dilemma. In order to resolve the issue, one of the sides is going to have to give up its idea: for Azerbaijan, the idea of restoring territorial integrity; for Armenia, the idea of a sovereign Nagorno-Karabakh. Neither is prepared to do so. Therefore, a final solution to the matter may be dragged out indefinitely. But this is not the end of the world. History is full of examples where some conflicts took decades – if not centuries – to resolve. The Nagorno-Karabakh conflict is actually a fairly new one – it's "merely" 20 years old. So it would be naïve to think that the Sochi negotiations, which were the initiative of [Russian President] Vladimir Putin, could offer a solution. Their main goal was to deescalate the situation in Nagorno-Karabakh, at least in the short term. It seems this has been achieved. Moscow has scored a few crucial points in the global arena as a vital and indispensable mediator in resolving the Nagorno-Karabakh conflict.

First, this is because while Western mediators pondered the reasons for the sudden escalation of tensions and philosophically suggested changing the category of the Nagorno-Karabakh conflict from "frozen" to "active," Russia suggested that the leaders of the two sides immediately sit down at the negotiating table.

Second, Moscow looks twice as efficient if you consider that shortly before the Sochi meeting, Baku and Yerevan ignored an analogous initiative from another mediator to the conflict resolution process – French President François Hollande. The proposal to meet in New York as part of a UN summit also met with ambiguous statements.

Third, Russia made it clear that if anyone thinks it's been too busy with the problem of Ukraine and Western sanctions to get drawn into the Nagorno-Karabakh issue, they should think again. Russia is closely following the events in the post-Soviet space and considers the Southern Caucasus an area of its geopolitical interests and responsibility. So, it is ready to give the region its attention and, if need be, other resources – such as peacekeeping forces. Of course, both Aliyev and Sargsyan turned down the latter, but that did not deprive the conflict of its uniqueness: This is the only confrontation where the belligerents are not separated by a third force, but are instead "eye to eye."

Fourth, Putin showed up analysts who maintained that in order to get Azerbaijan to join the Eurasian Economic Union, he would somewhat sacrifice the interests of his ally Armenia, recommending that it "ease up a bit" on the Nagorno-Karabakh issue.

Finally, [Putin] also managed to show up those who believed that with the world growing increasingly polarized, Moscow would resort to the approach of "if you're not with us, you're against us." Putin has demonstrated that Armenia is an ally and will remain one, and that Azerbaijan and its people are also important to Russia. Russia is very much interested in a stable Southern Caucasus, and is prepared to do whatever it takes to ensure that stability.

Russia's success, although local, could not but irritate some in light of its tense relations with the West – especially given that the attempts of Western politicians to bring the Armenian and Azerbaijani leaders to the negotiating table had proved unsuccessful (as noted above). This led one of the mediators to put forward a provocative theory regarding Nagorno-Karabakh: Supposedly, Yerevan and Baku were so agreeable because the recent exacerbation in tensions was just a ploy. Perhaps the supporters of this theory should spend a few weeks in the conflict zone – and we don't mean now, when, thanks to Moscow's timely intervention, the shooting there has stopped.

'UNBREAKABLE BROTHERHOOD' FOCUSES ON ARMENIA

By Vladimir Mukhin. *Nezavisimaya gazeta*, Sept. 30, 2015, p. 2.

The CSTO's Unbreakable Brotherhood peacekeeping exercises get under way today at Armenia's Bagramyan military training ground. The exercises were planned and had been known about since early 2015, but they have become even more relevant now that the situation in Nagorno-Karabakh has flared up. Officially, CSTO peacekeepers are rehearsing a joint peacekeeping operation in the Caucasus. This already has some experts talking about the real possibility of CSTO peacekeepers being deployed to Nagorno-Karabakh.

Artillery duels on the demarcation line between the parties to the conflict in Nagorno-Karabakh persist. But comprehensive solutions for settling the situation have yet to be articulated. So the backdrop for the CSTO peacekeeping maneuvers is very relevant and "hot," as it were....

The CSTO leadership has so far made no official announcement that the situation in Nagorno-Karabakh has deteriorated. Meanwhile, speaking about the goals and objectives of the organization's peacekeeping force, Russia's permanent representative to the CSTO Viktor Vasilyev said that "the CSTO member countries are primarily interested in participating in peacekeeping operations that concern our countries' interests. Unfortunately, such hot spots exist."...

The CSTO's peacekeeping force was established in 2007. Its formation took several years. According to Vasilyev, the peacekeeping force now numbers 3,500.

Not once in its eight-year history has it been used in an actual conflict. However, it has regularly honed its skills. The current CSTO peacekeeping exercises in Armenia are the fourth such maneuvers. CSTO press secretary Vladimir Zainetdinov said, "The main purpose of Unbreakable Brotherhood is to strengthen understanding and cooperation among the peacekeeping contingents of organization member states in preparing and conducting operations to curtail and localize a conflict." "Understanding and cooperation" are, apparently, key words with respect to the situation in which the CSTO peacekeeping exercises are taking place. In the southern Caucasus, the hottest hot spot is Nagorno-Karabakh, where the parties to the conflict are Armenia and Azerbaijan. But the CSTO countries (Armenia, Belarus, Kazakhstan, Kyrgyzstan, Russia and Tajikistan), with the exception of Armenia, have friendly relations with Azerbaijan. Russia is actively promoting military-technical cooperation with the current regime in Baku. Therefore, even a hypothetical peacekeeping scenario in which Azerbaijan may be an implied party to a conflict requires very clear political assessments and explanations for the CSTO peacekeepers.

Armenian expert Naira Airumyan believes that it is Russia that is now proposing the deployment of CSTO troops to the Karabakh conflict zone. This is purportedly necessary in order to "change the status quo in the region and to prevent 'foreign troops' from entering the region." "This option may not be to the liking of Armenia, or to the US and France," Airumyan believes. Lt. Gen. Yury Netkachev, who for a long time was deputy commander of Russian forces in the Transcaucasus Group, believes that "it is now unprofitable for Moscow to undertake a peacekeeping operation in Nagorno-Karabakh, since Russia is focused on Syria. But it could become a forced measure if real war breaks out between Armenia and Azerbaijan," he commented.

PUTIN, SARGSYAN DISCUSS SOUTH CAUCASUS

By Yury Roks. *Nezavisimaya gazeta*, March 11, 2016, p. 7.

Russian President Vladimir Putin and Armenian President Serzh Sargsyan met Thursday [March 10] in Moscow, where they discussed the Nagorno-Karabakh conflict, bilateral relations, and the enhancement of economic and humanitarian cooperation....

The same day Serzh Sargsyan visited Moscow, Azerbaijani President Ilkham Aliyev spoke in Baku at the fourth "Toward a Multipolar World" forum, where he asked the international community to step up pressure on Armenia to "liberate the occupied Azerbaijani territories." "Negotiations for a peaceful settlement are not making any headway.*** This is intolerable; the status quo must change. The heads of state of the countries cochairing the OSCE Minsk Group have said this time and again. Armenia must leave the captured land," Aliyev said.

Serzh Sargsyan, of course, has his own view of the situation and his own approach to it. Azerbaijan's latest surge in bellicose rhetoric and threats cannot but concern Yerevan. Moreover, they are now openly supported by [Azerbaijan's] ally Turkey, whose leaders are doing all they can to encourage Baku's aggressive statements regarding the Nagorno-Karabakh conflict. The time has come to liberate Nagorno-Karabakh from the Armenians; peace will come when the last Armenian is driven out of there, Turkish Prime Minister Ahmet Davutoglu said recently.

In that light, Armenia's alliance with Russia is doubly vital. At the same time, it seems Yerevan has realized that given the polarization in the world and the region in particular, there is no need to mince words about Russia's arms supplies to Azerbaijan. Until recently, Armenian leaders had no qualms explaining to the population, which is upset about this issue, that Azerbaijan would buy weapons regardless – so what difference does it make where it buys them? But after Baku's recent formal protestations to Moscow through diplomatic channels about [Russian] arms supplies to Armenia, Yerevan is apparently also ready to at last openly express dissatisfaction that the Azerbaijani Army is also getting Russian weapons. Albeit at a higher price. At any rate, ahead of Sargsyan's visit to Moscow, some media outlets with close ties to Armenian government agencies wrote that it is immoral to sell arms to your strategic ally's enemy. In Moscow, Sargsyan personally assured Putin of [Armenia's] commitment to resolving the [Nagorno-Karabakh] conflict peacefully.

It is important to Moscow to maintain balance and stability in the South Caucasus. "Russia seeks to pursue a balanced policy with regard to Azerbaijan. This course has already proved effective. If Moscow were to spoil relations with Baku, then given the deterioration of Russian-Turkish relations that came with the 'Syrian package,' it would have considerable problems in the Caucasus," said Sergei Markedonov, associate professor at the Foreign Policy and Regional Studies Department of the Russian State University for the Humanities. It follows from what the political analyst said that the deterioration of relations between Moscow and Baku could facilitate the formation of a tripartite alliance of Azerbaijan-Georgia-Turkey, which serves the interests of not only Ankara but also the West in general. This alliance could become a counterweight to Russian dominance in the Caucasus, which the West reluctantly accepted after the August 2008 [Russian-Georgian war] but would now like to minimize. "In this context, Baku's desire to move beyond the unequivocally anti-Russian stance that it has repeatedly demonstrated over the past six months is very important for Moscow. But this approach requires outlining exactly where [Russia] stands with Yerevan, including possible scenarios for military-technical cooperation with the two rival Caucasus republics," Markedonov believes.

Clearly, we are seeing the emergence of another axis (Russia-Armenia-Iran) to counterbalance the aforementioned one. For now, this concerns economic projects, which have become possible since the sanctions against Tehran were lifted: constructing a railway connecting Armenian and Iranian rail lines; exporting Iranian gas to Georgia and subsequently to Europe via Armenia; and establishing a free trade area for Iran with countries of the Eurasian Economic Union (EaEU). Armenia plays a key role in all of these projects. Russia is the de facto manager of Armenian infrastructure (pipelines and railways) and plays the main role in the EaEU. So naturally Sargsyan had something to discuss with Putin regarding major economic matters, not just the issue of lowering the price of Russian gas for Armenian consumers.

TRANSCAUCASUS 'FORK' FOR MOSCOW

By Aleksei Fenenko. *Nezavisimaya gazeta*, May 22, 2018, p. 5.

The Eurasian Economic Union summit that took place in Sochi on May 14 at first seemed positive for Russian-Armenian relations. New Armenian Prime Minister Nikol Pashinyan, who came to power on May 8 on a wave of six-week protest demonstrations, vowed to deepen economic cooperation with Russia. "This is the new Armenia, where all investments will be protected," he said. For his part, President Vladimir Putin said that Russia considers Armenia its "closest partner and ally in the region." These statements seem to give cause for optimism, especially since just prior to the Sochi summit, on May 11, Pashinyan also said that Yerevan will not change its foreign policy course. Nevertheless, Moscow still has reason to worry.

Over the past 10 years, Armenia continued to strengthen its pro-Western course. The ousted regime of Armen [sic; Serzh – *Trans.*] Sargsyan was not unequivocally pro-Russian. While talking about a partnership with Russia, it pursued rapprochement with the West. In 2014, Armenia signed a package of agreements with NATO, making it the CSTO country with the most military cooperation programs with the alliance. In December 2017, Armenia initialed an association agreement with the EU that the Armenian parliament ratified in April. American and European NGOs operated freely in Armenia. Sargsyan's government could not hinder their work because it had professed a pro-European course. Now, Sargsyan has been ousted by a mainly pro-Western opposition.

Armenia now has an entire generation of young (and not so young) politicians who have been brought up on American and European grants. This segment [of society] has cashed in on Russia's increasing alienation from Armenian society, which felt that Moscow did not offer Armenia sufficient support during the 2016 "April war" in Nagorno-Karabakh and the Yerevan CSTO summit. At the time, Russia stated that the CSTO's security guarantees apply to Armenia but not to Nagorno-Karabakh. This has been compounded by the social situation in the country, which further fueled protest sentiment. In a sense, Sargsyan repeated the fate of [former Georgian] president Eduard Shevardnadze, who first tried to balance between Russia and the West, and cultivated a pro-Western elite in the country that ended up ousting him. The current Armenian leadership tandem of [President

Armen] Sarkisyan and Pashinyan is most likely going to be more pro-Western than the fence-riding Sargsyan (otherwise, what was the point of ousting him?).

The new Armenian government includes officials whose careers are linked to international Western organizations. It's unlikely that this tandem will immediately sever ties with Russia. However, Armenia will most likely start to gradually drift away from "Eurasian organizations." This could result in several military-political crises. The first could concern the Eurasian Economic Union: The EU association agreement puts Armenia's membership in the EaEU in jeopardy. This is further compounded by growing criticism of the EaEU in Armenia, since several Armenian economists say it would hinder the nation's development. Armenia could change its membership format in the EaEU, from an associate membership to a complete exit. Such a situation could create a serious crisis for the newly created EaEU. If the EaEU ignores Armenia's association agreement with the EU, that could weaken [the union's] customs border checks.

At the same time, it would create a dangerous precedent for EaEU members making trade agreements with the EU, thus weakening [the EaEU's] role as an integration structure. However, if the EaEU issues Armenia an ultimatum on its EU association agreement, then Armenia could use that as a pretext to reconsider its participation in the EaEU.

The second crisis could start when settling the Karabakh issue. The new Armenian premier visited Nagorno-Karabakh on May 9, demonstrating a tougher approach than his predecessor. Pashinyan's government may propose to reevaluate the Vienna and St. Petersburg agreements of 2016 that serve as the foundation of the Karabakh peace process today. As cochairs of the OSCE Minsk Group, the US and France are likely to side with Armenia on this issue in order to further drive a wedge between Moscow and Yerevan. Russia will be faced with a difficult choice: Either to accept Armenia's westward drift, or to show more support for Yerevan than the West. A third crisis could concern the CSTO. Back in 2005, Armenia and NATO signed an Individual Partnership Action Plan. Yerevan's participation in it presumes holding periodic consultations with NATO on regional security issues, developing a security strategy and Armenia's military doctrine, and improving defense and budget planning processes as well as other issues.

Armenia also participates in NATO's peacekeeping missions in Kosovo and Afghanistan. Starting in October 2014, Armenia and NATO began drafting an annual individual cooperation "road map." The next step may be to boost coordination between Yerevan and Brussels regarding military personnel planning, which could conflict with Armenia's obligations within the CSTO.

Russia risks ending up in a politically difficult situation. Supporting the new pro-Western government in Yerevan would undo all the progress in the dialogue with Azerbaijan and Turkey that Moscow has been patiently building for 15 years. Armenia would continue to drift toward the West, growing increasingly distant from the EaEU and the CSTO. Essentially, Moscow would be supporting a government determined to move away from Russia and strengthen Western institutions in the Transcaucasus. In chess, a fork is when a player is forced to give up a piece. It happens when the opponent threatens two of the player's pieces at once, usually resulting in a checkmate. Regardless of what the player does, one of the pieces will be lost. Unfortunately, Russia could get "forked" in the Transcaucasus. So far, Moscow is cautiously optimistic about the developments in Armenia. But in the long term, they could create a serious strategic "fork" for Russia, and not only in the Transcaucasus.

WHO NEEDS THE RUSSIAN MILITARY BASE IN GYUMRI MORE?

By Aleksandr Khramchikhin. *Nezavisimaya gazeta*, Aug. 28, 2018, p. 7.

Russia's Southern Military District has three military bases located outside the country. Two of them are in Abkhazia and in South Ossetia (whose independence Moscow recognized following the 2008 [Russian-Georgian] war). These bases are fully integrated with the armed forces of the respective republics and are under Russian command. The Russian military's 102nd military base, stationed in the city of Gyumri, Armenia, is in a very different situation.

From a military standpoint, the 102nd military base is a motorized rifle brigade enhanced with operational-tactical missile complexes (OTMC), multiple-launch rocket systems (MLRS) and air defense systems – and not just land-based ones. The base's weapon systems include various armored vehicles, artillery systems, Iskander [tactical missile] and Smerch [MLRS] batteries, a Buk-M1 air defense division, as well as two divisions of S-300 surface-to-air missile systems that are combined with the Buk divisions of the 988th surface-to-air missile regiment.

Organizationally, the 102nd military base also includes the 3624th air base, located at the Erebuni airfield in Yerevan. It has 18 MiG-29 fighter jets (including two modernized MiG-29S fighters and four MiG-29UB combat trainers), four Mi-24 attack helicopters and seven multirole Mi-8 helicopters of the Russian Federation. This air base has a much higher [military] potential than the Armenian Air Force (especially in terms of air defenses).

Formally, the 102nd military base is not grouped with the Armenian Armed Forces, but they of course coordinate closely and hold joint exercises regularly. However, its situation is quite complex for geopolitical reasons.

Armenia is cut off from Russia by Georgia, which is completely hostile toward Russia, and by Azerbaijan, which is completely hostile toward Armenia. The military potential of the Azerbaijani Armed Forces is currently higher than even the combined potential of the armies of Armenia, the Nagorno-Karabakh Republic (NKR) and the 102nd military base (granted, the Armenian and Russian sides have a higher level of combat and mental preparedness). And Turkey, which is an ally of Azerbaijan and completely hostile toward Armenia, has overwhelming superiority over the Russian-Armenian forces. Moreover, due to Armenia's aforementioned geographical isolation, in the event of war, supplies from Russia could only reach the 102nd military base and the Armenian Army via a roundabout route through the Caspian Sea and Iran, which is very long, expensive and not very reliable (both politically and in purely military terms).

This means the 102nd military base has more political than military significance. It is located on the border with Turkey and guarantees that this country will not intervene on Azerbaijan's side in a new war over Nagorno-Karabakh, should one break out. Of course, the Russian base could not go up against the Turkish Army given the mismatched potentials, but under international law, an attack on it would be an act of aggression against Russia as a whole – i.e., this would ensure that Russia would go to war with Turkey.

Obviously, the Russian Army is not about to march on Ankara, but it would prevent a Turkish occupation (even partial) of Armenia. Russia is unlikely to go to war with Azerbaijan (unless Armenia itself is involved), but Armenian and NKR troops could still handle Azerbaijan on their own (because they are more prepared and have powerful defensive positions). The truth is, the more Azerbaijan arms itself, the less certain Armenia's victory becomes.

Thus, the 102nd military base is a guarantor of Armenia's existence. In other words, for Russia the base in Armenia is a matter of geopolitical ambition, while for Armenia it is a matter of survival. The Armenian authorities understand this – at least all the previous authorities have (it is not so clear if the new authorities do). So they not only allow Russia to use the base free of charge, but they pay it for being there (this might be the only such case in the world).

However, the attitude in Armenian society toward the presence of Russian troops is highly ambiguous. Anti-Russian sentiment is being very actively fanned both inside and outside the country, and it is eliciting a very clear response from Armenians. Therefore, it is difficult to say what the long-term prospects are for the 102nd military base's continued presence in Armenia. Although its departure would be suicide for Armenia, the world, unfortunately, has known more than enough examples of suicides of entire societies.

And Moscow is also playing its own political games, shaping the situation in the region. In particular, since mid-2016, Russia's policy in Syria has been based on an alliance with Turkey, and this alliance has ensured the majority of Russian-Syrian military victories. For Moscow, this is part of big geopolitics; moreover, its friendship with Ankara is for now not affecting the situation in the Caucasus, but Yerevan is extremely nervous about it. What has Armenians even more outraged (and understandably so) are deliveries of the latest Russian weapons to Azerbaijan – and in very large quantities. Moscow is pretending that the irreconcilable conflict between Armenia and Azerbaijan generally does not concern it, so it has no problem supplying arms to both sides (even though Armenia is a member of the CSTO and Azerbaijan is not).

However, the Armenians ultimately should only be offended at themselves. They were fully aware of their actions when they took a leading role in the process of dismantling the USSR. Armenia behaved in a more civilized and decent manner than many other former Soviet republics, but it did make a break for independence extremely actively and confidently. Its citizens should have been fully aware of the very complicated – mildly speaking – geopolitical situation Armenia might end up in after gaining independence. And that is exactly the situation it did end up in. There was no other possible outcome.

Today, Moscow and Yerevan are in completely different geopolitical weight classes and, consequently, addressing issues on completely different levels. Therefore, cognizant and grown-up Armenians must take a sober look at things and understand who needs the 102nd military base more.

NOTES

1. Aman Tuleyev, Russia's minister for CIS Affairs, was the first to publicly declare that Russian arms were being supplied illegally to Armenia.

Chapter 10 | Iran

VELAYATI'S MISSION TO NAGORNO-KARABAKH – Iran Trying to Become a Mediator Between Armenia, Azerbaijan

By staff correspondent Konstantin Eggert. *Izvestia*, Feb. 26, 1992, p. 1.

A 25-hour ceasefire in Nagorno-Karabakh was supposed to go into effect at 9 a.m. local time on Feb. 26. Both sides in the Armenian-Azerbaijani conflict took this step in order to allow Ali Akbar Velayati, Iran's minister of foreign affairs, to undertake an unexpected and dramatic attempt at mediation in the hope of bringing about a cessation of hostilities.

The chief of Iran's Ministry of Foreign Affairs held talks with President Mutalibov in Baku on Feb. 25, and he intended to visit Nagorno-Karabakh the next day before going to Yerevan. Reuters reports that at the end of the conversation with the Azerbaijani leadership, which both sides characterized as "encouraging," Velayati stated very emphatically that this was only Iran's "first step" toward settling the Karabakh conflict. In his words, the Iranian side has a number of effective proposals for stabilizing the situation in the region. Their specific content is unknown, but UPI, citing Radio Tehran, reports that in the first stage Azerbaijani control in Karabakh "will be maintained."

Officially, Velayati's mission was undertaken at the request of the Ministers of Foreign Affairs of Azerbaijan and Armenia. However, few people doubt that the real initiative here comes from Iran, which is trying to untie a knot of contradictions....

The supposition is being voiced that Iran is concerned by a war not far from its borders. I think that this is by no means the main consideration for the Rafsanjani government. Velayati's mediation should be viewed within the framework of a regional struggle for influence, primarily between Iran and Turkey, which the US recently has been increasingly setting up against Iran as a model for the new states on the CIS's southern flank. A more propitious moment could not have been chosen. Russia has demonstrated its inability to influence events, thanks largely to its image as an "imperial" state. Turkey's mediation would be rejected by Yerevan, and UN interference is unacceptable to Baku.

However, Velayati is a figure who is completely suitable to both sides – for different reasons, needless to say. Armenia sees Iran as a counterbalance to Turkish influence in the region, particularly in Azerbaijan. Incidentally, in this respect the opposition in the republic parliament is even more insistent than the government. In a conversation with me last summer, Ashot Navasardyan, the leader of Armenia's opposition Republican Party, spoke in favor of the all-out development of ties with Iran.

Baku's position can also be explained: Moslem Iran is the most preferable of all possible mediators. Any settlement plan emanating from Tehran will, needless to say, be more likely to be based on Azerbaijan's interests. Velayati cannot permit himself the luxury of absolute impartiality without risking a loss of support from the influential Azerbaijani diaspora at home. Yerevan cannot fail to understand this, too. Levon Ter-Petrosyan's government is probably prepared to make certain concessions, perhaps important ones, to Baku in the face of the danger of physical extermination that threatens the residents of Karabakh. Most likely, there will be talk of returning to plans for giving the province autonomous status within Azerbaijan, although it is not entirely clear what guarantees of the population's safety and ethnic balance Tehran could propose....

There is still another aspect to this situation: Both Azerbaijan and Armenia are members of the Conference on Security and Cooperation in Europe. ITAR-TASS reports that German Minister of Foreign Affairs Genscher reminded both sides of this fact in no uncertain terms when he demanded that they observe the entire set of obligations that they have accepted within the framework of the Helsinki process. The Armenian-Azerbaijani conflict will be discussed at a meeting of a committee of senior CSCE officials in Prague Feb. 27-28. For Europe and the US, needless to say, mediation by the UN or European security structures is preferable to the Iranian Minister's not disinterested mission. Therefore, one should expect closer attention to the problem of Nagorno-Karabakh on the part of international organizations in the near future.

However, the prospect of sending "blue helmets" [UN peacekeeping forces] seems unlikely at present, considering Baku's rejection of this idea and the international community's lack of any real levers for putting pressure on Azerbaijan. Therefore, even Velayati's initiative will be a step forward, if it stops the bloodshed....

VELAYATI CONTINUES MEDIATION EFFORTS – Will the New Ceasefire Hold?

By staff correspondent Konstantin Eggert. *Izvestia*, Feb. 27, 1992, p. 1.

Despite the failure of the first attempt to achieve a ceasefire in Nagorno-Karabakh, Iranian Minister of Foreign Affairs Ali Akbar Velayati is not losing hope in the success of his mission. It is expected that he will begin talks in Yerevan with President Ter-Petrosyan on the evening of Feb. 27. At the same time, UPI reports, citing IRNA, the official Iranian news agency, that a three-day ceasefire is supposed to go into effect in Karabakh at 9 a.m.

The first attempt to suspend combat operations, on Feb. 26, produced no results, since both Armenian and Azerbaijani officials denied that they knew anything about it. However, now a representative of the Iranian Ministry of Foreign Affairs has said that an accord on a ceasefire has been agreed upon by both sides....

Only the success of the three-day temporary truce proposed by Iran will allow Velayati to continue his mission. If the ceasefire falls through, the tour by Velayati will have been futile. A great deal depends on whether he is able to visit Nagorno-Karabakh before arriving in Yerevan. To this end, the Iranian minister has flown to Gyandzha, and from there he intends to go on to Shusha and Stepanakert.

Velayati's visit has evoked noticeable concern in Europe and the US, where any attempt to expand Iranian influence in the region is looked upon very unfavorably. The critical nature of the situation is increased by the fact that Iran's foreign minister has expressed an unambiguous desire to look into the situation on the spot, directly in the conflict zone, something that, one must admit, not one high-ranking leader of a Western state has risked doing.

ITAR-TASS reports that an official spokesman for the State Department in Washington has made a statement that, without commenting directly on Velayati's efforts, nevertheless expressed "firm support for the mediation efforts of the Russian Minister of Foreign Affairs," referring to Andrei Kozyrev's attempt last week to reach an agreement on a ceasefire with both the warring parties, an attempt that, unfortunately, ended in failure.

At virtually the same time that the spokesman for the American administration was speaking, France came out with its own peacemaking initiative. Its details have not yet been revealed; however, according to ITAR-TASS the plan is known to consist of four points and to provide for "intervention by international organizations" and the creation of "security corridors" for the evacuation of women and children and the delivery of emergency aid. For this purpose, Paris will send Bernard Kouchner, Secretary of State for Humanitarian Policy, to Karabakh. He will be in the conflict zone March 3-6. Evidently, the French initiative will be discussed at the two-day meeting of a committee of senior officials of the CSCE that will open in Prague on Feb. 27. A Russian delegation headed by Deputy Minister of Foreign Affairs Fyodor Shelov-Kovedyayev will take part in the meeting....

NAGORNO-KARABAKH: STEPANAKERT REJECTS RUSSIAN MEDIATION – It Likes Iran Better

By NEGA correspondent Lyudmila Khanbabyan. *Nezavisimaya gazeta*, April 24, 1992, p. 1.

Lately the leadership of Nagorno-Karabakh has been discussing the possibility of rejecting Russia's mediatory mission in settling the Karabakh conflict.

On April 21, Georgy Petrosyan, acting chairman of the Nagorno-Karabakh Republic Supreme Soviet, sent a letter to this effect to Russian Foreign Affairs

Minister Andrei Kozyrev, and on April 22 the press center of the Nagorno-Karabakh Republic Supreme Soviet released a statement setting forth the basic premises of the message. It says, in particular, that Russia's position in the conflict has appeared one-sided lately. The Russian army continues to give weapons and army property to the Azerbaijani armed forces. Every day Karabakh is subjected to barbaric shelling with rockets and projectiles seized from depots in Agdam. The residents of the Nagorno-Karabakh Republic also constantly see over their heads 16 Mi-24 combat helicopters that Russian units have given to the Azerbaijani army. One of the most recent incidents that was perceived extremely negatively in both Stepanakert and Yerevan was the dividing up of the Caspian Naval Flotilla, 25% of which was put under Azerbaijan's jurisdiction, appreciably strengthening its offensive might. There are also numerous documented cases in which Russian Federation officers and soldiers have participated in battles with the Nagorno-Karabakh forces on the side of Azerbaijan, acting as mercenaries. At the same time, any attempts by Armenia to take part in the process of dividing up the equipment and weapons of the former Soviet Army are encountering harsh resistance from Moscow.

Stepanakert believes that, in this light, Iranian mediation looks far preferable to Russian mediation, if only because Teheran is proposing significantly better starting conditions for the initiation of talks than Moscow is. For instance, the Iranians believe that there must be direct meetings between the leadership of Stepanakert and Baku as equal sides, while the Russian proposals talk only about participation by Baku and Yerevan. This, by the way, was one of the reasons why representatives of Nagorno-Karabakh declined to participate in the planned meeting in Mineralniye Vody that had been agreed upon by the foreign ministers of Russia and Azerbaijan.

If in the end Stepanakert really does refuse Moscow's mediation, Iran's position and standing in the region will unquestionably become significantly stronger, which will most likely allow it to gain a firm hold in the strategic areas that Russia is now abandoning.

AZERBAIJAN: BAKU, TEHRAN SEEK ECONOMIC COOPERATION – But Political Differences Are Getting in the Way

By Aidyn Mekhtiyev. *Nezavisimaya gazeta*, July 30, 1992, p. 3.

The government of Azerbaijan believes it is important to develop relations with Iran. This was stated by First Deputy Prime Minister Vakhid Akhmedov at a Cabinet of Ministers meeting on foreign policy.... It was noted at the government meeting that the Nakhichevan Autonomous Republic, which is periodically subjected to a transportation and communications blockade by neighboring Armenia, has a special need to expand cooperation with Iran. In the near future, plans call for building a 130-kilometer gas pipeline from Iran to Nakhichevan, as well as for completing the laying of a cable that will make it possible to set up telephone communications between the Iranian city of Rizaiyeh and Nakhichevan.

On July 22, Prime Minister Rakhim Guseinov signed a directive establishing the Iran-Azerbaijan Business Cooperation Council, whose main purpose is to promote the development of trade, economic, scientific, technical and cultural ties between the two countries....

However, political differences between Baku and Tehran could pose a serious obstacle to broader economic relations. Efforts to resolve conflicts that have arisen between the two countries over three main problems have so far been unsuccessful. These problems are: (1) the Iranian leadership's approach to the Armenia-Azerbaijan war; (2) Tehran's policy toward Azerbaijanis living in Iran; (3) the role of Islam in society. Azerbaijani President Abulfaz Elchibei, in his first public statements after being elected, accused Iran of violating its neutrality in the Karabakh conflict and of indirectly supporting Armenia. The Azerbaijani leader's position, in turn, forced Iran to abandon any attempts to launch new peacemaking initiatives to settle the Karabakh conflict....

Elchibei's sharp criticism of Tehran's domestic policies has also had repercussions within the Iranian leadership. As we know, after the 1979 Islamic Revolution, the clerical regime forbade any distinction between citizens on the basis of nationality. In reality, that led to discrimination against Iran's 25 million [sic] Azerbaijani citizens. The news that the president of the Republic of Azerbaijan (northern Azerbaijan) had spoken out in defense of the rights of residents of Iranian (southern) Azerbaijan quickly spread through every province in Iran, sharply increasing Elchibei's personal popularity among Azerbaijanis on the other side of the Aras River. The Iranian government then made some concessions and announced that, in addition to the Arab and Persian languages, the Azerbaijani language would be taught for the first time in Iran's schools and institutions of higher education in the new academic year. Textbooks are now being published in the Azerbaijani language for this purpose.

Presidents Elchibei and Rafsanjani also have serious differences over the role of religion in each country.... Elchibei is resolutely opposed to the forcible propagation of Islam in all areas of life, which is what he believes is happening in Iran....

Azerbaijan's new leadership, which has proclaimed its commitment to a secular society, is in no hurry to open its borders with Iran, fearing that the latter's top clergy will take advantage of the situation to propagandize Islamic fundamentalism in Azerbaijan. The fact that Islamic ideology has very little influence in Azerbaijan was demonstrated by a survey conducted by the republic Academy of Sciences' Institute of Law and Philosophy: Only 3% of the respondents said they prefer the Iranian state model. At the same time, in southern regions that border on Iran (Astara, Lenkoran, Massaly, etc.) and have large concentrations of Talysh, who are ethnically related to the Persians, the population has shown heightened interest in the Islamic religion.... [Azerbaijani Foreign Minister Tofik Gasymov believes] that at a time when Azerbaijan has no national currency and its citizens have no national passports, a policy of open borders could lead to a massive outflow of goods from

Azerbaijan and paralyze the economy. The fact that the Iranian ambassador [in Baku] has given Foreign Minister Gasymov a friendly message from the Iranian Ministry of Foreign Affairs proposing that he make an official visit to Iran could indicate a desire on Tehran's part to resolve all differences between the neighboring countries through negotiation.

150,000 REFUGEES ON AZERBAIJAN-IRANIAN BORDER

By Konstantin Eggert. *Izvestia*, Aug. 26, 1993, p. 1.

Some 150,000 residents of southwest Azerbaijan who fled approaching Armenian units are now pressing against the Iranian border. A crisis is brewing, the likes of which the Middle East hasn't seen for more than two years now, since the mass flight of Iraqi Kurds from Saddam Hussein's army.

The first refugees headed toward Iran back in the spring, after the Armenians took the city of Kelbadzhar. [The recent] fall of Dzhebrail and Fazuli triggered a mass exodus of tens of thousands of people who no longer felt safe on Azerbaijani territory. As Agence France-Presse reports, the front is essentially following right on their heels. Several shells have exploded on the Iranian bank of the Araz River, which forms the border. Fortunately, there were no casualties. Iranian Army units in the areas adjacent to the border have been put on heightened alert.

The refugees haven't attempted to begin a mass crossing of the border as yet. They are not sure how the Iranian authorities would receive them. For a quite some time now, officials in Tehran have warned the world community that if large numbers of Azerbaijani refugees wind up on their territory, the country will need material and financial assistance to accommodate them.

For not only economic but, mainly, political reasons, Tehran is hoping this won't happen: The refugees would end up on the territory of East Azerbaijan Province, which is populated mainly by Azerbaijanis. Ever since the USSR broke up and the former Union republics became independent, the possibility that separatist sentiments would appear among the influential and large (more than 10 million people) Azerbaijani community have been a source of concern for Tehran. An influx of refugees could only heighten nervousness in the community. This is why Iran has made a number of very tough statements to Armenia of late, asserting that it "will not tolerate aggression in direct proximity to Iran's borders."

Until recently Tehran had very good relations with Yerevan, pursuing its traditional strategy of opposing the spread of Turkish influence in the region. However, the threat of destabilization in the three northwestern provinces populated by Azerbaijanis, as well as the need to maintain "Muslim solidarity," has forced Hashemi-Rafsanjani's government to change its tone toward Armenia....

The question remains: How serious is Iran's threat against the Armenians? For the time being, the danger of a direct clash between the Iranian Army and Armenian units seems slight. But if tens of thousands of people stream across the border to flee shelling, the possibility cannot be ruled out that Tehran might decide to launch a limited military operation, such as an air strike.

Now that Fizuli and Dzhebrail have fallen, Azerbaijan's Kubatly and Zangelan Districts are threatened. The districts are under total siege. If they are occupied by Karabakh Armenian units, the stream of refugees heading toward Iran will increase, adding to the Iranian authorities' problems.

IRANIAN PRESIDENT VISITS AZERBAIJAN – Tehran, Baku Sign 14 Agreements

By Mekhman Gafarly. *Segodnya*, Oct. 30, 1993, p. 4.

As a result of the three-day visit by President Ali Akbar-Hashemi Rafsanjani of the Islamic Republic of Iran, 14 Azerbaijani-Iranian agreements, protocols and memorandums were signed in Baku on Oct. 28. They include a memorandum on principles of friendship and cooperation between Azerbaijan and Iran and agreements on economic, political and diplomatic relations, scientific and cultural exchanges, etc.

One important document that will shape the development of good-neighbor relations is an agreement allowing citizens of Azerbaijan and Iran citizens to freely enter each other's country. Iran is the third country (after Turkey and Britain) to which Azerbaijani citizens may travel without a visa.

A meeting between Rafsanjani and Aliyev touched on the question of Azerbaijani oil production. Answering questions about Azerbaijani oil contracts with foreign firms and a planned pipeline to export oil, Aliyev said no concrete decisions have been made as yet. He did not rule out the possibility that such an export oil pipeline could pass through Iranian territory. Hashemi-Rafsanjani gave assurances that the Iranian leadership would always be prepared to offer Azerbaijan that opportunity.

The Karabakh conflict remains one of the main problems of concern to the Presidents of the two neighboring countries. Speaking at a briefing, Aliyev said that he had asked the Iranian leader to exert influence on the Armenian leadership to stop the hostilities that resumed Oct. 21 in the Armenian-Azerbaijani conflict zone....

Mr. Rafsanjani contacted Armenian President Levon Ter-Petrosyan and reminded the latter of his statement that Armenian forces would not seize one inch of Azerbaijani land. Expressing hope for an improvement of the situation in the region, the Iranian leader stressed that Tehran "will not tolerate a dangerous turn in the situation on its borders." The Iranian leader stated that he "will try to avoid" providing military assistance to Azerbaijan, but he also noted that the "Islamic world will not allow open Armenian aggression against Azerbaijan."

Geidar Aliyev appealed for help to not only the Iranian President but also the UN Security Council. Mr. Aliyev urged the Security Council to condemn the Armenian Armed Forces' seizure of Azerbaijani territory, namely Zangelan District.

TEHRAN AND BAKU: CONFLICTS AGAINST BACKDROP OF GOOD-NEIGHBOR RELATIONS – Azerbaijani Leader Warned That Closer Relationship With Israel Is Undesirable

By Mamed Safarly. *Nezavisimaya gazeta*, July 5, 1994, p. 1.

Azerbaijani President Geidar Aliyev's four-day visit to Iran concluded with the signing of a joint statement by Aliyev and President Ali Akbar Hashemi-Rafsanjani of the Islamic Republic of Iran. In the document the sides declare their intention to deepen bilateral cooperation in politics, economics and culture. Eight other documents were also signed, providing for the joint construction of a water engineering system on the Araz River, the building of a railroad from Ordubad to Menjan and the laying of a gas pipeline from Khoy to Ordubad.

Judging from the Azerbaijani leader's statements, the visit to the Iranian capital was very productive. At a concluding press conference in Tehran, Aliyev said, "This visit is an important step in the development of relations between Iran and Azerbaijan." He succeeded in winning Tehran's support on the Karabakh issue. In discussing it, the Azerbaijani leader appealed to the idea of so-called Islamic solidarity....

At the same time, observers who followed Aliyev's visit to Tehran called attention to the fact that differences remain between the two capitals. First of all, the rights of the 20 million Azerbaijanis living in Iran is a sore point for Tehran. In 1992, then Azerbaijani President Abulfaz Elchibei openly accused the Iranian leadership of violating the Azerbaijanis' rights. More-over, a number of political parties and movements in Baku spoke of the need to discuss the "problem of South Azerbaijan" (territory that is part of Iran). Tehran rejected such claims and demanded explanations from official Baku. After Geidar Aliyev came to power in 1993, Azerbaijani-Iranian relations began to mend. But it took Aliyev a great deal of effort to convince Tehran that the Azerbaijani leadership has no claims against Iran. During the just-concluded visit, Aliyev emphasized unequivocally that the "territorial integrity of Iran is sacred to the Azerbaijani Republic." Nevertheless, the fact that during his visit to Iran, Aliyev had to cancel a trip to Tebriz, capital of South Azerbaijan (most likely at the Iranian side's insistence) suggests that Iran is still suspicious of Baku's intentions in this regard.

Another problem that has caused persisting tension in Azerbaijani-Iranian relations is the stepped-up cooperation between Tehran and Yerevan of late. During a recent visit to Tehran, Armenian Vice-President Gagik Arutyunyan discussed the possibility of building a gas pipeline from Iran to Armenia through the Megri corridor. Baku fears that Armenia, if it were to solve its energy problems with Iran's help, would step up the military pressure on Azerbaijan. During his visit to Tehran, Aliyev urged the Iranian leadership to refrain from cooperation with Armenia.

Tehran, for its part, warned Azerbaijan about the danger of the "Zionist plot," whose essence is to undermine the Muslim countries' attempts to establish close cooperation among themselves.... Despite Tehran's appeal, Aliyev avoided making any anti-Israel statements. Evidently, Azerbaijan is not the only country for which stepped-up cooperation with Israel could complicate relations with Iran. Israeli Foreign Minister Shimon Peres arrived in Tashkent on July 3 and declared right at the airport, in advance of a meeting with President Islam Karimov, that Uzbekistan and Israel are united by a common struggle against Islamic fundamentalism. If Karimov concurs with Peres's statement, a sharp exacerbation of Iranian-Uzbek relations will be inevitable.

ARMENIAN-IRANIAN COOPERATION IS PICKING UP

By Armen Khanbabyan. *Nezavisimaya gazeta*, Sept. 1, 1998, p. 5.

Yerevan – The results of a visit by Armenian Foreign Minister Vardan Oskanyan to Iran have pleased both sides. The Armenian minister held talks with Iranian President Mohammed Khatami, Majlis chairman [Ali Akbar] Nateq Nouri and Iranian Foreign Minister Kamal Kharrazi. Kharrazi declared: "Armenia is an important neighbor of Iran's, and official Tehran has always had a special liking for Yerevan." The statement takes on special significance in light of the continuing sharp deterioration of relations between Armenia and Turkey. As readers are aware, the Turks recently accused Yerevan of "spreading hatred of Turkey" and said they had no desire to consider ways of improving bilateral relations. Furthermore, Ankara intends to stick to this position until Yerevan stops insisting on international recognition of the 1915 Armenian genocide, something that Armenia can hardly be expected to do, needless to say. Armenian Foreign Ministry spokesman Arsen Gasparyan said: "Although Armenia, in the seven years since gaining independence, has not raised the genocide issue but instead pursued a policy aimed at normalizing its relations with Turkey, the Turkish side has nonetheless found a pretext to ignore Armenia's hand extended in goodwill, citing the Nagorno-Karabakh problem."

Under these circumstances, good-neighbor relations with Iran are increasingly important to Armenia. At the same time, bilateral economic cooperation is assuming a greater role. It was no coincidence that this aspect dominated the negotiation process, with special attention devoted to such issues as accelerating the construction of a gas pipeline from Iran to Armenia, establishing a policy of free trade between the two countries, and carrying out plans to erect a hydroelectric station on the Araz river, which forms the border between the two countries. In focusing on these issues, Yerevan is obviously trying to lessen its dependence on Georgia, through which the only gas pipeline leading to Armenia passes, together with the only railroad linking the country to the outside world. It should be pointed out that a potential exacerbation of the situation in Dzhavakheti – a Georgian region populated by Armenians – heightens Yerevan's risk of ending up under another transportation and energy embargo, something that the development of infrastructure ties with its southern neighbor will help in part to prevent.

By the way, the advantages of Armenian-Iranian cooperation are far from one-sided. Tehran is as interested as Yerevan in strengthening its international position and reinforcing its regional role. Kamal Kharrazi told Vardan Oskanyan he would like to revisit the issue of Iran's facilitating a settlement to the Karabakh problem, a desire that met with full understanding. Armenia's chief diplomat stressed that, in Yerevan's view, Iran "can play a key role in all regional processes." And so the Armenian-Iranian rapprochement that began in 1991, immediately after Armenia became independent, continues to gain momentum and appears to be reaching new political and economic levels. However, it remains unclear just how this circumstance will affect Yerevan's ties with the European community and the West as a whole.

WORLD WAR III COULD BREAK OUT IN THE SOUTH CAUCASUS

By Armen Khanbabyan. *Nezavisimaya gazeta*, Aug. 18, 2001, p. 5.

Three weeks ago, an Iranian Air Force jet invaded Azerbaijani airspace. Needless to say, Baku responded immediately with a forceful diplomatic demarche. In all honesty, however, it had no perceptible impact. Tehran didn't apologize. On the contrary, flights over Azerbaijani territory by Iranian fighters have become all but a regular occurrence of late. And the warplanes have been coming closer and closer to the Azerbaijani capital. Last time, residents of the district center of Salyany panicked when an Iranian attack plane overflew the town at low altitude. In addition, Iran has demonstrated its naval power – significantly, in the vicinity of the disputed oil fields.

It's no secret that ever since Azerbaijan gained independence, Baku's relations with its neighbor to the south have left much to be desired. Azerbaijani leaders have repeatedly provoked Tehran by hinting at the possibility of unification with their "brothers living in South Azerbaijan" (meaning Iran's northern provinces, which have a large population of ethnic Turks).... Nothing could irritate Iran more than even indirect hints of a threat to the country's territorial integrity.

Furthermore, Azerbaijan's pro-Western (in particular, pro-American) orientation, as well as its "special ties" with Turkey, have had and continue to have an extremely negative effect on its relations with Iran. There are deep-rooted conflicts between Iran and Turkey....

The Karabakh factor has also had a very significant impact on the situation all these years. Despite being a leader of the Islamic world, Iran has never tried to put any appreciable pressure on Armenia and the Nagorno-Karabakh Republic to force Yerevan and Stepanakert to make the concessions demanded by Azerbaijan. In contrast to Turkey, we should point out; the latter country refuses to establish diplomatic relations with Armenia to this day and continues to maintain a tight blockade on the republic's land borders. Furthermore, it is precisely Armenia's good relations with Iran that have largely helped Armenia minimize the consequences of the Turkish embargo....

Not even the haughty restraint traditionally characteristic of Iranian diplomacy could help completely muffle the fury that gripped Tehran after Azerbaijani President Geidar Aliyev declared on his return from the recent CIS summit in Sochi that Vladimir Putin had proposed that the upcoming meeting of Caspian nation presidents be held without Iran. Iranian Deputy Foreign Minister Ali Ahani was immediately dispatched to Moscow.... The Iranian diplomat was assured that "the Azerbaijani side's interpretation of the Russian president's statements was incorrect." In fact, it was after this that Iran, convinced the other Caspian states basically wanted to hoodwink it, began putting on its show of strength.

Baku was clearly rattled. On the one hand, as the Bilik Dunyasy news agency reported, Defense Minister Safar Abiyev "said that Iran is not a hostile country and so I didn't want to fire on its planes," and the president's chief of staff, Ramiz Mekhtiyev, urged a "peaceful dialogue" between the neighbors. On the other hand, President Aliyev's son Ilkham, one of the leaders of the pro-Aliyev party Yeni Azerbaijan, essentially expressed solidarity with the opposition, which has demanded a "fitting rebuff to Iran's encroachments."

The US and Turkey, by contrast, have made their positions crystal clear, without mincing words. Both Washington and Ankara harshly condemned Tehran's actions, and it is telling that, in the process, Turkey made direct threats against its eastern neighbor. For instance, the authoritative Hurriyet, which frequently reflects the views and thinking of official circles, published a front-page article under the banner headline "Note to Tehran: If You Touch Azerbaijan, You'll Have to Deal With Us." The article said, among other things, that "if necessary, Azerbaijan will be given support in any sphere." Other newspapers carried headlines such as "Azerbaijan Is Not Alone," "Iran Risks Colliding With a Rock" (meaning Turkey – A. Kh.), and so on. Furthermore, it was explained to the Iranians clearly and in detail exactly what kind of difficulties they might encounter in view of the fact that "Azerbaijanis account for 20% of Iran's population." Finally, Iranian Ambassador to Ankara Hussein Lavasani was summoned to the Turkish Ministry of Foreign Affairs, where he was officially told that "such actions will mainly hurt Iran itself."

Tehran took all of this with classic Eastern imperturbability. Not only did Iran not try to justify its behavior (something that, most likely, no one really expected it to do), but it didn't even furnish any evidence or arguments that it was in the right. Official Iranian Foreign Ministry spokesman Hamid-Reza Asefi issued a statement basically saying that absolutely nothing had really happened. Azerbaijani airspace was never violated, and any claims to the contrary are "hostile insinuations" that can only give rise to "bewilderment."

That response, intended to show that Tehran is not afraid of any threats, no matter where they might come from, appears to be more than just a poorly concealed taunt. Tehran also asserted that all flights by Iranian Air Force planes took place "over Iranian territorial waters in the Caspian." So such flights should not be viewed "as a threat to neighboring states." Azerbaijani officials were advised in this regard to "be vigilant" and take prompt action to put a stop to "trends that could damage friendly bilateral relations." Meanwhile, it was pointed out to Washington that, in supporting Azerbaijan, the US was engaging in "interference," "stirring up tension," and basically acting in a "provocative" and "unrealistic" manner.

After that rebuke, everything became perfectly clear both to the "friendly" Azerbaijanis themselves and to everyone else with an interest in the forthcoming division of the "Caspian pie." Tehran was simply demonstrating its belief that all the oil fields Azerbaijan is claiming belong indisputably to Iran. And that it has absolutely no intention of discussing the matter....

In light of this, there can be no doubt that the upcoming summit [of the five Caspian littoral states, scheduled for October] in Turkmenbashi (formerly Krasnovodsk) will be rather difficult. At any rate, it's doubtful that the idea, proposed by Viktor Kalyuzhny on Russia's behalf, of forming a new Caspian regional structure will be carried out. Moscow had probably hoped to use such a mechanism to strengthen its position, since it still has a great deal of leverage on the former peripheral Soviet lands, but Iran clearly fears that any such mechanism could lead to the emergence of a kind of "united front" against it, one in which, moreover, the positions of multinational oil and gas monopolies, and hence the West, would be very strong. That is why it decided to teach Azerbaijan a lesson, in hopes that conclusions would be drawn not only and so much by Baku as by the other, more powerful parties to Caspian oil intrigues.

But the possible failure of the Caspian summit is nothing compared to what might await the region if the numerous chronic conflicts that have manifested themselves sharply in recent times start to intensify and new ones emerge. In this regard, one can't help mentioning the unprecedented outpouring of militaristic rhetoric in both Azerbaijan and Armenia.... One might get the impression that the Nagorno-Karabakh peace process is not just spinning its wheels again but has reached a total impasse, and that the truce, now in its seventh year, is in serious jeopardy....

The authors of a [recent Pentagon] report argue that [in the event that Azerbaijan were to retake Karabakh, Armenia could attempt to occupy Nakhichevan, in which case,] under the 1921 Kars Treaty, Turkey and then Russia would be obligated to intervene in the conflict. It may be recalled that, under the treaty, Ankara is the guarantor of the existing status of Nakhichevan and must make every effort to prevent "its passing to any third party." This means Armenia, of which the region is a historical province. Moscow, in turn, would of course be obligated to respond in some way to Turkish use of force against its strategic ally, which hosts a Russian military base to boot. The potential response of Iran in such a scenario is also clear....

Chapter 11 | The United States

GEOPOLITICS: IF AMERICA TURNS AWAY FROM AZERBAIJAN, BAKU COULD TURN TO ISLAMIC STATES

By Aidyn Mekhtiyev. *Nezavisimaya gazeta*, Nov. 17, 1992, p. 1.

Bill Clinton's victory in the US presidential election lends a special urgency to the future of American-Azerbaijani relations. No matter how officials in Baku have tried, for some time, to persuade people in the republic that there are no insoluble problems in relations between the US and Azerbaijan, a recent decision of the American Congress is causing local commentators to have doubts. As we know, at the suggestion of the Bush Administration, first the Foreign Relations Committee and then the US Congress approved an amendment to the Freedom Support Act stipulating that no humanitarian aid will be provided to Azerbaijan until it "ends its policy of blockading Nagorno-Karabakh." The fact that the initiative for imposing economic sanctions on Azerbaijan came from the Bush Administration caused some bewilderment in Baku, to say the least. After all, after the People's Front came to power in Azerbaijan this June, President Abulfaz Elchibei made it clear that henceforth Azerbaijan would give priority in its foreign policy to relations with the US and the NATO bloc. One indication that Azerbaijan was ready to become a US ally in the region was official Baku's active campaign against Iran. In public statements, the Azerbaijani leader charged the Iranian regime with human rights violations.

The new emphasis in Azerbaijan's foreign policy did not go unnoticed by the American administration: In June, President Bush sent Elchibei a personal message in which he set forth the basic aims of US and NATO policy in the region. Bush's letter evoked a great deal of commentary in the Azerbaijani press. The hope appeared that by taking steps to accommodate each other, Baku and Washington would create the right conditions for a summit meeting. But the hopes of an imminent warming of bilateral relations proved illusory. The amendment to the Freedom Support Act essentially means that US public opinion has firmly come to view Azerbaijan as a country that is flagrantly violating the rights of Karabakh's Armenians. The Democratic Party candidate's coming to power in the US might only lead to a toughening of the new American administration's policy on Azerbaijan. For US Democrats have traditionally paid greater attention to the problem of protecting the rights of national minorities than Republicans have. It's no accident that Bill Clinton, during his campaign, criticized Azerbaijan's position in the Karabakh conflict. In a letter to Clinton, Yusif Samedoglu, chairman of Azerbaijan's parliamentary commission on foreign affairs, suggested that Clinton had been given distorted information about the real nature of events in the region.

During the Bush Administration, Azerbaijan could count on Turkey – a close military and political ally of the US for many years – to mediate problems in relations with Washington. It's no accident that at the conclusion of Operation Desert Storm, Bush called Turkey his "second home." But with Clinton's election to the US presidency, cracks could appear in the American-Turkish alliance. As we know, the Republicans' 12-year rule in the US coincided with the reforms of Turgut Ozal in Turkey. Ozal, who was prime minister from 1983 to 1989 and has been Turkey's president since 1989, achieved considerable success in relations with the US and won the Republicans' support in Ankara's confrontation with Greece over the Cyprus issue. The American administration also fully supported the Turkish government's struggle against Kurdish separatists in the southeastern part of the country. Since the US presidential election, the Turkish leadership has become seriously concerned. It is recalled there that Al Gore, the US vice-president-elect, was a cosponsor of a resolution adopted by Congress in the 1980s condemning Turkey's "genocide of Armenians in 1915." Moreover, Clinton himself, according to Turkish press reports, is strongly influenced by the Greek lobby in the US, which could lead to changes in the US approach to the Cypriot problem. Clinton's position on the Kurdish question is also causing concern in Ankara. While condemning the actions of Kurdish terrorists from the Kurdish Workers' Party, Clinton also supports the rights of the Kurdish minority in Iraq and Turkey.

Nevertheless, both Baku and Ankara hope that Bill Clinton will maintain continuity in US foreign policy.

A few days ago, President Elchibei told journalists that a worsening of American-Azerbaijani relations would not serve US strategic interests. But one cannot rule out the possibility that Azerbaijan, if it doesn't make any progress in its relations with Washington, could slam the door. This possibility was mentioned, in particular, by Isa Gambarov, the parliamentary chairman, at a press conference in Baku on Nov. 12. "If they lose faith in Western and US support," he said, "the Azerbaijani people could turn to the Islamic states."

That very scenario is the dream of Iranian leaders, who would like to see the ideas of Islamic fundamentalism spread in Azerbaijan.

ALIYEV, SHEVARDNADZE TRY TO TRADE MOSCOW FOR WASHINGTON – But White House Advises Them Not to Be in Too Big a Hurry

By Leonid Gankin and Gennady Sysoyev. *Kommersant*, Aug. 6, 1997, p. 4.

A visit to Georgia that John (Malkhaz) Shalikashvili, Chairman of the US Joint Chiefs of Staff, began yesterday and the president of Azerbaijan's trip to the US, which ended a few days ago, show that in their attempts to solve their internal problems, Tbilisi and Baku are relying more and more on Washington and less and less on Moscow. However, the Americans are not inclined to force the pace of events and jeopardize their relations with the Kremlin.

When he arrived in his ancestral homeland, Gen. Shalikashvili switched roles, as it were, with Georgian President Eduard Shevardnadze: Two weeks ago, the general cordially welcomed the Georgian leader during his official visit to the US. It's interesting to note that the Azerbaijani and Georgian Presidents' trips to that country were very much alike and had approximately the same outcomes.

Washington promised both Azerbaijan and Georgia expanded bilateral ties in all areas. Both leaders took home agreements on deeper military cooperation with the US. Incidentally, it was to follow up on these matters that Gen. Shalikashvili went to Georgia.

In addition, Geidar Aliyev took back to Baku an agreement on mutual investment protection, as well as four contracts (worth a total of about $8 billion) under which American oil corporations Exxon, Amoco, Chevron and Mobil will take part in developing Azerbaijan's oil resources.

For his part, Eduard Shevardnadze announced that a major American corporation planned to invest approximately $1 billion in the Georgian economy (in transportation, communications and machinery manufacturing). Shevardnadze also reported that the American Senate had approved a decision to give Georgia $100 million in aid. Aliyev was unable to boast of such a success: The US continues to maintain a ban that the US Congress imposed on financial aid to Azerbaijan because of the republic's conflict over Nagorno-Karabakh with neighboring Armenia.

Both Aliyev and Shevardnadze were particularly hopeful that the US would take a more active role in resolving problems that Baku and Tbilisi regard as top priorities namely, settlements in Karabakh and Abkhazia. While bidding to play the "American card," they had been in no hurry to consent to Moscow's proposals for resolving the conflicts, in the belief that Washington would come up with more favorable terms.

A Kommersant correspondent has learned from circles close to top officials of the Russian Foreign Ministry that Eduard Shevardnadze refused to sign a protocol drafted by Moscow and reconciled with Abkhazia on a settlement of the Georgian-Abkhaz conflict precisely because he expected, during his forthcoming visit to the US, to persuade the White House to take his side. And even after initially giving high marks to the Russian plan, Shevardnadze unexpectedly declared in the US that the "negotiating process has reached a dead end."

According to Kommersant's information, the Georgian leader offered Washington a choice between two options for replacing the Russian peacekeepers in the conflict zone: Either send a foreign contingent into Abkhazia to mount an operation to implement peace by force (along the lines of the Bosnian operation), or send UN troops there.

However, the US took a restrained view of both options, advising Shevardnadze "not to rock the boat" and to refrain from raising the issue of a withdrawal of Russian peacekeeping forces from the Inguri River basin.... The US fears that pulling out the Russian peacekeepers could lead to a resumption of fighting in the region, through which a "strategic oil pipeline is to pass" (the reference is to transporting so-called "main oil" via the Western route across Georgia and Turkey).

Having taken the US position under advisement, Shevardnadze last Monday offered an almost complete endorsement of the Russian plan for a peace settlement in Abkhazia and agreed that the Russian peacekeepers should stay in the conflict zone at least until the CIS summit in September.

Geidar Aliyev behaved much the same way, although he was more cautious in his statements. Despite having secured a promise from Boris Yeltsin that Russian Foreign Minister Yevgeny Primakov would wake up every morning thinking about Karabakh, Aliyev nonetheless considered it necessary to say in the US that a resolution of "this painful problem for Baku is overdue" and asked the Americans to step up their efforts in this area.

However, his American hosts made it known that they had no intention of replacing the Karabakh plan agreed upon by the Minsk group, which, in addition to the US, includes Russia and France. Perhaps that's why Aliyev, in concluding his American tour, stressed that "Russian interests in Azerbaijan will not suffer."...

The Russian Foreign Ministry didn't expect Shevardnadze's and Aliyev's trips to the US to have any other outcome. [Russian] diplomats say that the Georgian and Azerbaijani leaders had inflated expectations of the US's willingness to tackle their internal problems because it's difficult for the heads of state, who were former [Communist] party leaders, to entirely abandon their old stereotyped patterns of thinking. The rivalry between Moscow and Washington in international affairs does indeed continue. The US is not averse to establishing a presence in the Transcaucasus, but it prefers economic forms of penetration. Moreover, the rivalry no longer has the confrontational overtones of the cold war era. So it's hard to even imagine what one would have to promise the Americans to get them to sacrifice their partnership with Russia.

U.S. 'GOLD MINE' – Aliyev Knows What to Take to Washington

By Aleksandr Shinkin. *Rossiiskaya gazeta*, Aug. 6, 1997, p. 7.

Azerbaijani President Geidar Aliyev's official visit to the US has ended. Observers consider it a success.

There are a number of reasons for this. First of all, Aliyev's visit came at a time when the Transcaucasus region is assuming central significance in US strategy, the objective of which is to gain control of Caspian oil reserves. Aliyev was the second leader of a Transcaucasus country to visit Washington in the past month. He was preceded by Georgian President Eduard Shevardnadze.

Second, Geidar Aliyev himself put a lot of effort into his success. He went to the US with economic proposals that were very advantageous to the Americans. During the visit, he signed several oil contracts with various companies. The projects to develop the Apsheron, Nakhichevan and Oguz fields are worth a combined total of $10 billion.

In addition, Geidar Aliyev broadened the activities of American capital investors in Azerbaijan, signing a contract with a consortium of American companies on the joint exploration and development of several promising gold deposits. According to republic Prime Minister Artur Rasizade, the value of the contract is estimated at approximately $500 million and includes nine "gold sites."

While seeking to convince the US administration of the economic advantages of cooperating with Azerbaijan, Geidar Aliyev also tried to solve a number of his own problems. A ban imposed on American governmental assistance to Azerbaijan under Art. 907 of the Freedom Support Act is a stumbling block in American-Azerbaijani relations. The embargo was announced five years ago, at the height of the Karabakh conflict. Since then Baku has tried repeatedly to get it lifted, but to no avail. Now Azerbaijan has won the backing of American oil companies and a number of influential politicians. Among them, for example, is Zbigniew Brzezinski, the former presidential national security adviser, who is now a consultant to the Amoco oil and gas company. To all appearances, Bill Clinton also expressed support for lifting the sanctions. Geidar Aliyev's meeting with the President lasted about three hours instead of the planned one hour.

But the main purpose of Geidar Aliyev's visit was to try to make a breakthrough in settling the Karabakh conflict. The details of the two Presidents' discussion of this problem are not yet known....

At any rate, Geidar Aliyev returns to Azerbaijan having secured American recognition and refocused attention on the Karabakh conflict.

WASHINGTON STEPS UP AID PROGRAM FOR STEPANAKERT – American Legislation Doesn't Treat Nagorno-Karabakh as Part of Azerbaijan

By Arman Dzhilavyan. *Nezavisimaya gazeta*, April 21, 2000, p. 5.

The US government's Agency for International Development (USAID) recently released a special report on aid for Nagorno-Karabakh and victims of the Karabakh-Azerbaijani conflict. USAID has been implementing such programs under laws that were written by the US Congress and oblige the American government to provide direct assistance to Nagorno-Karabakh, as well as to carry out programs for the social, physical and psychological rehabilitation of the people of Nagorno-Karabakh itself and of the neighboring districts of Azerbaijan and Armenia once the conflict has been settled.

It is noteworthy that the US government report, like the relevant legislative acts, treats Nagorno-Karabakh as an independent entity. The documents speak of direct cooperation between US government organizations and the Nagorno-Karabakh authorities, as well as agencies of the Karabakh Cabinet of Ministers. In particular, they emphasize that the American humanitarian programs have been approved by the Nagorno-Karabakh Ministry of Public Health. Over the past three years, then, the US and Armenia have been the only countries providing official assistance to the government of Nagorno-Karabakh. This can only be interpreted as signifying the de facto recognition of the Nagorno-Karabakh Republic by those states.

It should be pointed out that the USAID programs are also of considerable humanitarian importance, both for the people of Nagorno-Karabakh and for citizens of Azerbaijan and Armenia hurt by the Karabakh conflict. In 1998-1999, according to the report, the US appropriated $11.8 million for programs within Nagorno-Karabakh, and $6.7 million for activities in adjacent areas that suffered during the armed conflict.... At present, only 70% of what was planned under these projects has actually been done. This is constant sore point for American lawmakers, especially members of the Armenian Caucus, a pro-Armenian congressional group. Representative Frank Pallone, the group's Democratic cochairman, recently leveled harsh criticism at USAID for its "sluggishness." The consistent stand taken by the congressmen has proven very fruitful. USAID has pledged to step up the American government's aid program for Nagorno-Karabakh. Not only is this of key importance for Nagorno-Karabakh from a socioeconomic standpoint; it will also yield obvious political dividends for the self-proclaimed republic.

However, the US government assistance programs for Nagorno-Karabakh have drawn an extremely negative reaction from the authorities in Baku. Commentators in Azerbaijan are talking more and more about "American treachery" and saying that America, "like Russia, has taken the Armenians' side." Azerbaijani politicians feel they can learn a great deal from the Armenians, who can teach Baku how to "sit on two stools at the same time: an American one and a Russian one." It is noteworthy that even official Yerevan now acknowledges this fact. Armenian Foreign Minister Vardan Oskanyan said recently that President Robert Kocharyan's policy of pursuing complementary foreign relations has become distinctly more popular lately. Oskanyan said that Azerbaijan is now inclined to take this route and is trying to balance its foreign policy. Many experts feel that this trend could ease tensions in the South Caucasus and foster better conditions for settling regional conflicts.

ANTICIPATING A KARABAKH BOOM – Washington Tries to Monopolize Role of Mediator Again

By Aleksandr Armand. *Nezavisimaya gazeta*, Nov. 3, 2000, p. 5.

An unexpected grand tour of Baku, Yerevan and Ankara by Stephen Sestanovich, the Clinton administration special envoy and adviser to the US secretary of state, has only further inflamed the domestic political situation in Azerbaijan. According to news reports from Baku, the main purpose of the American diplomat's visit was to strike a deal with the Azerbaijani authorities on the price that Baku will have to pay for silence on the part of the US and the international human rights institutions it controls, should Azerbaijan falsify the results of the upcoming Nov. 5 parliamentary elections. Most observers believe the Americans are asking for a moderation of Azerbaijan's position on the Nagorno-Karabakh conflict. Meanwhile, the official reason given for the Baku visit by Madeleine Albright's adviser was to discuss the prospects for a Karabakh settlement, and in particular for stepped-up bilateral dialogue between the presidents of Armenia and Azerbaijan. Characteristically, the US feels that this negotiating format is the most promising one, and Washington is confident that Armenian-Azerbaijani dialogue at the highest level will gain new momentum after Azerbaijan's parliamentary elections, as Sestanovich said after moving on to Yerevan. At the same time, it should be pointed out that the American diplomat is not as optimistic about the prospects for a resumption of negotiations under the main format for a Karabakh settlement the Minsk Group of the Organization for Security and Cooperation in Europe (the group is cochaired by Russia and France, as well as the US). Experts believe that Sestanovich's approach indicates that Washington intends to usurp the role of mediator and exploit the process of reaching a Karabakh settlement for the sole purpose of accomplishing the US's geopolitical objectives in the Greater Caucasus region....

Radio Liberty reports that Sestanovich made sure to lift slightly the curtain of confidentiality over the so-called problem of a potential exchange of territory between Armenia and Azerbaijan. After saying that there was no truth to speculation by the opposition that [Azerbaijani President] Aliyev and [Armenian President] Kocharyan had already reached agreement on one modification of the Goble plan, the American diplomat emphasized nonetheless that this plan and other proposals for achieving lasting peace and stability in the Transcaucasus "merit" serious discussion. Sestanovich could well attempt to conduct a key phase of that discussion in Ankara....

GUESTS OF GEORGE W. – After the Sultry Beaches of Florida, the Snows of the Swiss Alps Await Aliyev, Kocharyan

By Armen Khanbabyan. *Nezavisimaya gazeta*, April 11, 2001, p. 5.

After the Armenian and Azerbaijani presidents held an unprecedentedly lengthy summit in America's Key West to discuss a Karabakh settlement once more, Geidar

Aliyev and Robert Kocharyan were received by President George W. Bush at the White House. That in itself was intended to demonstrate Washington's high opinion of its own efforts in the peacemaking realm. The American president was known to have said beforehand that he would meet with the leaders of the opposing sides only if the talks in Florida were successful and productive.

No document was worked out in the course of the six-day talks: The sides only agreed to start working on yet another version of a possible accord. American diplomats are probably inclined to consider that an achievement, even though it's clear that this does not represent any real progress toward peace, only the preservation of the current status quo of "neither war nor peace."

Nevertheless, it can be assumed that Bush wouldn't really have passed up the chance to meet the presidents of Armenia and Azerbaijan and make their personal acquaintance, since such an opportunity might not present itself again for some time. Moreover, the meeting at the White House was meant to symbolize the American leader's deep personal interest in an early resolution of the Karabakh crisis. This is also consistent with the new Washington administration's desire to retain the initiative in the work of the cochairs of the OSCE Minsk Group on Karabakh at a time when Moscow and Paris are clearly stepping up their own activities. It's no accident that a White House spokesman hastened to emphasize that Vladimir Putin and Jacques Chirac are already actively engaged in a settlement process, "and now Bush and Secretary of State Powell have become directly involved in that process." According to ITAR-TASS, the spokesman added that "the work of the cochairs of the OSCE Minsk Group is an example of genuine partnership on the part of Washington, Moscow and Paris."

Geidar Aliyev and Robert Kocharyan each met separately with Bush and members of his team – Vice-President Richard Cheney, Secretary of State Colin Powell and National Security Adviser Condoleezza Rice. Both meetings were "held in an exceptionally warm atmosphere." The Azerbaijani president said that he had discussed with his American counterpart not only peacemaking issues, but also matters pertaining to the use of Caspian energy resources. Moreover, it was reiterated that relations between Washington and Baku are in the nature of a "strategic partnership" and will remain so.

Robert Kocharyan declined to share his impressions of the meeting with journalists, but Bush administration officials said during an unofficial briefing that the presidents had talked about the Karabakh conflict, the "historic ties between the American and Armenian peoples" and developmental prospects for the South Caucasus as a whole.

It was also learned that the next round of direct talks between Aliyev and Kocharyan would be held in Geneva in June, and that Colin Powell had already reached an agreement to that effect with his Swiss counterpart, who was also visiting Washington last week. However, it's quite likely that before that meeting, the presidents will visit Moscow in order to work toward agreement on a new set of proposals for settling the conflict that are already being drawn up by the foreign-policy departments of the mediating countries and of the opposing sides themselves.

IS WASHINGTON TURNING TOWARD BAKU? – Azerbaijan Pleased With the Bush Administration

By Asya Gadzhizade. *Nezavisimaya gazeta*, April 18, 2001, p. 5.

Baku – Geidar Aliyev is pleased with the results of the Karabakh peace talks held April 3-6 in Key West, in the American state of Florida, and with his meetings with the new US administration. Without going into detail, Aliyev told journalists in the Baku airport on Saturday [April 14] that the new US administration was working on the issue very actively and that this could help settle the conflict. It is worth noting that on March 30, just before the Key West talks, the US State Department released a background report on the Armenian-Azerbaijani conflict, including an assessment of it. For the first time, the State Department acknowledged that Azerbaijani territories were occupied by Armenian armed forces in conjunction with armed Karabakh separatists.

The report also includes a historical overview saying that large numbers of Armenians began settling in Karabakh after 1813, when the region was annexed to Russia, while the area's Azerbaijani population began declining. In addition, the report says that the city of Shusha, populated by Azerbaijanis, is the historical center of Karabakh. It also points out that the majority of the region's Azerbaijanis lived in Shusha, which was occupied by Armenian armed forces and Karabakh Armenians in May 1992.... The State Department report goes on to say that in 1993 the UN Security Council passed four resolutions urging an end to hostilities, the admission of international humanitarian forces to the region, and the deployment of peacekeeping forces there. The UN also called for the "immediate withdrawal of all Armenian forces from occupied territories of Azerbaijan."

Baku was clearly pleased with the State Department report, which was official Washington's first statement of facts of this nature. In contrast to the previous US administration, which took an ambiguous stance toward Azerbaijan, the new White House leadership is more forthright in assessing Azerbaijan's role in the Caucasus region. Behind all this, experts say, is a new approach on Washington's part toward the Caucasus region in general and toward Azerbaijan in particular. For example, Armenian sources say that the Washington administration has asked the US Congress to cut aid to Armenia in 2002 by 22% and to increase aid to Azerbaijan that year by 46%. If that happens, aid to Armenia will drop from $90 million to $70 million, while aid to Azerbaijan will go up from $34 million to $50 million.

The new approach in Washington was indirectly confirmed by a comment made by US Senator Richard Shelby of Alabama, who said at a meeting with Geidar Aliyev, "Although we have been friends with the Armenians for a long time, we must explain to the Armenian people that a continuation of this conflict promotes neither their short-term nor their long-term goals."...

BAKU BELIEVES THE AMERCANS ARE 'WRONG'

By Arkady Dubnov. *Vremya novostei*, Aug. 4, 2008, p. 5.

The latest meeting between Armenian and Azerbaijani Foreign Ministers Eduard Nalbandyan and Elmar Mamedyarov, which was held in Moscow on Aug. 1 and was devoted to searching for a compromise in resolving the Karabakh conflict, led to an uproar in Baku. It was caused not by the meeting itself, but by a statement made afterwards by the American cochairman of the Minsk Group, Matthew Bryza....

Nalbandyan said after the talks that he and his counterpart "were able to discuss all issues on the agenda at the meeting" and "when we say that the meeting was constructive, we are not just trying to put a good spin on things."...

The Azerbaijani minister was cautiously optimistic in his assessment of the Moscow talks: "I listened carefully to the Armenian side and we each understand where the other is coming from, but a breakthrough is still a long way off."...

Such a positive tone in the assessment of ministerial meetings between the two conflicting sides is quite unusual, and therefore encouraging. According to Nalbandyan, agreement was reached in Moscow to continue negotiations on the basis of the Madrid proposals for settling the Karabakh conflict within the framework of the OSCE Minsk Group, "in order to bring the sides' positions closer together."

But right after the ministers' meeting, when the American cochairman announced the proposals that he himself had allegedly presented to the two sides, Baku immediately cast doubt on Azerbaijan's willingness to accept them. In an interview with the BBC, Mr. Bryza said: "We proposed the withdrawal of Armenian troops from seven regions around Nagorno-Karabakh, the deployment of international peacekeepers, the return of internally displaced persons and refugees and the creation of an international corridor connecting Armenia and Nagorno-Karabakh.[1] There should also be a form of voting to determine the future of Nagorno-Karabakh." At the same time, the American diplomat admitted that "we don't know exactly when this will happen."

These proposals by the Minsk Group are well known, although previously, in compliance with agreements reached with the parties to the conflict, the Minsk Group's cochairmen had not disclosed them so openly and publicly. The uproar in Baku was caused by different words that Interfax quoted the American as saying: "The residents of Nagorno-Karabakh will decide for themselves whether the republic will be under Azerbaijan's jurisdiction or gain independence. A referendum will be conducted in which the people of Karabakh will determine their own fate."

Baku also noticed a report that was immediately posted on the Interfax Web site noting "the undisguised joy in Abkhazia and South Ossetia over Matthew Bryza's latest statement on Nagorno-Karabakh." In the unrecognized republics striving for independence from Georgia, any hint at the possibility of Nagorno-Karabakh's gaining state sovereignty will be received with delight as a precedent.

The key word in the diplomat's statement and the one that caused indignation in Azerbaijan was "republic," used in reference to Nagorno-Karabakh. Needless to say, Baku was also upset by his allowing for the possibility that the "republic" could gain independence....

One can only guess as to whether Bryza really did leak information from the confidential and very delicate Armenian-Azerbaijani talks on a Karabakh settlement. And if the answer is yes, what goal was he pursuing in doing so? What he said will hardly be a valuable political present for Azerbaijani President Ilkham Aliyev two and a half months before the presidential election, in which he will be running for a second term....

President Aliyev's position in the run-up to the election appears so unshakable that going up against him seems completely pointless. Therefore, it is easier to consider Bryza as "wrong when he pulls the idea of voting on the status of Nagorno-Karabakh out of the entire context of the talks," as is now being done in Azerbaijan.

ALIYEV SETS SIGHTS ON WASHINGTON

By Sokhbet Mamedov. *Nezavisimaya gazeta*, Jan. 24, 2017, p. 6.

On Jan. 20, Azerbaijan honored the memory of victims of the events of 1990, which went down in the country's history as Bloody January. But another event took place on this date [in 2017] that had Azeris just as riveted – the inauguration of the 45th US president. The fact of the matter is that under the Democrats, relations between Washington and Baku have not been as rosy as the country's authorities would have liked. Now, Azerbaijan's leaders have hopes for positive [developments].

Over the past few years, despite outwardly smooth relations, the previous White House administration surreptitiously sought to interfere in Azerbaijan's domestic affairs. However, all of those attempts were met with resistance and the independent policy of President Ilkham Aliyev. In retaliation, Washington repeatedly tried to resort to its cherished tactic of instigating a color revolution in Azerbaijan.

A few years ago, controversy erupted between Baku and Washington over the activities of the Azerbaijan representative office of the National Democracy Institute (NDI), a US organization. [Azerbaijani] authorities accused NDI of organizing a so-called Facebook revolution. It was established that between March 2, 2010, and Dec. 13, 2012, $1.7 billion had been withdrawn – without any indication for what purpose – from an account at the International Bank of Azerbaijan belonging to the head of the local NDI office. Those funds were entirely at the disposal and under the personal discretion of NDI's Baku office director Alex Grigorievs. Revolutionaries in Georgia call him "father"; in Moldova, they call him "commander in chief"; in Ukraine he is called a "purveyor of democracy"; and in Russia, he is known as the main [protest] rally theorist. These days, many experts agree that wherever this man who was seemingly past his prime would show up, riots would break out; wherever he would set foot, revolutions and tectonic processes would follow, resulting in a change in the sociopolitical formation. However, those plans ran up against a wall in Baku.

Against this backdrop, it is understandable why Azerbaijan is so attuned to the power change in Washington. Official Baku has said that it wishes to develop partner-like relations with the US. Aliyev expressed hope in his congratulatory letter to [US President] Donald Trump that bilateral relations between Azerbaijan and the US would continue to thrive. And Ali Gasanov, presidential aide in charge of public policy, said that Baku is hoping the US will step up efforts to settle the Nagorno-Karabakh conflict.

"There is cooperation between the two countries in many areas. This cooperation will continue," Gasanov stressed. According to him, Baku expects the new White House administration to support it on the Nagorno-Karabakh issue, and believes that the US will be more active in the OSCE Minsk Group.

It should be noted that most local analysts believe that several provisions of Donald Trump's inauguration speech jibe with Azerbaijan's foreign policy. According to philosophy professor Elkhan Aleskerov, head of the Baku Network expert council, "Many countries around the world, including Azerbaijan, expect the new US administration to restructure the world order, and reformat the outdated and inefficient UN system," as well as scale back White House "interventions in the domestic affairs of independent countries."

They also expect Trump to change the US's position on Islamic radical groups and to begin supporting secular countries with Muslim populations, of which Azerbaijan is a prime example.

According to Aleskerov, those issues unfortunately "went unnoticed" by some members of the previous administration, and "questionable bills, like the bill from New Jersey Congressman Chris Smith,"[2] aimed against Azerbaijan, were even initiated in the US Congress.

"However, US President Donald Trump's inauguration speech suggests that the Republicans who have come to power in Washington will not make the mistakes of the Democrats. The US leadership will value its partnership ties with Azerbaijan while avoiding the negative impact of anti-Azerbaijani forces on bilateral relations," the expert said.

NOTES

1. Bryza's actual phrase was "creation of a certain kind of communication between Armenia and Karabakh,"

2. Congressman Smith introduced a bill in December 2015 seeking to prevent top-level Azerbaijani officials from obtaining US visas because of what he called "appalling human rights violations" in Azerbaijan.

Part Four |

Revived Conflict and Ramifications

Chapter 12 | The Four-Day War

CEASEFIRE UNDER ATTACK

By Olga Kuznetsova and Ivan Safronov. *Kommersant*, April 4, 2016, p. 1.

Clashes have erupted in the Armenian-Azerbaijani conflict zone – the most serious since 1994, when the parties reached a ceasefire agreement halting the hot phase of the war over Nagorno-Karabakh. Dozens have been killed, and Yerevan, Baku and Stepanakert are reporting the destruction of enemy helicopters and armored vehicles. Despite the fierce fighting, most experts queried by Kommersant believe that a full-scale war will be avoided. Neither side is currently prepared for [war]. International mediators are actively seeking to reach a ceasefire: The OSCE Minsk Group will hold a consultation tomorrow in Vienna, and later, Russian Prime Minister Dmitry Medvedev will visit Yerevan while Foreign Minister Sergei Lavrov visits Baku.

The escalation began the night of April 1 along the entire line of contact between Armenian and Azerbaijani Armed Forces, and involved armored vehicles, multiple rocket launchers and aircraft. "I ordered [soldiers] not to succumb to provocations, but the enemy completely let loose," explained Azerbaijani President Ilkham Aliyev. The Armenian Defense Ministry announced "offensive actions by the Azerbaijani side" and condemned Baku for the decision "to penetrate the rear of the Nagorno-Karabakh Defense Army and assume strategic positions."

Moscow reacted swiftly to the escalation. According to a Kommersant Russian military source, President Vladimir Putin has been getting regular updates on the situation in Nagorno-Karabakh. "We have analyzed all possible scenarios," he said. The Kremlin announced Saturday afternoon [April 2] that the president "urges the parties to the conflict to cease fire immediately and exercise restraint to prevent further loss of life." According to Kommersant, the situation in Nagorno-Karabakh may be discussed at the next meeting of the Russian Security Council.

According to Kommersant, Mr. Putin subsequently instructed Russia's defense and foreign ministers to negotiate with their counterparts in Armenia and Azerbaijan. In the afternoon, it became known that Russian Defense Minister Sergei Shoigu had held urgent telephone conversations with [Armenian Defense Minister] Seiran Oganyan and [Azerbaijani Defense Minister] Zakir Hasanov, calling on the parties to take "immediate measures to stabilize the situation in the conflict zone." At the same time, Russian Foreign Minister Sergei Lavrov talked with [Armenian President] Serzh Sargsyan and [Azerbaijani Foreign Minister] Elmar Mamedyarov, stating the need to act to stop the violence.

Collective Security Treaty Organization General Secretary Nikolai Bordyuzha also held telephone conversations with Seiran Oganyan and with Armenian Foreign Minister Eduard Nalbandyan. According to Art. 4 of the Collective Security Treaty, any state that is attacked may ask other parties to provide necessary assistance, including military assistance. A Kommersant source in the Armenian Defense Ministry yesterday confirmed that if Azerbaijani Armed Forces invade the country, Yerevan would be ready to ask the CSTO to deploy [its] Collective Rapid Reaction Forces.

However, the active fighting is so far taking place in Nagorno-Karabakh and adjacent territories outside the area of the CSTO's responsibility. As for Armenia, Yerevan claims that Azerbaijani artillery is shelling border districts, but acknowledges that the opponent is not taking offensive actions. Accordingly, there is still no formal pretext for appealing to the CSTO. "But if the scenario unfolding in Nagorno-Karabakh is repeated on Armenian territory, Yerevan is guaranteed to ask the CSTO for help under the terms of the agreement," Kommersant's interlocutor in the Armenian Defense Ministry warned....

Although Baku announced a unilateral halt of all military operations on the line of contact at midday yesterday, Stepanakert denied this information, accusing the Azerbaijani side of new shelling. The Armenian Defense Ministry called Baku's statement about the suspension of fighting an "information trap." The fighting continued.

"For Azerbaijan, the flare-up is a peculiar form of capital that can be monetized," a high-ranking Armenian government official told Kommersant. "Fighting usually breaks out along the contact line ahead of important international events involving the Azerbaijani leadership." "There is no point for Yerevan to keep fighting any longer," director of Armenia's Caucasus Institute Aleksandr Iskanderyan told Kommersant. "The Armenians will maintain their positions; they have no temptation to seize Baku or carve out a corridor to the Caspian Sea."

Yerevan complains that there is no objective oversight mechanism on the contact line. Azerbaijani Foreign Minister Elmar Mamedyarov responded to this in a recent Kommersant interview. "Armenia is raising this issue to divert attention from the conflict and to continue to occupy Azerbaijani territory," he said. "Armenian troops should leave Azerbaijani territory; there would be no more incidents, and there would be nothing at all to investigate."

The flare-up along the contact line has encouraged international mediators to try to resolve the conflict through diplomatic channels. On Tuesday, the OSCE Minsk Group cochairs (Russia, France, the US) handling the Armenian-Azerbaijani conflict settlement will hold consultations in Vienna. Prior to this, the Minsk Group issued a statement condemning the use of force and calling on the parties to stabilize the situation.

Azerbaijan harshly criticizes the activities of the Minsk Group. Baku has repeatedly complained that [the Minsk Group's] efforts have stalled for good. During the previous flare-up on the contact line, Ilkham Aliyev called the organization "absolutely pointless" and accused it of trying to "freeze the conflict, not resolve it." The Azerbaijani president said yesterday that "the decisions of the Minsk Group have no effect on the Armenian leadership."

Yerevan has a different take. "The mediators' efforts should be aimed primarily at establishing dialogue, organizing meetings and bringing the positions of the sides closer together, rather than pressuring one side or the other," Armenian Foreign Minister Eduard Nalbandyan said in a recent interview with Kommersant.

Rasim Musabekov, a parliamentary deputy from [Azerbaijan's] opposition Musavat (Equality) party told Kommersant that the activities of the Minsk Group have been fruitless for a long time. "The Minsk Group must take a principled stance; [it must] require Yerevan to comply with UN Security Council resolutions and withdraw its Armed Forces from Azerbaijani territory." Under the current conditions, he said, "Azerbaijan has no other option but to rely on its own forces and on the right to ensure its territorial integrity."

As for Yerevan, it considers the Minsk Group "an effective instrument for maintaining security in the region." "There is no alternative to this mechanism," Aleksandr Iskanderyan believes....

Kommersant's interlocutors in Baku believe that Russia must jump-start efforts to resolve the Nagorno-Karabakh conflict.

"Moscow could facilitate the implementation of agreements that would get Armenia's Armed Forces to pull out of Azerbaijani territory," says Rasim Musabekov. "Only then would it make sense to convene a summit of the leaders of Russia, Azerbaijan and Armenia."...

Rasim Musabekov ruled out the possibility of returning to the 2011 agreements. "The [2011] summit in Kazan was supposed to formalize the existing status quo; Azerbaijan was asked to provide guarantees it would not use force even as its territory continued to be occupied indefinitely," he told Kommersant. "But in response, we heard only vague promises that someday the Armenian side would allegedly withdraw its Armed Forces." Yerevan's recollection of the Kazan talks is no more enthusiastic. "For us, a scenario where we would give the Azeris even three square meters on the contact line – to say nothing of six districts – is unthinkable," says Aleksandr Iskanderyan. According to him, the line of defense that was constructed over the years costs billions of dollars, and the Armenian side has no reason to modify its configuration, which would expose it to potential danger in the future....

RUSSIA'S ROLE IN SETTLING THE NAGORNO-KARABAKH PROBLEM

By Vladimir Mukhin. *Nezavisimaya gazeta*, April 4, 2016, p. 3.

The fighting that began on the night of April 1 in Nagorno-Karabakh, the most significant since the [1994] ceasefire, caused understandable concern among Russia's leadership. President Vladimir Putin and Defense Minister Sergei Shoigu urged the parties to the conflict to cease fire immediately. And now [Russia's] military-political leadership is planning to head to Baku for relevant negotiations. Last Sunday, even though both sides said that the hostilities were winding down, mutual shelling still continued along the line of contact between Armenian and Azerbaijani forces, albeit not as intensely.

The international community is naturally concerned; the most pessimistic development scenarios are being forecasted. And perhaps one of the main questions for the Russian leadership now is what to do next.

The answer to this question is very important, because Moscow is largely responsible for this conflict – not only as a cochair of the Minsk Group, but also as Baku's and Yerevan's main partner on military-technical cooperation. It is no big secret that over the past five or six years, Azerbaijan has tripled the volume of its weapons business with Russia, and the total cost of military contracts is estimated at about $4 billion. Russia is wrapping up delivery to this country of almost the entire list of key weapons for the Ground Troops (T-90S tanks, infantry combat vehicles, Msta-S self-propelled howitzers, TOS-1A heavy flamethrower systems, as well as Smerch multiple rocket launchers) – enough weaponry to equip several mechanized brigades. Meanwhile, Azerbaijan has already received two battalions of S-300PMU-2 air defense systems, several Tor-M2E air defense batteries, as well as a few dozen Mi-17V-1 military transport helicopters and Mi-35M attack helicopters.

Military-technical cooperation with Armenia is also in full swing. For example, in February 2016, an agreement entered into force to supply that country on a $200 million arms loan several divisions of Smerch multiple rocket launchers, Igla-S surface-to-air missile systems, RPG-26 grenade launchers, Dragunov sniper rifles, TOS-1A heavy flamethrower systems, etc.

A simple analysis of the information coming from the conflict zone in Nagorno-Karabakh shows that perhaps some of these weapons are already being used in combat. And this raises another question: Does this make Russia, shall we say, a stimulator of the conflict between Armenia and Azerbaijan?

As is known, this question is being discussed at the diplomatic level. And perhaps it's no coincidence that a month ago, when Russia's weapons contract with Yerevan went into effect, Azerbaijan's Foreign Ministry issued a note to Moscow demanding: "These weapons must not end up in the occupied territories of Azerbaijan" – i.e., these weapons must not be transferred to the Nagorno-Karabakh Defense Army. As Azerbaijani Foreign Minister Elmar Mamedyarov stated two weeks ago, this was one of the main topics of discussion when [Russian] Deputy Prime Minister Dmitry Rogozin paid an urgent visit to Baku in early March 2016. And Mamedyarov at the time claimed that Russia had "properly perceived" the foreign ministry's note.

As can be seen from the Kremlin's statements, Moscow opposes a military solution to the Nagorno-Karabakh conflict. And Russia's involvement in strengthening Azerbaijan's and Armenia's combat potential apparently comes with the caveat that they must not link their national defense problems to the territorial disputes that exist between them.

Military-technological cooperation is, of course, a very delicate business. However, it seems that Russia has chosen the correct position in its arms trade with Armenia and Azerbaijan. Without Moscow, the military-technological trading niche with Baku would be filled by other countries. (Azerbaijan currently ranks second in Europe in terms of arms procurement.) And then, of course, there is tough competition. In addition to Moscow, Baku is making arms deals with Turkey, Israel and some CIS countries. Russia's militarily assistance to poor Armenia is dictated by geopolitical interests – primarily to counter Turkey.

Armenia is Russia's ally. But Azerbaijan is by and large also a partner and an ally. And Moscow doesn't fight with allies. All it can do is once again try to reinvigorate the peace process, and wait for the parties to show good will and sit down at the table for constructive negotiations on resolving the conflict.

ARMENIA MAY ASK PARTNERS AWKWARD QUESTIONS

By Yury Roks. *Nezavisimaya gazeta*, April 7, 2016, p. 6.

... There has been more than 24 hours of calm in the unrecognized Nagorno-Karabakh Republic. The conflicting parties are starting to reach agreements through the Red Cross on exchanging the dead and are trying to learn what happened to the missing. The ceasefire is being generally observed. The results of the sudden military flare-up along the entire contact line are perhaps currently reduced only to the inevitable consequences of any military campaign. The positions held by the sides on the contact line have not changed. But there are some changes in political positions. Statements have begun to be heard in Baku that Azerbaijan has not assumed any obligations not to use force. Does this mean that Baku is ready to formally withdraw from the agreements ending the war in Nagorno-Karabakh, as outlined in the Bishkek peace agreement of May 5, 1994, and that it is also abandoning a number of high-level "pacifist" agreements on Nagorno-Karabakh signed in subsequent years? Obviously, this needs to be explained to the OSCE Minsk Group cochairs, who are preparing to visit the region.

Turkey has moved in the opposite direction. Ankara claims that the country's leadership not only did not encourage Baku's aggressive action, but in fact urged Russia to direct joint efforts at reducing tensions. If they say so. If this serves to strengthen peace in the region, it is possible to forget that Turkish Prime Minister Ahmet Davutoglu congratulated Azerbaijan's leaders on their military successes.

In Armenia, the Nagorno-Karabakh conflict underscored the issue of relations with its partners in the post-Soviet space. For example, the public is wondering whether the Eurasian Economic Union (EaEU) should continue to be considered a purely economic alliance. The decision to move the EaEU summit from Yerevan to Moscow, so that it did not look like the union supported one of the parties to the conflict, speaks to the contrary. In any case, the decision on the venue for the meeting was made long before the flare-up in Nagorno-Karabakh; one of the parties to the conflict is not an EaEU member; and Yerevan itself is a considerable distance from the fighting, so nothing did (or could have) threatened the security of the summit participants. Meanwhile, Kazakhstan's refusal to participate in the summit in the Armenian capital looked more like a boycott than anything else.

However, Kazakhstan's position did not particularly surprise anyone. [Kazakh] President Nursultan Nazarbayev has never concealed the fact that he believes the only way to resolve the Armenian-Azerbaijani problem is to restore Baku's jurisdiction over Nagorno-Karabakh. Moreover, both states, Kazakhstan and Azerbaijan, are bound by close economic cooperation, a number of interesting projects, and in addition, play leading roles in the Turkic Council.

But how does all this correlate with Armenia's and Kazakhstan's membership and partnership in the CSTO military-political bloc? Is it conceivable that, in a war between a NATO member and a non-NATO country, some alliance members would take the side of the "outsider," despite the well-known Art. 5 of the NATO Charter?[1] This "Art. 5," meanwhile, is expressed in almost identical terms in the very name of the CSTO. Yerevan, of course, is soberly assessing the situation – especially in light of the fact that hostilities broke out between Azerbaijan and Nagorno-Karabakh, which, despite [its] proximity to Armenia, cannot be identified with it. Therefore, the CSTO's military capabilities and jurisdiction do not extend to Nagorno-Karabakh. The Armenian side never expected or requested any help from Kazakhstan or any of its CSTO partners. But anti-Armenian political remarks from CSTO allies were an unpleasant surprise for Yerevan. And not just for Yerevan. Sometimes for rational reasons – such as to maintain the organization's image – its members have to refrain from statements that demonstrate anything but unity in the military (!) bloc that is vying to be an alternative to NATO. Yerevan was especially stung by a statement from Belarus, whose ambassador was summoned to the Armenian Foreign Ministry for clarification. Afterward, Minsk issued a new, markedly altered statement regarding the situation in Nagorno-Karabakh in which calls for peace prevailed....

BAKU INSISTS ON CHANGING STATUS QUO IN NAGORNO-KARABAKH CONFLICT

By Sokhbet Mamedov. *Nezavisimaya gazeta*, April 21, 2016, p. 6.

Baku – The situation at the line of contact in the areas of Azerbaijan occupied by Armenia remains troubled. The Azerbaijani Defense Ministry's press service reported to NG that, despite the ceasefire agreement initiated and brokered by Russia, Armenia continues to escalate the situation along the front line....

Meanwhile, Russian Foreign Minister Sergei Lavrov and Armenian President Serzh Sargsyan are visiting the Nagorno-Karabakh region on a peacemaking mission. Sargsyan's trip to the occupied territories to discuss military matters was characterized by Azerbaijan's Foreign Ministry as another provocative step that will further complicate an already trying situation.

"By taking such actions, [which are] contrary to the rules and principles of international law and the UN Charter, the Armenian leadership once again proves that it is pursuing a policy to annex the occupied territories of Azerbaijan," commented Khikmet Gadzhiyev, head of the Azerbaijani Foreign Ministry's press service. According to him, this irresponsible step by the Armenian leader is the latest confirmation that it was Yerevan that initiated the April 2 escalation of tensions along the contact line, which violated the [1994] ceasefire.

"In order to prevent a repeat of recent events, resolve the conflict and ensure security in the region, Armenian troops must withdraw from all occupied territories of Azerbaijan. The sooner the Armenian authorities realize this, the sooner peace will reign in the region," Gadzhiyev said. However, it seems that Yerevan does not want to listen to this advice. On the contrary, all Armenian forces, as well as the Armenian lobby abroad (including in Russia), are rallying to accuse Baku of aggression. Another such attempt was made in the German city of Leinsweiler, where the Parliamentary Assembly of the Organization for Security and Cooperation in Europe (OSCE PA) held a seminar on how the PA and its members could contribute to OSCE confliction resolution efforts – focusing particularly on protracted conflicts. Commenting on statements made by members of the Armenian delegation, Bakhar Muradova, deputy speaker of the Milli Majlis and head of the Azerbaijani delegation to the OSCE PA, told seminar participants about the true intentions of the Armenian Armed Forces' General Staff. She cited a February statement by Armenian Deputy Defense Minister David Tanoyan. The gist of the Armenian general's statement was that the Army needs to quickly adopt a conceptually new military doctrine that would expand the zone of occupation in the foothills as far eastward as possible, providing for preventive strikes [by Armenia] in the event of the slightest suspicion of Azerbaijani forces being mustered along the contact line.

According to Muradova, the recent outbreak of hostilities in the occupied areas was an attempt by the Armenian top brass to test out that very doctrine of a preventive strike.

"Everyone knows what happened next: The sudden strike failed. Instead, the Armenian troops not only met fierce resistance, but fled from a rapid counterattack by a limited contingent of the Azerbaijani Army," Muradova stated.

[OSCE PA] leaders are calling for immediate changes to the status quo in the Nagorno-Karabakh conflict, as are [other] prestigious international organizations. Similar thoughts were expressed a few days ago by Turkish Prime Minister Ahmet Davutoglu.

Speaking from the rostrum of the Parliamentary Assembly of the Council of Europe, Davutoglu urged the international community to warn Yerevan about the inadmissibility of armed provocations in the Karabakh conflict zone.

Meanwhile, recent events along the contact line have shown the world that the time has come to seriously address the protracted conflict. Otherwise, war will break out, leading to unpredictable consequences for all countries in the region. To prevent this from happening, said Azerbaijani Ambassador to Russia Polad Bulbuloglu in a recent statement, the root cause must be removed. That root cause is the Armenian occupation of Azerbaijani territory, which is an internationally recognized fact. The ambassador commented that Azerbaijan has long asked [Armenia] to start by releasing five districts (occupied by Armenia and adjacent to Nagorno-Karabakh – *Ed.*) and then begin peace talks on the future of Nagorno-Karabakh....

TRANSCAUCASUS HAS NO ALTERNATIVE TO RUSSIA

By political analyst Oleg Matveichev, professor at the National Research University Higher School of Economics. *Izvestia*, May 19, 2016, p. 6.

A ceasefire was reached at recent negotiations of the heads of Armenia and Azerbaijan with the participation of the OSCE Minsk Group cochairs. The parties agreed to return to the ceasefire agreement signed in 1994 with Russia's mediation. However, the question remains: How long will the truce reached in Vienna last?

The ethnic confrontation between Azerbaijan and Armenia escalated into armed clashes in 1991. The Nagorno-Karabakh Republic was then proclaimed in parts of the region following a referendum. In the last 10 years, the conflict has been frozen, primarily due to the efforts of the international mediators.

Why was the international community interested in ending the conflict? Russia, first and foremost, does not need a war in the Transcaucasus, especially since our country has established good relations with both Azerbaijan and Armenia.

For a certain period of time, this conflict was not in the interests of Russia's nearest neighbors, Turkey and Iran, either. Oddly enough, even the US (which usually relishes using conflicts in Eurasia in its interests) did not need the war in Nagorno-Karabakh. But this is a special case: American corporations that refine and trade oil are working in Azerbaijan, so [the US] is not interested in destabilization there. Therefore, the pressure of the oil companies and the Armenian lobby (the Armenian diaspora is one of the largest in the US) on Washington was so strong that the US sided with Armenia in the peace process. Some [US] states even recognized the independence of Nagorno-Karabakh despite Washington's position.

After the 1994 agreement was signed, it seemed that the conflict had died down and other options could be considered for resolving it, even though both sides continued to insist on pursuing their own interests. Baku would like to see Armenia unblock territory that belonged to [Azerbaijan] historically and where the population is predominantly Azeri. Armenia would like to receive assurances from Azerbaijan regarding the integrity of Nagorno-Karabakh.

In such a difficult situation, relations between the two states can only be balanced on the basis of mutual trust that is gained over time.

Then suddenly, the so-called four-day April war broke out, with each side accusing the other of starting it.

It is not hard to speculate that certain interests prompted the new stirring of the conflict – i.e., Turkey. After losing international standing, Turkish President Recep Erdogan decided to teach our country a lesson for our response to the downing of a Russian bomber, as well as for [Russia's anti-Turkish] sanctions.

It was easy for Erdogan to aggravate the conflict, since almost the entire Azerbaijani elite have close ties to Turkish businesses and the establishment. Azerbaijani banks cooperate with Turkish banks; the two countries have established agricultural ties and are developing close military cooperation. In addition, experts say that it remains to be seen who the Azerbaijani Army reports to – the Turkish or Azerbaijani leadership. Some believe that Turkish leader Recep Erdogan pressured some of the Azerbaijani military to provoke new tensions in the hot spot. Perhaps they're right.

But there is another viewpoint that is also plausible. Arguably, Ilkham Aliyev himself could have needed the conflict. An economic crisis related to a fall in oil prices has devalued the national currency, triggering a drop in living standards in Azerbaijan and a decline in the popularity of Aliyev, who has become hostage to oil politics and local nationalists. To restore his ratings, he needed to do something remarkable. It is hard to do that with the economy. At the same time, by participating in the territorial conflict, the Azerbaijani leader appears like a protector of his country's territorial integrity.

Therefore, in reigniting an old conflict, Erdogan sought to exact revenge on Russia, and Aliyev sought to boost his ratings.

The parties are complaining that they didn't even agree on a truce yet, and it is already being violated. But it is easy to assume that this situation will persist as long as Azerbaijan and Turkey are using the conflict in their interests.

It should be said that the US and the European Union are also trying to play their own card. The EU and the US need to redeem themselves after the embarrassment in Syria, where the main recipient of political dividends was Russia, which conducted a brilliant peacekeeping operation and scored a number of diplomatic victories. Hence the attempt to play on the Armenian-Azerbaijani conflict and bring the two heads of state to the negotiating table, seizing the chief peacemaker role from Russia.

That attempt failed, mind you. It was clear that the April war ended thanks to Moscow's efforts, and Russia's role at the Vienna talks proved decisive. So, they did not manage to usurp Russia's leading role in resolving this matter and [handling issues] in the Transcaucasus in general.

Moreover, the prospect of solving the problem of the Transcaucasus is only possible if our country's role is strengthened. Historically, Russia played the role of peacemaker in the region during the Russian imperial era and during the Soviet period. Incidentally, the demise of the USSR led to a flowering of nationalism, many conflicts and victims.

The former Soviet republics have tried to live differently. Georgia came under US influence, severing all ties with Russia. But after a serious drop in living standards, it is slowly but surely returning to the Russian fold. Surrounded by hostile Turkey, Iran and other countries, it has no other option.

Armenia has also experienced democratic or "electric" revolutions,[2] but the Armenian people are smart enough not to sever ties with Russia.

Azerbaijan also tried its game on the oil field with Iran, Turkey and others, but it began to lose prosperity. The frailty of the economy and the desovereignization of the state that have resulted from mixing the Azerbaijani and Turkish elites have become a real threat.

One way or the other, the Transcaucasus republics are beginning to recognize that there is no alternative to Russia. Armenia was the first to realize this, which is why it has been an EaEU member for a year now. Similar processes are likely in the near future for Georgia and Azerbaijan.

FROM TURKEY TO KARABAKH: WHAT'S BEHIND THE 'UPRISING' IN ARMENIA?

By Mikhail Tishchenko. *Slon.ru*, July 18, 2016, https://slon.ru/posts/70942.

On July 17, a group of armed men seized a police station in Yerevan. They rammed the gate with a truck, shot a police officer [dead] and took the others hostage. The attackers were supporters of Zhirair Sefilyan, a veteran of the Nagorno-Karabakh war and now an opposition figure who was recently arrested on charges of illegal possession of weapons. They demanded his release, which the authorities refused. The radical part of the Armenian opposition supported the act, describing it as the beginning of an "armed uprising." However, the rebellion – if one can call it that – has not gone any further as yet.

The hostages were taken by a group that calls itself Sasna Tsrer (Daredevils of Sasun, named for a national epic about heroes from Sasun, a region in historical Armenia; [the epic is] better known as "David of Sasun" – *Ed.*). The station was attacked by about 25 men, including Nagorno-Karabakh war veterans. They were reportedly well armed and refused to surrender.

The attackers are supporters of the Founding Parliament, an opposition movement created several years ago by Zhirair Sefilyan and others. Its representatives have staged events calling for "regime change" (they blame the regime for the systemic crisis that the country has ended up in), and urging the creation of "pockets of resistance throughout the country" and the formation of alternative bodies of power.

Movement activists have been repeatedly arrested on various charges, including illegal trafficking of ammunition and preparation of mass disturbances. The Armenian National Security Service has described those who attacked the police station as terrorists.

Zhirair Sefilyan is a native of Beirut (he was born into an Armenian family and was active in a local chapter of the Dashnaktsutyun party). He came to Armenia in the early 1990s as a military instructor. He fought in Nagorno-Karabakh and participated in fighting to take control of the city of Shusha. Later, he served in the army of the unrecognized Nagorno-Karabakh republic and after demobilization went into politics. He has been arrested a number of times. Last year, he told reporters that the government was weak and that if a people's uprising got under way, the Army would support it.

How are the authorities handling the current incident?

The police station has been cordoned off. Entry points to Erebuni Borough, where it is located, have been closed. Internal Troops and police forces, including armored vehicles, have been brought in. Residents of adjacent buildings have been evacuated.

On Sunday, July 17, there were reports that a storming operation had begun, but they were not officially confirmed (according to some sources, security forces tried to neutralize the attackers, but with no success). As of midday Monday, the authorities were continuing negotiations. Several hostages have been released, with five police officers still [being held] at the station, including two Armenian deputy police chiefs).

There have been mass detentions of opposition members in Yerevan and other cities (in particular Gyumri and Vanadzor). They are reportedly being questioned about involvement with the group that seized the police station, as well as with the Founding Parliament. The police detained a total of about 200 people. As of the morning of July 18, about 50 of them had been released.

What brought all this on?

The attack was prompted by Sefilyan's arrest, which took place about a month ago. It is difficult to say whether his associates believed they would be able to exchange him for hostages. According to journalist Aik Khalatyan, after his arrest, representatives of the Founding Parliament also felt threatened. It is possible that they were afraid they would be arrested too, and decided to "take preemptive action."

After the station was seized, the Founding Parliament announced that this was the beginning of an uprising. "Dear fellow citizens, considering the situation prevailing in the country, we have decided to ensure a free and worthy future for the next generation. We are starting an armed uprising," Varuzhan Avetisyan, one of its leaders, wrote on social media.

However, his claims regarding the supposed uprising (for example, the oppositionists had purportedly taken control of Erebuni Borough and enlisted the support of "members of the Armed Forces") have not been confirmed. Nor have the radicals received significant support from the public.

In recent years, the Armenian opposition has made several attempts to organize a [wave of protests like those on Kiev's] Independence Square. Even though there are quite a few war veterans among its supporters, including some who have access to firearms, these protests have mainly taken the form of rallies and pressure on the authorities, rather than attempts at an armed uprising (the 2008 public rallies that erupted after the presidential election grew into riots [only] after the police tried to disperse demonstrators).

According to Khalatyan, the level of discontent with the authorities in Armenia is high, but few support the radical opposition. The same goes for their recipes for a change of government. "The country is in a state of war with neighboring Azerbaijan, and under these circumstances, people do not want to provoke internal political upheavals in the country," he says.

The Nagorno-Karabakh conflict is a significant factor. Even if the uprising does result in a change of government, that could result in a civil confrontation. For Azerbaijan, which has often declared its willingness to recover its lost territory by any means, including military force, a crisis in Armenia would be a favorable opportunity to make such an attempt. A new government in Yerevan could be faced with the threat of a new war, the outcome of which would also determine its fate.

What's Turkey got to do with it?

The opposition announced the beginning of the "uprising" soon after the failed coup in Turkey. Some thought this was no coincidence. According to political commentator Andrei Buzarov, the Armenian opposition may have used the events in Istanbul merely as an excuse to attract additional attention: "They decided to promote themselves by claiming that a change of government was under way in the country."

There are also conspiracy theories linking the latest events to talks on the Nagorno-Karabakh conflict, the next round of which had been set for July 18. Purportedly, Turkey could have made certain concessions on Nagorno-Karabakh (it generally supports Azerbaijan, and its border with Armenia is closed). So certain forces tried to prevent that – first through the Istanbul uprising, then with the destabilization in Yerevan.

The events in Yerevan have also been linked to Nagorno-Karabakh in another sense. The Azerbaijani press views them as an attempt to prevent possible concessions by Yerevan in the conflict resolution talks. According to one theory, this was also the objective of the 1999 terrorist attack in the Armenian parliament that claimed the lives of members of the country's top leadership (the terrorist attack was preceded by negotiations that could have resulted in an exchange of territory with Azerbaijan).

Sefilyan and his supporters have repeatedly accused the authorities of intending to surrender the territory of Nagorno-Karabakh to Azerbaijan. Following the recent escalation of the conflict, when Azerbaijani troops occupied some positions on the line of contact and official Yerevan refused to recover them by force, the opposition leader said he was ready to organize an unofficial operation to "restore the integrity" of Nagorno-Karabakh. As a result, Sefilyan's supporters assert, the authorities chose to sideline him.

Granted, this is not the first time that rumors have circulated about Armenia's willingness to make concessions on the Nagorno-Karabakh conflict (according to one theory, Yerevan is being prodded by Moscow to make certain concessions – for example, to let Azerbaijan into the buffer zone around Nagorno-Karabakh). However, no territories have yet been transferred through negotiations. Such a decision would spark serious protests in Armenia, and not only on the part of the radical opposition. The authorities understand this.

"If so (i.e., if territory were ceded – *Ed.*), people would take to the streets," journalist Aik Khalatyan says. "This is the only issue that unites Armenian society as a whole.*** In addition, I want to underscore a very important point: In all previous cases, the authorities have been able to count on the loyalty of law-enforcement agencies, special services and the Army – but if the Armenian authorities decide to make concessions that Armenian society regards as unilateral, it is highly possible that there would be no [such loyalty]. Therefore, in this case, Armenia is faced with a real threat of internal political upheaval, including a change of government."

RADICALISM AS BACKLASH

By Polina Khimshiashvili. *RBC Daily*, Aug. 2, 2016, p. 6.

... On Sunday [July 31], all participants in the Sasna Tsrer (Daredevils of Sasun) group, who had seized a police station on July 17, surrendered to the authorities in Yerevan....

The group seized the station in the wee hours of July 17. According to Armenian media reports, the group consisted of 30 members. During the attack, one police officer was killed and six people, including five police officers, were injured. Seven people were taken hostage, including two city deputy police chiefs. All of them were released by July 23. The second group of hostages – doctors who arrived to help after the shootout – were seized on July 27, but all of them were also released by July 30. A second police officer was killed on July 30. Police said on Monday he had been killed by a sniper positioned at the station compound. The attackers demanded the release of Zhirair Sefilyan, the imprisoned leader of the Founding Parliament, an opposition movement; the resignation of President Serzh Sargsyan; and the formation of a new government.

Sefilyan is well known in Armenia. He was born in Lebanon and fought in the Nagorno-Karabakh war. In 2012, Sefilyan went into politics and became a cofounder and leader of the Founding Parliament, a movement campaigning for regime change. The organization's leader is Garegin Chukaszyan; he is currently on a wanted list. One-third of the group that seized the police station are Nagorno-Karabakh war veterans....

Since 2013, not a single summer in Armenia has passed without protest rallies. Last year, from June to September, there were protests against electricity rate hikes; in 2014, against pension reform; and in 2013, against public transit fare increases in Yerevan.

Street activism and influencing politics through public rallies is characteristic of Armenian political culture, says Aleksandr Iskandaryan, director of the Yerevan-based Caucasus Institute. However, this is the first time a government facility has been seized by an armed group, he points out. "One can say that protest sentiments are radicalizing and society is polarizing," the expert commented.

Public rallies in support of the group that seized the police station began almost immediately both near the building itself and on Svoboda [Freedom] Square. The Saturday event was attended by between 1,500 and 6,000 people, the [Web site] Kavkazsky uzel [Caucasian Knot] reported. The police tried to disperse the protesters. On July 29, a march in support of the rebels took place, and was dispersed by police near the seized building. According to the Public Health Ministry, 73 people sought medical assistance following the dispersal of the action....

Just as last year, the rallies, which featured the slogan "Serzhik [Sargsyan], go!" were attended by well-known public figures and actors not only from Armenia, but also from abroad. "The armed attack is the consequence of despair," said actress Arsinée Khanjian, the wife of Atom Egoyan, a famous Canadian filmmaker of Armenian descent....

On July 17, Armenian President Serzh Sargsyan, whose resignation the attackers demanded, held an emergency meeting on the situation, but made no statements at the time. Five days later, on July 22, he stated that such actions were unacceptable and also explained why the authorities were not taking tough action. "We are showing patience and this why we have not opted for the classic scenario. The life and health of every Armenian citizen are dear to us," the president said. He has not commented on the situation since. The authorities adopted the same wait-and-see tactics last summer.

Throughout these two weeks, the authorities conducted fruitless negotiations. As Zhirair Sefilyan, who is in prison, said on Saturday, over the past few days he was visited by "well-known and respected people," who had met with the president beforehand. According to him, he was told that Sargsyan had not changed his position – that he still believed all members of the Sasna Tsrer armed group must lay down their arms, and that he would not agree to meet with Sefilyan until then. The latter stated that he first needs to meet with "his boys," and only then with the president.

Like all members of Sefilyan's group, the president is a Nagorno-Karabakh war veteran. During the war with Azerbaijan in the early 1990s, he was head of the Nagorno-Karabakh self-defense forces committee and then became Armenia's defense minister. Talks between Sargsyan and Sefilyan were brokered by Vitaly Balasanyan, another Nagorno-Karabakh war hero, who is now a deputy of the un-recognized Nagorno-Karabakh Republic's parliament....

There are several factors working against the authorities that are increasingly difficult to dismiss, [political analyst Sergei] Markedonov points out: a change of generations [and] a failure to meet the demand for an alternative vision of the country's future. This is because the aspiration for change is practically nonexistent in Armenia's political elite, which is dominated by politicians who evolved back in the Soviet days and are focused on maintaining a complex bureaucratic balance, not toward development, the expert says. Hence the demand for radicalism, including violent action and terrorism, which threaten Armenia's very existence, the expert warns.

On Monday, President Sargsyan met with public and political figures, and said that reforms will be accelerated in response to recent events. "One thing is clear: It is necessary to speed up the process of radical changes in public and domestic political life. We have no right to tolerate even the thought of resolving problems through the use of force. The next [attempt] may be devastating for our country," the president warned (as quoted by Interfax).

The president explained the government reforms. "At this stage, our objective is to form a government of national unity where decisions will be implemented through a broad consensus. Constitutional reforms were carried out precisely with this aim in mind." ...

As for the attackers' demands regarding the country's domestic political life, they were all for naught, says [Caucasus expert Nikolai] Silayev. According to him, considering the difficult situation in Armenian society, the authorities' response is insufficient.

However, the rebels have been successful in terms of foreign policy, Silayev says: During the events in Yerevan, there was active discussion of Russia's purported proposal to resolve the Nagorno-Karabakh problem by returning part of its territory to Azerbaijan. Now the Armenian authorities have an opportunity to say that it is not possible to make any concessions, the expert believes.

The rebels' demands did not touch on Nagorno-Karabakh, but we know that Sefilyan's Founding Parliament is campaigning to make Nagorno-Karabakh part of Armenia. Sargsyan said on Monday that there will be no unilateral concessions on Nagorno-Karabakh.

NOTES

1. Art. 5 of the North Atlantic Treaty reads, in part: "The Parties agree that an armed attack against one or more of them in Europe or North America shall be considered an attack against them all and consequently they agree that, if such an armed attack occurs, each of them ... will assist the Party or Parties so attacked by taking ... such action as it deems necessary, including the use of armed force, to restore and maintain the security of the North Atlantic area."

2. An announced increase in electricity rates by 17% to 22% for Armenian households prompted thousands of people in Yerevan to protest in the streets in June 2015.

Chapter 13 | The Road to 2020

AZERBAIJAN ARMS ITSELF TO SUPREMACY

By Inna Sidorkova. *RBC Daily*, March 26, 2018, p. 5.

... An armed clash between Armenia and Azerbaijan over the status of Nagorno-Karabakh is inevitable. That was the conclusion of experts from the Center for Analysis of Strategies and Technologies in a report titled: "The Gathering Storm: Southern Caucasus" (RBC has obtained a copy). The conflict could escalate sharply for several reasons: Azerbaijan's technological superiority, a possible increase in oil prices, a demographic imbalance [between the two countries], and the impossibility of legally securing Armenia's claims to Azerbaijani territories it seized adjacent to the Nagorno-Karabakh.

Power of oil

During the decade following the Nagorno-Karabakh conflict (1991-1994), a balance of forces was maintained between Azerbaijan and Armenia/NKR (Nagor-no-Karabakh Republic). The American embargo in the 1990s on arms sales to Azerbaijan and Russia's support for Armenia created parity in the Southern Caucasus. This changed in the 2000s, following a jump in oil prices, experts say. The balance of forces shifted in favor of Azerbaijan, a country with a well-developed oil industry. The influx of petrodollars allowed Azerbaijan to boost military spending and increase the size of its Army. In 2001, its military budget was $300 million; in 2013, it reached $3.7 billion and equaled Armenia's entire budget, the report states. According to SIPRI, Azerbaijan's military spending in 2001 was about $300 million; in 2013, it was roughly $2.8 billion; and in 2015, it peaked at $3 billion.

In 2016, the size of Azerbaijan's Armed Forces reached 126,000 troops, according to Military Balance. "If you also count various [law-enforcement] agencies, the presidential guard and various paramilitary organizations, as well as reservists, the overall number of armed personnel in Azerbaijan is at least 250,000," CAST maintains.

Since 2002, Armenia's Armed Forces have stood at 45,000 people. The Nagorno-Karabakh Defense Army currently consists of about 20,000 troops, and half of them are conscripts from Armenia.

The influx of oil revenues facilitated a large-scale, albeit fairly disorganized rearmament of Azerbaijan's Army. It purchased large quantities of modern tanks, armored vehicles, antiaircraft missile systems, jets, helicopters, antitank guided missiles, artillery systems, detection devices (night vision equipment, laser reconnaissance instruments, infrared cameras) and unmanned aerial vehicles. The main suppliers were Israel, Ukraine, Belarus, Georgia, Turkey and Russia. Baku's new capabilities were demonstrated during the "April war" (four-day war in Nagorno-Karabakh in April 2016): Those clashes demonstrated that Azerbaijani forces, which were equipped with modern technology, had the advantage during nighttime fighting.

Azerbaijan's growing strength forced Russia to respond by increasing arms deliveries to Armenia starting in 2013. In 2016, [Armenia] was given a $200 million loan to finance arms purchases. Deliveries included Smerch multiple rocket launcher systems and the missiles that go with them; electronic reconnaissance equipment; TOS-1A heavy flamethrower systems; and firearms. In addition, following the "April war," Yerevan purchased personal night vision equipment and infrared cameras, motion sensors, laser reconnaissance devices and UAVs, which were in short supply in Nagorno-Karabakh.

And even though falling oil prices prompted Azerbaijan to curtail its military spending (since 2015, it has been between $1.55 billion and $1.7 billion a year), Armenia cannot match that spending in the medium and long-term perspective, CAST experts believe. In 2017, Armenia's military spending was $440 million; in 2016, it was $436 million.

Demographic crisis

In Soviet times, the populations of Azerbaijan and Armenia grew at a comparable rate. But the situation changed in 1993, experts say. Despite extensive emigration, Azerbaijan's population continued to grow by 1% to 2.5% a year. Armenia's population started to decline sharply, due to falling birth rates and even greater emigration, particularly of young people. From 1993 to 1995, its population declined by up to 3% each year. Given that Armenia had a smaller population to begin with, this only exacerbated the demographic imbalance.

In 1993, the population of Armenia and Nagorno-Karabakh was 3.6 million, compared to Azerbaijan's 7.44 million; in 2000, [the gap was] 3.37 million to 8 million; and in 2014 – 3.15 million to 9.5 million.

Azerbaijan's population also has a lot of young people fit for military service, while Armenia's population is growing older, the report's authors state. In 2016, Azerbaijan had 800,000 conscription-age individuals to Armenia's 225,000.

If these demographic trends continue, Armenia's population could drop to 3 million by 2030 and 2.7 million by 2050. The population of Azerbaijan, according to the UN's estimates, will grow to 10.7 million by 2030 and 11 million by 2050, the analysts report.

Social problems

Baku is faced with growing social tensions, resulting in part from population growth, the report states. An influx of disenfranchised rural young people carries serious domestic political risks.

Any sign of weakness from Armenia could serve as a pretext for Baku to resume military action in Nagorno-Karabakh. And if the attack is swift, Baku could win.

Don't expect a legal solution to the conflict, CAST analysts say. "Any discussion of the status of Karabakh is framed by Azerbaijan as a return of territories that were not part of the former Nagorno-Karabakh Autonomous Province. Meanwhile, even the prospect of returning just Agdam and Fizulin Districts [to Azerbaijan] would significantly undermine Armenian defense; returning Lachin or Kelbadzhar Districts would destroy it completely," the report's authors state.

"Karabakh lacks international legal recognition of its de facto status, so the Armenian side is being doomed to a permanent arms race against Azerbaijan with unequal economic and demographic resources," the military experts conclude.

The Russian factor

Today, Russian diplomacy is trying to solve the difficult problem of balancing relations with a valued partner and an inevitable ally, said CAST deputy director Konstantin Makiyenko.

Russia is currently participating in the Syrian conflict, and provocations in the Donetsk Basin are also highly likely, he recalled. "Russia does not need a third hot spot, given its far-from-unlimited resources. Meanwhile, as post-Soviet history teaches us, Moscow cannot afford to ignore crises in the Transcaucasus," Makiyenko believes. That is why the objective is to prevent a situation that would require a "ruinous and politically inexpedient military intervention that should be used only as a last resort," he said.

Of course, there is a danger that the conflict's unresolved status would spark active military conflict, deputy chairman of the Federation Council's international affairs committee Vladimir Dzhabarov told RBC. According to him, Russia is making every effort to resolve these issues via negotiations. "At the same time, I believe that settling this conflict is something for future generations to tackle. Right now, it is important to find a way out of the impasse, since each side is being intransigent," Dzhabarov said.

AZERBAIJAN AT A CROSSROADS

By Vakhtang Dzhanashia. *Ekspert*, April 16, 2018, p. 56.

The absolute predictability of the [presidential] election's outcome made the procedure for extending President Ilkham Aliyev's term a mere formality: 86% of voters opted for the incumbent president. The runner-up got a little over 3% of the vote.

Given such a wide gap, the explanations of Aliyev's opponents that they lost because the election date was moved up sound ridiculous. Supposedly the opposition did not have enough time to prepare an election campaign.

The official reason for moving the election from October [2018] to April 2018 was the festivities marking the 100-year anniversary of the Azerbaijan Democratic Republic (ADR). The ADR was established on May 28, 1918. However, celebrations marking the occasion are scheduled to run practically through the end of the year.

There is another reason for moving the election. Now, the president of Azerbaijan is elected to a seven-year term, so in this case – until 2025. If the next election were held in October 2025, it would coincide with constitutionally mandated parliamentary elections. Azerbaijan decided to set those elections at least six months apart. Of course, there are other reasons why the election was moved up that are not being mentioned.

The first is that Russia held a presidential election in March. Meanwhile, in April-May 2018, Armenia is to complete its transition from a presidential republic to a parliamentary one. Baku decided to synchronize its political processes with two of its main partners in the Karabakh negotiations to avoid accusations of dragging its feet on finding a peaceful resolution to the conflict.

The second reason is that experts predict a third devaluation in as many years of Azerbaijan's currency. Maintaining a stable exchange rate of the manat to the dollar is turning out to be too costly. In order to bring down the demand for dollars, the Central Bank of Azerbaijan has limited the supply of the national currency, thus making borrowing extremely difficult for commercial banks. And making businesses tighten their belts makes more sense after an election than before.

Bureaucratic clan battles

During his previous term, Ilkham Geidarovich Aliyev completed and started many important projects. The simplest one was extending the presidential term from five to seven years. At the same time, the post of vice-president was created, which was predictably taken by his wife, Mekhriban Aliyeva-Pashayeva. The creation of the post of vice-president is not so much a Constitutional [act] as a bureaucratic clan event. The beautiful Mekhriban gained authority in the country not only though a successful and (you could say) dynastic marriage, but real work as a UNESCO goodwill ambassador and chief of the Geidar Aliyev Foundation, which finances humanitarian and charity projects. In addition to that, Mekhriban is the leader of Azerbaijan's large, influential and aristocratic Pashayev clan....

Ilkham's marriage to Mekhriban did more than just expand his electoral base; the Pashayevs and clans close to them provided significant support for Ilkham Geidarovich. When he turned over power to his son in 2003, Geidar Aliyev assumed that the Nakhichevan-Yeraz clan he built up would serve as a support base for his heir. But for Geidar Aliyev's inner circle, Ilkham was just a kid, the son of the great *muallim* [teacher] Geidar with whom they had risen to power in Soviet Azerbaijan and survived perestroika-era persecution, reviving a republic that was destroyed by those reforms. In off-the-record conversations, they believed that if not for them, Ilkham would still be teaching at the Moscow State Institute of International Relations.

It was necessary for [Ilkham] to get rid of such an ambitious team. And in 2004-2005, Ilkham Aliyev, already president, started a purge and a personnel reshuffle within his team....

In early 2017, Ilkham Aliyev took a decisive step in his bureaucratic battle. By appointing his wife vice-president and thus protecting his new team and fledgling reform projects from oblivion in case a brick were to "accidentally" fall on his head, Ilkham Aliyev issued a decree dismissing the old presidential team and creating a new one....

Ilkham Aliyev is building a modern, efficient and politically neutral state with a nearly finalized team of young, Western-oriented technocrats. His fourth presidential term will undoubtedly accomplish a lot.

Locomotives of the economy

The economic situation will play a decisive role. The collapse of oil prices hit Azerbaijan hard, resulting in falling gross domestic product, economic stagnation, falling living standards, problems in the banking sector and so on. But signs of growth appeared in 2017. Most importantly, three projects were launched that will ensure the republic's prosperity and increasing international importance for decades to come.

In September 2017, a second "contract of the century" was signed to develop the Azeri-Chirag-Gunashli oil and gas fields. The "first contract of the century," signed in 1994, when independent Azerbaijan was just getting on its feet, have brought the republic $33 billion in investments and $125 billion in revenues over the course 23 years. About 440 million [metric] tons of oil have been produced.

The new agreement, which partners the State Oil Company of the Azerbaijan Republic (SOCAR) with BP, Chevron, Inpex, Statoil, ExxonMobil, TP, Itochu and ONGC Videsh, promises not only new technologies and job growth, but more than $40 billion of investment by 2050. Even with today's low oil prices, the oil produced will bring at least $180 billion in revenues, and according to the agreement, Azerbaijan will get 75% of that.

October also saw the launch of the Baku-Tbilisi-Kars railway. It stretches 850 kilometers and has the capacity to transport 35 million tons of cargo a year. This is a project of strategic significance, since it is the shortest and most reliable route linking Europe and Asia. It could potentially become part of China's New Silk Road megaproject.

The third global economic project is the Southern Gas Corridor (SGC), which the US, Germany and other European Union nations are pushing for with the aim to diversify gas supplies to Europe. The West has already issued billions in loans toward this project and continues to invest further.

These three projects paint an optimistic picture not only for Azerbaijan, but also for Ilkham Aliyev's position and his national reform projects. Global interest in the projects launched in 2017 will become an important factor for stabilizing the domestic situation – along with economic growth, which has more than tripled in the 15 years of Ilkham Aliyev's rule. Wages and pensions grew seven- to eightfold in that time.

At the same time, it must be said that all of Azerbaijan's projects continue to exacerbate the regional isolation of the country, which is in conflict with all of its neighbors. Russia, Armenia's ally, also ended up excluded from these projects and from the Caucasus.

Karabakh factor

This is not the time to engage is absurd arguments about who owns Nagorno-Karabakh. Karabakh is a distant, desolate and aid-dependent province. But for many Armenians, it's their homeland, while for many Azeris it is an ethnocultural center.

The loss of Karabakh would have zero economic impact on Azerbaijan. Moreover, experts in Baku and its ally Tbilisi are gloating about how Karabakh subsidies are ruining Armenia, once the most prosperous republic in the Soviet Transcaucasus, and how Karabakh natives who came to power in Armenia are bankrupting the republic, according to Armenian media outlets.

Azerbaijan is home to 178,000 Armenians – 30,000 of whom live in Baku. Meanwhile, following ethnic cleansing in 1989, there are no Azeris in Armenia, Nagorno-Karabakh or the neighboring regions that are under the control of the Armenian Army. Ethnic cleansing in regions bordering Karabakh had a very strong impact on local Kurds – the majority population in Kelbadzhar, Lachin, Kubatly and Zangelan Districts. The Kurdish elite is ignoring the ruin and exile of hundreds of thousands of Kurds, all for the sake of preserving an anti-Turkish alliance with Armenia. Baku, for its part, is not too concerned about the Kurdish problem. Meanwhile, hundreds of thousands of refugees from Agdam, Shaumyan, Fizuli and Dzhabrail Districts, not to mention Azeris expelled from Karabakh and Armenia, are a source of constant unrest and a factor in domestic instability. They also exert constant pressure on the republic's leadership, not only from the opposition but also from members of government agencies.

Baku, Tbilisi and Ankara are convinced that Russia has an entirely pro-Armenian stance and are ready to back this up with a lot of evidence. Nevertheless, Azerbaijan is trying not to aggravate relations with Russia. While still running for his first term, Ilkham Aliyev withstood tremendous pressure from the US, which was basically demanding that [Azerbaijan] allow it to deploy a full-scale military base either in Apsheron, near Baku, or near the city of Kazakh, at the intersection of the three Caucasus republics. At the same time, a "color revolution" was being openly prepared – Gene Sharp's how-to book was even translated into Azeri. The situation was saved by former [US] secretary of state Madeleine Albright, who met with the local opposition. She summed up her impression in just one word: "dumbfounded."

Azerbaijan has two reliable allies in its confrontation with Armenia: culturally close Turkey and geographically close Georgia, which has its own laundry list of grievances against Armenia. It must be said that in private conversation, Georgian politicians are much more hostile toward Armenia than their Azeri counterparts. The Georgians are furious that the economic situation in their country does not allow them to close off the only remaining transit route to Armenia even though Georgia's [transit] prices for that route essentially amount to highway robbery.

Relations with Europe and the US are driven by natural resources, which Azerbaijan has in abundance and Armenia basically lacks. Levon Ter-Petrosyan, Armenia's first president and a proponent of incorporating Karabakh into Armenia, publicly admitted 20 years ago (while still president) that the country lacked the resources to continue to wage a war to make Karabakh part of Armenia, so the conflict must be settled peacefully by recognizing Azerbaijan's territorial integrity. But where does that leave the Armenian security establishment and Karabakh field commanders, for whom the war is the only source of income? Even if they had professions at one point, everything has been forgotten during the past 30 years. How will the current Armenian leadership, which hails almost entirely from Karabakh, hang on to power?

The real danger for Azerbaijan is not the Armenian Army, but the legion of well-organized, coordinated, bankrolled and confident Armenian lobbyists in the US, France and especially Russia. The Armenian lobby is powerful. Only recently, the All-Russian Azerbaijani Congress was outlawed in Russia under a completely flimsy pretext. The organization, which united the Azeri diaspora across 70 Russian federation members, was created and supported by President Vladimir Putin and Geidar Aliyev.

Baku is not making any waves, since every day of confrontation is ruinous for Yerevan. In his postelection address to the people, Ilkham Aliyev stressed: "We have not ceded an inch of our principled position on resolving the Armenian-Azeri conflict over Nagorno-Karabakh.*** This conflict must be resolved by preserving the territorial integrity of our country; there is no other way." However, the current Karabakh leaders of Armenia have their backs against the wall. Giving up the "Karabakh idea" will not only bring them political ruin (as it did Ter-Petrosyan), but also make them responsible for Armenia's catastrophic situation, and the country's total dependence on Russia's willingness to sacrifice its interests in the region as well as its relations with Azerbaijan.

Azerbaijan's purchase of Russian arms is a sort of bribe to Russia in the hope that it won't intervene in case military operations resume – something that the [Azeri] parliamentary opposition has been demanding. But even its representatives are beginning to understand that Azerbaijan has zero chance of military victory until it wins the propaganda war. And here, Armenia has absolute superiority. No positive developments for Azerbaijan are evident on this front.

PASHINYAN'S PATH

By Arnold Khachaturov. *Novaya gazeta*, Aug. 10, 2018, p. 14.

Yerevan-Moscow – **Editors' Note.** – To learn what is happening in Armenia under the leadership of Prime Minister Nikol Pashinyan, whether the new government has a chance to boost economic growth, and how old conflicts within the country and along its borders are preventing that, we present an analysis of the situation by Novaya gazeta's special economics correspondent who visited Yerevan.

* * *

The State Control Service of Armenia, which was created to fight corruption, until recently has served purely a symbolic function, helping the authorities create the semblance of democracy. But after the April "velvet revolution," big changes have taken place....

Current Prime Minister Nikol Pashinyan, 42, aims to set accountability standards for society and the authorities through personal example. Pashinyan is known as the father of Armenian-style digital democracy. He was the first politician to start using Facebook Live video streaming to connect with the people, turning the social network into a communications channel for the street protests [that brought down the regime of Serzh Sargsyan]. After heading up the government, Pashinyan traded his selfie stick for a professional camera, and his signature baseball cap and fatigues for a power suit. He also started to make noticeably fewer live broadcasts. However, according to Pashinyan's supporters, his new government position has not prevented him from remaining loyal to the revolution's ideals.

Political analysts listed the success factors of Armenia's protest movement – from knowing how to effectively block streets in Yerevan to drawing on civil society's experience. But one of the more important fundamental reasons has been the natural change in political generations. "This is a common occurrence across the [former] USSR: The number of people without a Soviet history is increasing. Right now, Pashinyan is the only Eurasian Economic Union leader who is not a native Russian speaker: He studied it," says Aleksandr Iskandaryan, director of the [Yerevan-based] Caucasus Institute.

But an increasingly younger ruling class (some Armenian cabinet ministers are not even 30) is not enough to turn Armenia into a prosperous country. It is too early to talk about radical changes – it has only been about three months since former prime minister Serzh Sargsyan stepped down. Corruption and low wages remain problems despite the revolutionary euphoria. Nevertheless, Armenians are hoping that the first step, on the mental level, has been made: The Armenian people once again believe they are able to influence political processes and determine their own future.

The current feeling that a window of opportunity has opened up contrasts sharply with the political stagnation the country has experienced in the last 20 years. "During that time, Armenia had a complex system of stakeholders. Domestic and foreign policy was determined not so much by objective national interests as by the interests of major players – various oligarchic and security clans, and diasporas," says political analyst Areg Galstyan. That is why people viewed any talk by politicians about change as empty words from corrupt officials who usurped power. As the people's leader, Pashinyan is wildly popular; [the people] trust him and expect him to take concrete steps toward building a new state. But as always, the road to postrevolutionary reforms is fraught with pitfalls....

Reforms without a vendetta

Given that he has complete popular support, Pashinyan does not need to worry about behind-the-scenes intrigues. Nevertheless, he has a very difficult task ahead of him: to completely demolish the existing political system, and carry out constructive economic and political reforms. Many people I spoke with in Armenia said that regime change has already had a positive effect: With Pashinyan coming to power, many government agencies, from the Customs Service to the police and medical institutions, have cut back on bribes, simply because they once again believe in the power of the law. "The biggest effect from the regime change that is already noticeable is a reduction of the shadow economy's [share in the economy]. Over the past two months, tax revenues have grown by 20%," says Mesrop Arakelyan, an economic adviser to the Armenian prime minister....

But even as he carries out economic reforms, Pashinyan still has to contend with the interests of major businesses. When it comes to Armenia's economy, infringing on the interests of one oligarch could seriously damage the entire country, which is experiencing big problems attracting investment. "Protecting capital is a matter of principle, especially for small markets," says Armenian Deputy Prime Minister Mger Grigoryan. That is why Pashinyan's public message to Armenian oligarchs is that there will be no vendetta; return what you have stolen and continue to work legitimately. At the same time, many wealthy Armenians have invested in foreign assets, so repatriating [stolen funds] could be very difficult....

Another key question on the new authorities' economic agenda is "revolutionary" tax reform. "During the next two to three months, we plan to liberalize the Tax Code, reducing the number of taxes and tax rates. Right now, not only businesses but professional accountants can't make heads or tails of our tax system," adviser Arakelyan says.

Overall, the Armenian economy has very few potential sources of growth. This is due in part to geographic difficulties: Only two of its four borders are open – with Georgia and Iran. Moreover, Georgia does not have diplomatic relations with Russia, while Iran is just now starting to exit international sanctions. One solution is to develop industries that are not burdened with high logistics and energy costs, says Deputy Prime Minister Grigoryan. This means mostly IT, tourism and agriculture.

Everyone understands that Armenia won't become Switzerland in a year, or even 10 years. But under the right conditions, it is possible to significantly raise living standards in the country. The most important thing is not to delay reforms: Society's postrevolutionary enthusiasm will fade fast if the tactical fight against corruption fails to result in systemic changes. Right now, Armenian society is living with overinflated expectations, but by winter, political analysts expect Pashinyan's ratings will inevitably decline.

In Lukashenko's footsteps

Ideally, regime change must be followed by the establishment of new political institutions not contaminated by authoritarianism. However, Pashinyan is the type of politician who tears things down: He has been consistently fighting the existing political system since his student years. "Usually, such politicians totally destroy everything, leaving nothing but ruins and handing over the reins to the 'builders' – people who will create a new system. The big question is whether Pashinyan is able to play both roles," says political analyst Areg Galstyan.

The Armenian people will find out after the early [parliamentary] elections scheduled for next spring. Right now, Pashinyan's campaign platform looks fairly vague, which is hardly surprising – his team is currently busy trying to convert revolutionary success into electoral results in order to get a mandate for sweeping changes. In addition, the new authorities are refusing to have any ideological associations, saying that partisan divisions are obsolete. As a result, it is not always clear what Armenia's new economic course will look like, except that it will fight corruption....

Another problem is that Pashinyan does not yet have a team of professional managers, which is imperative for carrying out major reforms. The people Pashinyan has appointed to the cabinet are his fellow party members and supporters of the revolutionary movement; many of them have no managerial experience whatsoever. In addition to the parliamentary elections, Pashinyan has to generate a party list of several hundred names. What criteria will be used to draft it and how competent the new parliamentary majority will be are both big questions.

In the worst-case scenario, Pashinyan could completely usurp power – like [Belarussian President] Aleksandr Lukashenko, who won the presidential election 24 years ago on an anticorruption platform....

If elections were held in Armenia today, it would be a national catastrophe, agrees Stepan Grigoryan, head of the Analytical Center for Globalization and Regional Cooperation. Pashinyan would get over 80% [of the vote], and the party system simply cannot function like that. A multiparty system could only begin to take shape after a comprehensive reform of the Constitution and electoral law. Ultimately, everything depends on whether Pashinyan will be prepared to sacrifice his own power for the sake of strengthening the country's political institutions.

Considering that Pashinyan was not the sole protest leader and Armenian society has gotten much more demanding following the revolution, there is a good chance that he will step down amicably. "It is quite possible that the major reforms will be carried out by Pashinyan's team, while he takes a parallel route of securing the people's mandate through anticorruption investigations," says Galstyan.

Foreign policy trap

Another reform obstacle is the lack of flexibility in Armenia's foreign policy.

In particular, the country's transition to democracy looks somewhat contradictory, given that its main ally is a distinguished member of the authoritarian nations club. The Armenian authorities respond to that by stressing that the country's democratization is not tied to anti-Russian sentiments either among the ruling class or in its foreign policy. "This revolution is unique because we did not quarrel with anyone," one of the [revolution's] participants told Novaya. In order to avoid any unnecessary associations, Pashinyan refuses to call what happened a "color revolution."

Some members of the new government have noticeably softened their rhetoric on Russia and the EaEU after coming to power. Earlier, many of them perceived Kremlin projects as a threat to Armenia's sovereignty, but today, [they view] Russia as a loyal friend that is ensuring [Armenia's] military security and proposing unique possibilities for economic cooperation. Due to an unfortunate geographic location, Armenia is simply unable to seriously diversify its foreign policy.

The country last updated its National Security Strategy in 2007, Galstyan says, and there is no foreign policy strategy as such. Foreign policy strategy is limited to emotional and uncompromising divisions [of countries] into friends and enemies. The assumption that Russia's imperialist ambitions could go too far is met with a condescending smile by most Armenians. The only thing that could shake the "brotherly relations" is the fact that Russia sells offensive weapons to Azerbaijan. But there still are no alternatives. The EU cannot even in theory ensure Armenia's security in case the Nagorno-Karabakh conflict flares up. And in addition to military cooperation (a joint air defense system, the fact that Russia's 102nd military base is stationed in Gyumri, membership in the CSTO, supplies of [Russian] weapons at [Russian] domestic prices), Russia is also a major investor in the Armenian economy, with complete control over strategic infrastructure, from the gas market to railway transit. For its part, after the conflict with Georgia, Russia needs some way of maintaining its influence in the region.

These factors suggest that Armenia is not going away from Russia, even if it starts build a democracy under the guidance of the US State Department. Georgia, which has much better relations with its neighbors, paid the price of losing South Ossetia and Abkhazia for switching over to the Western camp, Galstyan recalls. For Armenia, the price would be prohibitively high....

'WE HAVE NO CHOICE; WE MUST CONDUCT SUBSTANTIVE NEGOTIATIONS WITH ARMENIA'

By Elnar Bainazarov. *Izvestia*, Oct. 17, 2019, p. 3.

Editors' Note. – Some progress has been achieved in negotiations between Baku and Yerevan to resolve the crisis in Nagorno-Karabakh, Azerbaijani Foreign Minister Elmar Mamedyarov tells Izvestia in an interview....

* * *

Question. – At an expanded meeting at the summit of CIS foreign ministers in Ashgabat, you and your Armenian counterpart were seated next to each other. Based on this, how do you assess the role of the CIS in resolving the Azerbaijani-Armenian conflict? Does it extend further into the practical field, or does it end merely with attempts to seat Baku and Yerevan at the same table?

Answer. – Initially, it was the UN that was working on reaching a settlement between our states. As you know, the UN Security Council was the main organization for maintaining peace and security between our countries. During the hot phase [of the crisis] in 1993, it determined the formats, laid the basis for resolving the conflict and adopted four resolutions. Then the peace initiative was handed off to the OSCE Minsk Group. It is working now to achieve a settlement between Baku and Yerevan in accordance with its mandate as an international organization.

The Minsk Group, led by three cochairs – Russia, the US and France – is the OSCE's principal agent for resolving this conflict. Of course, we briefly touched on this topic now (on the sidelines of the CIS Council of Foreign Ministers – *Ed.*). We all understand that unresolved conflicts in the CIS space only impede any activity, including economic, humanitarian, etc. And all 10 [CIS member] countries, including Azerbaijan and Armenia, acknowledged that a speedy solution to this conflict needs to be found. But it must be acknowledged that the main work on a settlement is taking place within the framework of the OSCE Minsk Group, not the CIS.

Q. – Over the past year, you met with your Armenian counterpart, Zograb Mnatsakanyan, seven times, including as part of trilateral negotiations involving the Russian Foreign Ministry in Moscow. Do these meetings bring any benefit? Is it possible to say that some progress has been made in resolving the conflict?

A. – We are still only waiting for results. The last time we met was in the US a month ago. I already said that, unfortunately, we should not say "negotiations" – it was really a meeting. Although the last such meeting with my Armenian counterpart was in New York with the participation of the Minsk Group, to be honest, I was a little disappointed with it.

If we want to move forward and actually find a political solution to this dispute, then, of course, we need to start what is called "substantive negotiations" – a favorite phrase of mine – so that there is some kind of substantive conversation. Yes, we were negotiating, but the Minsk cochairs at one point said, "But, you see, there are military operations on the line of contact."

But for the sake of objectivity, over the past few years (by the way, how many already?) [talks] were getting under way in Prague that then resulted in the Madrid document, and during all this time the contact line was quite hot. And yet we managed to solve problems, move forward and had quite serious, step-by-step negotiations on how to address current issues: First, to arrange for soldiers to return to their barracks, and for people displaced from their places of permanent residence to return home. And after that, all other issues could have been resolved.

What was spelled out in the Madrid document in 2008, then in its revised version in 2010, and again in the Kazan document – all this is being altered over and over, but in principle it remains the basis for negotiations. And we always tell our cochairs: We have no choice, we must sit down and conduct substantive negotiations with Yerevan on the document currently on the table....

TWO-DAY WAR

By Igor Karmazin and Aleksei Zabrodin. *Izvestia*, July 14, 2020, p. 4.

Editors' Note. – Armed clashes broke out between Armenia and Azerbaijan along their international border, far from Nagorno-Karabakh. Each side is blaming the other for initiating the altercation. Baku has acknowledged the deaths of three soldiers. Yerevan is not reporting any casualties. Izvestia examines the causes and possible implications of the incident.

* * *

What happened

The clashes between Azerbaijan and Armenia took place on July 12-13.

Baku reported that the enemy fired artillery rounds at Azerbaijani positions. Armenian Defense Ministry spokeswoman Shushan Stepanyan said that a group of Azerbaijani soldiers in a UAZ truck tried to cross the state border "for no apparent reason." After being warned [by the Armenian side], the Azerbaijanis abandoned the vehicle and returned to their positions. But an hour later, they opened artillery fire and attempted to capture an [Armenian] base. The advancing forces were repelled by return fire.

Baku said that the clashes left five people wounded and three soldiers dead....

Yerevan is denying reports of casualties on its side. It claims that only two police officers were slightly wounded....

On the afternoon of July 13, the sides reported the continuation of clashes. Armenia is saying that the enemy is firing artillery rounds every 15 to 20 minutes. Azerbaijan is saying that the Armenians have started using snipers and machine guns on the border, violating the ceasefire 70 times in 24 hours.

Azerbaijani President Ilkham Aliyev commented on the incident at a meeting of Azerbaijan's Security Council. "All [offensive] attempts by the Armenian side failed. Azerbaijan defended its state border, and Armenian soldiers failed to get even a centimeter beyond the border," he said.

At an emergency cabinet meeting, Armenian Prime Minister Nikol Pashinyan said Azerbaijan is to blame for the incident. "The opponent took provocative actions at the border. Azerbaijan's military and political leadership will be held responsible for exacerbating the regional situation," he said.

What triggered the incident?

The root cause of the flare-up is accumulated differences in Armenian and Azerbaijani society. The coronavirus pandemic has taken a major toll on the economies of both countries. Damage is estimated at $1.5 billion in Armenia. A state of emergency has been in effect since March and was recently extended until mid-August. In June, citizens were prohibited from leaving their homes without a face mask and documents, under penalty of fines. But officials have repeatedly been accused of violating the self-isolation regime, and fatality rates are still high. As a result, discontent with the authorities' actions is growing in the country, leading to protests.

Azerbaijan is in a similar situation. The coronavirus pandemic is hitting the republic hard. Azerbaijan's authorities instituted a special quarantine in the republic's seven largest cities from July 4 to July 20. Large shopping centers are closed, [public] transportation is suspended, and people's movements are restricted. An additional blow to the economy is the falling price of oil, which is the backbone of [Azerbaijan's] exports.

A contributing factor to the tension in Armenia is the battle between the authorities and their political opponents. In June, the country's parliament approved legislative changes allowing the Constitutional Court's head and judges to be replaced. Until recently, the Court had remained the last major state body to maintain independence from the team of Prime Minister Nikol Pashinyan. In addition, Armenia's National Security Service (NSS) has opened three criminal cases against opposition leader Gagik Tsarukyan.

"Both sides benefit from the armed clash. The authorities can use it to alleviate tension in society, distract from domestic problems and rally citizens," Nurlan Gasymov, a Caucasus expert, told Izvestia.

It is also significant that negotiations have stalled on Nagorno-Karabakh's status. The two leaders first talked with each other publicly in February, during the Munich Security Conference, but the conversation ended in recriminations. Nikol Pashinyan criticized Baku for being unwilling to conduct direct dialogue with Nagorno-Karabakh. Ilkham Aliyev responded by demanding that Yerevan stop funding "this illegal entity" and completely withdraw from Azerbaijani territory.

What's next?

The Russian Foreign Ministry expressed major concern about the altercation on the border of Armenia and Azerbaijan. "We consider further escalation that threatens regional security unacceptable. We urge the opposing parties to exercise restraint and strictly observe the ceasefire. For its part, the Russian Foreign Ministry is ready to provide necessary assistance to stabilize the situation," reads a statement published on the ministry's Web site.

Stanislav Zas, secretary general of the Collective Security Treaty Organization, convened an emergency meeting of the CSTO's permanent council.

Experts believe that the clashes are unlikely to turn into a full-blown conflict.

"There are no fundamental preconditions for war. But shelling and positional battles may increase. International observers should actively encourage the parties to negotiate," says Stanislav Pritchin, an associate at the Institute of World Economics and International Relations' Center for Post-Soviet Studies.

Konstantin Kosachov, chairman of the Federation Council's international affairs committee, comments that Russia will work to reconcile the sides.

"We are promoting reconciliation, not imposing our own position. We must determine what started this, how it progressed and what it led to. The status quo needs to be restored that precludes the use of military force," Kosachov says.

Denis Denisov, director of the Institute of Peacekeeping Initiatives and Conflict Studies, told Izvestia that such incidents are typical of partially settled, frozen conflicts.

"The fact that [the latest incident] happened not in Nagorno-Karabakh but on the Azerbaijani-Armenian border again testifies that these states' problems go beyond Nagorno-Karabakh," Denisov comments. He adds that negotiations must resume to resolve the situation.

"Russia can act as a guarantor who can help build such bridges," Denisov believes.

AZERBAIJAN RAISES THE STAKES

By Gleb Mishutin. *Vedomosti*, July 15, 2020, p. 2.

The clashes along the Armenian-Azerbaijani border that began on July 12 continued into the next day. On July 14, Baku acknowledged the death of Maj. Gen. Polad Gashimov, chief of staff of the Army corps located in the area [of the fighting], and several other senior officers. The Armenian Defense Ministry also acknowledged the loss of two officers. Azerbaijani Deputy Defense Minister Kerim Valiyev promised to "avenge the martyrs." And Khikmet Gadzhiyev, a foreign policy adviser to the Azerbaijani president, said that Armenia is trying to "get a military-political organization it participates in (i.e., the CSTO – Ed.) involved in the Armenian-Azerbaijani conflict." Kremlin spokesman Dmitry Peskov said on July 12 that Russia is urging both sides to exercise restraint and is willing to mediate.

Nikolai Silayev, a senior research fellow at the Moscow State Institute of International Relations' Institute for International Studies, says this is the largest armed clash since April 2016. The border had been relatively calm for a long time. According to him, the change of power in Yerevan in 2018 was expected to have a positive effect on negotiations, but now the situation is returning to its earlier phase, hopes of diplomatic success are fading, and the old logic of confrontation is starting to kick in. It is very important for Armenia and Nagorno-Karabakh to maintain the status quo: Azerbaijan has not controlled Nagorno-Karabakh for nearly three decades, and the status quo is solidifying over time, the expert says. He believes that Baku's objective is to ensure that no one grows accustomed to the status quo. Of the two alternatives – rigorous negotiations or military tension – Azerbaijan chose the latter to undermine this status quo that it finds unfavorable. But even constant military tension has become commonplace, so Baku is having to send stronger and stronger signals, Silayev says: "The fact that the conflict took place right on the Azerbaijani-Armenian border, not in Nagorno-Karabakh, sends a very strong signal. The incident concerns not Nagorno-Karabakh, which only Armenia recognizes; it concerns Armenia itself, which is in a military-political alliance with Russia and a CSTO member."

The border conflict has already drawn international attention. Russian Foreign Minister Sergei Lavrov held telephone talks with his counterparts from Armenia and Azerbaijan, and urged both sides to immediately cease hostilities, offering to resolve the conflict with the help of representatives of Russia, the US and France. However, the CSTO will avoid being drawn into this situation, Silayev believes. "One shouldn't expect it to respond. But Russia has deep and trusting relations with both countries, which the other mediators – the US and France, the cochairs of the [OSCE] Minsk Group – lack. This balance allows Russia to act as an intermediary. "The hostilities in April 2016 ended in Moscow; the chiefs of the general staff of both states met there," the expert recalled.

PEACE CAN'T BE FORCED

By Vladislav Zuyevsky. *Izvestia*, July 17, 2020, p. 2.

It will be difficult for Armenia and Azerbaijan to extinguish their latest flare-up without mediation. And Russia could play a key role in this regard, say politicians and experts interviewed by Izvestia. The escalation that began on the two countries' border on July 12 is already becoming internationalized, although so far only in rhetoric. According to political analysts, both sides are to blame.

They will not be able to handle this on their own.

The conflict between Armenia and Azerbaijan has long gone beyond the borders of Nagorno-Karabakh. The language of political and diplomatic enmity – which has at times varied in intensity – has for some 30 years been an integral part of discussions within both countries about their place in the world. So the July 12 border attacks troubled everyone, but surprised no one. And nobody was surprised when the fighting was still continuing on July 16....

Given how long the two countries have been at odds, not to mention the numerous rounds of high-level negotiations, it will be very difficult for Yerevan and Baku to extinguish the most recent outbreak of hostility on their own. And most importantly, there is no guarantee that the doused fire won't flame up again later. And what is perhaps most dangerous about the current situation is that the flare-up occurred not in Nagorno-Karabakh, but right at the border of the two states.

According to Grigory Karasin, a member of the Federation Council and former Russian deputy foreign minister, the OSCE Minsk Group, established in 1992, must play a role in reconciling the sides. The politician explained to Izvestia that the cochairs of the group – Russia, France and the US – are already working to resolve the conflict. He is confident that international players are obligated to do whatever they can to prevent a major conflict in this region.

But the Minsk Group has been around for a long time, and the ultimate goal – a complete settlement of the [Nagorno-Karabakh] conflict – has not been achieved, Leonid Kalashnikov, chairman of the State Duma's committee on CIS affairs, Eurasian affairs and liaison with compatriots, reminded Izvestia. According to him, back when it was established, the OSCE mechanism helped halt the bloodshed, but did not solve the problem. So now Yerevan and Baku need a mediator who can unwaveringly guide the parties toward a final reconciliation.

"The situation is unacceptable to both Azerbaijan and Armenia. Some international players are trying to back one side or the other, which is completely inappropriate. It doesn't help the search for a solution. Only Russia can play a truly positive role in a settlement. We could help resolve this conflict now that we aren't looking over our shoulder at the US and Europe and realize that, for them, it is better to maintain tension at our borders," the deputy said.

According to him, three people could settle the problem today: the president of Azerbaijan, the prime minister of Armenia and the leader of Russia, because Moscow wields "unconditional clout in these republics." The parliamentary deputy is confident that Russia can use its good relations not only with Yerevan and Baku, but also with Ankara, which has now taken an openly pro-Azerbaijani position, to help the sides finally come to terms.

"The end result could be new opportunities for everyone. For example, Azerbaijan could join the EaEU and Armenia's prospects could get expanded. This would serve as a model political and diplomatic approach to conflict resolution," Leonid Kalashnikov said.

The effect of a freeze

As long as the conflict over Nagorno-Karabakh remains frozen, without any positive developments, such flare-ups are inevitable, Denis Denisov, director of the Institute of Peacekeeping Initiatives and Conflict Studies, said in an interview with Izvestia. And it is not just the territorial dispute that is to blame, but the mutual negative atmosphere that has formed in Baku and Yerevan over several decades. Denisov believes that perhaps now Russia will demonstrate its clout and capabilities as a mediator capable of resolving the conflict.

But it is very difficult to understand who is at fault in the current incident. Both sides naturally blame each other. And any attempt to attribute the outbreak to one of the sides is perceived extremely negatively by the other. Moscow State Institute of International Relations Associate Professor Kirill Koktysh explained to Izvestia that some people in Yerevan are now calling to internationalize the conflict – to involve as many participants as possible in resolving it. This is confirmed by Armenia's appeal to the CSTO, of which it is a member, the political analyst believes. At the same time, the goal is not to trigger a major confrontation, but to attract the attention of international players.

"In any event, neither side wants war," the expert stressed.

Besides, now Armenia could, for instance, try to convert domestic problems into foreign ones, Kirill Koktysh said. For example, the country has been failing in its efforts to tackle the coronavirus epidemic, which continues to rage in the republic, but now the confrontation with Baku has taken over the entire agenda.

Azerbaijanis are also dissatisfied with the authorities' response to the pandemic in their country, Vladimir Yevseyev, an expert with the Institute of CIS Countries, reminded Izvestia. He says that Azerbaijan's leaders are also using the conflict to shift locals' attention away from COVID-19 and the tough quarantine measures, and toward the conflict with Yerevan. The expert believes that the current situation is extremely dangerous, because it could get out of control and escalate into a regional conflict, given Turkey's rhetoric. And if the situation takes a turn for the worse, it could affect Russia and even Iran. So the priority now is to put out this latest flare-up on the border and steer the parties back to seeking compromise, especially on the Nagorno-Karabakh issue.

Meanwhile, on July 16, Azerbaijani President Ilkham Aliyev dismissed Foreign Minister Elmar Mamedyarov, who has headed the Foreign Ministry since 2004. According to Interfax-Azerbaijan, the leader of the country had harshly criticized the minister the day before. On July 12, when the first border incident occurred, Ilkham Aliyev was unable to find the foreign minister at the ministry. What is more, the president was furious that amid the conflict with Yerevan, Elmar Mamedyarov was discussing cooperation on combatting the coronavirus with his Armenian counterpart.

Dzheikhun Bayramov, who previously served as education minister, is Azerbaijan's new foreign minister.

NUCLEAR GENOCIDE AND CRUSHED APRICOTS: WHAT KIND OF WAR IS THERE BETWEEN ARMENIA AND AZERBAIJAN AGAIN?

By Aleksandr Artamonov. *Republic.ru*, July 17, 2020, https://republic.ru/posts/97262.

The 30-year smoldering conflict between Armenia and Azerbaijan flared up again in mid-July. The two republics are exchanging artillery fire, disinformation and threats to trigger a humanitarian catastrophe on each other's territory, and Azerbaijanis and Armenians are quarreling at Moscow [outdoor] markets. At first glance, this all seems routine: Similar events last occurred in 2016-2017. But a closer look reveals alarming signs that the conflict between Baku and Yerevan is reaching a new level. For the first time, the clashes are in no way connected to Nagorno-Karabakh (which both countries are fighting to control) and are taking place outside that territory, giving it a broader geopolitical context than usual....

A hybrid war

Both sides are not only shelling each other's territories but actively carrying out cyberattacks.

As early as July 12, just hours after the first shots were fired, Azerbaijani hackers breached the Web sites of the Armenian government and prime minister. In response, Armenian hackers attacked Azerbaijani Wi-Fi networks and the [Azerbaijani] Navy's servers.

Representatives of the Armenian Defense Ministry said that on July 15-16, Armenians started receiving text messages and mass notifications via messenger services claiming that the Army is sustaining heavy losses, troops have been put on high alert, and civilians are being urged to donate blood for the injured. The military asked [Armenians] not to believe the fake reports that the Azerbaijanis are disseminating to spread fear and made assurances that the Army does not yet need active assistance from civilians.

For its part, the Azerbaijani military accused Armenia of publishing fake reports about downed unmanned aerial vehicles. For example, Azerbaijani Defense Ministry spokesman Vagif Dargyakhly claimed that the drone whose pictures the Armenian military used as proof of its success was shot down back in 2014, in Afghanistan.

The conflict between the two nations has even reached Russia. The Armenian Aizor news agency, citing the newspaper Graparak, reports that some of Moscow's Azerbaijani-owned markets have refused to sell Armenian produce. In a video currently circulating on social media, Azerbaijanis can be seen crushing several crates of Armenian apricots by stomping on them. According to Armenpress, in the early morning hours of July 17, truckloads of Armenian fruit and vegetables were turned away from Moscow's Food City [the largest wholesale food distribution center in Russia – *Trans.*]. The trucks were moved to an alternate parking lot, where much of the produce spoiled as a result.

Threats of total annihilation

Both sides have hinted that they are prepared to attack the enemy's major infrastructure facilities, which could have catastrophic consequences for the entire region.

The idea of a missile strike on the Mingechaur hydroelectric power station, the largest in the Transcaucasus, located on the Kura River in western Azerbaijan, began to be discussed in the Armenian media in early July. The power station generates over 400 megawatts of electricity and meets half of Azerbaijan's electrical power needs. It also supplies electricity to neighboring regions of Turkey, Georgia and Russia.

The Mingechaur reservoir holds about 16 billion cubic meters of water and is the second largest water body in the Transcaucasus. If the power station is destroyed, the region would suffer a major energy crisis, and water from the reservoir would flood vast areas of the mostly low-lying Aran region in central Azerbaijan, which is home to over 1 million people live, and could also reach Baku.

In response to that threat, on July 16 Vagif Dargyakhly hinted that Azerbaijan might launch a strike against the Metsamor Nuclear Power Plant (known as the Armenian Nuclear Power Plant in Soviet days), which "could be disastrous for

Armenia." Only one power-generating unit is currently operational, with a capacity of approximately half that of the RBMK-1000 reactor that exploded during the Chernobyl accident.

According to a study by Turkish geographer Tayfun Kindap, if an accident occurred at the Metsamor nuclear power station, all of eastern Turkey, along with Armenia, would be the center of radioactive contamination, and the radioactive cloud would envelop all of the Caucasus, Turkey and Iraq. Armenian representatives called these threats a "manifestation of international terrorism" and an "expression of Azerbaijan's genocidal intentions."

Mutual threats to destroy those two critical facilities are made whenever the conflict between Baku and Yerevan escalates. The last time politicians from both countries actively commented on this subject was in 2016-2017, when major armed clashes took place in Nagorno-Karabakh.

Reaction from other actors

The OSCE, the UN, the EU and the US State Department condemned the violence, and urged Baku and Yerevan to stop the escalation.

Russia is calling on both sides to settle their differences peacefully, but it is not taking sides....

"Armenia is Russia's ally in the region," said military expert Aleksandr Khramchikhin, deputy director of the Institute of Political and Military Analysis. "Russia simply had to respond to [the flare-up]. Moscow wants to calm the situation and prevent it from growing into full-blown combat operations, because otherwise Moscow would have to honor its commitments as an ally and somehow respond to another [Azerbaijani-Armenian] war. So it is better not to allow the conflict to turn into a war. Russia has enough problems right now."

Turkey supported the actions of "fraternal and friendly" Azerbaijan and condemned Armenia's "aggression" immediately after the conflict broke out. On July 14, Turkish Defense Minister Hulusi Akar said that the Turkish Army is ready to support its allies, "whom we treat in accordance with the 'one nation, two states' principle." Ismail Demir, head of [Turkey's] Defense Industry Development and Support Administration Office, promised that his agency will help Azerbaijan modernize its Army and supply it with advanced weapons. But Turkey's stance has so far been limited to rhetoric.

Why the conflict began

Determining exactly who provoked the confrontation is impossible. Military commentator Aleksandr Starver believes the conflict could have been caused by human error: The Azerbaijani soldiers may have crossed into Armenian territory by accident, but Armenian border guards justifiably treated that as a provocation.

"This is the kind of conflict that could rekindle with any degree of intensity at any moment, because it is still unresolved. I don't think it can be resolved without war," Khramchikhin said.

According to political commentator Vladimir Novikov, Azerbaijani President Ilkham Aliyev may have decided to escalate the conflict to boost his popularity, which has suffered significantly amid the [coronavirus] pandemic that has hit the country rather hard. "The constantly smoldering Nagorno-Karabakh conflict clearly fits the bill," Novikov said. Meanwhile, the coronavirus pandemic has hit Armenia even harder, and now, according to Novikov, the country is experiencing yet another domestic political struggle between the government and the opposition. "So Baku probably decided that now would be a good time to pull off a victorious military maneuver meant for the domestic audience," [Novikov said]....

Will there be war?

Most experts agree that the conflict is unlikely to go beyond the minor border skirmishes that have been constantly occurring for the past 25 years and turn into a real war. "The conflict is still unresolved. Baku is unhappy with the situation. The escalation on the border shows just that. [It's] nothing unique," Khramchikhin said.

He is echoed by Ismail Agakishiyev, head of Moscow State University's Center for Caucasus Studies: "A large-scale war benefits no one. It does not benefit Azerbaijan, because Azerbaijan is not claiming Armenian territories. Azerbaijan only wants its own territories liberated. Armenia also realizes that war does not benefit it, since CSTO members have put the issue on hold. The CSTO countries do not need this conflict amid the ongoing economic crisis and pandemic. As for Belarus, a [presidential] election is just around the corner."

Political analyst Sergei Markedonov offers a far more chilling forecast. In his opinion, the conflict risks moving beyond the bounds of Armenian-Azerbaijani relations in the context of the struggle for Nagorno-Karabakh. "Whereas Moscow is trying to reconcile the conflicting Caucasus countries, Ankara's stance is clearly and consistently pro-Azerbaijani. A border escalation may carry far greater negative consequences than an incident in Nagorno-Karabakh – especially considering that Armenian-Azerbaijani border demarcation issues are not part of the revised Madrid Principles (OSCE Basic Principles for settlement of the Nagorno-Karabakh conflict – *Ed.*), whose implementation has been the subject of negotiations for many years now."

FORGOTTEN WAR: UNFROZEN

By staff commentator Pavel Felgengauer. *Novaya gazeta*, July 20, 2020, p. 3.

The Azerbaijani-Armenian conflict, long forgotten by the international community, suddenly flared up with the largest armed clashes since April 2016. Over four years ago, hundreds of people were killed or injured on both sides in fierce fighting during the so-called four-day war, but on the fifth day, the sides agreed to a ceasefire with Moscow's mediation and pressure.

This time, the fighting is not as intense and there are fewer casualties (in the dozens), which may be why Russia and other world and regional powers are acting a bit more passively. Maybe the coronavirus pandemic is to blame, or perhaps there are just too many other wars, conflicts and disagreements going on in the world right now.

The Azerbaijani-Armenian artillery duels and exchanges that began on July 12 along the border of Armenia's Tavush Province and Azerbaijan's Tovuz District are continuing, interspersed with periods of calm: A quiet day is followed by shelling, but mutual belligerent threats are only growing.

Top officials on both sides, Ilkham Aliyev and Nikol Pashinyan, clearly do not want the conflict to escalate or spread. In the mountainous Tavush-Tovuz sector of the Armenian-Azerbaijani border, there is nowhere for anyone to advance and no reason for them to do so, nor are there any territorial claims there, and the sides are fighting from fixed positions.

But the public is far more belligerent than the leaders. Prowar demonstrations in Baku in support of an offensive operation and the liberation of Nagorno-Karabakh were so intense that water cannons had to be used to disperse demonstrators. Thousands of Azerbaijanis volunteered to go to the front. [People] in Armenia are convinced that the country's new leadership has shown toughness and punished the enemy, taking revenge for the humiliating tactical defeat in the four-day war (Azerbaijani Gen. Polad Gashimov was killed during the first day of shelling).

Tensions have been high since 1994, when the Nagorno-Karabakh war ended with Armenia's victory and a ceasefire – albeit a very unstable one, with sporadic clashes. There's neither peace nor war. But both sides have stockpiled weapons and long been mentally prepared for all-out war. The national leaders' desire to avoid unnecessary risks may prove insufficient to prevent an uncontrolled escalation.

Armenia (including Nagorno-Karabakh) has approximately the same number of tanks, artillery systems and other heavy equipment as Azerbaijan. However, thanks to its oil and gas exports, Azerbaijan has spent far more on defense and therefore enjoys a significant qualitative advantage. Armenia is buying a limited number of modern weapons only from Russia and on credit, while Azerbaijan is buying from Russia, Israel and countries all over the world, including systems that not even the Russian military has, let alone the Armenians. For example, the Erbit [sic; Elbit] Hermes 450 and 900 and IAI Heron strike and unmanned surveillance drones (Israel); and the Spike (Israel) and AT-1K Raybolt (South Korea) third-generation fire-and-forget antitank guided missiles tipped with a tandem high-explosive warhead. Turkey has announced that it will supply Azerbaijan with its strike drones, which have already demonstrated their effectiveness in Syria and Libya. [Azerbaijan] has signed a contract with South Korea for K2 Black Panther next-generation battle tanks. How well the Azerbaijani military has mastered the new systems and whether it will be able to effectively use them in combat is another story. However, Israeli and Turkish specialists and instructors in Azerbaijan would help if need be.

Russia's 102nd military base – about 4,000 personnel (a motorized rifle brigade) plus combat aviation and air defense systems – is stationed in Armenia. There are no [Russian] troops in Nagorno-Karabakh, nor does Russia have any obligation to defend it, but Armenia's internationally recognized territory is part of the Moscow-led CSTO military alliance. Since the most recent clashes took place along the Armenian border, and not in Nagorno-Karabakh, Yerevan has requested an emergency meeting of the CSTO Permanent Council. Originally scheduled for June 13, it was cancelled and subsequently held on June 14 as a regularly scheduled meeting, where it was announced that Armenia's allies "have taken notice of the reported armed clashes." If the Armenians were counting on solidarity, they were sorely disappointed. Needless to say, such illustrious STO members Kyrgyzstan, Kazakhstan, Tajikistan and Belarus have no intention of ever going to war in the Transcaucasus under any circumstances, since they do not have any vital interests there. For its part, Moscow is seeking to restore its dominant position in the region, which, of course, requires a balanced relationship with both Baku and Yerevan, and not getting involved in the conflict on one side or the other. As for the 102nd base, it is there to contain NATO (Turkey), not Azerbaijan.

But what would happen if escalation spun out of control?

Armenia has old Soviet R-17 (Scud-B) short-range ballistic missiles with a 300-kilometer range and a 1,000-kilogram warhead, but limited accuracy. There are also Russian Iskander operational-tactical high-precision quasi-ballistic missiles. Generally, these missiles can effectively engage almost any significant target in Azerbaijan – oil and gas infrastructure, government facilities in Baku or the Mingechaur dam on the Kura [River] with a 16-sq.km. reservoir.

For its part, Azerbaijan has 50 Israeli-made LORA [Long Range Attack] high-precision quasi-ballistic missiles with a range of 400 km and Belarussian Polonez missiles with a range of 300 km, as well as shorter-range Turkish and Israel missiles. During the four-day war in 2016, Armenian operational-tactical missiles were deployed but not used in Nagorno-Karabakh. Now Baku has said that it may retaliate by launching high-precision strikes against Armenia's Metsamor Nuclear Power Plant, the only nuclear power plant in the Transcaucasus, located 34 km from Yerevan, potentially triggering a nuclear disaster with massive radioactive fallout. But despite the mutual escalation in tension, that may still be avoided, with missiles launched not against the nuclear power plant but against other significant targets in and around Yerevan.

Turkish Defense Minister Hulusi Akar has said that the Turkish military "is ready to support the Azerbaijani Armed Forces against Armenian aggression." If mutual animosity gets to the point of unchecked escalation, Turkey may make good on its threats. Turkish troops could enter the Nakhichevan enclave and make their way to Yerevan. The 102nd base could mobilize. But what good is one Russian brigade of contract soldiers (mostly Armenians with Russian passports) against the might of the Turkish Army? Then, per Russia's official military doctrine, nuclear deterrence would have to be brought into play to prevent the catastrophic destruction of an ally. This is known as "escalation for the sake of escalation" – i.e., launching a limited nuclear strike (a couple of warheads) against Turkey to scare it and force it to retreat.

Of course, the situation is unlikely to become a nuclear disaster. The July 2020 escalation will end, and everything will return to the previous, slightly frozen state. The world will quickly move on, but the parties to it will not. There are no prospects for a political compromise to the Nagorno-Karabakh conflict. No one is working earnestly toward that end. Baku and Yerevan will continue to make [military] preparations and stockpile weapons until the next flare-up.

WHO'S IN THE CSTO: RUSSIA'S ALLIES OR POTENTIAL ADVERSARIES?

By Reserve Col. Vladimir Valentinovich Popov, Doctor of Historical Sciences, combat veteran. *Nezavisimaya gazeta*, July 24, 2020, p. 3.

As shells whizzed back and forth across the Azerbaijani-Armenian border, a lot of questions were raised about who could step in and separate the warring sides if need be. CSTO forces could help reconcile the situation, but CSTO officials have not put forward any meaningful proposals. It should be said that there is no precedent for CSTO involvement in resolving such disagreements. This repeat situation has once again raised the question of the organization's viability and who needs it.

Besides Russia, the CSTO currently includes Armenia, Belarus, Kazakhstan, Kyrgyzstan and Tajikistan. All of them are considered allies of Russia, which is generally believed to be interested in preserving the organization. What does Russia get out of it? No CSTO member followed suit when Moscow recognized the independence of Abkhazia and South Ossetia. Nagorno-Karabakh's status is still up in the air. Of all the disagreements involving the Collective Security Treaty, this territorial dispute is the quintessence, as it were. Armenia is a CSTO member, and Azerbaijan was a member before almost immediately withdrawing from the organization in 1994, apparently after Baku realized that 20% of Armenian-held territory in Nagorno-Karabakh was unlikely to go to Azerbaijan without a big bloody war. So a conflict exists, but the CSTO had no ready solutions to it.

If memory serves, there was talk back in the 1990s about deploying a collective CSTO peacekeeping force in Nagorno-Karabakh. Moreover, there is not a single instance of the organization participating in resolving similar disagreements. And there have been quite a few. In Tajikistan, there were the events of 2010 in the Fergana Valley. In June 2010, when disagreements between the Kyrgyz and Uzbek diasporas in effect brought Kyrgyzstan to the brink of civil war, the Committee of Security Council secretaries convened an emergency meeting to consider providing military assistance to Kyrgyzstan – namely, deploying Collective Rapid Reaction Forces (CRRF) in the country. Then-Russian president Dmitry Medvedev asked then-Kyrgyz president Roza Otunbayeva [to host CRRF forces], but the answer was no. Belarussian President Aleksandr Lukashenko then lambasted the CSTO for refusing to help address the situation in a CSTO member state. Perhaps that's why on June 28, 2012, Tashkent sent a note announcing the suspension of Uzbekistan's CSTO membership, which officially took effect on Dec. 19, 2012. There were other confrontations besides that: between Georgia, Abkhazia and South Ossetia in 2008, and in the Donetsk Basin in 2014. The CSTO's mission is to use the combined efforts of [members'] armies and auxiliary units to protect the territorial and economic space of member countries from any outside military-political aggressors, international terrorists, as well as major natural disasters. The CSTO, as a unified military-political alliance, has so far been doing all that virtually. The CRRF has never participated in combat operations.

At the same time, we see another example: actions by NATO's collective forces, which are active even in areas where Russia and its CSTO allies have geopolitical interests. Although there are certain disagreements among NATO member countries, there is no denying the combat effectiveness and cohesiveness of its actions in conflict zones. The bombing of Yugoslavia in 1999, the tearing away [from Serbia] of Kosovo, as well as the occupation of Iraq in the early 2000s, and subsequently of Afghanistan and Syria – these examples suggest that NATO is committed to its declared principles, no matter how we may view them.

But let's get back to discussing who benefits from the CSTO. We see that despite being CSTO members, Armenia and Kazakhstan are flirting with NATO. They are prepared to strengthen military-political ties with NATO and are even contemplating joining that bloc. How does this stack up with preserving the CSTO? Meanwhile, [CSTO] collective forces hold joint exercises every year and gather at the Moscow headquarters to discuss pressing issues. But, unfortunately, minimal real work is being done to protect member states' interests and resolve conflicts.

For now, there are only regular troop exercises. Moscow, of course, is the main driving force behind them. Beginning in 2005, Russia began to train CSTO soldiers at its military educational institutions for free. Soldiers from Kazakhstan, Belarus, Armenia, Tajikistan and Kyrgyzstan began studying in Russia in 2010. Several thousand of their soldiers are currently enrolled at [Russian] military academies. But does this collaboration make any sense and provide any benefit to our collective defense? Right now, given how relations are shaping up among the [CSTO] countries, it is unclear what armed conflicts the specialists who graduate from Russian military academies would be involved in and – most importantly – on whose side.

Chapter 14 | Karabakh War 2.0: Death of the Status Quo

Conflict Unfrozen

MOBILIZATION IN RESPONSE TO CONFRONTATION

By Yelizaveta Antonova, Kirill Sirotkin and Yevgeny Pudovkin. *RBC Daily*, Sept. 28, 2020, p. 6.

... In the early morning hours of Sunday, Sept. 27, fighting resumed along the Armenian-Azerbaijani border. Azerbaijan used Grad multiple-launch rocket systems to fire on the city of Stepanakert and other residential areas in Nagorno-Karabakh, said Vagram Pogosyan, press secretary of the unrecognized republic's president, in a Facebook post. The ombudsman of the Nagorno-Karabakh republic said a woman and a child were killed in the Azerbaijani attack. Armenia and Azerbaijan accused each other of violating the ceasefire. Baku said residential settlements along the border came under heavy shelling by Armenia....

For its part, the Armenian Defense Ministry blamed the clashes on Azerbaijan. According to Yerevan, the Azerbaijani Army launched strikes along the entire border and was the first to shell Nagorno-Karabakh's territory. The Armenian Armed Forces said two Azerbaijani helicopters and three drones were shot down. Baku confirmed the loss of one helicopter.

What now?

Azerbaijani President Ilkham Aliyev said there were casualties among Azerbaijani civilians and military personnel. "[The shedding of] their blood will not go unpunished," he said, adding that the Azerbaijani Army has destroyed a large amount of Armenian military hardware and equipment.

Nagorno-Karabakh has imposed martial law. Araik Arutyunyan, head of the unrecognized republic, has declared a full mobilization of men aged 18 [to 55].

Armenia has also imposed martial law and launched a general mobilization. "By the decision of the government, martial law and a general mobilization are declared in the Republic of Armenia," Armenian Prime Minister Nikol Pashinyan wrote on Facebook.

The international community's response

The Russian Foreign Ministry urged the [conflicting] sides to immediately cease fire and engage in talks to stabilize the situation. In a telephone conversation with the

Armenian prime minister, Vladimir Putin said it is necessary to end hostilities and avoid further escalation of the conflict.

Turkey has backed Azerbaijan in the conflict: Turkish presidential press secretary Ibrahim Kalin said Ankara supports Baku and condemns Yerevan for violating the ceasefire....

What now?

The current escalation is the most serious since the 1992-1994 war, Leonid Nersisyan, head of the defense studies department at the Armenian Research and Development Institute (ARDI), told RBC. "This is in fact a full-blown war: The conflict involves not just local clashes, but the entire line of contact," he said....

Despite the clashes, the sides hardly have the resources for a full-blown war, said Stanislav Pritchin, senior research fellow at the Center for Post-Soviet Studies at the Russian Academy of Sciences' Institute of Economics. "Even though Azerbaijan's economy is quite stable, the prospect of fighting along the entire border to the last bullet is a very costly option in terms of human resources and financial costs," he said, adding that Baku's current actions are most likely pursuing tactical goals – namely to retake Azerbaijani territory.

Still, the risks that the conflict will continue are high, Pritchin believes. First, the scale of the sides' military mobilization is quite impressive. Second, the danger of escalation makes it increasingly unacceptable for each side to come off as the loser in the conflict, the analyst added.

"As for Russia, it is in a difficult situation, since it is a key player both in the trilateral format for Nagorno-Karabakh settlement and in the OSCE format, where the parties are trying to work out a compromise with French and US mediation," Pritchin said. "Besides, right now, Moscow has no direct leverage over the sides," he added.

CSTO WILL NOT GO INTO BATTLE

By Aleksei Nikolsky and Svetlana Bocharova. *Vedomosti*, Sept. 30, 2020, p. 1.

On Sept. 29, the Armenian Defense Ministry announced that at 10:30 a.m. local time, a Turkish F-16 fighter jet shot down an [Armenian] Su-25 ground-attack plane on a combat mission in Armenian airspace. The pilot of the Su-25 died. According to the Armenian Defense Ministry, the F-16 took off from Gyandzha airport in northeastern Azerbaijan and hit the Su-25 with a missile from a distance of about 60 kilometers [sic; in a Facebook post, Armenian Defense Ministry spokeswoman Shushan Stepanyan said the Turkish F-16 was 60 km (37 miles) deep into Armenian airspace – *Trans.*].

The report was denied shortly afterward by the Turkish Defense Ministry, and then by the Azerbaijani Defense Ministry. Azerbaijani President Ilkham Aliyev said

Sept. 29 on the "60 Minutes" show on the Rossia 1 TV channel that "there are no F-16 fighter jets" anywhere near Nagorno-Karabakh. For his part, the Armenian prime minister said on the same show that Azerbaijan was attacking Armenian territory, and that there were casualties. On Sept. 28, the Armenian side said a military unit in the town of Vardenis came under attack and a bus was hit in the same area, killing the driver.

Armenia is a member of the Collective Security Treaty Organization (CSTO). Under Art. 4 of the treaty, "If one of the member states undergoes aggression (armed attack menacing [its] safety, stability, territorial integrity and sovereignty), it will be considered by the member states as aggression***against all the member states of this treaty." At the same time, CSTO member states, including Russia, do not officially recognize the territory of Nagorno-Karabakh, where fighting has been going on since Sept. 29, as Armenian territory. Clashes and incidents are also taking place along the Armenian-Azerbaijani border, as they did in the past, but this is the first time that Armenia has accused a third country, i.e., Turkey, of committing a hostile military act against its territory.

At a press briefing on Sept. 29 before the [F-16] incident, Russian presidential press secretary Dmitry Peskov refused to comment on the CSTO's response to the events in Nagorno-Karabakh.

Asked by Vedomosti after the incident whether Russia's stance on the CSTO's reaction could change as a result, Peskov said: "I still have no comment on that."

According to Aleksandr Yermakov, an expert with the Russian International Affairs Council, if the CSTO receives a request for assistance, as per the treaty, it would have to consider it, but a decision can be made only by consensus. "I believe it would be difficult for the organization to even go so far as to unanimously condemn Azerbaijan, let alone provide direct military assistance to Armenia: In terms of intrabloc discipline, the CSTO does not compare to NATO, and even [NATO's] unity is often in question," he said.

As for the wording of Art. 4 (aggression against one member country is considered aggression against the bloc), things are not so simple there, either, Yermakov says. Those opposed to punishing Azerbaijan might say that the current war is not aggression but the restoration of Azerbaijan's territorial integrity, and that it is not known exactly what happened to Armenia's Su-25, he added.

According to a Vedomosti diplomatic source, the most likely candidate for the role of such a brake in the CSTO mechanism is Belarus, despite the difficult situation that its president, Aleksandr Lukashenko, is in. The Belarussian president has openly said that Azerbaijan issued it a loan to pay for Gazprom gas deliveries 10 years ago. During this period, supplies of Belarussian weapon systems to Azerbaijan, primarily air defense systems and truck chassis, as well as Polonez long-range missile systems developed with China's assistance, have exceeded $1 billion, the source said.

Technically, Russia, which has an integrated air defense system with Armenia, could use that system or other reconnaissance assets to establish exactly what was responsible for the incident: a Turkish fighter jet, an Azerbaijan MiG-29 jet, or maybe even an Azerbaijani long-range air defense system, says a source close to the Russian Defense Ministry. But it is not known whether [Russia] has done that, nor is it clear whether Russia would make [its findings] public, he added.

SECOND NAGORNO-KARABAKH MOBILIZATION

By staff commentator Pavel Felgengauer. *Novaya gazeta*, Sept. 30, 2020, p. 2.

Over the past 26 years, there have been recurring clashes and exchanges of fire on the Nagorno-Karabakh fronts, with casualties and loss of equipment, but those were isolated incidents that did not substantially change the general lineup of forces. A significant flare-up took place in April 2016 – the so-called four-day war, when the Azerbaijanis suddenly mounted an offensive operation and seized several forward-based Armenian positions. The Armenians counterattacked, rectifying the situation somewhat. Hundreds of people were killed and injured. At the time, Armenia's health care system was overwhelmed, unable to cope with an influx of victims burned by Solntsepyok TOS heavy flamethrower systems made and supplied by Russia. But on the fifth day, with mediation and pressure from Moscow, the sides agreed to a ceasefire, and the war was over in four days.

Since 2016, the ceasefire remained frozen with sporadic minor clashes until July 2020, when a new conflict erupted not in Nagorno-Karabakh but right along the Armenian-Azerbaijani border in the mountainous Tavush-Tovuz area. The conflict was smaller in scale than the four-day one. After more than a week of shelling and fighting at the local level, hostilities stopped, but Armenian-Azerbaijani tensions in general continued to escalate, with official rhetoric and accusations of "provocations" on both sides becoming increasingly uncompromising. On Sept. 20, Azerbaijani President Ilkham Aliyev announced that the "Armenians are preparing for a new big war – we have intelligence to that effect," and that Armenia had provoked the July border conflict to "test the reaction of their CSTO allies." Aliyev added that "they must fully and unconditionally withdraw from our lands" in keeping with UN Security Council resolutions, and that this is the only condition for peacefully resolving the conflict. This may have looked like a rhetorical PR move, but a week later, war broke out without warning.

Needless to say, both sides accused each other of provocation and shelling, but it was the Azerbaijani Army that promptly mounted a decisive "counteroffensive" along the entire Nagorno-Karabakh line of contact, where no neutral observers have been permanently stationed over the past decades and where there are no demilitarized or arms limitation zones. So officially, there is no one to consult with about who exactly started the fighting. Granted, from a practical standpoint, this is no longer important. Regardless of who started it, the Azerbaijani Army seized the initiative.

In peacetime, defense in the Armenian-Azerbaijani conflict zone is not very deep. The Azerbaijani military managed to advance fairly rapidly and seize a number of positions in northern Nagorno-Karabakh, as well as in the south, in the Araz [River] valley along the Iranian border. The Armenian military put up active resistance and counterattacked, so right now the slight advance by the Azerbaijani Army as such does not have much tactical value. Even so, both sides are sustaining heavy losses of personnel and equipment. As is usual in any war, the figures reported by both sides are unreliable and are often later revised to underreport one's own losses and inflate enemy losses. Yet, it is clear that the fighting is intense: Within a couple of days, hundreds have been killed and injured.

The Armenian military is well armed, but with relatively obsolete equipment inherited from the Soviet Armed Forces or taken as trophies during the first war in Nagorno-Karabakh. There is a shortage of modern or substantially modernized weapons, since Armenia's budget is not very large and [military] deliveries to an isolated country are a logistical challenge. Rich Azerbaijan is buying weapons and equipment in Russia, Israel and all over the world, including systems that even the Russian military does not have, let alone the Armenians. That was already evident during the four-day war, and today Azerbaijan's strategy is built on military-technological superiority. On the very first day of fighting, the Azerbaijani military dominated Nagorno-Karabakh airspace, using armed unmanned aerial vehicles and piloted systems. The main priority was to suppress the Armenian air defense system. [Several] S-300 surface-to-air missile systems and up to 15 Osa SAM systems were reportedly destroyed with precision strikes. Baku claims to have fully suppressed Armenian air defenses in Nagorno-Karabakh.

Stepanakert's and Yerevan's response to the Azerbaijani offensive was extremely tough: On the very first day, they introduced martial law and declared a general mobilization of reservists aged 18 to 55. Azerbaijan also imposed martial law and a curfew, but declared only a partial military mobilization. These decisions will now predetermine the development of events and the course of the conflict. A general mobilization is an expensive and challenging undertaking. Israel, where the call-up of reservists and the deployment of reserve subunits is a well-organized and coordinated process, has declared a general mobilization only three times – in 1956, 1967 and 1973. A general mobilization drastically disrupts any country's economic and social life. It is impossible to maintain it without fighting, and subsequent mass demobilization also requires time, resources and money. It's like rules for courtyard chess: If you touch a piece [on the board], you must move that piece. Now the Armenians have no choice: It is practically impossible to call off the current general mobilization. Doing so would create a logistical mess that would take months to sort out, and all that time the country would be essentially defenseless. Amid the general uptick in patriotic sentiment, any attempt by Aliyev or Pashinyan to backpedal would lead to a political crisis and [their] possible overthrow, whereas mobilization has in effect cemented [their] positions.

For a small country like Armenia, mobilization is the only chance to match the opponent. A general mobilization would multiply the power of the Armenian Armed Forces: Together with the Nagorno-Karabakh Army, between 240,000 and 300,000 men could be called to arms. But it is impossible to send them all to the eastern front in Nagorno-Karabakh. Armenia has a second front in the west – i.e., against Turkey and Azerbaijan's Nakhichevan Province, and some forces have to be deployed there even if no war is going on there yet. Even so, a battle group could be raised in Nagorno-Karabakh superior to Azerbaijani forces that would mount a decisive counteroffensive, which should be expected very soon. The task would be not just to force the Azerbaijanis from their positions, but to rout them completely, as in the victorious [war of] 1993-1994.

This seems to be the basis of Azerbaijani strategy – namely, to goad the Armenians, provoke mass mobilization to bring Armenian men out into the battlefield for a decisive attack (thus draining the Armenian economy of its life force), and expose them to precision-guided armed drones and Israeli-made Spike and South Korean AT-1K Raybolt third-generation fire-and-forget antitank guided missiles tipped with a tandem high-explosive warhead that would burn [Armenian] armor. The [expected] social, political, and economic crisis would then undermine the Pashinyan regime and demoralize the Armenian Army.

Except for Turkey, which is actively supporting Baku, the rest of the world, including Russia, is unanimously urging all conflicting parties to deescalate, cease fire and engage in talks. But these good intentions have had no impact on the lineup of forces on the Nagorno-Karabakh fronts.

KARABAKH COLLAPSE

By Aleksandr Atasuntsev. *RBC Daily*, Oct. 1, 2020, p. 4.

... Yesterday, the conflict in Nagorno-Karabakh went beyond the Armenian-Azerbaijani confrontation. Yerevan officially announced that a Turkish F-16 fighter jet (Azerbaijan does not have such aircraft) shot down an Armenian Su-25 near the city of Vardanis – i.e., in Armenian airspace. At the same time, there is mounting evidence that Syrian mercenaries are fighting on the Azerbaijani side. For example, the Syrian newspaper Jesr Press published a photo of a mortally wounded fighter from Homs. The day before, Reuters and The Guardian reported that militants from Syria are fighting on the side of Baku.

Also on Sept. 30, the Armenian Defense Ministry said Azerbaijan had handed control of the offensive operation against Nagorno-Karabakh to the Turkish Air Force. As of 10 a.m., Turkish F-16s and Azerbaijani Air Force Su-25s jointly attacked Martakert, including civilian facilities. Their actions were directed from the E7T command and control center based in Erzurum, Turkey, said [Armenian] Defense Ministry spokesman Artsrun Avannisyan. Baku and Ankara earlier denied reports of Turkey's involvement in the conflict.

Later in the evening, Russian Foreign Minister Sergei Lavrov and Armenian Foreign Minister Sograb Mnatsakanyan talked by phone. Lavrov indicated the unacceptability of Turkey's involvement in the conflict and added that militants have been deployed to Azerbaijan. The ministers said the participation of third forces in the conflict is unacceptable, according to a statement published on the Armenian Foreign Ministry's Web site. After the conversation, the Russian Foreign Ministry said it was willing to provide a platform in Moscow for contacts to resolve the conflict.

Before the conversation between the Russian and Armenian foreign ministers, Azerbaijani President Ilkham Aliyev said Baku would agree to a ceasefire in Nagorno-Karabakh only if the Armenian Armed Forces withdraw from there. "Our mission is just. We want to restore our territorial integrity, and we will do that," he said.

Since 1991, Armenia has never asked for a ceasefire in Nagorno-Karabakh, Vagarshak Arutyunyan, chief adviser to the Armenian prime minister, told RBC. "It has always been Baku requesting a ceasefire – in 1992, 1993, twice in 1994, and in 2016," he said.

So far, contacts between Russian officials and the Turkish side have produced no results. Turkish Foreign Minister Mevlut Cavusoglu said Ankara has discussed with Moscow ways of resolving the conflict in Nagorno-Karabakh "like in Syria." The Turkish minister noted that talks on this issue were held with Russian President Vladimir Putin and Sergei Lavrov. "We tried to cooperate here (in Nagorno-Karabakh – *RBC*) just as we are cooperating on Syria, but it did not work out. They are saying, 'end the war.' So end it. A ceasefire needs to be declared, but Armenia would have to withdraw from the occupied territories. Is that being said? No. So how can this issue be resolved?" Cavusoglu said.

Yerevan views Russia as a mediator. If Moscow were to take sides, it would lose that status, Arutyunyan said. Russia was the first among the cochairs of the OSCE Minsk Group [on Nagorno-Karabakh] to respond to the escalation, he added. Lavrov had telephone conversations with his Armenian and Azerbaijani counterparts on Sunday, hours after the flare-up.

Why isn't Armenia asking for help?

During Nikol Pashinyan's talks with Vladimir Putin on Sept. 27 and Sept. 29, the possibility of Russia's military intervention was not discussed, the Armenian prime minister told RBC. Moreover, Armenia so far sees no need to ask the CSTO for assistance, either. "At this stage, the Armenian Armed Forces are in a position to ensure the country's security, and we believe we are not in a situation where we would need to make such a request," Pashinyan said....

If the situation drastically deteriorates and if Armenia is attacked, Yerevan has other options. For example, Russia's 102nd military base could be brought into play not only under the CSTO Treaty, but also in accordance with the Russian-Armenian Treaty on Friendship, Cooperation and Mutual Security, the expert explained.

Azerbaijani Ambassador to Russia Polad Byulyulogly told RBC on Wednesday that the CSTO is staying out of the conflict "because fighting is taking place on Azerbaijani territory," and "if the CSTO intervenes, then our ally Turkey may also intervene."

Yerevan may also recognize Nagorno-Karabakh's independence or sign an agreement on strategic cooperation between Armenia and Nagorno-Karabakh, as well as a security and defense cooperation treaty, Pashinyan said on Wednesday. That decision would allow the Armenian Armed Forces to become openly involved in the conflict: Right now, the unrecognized republic is being officially defended only by the Nagorno-Karabakh defense army, which is comprised of Nagorno-Karabakh troops and hundreds of Armenian volunteers who went to the conflict zone after Sept. 27. For its part, Azerbaijan is saying that Moscow's recognition of Nagorno-Karabakh's independence "would be the last bridge they would burn," and then the war would continue until the "victorious end."

ANKARA IMPOSING A SYRIAN SCENARIO ON MOSCOW IN TRANSCAUCASUS

By Vladimir Mukhin. *Nezavisimaya gazeta*, Oct. 2, 2020, p. 1.

The OSCE Minsk Group cochairs finally turned its attention to the military confrontation in the Nagorno-Karabakh conflict zone. Russian President Vladimir Putin, US President Donald Trump and French President Emmanuel Macron issued a joint statement calling for an immediate cessation of hostilities between the military forces of the parties to the conflict. This is the first collective statement by world leaders on the Nagorno-Karabakh problem in modern history.

But will the conflicting sides and their allies heed this call? In Ankara, almost at the same time as the Russian, US, and French leaders released their statement, Turkish President [Recep] Tayyip Erdogan criticized the OSCE Minsk Group for urging a ceasefire in Nagorno-Karabakh, saying that it was unacceptable. The war in the Transcaucasus continues.

Reports of fighting from fixed positions in the conflict zone are accompanied by information about Syrian militants fighting there. The Russian Foreign Ministry expressed concern over this situation.

"According to incoming data, militants from illegal armed groups, in particular from Syria and Libya, are being sent to the Nagorno-Karabakh conflict zone to directly participate in the hostilities," the Russian foreign policy agency's press and information department said in comments published last Wednesday....

The Armenian Foreign Ministry also said that Syrian fighters are involved in hostilities in the Nagorno-Karabakh conflict zone. The media quoted an informed source in Yerevan who said on condition of anonymity that "Turkey dispatched to Azerbaijan between 2,000 and 3,000 mercenaries consisting of Turkoman proxy units from Syria's Idlib and Afrin, which have also fought in Libya." Meanwhile, influential Western media outlets (the BBC, The Guardian, The Times, etc.) have interviewed mercenaries who are present at the Nagorno-Karabakh front....

Turkish Foreign Minister Mevlut Cavusoglu has also presented his version [of events] in an interview with the Anadolu state news agency. "I spoke with Putin [and] Lavrov. We tried to cooperate here (in Nagorno-Karabakh – *RBC*) just as we are cooperating on Syria, but it did not work out. They are saying, 'end the war.' So end it." From Ankara's perspective, a ceasefire needs to be declared. But at the same time, Turkey's chief diplomat believes a settlement in Nagorno-Karabakh is possible "only if Armenia withdraws from the occupied territories." Earlier, Cavusoglu said that "Turkey will support Azerbaijan both at the negotiating table and on the battlefield."

The Anna-news.info portal has offered this explanation for the Turkish leadership's stance: "Ankara is seeking to become a direct participant in the events on the ground in the South Caucasus, and acquire a status on a par with Russia. But the Syrian settlement model used in Idlib that Turkey is trying to project onto Nagorno-Karabakh has demonstrated Ankara's inability to honor its own commitments. For example, it has yet to ensure the withdrawal of all terrorists and moderate militants from areas south of the M4 highway (Aleppo-Latakia) in the Idlib deescalation zone, even though that was one of the main provisions of the Russian-Turkish agreements that were reached in early March."

This view is echoed by Lt. Gen. Sergei Chvarkov (Ret.), former head of the Russian reconciliation center for Syria: "Currently, Turkey is actively establishing pro-Turkish autonomous districts in northern and northwestern Syria, effectively indicating that they have come to that country to stay." In his opinion, this is precisely the reason for Turkey's passive stance on the implementation of the September 2018 agreements with Russia on Idlib, the militants' last major stronghold in Syria.

Besides, Chvarkov noted, many experts get the impression that as part of establishing operational command for Operation Peace Spring, Turkey is laying the groundwork for legitimizing and coordinating joint military operations with moderate and intransigent opposition groups in Syria.

Once they get to Azerbaijan, the consequences of Syrian fighters' involvement in patrolling the so-called legitimization zones in Nagorno-Karabakh could be unpredictable.

Meanwhile, a number of military experts believe that the Russian military [base] in Gyumri could become a guarantor of starting a peaceful dialogue on Nagorno-Karabakh conflict settlement.

In a conversation with NG, Lt. Gen. Yury Netkachev, who in the 1990s was deputy commander of the Group of Russian Forces in the Transcaucasus and in charge of Russia's 102nd military base in Armenia, stressed that "subunits of the Russian Armed Forces can ensure a ceasefire in the Nagorno-Karabakh conflict zone if political agreements on the issue are achieved with the mediation of Russia and other relevant countries." The general recalled that this scenario had been considered earlier, when a ceasefire was reached after prolonged hostilities between the conflicting parties in Nagorno-Karabakh in 1994. This resulted in the signing of the Bishkek Protocol on a truce and cessation of hostilities between Armenia and the self-proclaimed Nagorno-Karabakh republic, on the one side, and Azerbaijan, on the other.

"I believe that Armenian Prime Minister Nikol Pashinyan has somewhat incorrectly described the Russian military base in the republic as an 'inalienable part of Armenia's security system,' saying that 'the base's potential should be leveraged in certain situations,' " said Netkachev. The general said that Russia has taken a neutral stance on the Nagorno-Karabakh conflict and is urging the conflicting sides to cease fire. "The 102nd base will not become involved in this conflict. Its principal function is to ensure the security of the CIS's Transcaucasus front against external aggression. Just as in Syria, it could become a reconciliation center for Nagorno-Karabakh. The Russian soldiers' mission is to bring peace, not to fight."

THERE IS ONLY PEACE

By Elnar Bainazarov, Anton Lavrov and Denis Kulaga. *Izvestia*, Oct. 6, 2020, p. 1.

Neither Baku nor Yerevan has heeded the urging of the OSCE Minsk Group cochairs to start peace talks without preconditions. Both Armenia and Azerbaijan have advanced their own proposals for resolving the conflict....

On Oct. 3, Armenian Prime Minister Nikol Pashinyan said that Nagorno-Karabakh peace talks are possible only if Azerbaijan stops fighting.

Baku does not consider continuation of the military phase a problem, and sets the following condition for a ceasefire: Nagorno-Karabakh mediators must provide guarantees of the "withdrawal of Armenian troops" from the [disputed] territories. That was announced on Oct. 5 by President Ilkham Aliyev. He also stressed that Turkey should play a role in the settlement process.

The Nagorno-Karabakh foreign ministry put forward its own condition ahead of the peace negotiations: It reported having submitted a statement to the OSCE on the need to recognize the republic's independence as a prerequisite for restoring peace.

Meanwhile, in response to Baku's and Yerevan's unwillingness to sit down at the negotiating table, the foreign ministers of the countries cochairing the Minsk Group issued a joint statement condemning the unprecedented and dangerous escalation of violence in and beyond the conflict zone.

Nikol Pashinyan called Vladimir Putin late in the evening. The leaders discussed the escalation of the conflict, "which has become large-scale and is leading to significant losses on both sides, including civilian casualties," the Kremlin press service said. The Russian leader stressed that the fighting must end without delay.

The day before, in an interview with Al Arabiya TV, Ilkham Aliyev said that he does not agree that the conflict has no military solution.

"If there is no military path, then give us a nonmilitary path – a diplomatic path. Implement the UN Security Council resolutions," the Azerbaijani president said. "If the international community cannot ensure the implementation of international resolutions, then Azerbaijan will do so on its own, and that is happening now."

But Russia does not agree with that position. There is no use-of-force solution to the Nagorno-Karabakh conflict, Konstantin Kosachov, head of the [Russian] Federation Council's international affairs committee, told Izvestia. He also commented that Russia is not remaining a passive observer in the Nagorno-Karabakh conflict and continues to actively urge both sides to hold peace talks.

"This is a false impression (that Moscow is observing the conflict from the sidelines – *Iz.*). But with respect to peacekeeping, it will be called for and effective only if all parties to the conflict are interested in it. Until that happens, I am afraid that the chances of such an operation are slim, since the opposing side would perceive it not as peacekeeping but as strengthening the position of the other side," the parliamentarian explained.

Izvestia spoke with politicians from both countries to clarify why both sides continue to put forward conditions and refuse to lay down their arms. Deputy speaker of the Armenian parliament Alen Simonyan, in an interview with Izvestia, stressed that it will be impossible to resolve the conflict at this stage without third-party mediation, since Baku is still saying that it will continue to address the issue militarily.

"What can you say when a republic with a population of 150,000 is attacked by a country with a population of 10 million, and a country with a population of 90 million, Turkey, is helping it, while third countries are merely calling for peace and not taking any active steps to halt the aggression? Naturally, it will be impossible to resolve the conflict without third-party intervention," the politician commented.

Sabir Gadzhiyev, a deputy of the Azerbaijani Mejlis (parliament), explained to Izvestia that from Baku's standpoint, to start the negotiation process, guarantees are needed that the OSCE Minsk Group will ask Yerevan to comply with the Bishkek Protocol. The latter, the politician recalled, envisaged the withdrawal of Armenian troops from the territory of seven regions of Azerbaijan that were not part of the Nagorno-Karabakh Republic during the Soviet period.

"The international community should press harder on the question: Why isn't Armenia lifting its occupation of the territories?" the parliamentarian said....

THIS WAR IS BASICALLY CHANGING THE ENTIRE CONTEXT OF THE CONFLICT

By Aleksandr Atasuntsev. *RBC Daily*, Oct. 8, 2020, p. 4.

Editors' Note. – Since Sept. 27, fierce fighting has been taking place in Nagorno-Karabakh. In an interview with RBC, Armenian Prime Minister Nikol Pashinyan speaks about the tactics of the Nagorno-Karabakh Army, the topic of his conversations with the Russian president, and conditions for recognizing the NKR.

* * *

'A real foundation for the final victory of the Nagorno-Karabakh Army is being laid'

Question. – You have returned from Nagorno-Karabakh. What is the situation there now?

Answer. – I was in Stepanakert, the capital of Nagorno-Karabakh. Stepanakert is under almost round-the-clock rocket fire, and, of course, civilians are suffering there. And that is beyond the pale. You understand that if Azerbaijan insists that Nagorno-Karabakh is part of its territory and really thinks that the people of Nagorno-Karabakh and Azerbaijan can live with each other – well, then they would be destroying their own cities. What is Ilkham Aliyev thinking? Does he think that he can bomb Stepanakert and after that the people of Nagorno-Karabakh will live as part of Azerbaijan? This approach once again underscores that Nagorno-Karabakh cannot and never will be part of Azerbaijan. That has already been ruled out – 100%. And Azerbaijan's actions attest to that.

Q. – In recent days, Azerbaijan has been declaring successes at the front – for example, the capture of several villages on the line of contact. Is this true?

A. – Considering the reports that have been coming in since early this morning, we can say that the Nagorno-Karabakh commanders' idea worked: They took tactical [backward] steps in the south, left a corridor [open] and lured a contingent of Azerbaijani troops there. Literally this very second, that contingent is falling under a crushing attack. And I think this will be the key moment of the entire operation. Right this minute, according to my information, a real foundation for the final victory of the Nagorno-Karabakh Army is being laid.

Q. – Why do you say that?

A. – Because Nagorno-Karabakh and Armenian commanders had a plan to retreat toward Dzhebrail and lure large forces of the Azerbaijani Army there. Yesterday evening, [Azerbaijani forces] entered there in large – very large – numbers, and this morning, a crushing attack was launched against them, and the operation is going extremely well.

Q. – Is there any information about the Azerbaijani side's losses?

A. – Yes, there is already an official statement from the Armenian Defense Ministry, and it is very significant that Azerbaijan sent a lot of [military] equipment into [the ambush]. Most of it was destroyed or simply abandoned by the fleeing Azerbaijanis. So I think the Nagorno-Karabakh Army will have a lot of equipment today.

Q. – A few days ago, there were reports about a missile strike on the city of Gyandzha, [Azerbaijan]. Could fighting spill into Azerbaijan?

A. – [Yes,] if today's operation ends as it began, and I think that is very likely. Because after such a success, the Nagorno-Karabakh Army will not just sit and wait for Azerbaijani forces to regroup. And I think that if they succeed today, they will try to build on their success.

Q. – So, go on the offensive in Azerbaijan?

A. – I can't speak for them. Those decisions are made by Nagorno-Karabakh's military leaders. I'm assessing the overall situation.

'We are discussing he situation in our region, especially the presence of terrorists.'

Q. – You have spoken by phone with Vladimir Putin several times since the conflict broke out. What are you discussing? Are you talking about the supply of military equipment from Russia to Armenia?

A. – We are discussing everything. But the main topic of discussion is the situation in our region, especially the presence of terrorists in the South Caucasus. Because, you know, if Nagorno-Karabakh and Azerbaijan, or Armenia and Azerbaijan, are simply fighting, that is one situation. But if terrorists from specific terrorist groups are involved in the fighting (and, incidentally, yesterday, Russian officials mentioned specific terrorist organizations whose members are fighting in the conflict zone), this is a completely different situation. This is not just about Nagorno-Karabakh, but about security in our region in a broader sense – the security of Russia and Iran. This is basically a global security issue. Because it means that terrorists are expanding their range. It turns out that with the help of Turkey and Azerbaijan, terrorists have new territories where they can prove themselves. Let's imagine this conflict ends somehow; what would [the terrorists] do after that? Some of these terrorists would undoubtedly stay in the region and operate there. We are getting information that these terrorists are already instituting their own rules and practices in some Azerbaijani villages. And that raises the question: To what extent are the Azerbaijani authorities in control of the situation in their own country? Because if terrorists are operating somewhere in any normal country, a normal government is supposed to work to destroy them, not give them the opportunity to act unchecked and institute their own rules and practices.

Q. – In this changed context, was Armenia given guarantees of Russian military intervention?

A. – Russia is a strategic ally of Armenia, and we have specific security agreements. For example, we have a common air defense.

Q. – Are air defenses involved now?

A. – Yes, of course.

Q. – In the fighting, too?

A. – No, not in combat. I'm referring to the territory of the Republic of Armenia. But if there is a threat to Armenia from the air, then our joint forces must get involved. And that is stipulated by our agreements, statutes and other documents.

Q. – But the terrorist threat, as you said, is in Nagorno-Karabakh, and the issue of guarantees has to do with Russian military intervention.

A. – Right. And that guarantee applies to the territory of the Republic of Armenia.

Q. – Were those guarantees confirmed during your most recent conversations with Moscow?

A. – You know, we did discuss those topics in recent conversations, but since all this is stipulated in our agreements, there is no need to confirm it every time. This is an established fact, and we discussed some of the nuances in this area.

Q. – Still, are you expecting supplies of military equipment from Russia to Armenia?

A. – As I said, Russia and Armenia have allied relations, an integral component of which is also military-technical cooperation.

Q. – Will there be new supplies in connection with this conflict?

A. – That is a different matter, which I cannot discuss openly. Especially in this situation.

'This is an antiterrorist war'

Q. – Do you agree that this conflict has pushed back the negotiation process for years, if not decades? Is any compromise at all possible now? For example, would Yerevan agree to the transfer of some districts or some new formulas?

A. – I don't think it's appropriate to discuss that now. You asked if I think this war has pushed back the negotiation process for decades. I think that this war basically changes the context, the whole context of this conflict. Because this is no longer a conflict in Nagorno-Karabakh. This is an antiterrorist war being waged by Nagorno-Karabakh and Armenia. This is a terrorist attack against Nagorno-Karabakh initiated by Azerbaijan and organized by Turkey. This is no longer a threat to just Nagorno-Karabakh; it is a specific threat to Russia. And the fact is that Russia, too, is thinking about the situation in more or less those terms. And if you have been following official statements from Moscow in recent days, it is obvious that Russia, if not 100%, then 80%, perceives the situation roughly the same way.

Q. – So the war can end only if Azerbaijan surrenders unconditionally?

A. – No, the war can end only if the terrorist groups surrender unconditionally. Because the objective of Armenia and Nagorno-Karabakh is not the unconditional surrender of Azerbaijan; the objective is the unconditional surrender of the terrorist groups operating in the conflict zone.

Q. – But that would not remove the issues between Yerevan and Baku.

A. – Of course. I have already said that [the terrorists'] presence, and in general the presence of Turkey in the region, changes the context. Why did Turkey return to the South Caucasus a hundred years later? For two reasons. The first is to continue the policy of Armenian genocide. You understand that if something goes wrong, a genocide will begin of Nagorno-Karabakh Armenians, at the very least. That is no exaggeration.

But why is it important for Turkey to continue the policy of genocide? Because the Armenians of the South Caucasus are the last obstacle to Turkish expansion to the north and east. And if we look at this situation in the context of Turkey's policy in the Mediterranean region with respect to Greece, with respect to Cyprus, in the context of the policy that Turkey is pursuing in Iraq and Syria, the picture will become clearer. This is an imperialistic policy that threatens not only Armenia and Nagorno-Karabakh, but also a lot of countries quite far from here.

Q. – So, do I understand correctly that negotiations with Azerbaijan on settling the situation in Nagorno-Karabakh are possible only if all terrorist groups leave the line of contact [and] leave Azerbaijan's territory?

A. – Negotiations are a separate topic. Because there are the cochairs of the OSCE Minsk Group – Russia, the US and France. And they are working to restore the negotiation process. They issued a statement on the situation. They said that the violence, shelling and military operations must stop. Armenia welcomed that statement. In any situation, the ability to negotiate and the negotiating process are, of course, important. And we are very appreciative of the OSCE Minsk Group cochairs' efforts, and we, of course, will be as constructive as possible in working with the cochairs.

'It is wrong to take the Nagorno-Karabakh issue and discuss its individual details'

Q. – This negotiation process has been going on for over 25 years. As we can see, it has not led to anything, and Stepanakert has been under constant shelling for a seventh day. What must happen for Yerevan to recognize the NKR's independence?

A. – We are discussing this and have said that this issue is on our agenda. But this is not a situation that allows us to make specific explanations or plans – to say "if X, then Y." Given the situation, we are discussing several possible courses of action, but there is also a caveat: We are doing everything to be as constructive as possible even in the worst situation, and primarily in our relations with the OSCE Minsk Group cochairs.

Q. – Are the OSCE Minsk Group cochairs or your allies in the CSTO asking you not to recognize the NKR?

A. – No, there has been no such request. I'll tell you honestly, from the moment we said that we were discussing this issue, no one has asked us not to do that. No one ever has.

Q. – Why don't you recognize the NKR? Because that would mean the end of negotiations?

A. – It would not mean the end of negotiations. It would depend on the specific situation – how and when this decision is made or not.

Q. – Are you closer to recognizing the NKR now than at the beginning of the week?

A. – As I said, this issue is on our agenda. But that does not mean we will definitely make such a decision. But it does not mean that we won't, either. We are discussing it.

Q. – Explain your position on peacekeeping forces. Are you in favor of their deployment at the line of contact?

A. – You know, it is wrong to take such a big issue, the Nagorno-Karabakh issue, and discuss its individual details – details of a possible settlement. You need to look at all this in the chain of cause-and-effect relationships.

Q. – But then only war remains if you do not find some way to solve the problem right now, be it recognizing Nagorno-Karabakh, deploying peacekeepers, transferring regions or some other measures.

A. – All these issues must be discussed during negotiations, which should take place among the OSCE Minsk Group cochairs.

Q. – Do you think that this negotiation process will begin only when Azerbaijan is weak enough to want to return to the negotiating table?

A. – If you look at this issue broadly, the negotiation process is continuing even now. Our minister is in constant touch with the OSCE Minsk Group cochairs. As far as I know, the cochairs are keeping in touch with the Azerbaijanis, too. So the conversation is ongoing. The negotiation process has never stopped and never does. But, of course, in the current situation it is impossible to discuss the details of a conflict settlement. Right now, there is war, and the main question is how to stop it.

Q. – There have been no contacts between Yerevan and Baku all these days of fighting?

A. – Nope, none.

YEREVAN, BAKU UNDER ATTACK?

By staff commentator Pavel Felgengauer. *Novaya gazeta*, Oct. 9, 2020, p. 2.

The war in Nagorno-Karabakh has been going on for two weeks now, and all this time the Azerbaijani Armed Forces have firmly maintained the upper hand on the battlefield but have yet to make any territorial breakthroughs. Every day, both sides are reporting huge enemy losses and sometimes their own, clearly smaller losses. During the first few days of fighting, PR services took such a heady dose of patriotism that the total number of destroyed Armenian and Azerbaijani tanks and other armor on paper reached 500 – and that is in addition to the many downed aircraft, helicopters and drones, as well as thousands of military casualties. If only half of it were true, the war would probably have already ended from lack of fighters. The fanciful PR campaign notwithstanding, the meat grinder of the second Nagorno-Karabakh [war] is in fact mincing people and equipment daily.

As often happens, the Armenian military-political leadership was preparing not for this war but the previous one (the first Nagorno-Karabakh war), which Armenia won convincingly. Objectively, by Sept. 27, 2020, the Armenian and Nagorno-Karabakh Armed Forces were far stronger than the semi-guerrilla detachments that won the first Nagorno-Karabakh war in 1993-1994. Armenia has amassed a large number of tanks and other combat equipment, [and] stocked up on ammunition and other supplies, as well as spare parts, tools and accessories – everything it frequently lacked during the first war. It has established an effective system for training military personnel and preparing reservists for mobilization. And Moscow recently delivered to Yerevan on credit several modern Su-30SM fighter jets, a couple dozen T-90 tanks, Iskander high-precision aeroballistic missiles, and Solntsepyok TOS heavy flamethrower systems to breach permanent defenses.

Of course, Azerbaijan has spent dozens of times more petrodollars to buy new [combat] equipment and ready its Armed Forces, but until Sept. 27, the general opinion in Yerevan (as well as in Moscow) was that nothing had fundamentally changed over the past 26 years. Few people took seriously Baku's stern warnings that "Azerbaijani lands will be liberated from the occupiers." It was assumed that if elite Azerbaijani units attempted to breach the front (the line of contact) in Nagorno-Karabakh, they would be stopped, dispersed and routed by Armenian counterattacks. And then Armenian units, deployed at wartime staffing levels after the mobilization of reservists, would mount an all-out counteroffensive. Second-echelon Azerbaijani units would flee as before, abandoning their much-touted Israeli, Turkish, South Korean and Russian equipment, which would be used to reoutfit the Armenian Army. The conflict would quickly end with a new truce brokered by the great powers.

But it turned out that the Azerbaijanis, the losers in the first Nagorno-Karabakh war, managed to prepare for the second war far better: They consolidated and equipped an army capable of waging modern warfare, using primarily unmanned [aerial] systems for data processing and high-precision target designation in real time. This disrupted Armenia's preconceived strategy of winning a regional conflict. Armenia's counterattacks in the initial days of fighting proved ineffective, and it failed to mount a victorious counteroffensive. The Armenian military has major problems in Nagorno-Karabakh amassing forces and assets for an effective counterstrike (in keeping with Soviet military science), since their actions and any movements day and night are detected by reconnaissance drones and preempted by high-precision shelling – also at any time of day.

Of course, based on their own bitter experience and in the course of the [current] war, competent [Armenian] commanders may wise up and teach their soldiers to better camouflage, maneuver and disperse, acting asymmetrically against a high-tech adversary, like Hezbollah in southern Lebanon or the Taliban in Afghanistan. But then how will it prepare and launch the much-coveted victorious counterstrike? Armenia's current Armed Forces are regular troops, not guerrillas. They are a good army, but it is simply unprepared for the modern warfare unleashed on them by the Azerbaijanis, who were trained and armed by Israeli and Turkish specialists.

It is impossible to win [a war] only by defending oneself and not seizing the upper hand, so the Armenian command is looking for an opportunity to launch a massive counterstrike and avoid imminent defeat. On the southern flank, Azerbaijani tanks and motorized infantry have advanced westward along the Araz valley near the Iranian border in the Dzhebrail District. The Armenians are shelling them with artillery and multiple-launch rocket systems, hoping to push them back to the river so that they flee to Iran to be interned, as was the case here in 1994 during the final stage of the first war. Such a victory could boost the Armenian units' broken morale. Armenian Prime Minister Nikol Pashinyan was quick to describe a supposed local tactical success in the south on Oct. 7 as a "real foundation for the final victory," but this exaggeration rather reflects the growing despair of the Armenian leadership. According to Pashinyan, "the situation in certain sectors is extremely difficult," and he asked soldiers who were demobilized a year ago to return to service voluntarily, since by law he cannot mobilize them now.

Armenia is in almost complete geographical isolation. The only air corridor for military transport aircraft carrying essential war supplies from Russia passes over the Caspian [Sea] and Iran. But in the past few days, the not particularly accurate Armenian [artillery] shells and rockets have started flying over to Iran during border clashes in Dzhebrail District. Tehran has already protested to both sides, and its tacit support for Yerevan may change if [Armenia's] defeat becomes obvious.

Azerbaijan has far better capabilities for receiving military supplies, and it has regular air links with Turkey. From day one, Azerbaijan has had qualitatively superior modern weapons. In the course of the new war, the Azerbaijani Armed Forces have taken and are maintaining the lead on all Nagorno-Karabakh fronts. Armenia faces long odds in a protracted war of attrition. Ankara fully supports Baku's determination to resolve the Nagorno-Karabakh problem militarily. Russia – Armenia's CSTO ally – has said that its obligations [to Yerevan] do not apply to Nagorno-Karabakh. It is important for Moscow to maintain a balanced relationship with Baku and Yerevan, and prevent the deployment of large Turkish forces in the Transcaucasus, [which could lead to] the entire region winding up in the Turkish zone of influence. Yerevan is getting some assistance and support, but unofficially. So far, Moscow is not prepared to intervene and make threats, demanding an immediate ceasefire.

Under the circumstances, a so-called "war of cities" could begin – i.e., an exchange of missile strikes on strategically important installations in Azerbaijan and Armenia, including cities – possibly even capitals. Both sides have the necessary operational-tactical missiles of various ranges and may soon want to use them – for example, to activate Moscow's CSTO obligations if Yerevan comes under attack.

If the Armenians lose the war and part of Nagorno-Karabakh – or even all of it, as Aliyev, with Recep Erdogan's backing, is demanding – then the Pashinyan regime in Yerevan would fall. Moscow might not strongly object to having the old Nagorno-Karabakh thorn removed and the problem resolved (even by force), with the fall of the potentially pro-Western (in Moscow's view) regime in Armenia coming as an additional bonus.

(Editorial) – IS RUSSIA OBLIGATED TO MAKE A CHOICE IN KARABAKH?

Nezavisimaya gazeta, Oct. 16, 2020, p. 2.

The war in Nagorno-Karabakh is continuing, and Russia is still maintaining equal distance from – or closeness to – Baku and Yerevan. How long will it be able to maintain neutrality? ...

Russia's desire to remain equidistant from Azerbaijan and Armenia on the Karabakh issue is understandable. A solution to the conflict in favor of one party would automatically turn the other away from Russia.

If Baku were to get Karabakh, then Yerevan would have more reason to move away from Moscow. And it would move in only one direction – toward the West. Questions would arise, for example, about why a Russian [military] base is needed in the republic. And [Armenia's] plans for cooperation with NATO would accelerate. In other words, [relations between Russia and Armenia] may follow the Georgian scenario.

The Turkish factor has lately been influencing Russia's relations with Azerbaijan. Ankara has announced the beginning of a rebuilding of a Turkic neo-empire from the Balkans to China. Just a few days ago, on the shores of the Bosporus, representatives of interested countries discussed creating a unified Turkic-speaking army. In this light, Azerbaijan's fallback to Turkey seems irreversible, and a possible success in the Karabakh campaign would slow this process only slightly. First, Baku will be grateful to Moscow for not interfering in the conflict on Armenia's side. Second, it will be necessary [for Azerbaijan] to calmly gain a foothold in the conquered territory. But as a result, Russia's sphere of influence in the South Caucasus may be reduced to the partially recognized Abkhazia and South Ossetia. But how absolute [that influence] will be is hard to say, given the role that the prominent Abkhaz diaspora in Turkey plays in the affairs of its historical homeland. Plus, Moscow has never managed to install the most convenient politician for Russia as president in Abkhazia, and [only] did so with great difficulty in South Ossetia. (And these are republics whose peace and existence Russia agreed to guarantee.) But given the concurrent growth of Turkey's influence in the South Caucasus, it is unlikely that anyone would undertake to guarantee Moscow peace in the North Caucasus, and subsequently in Bashkiria and/or Tatarstan.

Russia is in a position where it would better for it not to get involved in the Karabakh situation on its own. The regulator will face flak no matter what. It will also be impossible to employ Moscow's traditional policy and freeze the conflict: Azerbaijan's position and the situation on the battlefield are such that there is no longer any hope of maintaining the status quo. That is why the only option now is to leverage international diplomacy to the max. Russian President Vladimir Putin and Turkish leader Recep Tayyip Erdogan recently talked by phone and advocated stepping up the political process – for example, based on the work of the OSCE Minsk Group. And the Russian leader expressed hope that Turkey, as a member of the group, would "make a constructive contribution" to deescalating the conflict. Maximally involving all centers of influence – from Ankara to Paris and Washington – as well as striving to actually solve the problem will allow Russia to validate its aspirations as a significant regional state capable of using its clout and influence to maintain peace along its border, the longest in the world. And that is what makes Russia a world power.

ERDOGAN DRAWS A RED LINE FOR PUTIN

By Gennady Petrov. *Nezavisimaya gazeta*, Oct. 29, 2020, p. 1.

The Turkish president has told Moscow what it should and should not do in Syria and Nagorno-Karabakh.

Turkish President Recep Tayyip Erdogan's remarks at a meeting of the ruling Justice and Development Party faction unexpectedly made a lot of noise and caused a stir. Speaking at a routine event where it is more customary to discuss domestic political affairs, he attacked Russia. Erdogan condemned Moscow for not seeking peace in Syria, and at the same time declared some kind of red line in Nagorno-Karabakh that must not be crossed.

The Turkish president considered it necessary to reveal details about the telephone conversation he had had the day before with Russian President Vladimir Putin. According to the Kremlin press service, the conversation was initiated by the Turkish side. "I had a good talk with Putin. [We] discussed Nagorno-Karabakh in detail. We said: Let's put an end to this in the Caucasus. If you want, we can take joint steps [and] hold talks with the parties concerned. But right now it is important for us to finally decide whether we will work to resolve this problem or not," Erdogan said.

Then the Turkish president announced that he had notified Putin "about Ankara's red line on this issue." Erdogan did not elaborate. He said he had informed Putin about 2,000 Kurdistan Workers' Party (PKK) militants fighting in Nagorno-Karabakh on the Armenian side.

There has long been talk in Ankara that the PKK, which is designated a terrorist organization in Turkey (but not in Russia or Armenia), is involved in hostilities in the Transcaucasus. However, there is practically no proof of that involvement. There are many foreign reporters working in Armenia, and they are subject to less censorship than in Azerbaijan.

However, they have found no signs of Kurdish participation in hostilities. The only evidence that might confirm Erdogan's allegations about PKK fighters is the testimony of Armenian prisoners captured by Azerbaijanis – in other words, a very dubious source. But on the other hand, there is ample proof of Syrians from pro-Turkish groups (the Hamza Division and the Sultan Murad Brigade) being involved in hostilities in Nagorno-Karabakh. They themselves are taking photos and videos, and posting them on the Web. There is even public knowledge of the amounts of money being paid to Syrians willing to fight in Nagorno-Karabakh....

"One gets the impression that Erdogan is losing his sense of proportion. Simply put, he has gone too far. This has been happening with him since Nagorno-Karabakh. He has decided to clash with everyone at once – Russia, France, the US and Arab countries. If he thinks the Muslim world will support his stance, he is mistaken. He will find no understanding even at home. As for Russia, we objectively need to reach agreement with Turkey. Let's wait two or three days. I think Erdogan will back down, saying he was misunderstood," Aleksei Malashenko, chief researcher at the Dialogue of Civilizations Research Institute, told NG.

Truce or Peace? And for How Long?

A DIFFICULT SURRENDER

Story by Dmitry Kuznets. Translation by Kevin Rothrock. *Meduza*, Nov. 9, 2020, https://meduza.io/en/feature/2020/11/10/a-difficult-surrender.

Editors' Note. – Armenia and Azerbaijan have agreed to a Moscow-brokered truce in Nagorno-Karabakh. Azerbaijani President Ilkham Aliyev and Russian President Vladimir Putin signed the agreement during a live video stream late on Monday [Nov. 9], but Armenian Prime Minister Nikol Pashinyan (who announced the "painful" settlement in a Facebook post) did not attend the streamed signing. Meduza summarizes what has been agreed upon in the contested Karabakh region and tracks the violent reactions from angry critics in Yerevan.

* * *

Yerevan and Baku agreed to the following main points:

Russian peacekeepers will be deployed to the "contact line" between the two opposing sides.

Armenian Karabakh does not cease to exist physically, but the future status of the unrecognized breakaway republic is mentioned nowhere in the truce.

Armenia must return to Azerbaijani control the territories it seized in the early 1990s that were not part of the Soviet Nagorno-Karabakh [Autonomous] Province. These lands, still currently occupied by Armenian forces, must be handed over to Baku between Nov. 15 and Dec. 1.

Baku will retain control over the districts in the unrecognized Nagorno-Karabakh Republic that Azerbaijani troops seized during the 2020 war. This apparently includes the strategically and symbolically significant city of Shusha, which Azerbaijani troops captured on Nov. 9.

The Nagorno-Karabakh Republic's capital, Stepanakert (just six miles from Shusha), effectively remains under Armenian control. The city will remain connected to Armenia by the Lachin Corridor mountain pass, which will be guarded by Russian peacekeepers.

In exchange, Baku obtained guarantees that Russian peacekeepers will also guard a corridor to the Nakhichevan Autonomous Republic, Azerbaijan's exclave separated by Armenia.

The signatories also agreed to refugees' right of return. Given that Azerbaijani territories are returning to Baku's control, this means Azerbaijanis will have the right to return to the Armenian parts of Karabakh, where an Azeri ethnic minority lived before war broke out in the early 1990s. The UN will play a role in the return process.

There will be a "center of peacekeeping forces" that will include a role for Turkey, Azerbaijan's main strategic ally, according to President Aliyev. Although Ankara was not formally part of the trilateral truce, Turkey was where initial rumors about an impending settlement started circulating, indicating President Erdogan's involvement in the negotiations.

The settlement's text does not clarify what rights exactly the Armenian enclave in Karabakh will enjoy. Aliyev said he "offered them autonomy, but they wanted independence." "Well, what do you say now, Pashinyan?" the Azerbaijani president said tauntingly in a national address on Monday night. "Karabakh is ours!" he declared at the end of his speech.

The agreement will last five years and can be extended if neither side withdraws from the settlement.

Civil unrest erupted in Yerevan after Prime Minister Pashinyan announced the "extremely painful decision" to accept the settlement's terms. Hundreds of protesters flooded the capital's streets, stormed the House of Government and vandalized the building's interior. Angry demonstrators shouted condemnations of the prime minister and marched toward his official residence, seeking an audience. An angry mob also attacked Armenian parliamentary speaker Ararat Mirzoyan and beat him unconscious.

On Telegram, popular channels urged Armenians to join street protests against the truce with Azerbaijan. Seventeen opposition parties have also called for Pashinyan's resignation and advocated a transfer of executive power to a temporary governing body until fighting ends in Karabakh.

Meanwhile, President Aliyev and sources in Armenia have indicated that Pashinyan, despite his Facebook announcement, actually refused at the last moment to sign the trilateral agreement. It is unclear whether the prime minister's signature will appear in the future, given that the news of the truce has provoked widespread unrest in Yerevan against Armenia's "capitulation" to Azerbaijan. Pashinyan later spoke in a live broadcast on Facebook where he argued that he had no alternative but to sign the settlement. He promised to report the details of his negotiations with Moscow and Baku in the coming days....

RUSSIA, TURKEY WIN BATTLE FOR KARABAKH

By Polina Khimshiashvili. *RBC Daily*, Nov. 11, 2020, p. 4.

On Tuesday, Russia began to deploy peacekeepers in Nagorno-Karabakh. That came as a result of an agreement between the Armenian, Azerbaijani and Russian leaders. However, Armenia is unhappy with the terms of the deal.

In the early hours of Nov. 10, the leaders of Armenia, Azerbaijan and Russia said that they had reached an agreement on a ceasefire in the unrecognized Nagorno-Karabakh Republic. Fighting has been going on there since Sept. 27, with several thousand casualties on both sides (according to Russian data).

Azerbaijani President Ilkham Aliyev hailed the agreement as a victory, [but] Armenian Prime Minister Nikol Pashinyan said that he was forced to sign it due to the situation at the front. Russian President Vladimir Putin said that the agreed-upon provisions will create the "necessary conditions for a lasting and comprehensive settlement of the crisis around Nagorno-Karabakh on an equitable basis."

The agreement provides for a complete cessation of hostilities in the conflict zone at midnight on Nov. 10, Moscow time. Azerbaijani and Armenian troops will remain in their positions. A Russian peacekeeping contingent will be deployed immediately: 1,960 troops with light weapons, 90 armored personnel carriers, [and] 380 motor vehicles and units of special equipment. A [joint Russia-Turkey] cease-fire monitoring center will be set up.

Armenia will also begin to hand over territories to Azerbaijan.

What Armenia loses

Under the agreement, Armenia will return to Azerbaijan more territory than was envisioned under earlier peace settlement plans. As a result of the 1992-1994 war, Armenia established control over not only the Nagorno-Karabakh Auton-omous Province, which was part of Azerbaijan, but also seven other districts of the [former] Azerbaijani SSR. In previous years, recalls Armenian political com-mentator Aleksandr Iskandaryan, there had been discussions about the handover of the seven districts: Dzhebrail, Fizuli, Lachin, Zangelan, Kelbadzhar, Agdam and Kubatly. Under the agreement, all of those districts will come under Azerbaijan's control, because some of them were already seized [by Azerbaijan] (for example, Dzhebrail and Zangelan) and some are to be surrendered (for example, Lachin and Kelbadzhar). In addition, the city of Shusha and some areas that have been recaptured since Sept. 27, including parts of the Gadrut and Martuni districts, will pass to Baku's control, Iskandaryan explained....

The agreement will significantly impact [Armenia's] domestic stability. Arme-nia's current prime minister, Nikol Pashinyan, came to power in spring 2018 as a result of mass protests (in the fall 2018 elections, his party bloc My Step won a parliamentary majority, 88 seats out of 132). He received support for his struggle against [then] president Serzh Sargsyan, who had ruled for 10 years. [Pashinyan] changed the Constitution, and became prime minister following the country's transition to a parliamentary republic. But as hostilities escalated and territories were lost, opposition politicians began to criticize the Pashinyan government's actions. On Nov. 9, 17 opposition parties, including Sargsyan's Republican Party and Prosperous Armenia, the second largest party in parliament (24 seats), demanded his resignation. On the morning of Nov. 10, Pashinyan assured everyone that he was still in Armenia and called for calm. However, President Armen Sarkisyan's statement testified to a split within the ruling establishment. He said that he had learned about the substance of the agreement from the media. The domestic political situation in Armenia is becoming one of the main factors in the implementation of the agreement. By accepting this agreement, Pashinyan "has signed his own death warrant," said political analyst Stanislav Pritchin.

There are no references to Nagorno-Karabakh's future status. There are no in-dications in the agreement that its status is to be determined in the future, nor is there any mention of the OSCE Minsk Group, where all recent peace talks have been held. "This may still be under consideration," Pritchin suggested. Now it was more important to cease hostilities, because the seizure of Shusha gave Azerbaijan the possibility of taking Stepanakert, experts pointed out. Responding to a question about Nagorno-Karabakh's future status, Russian presidential press secretary Dmitry Peskov said that all previous legal acts, including UN Security Council resolutions, are still in force. They declare commitment to Azerbaijan's territorial integrity.

In Armenia, the agreement has sparked protests. This evening, crowds broke into government and parliament buildings, beating up [parliament] speaker Ararat Mirzoyan, a member of the My Step ruling bloc.

What Azerbaijan gets

Azerbaijan has secured the return of a significant amount of territory – not only the [seven] districts and Shusha, but also the restoration of direct land access to Nakhichevan. The agreement provides for unblocking all economic and transportation links in the region. Armenia is to ensure transportation routes between western Azerbaijan and the Nakhichevan Autonomous Republic. Transportation routes will be guarded by the Russian FSB [Federal Security Service] Border Service.

The agreement consolidates Ilkham Aliyev's role as head of state, Pritchin said. Aliyev, 58, has been running the country since 2003. Prior to that, his father, Geidar Aliyev, had been president (from 1993). Geidar Aliyev came to power amid domestic political instability created by the war in Nagorno-Karabakh, but failed to achieve victory in the war. Ilkham Aliyev is fulfilling his father's promise to regain Nagorno-Karabakh. Considering the significance of the issue, power will be concentrated around him for the next 20 to 30 years, the expert said.

[Azerbaijan's] alliance with Turkey has strengthened. Ankara has been providing Baku with active military and technical assistance since the outbreak of hostilities. [Turkish] President Recep Tayyip Erdogan has been upholding at the diplomatic level Azerbaijan's right to use military force to recapture its territories. Turkey has sent fighters from Syria.

What Russia gets

Since the start of the conflict, experts have noted the Kremlin's restrained position. It urged both sides to cease fire. The first truce was signed in Moscow (on Oct. 10), but it did not hold even a day.

The current agreement restores Moscow's leading role in the South Caucasus. This outcome is quite successful for Russia, Fyodor Lukyanov, editor in chief of the journal Rossia v globalnoi politike [Russia in Global Affairs], says with confidence. "It was impossible to preserve the status quo after it turned out that the Armenian side was no longer able to achieve military victory. Until now, it was presumed that the Armenians would prevail, but this time the Azerbaijanis were better prepared, and when there is not enough military might, the entire configuration that had established itself in recent years falls apart," the expert explained.

The new model is favorable for Russia. It remains the main player in the region, and Armenia is becoming increasingly dependent on its presence, Lukyanov believes. There is reason to say that the OSCE Minsk Group has effectively ceased to exist, the expert commented. The agreement makes no mention of the OSCE, nor were its cochairs – France and the US – mentioned as active participants in drafting [the agreement].

Moscow will also bear the brunt of the costs to implement the plan. Peacekeepers will be deployed in Nagorno-Karabakh for at least five years, with the possibility of extending the term. It will also be up to Russian border guards to secure the transportation corridor to Nakhichevan.

What Turkey gets

Turkey has strengthened its foothold in the South Caucasus. "Turkey's gains are perfectly obvious. It has achieved spectacular successes [and] become a party to a major regional conflict. In recent years, Turkey has in one way or another expanded its influence throughout the former Ottoman Empire. In Nagorno-Karabakh, it played a great game without incurring any particular risks or costs," Lukyanov said.

"Over the past decade, Turkey has once again shown itself as a country that is not only laying claim to being a regional power center, but also a state that is capable of defending this claim to leadership and strengthening it in practice," said Yury Mavashev, director of the Russian Center for the Study of Modern Turkey. "Turkey's energy security is inconceivable without control in the South Caucasus. This primarily applies to [natural gas] pipelines – both existing pipelines (TANAP [Trans-Anatolian Natural Gas Pipeline] and Baku-Tbilisi-Ceyhan) and future ones with Central Asian countries," Mavashev explained. Moreover, without control in the South Caucasus, Turkey will not be able to become a full-fledged master of the Middle East, he commented.

Point 5 of the agreement is still a source of controversy. Aliyev said that it provides for a joint Russian-Turkish peacekeeping mission. Russian Foreign Ministry spokeswoman Maria Zakharova insists that there will be only Russian peacekeepers (she said this on Ekho Moskvy radio).

KARABAKH: THE PRICE OF PEACE

By Anatoly Tarasov. *Sovetskaya Rossia*, Nov. 12, 2020, p. 7.

... The [ceasefire] agreement was signed immediately after Azerbaijan said that it had taken control of the key city of Shusha, allowing [Azerbaijani] troops to train their fire on Stepanakert, the capital of the Nagorno-Karabakh Republic, and the road connecting the NKR with Armenia.

Before the agreement was signed, it became known that, as the Russian Defense Ministry put it, "a Russian Mi-24 helicopter was shot down from a man-portable surface-to-air missiles system near the Armenian-Azerbaijani border. Two crew members were killed." The Azerbaijani Foreign Ministry subsequently released its own statement: "According to information received from the Azerbaijani Defense Ministry, a Russian Mi-24 military helicopter was shot down on Nov. 9, 2020, at 6:30 p.m. in the Nakhichevan section of the Armenian-Azerbaijani border. In this regard, the following should be emphasized:

- The helicopter was flying in close proximity to the Armenian-Azerbaijani state border amid ongoing, active military clashes in the Armenian-Azerbaijani Nagorno-Karabakh conflict zone.

- The helicopter was flying in the dark, at low altitude, outside the air defense radar detection zone.

- Russian Aerospace Defense Force helicopters have not previously been seen in the specified area.

"Given these factors, and in the light of the tense situation in the region and heightened level of combat readiness in connection with the possibility of provocations by the Armenian side, the combat crew on duty decided to shoot to kill. The Azerbaijani side apologizes to the Russian side over this tragic incident, which was accidental and not directed against the Russian side. The Azerbaijani side expresses its sincere condolences to the families of the killed crew members and wishes a speedy recovery to those who were injured. The Azerbaijani side declares its readiness to pay appropriate compensation."

The way the Russian leadership is acting, they consider this incident over and done with. But that makes it even more bewildering. The Azerbaijani military shot down our helicopter. Russian pilots were killed. Russia is said to have made a mistake. Excuse me, but a great power does not have its planes or helicopters shot down or its ambassadors killed! If Russia were great, strong and powerful, then, first, no one would have thought of committing such a provocation, brazen act, sucker attack – whatever you want to call it. And second, even if the downing was accidental, the Azerbaijani ambassador would have been immediately summoned to the Russian Foreign Ministry. And the very next day, the soldier who pulled the trigger, his comrades who saw him do it (and didn't stop him), that soldier's immediate commander, that commander's immediate superiors, and the Azerbaijani defense minister would sit down in Moscow and personally apologize to the victims' relatives. Then there would be a Russian trial and a harsh punishment. Why? To ensure that there are no accidents in a war with a great power. After this, others would really play it cool. They would think long and hard about who they are shooting at before pulling the trigger. But, alas, Russia is no longer a great and strong power.

And today, Turkey basically won in Karabakh after its opponents surrendered....

The turning point was the loss of Shusha. Basically, all military experts said that the loss of Shusha would mean Karabakh's complete and unconditional defeat. The Russian helicopter shot down "by accident" 200 kilometers from the combat zone was just a pretext [for getting the parties to sign a ceasefire] and a clear hint.

Incidentally, it's by no means certain that it was the Azerbaijanis who shot down the helicopter.

Most experts believe that if that were the case, then Turkey would get the right to bring its forces into Azerbaijan as peacekeepers and stay in the Transcaucasus indefinitely. Aliyev said Turkey will also be present in the conflict zone as a peace-keeping force. Turkey's military and political presence in the region is a much more important objective than Karabakh itself. Turkey defended the most vulnerable section of the Southern Gas Corridor and gained a toehold for accessing the Caspian Sea and Central Asia. Armenia's defeat in the war with Azerbaijan will undoubtedly bring a host of negative consequences for Russia. And the main one is that Turkey has shown it is ready to resolve conflicts on the territory of the former USSR. Where the Kremlin pursued a vague policy, looking to save its own skin, the Turks acted un-equivocally, cutting to the chase. In the Karabakh war, [the Turks] became basically an organizing and motivating force. The direct participation of their troops in the fighting, if it was even detected, was strictly in the form of "*ikh tam net.*"[1] Turkish objectives were achieved by "native" troops. The Turks merely tallied the spoils.

Erdogan appears to have done a bang-up job as a political grandmaster. He achieved what he was after in absolutely all his military exercises at the preliminary stage. And he did not draw out any of his military operations longer than necessary. He settles for an interim result as soon as an operation begins to lose steam. That has always afforded him the opportunity to quietly retreat without losing the main prize. That is incidentally what happened in Idlib. In any case, Armenia's defeat is a trend that is most likely impossible to reverse now.

'TURKEY GETTING DOMINANT ROLE IN SOUTH CAUCASUS'

By Vyacheslav Polovinko. *Novaya gazeta*, Nov. 11, 2020, p. 6.

Editors' Note. – Political analyst Arkady Dubnov comments on the winners and losers in the second Nagorno-Karabakh war.

* * *

Question. – Did Pashinyan have any other choice but to concede defeat?

Answer. – I don't think so. He had to do it, and I would describe his decision as the best of the worst. Pashinyan cited military [commanders] when he said that the Army had practically no resources left for the war – neither manpower nor weapons. That statement carries a lot of weight: Army commanders know the cost of war better than anybody else.

Q. – Judging by what happened overnight in Yerevan, this decision is considered the worst of the worst in Armenia. Could public opinion in the country change the script of the agreement if Pashinyan were to resign? Armenia would just go ahead and pull out of the agreement, [right?].

A. – I don't think that what happened overnight, when the presidential residence in Yerevan was stormed and looted, including Pashinyan's personal belongings, fully reflects Armenian society's attitude toward what is happening. There is always a group [of people] that feels humiliated and insulted by defeat in a war, but it seems that they do not express the general opinion of the country's population. To me, this is not an indicator. In this case, the Armenians looked more like the Kyrgyz on the night they stormed their White House, and they will one day feel ashamed of what happened. Pashinyan, who is not a military leader or a very experienced politician, has already saved many Armenian lives with his decision.

Nor do I think that the Armenians would be able to turn the tide on the battlefield even if they wanted to. They have neither the strength nor the opportunity to do that. The nation is tired. I should add that when I was asked at the very start of the war when it would end, I was way off when I said two weeks. It lasted a month and a half, but ended just as I had expected: One of the sides ran out of resources.

Q. – What kind of Pashinyan does the Kremlin need right now: a weak but sitting prime minister, or a former prime minister?

A. – If Moscow chooses in some way to state its position, it will say diplomatically that "the region's stability and prosperity are important to us." But as a matter of fact, a battle-scarred, experienced and still popular Pashinyan should be more useful to a sensible Russian leadership – that is, of course, unless Moscow is out to get the Armenian leader.

In this context, I must say that President Ilkham Aliyev's reaction was revoltingly indecent. In his address, Aliyev taunted and mocked his defeated opponent: "Pashinyan, where is your status? This is the status you get!" and so on. This is unbecoming, first, of the [Army] officer that Aliyev thinks he is, and second, of a man who has left the battlefield. It is totally wrong to mock and gloat over a defeated opponent. At this moment, I believe those who are showing videos of dead Armenian soldiers with their ears cut off and their eyes gouged out. This is inappropriate behavior – regardless of the fact that the outcome of the war waged by the Azerbaijani-Turkish bloc against incomparably weaker and effectively defenseless Armenia was a foregone conclusion.

Q. – Is this a total victory for Aliyev? The fact that part of Nagorno-Karabakh will remain under Armenia's control looks like a winner's concession.

A. – Absolutely right. Victory is what you say it is. Everything is being portrayed as a total victory, because even without the dramatic disaster involving the Russian helicopter, which made Azerbaijan cool off a bit, Baku still would not have advanced on Stepanakert, even though doing so would not have been very difficult militarily. What would Aliyev have done with a defeated Karabakh as a territory? Then – regardless of whether Aliyev wanted it or not – a humanitarian disaster for Nagorno-Karabakh's very few remaining residents would have been unavoidable. The downed helicopter simply saved Aliyev from a Pyrrhic victory.

Q. – What is Azerbaijan going to do about Nagorno-Karabakh during the five years peacekeepers will be deployed there? Will it try to develop infrastructure, or are constant preparations for a new war in store for Nagorno-Karabakh?

A. – I believe the second scenario is out of the question. Azerbaijan will not prepare for a new war if it gets all the areas specified in the agreement. Baku needed victories, not those territories per se. Aliyev needed to build up his image as the leader of a country that has long been in a state of frustration over the war that it lost in the 1990s. He has mercilessly exploited the Nagorno-Karabakh issue, thus justifying the harsh ruling regime that he established in the country. Now that Nagorno-Karabakh is in Aliyev's hands, decades will pass before these areas begin to return to normal life – if we disregard the refugees who I believe will be forcibly brought to Nagorno-Karabakh to demonstrate that life is returning to normal in what is now Azerbaijani territory. For now, Aliyev is fine with Nagorno-Karabakh's current status. It essentially has no status at all, but the most important thing is that it is not Armenian. That is Baku's logic.

Incidentally, the status of discussions on this problem has changed. Everyone immediately forgot about the [OSCE] Minsk Group: There is no mention of it in the ceasefire agreement. As a matter of fact, there are many gaps and ambiguities there, but by all indications, the formula – for now a trilateral one – will be expanded by including Turkey, whose peacekeeping forces Aliyev is persistently talking about.

Q. – The agreement was signed by three sides, but Aliyev's remarks that Erdogan will now definitely be a player as well seemingly took the Kremlin by surprise: Apparently, that was not part of the deal.

A. – Everyone is playing [their own game] – and also playing the fool a bit. When Moscow sends signals that this was not part of the deal, the exact opposite is true. This means that Turkey is giving Moscow an opportunity to play the role of the main peacemaker [and] giving Putin a chance to show himself as a great Russian tsar who has once again reconciled everyone and is regaining the role of the principal guarantor of security in the South Caucasus.

But on the other hand, Turkey cannot fail to benefit from its blood brothers' victory. I am absolutely positive that Moscow anticipated this course of events, but for now, this game will continue – primitive, understandable to all, and a bit like a card game where everyone is cheating a little but at the same time playing up to each other. That is par for the course. Likewise, when the war was starting, Baku and Ankara knew that Moscow would not intervene. It would make resounding statements, calling for peace [and] establishing official ceasefire regimes, but not lift a finger until the Armenian presence in Nagorno-Karabakh was in jeopardy. That is exactly what happened: Moscow intervened when – just like with a chess clock – the minute hand began to approach 12 o'clock, and the flag was just about to fall.

Q. – How will Russian and Turkish peacekeepers interact when they are deployed in Nagorno-Karabakh? Will this be a business-like relationship, or will they be like cats and dogs?

A. – It doesn't matter. Turks will be there together with Russians, and even if conflicts flare up at some point, eventually they will find a modus vivendi. This is a long-term arrangement: five years, which will be extended. A new status quo is being established in the South Caucasus, where Turkey is effectively taking on the role of a dominant player, or at least a player on a par with Russia. There is nothing Moscow can do about it. It will have to put up with a Turkish presence. As a matter of fact, this is a global change that has yet to be analyzed. As for how they adjust to each other, that is of secondary importance. After all, Russia and Turkey share dramatic experience of interacting in Syria.

Q. – Is it correct to say that Russia no longer has leverage over Aliyev?

A. – Did it have that leverage before?

Q. – Before, it could at least urge him to do something – try to persuade him of something. But now if Moscow wants to get anything from Aliyev, it will have to consult with Turkey.

A. – There is another answer to this question. Previously, Russian-Azerbaijani relations could be described as the "tail wagging the dog." Now the "tail" has become its own entity, and the "dog" has to reckon with this "tail."

Q. – The "tail" has its own teeth.

A. – Now it's up to the "tail" to decide when to wag and when to curl.

Q. – It seems that Russia, as Armenia's defender, has lost in this conflict, but Putin has won. Would that be fair to say?

A. – Yes, that's one way to describe the situation. The Armenians' attitude toward Russia has sharply changed for the worse compared to what it was before the war. Bitter disappointment with Russia is obvious. Armenia's tilt toward "those undesirable to Russia" – i.e., the West – will increase. Yes, Putin rode in on a white horse, and just a second before the flag fell, he made his move, sending the 15th [Motorized Rifle] Brigade to Nagorno-Karabakh. [He] needed a casus belli, and it came in the form of a downed helicopter – however, not to intervene in the war, but to disengage the [conflicting] sides.

As far as the outcome of the war is concerned, it is also important to say this: It has come as a great ideological and philosophical disappointment to me. I did not think that [political] figures like Aliyev would be willing to fight for territory and for their flag over that territory at the cost of thousands of lives. This is an existential shock. Because of this naïveté of mine, my forecasts over the past weeks were often wrong.

The victory of the incomparably more powerful Turkic-Islamic alliance (let's call a spade a spade) over Christian Armenia will have a tremendous impact on the global Islamic Ummah. Humiliated and insulted by attacks from all parts of the world, the Ummah was desperate for triumphant news. This victory gives the Ummah an opportunity to hold its head high. Now it can say that it is ready to fight its wars out in the open.

NIKOL PASHINYAN REFUSES TO SURRENDER, AGAIN

By Aleksandr Atasuntsev. *RBC Daily*, Nov. 18, 2020, p. 4.

The signing of the Nov. 10 Nagorno-Karabakh trilateral ceasefire agreement, which basically spells out Armenia's military capitulation, triggered a political crisis in the country. On the night that it became known that Russian, Azerbaijan and Armenia had signed an agreement, an angry mob in Yerevan ransacked government and parliament buildings, and beat up parliamentary speaker Ararat Mirzoyan; members of the My Step ruling party avoided making so much as a statement, let alone a public appearance. Then several deputies left the faction and the Armenian foreign minister resigned, as did some other cabinet members.

The opposition calls for the government to step down

Right now, hundreds of people unhappy with the ceasefire terms accepted by Prime Minister Nikol Pashinyan and demanding his resignation are converging on central Yerevan. Police are detaining protesters: Even though the war is over, Armenia remains under martial law. At the same time, none of the opposition leaders have stated their willingness to lead the government: In part, this has to do with the fact that any politician who comes to power now would have to honor the terms of the controversial agreement.

Armenia's former presidents Robert Kocharyan and Serzh Sargsyan have not publicly commented on the deal.

Apart from the prime minister's resignation, the opposition is demanding the formation of a government of national accord and new parliamentary elections. Moreover, it is expecting to get some points of the Nov. 10 agreement reevaluated, but no one has any idea how to do that. Pashinyan's opponents are constantly trying to call parliament into session to discuss the prime minister's resignation and lift martial law, but are unable to get a quorum: Deputies of the My Step faction, which has more than 80 out of 132 seats in the National Assembly after the 2018 elections (the first since the revolution [that swept Pashinyan into power – *Trans.*]), are not attending parliamentary sessions.

The president calls for snap elections

On the evening of Nov. 15, Pashinyan wrote on Facebook that he had watched dozens of videos in his support posted by frontline soldiers: "I was amazed by their wisdom. Guys, you are right. I am waiting for you in Yerevan to finally deal with the dogs barking outside."

Both Pashinyan's parliamentary opponents and supporters saw his remarks as a step toward a civil war. At the same time, Armenian society is divided; Pashinyan still has many loyal supporters who are afraid that if he goes, power would be seized by the "old clans," namely by Kocharyan's and Sargsyan's people.

Four deputies left the My Step faction within 30 minutes after those remarks were posted. On the morning of Nov. 16, [Pashinyan] tried to clarify his stance: He assured everyone that he was not calling for violence and that he was waiting for soldiers in Yerevan to have a personal meeting with them. "I am calling on you, pleading, demanding not to view these remarks in the context [of a civil war – *Trans.*]. If that's the impression you get from any of my statements, it's wrong," he wrote on Facebook.

Later in the day, the prime minister gave a press conference. "There is only one item on my agenda: ensuring stability in the country. There is no other item on my agenda," he said, responding to a question about his resignation. He also said he was responsible for the situation in Nagorno-Karabakh.

On Monday evening, Armenian President Armen Sarkisyan called on the government to prepare for snap parliamentary elections. "Over the past several days, I have held dozens of political consultations with parliamentary and nonparliamentary forces, various nongovernmental organizations and individuals. The absolute majority of participants agree on one thing: The prime minister must resign in accordance with the Constitution, to be followed by early parliamentary elections," Sarkisyan said. He added that snap parliamentary elections are inevitable. During the period between the government's resignation and new, early elections, the country would be run by a government of national accord, the president said.

Foreign Ministry argues with prime minister

On Monday, after his press conference, Pashinyan addressed parliament, making a new resounding statement – namely, that handing over [the city of] Shusha had been a subject of negotiations between the parties to the conflict and Russia from the very start. "It was the same logic as before the war – the handover of territories to Azerbaijan, including Shusha," he said. "It was the same before the war – it has been [the same] since 2016 [i.e., the last time fighting erupted over Nagorno-Karabakh – *Trans.*]," the prime minister said.

"The transfer of Shusha was not up for discussion at any stage of the peace process," Armenian Foreign Ministry press secretary Anna Nagdalyan immediately posted on Facebook. [Her] statement, which refuted the prime minister's remarks, had been approved by Foreign Minister Zograb Mnatsakanyan, RBC's source at Armenia's Foreign Ministry said.

Right after Pashinyan's speech, the Armenian foreign minister announced his resignation. Pashinyan threw the entire diplomatic corps under the bus and insulted diplomats, even though they had not known about the upcoming agreement, RBC's source said, adding that final decisions on the document were made by three people – Pashinyan, [Armenian Armed Forces] General Staff chief Onik Gasparyan and Nagorno-Karabakh Republic head Araik Arutyunyan. "[After the peace deal was signed,] the Foreign Ministry asked [Pashinyan] not to make any statements [on the rationale behind the agreement], but to give [the Foreign Ministry] a chance to save the document and not turn the matter into a domestic policy issue," RBC's source said.

Experts predict confrontation will continue

Even if the issue of handing over Shusha was raised [at the peace talks], it was only in the course of direct contacts among the three countries' leaders and in the very last days of the conflict, RBC's source is confident. In any case, contrary to what Pashinyan said, the issue was not discussed at the meetings between Armenian and Azerbaijani foreign ministers on Oct. 10, Oct. 17 and Oct. 25. Meetings at the start of the war focused on the creation of a verification mechanism, and then on introducing peacekeepers. Azerbaijan, which was winning the war, refused to agree to anything. It was only with Russia's assistance that peace was achieved, but RBC's source said he did not know how.

Pashinyan's team is currently coming under significant pressure, but it isn't enough to make the prime minister step down, said Armenian political analyst Aleksandr Iskandaryan. "The turnout at rallies is 10,000 people at most. It is extremely difficult to legally do what the opposition wants: In order to lift martial law, at least 50% of deputies need to vote in favor. As for launching impeachment proceedings, [only] one-third of deputy votes are needed for that, but the opposition does not even have that," he explained. There is no united, established opposition in Armenia that can demand the prime minister's resignation, "and all of these conditions give Pashinyan an opportunity to hold on to power for now," the expert said. "Of course, the authorities have been greatly weakened, but obviously the Pashinyan team realizes that not all is lost yet," Iskandaryan concluded.

WHY THERE ARE NO CSTO PEACEKEEPERS IN NAGORNO-KARABAKH

By Vladimir Mukhin. *Nezavisimaya gazeta*, Nov. 18, 2020, p. 1.

The events in Nagorno-Karabakh have shown that the collective security system in the post-Soviet space is not working. Interethnic and regional conflicts that arise on the territory of the former Soviet Union are in effect ignored by the CSTO, which was supposedly created to prevent and resolve them. For example, a Russian peacekeeping mission is being deployed in Nagorno-Karabakh, but CSTO forces are not involved. Why?

There is no clear answer to this question. It is equally unclear why the countries that comprise the CSTO (Armenia, Belarus, Kazakhstan, Kyrgyzstan, Russia and Tajikistan) won't dissolve this organization, given its ineffectiveness. That can only mean that the CSTO's existence is of some benefit to someone. While Moscow is taking large-scale and very costly peacekeeping steps in Nagorno-Karabakh that aim to separate the warring parties, facilitate the return of refugees, establish observation posts, carry out demining efforts, and so on, the security council secretaries of CSTO member states supposedly discussed all those issues remotely on Tuesday [Nov. 17].

According to CSTO press secretary Vladimir Zainetdinov, pressing collective security issues were discussed via videoconference. Those included "defense cooperation, peacekeeping forces, supplying and equipping the Collective Rapid Reaction Forces (CRRF), and the CSTO's antinarcotics strategy."

Readers are reminded that when creating the collective peacekeeping forces, CSTO leaders even planned [for them] to participate in UN [peacekeeping] missions, preparing a special blue helmet battalion to that end. But where are these battalions now?

Exactly a month ago, a CSTO peacekeeper training exercise was held in Belarus, called Unbreakable Brotherhood 2020. It included CSTO peacekeeping battalions, including Russian Defense Ministry brigades that are currently on the ground in Nagorno-Karabakh. Belarussian Defense Minister Maj. Gen. Viktor Khrenin, who supervised the maneuvers, reported that as part of the exercises, CSTO forces "practiced conducting peacekeeping operations: Escorting convoys, carrying out patrols, and defusing improvised explosive devices." Now, Russian peacekeepers are carrying out these tasks in the Transcaucasus, namely in the Nagorno-Karabakh conflict zone. No blue helmets from other CSTO countries are present.

In summing up the maneuvers, Gen. Khrenin said that "the exercises took place against the backdrop of difficult situations in certain countries and regions. Unfortunately, we are constantly witnessing the emergence of new risks and threats to peace and security. In light of that, it is especially important to consolidate efforts among allies, and international and regional organizations." However, Russia's CSTO allies are failing to show such consolidation in Nagorno-Karabakh.

In October 2020, when the Karabakh war was at its peak, CSTO secretary general Stanislav Zas stated that "the organization will provide military assistance to Armenia in the event of a real threat to its territorial integrity or a direct military attack." However, according to him, Yerevan never requested such help from the CSTO. On Nov. 11, the CSTO secretary general welcomed the deployment of Russian peacekeepers in Nagorno-Karabakh, but for some reason did not say a word about other CSTO members' readiness to do the same.

In this situation, Turkey's position has been completely different: It announced its participation in the Nagorno-Karabakh peacekeeping process without asking for Moscow's opinion. Turkish President Recep Tayyip Erdogan recently signed a decree to send Turkish troops to Azerbaijan. It is still unclear where the Turkish troops will be stationed, and how a joint center that Ankara created together with Moscow to oversee the ceasefire will function.

The OSCE Minsk Group cochairs are also unclear on that. Apparently that's why the US State Department stated that Washington and Paris would like to clear up the parameters of the agreement on resolving the situation in Nagorno-Karabakh, and to understand Turkey's role in this matter.

Commenting on the situation, political analyst and CIS expert Arkady Dubnov said: "Russia cannot risk worsening its relationship with Turkey. This [relationship] is such a huge bonus that it clearly trumps the fact that [Russia] could have nipped Turkey's efforts to help Azerbaijan in the bud. Apparently, for Moscow, the times are such that instead of being primarily an ally, [Russia is] becoming a merchant and a partner. The CSTO has demonstrated its utter unviability in the situation. [Russia] understands that."

The expert believes that Yerevan did not ask the CSTO for help because it realized that such a move would be an "anachronism." "There's an organization called the Turkic Council, which unites three Central Asian nations – Kazakhstan, Kyrgyzstan and Uzbekistan – as well as Azerbaijan and Turkey. And this Council, currently headed by a Kazakh diplomat, sided with Azerbaijan in the war against Armenia. Thus, three members of the CSTO are members of an organization that supports a country that's at war with another [CSTO] member," said Dubnov.

"Neither Russia nor Armenia wants Turkic-speaking CSTO member states to take part in resolving the Karabakh conflict. Meanwhile, the Army of Belarus, Russia's only Slavic collective defense ally, has its hands full right now, so to speak. That is why Moscow took it upon itself to conduct the peacekeeping mission," military expert Lt. Col. Aleksandr Ovchinnikov told NG. In his opinion, Russia needs the CSTO to give it an image boost in the world, and to have the potential to deflect possible Western aggression.

"Meanwhile, other member states need the CSTO to get weapons from Moscow either at a discount or free of charge as part of collective defense. But as the war in Karabakh has shown, such assistance is a double-edged sword: The Armenian forces, which were armed practically with only Russian and Soviet weapons, lost the war. These weapons are somewhat outdated. As for new weapons, like the attack drones used by Azerbaijan, even Russia has very few of them," Ovchinnikov said.

EVEN MOSCOW LIKES A PAT ON THE HEAD

By Yelena Chernenko. *Kommersant*, Nov. 19, 2020, p. 6.

... On Wednesday, Sergei Naryshkin, [director of the Russian Foreign Intelligence Service, aka SVR], made a surprisingly harsh statement. According to him, the leading NATO countries "are trying to hide their irritation over the Nagorno-Karabakh ceasefire [agreement] between Azerbaijan and Armenia that was reached with Russia's active participation." "The US and its allies are frustrated that the war was ended with Moscow's mediation. After all, this basically undoes their years-long work to push Russia out of the Transcaucasus," the SVR chief said. "Neither Washington nor 'united Europe' wants to accept the current balance of forces in the region. In order to destroy [that balance], they couldn't come up with anything better than to try to stoke enmity between the peoples of Azerbaijan and Armenia."

According to the SVR, "Certain Western countries are provoking Armenian and Azerbaijani nationalists to discredit and derail the ceasefire agreement. [They] are trying to convince Armenians that peace in Nagorno-Karabakh is a defeat for Yerevan, and are promoting the idea of 'fighting to the victorious end.' [They are] also telling Azerbaijanis that the Kremlin stole their victory when the Azerbaijani Army was a step away from taking Stepanakert." According to Sergei Naryshkin, "such actions are only further evidence that, as always, the US and its European friends are solving their problems at the expense of the interests of ordinary people, this time – the Azerbaijanis and Armenians." "The Americans and Europeans are not concerned that their provocations could result in more bloodshed and plunge the region into a major military conflict," he concluded.

Speaking about the US's European allies, Sergei Naryshkin did not specify which countries [he was alluding to], but Kommersant's sources in the Russian government have named Great Britain, for one.

The SVR director's statement contradicts the public remarks on the actions of Western countries made by other Russian officials, including Vladimir Putin. Just the day before, [Putin] gave an extensive interview to the Russian media, where he gave a fairly favorable assessment of the role of the US and France, which are cochairs, along with Russia, of the OSCE Minsk Group for resolving the Nagorno-Karabakh conflict. Explaining why Moscow acted alone to reach the ceasefire agreement between Yerevan and Baku, he said that the Russian side "proceeded from battlefield realities." "We had mere hours," [the Russian president said], and there was no time to consult Western partners. Vladimir Putin gave high marks to the role of the US and France, adding that they "always" sought to resolve the Nagorno-Karabakh problem. According to him, starting in 2013, when Russia proposed a new format for a future settlement, "both France and the US generally supported the Russian proposal and cooperated on the issue."

Vladimir Putin emphasized that the agreements reached on Nov. 9 are in line with the Minsk Group's proposals. Because of that, he said that the Western cochairs have no reason to feel slighted. "When issues are resolved at such a [high] level and in such a context; when we are talking about the life, wellbeing and fate of millions of people for the foreseeable future, there's no room for pouting or resentment," he said on Tuesday night.

For their part, neither American nor French representatives said anything about resenting Russia – at least not publicly. Of course, they also did not enthusiastically support the agreement reached on Nov. 9; instead, they just said they welcomed the ceasefire and mentioned some remaining "unresolved issues." According to Kommersant's diplomatic source familiar with the position of Washington and Paris, those concern mostly the Russian peacekeeping mission in Nagorno-Karabakh (bringing in peacekeepers was discussed by the Minsk Group, but there was no clear decision), Turkey's role in the agreement (the US and France took a much harsher stance on its actions than Moscow, openly accusing Ankara of fueling the Karabakh conflict), and the Minsk Group's future.

To get answers to these questions, representatives of the Minsk Group cochairs were dispatched to Moscow on Wednesday: [They included] Andrew Schofer for the US and Stéphane Visconti for France. They met with Russian Foreign Minister Sergei Lavrov. Igor Popov, Russian ambassador at large, and Andrzej Kasprzyk, the OSCE's special representative to the Minsk Group, were also present at the meeting. The meeting was closed to the press. Afterward, the [Russian] Foreign Ministry released a brief statement that just said that "issues of coordinating future mediation by third countries were discussed." Earlier, Sergei Lavrov said that "from the very start of Russia's efforts to end the acute phase of the conflict, Moscow has been in very close contact with the Minsk Group cochairs." In a recent Kommersant interview, he said that replacing the [OSCE] format with some other mechanism (one that would involve Turkey, for instance) was not under discussion.

Neither Vladimir Putin nor Sergei Lavrov spoke about the US and the Europeans trying to squeeze Russia out of the Transcaucasus, or trying to undermine the agreements reached with [Moscow's] mediation.

Kommersant's sources in the Russian government had this to say about this game of "good cop/bad cop": Moscow worked alone to achieve a truce in the Transcaucasus because that way was faster and turned out to be more effective, but it always did its best to keep its Minsk Group partners in the loop. Overall, the agreement is in line with that the Western mediators were trying to accomplish. Russia does not agree that the communication was insufficient, and will not allow anyone to question the legitimacy of its increased role in the region. Moscow intends to work with its Western partners in the Transcaucasus, but if they are not interested, it will act without getting their permission.

Meanwhile, the position of the US and France is important in terms of the international community, namely the UN Security Council recognizing and supporting Russia's efforts. Last week, Sergei Lavrov said during a press briefing that Russia "proposed that the UN Security Council welcome the ceasefire agreement." As Kommersant has already written, it is not yet clear how this will be done and when. Russia does not expect to get a UN mandate for its peacekeeping mission in Karabakh. Of course, the lack [of such a mandate] hasn't stopped Moscow's activities in other regions (Transnistria, South Ossetia, Abkhazia). It follows from Sergei Lavrov's statement that Moscow would be happy if the Security Council simply welcomed the agreement that was reached with Russia's mediation. However, judging by Moscow's tactics and rhetoric, it's ready to do without it.

RUSSIA PREPARES KARABAKH FOR WINTER

By Gleb Mishutin. *Vedomosti*, Nov. 26, 2020, p. 3.

Russian presidential press secretary Dmitry Peskov denied reports that Russian peacekeeping forces are expanding their mission in Nagorno-Karabakh. That is a mistaken impression, he told journalists on Nov. 25. The humanitarian centers Russia is creating are aimed at solving the numerous problems that have been exacerbated by the war.

On Nov. 19, on orders from Russian Defense Minister Sergei Shoigu, five additional humanitarian centers were created in Nagorno-Karabakh for demining, reconciliation, transportation support, medical [assistance], and trade and administrative support. These centers were established under the aegis of an interagency humanitarian response center created on Nov. 13 by decree of Russian President Vladimir Putin. According to the text of the decree, which was published on the official Kremlin Web site, the interagency center's goals are to assist refugees, help the Armenian and Azerbaijani leadership rebuild civilian infrastructure, and create normal living conditions for the local population.

Additionally, Russian Deputy Prime Minister Aleksandr Novak has been tasked with preparing Karabakh for winter. According to Sputnik Armenia, on Nov. 20, Putin instructed him to coordinate this issue with the Armenian side. Novak traveled to Baku and Yerevan on Nov. 21 as part of an interagency delegation headed by Russian Foreign Minister Sergei Lavrov. Besides Novak, who oversees relations with the CIS countries, [the delegation] included Deputy Prime Minister Aleksei Overchuk, Health Minister Mikhail Murashko, Emergency Situations Minister Yevgeny Zinichev and Anna Popova, head of Rospotrebnadzor [Russian Federal Oversight Service for Consumers' Rights and Human Welfare]. The delegation arrived in Baku from Yerevan, where on the same day Sergei Lavrov held talks with Armenian Prime Minister Nikol Pashinyan. Russian Defense Minister Sergei Shoigu also held talks with the leaders [of Armenia and Azerbaijan] that day.

Konstantin Makiyenko, an expert with the Center for the Analysis of Strategies and Technologies, says that the cost of stationing a Russian peacekeeping contingent in Nagorno-Karabakh and providing potential humanitarian and other aid [to the region] could amount to several billion rubles a year. But this is a justified expense, since a completely pro-Turkish Azerbaijan and an anti-Russian Armenia would be much more costly.

According to political analyst Aleksei Malashenko, today, Russia's peacekeeping mission in Karabakh is fully justified – without Russia's military presence, the war would have continued, resulting in a humanitarian disaster for the region. At the same time, this in no way implies that Russia is establishing a military protectorate in Karabakh. "Russia's presence is completely natural. Right now, it's important to avoid provocations, which is the Russian peacekeepers' main task. A protectorate would mean de facto recognition of Karabakh as a quasi-independent territory, which doesn't suit anyone," Malashenko said.

The expert believes that a joint Russian-Turkish mission would have been an unofficial provocation, since Moscow would have represented Armenia, and Istanbul – Azerbaijan. In his opinion, it's too early to talk about the region's future, but Karabakh has become another area of Russian military presence – and it seems for a long time to come. "[Instead,] we need to discuss how relations will develop between residents of Karabakh, and between Armenia and Azerbaijan, given the disengagement [of forces] and the presence of almost 2,000 Russian troops," the expert said.

Russia's civilian and military presence in Karabakh is not involved in the region's administration, even though it may create that impression. [Rather,] its goals are to help the [local] population find a way to coexist with Azerbaijan and Armenia, a source close to the [Russian] Defense Ministry said.

As of 2018, according to the authorities of the unrecognized Nagorno-Karabakh Republic, the population of the region was 148,000, while its gross domestic product for January-March 2020 was about $120 million. By comparison, South Ossetia's population in 2016 was 53,500, and Abkhazia's in 2019 was 245,500 (according to the authorities of both republics).

WHY ERDOGAN SENT ELITE SPECIAL FORCES TO NAGORNO-KARABAKH

By Vladimir Mukhin. *Nezavisimaya gazeta*, Dec. 2, 2020, p. 1.

Ankara is beginning to crowd Russia in the Nagorno-Karabakh conflict zone. In light of the Turkish National Defense Ministry's announcement that an agreement was signed to set up a joint [ceasefire] monitoring center, Baku said that Turkish military personnel are already acting in Nagorno-Karabakh as sappers. The Voice of Turkey Telegram channel published a photo of one such group, suggesting that it is a Turkish special forces detachment. Plans call for the center to use drones to "collect, analyze and verify data about the parties' compliance with the ceasefire." It was never presumed that the Turkish military, let alone special forces, would operate in the conflict zone.

Now, by all indications, apart from monitoring, Ankara, with Baku's support, will also use its military to pursue other objectives in Nagorno-Karabakh. There is reason to believe that not only sappers but also commandos from the Turkish Armed Forces' Special Operations Forces (SOF) are active in the region. In June 2020, the Voice of Turkey published a photo of a "demining team from the naval special forces subunit" that was sent from Turkey to southern Tripoli. It was reported at the time that the team was to help Government of National Accord (GNA) forces secure liberated territories. Later, it turned out that the special forces were engaged not so much in demining efforts as in training Libyan elite commandos to fight the Libyan National Army (LNA), which opposes the GNA. A study by the Institute of the Middle East titled "The Intelligence Community of the Turkish Republic" says that missions of Turkish SOF subunits abroad include "reconnaissance and diversionary operations, counterterrorism operations and raiding operations behind enemy lines." They "perform search and rescue functions," including mine clearance, only when absolutely necessary, as a cover.

It should be noted that photos from Nagorno-Karabakh show Turkish soldiers with spot mine clearing equipment. At the same time, Russia has the most powerful grouping in the conflict zone. The grouping was formed on the basis of the International Mine Action Center and has accumulated extensive experience in demining operations in Syria, Laos and other countries. In Nagorno-Karabakh, Russian forces have demined 24 hectares of terrain and eight kilometers of roads, removing 750 explosive devices in two weeks.

Analysis of Voice of Turkey publications, which are generally topical and credible, indicates that this Internet platform is close to Turkey's propaganda services that are working to build a favorable image of their country in the eyes of Russians. In this case, reports of the Turkish special forces' presence in Nagorno-Karabakh can be seen as evidence of Ankara's victories, and the futility of Moscow's attempts to hinder the Turkish leadership from achieving its geopolitical goals in the post-Soviet Transcaucasus.

NG has already written about disagreements between Moscow and Ankara over Turkey's participation in the peacekeeping process in Nagorno-Karabakh. After

Moscow, Baku and Yerevan signed a trilateral ceasefire agreement on Nov. 9, Turkish Foreign Minister Mevlut Cavusoglu insisted that "along with the Russian-Turkish ceasefire monitoring center in Nagorno-Karabakh, separate Turkish observation posts will be set up on the ground." Azerbaijani President Ilkham Aliyev said practically the same thing on Nov. 10. Russian presidential press secretary Dmitry Peskov acknowledged that [Moscow and] Ankara have different approaches toward a settlement in Nagorno-Karabakh. But Moscow continues to insist that there will be no Turkish troops in Nagorno-Karabakh, and that the Turkish presence will be limited to work at the Nagorno-Karabakh joint ceasefire monitoring center that will be based on Azerbaijani territory outside the conflict zone. Earlier, Turkey's political leadership made a snap decision to send troops to Azerbaijan. On Nov. 22, Turkish Defense Minister Hulusi Akar said subunits of the Turkish Armed Forces ground troops would be sent there.

"You can always conceal special forces among infantry," Lt. Gen. Yury Netkachev (Ret.), former deputy commander of the Group of Russian Forces in the Transcaucasus and unofficial defense minister in the Adzharian government, which was in opposition to official Tbilisi after the breakup of the USSR, told NG. "From the Sukhumi experience, I know what role special forces can play in destabilizing the situation [and] dealing with political issues in a separatist region. At that time, [then-Georgian president Mikhail] Saakashvili's special forces fought against [then-Adzhar leader Aslan] Abashidze. Today, Aliyev in Baku is unofficially supported by Turkish special forces," the expert said.

According to Netkachev, Turkey's objective is to crowd Russia out of Nagorno-Karabakh and the Transcaucasus. "This could be done with the participation of Turkish special forces through diversionary activities, by setting the local population against Russian peacekeepers, and so on," Netkachev commented. He recalled that before the outbreak of the Nagorno-Karabakh war, anti-Russian demonstrations took place in Azerbaijan, where protesters waved Turkish flags alongside Azerbaijani ones. "Right now, supplies for the peacekeeping forces in Nagorno-Karabakh are being transported via Azerbaijani territory. Tellingly, Russian convoys are moving along the country's roads, escorted by the local police and without Russian state symbols. I believe this is being done to avoid attracting the attention of locals, including those who are not very happy with what Russia is doing," Netkachev believes.

The Azerbaijani Armed Forces' Telegram channel reported on Tuesday [Dec. 1]: "Armenian and certain pro-Armenian Russian media outlets are disseminating information that the Azerbaijani public is supposedly expressing discontent with the Russian peacekeeping contingent, with calls to expel Russians from Nagorno-Karabakh, including by military force." "It is highly unlikely that Russian or Armenian media are behind these attempts to egg on the Azerbaijanis. I believe that Turkey stands to gain from this, and this is the work of its propaganda machine," Netkachev said.

AFTER KARABAKH

By Aleksandr Vorobyov, director of the Center for Investment and Integration Cooperation. *Nezavisimaya gazeta*, Nov. 30, 2020, p. 11.

To the average observer, the bloody outbreak of violence in Nagorno-Karabakh ended just as suddenly as it began. The parties to the conflict signed a Russia-brokered ceasefire, which was announced on Nov. 10. The cessation of hostilities shifted attention from the course of events and the sides' tactics to the evaluation of the war's outcome. At first glance, Azerbaijan is the winner in the conflict [and] Turkey, which supported it, a major beneficiary. Armenia lost the war and Russia strengthened its position as a peacekeeper in the South Caucasus. Overall, that is a fairly objective interpretation of the outcome of the war. But a closer analysis reveals additional aspects.

There is no doubt that Azerbaijan reaped quite a few benefits, winning a convincing military victory. Baku retook a significant chunk of Armenian-controlled territory: seven Azerbaijani districts, as well as a significant part of Nagorno-Karabakh itself, including the city of Shusha. The agreements signed by the conflicting sides stipulate unblocking transportation links with Azerbaijan's Nakhichevan Province, a landlocked exclave bordering Armenia. The Azerbaijani authorities have also reaped substantial political dividends. The surge of patriotism and national unity have sidelined economic problems caused by falling oil prices, the coronavirus pandemic and lockdowns. The upbeat public mood is likely to ensure political stability and public consensus in Azerbaijan for years to come....

What will be a long-term controversy for Baku is the appearance on Azerbaijani territory following the conflict of foreign troops – i.e., Russian peacekeepers and Turkish soldiers. Indeed, their status and their objectives are not hostile to Azerbaijan, and their deployment was approved by the Azerbaijani side. But the presence of foreign forces on [Azerbaijan's] territory still limits the state's flexibility on the international arena. This situation could become a problem if relations between the two major players in the South Caucasus – i.e., Russia and Turkey – lose their constructive character for whatever reason and become acutely competitive or, in the worst-case scenario, antagonistic.

In light of this, Azerbaijani President Ilkham Aliyev's flexible policy of maneuvering between Russian and Turkish interests may fail: The Azerbaijani authorities risk ending up between a rock and a hard place. The pro-Turkish and nationalist-minded segment of the Azerbaijani public may have a bone to pick with President Aliyev over his "pro-Russian course," specifically the deployment of Russian peacekeepers in Nagorno-Karabakh – i.e., within Azerbaijan's internationally recognized borders. Questions may also arise over the fact that Baku ended a victorious war too soon and without achieving the main objective – i.e., putting [all of] Nagorno-Karabakh back under Azerbaijan's control. At the same time, it is clear that if Baku turns into Ankara's obvious satellite, Moscow will have to toughen its stance toward Azerbaijan.

The outcome of the conflict for Armenia seems to be more disappointing, but at the same time more unequivocal. Yerevan was inferior to the Azerbaijani side in firepower and combat tactics, losing air superiority. As a result, control over a substantial part of Nagorno-Karabakh territory and seven Azerbaijani districts was lost. The country has plunged into a political crisis with the Armenian public showering accusations on Russia of failing to deliver on its allied commitments – if not legal, then moral.

Still, while the current situation is bad for Yerevan, it is not catastrophic. First, Armenia has retained control of Armenian territory as such, and has preserved its zone of influence in Nagorno-Karabakh and its economic potential. [Armenia's] defeat in the war is likely to spur economic reforms and a change in the lineup of political forces in the country. The situation will also require [Armenia] to reevaluate its stance on the Nagorno-Karabakh issue. After all, the passive reaction of the international community to the war in Nagorno-Karabakh was partly due to the fact that although Armenia retained control of Nagorno-Karabakh, as far as the global community is concerned (and this includes Russia), Nagorno-Karabakh has remained Azerbaijani territory in terms of international law. This made it rather difficult to support Yerevan's position on Nagorno-Karabakh. If the Armenian leadership draws the necessary conclusions from the situation, modernizes the Army and the economy, builds a more sensible relationship with Russia and a constructive relationship with Western countries (but not at the expense of its relations with Moscow), then Yerevan will eventually restore its international standing.

The bitter conflict in Nagorno-Karabakh has put Moscow in a tough spot. On the one hand, the position of the Armenian leadership and Prime Minister Nikol Pashinyan toward Moscow was not very constructive, and was criticized for its "overly pro-Western course." So a segment of Russia's expert community perceived Armenia's defeat in the war as a defeat of the "West's client." But it should not be forgotten that Yerevan has been and remains a member of the CSTO and the EaEU – in other words, the country is in a close military and political alliance with Moscow, and is more like its client [instead of the West's]. So, in one way or another, Yerevan's defeat in the war resulted in political and image losses for Russia.

If we look at the Russian leadership's actions after the start of the active phase of combat operations, we can see that they were commensurate with the situation and well balanced. Moscow stated that it was equidistant from both parties to the conflict, focused on the unacceptability of military and civilian deaths, and called on the [conflicting] parties to exercise restraint and end the conflict as soon as possible. Thus, Russia managed to maintain the necessary balance. The decision to send Russian peacekeepers to the Nagorno-Karabakh conflict zone, which was announced in November, can also be considered a success of Russia's policy in the region.

Turkey was another party actively involved in the conflict. Ankara can be considered a beneficiary of the 2020 war in Nagorno-Karabakh. Turkey has consolidated its own military-political positions in the South Caucasus; the Turkish authorities have strengthened their influence on Azerbaijan's political and military leadership, and pro-Turkish sympathies in Azerbaijani society have grown, although they were strong already. There are also signs of a rise in pan-Turkic sympathies in the post-Soviet space. But Turkey will hardly be able to parlay those sympathies into political, economic or military bonuses.

At the same time, Ankara will likely reap certain economic benefits from the end of the war in the South Caucasus on terms that are favorable to it. Turkey may make additional efforts to improve infrastructure and transportation connectivity in the South Caucasus, based on the Turkish-Azerbaijani [transport] corridor that will subsequently extend to the opposite coast of the Caspian Sea in the east, and southeastern Europe in the west. The Central Asian countries (primarily Kazakhstan), China and European countries are all interested in better transportation links in the South Caucasus.

But Ankara may encounter serious obstacles with regard to its own foreign policy activities. Turkey's assertive policy, often uncompromising rhetoric and worsening relations with its Western partners have led to a lack of trust in relations with its partners, foreign capital flight from Turkey and the overall overstraining of the Turkish economy. The Turkish lira has lost 10% [sic; more than 25% – *Trans.*] of its value in 2020 and, according to Bloomberg, is the "worst-performing currency [in emerging markets after the Brazilian real]." Turkey's gold and foreign-exchange reserves have been significantly depleted. Economic factors, the need to maintain constructive relations with major international players and the Turkish public's discontent with socioeconomic difficulties may compel Ankara to adjust its foreign policy course.

KARABAKH SUMMONED ONCE AGAIN

By Sergei Strokan and Aik Khalatyan. *Kommersant*, Dec. 8, 2020, p. 6.

Ara Aivazyan, Armenia's new foreign minister, held talks on Monday [Dec. 7] with Russian Foreign Minister Sergei Lavrov as part of a two-day working visit to Russia....

This was their second in-person meeting. Their previous meeting took place during the visit of a Russian interdepartmental delegation to Yerevan on Nov. 21, just three days after the sudden replacement of Armenia's foreign minister, Zograb Mnatsakanyan.

When dismissing Mnatsakanyan, Armenian Prime Minister Nikol Pashinyan said that "the [ceasefire] negotiations irrevocably led to the surrender of territories," including Shusha, Nagorno-Karabakh's second largest city, to Azerbaijan.

But according to the previous leadership of the Armenian Foreign Ministry, surrendering Shusha was never discussed.

Zograb Mnatsakanyan's contradiction of Nikol Pashinyan led to the Armenian foreign minister's resignation. Aivazyan, who previously served as ambassador to

Lithuania, Latvia, Estonia, Mexico, Costa Rica, Honduras, Guatemala, Panama and Cuba, is taking the helm of the Foreign Ministry at a critical time. Soon after taking office, he made the sensational remark that "Armenia failed not on the diplomatic field" but on the battlefield, because the balance of forces was disparately tipped in the enemy's favor.

Outlining the agenda of the talks in Moscow, Russian Foreign Ministry spokeswoman Maria Zakharova said that the main topic was the "implementation of the Nov. 9 statement from the leaders of Russia, Azerbaijan and Armenia, with an emphasis on providing humanitarian assistance, restoring infrastructure, and unblocking transportation corridors in the region." The Russian side acknowledged that exchanging prisoners of war and dead bodies is imperative.

The Russian Foreign Ministry said that a Russian peacekeeping mission is using state-of-the-art technology to help search [for dead bodies].

Another topic discussed at the talks in Moscow was the resettlement of refugees (more than 33,000 civilians have returned to their places of permanent residence in Nagorno-Karabakh since the start of the peacekeeping operation)....

Assessing the situation in the conflict zone after the signing of the trilateral agreements between the leaders of Russia, Azerbaijan and Armenia, the Russian foreign minister said: "We are unanimous that the Nov. 9 statement creates all the necessary conditions for a fair, long-term settlement of the Nagorno-Karabakh conflict in the interests of Armenians and Azerbaijanis, and will serve to stabilize the situation in the South Caucasus." Nevertheless, Sergei Lavrov considered it necessary to reiterate: "We are just now exiting the acute phase of the Nagorno-Karabakh conflict."

For his part, at the final press conference with Sergei Lavrov, Aivazyan stressed the importance of exchanging prisoners and dead bodies. "Locating missing soldiers and exchanging prisoners and dead bodies is a very sensitive issue that requires prompt resolution. This is especially true given reports about numerous and confirmed instances of the barbaric – in the literal sense – treatment of prisoners of war and others. Preserving Armenian religious and cultural sites is another such issue," he stressed....

It is noteworthy that the Russian and Armenian foreign ministers did not say a word at the joint press conference about the future status of Nagorno-Karabakh, which remains a bone of contention between Yerevan and Baku.

Speaking last week at the OSCE Ministerial Council, Aivazyan said that a long-term settlement in the region must include "a status for Artsakh (the Armenian name for Nagorno-Karabakh – K) based on the right to self-determination." Aivazyan also touched on the issue of Nagorno-Karabakh's status in an interview with the Armenpress agency before his visit to Moscow. "The brutal military force used against the people of Artsakh has further strengthened support for recognizing the right of the people of Artsakh to self-determination, and we are seeing some new approaches in this area," he said.

For its part, the Azerbaijani side considers the issue of Nagorno-Karabakh's status closed.

A line from President Ilkham Aliyev's address to the nation after Armenia's defeat has become a catchphrase in the country: "Pashinyan, where is your status?"

When asked last week whether Russia's position on Nagorno-Karabakh's status had changed, Dmitry Peskov, the Russian president's press secretary, commented that it had not, recalling "the relevant UN Security Council resolutions, which have been in force for some time." "Russia has not changed anything [in its position] – actually, no country has. In fact, even President Putin has said that Nagorno-Karabakh***has never been recognized. It has not been recognized even by Armenia. President Putin has said that," Dmitry Peskov explained (UN Security Council Resolution No. 853, adopted in 1993, confirms the sovereignty and territorial integrity of Azerbaijan and of all other states in the region).

Aivazyan's diplomatic mission in Moscow was complicated by the extreme circumstances surrounding his talks with Sergei Lavrov; the Armenian opposition is accusing Prime Minister Pashinyan of losing control of the situation and is demanding his resignation by noon Tuesday.

So when Aivazyan set out for Moscow, he could not be 100% certain that Pashinyan would still be prime minister when he returned.

One of the Armenian opposition's main grievances with Prime Minister Pashinyan is the failure of [his administration's] Russia policy. Former president Robert Kocharyan said that "Armenia needs a swift change of power," because the country "must have a government that has complete confidence that relations with Russia are built properly." Meanwhile, the united opposition's candidate vying to replace Pashinyan, former prime minister Vazgen Manukyan, called for "restoring relations with allies" who have lost confidence in Yerevan....

NIKOL PASHINYAN WEATHERS ULTIMATUM

By Aleksandr Atasuntsev. *RBC Daily*, Dec. 9, 2020, p. 4.

The Armenian opposition's ultimatum to Prime Minister Nikol Pashinyan expired at noon on Dec. 8. After the six-week Nagorno-Karabakh war, the prime minister agreed to cede to Azerbaijan the territories that Armenia had conquered during the first Karabakh war. Now his opponents believe he is no longer fit to lead the country and must voluntarily resign. They are vowing mass protests and road closures if he does not.

Several thousand people did in fact rally, blocking several streets in Yerevan. And one group [of protesters] held up the subway system for several hours. Protesters went down to one of the stations and stood in the doorways of subway trains, blocking their movement. Several dozen people were detained, and by evening the protests had subsided.

After coming together to form the Fatherland Salvation Movement, Pashinyan's opponents last week nominated a consensus candidate for the country's prime minister. It took more than three weeks to find a candidate who would satisfy all the members of the anti-Pashinyan alliance. They settled on 74-year-old Vazgen Manukyan, who headed the republic's government a very long time ago, in 1990-1991. In 1992-1993, at the height of the first Karabakh war, Manukyan served as defense minister. He then headed Armenia's Public Council for many years.

At a Dec. 5 rally in downtown Yerevan, where several thousand people had gathered (a record 40,000, according to the opposition) and an ultimatum to the prime minister was finally formulated, Manukyan said that if Pashinyan did not leave on his own accord, he would be forced to do so: "Pashinyan must understand that this movement presents him with a chance to leave in a civilized manner. If the movement loses, enraged Armenians will rip him to shreds." Manukyan said that he is willing to lead the country during a transition period until early parliamentary elections can be held, in which he promised not to run.

He acknowledged that Armenia would not be able to back out of the Nov. 10 agreement with Russia and Azerbaijan on Nagorno-Karabakh. "We will never come to terms with this declaration, but it is de facto now in effect. We cannot renounce it, as that would mean resuming war with Turkey and Azerbaijan,***but the agreement was drawn up sloppily. There are many ambiguities; the new government must clear up all the nuances and resolve issues in our favor," he explained the tasks of the future cabinet.

Meanwhile, Pashinyan is showing no sign of leaving. Before Saturday's opposition rally, he went live on Facebook and said that he could not be legally removed, since he came to power legitimately after "the only uncontested parliamentary elections in [Armenia's] history." "The point of some political processes taking place in Armenia today is clear. Some circles want to do everything to make this the last such [i.e., uncontested – Trans.] election. We will not allow that. The power of the people cannot be questioned," the prime minister said.

On Tuesday, Pashinyan met with US Ambassador Lynne Tracy to discuss relations between the two countries and the situation in Nagorno-Karabakh.

But pressure on the head of government is growing by the day. On Tuesday, head of the Armenian Apostolic Church Garegin II urged him to resign. Earlier, the [Armenian] National Academy of Sciences, Yerevan State University, a number of public organizations, mayors and community leaders called for his resignation. All the leaders of independent Armenia, who ruled the country from 1991 to 2018, demanded that he resign as prime minister: [They include] Levon Ter-Petrosyan, Robert Kocharyan and Serzh Sargsyan. Earlier, President Armen Sarkisyan also called for early parliamentary elections (after the 2015 reform, the president lost some powers, and the country became a parliamentary republic).

"All of independent Armenia's previous governments will go down in history as governments that won and liberated lands, and defended their homeland with dignity. But you, a leader who dishonorably suffered defeat in war for the sake of his own post and who surrendered the lands of Artsakh, are not fit to negotiate," Sargsyan told the prime minister. Sargsyan was forced to relinquish power in 2018 due to mass protests initiated by Pashinyan. Ex-president Kocharyan, who, after

Pashinyan came to power, was accused of trying to overthrow the state, said that Pashinyan could be given security guarantees if he resigned.

Pashinyan is not going to give up, Armenian political analyst Aleksandr Iskandaryan told RBC in an interview. He said that it is practically impossible to legally oust the prime minister. "The Constitution was created by Serzh Sargsyan for the Republican Party, and it has now proved very convenient for Pashinyan. Under the current configuration, where the ruling party holds more than two-thirds of the seats in parliament, it is impossible to dismiss him. It is impossible even to abolish martial law, which is still in place in the country: Doing that requires the consent of more than 50% of the deputies. Even launching impeachment proceedings requires the support of one-third of deputies, and the parliamentary opposition does even not have that," Iskandaryan said.

Of the 132 deputies in the national parliament, 85 are in the pro-Pashinyan My Step bloc. The second largest faction is the opposition Prosperous Armenia party, but it has only 24 deputies. Three deputies have left My Step since Nov. 10; on Dec. 8, another member of the faction, Aram Khachatryan, submitted a resignation statement. No reason for the resignation was given.

According to Iskandaryan, only large-scale protests can make the prime minister leave. But so far, the protest movement is drawing big names more than big crowds. "There still aren't enough people taking to the street. And the challenge is to make the protest massive," he says. In addition, public apathy is playing in Pashinyan's favor: "People are tired and not ready to start another revolution two years after [the first one]."

OLD PRESIDENTS ARE WORSE THAN A FIRE:[2] HOW PASHINYAN WON THE ELECTION AFTER LOSING IN KARABAKH

By Aleksandr Artamonov. *Republic.ru*, June 21, 2021, https://republic.ru/posts/100785.

After signing the humiliating peace agreements following the war in Karabakh, it seemed to many that Nikol Pashinyan's days were numbered. This is generally the natural order of things – as a rule, a democratic leader who has lost a serious war is not reelected. However, it turned out quite differently.

Under pressure from the opposition, Pashinyan called new parliamentary elections, which were held on June 20. The results of the vote came as a huge surprise – the prime minister's Civil Contract party received almost 54% of the votes and will again be able to form a government without the participation of other forces. How did the Armenian prime minister manage to hold on to power?

Election results

All in all, three parties made it into parliament:
Nikol Pashinyan's Civil Contract – 53.92%;

Ex-president Robert Kocharyan's (1998-2008) Armenia bloc – 21.04%;

Ex-president Serzh Sargsyan's (2008-2018) and former head of the National Security Service Artur Vanetsyan's I Have Honor bloc – 5.23%. This party did not overcome the 7% entry barrier, but will still get mandates, as by law there can be no fewer than three parties in the parliament.

A total of 25 parties and blocs took part in the elections, and the results for the vast majority of them were within the margin of statistical error. In total, the parties that did not enter parliament gained 19.8%.

Some political analysts were quick to say that the support of 54% of the deputies was needed in order to form a government, but that Pashinyan's party had received 0.08% fewer votes and would be forced to join the coalition. This is not the case: The parties that got into parliament will gain additional mandates at the expense of those that did not clear the entry barrier. The exact distribution of mandates is not yet known, but Civil Contract will be able to form a government independently – this was confirmed by Tigran Mukuchyan, the chairman of the Armenian Central Electoral Commission (CEC).

Turnout was 49.4%, which is 1% more than in the early parliamentary elections of 2018 in which Pashinyan's bloc received 70%, and about 12% less than in the elections during the Sargsyan era. Many observers predicted that the turnout would be much lower – after the military defeat and the protracted crisis, Armenians are tired of politics.

Civil Contract received the most votes in rural areas, and the least in Yerevan – 41% vs. 27% for Kocharyan's party. Even in Syunik Province, which was recently invaded by Azerbaijani troops and where Pashinyan had rotten eggs thrown at him, his party received 53.5% of the votes. The majority of voters chose him even in the village of Shurnuch, part of which came under the control of Azerbaijan in January under the Karabakh ceasefire agreement.

The election results came as a big surprise. Until the counting of votes began, it was not clear who would win, but even Pashinyan's most loyal supporters hardly expected that his party would win so many.

The companies that conducted the polls were playing on the side of one of the candidates – most often Kocharyan – and predicted a crushing victory for him. The results of independent polls were also wrong. For example, pollsters from Russia's RIA Novosti predicted a Kocharyan victory with 32% against Pashinyan's 24%. Gallup's Armenian branch conducted a poll that showed Pashinyan's and Kocharyan's parties receiving about the same number of votes – 25% and 28%, respectively.

Observers from the CIS and the OSCE recognized the elections as competitive and fair. Serious irregularities have been ruled out – the Armenian CEC uses a complex system of voter identification involving a fingerprint scanner. However, the opposition has not acknowledged the results of the elections.

Representatives of the Armenia bloc accused the authorities of forced voting in the Army, as well as interference in the electronic counting process. In addition, electricity was cut off soon after the closure of the polling stations in some major cities of Armenia. The opposition suspects that the authorities used this moment for falsification. Tomorrow, Kocharyan's party will hold a press conference at which it is likely to announce the start of a new protest campaign. In addition, the Armenia [bloc's] lawyers are going to challenge the election results in the Supreme Court.

One new friend is better than two old ones[3]

Immediately after the signing of the truce between Armenia and Azerbaijan in November 2020, protests began in the Armenian capital in which the participants insisted on the continuation of the war, called Pashinyan a traitor to the nation and demanded his resignation.

The demonstrations never became a real mass phenomenon. Opponents of the prime minister did not even come close to the level of protest mobilization with which Pashinyan himself toppled Sargsyan in 2018. But the prime minister's approval rating plummeted.

The protest campaign was led by people close to two ex-presidents of Armenia: Sargsyan, who was overthrown by the popular movement under Pashinyan's leadership in 2018 after trying to "zero out" [avoid term limits by restarting at zero – Trans.] and his predecessor, Robert Kocharyan.

Both former presidents criticized the prime minister from similar patriotic and irredentist positions, but they did not join forces – there is a personal animosity between them. Kocharyan hinted that he would be able to change the terms of the ceasefire in Karabakh to be more favorable for the Armenians. His friendship with Putin was supposed to help him.

In February, the Armenian General Staff joined the opposition. Pashinyan had made a big public mistake: He said that Armenia used Russian Iskander [missile] complexes during the war, but that only 10% of their missiles reached the target, and he also called them "weapons from the 80s" (Iskanders were developed in 1999). The next day, deputy chief of the General Staff Tigran Khachatryan ridiculed the prime minister, for which he was dismissed by decree of President Armen Sarkisyan, who was asked to do so by Pashinyan. The General Staff opposed the decision and demanded the immediate resignation of the prime minister; Pashinyan called this démarche an attempt at a coup. As a result, the General Staff calmed down, and the firings were brought to an end....

During the political crisis, the two sides slung a lot of mud at each other, but the conflict never went beyond the bounds of democracy. The opposition and the military did not dare to fight Pashinyan by force, and he eventually agreed to resign and [call] early elections, which he was supposed to lose.

How Pashinyan won

First of all, Pashinyan was greatly helped by the low turnout. Many of those who did not come out to vote view him negatively, but they do not sympathize with his opponents. The more voters that had come to the polls, the lower the share of the votes for Civil Contract would have been.

Secondly, the opposition could have achieved a much higher result if it had consolidated and presented a coherent political agenda. Instead, it chose to yell at Pashinyan nonstop while being mired in internal strife.

The main approach taken by Sargsyan's and Kocharyan's parties to fighting the prime minister was nationalist and revanchist rhetoric, as well as nostalgia for the old days when they were in power. However, the proportion of Armenians susceptible to such an agenda was much lower than expected.

Thirdly, many Armenians who are unsympathetic to Pashinyan view the corrupt "old guard" represented by Sargsyan and Kocharyan as a much greater evil. And even defeat in the war could not change their minds.

"The slogan 'It will be like it was in grandpa's day' (from Robert Kocharyan, one of the leaders of Nagorno-Karabakh during the victorious war of 1992-1994 – Ed.) failed to sway Armenians since, along with the obvious m-ilitary successes in Karabakh, there were blockades, mass emigration, isolation of the country, poverty and corruption," says political analyst Sergei Markedonov. "Over time, the universal 'Karabakh logic' ceased to work. And the [2020] war did not cause that; it only highlighted it. Armenian society is not happy about the heavy defeat, which is very clear. But it is not ready, for the sake of a phantom rematch (and even opponents of Pashinyan are not ready to cancel the agreement of Nov. 10), to return either to those who have been rejected (Sargsyan), or to representatives of the past, even a heroic [past] (Kocharyan)."

Fourthly and finally, Russia did not help any of the candidates. During the election campaign, all the politicians, including Pashinyan, tried their best to demonstrate their loyalty to Moscow. However, only Kocharyan, who is strongly associated with Putin's elite, could seriously claim direct political assistance from the Kremlin. The Russian leadership chose not to interfere.

Before the war in Karabakh, the Kremlin viewed Pashinyan negatively and with suspicion as a leader who was too pro-Western and democratic. Such a position can hardly be called justified: Pashinyan did appoint a group of employees of Western NGOs to lead the country, but in general he did not give up the traditional pro-Russian course of all Armenia's leaders.

However, after the end of the war, Pashinyan became the main guarantor of the implementation of the ceasefire agreements, because his signature is on them. Russia is motivated to have the agreements implemented, and "the most pro-Russian" Kocharyan has been hinting at the possibility of regaining Karabakh, so he may take unpredictable steps and attempt to challenge the conditions of peace. So, keeping Pashinyan in power is more beneficial to Russia today.

NOTES

1. The Russian phrase *ikh tam net* ("they aren't there") refers to the Russian government's denial that the soldiers in unmarked green army fatigues carrying modern Russian military equipment who appeared in the Crimea in 2014 were active-duty Russian soldiers.

2. A play on words based on the Russian saying, "Moving house twice is worse than a fire."

3. A reversal of the rhymed Russian saying, "One old friend is better than two new ones."

Index

About the Editor

Artyom Tonoyan is a research associate at the University of Minnesota's Center for Holocaust and Genocide Studies. His research interests include sociology of religion, religion and politics in the South Caucasus, and religion and nationalism in contemporary Russia. He received his Ph.D. from Baylor University.